T0214492

Communications in Computer and Information Science 1083

Commenced Publication in 2007
Founding and Former Series Editors:
Phoebe Chen, Alfredo Cuzzocrea, Xiaoyong Du, Orhun Kara, Ting Liu,
Krishna M. Sivalingam, Dominik Ślęzak, Takashi Washio, and Xiaokang Yang

More information about this series at http://www.springer.com/series/7899

Alla G. Kravets · Peter P. Groumpos ·
Maxim Shcherbakov · Marina Kultsova (Eds.)

Creativity in Intelligent Technologies and Data Science

Third Conference, CIT&DS 2019
Volgograd, Russia, September 16–19, 2019
Proceedings, Part I

 Springer

Editors
Alla G. Kravets 🔾
CAD & Research Department
Volgograd State Technical University
Volgograd, Russia

Peter P. Groumpos 🔾
Electrical and Computer Engineering
University of Patras
Rion, Patras, Greece

Maxim Shcherbakov 🔾
Volgograd State Technical University
Volgograd, Russia

Marina Kultsova 🔾
Volgograd State Technical University
Volgograd, Russia

ISSN 1865-0929　　　　　　　　ISSN 1865-0937　(electronic)
Communications in Computer and Information Science
ISBN 978-3-030-29742-8　　　　ISBN 978-3-030-29743-5　(eBook)
https://doi.org/10.1007/978-3-030-29743-5

This Springer imprint is published by the registered company Springer Nature Switzerland AG
The registered company address is: Gewerbestrasse 11, 6330 Cham, Switzerland

Preface

In the era of digitalization and raise of artificial intelligence, creativity is still a crucial and essential ability for humankind. Creativity is the process of breaking out of established patterns; it is the reorganization, recombination or reinterpretation of concepts and ideas for getting something unique and previously unknown. Creating intelligent systems and artificial intelligence approaches is one of the most creative activities that humans undertake. It is developed for people and by people and people's creativity can be a good source to improvise solutions to problems for dominating complex systems such as intelligent system design and development. These actions merge science and art.

This book includes the proceedings of the third Conference on Creativity in Intelligent Technologies and Data Science (CIT&DS 2019), continuing the successful series of previous conferences, which took place in 2017 and 2015. The main objective of CIT&DS 2019 is to bring together researchers and practitioners to share ideas in using creativity to theory and practice in software and intelligent systems engineering as well as data science and decision-making support solutions. Readers will find results of creating cutting-edge intelligent technologies based on state-of-the-art research.

The conference has three main groups of topics. The first one is called "Artificial intelligence and Deep Learning Technologies for Creative Tasks." This chapter includes papers related to the following topics: (a) Knowledge Discovery in Patent and Open Sources; (b) Open Science Semantic Technologies; and (c) Computer Vision and Knowledge-Based Control. The second chapter unites articles in the framework of "Cyber-Physical Systems and Big Data-Driven World." In particular, findings related to the following are highlighted: (a) Pro-Active Modeling in Intelligent Decision-Making Support; (b) Design Creativity in CASE/CAI/CAD/PDM; and (c) Intelligent Internet of Services and Internet of Things. The last chapter is titled "Intelligent Technologies in Social Engineering," and contains contributions on the topics: (a) Data Science in Social Networks Analysis; (b) Creativity and Game-Based Learning; and (c) Intelligent Assistive Technologies: Software Design and Application.

July 2019

Alla Kravets
Maxim Shcherbakov
Marina Kultsova
Peter Groumpos

Organization

General Chairs

Vladimir Lysak   Volgograd State Technical University, Russia
Igor Kalyaev   Research Institute of Multiprocessor Computing
     Systems, Russia
Dmitriy Novikov   Institute of Control Sciences of Russian Academy
     of Science, Russia

Program Chairs

Alla Kravets   Volgograd State Technical University, Russia
Peter Groumpos   University of Patras, Greece
Maxim Shcherbakov   Volgograd State Technical University, Russia
Marina Kultsova   Volgograd State Technical University, Russia

Program Committee

Julio Abascal   University of the Basque Country, Spain
Abdul Hamid Abu Bakar   Putra Business School, Malaysia
Mohammed Al-Gunaid   Volgograd State Technical University, Russia
Yasemin Allsop   University College London, UK
Andrey Andreev   Volgograd State Technical University, Russia
Anton Anikin   Volgograd State Technical University, Russia
Danish Ather   Teerthanker Mahaveer University, India
Bal Krishna Bal   Kathmandu University, Nepal
Fernando Paulo Belfo   Polytechnic Institute of Coimbra, Portugal
Olga Berestneva   Tomsk Polytechnic University, Russia
Igor Bessmertny   ITMO University, Russia
Alexander Bozhday   Penza State University, Russia
Adriaan Brebels   KULeuven, Belgium
Germanas Budnikas   Kaunas University of Technology, Lithuania
Leonid Chechurin   LUT, Finland
Satyadhyan Chickerur   KLE Technological University, India
Yury Danilovsky   QM&E, South Korea
Maria Dascalu   Politehnica University of Bucharest, Romania
Jan Dekelver   Thomas More University, Belgium
Nuno Escudeiro   IPP-ISEP, Portugal
Demetra Evangelou   Democritus University of Thrace, Greece
Alexey Finogeev   Penza State University, Russia
Dragoi George   UPB-FILS, Romania
Olga Gerget   Tomsk Polytechnic University, Russia

Eduardo Sarmento	ULHT, Portugal
Sergey Serebryakov	Hewlett Packard Enterprise, USA
Olga Shabalina	Volgograd State Technical University, Russia
Sergiy Shevchenko	National Technical University "Kharkiv Polytechnic Institute", Ukraine
Olga Shikulskaya	Astrakhan Civil Engineering Institute, Russia
Vadim Stefanuk	Institute for Information Transmission Problems of RAS, Russia
Ilya Stepanchenko	Kamyshin Technological Institute VSTU, Russia
Pham The Bao	Sai Gon University, Vietnam
Florica Tomos	University of South Wales, UK
Victor Toporkov	National Research University MPEI, Russia
Uranchimeg Tudevdagva	TU Chemnitz, Germany
Anton Tyukov	Volgograd State Technical University, Russia
Joao Varajao	University of Minho, Portugal
Pavel Vorobkalov	Yandex, Russia
Hironori Washizaki	Waseda University, Japan
Vibhash Yadav	Rajkiya Engineering College, India
Rihito Yaegashi	Kagawa University, Japan
Hongji Yang	Leicester University, UK
Nadezhda Yarushkina	Ulyanovsk State Technical University, Russia
Alena Zakharova	Bryansk State Technical University, Russia
Andrius Zhilenas	INVENTSHIP, Lithuania

Contents – Part I

Cyber-Physical Systems and Big Data-Driven World. Intelligent
Internet of Services and Internet of Things

Contents – Part II

**Artificial Intelligence and Deep Learning Technologies
for Creative Tasks. Computer Vision and Knowledge-Based Control**

Intelligent Technologies in Social Engineering. Data Science in Social Networks Analysis and Cybersecurity

Intelligent Technologies in Social Engineering. Creativity and Game-Based Learning

Intelligent Technologies in Social Engineering. Intelligent Assistive Technologies: Software Design and Application

Keynotes

Designing AI Futures: A Symbiotic Vision

Karamjit S. Gill[✉]

Human Centered Systems, University of Brighton, Brighton, Great Britain
editoraisoc@yahoo.co.uk

Logic will get you from A to B. Imagination will take you everywhere
Albert Einstein

It takes something more than intelligence to act intelligently
Fyodor Dostoyevsky

Abstract. The new "AI spring" of Machine Learning and Deep learning, backed by Big Data and immense computational power, is opening up potential for innovation of new drugs, medical diagnosis, social robots, 'Robo-Nurse' and virtual assistants, but there are also imponderable existential downsides and deep anxiety that AIs are going to take over our jobs, our interaction with societal institutions and our lives. With the accelerated integration of powerful artificial intelligence systems into core social institutions and in our everyday lives, we are confronted with an electronic world where digital bots or electronic 'agents' are already representing us in our interactions. We face a challenge of the untamed integration of AI to come up with possible human-machine futures that mitigate the impact of the instrumental models of AI tools and systems. How can we transcend 'machine thinking' to mold technological futures for the common good? We need to address questions such as, can we harness collective intelligence as a transforming tool for addressing unpredictable problems of complex social systems? What are the possibilities and limitations of designing creative intelligent systems that are shaped by purpose and judgment, transcending instrument reason of the causal model? The talk will explore these issues, drawing upon current AI narratives of the relations between society and the scientific project of AI and the challenges it poses for us to come up with possible symbiotic AI futures.

Keywords: AI narrative · AI futures · Augmentation · Collective intelligence · Creativity · Existential risk · Human-centred systems · Instrumental reason · Judgment · Thinking machine · Wisdom

1 AIs Pandora's Box

When we open the AIs Pandora's Box, we find promotion of the automation agenda of the technological dream of Big Data, Machine, Deep Learning, and predictive algorithms. Beyond the headline of the thrill engendered by this technological dream, what

---

Editor, AI & Society: Journal of Knowledge, Culture and Communication.

A. G. Kravets et al. (Eds.): CIT&DS 2019, CCIS 1083, pp. 3–18, 2019.
https://doi.org/10.1007/978-3-030-29743-5_1

are we to make of artificial intelligence? We ask questions such: what if the machine replace humans? Can humanity live in a simulated state of digital being? Or the next step in evolution is the one in which technology finally asserts its mastery over us? What we are offered instead is the mirage of the digital futures, a digital marketplace of ideas, knowledge, innovations, skills, products, and services. Or maybe Artificial intelligence in its many faces become the source of redemptive systems. What are the crises and shocks of the AI machine that will trigger fundamental change and how should we cope with the resulting transformation? In exploring such questions we need not only cross the binary divide of system design but also seek alternatives to the cognitive driven deep learning, thereby mitigating turning life into a game of chess.

Smith [34] draws our attention to the implications and challenges of 'automated reckoning systems' in transforming human existence. What captures our imagination, he says, is not so much awe, this time, as the consequence. The exhilaration of world-beating Go programs, serviceable machine translation, and uncanny image recognition are being replaced by the terror that new and perhaps alien AIs are going to take over our jobs, our lives, and our world. If we are to assign tasks to cultivate intelligent human-machine collaboration, we need to understand what kinds of work require what kinds of capacity and this requires an understanding of intelligence and how should we want to live with other forms of intelligence. He says that to address such questions of the future, we need a grip on the past. This requires moving beyond Descartes's idea that understanding must be grounded on "clear and distinct ideas". However, when design creativity is rooted in cognition, it follows the Cartesian thesis of mind-body dualism together with the epistemological thesis of 'objectivity'. Although the Cartesian thesis of objectivity is at the root of the dominant computational paradigm, Simmons [32] takes a broader view Cartesian thesis that moves beyond the aggregate argument of mind-body dualism, and calls our attention to "the mind-body union that constitutes the human being and the role of the senses and passions in serving as the guardians of that union". Simmon's integrative view of Cartesian thesis takes us to the realm of human values and how these values could be reconciled in designing intelligent computer systems.

In seeking to shed a light on the Pandora Box of the Cartesian thesis, the computer scientist Stuart Russell puts forwards a utilitarian argument on the alignment of intelligent machines with human values [36]. The argument is that to the extent that our values are revealed in our behavior, there is a possibility that the machine will be able to "get" most of it. This is not to say that human values will not remain mysterious or that we would agree among ourselves on the nature of values. The issue remains how to deal with differences in human values. Even if a machine is extremely good at optimizing some utility function, the utility function may not align with the human value of utility. Even if we are able to define human values, the issue then is how to encode human values in a programming language, especially when humanity does not agree on common values and even parts we do agree on change with time. Just because there is the potential to create AI aligned systems, it does not mean that we should go ahead with them.

Collins [7] gives us a deep insight into the evolution of AI narratives. He says that there has been a long tradition of philosophical thought about artificial intelligence that has pushed us into thinking about computers as 'artificial brains'. This leads to the AI narrative: if we build machines that approach the complexity and power of the brain, we will have created artificial intelligence. Collins (ibid. 15) sees through the limit of deep learning as evolutionary algorithms when he argues that human evolution works because the conditions of success are set by nature - the survival of the fittest- a 'bottom-up' process, whereas cultural forces are a 'top-down' process. Evolutionary algorithms, however powerful they may be, are essentially 'bottom-up' data processing machines- a brute force- without sensitivity to contexts- social and cultural- i.e. without the socialization process of reaching the level of human intelligence. Smith [34] alerts us that ML architectures of AI, weave the 'world together into an integrated "sub-conceptual" whole' that is the world with which intelligence must come to grips. This integrative conception raises the question as to how to hold thinking and intelligence accountable to the fabulously rich and messy world we inhabit. Smith posits that this integrative goal, however, is starting to be recognized as a necessary ingredient for third-wave AI.

2   Common and Uncommon Voices of AI Futures

On opening the Pandora's box, we hear voices of concerns about the impact and implication of super AI, voices of redemption that seek possible potentials of AI while taming its harmful impact through human intervention, and voices of future with AI that promote AI benefits whilst minimizing adverse impact through algorithmic optimization. Sir Martin Rees [28] of the Centre for the Study of Existential Risk (CSER) [5] reminds us of the existential risk. In the midst of powerful AI technologies, he reminds us of the dangers of new cognition-enhancing drugs, genetics, and 'cyborg' techniques that have the capacity to alter human beings themselves, and alerts us that these dangers aren't of purely scientific concerns but these involve ethics, economics and social policies as well. He further notes that although creativity in science and the arts is open to creative and imaginative innovations, the stakes are now much higher than in the past.

Kevin Rose (2019) notes that whilst the automation of work and elimination of jobs continue to happen quietly out of public view, public mantra of automation agenda continues to focus on building "human-centered A.I.", the "Fourth Industrial Revolution", releasing Workers from onerous, repetitive tasks, using buzz words such as creativity over routine jobs. The AI Now Report [41] provides an insight into social challenges arising from the accelerated integration of powerful artificial intelligence systems into core social institutions. The report highlights the way the manipulation of big data by the Tech elites and law enforcement agencies undermine questions of ethical and meaningful accountability. For example, the report notes some of the serious consequences of testing of AI systems on live populations. These include voice recognition system in the UK designed to detect immigration fraud that ended up cancelling thousands of visas and deporting people in error; the "unsafe and incorrect" cancer treatment recommendations produced by the IBM Watson; the revelation of collaboration of IBM with the New York City Police Department (NYPD) to build an "ethnicity detection" feature to search faces based on race; and deep concerns on the involvement of autonomous cars in killing of drivers and pedestrians. The Report notes that the significant barrier to accountability is the industrial culture of legal secrecy that dominates the "black boxes" culture of AI development in the image of the industrial cultures that create them. This, the Report says that one way to address the questions of social impact and biases in AI systems is to create 'new coalitions between researchers, activists, lawyers, concerned technology workers, and civil society organizations to support the oversight, accountability, and ongoing monitoring of AI systems.' This would cultivate a decision-making process that would go 'beyond a focus on discrete technical fixes to systems', thereby gaining a deeper understanding of the various social contexts to shape the development and use of AI systems. The various perspective of the myths and reality of AI are explored in the international journal, AI&Society [14–16, 19].

3   Narrative of Rational Reason

The voices of rational reason keep reminding us that while new technologies of artificial general intelligence (AGI), synthetic biology, geo-engineering, distributed manufacturing will have very large benefits to humankind, these also pose existential risks for human societies. Knight (2015) says that debates on self-driving cars, robotics, deep learning, and super-artificial intelligence, promoting machine learning and biological networks alert us to the existential threat posed by future AI. These risks include «the creation of new weapons of mass destruction or catastrophe through accidental misuse». Moreover, artificial general intelligence "underlies human capabilities in strategizing, social manipulation, hacking, technology research, and economic productivity». Since the nature of this technological progress is unpredictable, there is a need to undertake proactive policy measures and a regulatory framework to mitigate the risks, even if no such breakthroughs currently appear imminent. Geist [13] says that while recognizing the limitations of the super-intelligence machine, AI-enhanced technologies might still be extremely dangerous due to their potential for amplifying human stupidity. So far as the existential risk is concerned, just by enhancing the familiar twentieth-century technologies, AIs of the future can endanger the future survival of existing societal structures by undermining their precarious strategic balances, for example by making the existing technologies much faster, cheaper and deadlier. If anything, Geist says that machines capable of conceiving and actualizing elaborate plans but lacking self-awareness could be far more dangerous than mechanical analogs of human minds. Voices of reason would also have us see AI in terms of cognitive intelligence, arguing that 'the characterization of intelligence as a spectrum grants no special status to the human brain'. The argument is that 'to date human intelligence has no match in the biological and artificial worlds for sheer versatility, with the abilities "to reason, achieve goals, understand and generate language, perceive and respond to sensory inputs, prove mathematical theorems, play challenging games, synthesize and summarize information, create art and music, and even write histories." This thus makes human intelligence a natural choice for benchmarking the progress of AI [9].

4   Narrative of Instrumental Reason

For data scientists, our brain is constantly required to adapt in a rapidly changing data-driven environment. When seen as predictive analytics, our brain is just a complicated learning machine whose main goal is data compression and interpretation. In the realm of data science, this data processing, occurring automatically in our brains billion of times each second, is seen an elementary step in many data analysis applications. Data science algorithms can be used to scan the data for meaningful patterns in all the different directions and extract the features' combinations along which the separation to meaningful clusters is the most prominent. Davies [12] gives us an insight into the impact and implication of the shifting power of data, when he says that the majority of us are entirely oblivious to what all this data says about us, either individually or collectively. As personal data are becoming a huge driver of the digital economy, the data corporations are becoming 'more and more skillful at tracking our habits and subtly manipulating our behaviors'. In providing personal data to digital corporations in exchange for service, we are not only sacrificing our privacy rights but in the process, we are also allowing 'our feelings, identities, and affiliations to be tracked and analyzed with unprecedented speed'. Moreover, anonymity and secrecy in which personal data are manipulated leave little opportunity to anchor this new capacity of the digital driver in public interest or public debate. Whilst until recent statistic provided a quantitative tool for calculating, measuring and comparing alternative options for public scrutiny and debate, what is most politically significant about the recent shift from a logic of statistics to one of the data, says Davies, is how comfortably it sits with the rise of new digital elite, 'who seek out patterns from vast data banks, but rarely make any public pronouncements, let alone publish any evidence'. It will be tragic if the new digital elite is not aware, let alone rising to the danger of ignorance of social implications of the secrecy of the data and the consequence of its default analysis. In the world of data analytics where secrecy surrounding methods and sources of data is regarded as a competitive advantage, it is doubtful that the 'big data elite' would easily give up their hold of data in favor of public interest and social benefit. In the face of this dominance of data accumulation, he indicates that it is encouraging to note that public bodies such as the Open Data Institute, co-founded by Tim Berners-Lee, have launched campaigns to make data publicly available [35]. Davies says that in spite of the pessimism of credible leverage over the data analytic corporations, there may still be hope that privacy and human rights law could represent a potential obstacle to the extension of data analytics.

As machine learning algorithms manipulate data to support and control institutional and organizational structures, they move beyond their role as computational artifacts, raising concerns about the limits of our 'entrenched assumptions about agency, transparency, and normativity'. Moreover, as Introna [22] observes, algorithms and their actions, are seen as problematic because they are inscrutable, automatic, and subsumed in the flow of daily practices. Although these concerns are voiced in terms of designing algorithmic transparency and openness, others have argued for a more democratic or value-centered design of such actors. Crawford [10] draws our attention to the working of algorithms within 'highly contested online spaces of public discourse, such as YouTube and Facebook, where incompatible perspectives coexist. Yet algorithms are designed to produce clear «winners» from information contests, often with little visibility or accountability for how those contests are designed'. She says that if we widen our perspective beyond the isolated idea of a nonnegotiable algorithmic «black box» to the idea of agonistic pluralism as both a design ideal for engineers and a provocation to understand algorithms in a broader social context: rather than focusing on the calculations in isolation, we need to account for the spaces of contestation where they operate. Ananny [1] proposes a possible approach to move beyond the isolated 'black box' algorithm, to the idea of a networked information algorithms (NIAs) as assemblages of institutionally situated code, practices, and norms with the power to create, sustain, and signify relationships among people and data through minimally observable, semiautonomous action. He argues for 'an empirically grounded, pragmatic ethics of algorithms' that draw on 'algorithmic actions based on perceived similarity and probability'. He observes that 'Algorithmic ethics resemble actuarial ethics: a prediction's legitimacy is based not only on the probable correctness of a current calculation but also on the risk of applying that calculation in the future'.

5 Narrative of Redemptive Reason

From a boarder societal perspective, the future of AI poses challenges of democratic politics, including questions of political agency, accountability, and representation. These matters: how we talk about new technologies and their risks and benefits can significantly influence their development, regulation, and place in public opinion. Balancing AI's potential and its pitfalls, therefore, require navigating this web of associations. Stephen Cave [4] of the Leverhulme Centre for the Future of Intelligence (CFI) [23] visualizes a redemptive curve on the horizon while asking us to take a note of the serious consequences of untamed AI and argues for developing a framework for responsible innovation that seeks to maximize the societal benefit of AI. He cautions that intelligence equal to our own will be created in computers, perhaps within this century. Freed of biological constraints, such as limited memory and slow biochemical processing speeds, machines may eventually become more intelligent than we are – with profound implications for us all. He cites Stephen Hawking as he has put it, "when it eventually does occur, it's likely to be either the best or worst thing ever to happen to humanity, so there's huge value in getting it right." However innovation frameworks have in the past fallen short of technological expectation, raising concerns such as how to engage AI community, social actors, policy makers and commercial sectors in working towards the balance near-term technological benefits and long term social challenges, and how to shape the role and prospects of regulation for social and ethical responsibilities. The connecting of diverse actors from diverse disciplines raises the issue of the 'Value Alignment' as to how to design AI systems that do not inadvertently act in ways inimical to human values.

In the very cognitively rational tradition of the Californian Silicon Valley, the Stanford report [38] quotes Nils J. Nilsson: "Artificial intelligence is that activity devoted to making machines intelligent, and intelligence is that quality that enables an entity to function appropriately and with foresight in its environment." The Report paints a rather rosy picture of AI when it notes that the field of AI is a continual endeavor to push forward the frontier of machine intelligence. It recognizes that "Intelligence" remains a complex phenomenon whose varied aspects have attracted the attention of several different fields of study, including psychology, economics, neuroscience, biology, engineering, statistics, and linguistics. Naturally, it says, that the field of AI has benefitted from the progress made by all of these allied fields. For example, the artificial neural network, which has been at the heart of several AI-based solutions, was originally inspired by thoughts about the flow of information in biological neurons. In the spirit of the narrative of redemptive reason, Pearl and Mackenzie [25] engage us in the discussion for making machines that think, provided we can make machines that are capable of distinguishing between good and evil, at least as reliably as humans. Pearl reminds us of the human intuition of continuing to make changes to the natural world with incredible speed, using our imagination to survive, adapt, and ultimately take over. In taking a creative turn on causality, we are asked to concur that human intuition is grounded in causal, not statistical logic. Although Pearl and Mackenzie conclude with the vision of a thinking machine as a 'wonderful companion for our species' and a 'best gift to humanity', we are reminded of the limit of the rhetoric and the endless touting of the possibilities of Big Data and deep learning. They question the blind faith in Big Data solutions to our societal problems and say that when adaptability is seen through the lens of 'causal blindness', we can see through the flawed mantra that 'correlation is causation'. This questioning of the folklore of machine learning and Big Data coming from an eminent insider of the computer science community is a most welcome contribution to the debate on AI Futures. Although we may admire the historical narrative of causality, the algorithmic vision of redemption would continue to keep human intuition bound by instrumental causality, rather than let it flourish in the tacit dimension

6 Life Is not a Game of Chess

Penny [26] reminds us that chess is a game for which rules can be entirely stated in logical terms within a logically defined closed universe that is endearing to AI in solving logical problems in closed, known, and fully defined formal logical domains. However, not all problems in life are amenable to this closed logical universe. We see this logical conception in critical discourses around computer culture that has centered on networking, databases, interactivity, and subthemes such as collaborative work. These approaches miss a fundamental point: A computer is a machine for manipulating symbols. Implicit in this are two dangerous ideas: that sensing, thinking, and action are separate and separable operations; that thinking happens in an enclosed, abstract, quasi-immaterial space of computation isolated from the world, where symbolic tokens are manipulated per mathematical rules. However, the world is not symbols; we turn the world into symbols for the computer. Humans are the analog to digital interface between the world and the Internet. The world remains outside the computer and outside the symbolic representation. Penny says that the hegemony of the digital and computer products with the world suffocates the broader conception of cognition. He argues that we need to abandon these ideas of dualism if we are to come to grips with the nature of our existence in the world and generate a new discourse on creative cultural practices of arts and science. Penny concludes that postcognitivistic ideas provide a new way of understanding of embodied, mediated and extended interactions- a 'complete understanding of cognition'. As social and cultural milieu accommodates the integration of art and technology, there emerge new cultural practices that incor- porate technologies. But how did we come to the binary division of arts and sciences, thus the narrowing of cognition and commitment to instrumental reason? Penny [26] notes that Enlightenment humanism had played a crucial role in the separation of arts and the sciences, as between passion and reason, thereby leading to the automation of reason and the rise of the digital computer. Citing Antonio Damasio on Descartes' Error, he reminds us of the same propagation of dualism in cognitivism, promulgating cognitivist notions like "thinking is reasoning" and "the brain is a computer". Penny's argument is that: Cognitivism assumes that intelligence consists of logical, mathe- matical manipulation of symbols in an abstract reasoning space, without accommo- dating the possibility of intelligence occurring in the process of ongoing embodied and environmentally engaged doing. Although the functionalist, representationalist, cog- nitivist, computationalist approaches seem to deliver intelligence-as-reasoning, they fail in situated and embodied contexts. He further notes that even when we abandon the distinction between intelligence and skill and accept that much of intelligence is not driven by abstract reasoning of symbols, we are still left to grapple with the perfor- mative and representational modes of embodied human practices, including artistic practice. He alerts us to the danger of slipping into objectivity by calling experience as content since, in any interactive artistic and performative action, the experience of the work is also part of the reflective experience of the activity of the spectator. It is this perspective of interactive performance that transcends the conception of the beliefs of the separation of the self from the world and of the observer and the observed, inherent in the humanistic dualism in science and art. Penny [26: 335] further says that as we exploit computers as tools and resources for artistic/creative/cultural ends or purposes, it behooves upon us to pursue an exploration of these deeper ramifications of values that underlie computational technologies and that insinuate themselves into daily life.

7 AI Futures: Creative Architecture

In seeking insight into creativity and computers, we turn to Maggie Boden [3], who says that computers and creativity make interesting partners, both for understanding human creativity and the production of machine creativity – or 'rather machine 'cre- ativity' – in which the computer at least appears to be creative to some degree.' Boden defines creativity as the ability to come up with ideas or artifacts that are new, sur- prising and valuable. 'Ideas' here include concepts, poems, musical compositions, scientific theories, cookery recipes, choreography, jokes – and so on. 'Artefacts' include paintings, sculptures, steam engines, vacuum cleaners, pottery, origami, penny whistles – and many other things you can name. She says that creativity is grounded in everyday abilities such as conceptual thinking, perception, memory, and reflective self- criticism. Creativity comes in three types: making unfamiliar combinations of familiar ideas, exploration, and transformation. Creative combinations, such as poetic imagery, collage in painting or textile art, and analogies require a rich store of knowledge in the person's mind, and many different ways of moving around within it. Moreover, these novel combinations have to have some intelligible conceptual pathway between them for the combination to 'make sense'. Exploratory creativity of conceptual spaces enables us to see possibilities that we hadn't glimpsed before, and these are normally picked up from one's own culture or peer group but are occasionally borrowed from other cultures. Boden cites the example of a driver who may explore spaces in the countryside rather than driving on the motorway, street artists may add a new trick to their existing repertoire in producing new portraits, or new caricatures, in a way that fits their style. Transformative creativity involves thinking about something, which we couldn't have thought before. This 'impossible' idea can come about only if the creator changes the pre-existing style in some way. For example, a driver rerouting from the motorway to a country road may find certain unexpected restrictions such an animal crossing or certain sections blocked and rerouted, leading to new ways of handling such restrictions. The link between computers and creativity raises a number of issues such as that of whether it is the creativity of the program or the computer, machine consciousness, values, desires or judgment.

As we move from individual connectivity to shared connectivity, from individual focus of human-machine interaction to collective and shared interaction, we move from the notion of intelligence rooted into the individual to collective intelligence rooted and located in the shared collective. Mulgan [24] notes that the 'earlier generation of work on collective intelligence focused primarily on the aggregation of individual insights and inputs for citizen science, web projects such as Wikipedia and crowd-sourcing ideas.' We now see increasing recognition of the limits of the aggregation thesis and the opportunity to explore the symbiotic architecture of collective intelligence emphasizes the combination of 'functional elements of intelligence (models, observation, creativity, memory, judgment, etc.)' and shared action and learning. This symbiosis valorizes 'everyday intelligence for ways of combining formal and informal, codified and tacit, whether in the hospital, classroom or political decision-making.' From Mulgan's argument, we note that formal knowledge has been historically associated with external observation, external power and in the computational realm with representation, whilst the tacit dimension has been seen inaccessible to representation and thus outside the design of formal architectures. The challenge is to design collective intelligence architectures that seek 'new accommodations between formal and tacit, and find new ways to get below the surface of data, and to reconcile the internal and external.'

Creative architectures thus need a better understanding of the transformative and shared experiences of users and designers rather than the algorithmic control and big data. This focus on algorithmic control risks overlooking the central importance of the tacit dimension of knowledge that lies at the root of the cultivation of shared experiences within societal contexts [20]. Tony Simpson [33] notes that in the real business the significance of shared experiences is well understood by companies such as Facebook Data Team researchers and further says that "without the widespread cultivation of shared experiences" there would be no business. Although this sharing model is limited to the business world, it provides an exemplar to design creative architectures for complex social systems such as health, welfare, learning, and training.

Chung and Ng [6] discuss the ways the digital technologies are shaping the nature of the modern self as a transition between the physical and the virtual self that is constructed from multifaceted translations and contributions of lived experiences and personal anecdotes. By considering the transitional self of millennials, they discuss the way this group, 'pegged for their digital adeptness and dependency, have come to embrace the virtual self, an expedited digital presence and a more fluid recognition of spatial inhabitation as part of their ways of being in the digital age.' They observe the way online platforms enable the many facets of reciprocal engagement in the form of one-to-one, one-to-many, many-to-many and many-to-one connections. These interactions provide opportunities to engage in extended social activities in the physical environment concomitant to virtual interactions, becoming a vehicle for the formation and curation of multiple identities of the self and the other. It would be interesting to explore in what ways the interaction of the self with the 'other' is impacted by the increasing convergence of physical and virtual world, and in what ways multiple digital technologies impact the design of creative interaction architectures for collective intelligence in the physical realm.

Commenting on the digital self, Sajber [31] argues that digital platforms – social media, augmented reality games, virtual reality spaces – intend to bring us closer together, but the selves they bring together our selves we can barely recognize. Beyond being networked, and beyond having to resort to a version of selfhood contingently rooted in interaction, we are hardly ever just "one" in digital communications. To frame our technologically-augmented selves amounts to curating a multiplicity: a collection of selves issuing from within and without, assembled both by personal concerns and by the possibilities opened up through the platforms upon which our virtual selves are projected. Such a curation would need to explore the way this interaction impacts in practice, for example, contribute to users' 'deep situated knowledge' in collaborative interaction that may itself be impacted by computational design process as well by the tacit dimension of interactive environment. The 'Re-' Interdisciplinary Network at University of Cambridge provides a framework for exploring wider perspective of curation that lies in questions such as asking 'how and why we repeat, revive, re-enact, restage, reframe, remember, represent, and refer – to whom, when, where and why – and why this a topical question in a digital era [27]. This curation thus 'extends beyond traditional disciplinary boundaries and the university/public divide.' The network recognizes the importance of understanding the mechanisms of translation, adaptation, preservation, memorial, and ritual to brand and social media 'sharing' and the need to 'explore whether different socially-driven practices of repetition might have meaningfully related structures, implications, and dynamics.' The curation of collective intelligence thus needs to bring different knowledge systems and approaches together, new questions, principles, and narrative that might emerge, the role of agency in creating coherence that may exist 'in reciprocity with its own notoriety?'

8 Seeking Creative Milieu

In seeking creative milieu for the curation of collective intelligence, we turn to art and music.

The artist, Ghislaine Boddington [2] sees the digital world in terms of rapidly extending digital connectivity between objects - virtual and physical. She notes that creative industries are developing connected products and services of all types and finally clarity is emerging on the need for technology to compliment us as living physical beings, as industry shifts to a more 'human first' approach. As the Internet of Things (IoT) acquire the potential to link "all the stuff" around us to the "all the stuff" around us, we start to see the evolution of linkage between our bodies, directly to machine interfaces, to data transference, and to interactivity. She calls this the 'Internet of Bodies' - digital linkage between the physical and virtual, human and machine - alive, connected and collective. She explores the development of connected interfaces through a burgeoning cyborg culture and the way this culture is starting to physically integrate with technologies inside their bodies, giving rise to a new space for positive collective intelligence. This visualizing of interaction space challenges the traditional dualism of the brain and body and acknowledges the tacit involvement of holistic body/mind interfaces, the physical with the mental, into all forms of future intelligence.

Vibeke Sorensen [37] posts if computers were developed to augment the Brain, the implication is that the human brain has become part of a system with greatly enhanced data processing and expanded memory. Today, with physical computing and biological sensors as interfaces, 'augmentation' extends beyond the brain to include the entire individual, body, and mind, and beyond the individual to the social group, and beyond that to the natural and built environment, thus encompassing a hybrid physical-digital 'eco-system' on a global scale. It is an increasingly sentient environment that is vast and complex, one we are engaging through sensors and databases, including Big Data, AI, and the Internet of Things (IoT). Are we headed towards a future of the Internet of Living Things (IoLT)? With all living things, there are important ethical issues to be considered as well as concerns for freedom of thought and movement, and intangible qualities such as emotion, empathy, and respect. In design and art, aesthetic concerns fundamentally involve ethics and emotion, as the design must respect and enhance the quality of life for all living things.

Marleen Wynants (2019) asserts that mediation and participation are a core condition for the design of knowledge and engagement since without informed consent and participants understanding the nature of the process, no change is possible. The more individuals express and explore their knowledge through social encounters, narratives, and dialogues, the more crucial tacit knowledge can be shared. Making things disputable is another responsibility. Sharing a space without necessarily having to agree. In society at large, there are very few examples where people feel interconnected and yet at the same time can disagree. In this world of connectedness and non-connectedness but still being critical as it were a shared space of discourse, technical shortcuts to creating and designing collaborative engagement architectures often result in dead-end streets.

Marcelo Velasco et al. [39] explore the effectiveness of mediated communication (internet communication via Tablet) in the context of tacit engagement and mental health. By creating a participatory discourse between interface designers, patients (adult women living with chronic mental health) interacting with their families and friends, students (art and media faculty) acting both as witnesses and participants, policymakers as witnesses, they have designed an exemplar of a mediated architecture for collective intelligence within a broader vision of tacit engagement in mental health. The exemplary illustrates how a creative technological mediated architecture can be used to provide external social support and contact with the outside world, in which these pieces of plastic (laptops-tablets) act as "portals" for the patients to access the outside world. This collaborative architecture may open up opportunities for community engagement to tackle the isolation suffered by mental health patients.

9 Towards a Symbiotic Vision

The deep concern of instrumental reason articulated by Weizenbaum [40] continues its march in the guise of Big Data machine learning algorithms. We see an increasing manipulation of data to support and control human interactions, institutional and organizational structures. Moving beyond their (algorithms) role as computational artifacts, what concerns us is how these algorithms take account of the limits of our 'entrenched assumptions about agency, transparency, and normativity'. Reflecting on these issues Gill [14, 17, 18] draws our attention to data manipulation practices as problematic because they are inscrutable, automatic, and subsumed in the flow of daily practices. Beyond the issues of algorithmic transparency and openness, calculative practices have a serious impact on how domains of knowledge and expertise are produced, and how such domains of knowledge become internalized, affecting institutional governance. Moreover, these algorithms not only work within 'highly contested' online spaces of public discourse, they often perform with little visibility or accountability. This is an argument to move out of the 'black box' notion of the algorithm, and promote the idea of 'networked information algorithms' (NIAs); assemblages of institutionally situated code, practices, and norms with the power to create, sustain, and signify relationships among people and data through minimally observable, semi-autonomous action. If AI reflections are to move out of the 'black box' of instrumental reason, we need to learn from the performance practices of artists, where the performance of data is seen not just in terms of its transformation into information, but also in terms of the interactivity between the artist and the audience. This interactivity itself becomes a tool for the continued evolution of an artist and a scientist and the amalgamation of their partnership. In the end, performance is about raising awareness of the interconnectivity of everything and everyone. Technology is or should be utilized to amplify the experience and/or the range of influence. In the midst of the fascination with digital technology, we are cautioned to remember that performance of data in the hands of creative artists and scientists embodies social/cultural and spatial intelligence that conforms to the living. The single story of the universality of instrumental reason [40] has so penetrated the culture of computation and machine learning that questions and challenges of human purpose are either ignored or misrepresented as if every aspect of the real world can be formalized and represented in term of a logical calculus. Weizenbaum [40] points out that those who aspire to equate machine intelligence to human intelligence keep convincing themselves that by outplaying human go players, composing music or creating human-like social robots, machines have either already or soon going to outsmart human beings. This belief in machine intelligence sees no distinction between the functional machine and the knowing and imaginative human being. It seems that in this pursuit of machine intelligence, the validation of human intelligence has been reduced to the display of technological wonders, just as scientific knowledge has been reduced to wonders of data science.

Cooley [8] and Rosenbrock [30] concur with Weizenbaum's concerns and misgivings of instrumental reason and propose an alternative human-centered paradigm of intelligent systems design. This paradigm, rooted in 'purpose' enshrines the richness of the tacit dimension of the knowledge thereby overcoming the instrumental limits of the 'causal model'. In this human-centered paradigm, humans and machines collaborate in ways that make the best of the computational capacity of the machine and knowledge of the human - in other words, the human and machine enter and act in a symbiotic and interactive relationship that valorizes human knowledge and computational resources. Cooley (ibid.) draws our attention to data-information-knowledge-wisdom-action cycle when he says that data (calculation end) suitably organized and acted upon may become information. Information absorbed, understood and applied by people, may become knowledge. Knowledge frequently applied in a domain may become wisdom, and wisdom (judgment end) the basis for positive action. Howard Rosenbrock reflects on his LuShi Hill journey and wonders what would have happened if science had followed the path of 'purpose' rather then the 'causal' road. In this human-centered vision, the choice of purpose and intelligent design is facilitated by judgment, which in turn is enriched by cultural wisdom. To the followers of Tao, making a choice (decision making) is part of the analytical judgment process [11]. Options and choices are subliminally analyzed and the best alternative is selected in the given circumstances. In this sense, decision-making is data and evidence-driven while judging is "impression" driven. Decision-making process is result oriented while judging is person oriented. Moreover, when giving judgment, you are not a part of the issue and supposed to be an outsider and with no bias. You are supposed to hear both the sides and tell who is right or wrong. Here, you do not choose what is right for you but tell who is right. Again to followers of Tao, Judgment is a social invention: societies use systems of judgment to maintain "order" and a balance between its membership [29]. Judgment is all about measuring what is right and what is wrong. No human judgment system can be perfect. When perfect, it would absolutely mean no free will could exist. When perfect, there would be no questions, no grey areas, no wrong actions, merely only always right actions. Groumpos [21] alerts us to the limit of judgment without wisdom. He says that many times in human history people have ignored and buried memories, knowledge, experiences, practices and habit of the past and have focused on the new and previously unimaginable bright future on the horizon. Whilst judgment can be seen as the application of knowledge to differentiate between the "right" and "wrong" facts, wisdom is about the use of knowledge to perceive and choose the "right" action or to avoid the "wrong" action. Wisdom here may involve factors such as speculation, feelings, and moral or ethical values not only of self but also of the other. Citing the example of dropping atomic bombs on Hiroshima and Nagasaki, Groumpos [21] notes that in terms of applied knowledge, the judgment of dropping the bomb may be obvious to their creators (self), but in terms of whether applying that knowledge was wise or not is still unclear and subject to intense debate when seen from the gaze of the other (those affected by it). The challenge of creating frameworks and models of wise decision-making and wise judgments is that we should never witness humanity becoming too trapped by its artifacts judgment systems, especially at risk of being trapped by codified judgment systems.

10 Conclusions

Whilst the accelerated integration of powerful artificial intelligence systems into our world opens up opportunities for harnessing their potential for creative innovations, we also face challenges of existential risk by our paying 'misplaced deference to machines'. As AI technologies penetrate in the functioning of our societies, they offer the potential for the transition from individual connectivity to shared connectivity, from the individual focus of human-machine interaction to collective and shared interaction. This transition provides a challenge and opportunity to design creative intelligent tools and move beyond the notion of intelligence embodied into the individual to collective intelligence embedded in the shared collective. However, Once Pandora's box of the technology of 'Reckoning' and the instrumental reason is open, we would require creative intelligence and judgment to harness its potential and wisdom to shape it. From a broader societal horizon beyond the conceptual and methodological preoccupation of academic circles, there is a need for an ongoing conversation between technology and society. This then also poses a challenge to the design of intelligent interactive and collaborative tools and systems that facilitate this conversation. Ultimately the AI machine raises the question of values we hold and judgments we make about shaping the nature and path of technology. The human-centered paradigm, rooted in the notions of purpose, tacit dimension and symbiosis provides a framework for designing intelligent system for facilitating creativity and judgment. In pursuing the current dream of the AI heaven, we need to be vigilant of not making the Baconian error of technological interventions without tempering them with human wisdom and mitigating their 'unwanted but foreseeable side effects.' The challenge is that we should mold AI futures for the common good of people and societies rather than letting technological determinism becoming a single story of 'singularity'.

Learning never exhausts the mind
Leonardo Di Vinci

References

1. Ananny, M.: Toward an ethics of algorithms: convening, observation, probability, and timeliness. Sci. Technol. Human Values **41**(1), 93–117 (2016). https://doi.org/10.1177/0162243915606523
2. Boddington, G.: The Internet of bodies. In: Tacit Engagement in the Digital Age, International Conference, University of Cambridge, 26–28 June 2019. www.crassh.cam.ac.uk/evets/28385
3. Boden, M.A., Research Professor of Cognitive Science Margaret A Boden: The Creative Mind: Myths and Mechanisms. Routledge, London (2004)
4. Cave, S.: Leverhulme Centre for the Future of Intelligence. http://lcfi.ac.uk/
5. Centre for the Study of Existential Risk (CSER). http://cser.org/
6. Chung, S., Ng, M.: Engagements across a multiplicity of millennial identities. In: Tacit Engagement in the Digital Age, International Conference, University of Cambridge, 26–28 June 2019. www.crassh.cam.ac.uk/evets/28385
7. Collins, H.: Artifictional Intelligence: Against Humanity's Surrender to Computers. Polity Press, Cambridge (2018)
8. Cooley, M.J.: Architect or Bee? Hogarth Press, London (1987)
9. CRASSH: A symposium on technological displacement of white-collar employment: political and social implications. Wolfson Hall, Churchill College, Cambridge (2016)
10. Crawford, K.: Can an algorithm be agonistic ten scenes from life in calculated publics. In: Ziewitz, M. (ed.) Governing Algorithms, Special Issue of Science, Technology, and Human Values (STHV), vol. 41, issue 1. SAGE Publications, London (2016)
11. Daily Tao/136 – Judgement [Web log post], 16 May 2013. https://mymostlyunfabulouslife.com/2013/05/16/daily-tao-136-judgement/
12. Davies, W.: How statistics lost their power – and why we should fear what comes next. The Guardian (2017). https://www.theguardian.com/politics/2017/jan/19/crisis-of-statistics-big-data-democracy. Accessed 28 Apr 2017
13. Geist, E.M.: Is artificial intelligence really an existential threat to humanity? (2015). http://thebulletin.org/artificial-intelligence-reallyexistential-threat-humanity8577. Accessed 8 Jan 2016
14. Gill, K.S.: Artificial super intelligence: beyond rhetoric. AI Soc. **31**(2), 137 (2016). https://doi.org/10.1007/s00146-016-0651-x
15. Gill, K.S.: Artificial intelligence: looking though the Pygmalion Lens. AI Soc. **33**(6), 459–465 (2018). https://doi.org/10.1007/s00146-018-0866-0
16. Gill, K.S.: Hermeneutic of performing knowledge. AI Soc. **32**(2), 149–156 (2017)
17. Gill, K.S.: Preface. AI Soc. **21**(1–2), 5–6 (2007)
18. Gill, K.S. (ed.): Human Machine Symbiosis. Springer, London (1996). https://doi.org/10.1007/978-1-4471-3247-9
19. Gill, K.S.: Artifictional intelligence: against humanity's surrender to computers. AI Soc. (2019). https://doi.org/10.1007/s00146-018-0873-1
20. Gill, S.P.: Tacit Engagement: Beyond Interaction. Springer, Cham (2015). https://doi.org/10.1007/978-3-319-21620-1
21. Groumpos, P.: Deep learning vs. wise learning: a critical and challenging overview. In: IFAC International Conference on International Stability, Technology and Culture, TECIS 2016, Durres, Albania, 26–28 October 2016

22. Introna, L.: Algorithms, governance, and governmentality on governing academic writing. In: Knight, W. (ed.) What Robots and AI Learned in 2015, 29 December 2015. MIT Technical Review (2016). http://www.technologyreview.com/news/544901/what-robots-and-ai-learned-in-2015/. Accessed 5 Jan 2016

23. Leverhulme Centre for the Future of Artificial Intelligence. http://cser.org/leverhulme-centre-for-the-future-of-intelligence/

24. Mulgan, G.: The dialectics of tacit and formal knowledge: or how can collective intelligence orchestrate tacit knowledge of different kinds? In: Tacit Engagement in the Digital Age, International Conference, University of Cambridge, 26–28 June 2019. www.crassh.cam.ac.uk/evets/28385

25. Pearl, J., Mackenzie, D.: The Book of Why: The New Science of Cause and Effect. Basic Book, New York (2018)

26. Penny, S.: Making Sense: Cognition, Computing, Art, and Embodiment. The MIT Press, Cambridge (2017)

27. 'Re-'Interdisciplinary Network 2018 (n.d.). http://www.crassh.cam.ac.uk/programmes/re-interdisciplinary-network

28. Rees, M.: The global village will have its village idiots. Conversation with Sir Martin Rees (2012). https://www.theeuropean-magazine.com/31-rees-sir-martin/920-existential-risks-and-the-fear-of-global-apocalypse

29. Releasing Judgment – Living with No Judgement [Web log post], 9 July 2019. https://personaltao.com/taoism/no-judgement-releasing-judgment/

30. Rosenbrock, H.: Machines with a Purpose. Oxford University Press, Oxford (1990)

31. Sajber, K.: The expressivity of virtual selves. In: Tacit Engagement in the Digital Age, International Conference, University of Cambridge, 26–28 June 2019. www.crassh.cam.ac.uk/evets/28385

32. Simmons, A.: Re-humanizing descartes. Philos. Exch. **41**(1) (2013). Art. 2

33. Simpson, T.D.: The subjectless shared experiences of lookalike audiences. In: Tacit Engagement. Tacit Engagement in the Digital Age, International Conference, University of Cambridge, 26–28 June 2019. www.crassh.cam.ac.uk/evets/28385

34. Smith, B.C.: The Promise of Artificial Intelligence: Reckoning and Judgment. MIT Press (2019, forthcoming)

35. The ODI – Open Data Institute. (n.d.). https://theodi.org/

36. Wolchover, N.: Concerns of an artificial intelligence pioneer. Quanta Mag. (2015). https://www.quantamagazine.org/artificial-intelligence-aligned-with-human-values-qa-with-stuart-russell-20150421/

37. Sorensen, V.: Art, technology, and the Internet of Living Things (IoLT). In: Tacit Engagement in the Digital Age, International Conference, University of Cambridge, 26–28 June 2019. www.crassh.cam.ac.uk/evets/28385

38. Stanford University: "Artificial Intelligence and Life in 2030." One Hundred Year Study on Artificial Intelligence: Report of the 2015–2016 Study Panel, Stanford University, Stanford, CA, September 2016. http://ai100.stanford.edu/2016-report. Accessed 9 July 2017

39. Velasco, M., et al.: Machine learning and social good - a Chilean experience. In: Tacit Engagement in the Digital Age, International Conference, University of Cambridge, 26–28 June 2019. www.crassh.cam.ac.uk/evets/28385

40. Weizenbaum, J.: Computer Power and Human Reason: From Judgment to Calculation. W. H. Freeman, Francisco (1976)

41. Whittaker, M., et al.: AI Now Report 2018. AI Now Institute, New York University (2018). https://ainowinstitute.org/AI_Now_2018_Report.pdf

Artificial Intelligence: Issues, Challenges, Opportunities and Threats

Peter P. Groumpos[✉]

Laboratory for Automation and Robotics, Department of Electrical
and Computer Engineering, University of Patras, 26500 Rion, Greece
groumpos@ece.upatras.gr

Abstract. The world is experiencing a period of instability in a range of pillar institutions in the international system. These instabilities and unsustainable systems may have serious implications for humanity. Catastrophic physical phenomena are on the rise, lately and many say that this is due to human disrespect to the environment. Urgently valuable and sustainable solutions are needed. One scientific approach to address these challenging questions is Artificial Intelligence (AI). Theories of AI are reviewed. Machine learning (ML), Neural Networks (NN) and Deep Learning (DL) are briefly presented. Certain criticisms of AI and DL are carefully analyzed. A number of challenges and opportunities of AI are identified. The future of AI and potential threats of it are discussed. Artificial Intelligence (AI) and Deep Learning (DL) are relying mainly on data analysis without taking into consideration the human nature. Theories of Fuzzy Cognitive Maps (FCM) seem to provide a useful tool in developing new AI theories answering this problem.

Keywords: Fuzzy Cognitive Maps · Decision making · Energy efficiency · Human cognition

1 Introduction

Everybody looks back to a world that does not remain the same. Furthermore no one can deny that the world is changing and changing very fast. Technology, education, science, environment, health, communicating habits, entertainment, eating habits, dress - there is hardly anything in life that is not changing, some changes we like, while others create fear and anxiety. Everywhere there is a feeling of insecurity. What will happen to us tomorrow? What will happen to our children? are questions that frequently been asked, [1]. Either we like it or not one thing, however, is clear. It is no more possible to live in the way we have been living so far. It seems that now the entire fabric of life will have to be changed. Life will have to be redesigned. The life of the individual, the social structure, the working conditions and governance—all will have to be replanned [1]. Why all these are happening? The human world evolves and progresses by applying knowledge either been known for long time or of new one been generated every day. The knowledge been used is derived from studying, analyzing, observing, experimenting, simulating the phenomena of nature and the human processes. The human's perceptions, understanding and ability to model real complex

© Springer Nature Switzerland AG 2019
A. G. Kravets et al. (Eds.): CIT&DS 2019, CCIS 1083, pp. 19–33, 2019.
https://doi.org/10.1007/978-3-030-29743-5_2

dynamic systems enable us to develop theories, methods, products and processes, and make the necessary policies and decisions that are needed to solve the problems of our everyday life. One main reason is that new scientific and technological results and thus new knowledge are developed at an exponential rate. As a result of this, large amount of data is created every day. Digital data is now everywhere—in every scientific and technical sector, in every economy, in every government, in every "organization" and user of digital technology. The flood of data can overwhelm human insight and analysis, but the computing advances that helped deliver it have also conjured powerful new tools for making sense of it all. It is clear that keeping up with the rate of digital advancement - for example, automation, harnessing big data, emerging technologies and cyber security as well other issues such: innovation, regional development, international stability, global coherence and sustainable growth- will pose significant challenges for the future [2]. We will need dynamic thinkers and policymakers to balance established needs, technological growth and provided technological advances.

Our objective is either to control (and exploit) the natural phenomena, or to create human-made "objects" with the desired characteristics and properties which essentially will be useful to humankind. In order to address all these challenges new scientific fields have been emerged during the last 50 years or so. Artificial Intelligence (AI) is one of them. [3–9]. Many believed (and still do) that AI will provide solutions to all problems of the world. However, is it so? In this invited plenary paper, a critical overview of AI is attempted and presented. In Sect. 2, a historical review of AI is presented. In Sect. 3 the basics of AI are presented and in Sect. 4 Deep Learning is described. In Sects. 5 and 6 issues concerning opportunities and threats of fuzzy logic and finally in Sects. 7 and 8 the author attempts to answer issues raised in the previous sections and useful conclusions are offered.

2 Artificial Intelligence- The Origin Story

2.1 The Idea of AI- The Myth

The idea of Artificial Intelligence (AI) was not born in the modern era. In fact, its origins could be traced back to Greek mythology or even before. Indeed, the history of Artificial Intelligence (AI) began in antiquity, with myths, stories and rumors of artificial beings endowed with intelligence or consciousness by master craftsmen. AI began with "an ancient wish to forge the gods. Aristotle (384–322 B.C.) was the first to formulate a precise set of laws governing the rational part of the mind. He developed an informal system of syllogisms for proper reasoning, which in principle allowed one to generate conclusions mechanically, given initial premises. "Logic is new and necessary reasoning", Aristotle [10, 11].

Symbolized with a hammer, Hephaestus the Greek god of blacksmiths, sculptors, metallurgy, fire and volcanoes. He is the blacksmith of the Olympus and makes weapons for all gods. He has invented countless interesting "machines," which made his legendary stories all the more intriguing. Hephaestus was the son of Hera and Zeus. He was born weak and crippled, displeasing Zeus, so much, so that he was thrown down the Mountain of Olympus. He was saved by people of the Aegean island Lemnos and grew up to become a blacksmith. As revenge, Hephaestus made a magical throne that trapped whoever sat on it. The throne trapped Hera successfully and helped Hephaestus return to Olympus. The idea of a machine throne has characteristics of artificial intelligence (AI): to be helpful for people to achieve a certain goal, be able to operate automatically and be programmed in advance to react in different ways depending on the situation.

Thus, the idea of artificial intelligence (AI) was not born in the modern era. In fact, its origins could be traced back to Greek mythology. The seeds of modern AI were planted by classical philosophers who attempted to describe the process of human thinking as the mechanical manipulation of symbols. This work culminated in the invention of the programmable digital computer in the 1940s, a machine based on the abstract essence of mathematical reasoning [12, 13]. This device and the ideas behind it inspired a handful of scientists to begin seriously discussing the possibility of building an electronic brain.

2.2 The New Era-AI as a Scientific Field

In spite of all the current hype, AI is not a new scientific field of study, but it has its ground in the fifties. If we exclude the pure philosophical reasoning path that goes from the Ancient Greek philosophers (Aristotle, Plato..) to Hobbes, Leibniz, and Pascal, AI as we know it (as was discussed above in Sect. 2.1) has been officially started in 1956 at Dartmouth College, where the most eminent experts gathered to brainstorm on intelligence theories and simulation. But even before this workshop that gave birth officially to AI there are other related studies that can be considered as the front runners of the AI. In 1308 Catalan poet and theologian Ramon Llull publishes *Ars generalis ultima* (The Ultimate General Art), further perfecting his method of using paper-based mechanical means to create new knowledge from combinations of concepts. In 1666 mathematician and philosopher Gottfried Leibniz publishes *Dissertatio de arte combinatorial* (On the Combinatorial Art), following Ramon Llull in proposing an alphabet of human thought and arguing that all ideas are nothing but combinations of a relatively small number of simple concepts.

3 Basics of Artificial Intelligence

Just what do people mean by Artificial Intelligence (AI)? The term has never had clear boundaries. The concept of what defines AI has changed over time, but at the core there has always been the idea of building machines which are capable of thinking like humans. When it was introduced at a seminal 1956 workshop at Dartmouth College, it was taken broadly to mean making a machine behave in ways that would be called intelligent if seen in a human. It is true that human beings have proven uniquely capable of interpreting the physical world around us and using the information we pick up to effect change. If we want to build machines at least to help us do this more efficiently, then it makes sense to use ourselves as a blueprint. Artificial Intelligence's progress has been staggering. Efforts to advance AI concepts over the past 40–45 years have resulted in some truly amazing innovations. Medical diagnosis, electronic trading, e-learning, speech recognition, smart cities, robot control, remote sensing, healthcare, manufacturing, education, transportation, Big data, data mining, deep learning and autonomous vehicles are just some of the incredible applications emerging from AI development.

To understand some of the deeper concepts, such as data mining, natural language processing, and driving software, we need to know the three basic AI concepts: (1) Machine Learning (ML) (2) Neural Networks (NN) and (3) Deep Learning (DL).

3.1 Machine Learning

Machine learning is one of the fastest growing and most exciting fields out there, and deep learning represents its true bleeding edge. Machine Learning (ML) is a branch of the larger discipline of Artificial Intelligence (AI), which involves the design and construction of computer applications or systems that are able to learn based on their data inputs and/or outputs. Basically, a machine learning system learns by experience; that is, based on specific training, the system will be able to make generalizations based on its exposition to a number of cases and then be able to perform actions after new or unforeseen events.

Artificial Intelligence (AI) and Machine Learning (ML) are the two trending topics for the last 30 years. Both terms pop up frequently now days, especially when discussing Big Data, analytics and other very interesting and challenging topics. Even these are very different; many sources seem to use them interchangeably. However, are different.

Artificial Intelligence (AI) is the broader concept of machines that are able to carry out tasks in a way we would consider intelligent, while Machine Learning (ML) is one of the current applications of Artificial Intelligent based on the idea that we should be able to give machines data access and with that information, machines should be able to learn more themselves. The discipline of Machine Learning (ML) also incorporates other data analysis disciplines, ranging from predictive analytics and data mining to pattern recognition. And a variety of specific algorithms are used for this purpose, frequently organized in taxonomies, these algorithms can be used depending on the type of input required (a list of algorithms can be found in Wikipedia based on their type). Machine learning, along with many other disciplines within the field of artificial intelligence and cognitive systems, is gaining popularity, and it may in the not so distant future have a colossal impact on the software industry.

3.2 Neural Networks

The development of neural networks is the key to make machines understand the world as we do, without losing the speed, accuracy and lack of bias. Neural networks are a set of algorithms, modeled loosely after the human brain, that are designed to recognize patterns. They interpret sensory data through a kind of machine perception, labeling or clustering raw input. The patterns they recognize are numerical, contained in vectors, into which all real-world data, be it images, sound, text or time series, must be translated. Over the last few decades, neural network (NN) has seen successful development that has wide applications due to the effort of industrial and academic communities. With the powerful approximation ability of NN, it has been evolved into many promising fields, such as modeling and identification of complex and nonlinear systems and optimization and automatic control.

Specifically, the state-of-the-art deep learning NN, allows richer intermediate representations to be learnt, eliminating the effort of feature engineering. For different theories and applications, the design philosophy of NN architecture can be different. Nevertheless, generally NN can be expressed as a weighted sum of several kernel functions, of which the weights can be tuned to approximate an arbitrary smooth or continuous nonlinear function. However, to reveal the fundamental representations and behaviors of NN as a complex system while it is applied into real-world control applications is still a problem to be explored. Understanding this problem could not only promote better understanding of the underlying mechanisms of NN, but also provide a possibility to design a universal NN solution in various real-world applications.

3.3   Deep Learning

Today Deep Learning (DL) is believed by most people that is the new big trend in machine learning [14]. But is it so? It had many recent successes in computer vision, automatic speech recognition and natural language processing. DL is a branch of machine learning based on a set of known algorithms that attempt to model high-level abstractions in data, by using multiple processing layers, with complex structures or otherwise, composed of multiple non-linear transformations [15]. Research in this area attempts to make better representations and create models and particularly software tools that learn these representations from large-scale unlabeled data. Deep Learning (DL) software attempts to mimic the activity in layers of neurons in the neocortex, the wrinkly 80 percent of the brain where thinking occurs [16]. The software learns, in a very real sense, to recognize patterns in digital representations of sounds, images, and other data.

The basic idea - that software can simulate the neocortex's large array of neurons in an artificial "neural network" - is decades old, and it has led to as many disappointments as breakthroughs. But because of improvements in mathematical formulas and increasingly powerful computers, computer scientists can now model many more layers of virtual neurons than ever before. DL actually is visiting again Artificial Intelligence (AI) and Artificial Neural Networks (ANN) with the objective to reformulate them given all recent scientific developments. Indeed, DL has been characterized as a buzzword, or a rebranding of neural networks and Artificial Intelligence [14] and [15].

Some of the representations are inspired by advances in neuroscience and are loosely based on interpretation of information processing and communication patterns in a nervous system, such as neural coding which attempts to define a relationship between various stimuli and associated neuronal responses in the brain. There are various DL architectures such as deep neural networks, convolutional deep neural networks, deep belief networks, recurrent neural networks among other ones which are actually the same ones as those was developed in AI and ANN. A number of reviews of DL and for certain branches of AI has been reported recently. A recent one, "Deep Learning in neural networks: An overview", by Schmidhuber provides a thorough and extensive overview [17].

This historical survey compactly summarizes relevant work, much of it from the previous millennium. Shallow and Deep Learners are distinguished by the depth of their credit assignment paths, which are chains of possibly learnable, causal links between actions and effects.

4 Deep Learning

Some believe that Deep Learning (DL) is a new area of Machine Learning research. It has been introduced with the objective of moving ML closer to one of its original goals: Artificial Intelligence. Deep Learning is nowadays one of the most highly sought-after skills in tech. In this section we aim to give an insight on what deep learning is and how it can promote or not the development of Artificial Intelligence.

Extending deep learning into applications beyond speech and image recognition will require more conceptual and software breakthroughs, not to mention many more advances in processing power. And we probably won't see machines we all agree can think for themselves for years, perhaps decades—if ever. But for now, says Peter Lee, head of Microsoft Research USA, "deep learning has reignited some of the grand challenges in artificial intelligence."

While AI and machine learning may seem like interchangeable terms, AI is usually considered the broader term, with machine learning and the other two AI concepts a subset of it. However lately, Deep Learning (DL) has been promoted as a new scientific field which according to Peter Lee, head of Microsoft Research USA, "deep learning has reignited some of the grand challenges in artificial intelligence."

4.1 Architectures and Methods

The two key aspects of DL are: (1) models consisting of multiple layers or stages of nonlinear information processing; and (2) methods for supervised or unsupervised learning of feature representation at successively higher, more abstract layers. DL is in the intersections among the research areas of neural networks, artificial intelligence, graphical modeling, optimization, pattern recognition, and signal processing. Three important reasons for its popularity of today are the drastically increased chip processing abilities (e.g., general-purpose graphical processing units or GPGPUs), the significantly increased size of data used for training, and the recent advances in machine learning and signal/information processing research. These advances have enabled the DL methods to effectively exploit complex, compositional nonlinear functions, to learn distributed and hierarchical feature representations, and to make effective use of both labeled and unlabeled data [18].

There are various DL Methods and architectures:

1. Artificial neural networks (ANN)
2. Deep neural networks (DNN)
3. Convolutional deep neural networks (CDNN)
4. Deep belief networks (DBN)
5. Recurrent (or recursive) neural networks (RNN) and
6. Long short-term memory (LSTM).

The above six and more DL methods are fully analyzed and presented on a number of books and/or articles [15, 19–26].

4.2   A Historical Overview

Although a historical survey is usually given in the beginning of a thematic topic, here, a historical perspective was chosen to be given at the end of this DL overview. This is due to the fact that it will be shown the deep roots and strong relations of DL to AI and ANN. The first general, working learning algorithm for supervised deep feedforward multilayer Perceptron was published by Ivakhnenko [27]. A paper again by Ivakhnenko already described a deep network with 8 layers trained by the Group method of data handling algorithm which is still popular in the current millennium [28]. Thus, deep learning (DL) is an upspring scientific field from AI and ANN. These ideas were implemented in a computer identification system "Alpha", which demonstrated the learning process. Other DL working architectures, specifically those built from artificial neural networks, date back to the Neocognitron introduced by Kunihiko Fukushima (1980) [29]. Actually, the ANNs themselves date back even further. Warren McCulloch and Walter Pitts (1943) created a computational model for neural networks based on mathematics and algorithms called threshold logic and further are inspired by the 1959 biological model proposed by Nobel laureates David H. Hubel & Torsten Wiesel (1959), who found two types of cells in the primary visual cortex: simple cells and complex cells. Many artificial neural networks can be viewed as cascading models of cell types inspired by these biological observations. The challenge was how to train networks with multiple layers [30, 31]. In 1989, Yann LeCun et al. (1989) were able to apply the standard backpropagation algorithm, which had been around as the reverse mode of automatic differentiation since 1970, to a deep neural network with the purpose of recognizing handwritten ZIP codes on mail. Despite the success of applying the algorithm, the time to train the network on this dataset was approximately 3 days, making it impractical for general use.

In 1993, J. Schmidhuber's neural history compressor Schmidhuber implemented as an unsupervised stack of Recurrent Neural Networks solved a "Very Deep Learning" task that requires more than 1,000 subsequent layers in an RNN unfolded in time [32]. In 1995, Brendan Frey demonstrated that it was possible to train a network containing six fully connected layers and several hundred hidden units using the wake-sleep algorithm, which was co-developed with Peter Dayan and Geoffrey Hinton [33]. However, training still took two days.

The real impact of DL in industry apparently began in the early 2000's, when CNNs already processed an estimated 10% to 20% of all the checks written in the US in the early 2000's. However industrial applications of large-scale speech recognition started around 2010. In late 2009, Li Deng invited Geoffrey Hinton to work with him and colleagues at Microsoft Research to apply DL to speech recognition. They co-organized the 2009 NIPS Workshop on DL for Speech Recognition. The workshop was motivated by the limitations of deep generative models of speech, and the possibility that the big-compute, big-data era warranted a serious try of deep neural nets. It was believed that pre-training DNNs using generative models of deep belief nets would overcome the main difficulties of neural nets encountered in the 1990s. However, this could not be scientifically proven although the findings were very promising.

This finding was verified by several other major speech recognition research groups. Further, the nature of recognition errors produced by the two types of systems was found to be characteristically different, offering technical insights into how to integrate DL into the existing highly efficient, run-time speech decoding system deployed by all major players in speech recognition industry [34]. The history of this significant development in DL has been described and analyzed in recent books and articles as is the case with the article of Deng and Yu [11]. The last 2–3 years advances in hardware have also been important in enabling the renewed interest in DL. In particular, powerful graphics processing units (GPUs) are well-suited for the kind of number crunching, matrix/vector math involved in machine learning. GPUs have been shown to speed up training algorithms by orders of magnitude, bringing running times of weeks back to days. All the above historical remarks make DL not a totally new scientific field.

4.3   Discussions and Some Criticism on Deep Learning

As it was said before, many scientists strongly believe that DL has been characterized as a buzzword, or a rebranding of neural networks and AI.

Given the far-reaching implications of artificial intelligence coupled with the realization that DL is emerging as one of its most powerful techniques, the subject is understandably attracting various discussions, criticism and comments, in many cases, in a very complicated ensemble of techniques, ranging from the statistical technique of Bayesian inference to not only from outside the field of computer science itself but also from the computer science.

A main criticism of DL concerns the lack of a fundamental theory surrounding many of the methods. Learning in the most DL architectures is implemented using gradient descent; while gradient descent has been understood for a while now, the theory surrounding other algorithms, such as contrastive divergence is less clear. (i.e., Does it converge? If so, how fast? What is it approximating?). DL methods are often looked at as a black box, with most confirmations done empirically, rather than theoretically.

Other scientists point out that DL should be looked at as a step towards realizing a strong AI, and not as an all-encompassing new method. Despite the power of DL methods, they still lack much of the functionality needed for realizing this goal entirely. Research psychologist Gary Marcus has noted that: "Realistically, DL is only part of the larger challenge of building intelligent machines. Such techniques lack ways of representing causal relationships, have no obvious ways of performing logical inferences, and they are also still a long way from integrating abstract knowledge, such as information about what objects are, what they are for, and how they are typically used. The most powerful A.I. systems, like Watson, use techniques "like DL as just one element deductive reasoning." [35].

To the extent that such a viewpoint implies, without intending to, that DL will ultimately constitute nothing more than the primitive discriminatory levels of comprehensive future machine intelligence, a recent pair of speculations regarding art and artificial intelligence offers an alternative and more expansive outlook [36]. The first such speculation is that it might be possible to train a machine vision stack to perform the sophisticated task of discriminating between "old master" and amateur figure drawings; and the second is that such sensitivity might in fact represent the rudiments of non-trivial machine empathy.

Nevertheless, Deep Learning is a very useful tool in creating new knowledge.

5 Challenges and Opportunities of Artificial Intelligence

Artificial intelligence capabilities are growing at an unprecedented rate. Also, all other related to AI technologies (machine learning, neural networks), are following the same speed of advancement. These technologies have many widely beneficial applications, ranging from machine translation to medical image analysis. Countless more such applications are being developed and can be expected over the long term. Less attention has historically been paid to the ways in which artificial intelligence can be used maliciously. This report surveys the landscape of potential security threats from malicious uses of artificial intelligence technologies, and proposes ways to better forecast, prevent, and mitigate these threats. We analyze, but do not conclusively resolve, the question of what the long-term equilibrium between attackers and defenders will be. We focus instead on what sorts of attacks we are likely to see soon if adequate defenses are not developed.

Artificial Intelligence (AI) presents an important and remarkable paradigm shift for science. Science is traditionally founded on theories and models, most often formalized with mathematical formulas and complex equations handcrafted by theoretical scientists and refined through observations and experiments. Machine learning, an important branch of Artificial Intelligence (AI), focuses on learning from data. Similarly, data mining and deep learning (DL). This leads to a fundamentally different approach in modeling complex dynamic systems (CDS): we step back and focus on the design of algorithms capable of building models from data. While in general are developed by humans lately many models themselves are designed by machines and independently of humans. This has been more obvious lately with deep learning (DL), which requires little engineering by humans and is responsible for many of Artificial Intelligence's spectacular successes the last few years.

In contrast to logic systems, knowledge from a deep learning (DL) model are difficult to understand, reuse, and may involve up to a billion parameters. On the other hand, probabilistic machine learning techniques such as deep learning offer an opportunity to tackle large complex problems that are out of the reach of traditional theory-making. It is possible that the more intuition-like reasoning performed by deep learning systems is mostly incompatible with the logic formalism of mathematics. Yet recent studies have shown that deep learning can be useful to logic systems and vice versa. Success at unifying different paradigms of Artificial Intelligence from logic to probability theory offers unique opportunities to combine data-driven approaches with traditional theories. These advancements are susceptible to impact significantly biological sciences, where dimensionality is high and limit the investigation of traditional theories.

6 Threats of Artificial Intelligence

The growth of artificial intelligence (AI) is not only unbelievable but also an exciting yet terrifying prospect. While there may be dramatic productivity gains as it transforms the workplace and our everyday life, there's always the worry of what AI could do in the wrong hands. The 2014 Hollywood blockbuster Transcendence movie, heavily based on AI, with showcasing clashing visions for the future of humanity, it's tempting to dismiss the notion of highly intelligent machines as mere science fiction. But this would be a mistake, and potentially our worst mistake in history. In May 2014, the world received a wakeup call from one of the most influential physicists of the twentieth century and perhaps the most celebrated icon of contemporary science, the famed, Stephen Hawking, (1942–2018). Together with three respected AI researchers, the world's most renowned scientist warned that the commercially-driven creation of intelligent machines could be "potentially our worst mistake in history. Later on, in January 2015 Stephen Hawking, Elon Musk, and dozens of artificial intelligence experts [1] signed an open letter on artificial intelligence calling for research on the societal impacts of AI. The letter affirmed that society can reap great potential benefits from artificial intelligence, but called for concrete research on how to prevent certain potential "pitfalls": artificial intelligence has the potential to eradicate disease and poverty, but researchers must not create something which cannot be controlled. [1] The four-paragraph letter, titled "Research Priorities for Robust and Beneficial Artificial Intelligence: An Open Letter", lays out detailed research priorities in an accompanying twelve-page document.

Comparing the impact of AI on humanity to the arrival of "a superior alien species," Hawking and his co-authors found humanity's current state of preparedness deeply wanting. "Although we are facing potentially the best or worst things ever to happen to humanity," they wrote, "little serious research is devoted to these issues outside small nonprofit institutes."

That was two years ago. So where are we now?

7 The Future of Artificial Intelligence

Depending on whom you ask, advances in artificial intelligence are either humanity's biggest threat or our best shot at curing diseases. 90% of the world's data was generated in the last two years along with apps and devices that have helped to make sense of data. By 2020, 57% of business buyers will depend on companies to know what they need before they ask for anything. IBM Watson has a 90% success rate in diagnosing cancer compared to a rate of 50% for human doctors. Chatbots will power 85% of customer service by 2020.

AI isn't just a headline, it's a breakthrough that is revolutionising every industry. Customers are experiencing incredible competitive advantages in marketing, supply chain management, single client targeting, fraud detection and more. However, this influx of information must be sorted appropriately to ensure consumers are getting the services they need. Thanks to machine learning, the accuracy of predictive algorithms can be relied on to help streamline this process. But how the scientists will answer to the questions rising from the concerns raised in the previous section? What is the key that will unlock the full potentional of Artificial Intelligence while on the same time keeping it safe for humans?

There is no simple answer to that question. And this issue is definitely not one that can be solved within the contents of this paper. But also, this paper cannot end without a proposal, one that will offer an optimistic outcome. For the author of this paper the balance of the use of AI lies in the research of how to effectively combine data mining with the human factor. For this reason, the Fuzzy Cognitive Maps (FCM) methodology is proposed. A methodology of modelling and potentially controlling systems using the human way of thinking. In FCM the human factor and data mining/ machine learning techniques co-exist.

7.1 Fuzzy Cognitive Maps

Fuzzy Cognitive Maps (FCMs) constitute a computational methodology that is able to examine situations during which the human thinking process involves fuzzy or uncertain descriptions. A FCM presents a graphical representation through a signed directed graph with feedback consisting of nodes and weighted arcs. The nodes of the graph stand for concepts that are used to describe, via cause and effect, the relations and behavior of a system in a simple and symbolic way. They are connected by signed and weighted arcs which represent the causal relationships that exist between the concepts (Fig. 1). Each concept Ci (variable) is characterized by a number that represents its values and is calculated through the transformation of a fuzzy value or the fitting of a numeric value, to the desired interval, [0, 1]. The values of the interconnections', weights, are initially linguistically defined by experts and then transformed into values which belong to the interval [−1, 1] through a specially designed algorithm. In this way FCMs embody the accumulated knowledge and experience from experts who know how the system behaves in different circumstances.

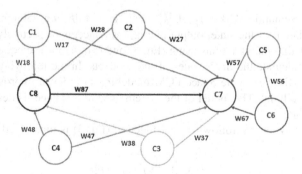

Fig. 1. Graphical representation of Fuzzy Cognitive Maps

The sign of each weight represents the type of influence between concepts (positive, negative, or zero). The degree of influence between the two concepts is indicated by the absolute value of W_{ij}.

Fuzzy Cognitive Maps have been thoroughly reviewed the last three years and many new forms have been proposed. In this section we will briefly describe the State FCM a new form of FCM which facilitates the use of learning algorithms for the more accurate modelling and control of systems.

7.2 State FCM

As stated in the introduction the FCM is a modelling methodology which is very promising when we need to model complex systems, which are highly non-linear and involve fuzzy or uncertain situations. State Fuzzy Cognitive Maps are an evolution of the classic methodology which can help model and give more accurate results for a large variety of complex systems. This methodology which is thoroughly analyzed in [37] has the following advantages. It improves the knowledge of the system by dividing the concepts into input, state and output concepts.

With the change of the calculation equations the model has a higher convergence speed and yields more accurate results. The State FCM methodology is mathematically described by the following equations (Eqs. 1–4).

$$x[k+1] = x[k] + \frac{\Delta x[k+1]}{\sum_{j=1, j\neq i}^{n} |w_{ji}|} \tag{1}$$

$$y[k+1] = y[k] + \frac{\Delta y[k+1]}{\sum_{j=1, j\neq i}^{n} |w_{ji}|} \tag{2}$$

Where

$$\Delta x[k+1] = A\Delta x[k] + B\Delta u[k] \tag{3}$$

$$\Delta y[k] = C\Delta x[k] + D\Delta u[k] \tag{4}$$

In this representation $\Delta x[k+1]$, $\Delta x[k]$, $\Delta y[k]$ and $\Delta u[k]$ are column vectors that contain the variation of the state, output and inputs concepts respectively.

After calculating the variations using (Eq. 3) and (Eq. 4) we use equations (Eq. 1) and (Eq. 2) to calculate the final values of the concepts. In the following sections we are going to use the new State Space FCM modelling in order to improve the energy efficiency of a building. The model of the system used in this paper is described in the following section.

Condition 1: When the following cost function (Eq. 5) is minimized.

$$F_1 = \sqrt{\sum \|C_j(k) - T_j\|^2} \tag{5}$$

where T_j is the mean target value of the concept C_j, e.g. $T_j = \frac{C_j^{max} - C_j^{min}}{2}$. For m concepts which we want to act as termination concepts Eq. 5 becomes

$$F_1 = \sqrt{\sum_{i=1}^{m} (C_i(k) - T_i)^2} \tag{6}$$

Condition 2: When the variation between two consequent values of a concept becomes very small (Eq. 7).

$$F_2 = \left| C_j^{n+1} - C_j^n \right| \leq \varepsilon \tag{7}$$

7.3   Fitting of the Inputs and Interpretation of Results

In order to apply the FCM methodology the values of all the input concepts must be between the interval [0, 1], where 0 denotes that the value of the concept is very small and 1 that the value is very big. For this reason, we use the following sigmoid function (Eq. 8) to fit the values to the desired interval; the slope of the curve changes depending on the variable we want to fit. The reverse action is followed in order to obtain the real value of a concept (Eq. 9)

$$f(x) = m + \frac{M - m}{1 + e^{-r(x - t_0)}} \tag{8}$$

where $x \in R$ and $f(R) = (m, M)$

$$f^{-1}(x) = t_0 - \frac{1}{r} \ln(\frac{M - x}{x - m}) \tag{9}$$

where $x \in (m, M)$ and $f^{-1}((m, M)) = R$. In the above-mentioned equations: m is the lower limit of the curve, M is the upper limit of the curve, r is the slope of the curve and t_0 is the symmetry to the y axis. More details concerning the State FCM methodology can be found in [37–39].

8   Conclusions

Today humankind is facing an unprecedented set of many difficult problems and challenges that have never been encountered before. They urgently need realistic and long lasting solutions. In this paper the very complex and challenging problem has been considered: can and how AI can address these problems? There is only one way to address, study and analyze systematically and mathematically correct: by using wisely existing knowledge and also creating new knowledge. How knowledge is created from the Big Data Driven World and the Cyber-Physical Systems? The basics and challenges as to how new knowledge is created in general was briefly reviewed by presenting definitions and theories of AI, ML and DL. There is no doubt that knowledge has been all around us for millions of years since the creation of the universe. All humans naturally desire knowledge. One main way creating "Knowledge" which is useful for the society is through Learning. AI presents many new ways. Artificial intelligence (AI) has become a crucial part of daily human lives today and it assists in almost every scenario—whether we realize it or not. However, at the same time AI has many weaknesses and provide many threats to our everyday life. This papers have raised a few. Much more serious work is needed to be done in the near future. But above all the human factor cannot and should not be left out from all future studies. Despite the dire state of the world today—and the stereotype that millennials are selfish and apathetic—the generation aged 18 to 35 cares deeply about global issues, and they're determined to tackle them. These people cannot be ignored from future decisions taken by the authorities.

References

1. World Economic Forum: The global risks Report 2017, Annual report 2017
2. OECD: Innovation and Growth Rationale for an Innovative Strategy. Paris, Organisation for Economic Cooperation and Development (2007)
3. Nilsson, N.: Principles of Artificial Intelligence. Tioga Press, Paolo Alto (1980)
4. Luger, G.F.: Artificial Intelligence: Structures and Strategies for Complex Problem Solving. Addison-Wesley, Boston (2005)
5. Warwick, K.: Artificial Intelligence: The Basics. Routledge, Abingdon (2011)
6. Shcherbakov, M., Groumpos, P.P., Kravets, A.: A method and IR4I index indicating the readiness of business processes for data science solutions. In: Kravets, A., Shcherbakov, M., Kultsova, M., Groumpos, P. (eds.) CIT&DS 2017. CCIS, vol. 754, pp. 21–34. Springer, Cham (2017). https://doi.org/10.1007/978-3-319-65551-2_2
7. Groumpos, P.P.: Creativity, innovation and entrepreneurship: a critical overview of issues and challenges. In: Kravets, A., Shcherbakov, M., Kultsova, M., Groumpos, P. (eds.) CIT&DS 2017. CCIS, vol. 754, pp. 3–20. Springer, Cham (2017). https://doi.org/10.1007/978-3-319-65551-2_1
8. Groumpos, P.P.: Why model complex dynamic systems using fuzzy cognitive maps? Int. J. Robot. Autom. 1(3), 1–13 (2017)
9. Groumpos, P.P.: Deep learning vs. wise learning: a critical and challenging overview. IFAC-PapersOnLine 49(29), 180–189 (2016)
10. Ackrill, J.L.: Aristotle's Categories and De Interpretatione, Clarendon Aristotle Series. Clarendon Press, Oxford (1961)
11. Aristotle's Logic, Stanford Encyclopedia of Philosophy, First published Sat Mar 18, 2000; substantive revision Fri Feb 17, 2017
12. Buchanan, B.G.: A (very) brief history of artificial intelligence. AI Mag. 26, 53–60 (2006)
13. Turing, A.: Computing machinery and intelligence. Mind 49, 433–460 (1950)
14. Bengio, Y.: Learning deep architectures for AI. Found. Trends Mach. Learn. 2(1), 1–127 (2009)
15. Deng, L., Yu, D.: Deep learning: methods and applications. Found. Trends Sig. Process. 7 (3–4), 197–387 (2014)
16. Riesenhuber, M., Poggio, T.: Hierarchical models of object recognition in cortex. Nat. Neurosci. 2(11), 1019 (1999)
17. Schmidhuber, J.: Deep learning in neural networks: an overview. Neural Netw. 61, 85–117 (2015)
18. Gybenko, G.: Approximation by superposition of sigmoidal functions. Math. Control Signals Systems 2(4), 3–314 (1989)

19. Friedman, J.M., Halaas, J.L.: Leptin and the regulation of body weight in mammals. Nature **395**, 763–770 (1998)
20. Simon, H.: Neural Networks: A Comprehensive Foundation. Prentice Hall, Upper Saddle River (1999)
21. Hassoun, M.H.: Fundamentals of Artificial Neural Networks. MIT Press, Cambridge (1995)
22. Hochreiter, S., Schmidhuber, J.: Long short-term memory. Neural Comput. **9**(8), 1735–1780 (1997)
23. Hinton, G.E.: Deep belief networks. Scholarpedia **4**(5), 5947 (2009)
24. Bryson, A.E., Gross, R.W.F.: Diffraction of strong shocks by cones, cylinders, and spheres. J. Fluid Mech. **10**(1), 1–16 (1961)
25. Russell, S., Norvig, P.: Artificial Intelligence: A Modern Approach, 3rd Edn. (2010)
26. Murphy, K.P.: Machine Learning: A Probabilistic Perspective. MIT Press, Cambridge (2012)
27. Ivakhnenko, A.G., Lapa, V.G.: Cybernetic predicting devices. No. TR-EE66-5. Purdue Univ Lafayette Ind School of Electrical Engineering (1966)
28. Ivakhnenko, A.G.: Polynomial theory of complex systems. IEEE Trans. Syst. Man Cybern. **SMC-1**(4), 364–378 (1971)
29. Fukushima, K.: Neocognitron: a self-organizing neural network model for a mechanism of pattern recognition unaffected by shift in position. Biol. Cybern. **36**(4), 193–202 (1980)
30. McCulloch, W.S., Pitts, W.: A logical calculus of the ideas immanent in nervous activity. Bull. Math. Biophys. **5**(4), 115–133 (1943)
31. Hubel, D.H., Wiesel, T.N.: Receptive fields of single neurones in the cat's striate cortex. J. Physiol. **148**(3), 574–591 (1959)
32. Schmidhuber, J., Prelinger, D.: Discovering predictable classifications. Neural Comput. **5**(4), 625–635 (1993)
33. Hinton, G.E., et al.: The"wake-sleep" algorithm for unsupervised neural networks. Science **268**(5214), 1158–1161 (1995)
34. Deng, L., Hinton, G., Kingsbury, B.: New types of deep neural network learning for speech recognition and related applications: an overview. In: IEEE International Conference on Acoustics, Speech and Signal Processing. IEEE (2013)
35. Marcus, G.: Deep learning: a revolution in artificial intelligence (2012)
36. Smith, G.W.: Art and artificial intelligence. ArtEnt (2015)
37. Mpelogianni, V., Groumpos, P.P.: Re-approaching fuzzy cognitive maps to increase the knowledge of a system. AI & Soc. **33**(2), 175–188 (2018)
38. Vassiliki, M., Groumpos, P.P.: Increasing the energy efficiency of buildings using human cognition; via Fuzzy Cognitive Maps. IFAC-PapersOnLine **51**(30), 727–732 (2018)
39. Groumpos, P.P.: Intelligence and fuzzy cognitive maps: scientific issues, challenges and opportunities. Stud. Inform. Control **27**(3), 247–264 (2018)

On Approach for the Development of Patents Analysis Formal Metrics

Alla G. Kravets[✉] [iD]

Volgograd State Technical University, Volgograd, Russian Federation
agk@gde.ru

Abstract. Analysis and modeling of the cross-thematic states of the world prior-art is a voluminous task that includes many subtasks. In order to assess the prior art, build forecasts and carry out analysis, it is necessary to develop and construct cross-thematic relationships between patents within an array in many ways. The scientific result of the work was the first developed formal metric "belonging to the technological epoch" for assessing the cross-thematic states of the world prior art, as well as the technique and method of applying formal metrics. This paper presents the development of a software module based on the developed metric.

Keywords: Formal metrics · World prior art · Patents · Cross-thematic search · Technological epoch

1 Introduction

Evaluation of cross-thematic relationships between the domains in relation to the development of engineering and technology at the global level requires the formalization of the subjective conclusions of the patent office expert, who is considering applications for inventions. When processing a patent or patent application, an expert needs to evaluate three parameters [1]:

1. Novelty
2. Industrial applicability
3. Inventive step

Assessing the novelty, the expert compares the patent application with the already existing patents for their differences from each other. At the same time, IPC of inventions is used to identify analogs on the world level. If there are few differences or the application repeats already existing patents in its content, it will be rejected at the "substantive consideration" stage.

Industrial applicability is the set of factors that allow using the invention in the near future to establish mass production of products or to modernize technological processes. At the same time, the possibilities of implementing the invention for the current level of scientific and technological development are assessed.

Assessing the inventive step, the expert makes a conclusion about how obvious and intuitive the intended invention was - from the standpoint of technological and structural complexity.

To automate a patent examiner, each of these three areas of work needs to be formalized. Despite the fact that for expert assessments there are specialized guidelines (prescriptive criteria for assessments [2]), this activity is time-consuming [3], and it requires significant intellectual labor. Moreover, its results have a large share of subjectivity. Automation of this activity will significantly reduce the time [4] and economic costs; greatly reduce the influence of the human factor in the processing of patent applications. However, to automate the activities of a patent examiner, a three-step approach is required [5] - so that each of the three points listed above can be formalized. Existing developments in this area are mainly based on the analysis of the text of a patent or patent application [6].

Therefore, the purpose of this work was to create (develop) more advanced methods using other approaches to this problem, namely, formal metrics [7] suitable for evaluating the invention at the initial stages of the examination.

2 Text Processing Approach for Patent Application Analysis

Many scientists tried to solve patent prior-art search task. The main research in patent retrieval started after the third NTCIR workshop [8]. There is an annual track CLEF-IP, which was created to compare different approaches in different tasks related to patent applications examination process, including the prior-art search task. Xue proposed a method based on machine learning [9], D'hondt tried to use syntactic relations [10], Verma approach is based on citations and patent classes [11], Robertson created a search query from the patent's text and tried to extract granted patents using this query and to rank them using BM25 [12], Mahdabi used patent's summary as a query to search for relevant patents [13], Magdy used an approach based on unigrams and bigrams [14], Graf tried to use external knowledge bases [15].

Existing automated systems for analyzing arrays based on text processing, as will be shown below, are applicable only within the framework of individual scientific disciplines and do not take into account cross-state conditions. This state of affairs leads to the conclusion that it is necessary to develop new general approaches to the analysis of the world prior-art (WPA), taking into account its cross-thematic states.

Automatic positioning system for the application materials to obtain a patent for an invention in the global patent space based on statistical and semantic approaches E-patent Examiner (EPE) - a system for expert decision-making in the examination of a patent application. The EPE was developed in the period of 2015–2017 to implement the cross-thematic methodology (Fig. 1). EPE developers [16] believe that new positions and results have been obtained in their work, which can be applied in the following areas:

1. Search for new scientific and technical solutions: technology and automated system, as a search and analytical toolkit.

2. Examination of application materials for obtaining a patent for an invention: technology and an automated system, as an expert decision-making support system.
3. Preparation of application materials for obtaining a patent for an invention: an automated system, as a tool for searching for analogs and analyzing the text of the Application.

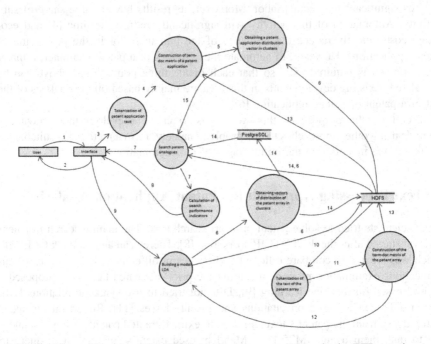

Fig. 1. The architecture of the EPE for analyzing a patent array in the DFD notation.

Figure 1 shows the figures for data flows: 1 - patent application, clustering parameters; 2 - found patents analogues, search performance indicators; 3 - patent application; 4 - tokenized patent application; 5 - term-document matrix of the patent application; 6 - LDA model; 7 - patent analogues; 8 - search performance indicators; 9 - clustering parameters; 10 - patent array; 11 - tokenized patent file; 12 - term-document matrix of the patent array; 13 - dictionary of words of the patent array; 14 - distribution vector of the patent array in clusters; 15 - vector of patent application distribution by clusters.

The study of existing systems for analyzing the states of the world prior art shows that all existing systems, in one way or another, use either the statistical or morphological properties of the states of the WPA. Existing systems may differ in performance, functionality, the number of connected databases, the availability and amount of processed information. Existing systems may even differ significantly from each other in architecture.

However, the next system based on statistical and morphological methods of text processing, cannot give, a significant qualitative breakthrough in the field of analysis of the states of WPA.

Thus, the need arose in the search for new methods for analyzing the states of the WPA. Statistical and morphological methods are too narrowly specialized and cannot be used for inventions in general. Therefore, the aim of this paper was to create more sophisticated methods using different approaches to this problem.

3 The Formal Metric of Belonging to the Technological Epoch (TE)

The main idea of this method is that each patent application or publication has a set of key terms [17], each of which can be attributed to any period of technological development of mankind. For example, computer technologies can certainly be attributed to modern (informational) TE, and a new model of a production machine, if it does not use any innovative solution, can be attributed to industrial (scientific and technical) TE (Table 1) - this corresponds to the first half of the twentieth century.

Table 1. Connection of technological revolutions with the growth of knowledge [18].

Start year	Technological epoch	N, billion	Z, Mill. c. b.	Growth Z	Growth N
52	Pre-feudal	0,1	0,11	1,54	1,41
630	Feudal	0,14	0,18	1,54	1,41
1038	Pre-craft	0,2	0,27	1,54	1,41
1325	Handicraft (proto-Renaissance)	0,29	0,42	1,54	1,41
1530	Renaissance	0,40	0,64	1,54	1,41
1674	Classical science	0,57	1	1,54	1,41
1776	First industrial	0,8	1,5	1,54	1,41
1848	Second industrial	1,13	2,3	1,53	1,41
1899	Harbinger NTR	1,59	3,6	1,53	1,4
1935	Science and technology	2,22	5,4	1,52	1,4
1961	Ancestry cybernetic	3,13	8,3	1,53	1,41
1979	Cybernetic	4,38	12,7	1,53	1,4
2005	Pre-biotech	6,45	20,6	1,62	1,47
2038	Biotech	8,74	30	1,46	1,35

Note: growth for the period corresponding to the technological epoch.

The indicators given in Table 1 correlate the number of humanity N and the volume of its knowledge Z; allow you to make estimates of these values in the periods corresponding to different TE; identify patterns of changes in these values. N is measured in billions of people; "Growth of N" and "growth of Z" are dimensionless values; Z - is measured in "conditional books" (c.b.). [Z] = c.b. One conditional book is equal in volume to the knowledge corresponds to the book, which after digitization will contain the amount of information in the amount of 1 MB. It can be seen that for each TE, the number of humanity increased by about 1.41 times, and the amount of knowledge - by 1.54 times. The deviation from this pattern to the "demographic transition" [19] does not exceed 0.01, and this error is associated with the use of integer values of years. Thus, there is a very interesting and, presumably, fundamental pattern of increasing the amount of knowledge and the number of people for periods corresponding to TE, by a constant number of times.

Inventions reflect the processes of fixing the intellectual achievements of mankind in the process of its development during each of the technological epochs. If in the text of an application for an invention, the number of matches of key terms is greater than a certain threshold value (k_N) set by us in the thesaurus of the newest technological epoch (in the modern world it is a pre-biotechnological epoch), then most likely this invention is new ($k_i > k_N$). If the newest keyword in the application text has long been known, for example, it belongs to the pre-Cybernetic technological epoch, and has a rich patent history (that is, humanity has already accumulated thousands of patents on this key term since its inception), then you can say that this invention has no novelty ($k_i < k_N$).

To implement the metric of technological epochs, several key decisions need to be developed.

1. Develop (form) a thesaurus – manually or by automated methods [20] to produce temporal markings on technological epochs of key terms found in the corpus of patent texts.
2. Determine the coefficients k_i that will allow ranking the corpus of patent texts by technological epochs.
3. Experimentally determine the threshold coefficient k_N, which will allow evaluating the novelty of the invention.

However, the described approach for metric definition has a significant drawback. This is the problem of "windmills". For example, wind generators - sources that convert wind energy into electrical energy, without a doubt, are modern high-tech devices. However, they use the principle of operation known to mankind since the invention of windmills, which can be attributed to the crafted technological epoch. This situation gives rise to a contradiction.

In addition, there is a scientific and technical problem of creating temporally labeled language buildings, the solution of which is probably the key to the implementation of the proposed formal metric in automated systems.

4   TE Metric Implementation and Software Development

To implement an automated analysis system and cross-thematic states of the world prior-art, it is necessary to programmatically implement software modules for the developed formal metric. As part of this study, it was decided to implement a software module based on the formal metric of belonging of the invention or the scientific term to a certain technological epoch. Since the remaining metric may be associated with technological epochs in the future.

The key point for the implementation of the TE metric is the scientific and technical problem of creating temporally-marked language corpus, the solution of which lies at the heart of the metric.

This means that, first of all, it is necessary to implement a method that will allow us to develop (form) a thesaurus by automated methods - to make temporal markup on technological epochs of key terms found in the corpus of patent texts.

For the full and convenient operation of the module, it is necessary to implement such functions as:

− implementation of the extraction of the invention name from the sample file;
− implementation of access to the information resource on the name of the invention;
− implementation of the extraction of the necessary information on the name of the invention from the information resource;
− search and retrieval of temporal elements;
− calculation of the temporal key by temporal elements;
− assignment of a technological epoch to a temporal sampling element according to a temporal key;
− write data to the temporal dictionary;
− analysis of the temporal dictionary for errors and repetitions;
− delete doubles in the temporal dictionary;
− sort the elements of the temporal dictionary in alphabetical order.

As an information resource, it was decided to use the Internet resource "Wikipedia". Since this resource differs in the frequency of updating information, contains the most complete database of scientific terms and inventions, it is notable for its convenience in working with the resource, including software, it does not overload the text of the page with an abundance of unnecessary information. Table 1 is used as a table of technological epochs' periods.

4.1   Development of Software Algorithm

The implemented software module forms a temporally tagged dictionary of scientific and technical terms based on the formal metric of technological epochs. For the software work, a text document containing the corpus of marked words or phrases is required. Such an input sample can be formed manually and must meet the requirements specified in the technical specifications for the software module.

The software checks the input document for the presence of words in it and extracts the elements of the input sample from the document if they are present, line by line (Fig. 2).

To solve the sorting problem, these three stages look like this:

1. The sorted array is divided into two parts of approximately the same size;
2. Each of the resulting parts is sorted separately, for example - by the same algorithm;
    1. - 2. Recursive splitting of a task into smaller ones occurs until the size of the array reaches one (an array of length 1 can be considered ordered).
3. Two ordered half size arrays are combined into one.
    3.1. Connect two ordered arrays into one.

The basic idea of merging two sorted arrays can be explained with the following example. Suppose we have two already sorted by non-decreasing subarray. Then:

3.2. Merge two subarrays into the third result array.

At each step, we take the smaller of the first two elements of the subarrays and write it into the resulting array. The counters of the numbers of the elements of the resulting array and the subarray from which the element was taken are increased by 1.

3.3. Combining residues. When one of the subarrays is over, we add all the remaining elements of the second subarray into the resulting array.

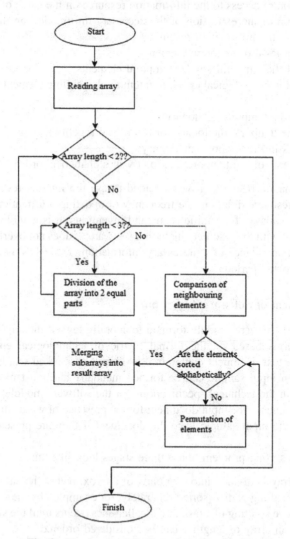

Fig. 2. The temporal dictionary sorting algorithm

5 Experiments and Results

5.1 Experiment 1. Correspondence of the Sampling Elements to the Assigned Technological Epochs

Input: a set of elements of the sample.

Output data: conclusions on the compliance of the sampling elements with the assigned technological epochs.

For a computational experiment, it is necessary to form a selection of elements for a temporal dictionary.

Based on the data in the compliance model is trained. Based on the trained models, relationships for the temporal dictionary are built.

Results.

Inputs: For this experiment, a sample of 100 elements was taken. The sample is presented in a text document format with line items sampled line by line. The sample contains randomly represented, in the form of words and phrases in Russian and English, scientific terms, names of inventions and technological products.

Output data: Output data are generated in the form of a temporal dictionary. The temporal dictionary is presented in the form of a text document with temporal connections written by line (the sample element is the technological epoch corresponding to the sample element).

Experiment Description: After processing the input data, the temporal dictionary should be analyzed by an expert on the correctness of the relevant sample elements and technological epochs.

As a result of the experiment No. 1, it was found that in the compiled temporal dictionary a complete and correct correspondence was reached between the elements of the temporal dictionary. The correctness of the correlation of the technological epoch to the sample element is 95%.

5.2 Experiment 2. Check the Temporal Dictionary for Errors and Repetitions

Input: sample for the temporal dictionary.

Output: temporal dictionary.

For a computational experiment, it is necessary to check the operation of the module on samples separated into different documents and check the dictionary for errors in the sorting algorithm and the avoidance of duplication.

Results.

Input data: For this experiment, a 100 elements sample was taken. The sample is presented in a text document format with line items sampled line by line. The sample contains randomly represented, in the form of words and phrases in Russian and English, scientific terms, names of inventions and technological products.

Output data: Output data are generated in the form of a temporal dictionary. The temporal dictionary is presented in the form of a text document with temporal connections written by line (the sample element is the technological epoch corresponding to the sample element).

Experiment Description: After processing the input data, the temporal dictionary should be analyzed for errors in sorting and doubles.

As a result of experiment No. 2, no sorting errors and repetitions were found in the temporal dictionary.

5.3 Analysis of the Novelty of the Invention Using the Software Module of the Automated Filling of the Temporal Dictionary

To use the formal metric of technological epochs and analyze the novelty of the invention, first of all, it is necessary to manually examine the patent application and on its basis form a document with input data. The document must contain a set of keywords or terms found in the patent application (Fig. 3).

```
Cannon
Airplane
Laser
Robot
Windmill
Internal combustion engine
Transistor
Electrical telegraph
Cinematograph
Telephone
Submarine
Radio broadcasting
Computer
Mirror
Crossbow
Printing
Periodic table
Electricity
Telescope
Train
```

Fig. 3. Example of the input document

If the collected information for the analysis of a patent application is sufficient to use a formal metric, and they can be applied within the framework of the task, then the execution of the program module should be started using the command line. It is important that the program module file and the input document in the .txt format are located in the same directory, and also that the elements of the sample are written line by line.

After starting the program module via the Windows operating system command line, error messages and processing of elements of the input document will be displayed on the command line. If there are no errors, after processing all elements of the input sample, a corresponding message will be displayed on the screen, the program module will be suspended, and the operating system command line will wait for the next command (Fig. 4). After stopping the execution of the work of the program

```
C:\Users\eisberg\TermsClassifier v1.0.1\TermsClassifier\TerminsClassifier\releas
e> java -jar TerminsClassifier1.1.jar tech.txt out.txt
Reading input file.....
There is no classified terms file. It will be created.
Classifying term 'Cannon'
Classifying term 'Airplane'
Classifying term 'Laser'
Classifying term 'Robot'
Classifying term 'Windmill'
Classifying term 'Internal combustion engine'
Classifying term 'Transistor'
Classifying term 'Electrical telegraph'
Classifying term 'Cinematograph'
Classifying term 'Telephone'
Classifying term 'Submarine'
Classifying term 'Radio broadcasting'
Classifying term 'Computer'
Classifying term 'Mirror'
Classifying term 'Crossbow'
Classifying term 'Printing'
Classifying term 'Periodic table'
Classifying term 'Electricity'
Classifying term 'Telescope'
Classifying term 'Train'
Writing data to output file.....
Done!

C:\Users\eisberg\TermsClassifier v1.0.1\TermsClassifier\TerminsClassifier\releas
e>
```

Fig. 4. Logging of the data processing

module, it will generate a document with the result of the program. The generated document contains a temporal dictionary - the distribution of the elements of the input sample according to the corresponding technological epochs (Fig. 5).

```
Airplane - Harbinger NTR
Cannon - Pre-craft
Cinematograph - Second industrial
Computer - Cybernetic
Crossbow - Handicraft (Proto-renaissance)
Electrical telegraph - First industrial
Electricity - Science and technology
Internal combustion engine - Second industrial
Laser - Science and technology
Mirror - Pre-biotech
Periodic table - Unknown
Printing - Pre-craft
Radio broadcasting - Pre-cybernetic
Robot - Pre-biotech
Submarine - cybernetic
Telephone - Science and technology
Telescope - Harbinger NTR
Train - Cybernetic
Transistor - Harbinger NTR
Windmill - Pre-craft
```

Fig. 5. Formed temporal dictionary

After the completion of the program module, you should examine the generated temporal dictionary. It is possible to assert that the invention is new in relation to the world technical level, only if a significant proportion of the elements of the input sample from the patent application belongs to the pre-biotechnological TE. In this case, it follows that the patent application and the invention is new in relation to the current state of the world prior art.

6 Conclusion

The developed formal metric for the automated assessment of a patent application allows the invention to be positioned relative to the world technical level; facilitate decision making for a patent examiner; reduce the influence of subjectivity on the assessment of the patent examiner; predict the development of technology. The totality of the identified promising technologies will allow for the prediction of the world technical level as a whole.

Within the framework of the study, the TE formal metric for evaluating inventive activity was developed and analyzed.

Thus, the proposed metric complement the existing approaches to automation the activities of patent examiners; open up new opportunities for forecasting the development of technology; create opportunities for cross-modeling of new technical solutions; deepen our understanding of the nature of technological processes and inventive activity.

During the experiments, it was revealed that the accuracy of the classification of the elements of the sample according to technological epochs is 95% and cannot be increased within the framework of the method used. The increase can be accurately achieved using machine learning algorithms [21].

The software was implemented on the basis of the formal metric of belonging to the technological epoch.

Acknowledgments. This research was supported by the Russian Fund of Basic Research (grant No. 19-07-01200).

References

1. WIPO. World Intellectual Property Organization. Infographics systems (2016). Official Site. http://www.wipo.int/export/sites/www/ipstats/ru/docs/infographics_systems_2016. pdf#page=1. Accessed 22 Sept 2018
2. Federal Service for Intellectual Property (Rospatent), Moscow (2004). Official Site. http:// www.rupto.ru/docs/other/ruk_mejd_poisk. Accessed 22 Sept 2018
3. Mironenko, A.G., Kravets, A.G.: Automated methods of patent array analysis. In: 7th International Conference on Information, Intelligence, Systems & Applications (IISA). Institute of Electrical and Electronics Engineers (IEEE), Greece, 13–15 July 2016. IEEE (2016). https://doi.org/10.1109/IISA.2016.7785341
4. Kravets, A., Shumeiko, N., Lempert, B., Salnikova, N., Shcherbakova, N.: "Smart Queue" approach for new technical solutions discovery in patent applications. Commun. Comput. Inf. Sci. **754**, 37–47 (2017)

5. Korobkin, D.M., Fomenkov, S.S., Kravets, A.G., Kolesnikov, S.G.: Prior art candidate search on base of statistical and semantic patent analysis. In: Proceedings of the International Conferences on Computer Graphics, Visualization, Computer Vision and Image Processing 2017 and Big Data Analytics, Data Mining and Computational Intelligence 2017. Part of the Multi Conference on Computer Science and Information Systems 2017, pp. 231–238 (2017)

6. Korobkin, D., Fomenkov, S., Kravets, A., Kolesnikov, S.: Methods of statistical and semantic patent analysis. Commun. Comput. Inf. Sci. **754**, 48–61 (2017)

7. Kravets, A.G., Legenchenko, M.S.: Formal metrics for automated assessment of inventions. Caspian J. Manage. High Technol. **3**(39), 8–19 (2017). (in Russian)

8. Iwayama, M., Fujii, A., Kando, N., Takano, A.: Overview of patent retrieval task at NTCIR-3. In: Proceedings of NTCIR Workshop (2002)

9. Xue, X., Bruce Croft, W.: Automatic query generation for patent search. In: Proceedings of the 18th ACM Conference on Information and Knowledge Management, New York, NY, USA, pp. 2037–2040 (2009)

10. D'hondt, E., Verberne, S., Alink, W., Cornacchia, R.: Combining document representations for prior-art retrieval. In: CLEF Notebook Papers/Labs/Workshop (2011)

11. Verma, M., Varma, V.: Exploring keyphrase extraction and IPC classification vectors for prior art search. In: CLEF Notebook Papers/Labs/Workshop (2011)

12. Robertson, S.E., Walker, S., Beaulieu, M.M., Gatford, M., Payne, A.: Okapi at TREC-4. In: Proceedings of the 4th Text REtrieval Conference (TREC-4), pp. 73–96 (1996)

13. Mahdabi, P., Andersson, L., Hanbury, A., Crestani, F.: Report on the CLEF-IP 2011 experiments: exploring patent summarization. In: CLEF Notebook Papers/Labs/Workshop (2011)

14. Magdy, W., Jones, G.J.F.: Applying the KISS principle for the CLEF-IP 2010 prior art candidate patent search task. In: Workshop of the Cross-Language Evaluation Forum, LABs and Workshops, Notebook Papers (2010)

15. Graf, E., Frommholz, I., Lalmas, M., van Rijsbergen, K.: Knowledge modeling in prior art search. In: Cunningham, H., Hanbury, A., Rüger, S. (eds.) IRFC 2010. LNCS, vol. 6107, pp. 31–46. Springer, Heidelberg (2010). https://doi.org/10.1007/978-3-642-13084-7_4

16. Kravets, A.G., Korobkin, D.M., Dykov, M.A.: E-patent examiner: two-steps approach for patents prior-art retrieval. In: IISA 2015 - 6th International Conference on Information, Intelligence, Systems and Applications: Conference Proceeding. Ionian University, Institute of Electrical and Electronics Engineers (IEEE), Piscataway, USA, Corfu, Greece, 6–8 July 2015 (2015). https://doi.org/10.1109/IISA.2015.7388074

17. Kravets, A.G., Mironenko, A.G., Nazarov, S.S., Kravets, A.D.: Patent application text pre-processing for patent examination procedure. Commun. Comput. Inf. Sci. **535**, 105–114 (2015)

18. Orekhov, V.A.: Forecasting the development of mankind, taking into account the knowledge factor (2015). ISBN 978-5-85689-102-6

19. Wikipedia: Demographic transition (2017). https://ru.wikipedia.org/wiki/Demographic_transition. Accessed 22 Sept 2018

20. Korobkin, D.M., Fomenkov, S.A., Kravets, A.G., Golovanchikov, A.B.: Patent data analysis system for information extraction tasks. In: Weghorn, H. (ed.) Applied Computing 2016: Proceedings of 13 International Conference. IADIS - International Association for the Development of the Information Society, Mannheim Germany, 28–30 October 2016, pp. 215–219 (2016)

21. Kravets, A.G., Kravets, A.D., Rogachev, V.A., Medintseva, I.P.: Cross-thematic modeling of the world prior-art state: rejected patent applications analysis. J. Fundam. Appl. Sci. **8**(3S. C.), 2442–2452 (2016)

Cyber-Physical Systems and Big Data-Driven World. Pro-active Modeling in Intelligent Decision Making Support

A New Approach to Reduce Time Consumption of Data Quality Assessment in the Field of Energy Consumption

Alexander Sokolov$^{(\boxtimes)}$ ⓘ, Maxim V. Shcherbakov ⓘ,
Anton Tyukov ⓘ, and Timur Janovsky

Volgograd State Technical University,
28, Lenin avenue, 400005 Volgograd, Russia
alexander.sokolov.it@gmail.com,
maxim.shcherbakov@gmail.com, anton.tyukov@gmail.com,
janovsky@yandex.ru

Abstract. This paper is devoted to solving the problem of reducing the time costs of the process of data quality assessment. The data describe energy resources consumption of various enterprises and institutions. The first part of the paper contains a review of recent data quality assessment studies was made. The analysis describes the problems of this process and the characteristics of the data, metadata and the algorithms used in it. The next part of the paper shows a new approach to reduce the time consumption of the process of assessing the data quality, which differs from the existing ones by the presence of a data-packaging and decision-making support using the oDMN+ notation. Finally, this paper presents an implementation example of the oDMN+ model for data on the energy consumption of the Volgograd hardware plant. The results showed that the use of data packaging and modeling the assessment process is a promising approach for modeling and reducing time costs in the process of data quality assessment for energy management systems used in the enterprises and institutions.

Keywords: Data quality · Energy management · Data packaging ·
Decision support · oDMN+ · Data collection

1 Introduction

Nowadays, energy management systems are being applied to a variety of modern enterprises and in various institutions. They are used to analyze and control the process of providing enterprises and institutions with energy resources [1]. These systems operate in real time with a large amount of different data. Most of this data describes the consumption of energy resources, environmental parameters, as well as the infrastructure parameters of an enterprise or institution [2]. This data comes from a variety of different sources: (1) meters, sensors and controllers using automated data collection and transmission systems (ADCTS) and the Internet of Things [3]; (2) external services, for example, providing weather data; (3) program tools for manual data and files input [1]. Data are collected in the form of time series. The most common collection interval is 15 min [1].

© Springer Nature Switzerland AG 2019
A. G. Kravets et al. (Eds.): CIT&DS 2019, CCIS 1083, pp. 49–62, 2019.
https://doi.org/10.1007/978-3-030-29743-5_4

Recently, many new data analysis algorithms (including visualization, knowledge extraction, decision support) and energy consumption data-driven control algorithms have been developed for energy management systems. In this article, they are referred to as the data analysis and control algorithms (DACA). These algorithms set certain quality requirements which the data used should meet [4]. The data quality (DQ) is the degree of compliance of the data characteristics with the specified requirements. It is set both for individual data points (DP) and for data packages, collected for specific periods of time, grouped and possibly processed.

As the number of data sources grows, it is more likely that incorrect or misleading data will be available, leading to erroneous decisions and incorrect analysis results. At the same time, it is often necessary to run DACA without a long wait for the DQ assessment. DQ allows: (1) to decide whether to run certain DACA with the available data; (2) to decide whether to process and improve DQ; (3) to identify the causes of the DQ decrease [3]; (4) inform decision makers (DM) about problems [4]. Most of the data sources described above provide information about the characteristics of the collected data in the form of metadata. Metadata are recorded in parallel in the ADCTS, complementing each DP. They are used in the algorithms of DQ assessment [5]. Also, an increase in the amount of metadata can slow down both the data collection process and the process of DQ assessment.

Thus, especially considering the trend of digitalization of enterprises and institutions, the problem of reducing the time costs of the process of automated DQ assessment in the field of energy consumption is urgent. Different applications, tasks, and specifically DACA need different levels of DQ, different sets of metadata, different assessment algorithms and data processing time consumption requirements. DQ is assessed by different experts in different ways. To reduce the time spent on the DQ assessment process, it is necessary to eliminate the subjectivity of this process, the choice of the algorithms for assessing DQ, data processing and DACA [6] through the decision-making support.

The rest of the paper is organized as follows. Section 2 deals with recent works on the DQ assessment. Section 3 proposes a new approach to reducing the time spent on the process of assessing the quality of data on energy consumption. Section 4 considers an example of the implementation of the proposed approach and the last section contains the conclusions made in this paper.

2 Background

Currently, two approaches are used for DQ assessment: (1) algorithmic and (2) based on machine learning (ML) methods. In this paper, the following solutions proposed in the first approach were examined. The papers [7, 8] described frameworks that assess the quality of data from the Internet of Things sensors. The paper [9] proposes a platform for automatic DQ assessment using Fuzzy Logic to form a continuous DQ scale. They, like many other similar solutions, are used in areas of research that differ from the energy management of enterprises and institutions. However, the algorithms, the obtained results and the best practices from these papers should be considered for transfer to the current field, which requires additional research. In [10], the DQ control of data streams includes, in addition to checking DP for compliance with pre-established standards, a comparison of DP with simultaneously obtained from duplicate sensors. However, the presence of duplicate data sources is not always possible and costly for enterprises and institutions, and it is also difficult to obtain correct data for comparison.

As the common disadvantages of the algorithmic approach are the following. (1) The use of a set of functions for evaluation and "if-then" rules adversely affect the accuracy of the result and the time costs of decision-making in the process of evaluating DQ [11]. (2) The use of statistical methods can be time-consuming. (3) Algorithmic DQ assessment methods are based on user experience or previously established business rules, which limits productivity and is a time-consuming process, often with low accuracy [12].

The increasing popularity of machine learning (ML) has a significant impact on the time consumption and accuracy of new methods for assessing DQ. The process of DQ assessment can be automated by "training" the ML model to identify nonconformities with DQ requirements [13]. Many papers, such as [10, 12, 14], suggest ML methods for assessing the quality of data from sensor networks and the Internet of things. Assessments are used to determine changes in data profiles and to identify anomalies. A paper [15] shows the strategy of detecting anomalies, assessing and improving the quality of data on the energy consumption of private and public buildings using the ML tools. However, in the papers described above, the DQ assessment process is mainly used only to detect anomalies.

The common shortcomings of ML methods can be identified as follows. (1) They require high-quality data for training models, which is not always possible in an industrial enterprise or a state-funded institution. This problem may occur in the process of deployment of ADCTS, when the DQ may be low in the initial stages. It is necessary to wait until the data collection processes become stable, while the DQ assessment system should provide support in this process [14]. (2) When the consumption profile, establishment schedule, or the composition of the equipment change at the facility, the model must be retrained, which can take a lot of time with a large amount of training data. (3) Decisions issued by models are often difficult to interpret to identify the causes of DQ degradation since the models used are often "black boxes".

In several reviewed papers [1, 2, 16, 17], the necessary stage in the implementation of the DQ assessment process is the formation of the following sets: (1) characteristics of the data sources; (2) DPs characteristics; (3) the required DQ assessment algorithms; (4) the required values of the characteristics of the data on which the assessments are based; (5) DACA algorithms and (6) their requirements for the set of data used and for the DQ. In this paper, it is also necessary to form these sets. This task is time-consuming. In addition, the monitoring of production processes in enterprises is characterized by frequent changes in information requirements. An effective mechanism is needed for rebuilding the process for DQ assessment [18]. Also, the task of forming a visual connection between the above sets is important. In the process of formation of the sets of the above characteristics and the time-optimal algorithms for DQ assessing and data improving, decision support is needed. The decision support should provide the acceptable sets in accordance with the DQ requirements of DACA algorithms, as well as it should help to identify the sources of problems with DQ in the

ADCTS and other factors affecting the DQ. In this paper, it is proposed to keep the focus on the algorithmic DQ assessment. To eliminate the above-described disadvantages of this approach, associated with low speed and accuracy of the DQ assessment, and solving the above tasks, this paper proposes the development of a new approach to reducing the time spent on the DQ assessment process. This paper will use and improve the previously proposed method in [4], as well as the results of [11].

In this paper, time savings will be achieved by applying an effective data import method where the raw data comes from sources, caching it, and then complementing it with DQ assesses (and, possibly, new metadata), improving, packaging, and writing to the database [19]. Also, effective methods of data packaging were previously described to speed up data ingestion in the field of time series databases [20].

3   The Proposed Approach

In this paper, a new approach to reducing the time spent on the process of DQ assessment is proposed, which consists of the preparatory and main stages. The purpose of the first stage is to form the following sets: (1) algorithms for preliminary and detailed DQ assessment and data improvement; (2) requirements for the metadata for the above algorithms; (3) settings for data collection and decision makers. The BPMN (Business Process Model and Notation) diagram of the main stage is shown in Fig. 1.

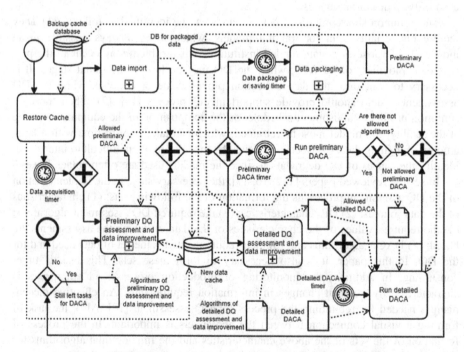

Fig. 1. BPMN diagram of the main stage of the proposed approach

In the main stage, the process of DQ assessment and data improvement, as well as the running DACA, are divided into preliminary and detailed. Data sets are formed for each individual DACA.

Since a large amount of data can arrive at short intervals of time, to reduce the load on the user database and speed up further interaction with new data, they are cached in RAM (random-access memory). The subprocess of data import is shown in Fig. 2.

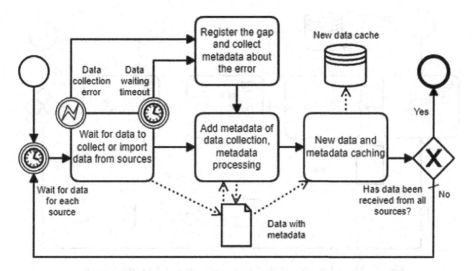

Fig. 2. The raw data import subprocess

New data from the cache is periodically written to the backup cache database (which is shown in the subprocess of data packaging, see below) to prevent their loss in the event of server work interruption. The cache is restored from the backup database when the system is started on the server (see Fig. 1). In parallel with the data import, a subprocess of the preliminary DQ assessment and data improvement is performed, which reads the available data from the cache and packaged data from the DB for packaged data (see below). The subprocess itself is universal for the preliminary and detailed subprocess. They receive various sets of algorithms and data with metadata. This subprocess is shown in Fig. 3. The subprocess of preliminary DQ assessment and data improvement is designed to quickly supplement these data with DQ assessments. There also are decision making which of the DACA can be performed. There are used the simplest and operational measures to improve the data (converting data to other format or unit of measure, aggregation, quick elimination of gaps and anomalies, if possible, etc.). If necessary, DQ assessments can be reevaluated after data improvement. In the process of improving data, values can be changed and supplemented with new metadata. In parallel with the process of the running of preliminary DACA, as well as the subprocess of the detailed DQ assessment, an improved method of data packaging is performed with an assessment of the quality of the data packages (see Fig. 4). The packaging is needed to speed up access to large amounts of data at times when they are needed. The method improvement consists of using the cache described above, from which new packages are formed instead of using the raw data database. Each data package has its own overall DQ assessment, calculated, for example, as the average value of the DQ assessments of each DP in it or the nested packages included in it. The assessment is calculated during the packaging process. A detailed description of the package was given in [4].

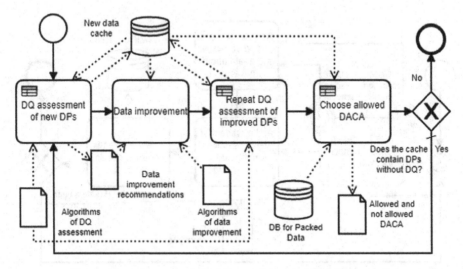

Fig. 3. The subprocess of the DQ assessment and data improvement

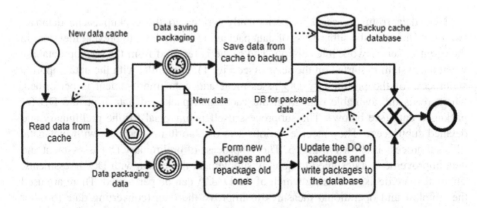

Fig. 4. Subprocess of data packaging and saving the cache to the backup database

During the detailed DQ assessment and data improvement, which subprocess is like that shown in Fig. 3, the algorithms that take a long time are executed. Here, improving the data may also include sending notifications with recommendations for eliminating problems due to which DQ has got worse. For example, an indication which stages of data collection in the ADCTS have failed. After the execution of this subprocess, detailed DACA is performed, which are more demanding to the DQ and are also more time-consuming. This process can be skipped if it is not necessary to divide the algorithms into preliminary and detailed ones.

As shown in Fig. 3, the processes "DQ assessment of new DPs" and "Choose allowed DACA" are processes of business rules in DMN (Decision Model and Notation). In the first, decisions are made on the DQ assessments of individual DP, and measures are chosen to improve the data. In the second, decisions are made about the possibility of using certain DACA. However, this notation does not allow a clear representation of the relationship between the data necessary for DQ assessment, data sources, and metadata. In this paper, we propose to use the oDMN+ notation described in [18], which is an extension of the DMN notation and eliminates this disadvantage. An example of the DRD diagram (DMN requirements diagram) included in the oDMN+ notation for the process "DQ assessment of new DPs" is shown in Fig. 5.

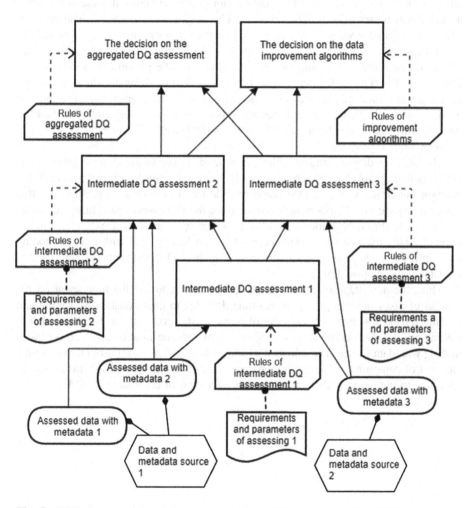

Fig. 5. DRD diagram of the "DQ assessment of new DPs" process in the oDMN+ notation

The process of "Choose allowed DACA" includes only one decision table of the oDMN+ diagram used the DQ assessments calculated in the previous process.

In this paper, a model for describing the set of DPs from a specific source is proposed, which has n characteristics, in the form of a tuple $\{C, D\}$, where:

$C = <c_1, \ldots, c_k>$, where c_i is one of the k characteristics of the data source, $i = 1, k$;

$D = <d_1, \ldots, d_l>$, where d_i is one of l DP of the given set, $i = 1, l$;

$d = \{t, val, M, E, e_a\}$, where t is the time stamp for collecting the i-th DP;

val is the obtained value of the i-th DP;

$M = <m_1, \ldots, m_n>$, where m is one of the n items of the metadata set M;

$E = <e_1, \ldots, e_o>$, where e is one of o DQ assessments for DP from the E set;

e_a is an aggregated DQ assessment for the DP.

The input of each decision table is the values of t and val, some m metadata of the DP, as well as some e, obtained from the previous decision tables. If some m is absent, its value will be set to the *NULL* constant. The output of each intermediate decision table is calculated e value. The output of this process is (1) the values of E and e_a, which is added to the DP and (2) a set of measures identifiers (data processing algorithms, notifications to decision makers, etc.) that must be performed to improve the DQ of this DP. For each intermediate DQ assessment, e is set by the scale of the resulting values at different intervals in accordance with the characteristic from bad to good, for example [0; 10], where 0 corresponds to the worst quality and 10 is the best. An assessment can also be a value from the set ("Excellent", "Good", "Bad") or a Boolean value ("yes"/"no").

The oDMN+ diagram and its tables can be made in one of the many existing visual DMN modeling tools (since there is currently no visual editor for diagrams in oDMN+ notation but future works in [18] could include the design of a supporting tool that makes the usage of oDMN+ easier). To calculate the DQ assessments, many functions of the FEEL (Friendly Enough Expression Language), used by DMN to formalize decision logic, may be used [21]. These tables can be exported with minimal coding costs into the decision-making software tool of the DQ assessment system that will implement the proposed approach.

Thus, the advantage of the proposed approach is reducing the time spent on the process of assessing the quality of real-time data due to their constant packaging and caching. Also, this approach uses the oDMN+ model and notation for the decision-making process. This eliminates the subjectivity of decision-makers, connects decision-making with data sources and allows decision-makers to make the best in terms of time and cost of computing resources the process of assessing the DQ of DP, the choice of measures to improve the data, as well as the selection of acceptable DACA.

4   Implementation

To implement the decision-making process in the proposed approach, a model and an oDMN+ diagram were developed for the data on the electricity consumption of the Volgograd hardware plant, shown in Fig. 6. For modeling the following diagrams and decision tables Camunda Modeler was used [22]. Conversions from DMN to oDMN+ diagrams were made manually. The key tables for this diagram are shown in Figs. 7, 8, 9, 10, 11. For the table of reliability assessment, the input is the follows metadata: data source name, battery level of a data source device, a wireless connection signal strength of the data source device and the number of attempts of connection to the data source device.

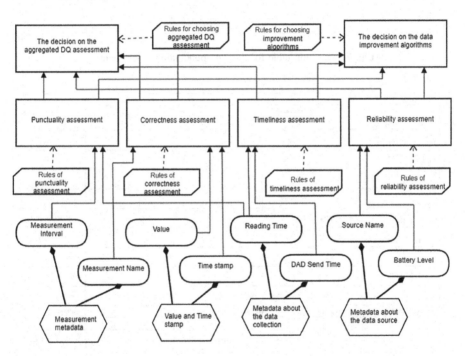

Fig. 6. oDMN+ diagram for assessing the quality of data on the energy consumption of the Volgograd hardware plant

The possible reliability assessments are "Excellent", "OK", "MeterProblem", "DeviceLowBattery", "BadWirelessConnection", "DeviceProblem". For the table of timeliness assessment, the input is the follows metadata: a request to a data source time, reading from the data source time, a time when a data acquisition device sends data to a

C+	Input			Output
	MeasurementInterval	ReadingMinute	ReadingSecond	Punctuality
	string	integer	integer	string
1	"min15"	0, 15, 30, 45	[0..5]	"Excellent"
2	"min15"	0, 15, 30, 45	[6..10]	"OK"
3	"hour1"	0	[0..10]	"Excellent"
4	"hour1"	0	[11..15]	"OK"
5	"min1"	-	[0..1]	"Excellent"
6	"min1"	-	[2..5]	"OK"
7	"min15"	not(0, 15, 30, 45)	-	"DataTransferProblem"
8	"min15"	not(0, 15, 30, 45)	-	"DataTransferProblem"
9	"hour1"	> 0	-	"DataTransferProblem"
10	"hour1"	> 0	-	"DataTransferProblem"
11	"min1"	-	> 5	"DataTransferProblem"
12	"min1"	-	> 5	"DataTransferProblem"

Fig. 7. Decision table for the data punctuality assessment

C+	Input				Output
	SourceName	MeasurementName	Value	Hour	Correctness
	string	string	double	integer	string
1	"Hardware shop", "Spring Shop"	"Electricity", "ColdWater"	NULL	-	"Gap"
2	"Hardware shop", "Spring Shop"	"Electricity", "ColdWater"	NAN	-	"DeviceError"
3	"Hardware shop", "Spring Shop"	"Electricity", "ColdWater"	ERROR	-	"MeterError"
4	"Hardware shop", "Spring Shop"	"Electricity", "ColdWater"	INF	-	"DeviceError"
5	"Hardware shop", "Spring Shop"	"Electricity", "ColdWater"	< 0	-	"ProblemLower"
6	"Hardware shop", "Spring Shop"	"Electricity", "ColdWater"	< 999999	-	"AnomalyLower"
7	"Hardware shop", "Spring Shop"	"Electricity"	> 2000	-	"ProblemUpper"
8	"Hardware shop", "Spring Shop"	"ColdWater"	> 100	-	"ProblemUpper"
9	"Hardware shop", "Spring Shop"	"Electricity", "ColdWater"	> 999999	-	"AnomalyUpper"
10	"Hardware shop"	"Electricity"	[2..20]	[0..7]	"Excellent"
11	"Hardware shop"	"Electricity"	[2..20]	[18..24]	"Excellent"
12	"Hardware shop"	"ColdWater"	[0..1]	[0..7]	"Excellent"
13	"Hardware shop"	"ColdWater"	[0..1]	[18..24]	"Excellent"
14	"Hardware shop", "Spring Shop"	"Electricity", "ColdWater"	-	-	"OK"

Fig. 8. Decision table for the data correctness assessment

U	Input +				Output +
	Punctuality	Correctness	Timeliness	Reliability	AggregatedAssessment
	string	string	string	string	string
1	"Excellent"	"Excellent"	"Excellent"	"Excellent"	"Excellent"
2	"OK"	"Excellent"	"Excellent"	"Excellent"	"OK"
3	"Excellent"	"OK"	"Excellent"	"Excellent"	"OK"
4	"Excellent"	"Excellent"	"OK"	"Excellent"	"OK"
5	"Excellent"	"Excellent"	"Excellent"	"OK"	"OK"
6	"OK"	"OK"	"OK"	"OK"	"OK"
7	"DataTransferProblem"	"Excellent", "OK"	"Excellent", "OK"	"Excellent", "OK"	"Satisfactory"
8	"Excellent", "OK"	not("Excellent", "OK")	"Excellent", "OK"	"Excellent", "OK"	"Bad"
9	"Excellent", "OK"	"Excellent", "OK"	not("Excellent", "OK")	"Excellent", "OK"	"Satisfactory"
10	"Excellent", "OK"	"Excellent", "OK"	"Excellent", "OK"	not("Excellent", "OK")	"Satisfactory"

Fig. 9. Decision table for choosing the aggregated assessment

C+	Input +				Output +
	Punctuality	Correctness	Timeliness	Reliability	Actions
	string	string	string	string	string
1	"Excellent", "OK"	"Excellent", "OK"	"Excellent", "OK"	"Excellent", "OK"	-
2	-	"Gap"	-	-	"GapFilling"
3	-	-	-	"MeterProblem"	"MeterMaintenance"
4	-	"MeterError"	-	-	"MeterMaintenance"
5	-	-	"ReadingProblem"	-	"MeterMaintenance"
6	-	"ProblemLower", "AnomalyLower", "ProblemUpper", "AnomalyUpper"	-	-	"MeterMaintenance"
7	-	-	-	"DeviceLowBattery", "DeviceProblem"	"DADMaintenance"
8	-	-	"DADProblem"	-	"DADMaintenance"
9	-	"DeviceError"	-	-	"DADMaintenance"
10	-	"AnomalyLower", "AnomalyUpper"	-	-	"DataTransferMaintenance"
11	"DataTransferProblem"	-	-	-	"DataTransferMaintenance"
12	-	-	-	"BadWirelessConnection"	"DataTransferMaintenance"
13	-	-	"ServerProblem", "DatabaseProblem"	-	"ServerMaintenance"
14	-	-	"SystemProblem"	-	"SystemMaintenance"
15	"DataTransferProblem"	"DeviceError"	"DADProblem"	"DeviceProblem"	"SystemMaintenance"

Fig. 10. Decision table for choosing the data improvement algorithms

server, a time when the server receives data, a time of writing data to the database. The possible timeliness assessments are "Excellent", "OK", "ReadingProblem", "DADProblem", "ServerProblem", "DatabaseProblem", "SystemProblem". The contents of the remaining tables are shown above and below.

U	Input +		Output +
	NewDataAssessment	GroupAssessment	ControlAnalyze
	string	string	string
1	"Excellent"	"Excellent"	"PredictiveAnalytics", "SystemReport", "HistoricalReport", "CostCalculation"
2	"OK"	"OK"	"CostCalculation" "SystemReport", "HistoricalReport"
3	"Bad"	"Excellent", "OK"	"Alarm", "SystemReport"
4	"Satisfactory"	"Satisfactory"	"SystemReport", "HistoricalReport"
5	not("Bad")	"Bad"	"TotalReport"
6	"Bad"	"Bad"	"SystemMalfunction"

Fig. 11. Decision table for choosing DACA

5   Conclusion

This paper presents a new approach to assessing the quality of data on energy consumption in the form of time series with metadata. The presented example of the implementation of the oDMN+ diagram shows the applicability of this method and the high visibility of the relationship between data quality estimates and data sources. One of the ways for further development of this approach is to add a coefficient of the confidence to the results of the DACA that use the assessed data. This decision can also be made using the oDMN+ table. Thanks to this coefficient, it is possible not to limit the usage of specified DACA, however, it should be borne in mind that the results of these algorithms can be trusted considering this coefficient. Further research is also needed on the possibility of implementing more complex DQ assessments using the oDMN+ notation.

Thus, it can be concluded that, although the developed model is simplified for a preliminary study of its potential, the results show that the use of oDMN + and the improved data packaging algorithm is a promising approach for assessing the quality of data in energy management systems of enterprises and institutions. Using this approach, the time spent on the data quality assessment process can be reduced. Although the approach is focused on the quality of data on energy consumption, the authors believe that with minor changes it can be implemented for other areas of data collection and analysis.

Acknowledgments. The reported study was supported by RFBR, research project No. 19-47-340010/19.

References

1. Tyukov, A., Brebels, A., Shcherbakov, M., Kamaev, V.: A concept of web-based energy data quality assurance and control system. In: 14th International Conference on Information Integration and Web-based Applications & Services (IIWAS 2012), pp. 267–271. ACM, New York, NY, USA (2012)
2. Fu, Y., Li, Z., Feng, F., Xu, P.: Data-quality detection and recovery for building energy management and control systems: case study on submetering. Sci. Technol. Built. Environ. **22**(6), 798–809 (2016)
3. Mohammadi, M., Al-Fuqaha, A., Sorour, S., Guizani, M.: Deep learning for IoT big data and streaming analytics: a survey. IEEE Commun. Surv. Tutorials **20**(4), 2923–2960 (2018)
4. Tyukov, A., Khrzhanovskaya, O., Sokolov, A., Shcherbakov, M., Kamaev, V.: Fast access to large timeseries datasets in SCADA systems. Res. J. Appl. Sci. **10**(1), 12–16 (2015)
5. Aljumaili, M., Karim, R., Tretten, P.: Metadata-based data quality assessment. VINE J. Inf. Knowl. Manag. Syst. **46**(2), 232–250 (2016)
6. Aquino, G., Farias, C.M., Pirmez, L.: Data Quality Assessment and Enhancement on Social and Sensor Data. BiDu-Posters@VLDB (2018)
7. Kuemper, D., Iggena, T., Toenjes, R., Pulvermueller, E.: Valid.IoT: a framework for sensor data quality analysis and interpolation. In: 9th ACM Multimedia Systems Conference (MMSys 2018), pp. 294–303. ACM, New York, NY, USA (2018)
8. do Nascimento, N.M., de Lucena, C.J.P.: FIoT: an agent-based framework for self-adaptive and self-organizing applications based on the Internet of Things. Inf. Sci. **378**, 161–176 (2017)
9. Timms, G.P., de Souza, P.A., Reznik Jr., L., Smith, D.V.: Automated data quality assessment of marine sensors. Sensors **11**(10), 9589–9602 (2011)
10. Campbell, J.L., et al.: Quantity is nothing without quality: automated QA/QC for streaming environmental sensor data. Bioscience **63**(7), 574–585 (2013)
11. Sokolov, A., Scherbakov, M., Tyukov, A., Janovsky, T.: Data quality and assurance framework for sensor-driven applications. In: Mathematical Methods in Engineering and Technology (MMTT-31), pp. 87–97. St. Petersburg State Technological Institute, St. Petersburg (2017)
12. Dai, W., Yoshigoe, K., Parsley, W.: Improving data quality through deep learning and statistical models. In: Latifi, S. (ed.) Information Technology - New Generations. AISC, vol. 558, pp. 515–522. Springer, Cham (2018). https://doi.org/10.1007/978-3-319-54978-1_66
13. Using Machine Learning for Data Quality. https://www.talend.com/blog/2017/03/20/machine-learning-impact-data-quality-matching-transfered/. Accessed 06 May 2019
14. Rahman, A., Smith, D.V., Timms, G.: A novel machine learning approach toward quality assessment of sensor data. IEEE Sens. J. **14**(4), 1035–1047 (2014)
15. Kontokosta, C.E.: DataIQ – a machine learning approach to anomaly detection for energy performance data quality and reliability. In: ACEEE Summer Study on Energy Efficiency in Buildings (2016)
16. Vale, S.: Statistical Data Quality in the UNECE. United Nations Statistics Division (2010)
17. Vetrò, A., Canova, L., Torchiano, M., Minotas, C.O., Iemma, R., Morando, F.: Open data quality measurement framework: definition and application to open government data. Govern. Inf. Q. **33**(2), 325–337 (2016)
18. Horita, F.E.A., de Albuquerque, J.P., Marchezini, V., Mendiondo, E.M.: Bridging the gap between decision-making and emerging big data sources: an application of a model-based framework to disaster management in Brazil. Decis. Support Syst. **97**, 12–22 (2017)

62   A. Sokolov et al.

19. Envelope Design Pattern. https://www.marklogic.com/blog/envelope-design-pattern/. Accessed 06 May 2019
20. Dunning, T., Friedman, E.: Time Series Databases: New Ways to Store and Access Data, 1st edn. O'Reilly Media Inc, Sebastopol (2014)
21. Friendly Enough Expression Language (FEEL). https://docs.camunda.org/manual/7.4/reference/dmn11/feel/. Accessed 06 May 2019
22. Camunda Modeler. https://camunda.com/download/modeler/. Accessed 06 May 2019

Decision Support System for the Socio-Economic Development of the Northern Part of the Volga-Akhtuba Floodplain (Russia)

Inessa I. Isaeva(iD), Alexander A. Voronin(iD), Alexander V. Khoperskov$^{(\boxtimes)}$(iD),
Konstantin E. Dubinko(iD), and Anna Yu. Klikunova(iD)

Volgograd State University, Volgograd, Russia
khoperskov@volsu.ru
http://www.volsu.ru

Abstract. In this paper we present a decision suppost system for the socio-economic development of the northern part of the Volga-Aktuba floodplain. It provides data, algorithmic and instrumental tools for searching, modeling, analyzing and evaluating the scenarios of the socio-economic development and the spatially localized and integral characteristics of the floodplain state. We show that mutual dependence of the floodplain hydrological and nature and socio-economic structures requires their target changes coherence in the effective scenarios of its development. The main role in these changes is played by hydrotechnical projects. Their implementation creates a new hydrological structure of this territory, contributing to its socio-economic development.

Keywords: Development scenarios · Hydrotechnical projects ·
Simulation modeling · Multi-criteria evaluation

1 Introduction

The Volga-Akhtuba floodplain (VAF) is a unique natural formation located in the south of Russia [1, 2]. The floodplain natural landscape is due to spring high water flooding a substantial part of its territory. The VAF ecosystem is assigned the first category of international significance. In the course of the last half-century spring floods in the VAF are fully regulated by releasing water through the dam of the Volga Hydroelectric Power Station (VHPS). Its establishment

AAV, KED and III are grateful to Russian Science Foundation (grant No. RFBR 18-41-342001) for the financial support of designing dam placement in the small channels of the northern part of the Volga-Akhtuba floodplain. AVK and AYK acknowledge Ministry of Science and Higher Education of the Russian Federation (government task, project No. 2.852.2017/4.6) for the financial support of the software and numerical simulations development.

© Springer Nature Switzerland AG 2019
A. G. Kravets et al. (Eds.): CIT&DS 2019, CCIS 1083, pp. 63–77, 2019.
https://doi.org/10.1007/978-3-030-29743-5_5

has led to changes in the channel-forming processes downstream, which became the main factor of the VAF natural system progressive degradation. In the VAF territory economic activity is conducted and urbanization processes are actively developing. Reinforcing each other, these factors contribute to the progressive decrease of the floodplain flood area. An additional risk factor is a threat of extreme floods [3, 4].

The issues of designing (creating) decision support systems (DSS) for river water resources distribution are the subject of intensive research. The DSSs described in [5–8] contribute to solving the problem of river water resources shortage for socio-economic demands. The DSSs in [9–12] deal with the problem of a rational balance between socio-economic and ecological needs. The DSS presented in [12] includes long-term natural and technogenic changes in the landscape. Methods and technologies used in these DSSs include interdisciplinary modeling, GIS technologies, scenario approach, multicriteriality. The need for an interdisciplinary approach is a common research problem for intensively managed hydrologic systems [13].

One of the major facts is that the problem under consideration requires the development of management standards for lands adjacent to river systems [14, 15]. The policy of protecting coastal areas should be strictly differentiated and depend on the form of ownership, land use and river system parameters.

Current attempts to supply the northern part of the VAF (NVAF) with water will not obviously change the instability of its socio-economic situation. In order to stabilize the floodplain ecosystem and sustainable socio-economic development one needs a scientifically based system of mutually agreed decisions on the hydrological and socio-economic restructuring of the NVAF territory. As a part of this system we propose the DSS for the socio-economic development of the NVAF in this paper.

2   The DSS Aims and Objectives

The main aim of the DSS is to provide data, algorithmic and analytical tools for searching, analyzing and evaluating scenarios of the NVAF socio-economic development. The scenarios are based on a combination of integrated hydrotechnical projects aimed at targeted flooding and hydrological safety of the territories and also projects of the NVAF socio-economic exploitation. A related aim of the DSS is to provide information about a current and forecast state of the system, considering the decisions taken in the course of its socio-economic development, to individuals and legal entities to increase their activity effectiveness.

The DSS addresses two following objectives:

- description, modeling and evaluation of modern and forecasting the future state of the NVAF, its hydrological and natural and socio-economic structures;
- simulation modeling, analysis and evaluation of the NVAF socio-economic development scenarios.

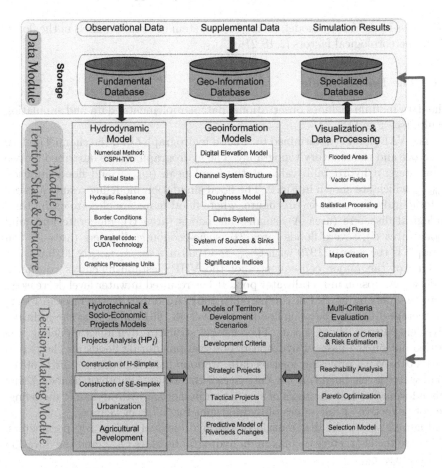

Fig. 1. The framework of the DSS for the NVAF development, including the main components and their relations.

3   The DSS Structure and Functions

A structural and functional model of our DSS is presented in Fig. 1.

We use both standard services of geoinformation technologies for working with spatial data and original approaches based on morphostructural analysis of a digital elevation model (DEM), new GPS measurements, vectorization of satellite images. Geoinformation systems are fundamental tools of decision support systems for environmental water management tasks [16]. A method of DEM creation is described in [17,18]. This method is based on an iterative procedure and uses all available spatial data.

An important component of the DSS is software for hydrodynamic modeling of surface water flows based on the equations of Saint-Venant and parallel methods for Graphics Processing Units (GPUs) [19,20]. We take into account realistic topography, hydraulic resistance to flow, using a non-uniform distribution of roughness in the Chezy model, hierarchical system of small channels in the flood-plain, meteorological factors [2, 18, 21].

3.1   The Data Module

The data module includes observational data, supplemental data and simulation results (see Fig. 1).

The VAF flood is determined by a flood hydrograph $Q(t)$, the channel system structure and the territory topography. The hydrograph can be described by two parameters: a hydrograph value at the flood peak (Q_{max}) and flood duration (τ_{max}), which are shown in Fig. 2. The flood simulation modeling results allowed us to identify five areas in this figure, where flood maps are close to each other: ecological disasters (area A), small-scale floods (area B), moderate and mild floods (area C), severe floods (area D), socio-economic disasters (area F) (an example is the year of 1979 with $Q_{max} \simeq 40\,000\,\mathrm{m}^3 \cdot \mathrm{sec}^{-1}$, $\tau_{max} \simeq 20$ days).

One of the major consequences of the VHPS establishment is continued underwater erosion in its tailwater pool. It has resulted in water level decrease in main channels by 1.2–1.4 m compared to 1961. According to the inset in Fig. 2, the average difference between flood water levels in 1961 and 2018 at the Akhtuba River entrance is about 1.3 m. The channel structure dynamics modeling was carried out on the basis of hydroposts observations during floods for the period 1961–2018. With provision for this data, we found the dependence $\Delta h(t)$ of the flood water levels height at the entrance of the Volga-Akhtuba Channel. Using this information and the tools of simulation numerical hydrodynamic modeling, we got "effective" peak values of hydrographs for different years Q_{max}^{eff}.

Figure 2 shows the distribution of two hydrological regime key parameters, which are the characteristic maximum hydrograph values Q_{max} and the duration of this stage τ_{max}.

Using the territory cadastral map, we created a digital map of social, economic and ecological indices, which reflect the significance of the corresponding territories. For illustrative purposes in Fig. 8 we combine the first two types of indices.

3.2   The Module of the Territory State and Structure

The hydrodynamic flood modeling block is based on numerical integration of Saint-Venant equations:

$$\frac{dH}{dt} = -H \cdot \nabla u + Q^{(+)} - Q^{(-)}, \tag{1}$$

$$\frac{d(Hu)}{dt} = -gH\nabla(b + H) - H\,|u|\,u\frac{gn_M^2}{H^{4/3}} + P_Q, \tag{2}$$

where $\dfrac{d}{dt} = \dfrac{\partial}{\partial t} + u \cdot \nabla$ is a total continual derivative, $\nabla = e_x \cdot \dfrac{\partial}{\partial x} + e_y \cdot \dfrac{\partial}{\partial y}$ is a 2D operator nabla, $H(x, y, t)$ is depth, $u(x, y, t) = e_x u_x + e_y u_y$, $b(x, y)$ is topography,

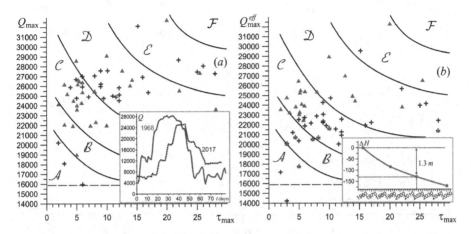

Fig. 2. The hydrograph parameters distribution on the plane $Q_{max} - \tau_{max}$ for the period 1961–2018. A sample group for the period 1961–1989 is marked by triangles and a sample group for the period 1990–2018 is marked by crosses ($[\tau_{max}] = $ days, $[Q_{max}] = $ m$^3 \cdot$ s^{-1}). Dashed line indicates critically low hydrograph level leading to catastrophic situations in the floodplain. a—for the modern topography with no correction for underwater topography change. b—with a correction for underwater topography change.

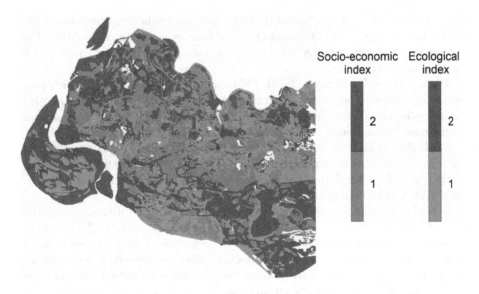

Fig. 3. The map of the NVAF nature and socio-economic indexes.

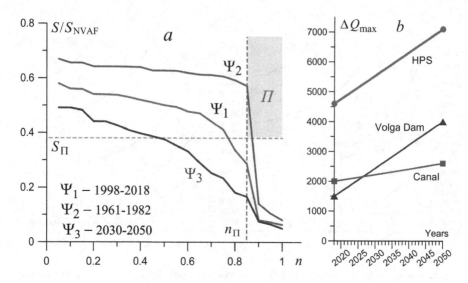

Fig. 4. (*a*) The cumulative distribution functions of the relative flood area in the NVAF: Ψ_1 is a curve for the period 1998–2018; Ψ_2 is a curve for the period 1961–1981; Ψ_3 is a forecast curve for the period 2030–2050. (*b*) Projections of increasing the maximum hydrograph values needed to maintain the stably flooded areas (See domain Π) in case of increasing the water release through the dam of the VHPS, in case of implementing projects: building a bypass canal to the Akhtuba River (HP_1) and building a dam on the Volga River (HP_2).

$n_M(x, y)$ is the Manning coefficient characterizing hydraulic resistance due to the earth's surface properties, $Q^{(+)}$ and $Q^{(-)}$ are sources and sinks respectively, $\boldsymbol{P}_Q$ is the momentum change due to the presence of the sources and sinks, g is a gravitational acceleration.

We use the well-balanced CSPH-TVD numerical scheme [2, 20], which provides conservatism and allows performing end-to-end calculation of the nonstationary dynamics of the water-dry bottom boundary. The system of equations (1) program realization is based on parallelizing with CUDA technology [19].

With the obtained results and the data on flood hydrographs presented in Fig. 2 we construct a modern (curve Ψ_1), a retrospective (curve Ψ_2) and a prognostic (curve Ψ_3) cumulative distribution functions of the relative flood area in the NVAF for the corresponding 20-year periods (Fig. 4).

In addition, in Fig. 4, we indicate threshold values of the frequency and the stably flooded territory area, found with the help of expert analysis. These values provide stable reproduction of the floodplain ecosystem. Figure 5 presents maps of stably (with frequency $n_\Pi = 0.85$) flooded areas corresponding to curves Ψ_1 and Ψ_2 in Fig. 4. As one can see, the territory, which is considered as a biotope of a modern floodplain ecosystem and has been stably flooded over the past 20 years, has significantly reduced its area and lost its compactness compared to 1961. Computational experiments have shown that this compactness can be significantly restored when S_Π reaches a value 0.38.

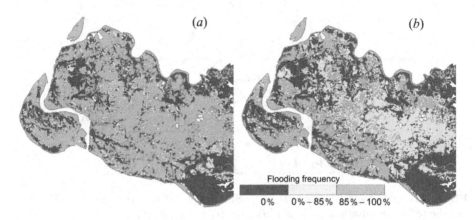

Fig. 5. The hydrological structure of the NVAF for the period: (a) 1962–1982, (b) 1998–2018.

The model of the NVAF channel structure is created for effective simulation modeling of hydrotechnical projects. It provides possibilities for storage, visualization and editing it as a hierarchical network graph containing 258 vertices and 6 hierarchical levels. Figure 3 presents the map of nature and socio-economic indexes (NSE-structure) of the NVAF. The models of aggregated hydrological and NSE structures of the NVAF are used for evaluation its current and target states. The vector $\boldsymbol{\mu} = (\mu_1, \mu_2, \mu_3)$ represents the aggregated hydrological structure of the floodplain territory. The vector components are determined by areas of stably (S_{st}), unstably (S_{un}) flooded and non-flooded (S_{not}) territories respectively. The aggregated NSE structure is set by a vector of relative areas of the territories $\boldsymbol{\varphi} = (\varphi_1, \varphi_2, \varphi_3)$ identified as ecological, social or economic territories due to their cadastral type by expert analysis. An important feature of the area under study is the cadastral type uncertainty of its substantial part (45%), which is the resource of the socio-economic development. The described aggregated structures are presented as a point and a region, respectively, on the corresponding simplexes in Fig. 6. At the simplex of the hydrological structure we show its dynamics trajectory for the period 1961–2018 and the forecast trajectory up to 2050.

4   The Decision-Making Module

4.1   Hydrotechnical and Socio-Economic Project Models

Since the Volga River pristine topography recovery requires unacceptably high costs, the hydrotechnical projects should alternatively change the channel structure in other parts of the NVAF, maintaining or restoring the flood hydrographs effectiveness.

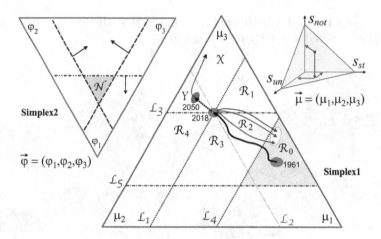

Fig. 6. The hydrological (Simplex1) and NSE (Simplex2) structures of the VAF. We use the following notation: $\mu_1 = S_{st}/S_{NVAF}$, $\mu_2 = S_{un}/S_{NVAF}$, $\mu_3 = S_{not}/S_{NVAF}$, $\varphi_1 = S_{ecol}/S_{NVAF}$, $\varphi_2 = S_{soc}/S_{NVAF}$, $\varphi_3 = S_{econ}/S_{NVAF}$. The symbol $\mathcal{N}$ indicates the territory with an undefined cadastral type.

The presented DSS includes simulation and optimization hydrotechnical project models of the following types:

HP_1. A bypass canal construction from the Volgograd Reservoir to the Akhtuba River.

HP_2. Flood dams installation on the Volga Channel.

HP_3. Flood dams installation on the Akhtuba Channel.

HP_4. Flood dams installation on the NVAF small channels.

HP_5. The NVAF small channels deepening.

The hydrotechnical projects that change the vector $\boldsymbol{\mu}$ as a result of their implementation are strategic. The projects changing only the plot of the function Ψ, but preserving $\boldsymbol{\mu}$ are tactical. The projects that save Ψ are called local.

The results of projects HP_1–HP_5 research demonstrate that the projects HP_1 and HP_2 are strategic [4,22–24].

Figure 7 shows the simulation results for the HP_1 project. The effectiveness of the bypass channel from the Volgograd reservoir to the River Akhtuba is greatly impaired by the possible return flow from the Akhtuba River to the Volga River, which requires an additional regulating dam between the Volga River and the Akhtuba River.

The projects HP_3, HP_4 and HP_5 are tactical or local [23,24]. We will describe the project HP_4 in more detail. The mathematical problem of targeted stable flooded area increasing by installing flood dams has the form:

$$S(\nu, Q, t) \geq S_{\Pi}, \quad n \geq n_{\Pi}, \quad \nu = (\nu_1, ..., \nu_k), \quad \nu_i = \{0; 1\}, \tag{3}$$

where k is a number of channels and virtual dams, $\boldsymbol{\nu} = (\nu_1, \nu_2, ..., \nu_k)$ is a dam configuration vector ($\nu = (1, 0)$ dam is/is not on a channel). In (3) a value of the flood hydrograph first stage actually sets a lower limit of the flooded area increase ΔS, which, with the territory relief, implicitly determines the target increment of the project flood map and water volume $\Delta V(\Delta S)$.

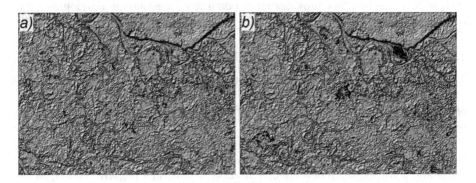

Fig. 7. (a) The red color shows areas of additional flooding from the implementation of the project of the bypass channel "Volgograd reservoir – Akhtuba". (b) The project of a new dam at the beginning of the River Akhtuba: red color indicates areas of additional flooding, blue color shows areas of negative impact of this dam. (Color figure online)

The algorithm for solving this problem is based on maximizing the upper estimate $\Delta V(\Delta S)$. Considering the flood analysis in the project target area, we define groups of acceptor channels, which serve as the source of its flooding, for a potential increase in the water volume passing through them. The number of elements s in a group is an internal parameter of the algorithm. We use two methods of selecting channels in groups. In the first method, we calculate the index of channel proximity to the target area. In the second method, we calculate the ratio of this index to the channel length.

For each group, using the channel structure model, we define a group with a maximum number of donor channels $m(s)$. Their capacity limitation may potentially contribute to an increase in the water flow in the acceptor channels group. Then we calculate the upper estimate of this variant effectiveness $\Delta V(s)$. For each s value one can determine the largest upper estimate value $\Delta V^*(s)$ ($s = 1, ..., n$) and the corresponding optimal groups of the acceptor and donor channels. Figure 8 shows the algorithm results as the NVAF map, which indicates threshold flooded areas (light-blue), the target area flooded with a frequency of $0.65 \div 0.85$ (blue), the optimal group of the donor channels (red) and the acceptor channels (green). Figure 8 corresponds to the case of $s = 27$.

The socio-economic projects are urbanization and agricultural territory expansion. The urbanization project of the NVAF was studied in [8]. In this work authors presented the spatially distributed and aggregated project change results and the permissible flooded area decrease as functions of control objectives.

The economic development projects are due to stabilization of filling the channels with water for agricultural lands irrigation. Using dams in small channels, we investigated the project for flooding one part of the territory. The side effect of that was stable filling the channels of the other part of the territory with water. The last fact provides an opportunity for economic development in this territory.

4.2   The Models of the Territory Development Scenarios

The criteria for the socio-economic development level are the values of aggregated social, economic and ecological criteria as well as the values of corresponding risks of reducing them in the future. In case of the floodplains, they are accompanied by the extreme flood risk.

A substantial peculiarity of the floodplain areas is mutual dependence of their hydrological and NSE structures. A change in one structure can be both a cause and a consequence of a change in another one. The negative consequence of the socio-economic expansion is the potential restriction of the safe flood parameters range and, as a result, the environmental and social risks growth. A counteraction is implementation of the hydrotechnical flooding and flood safety projects in this territory. However, the considerable dependence of the latter on the hydrological structure can significantly reduce their effectiveness for many options of such expansion. On the other hand, the aggregated nature of the socio-economic criteria makes possible a great variety of their territorial distribution.

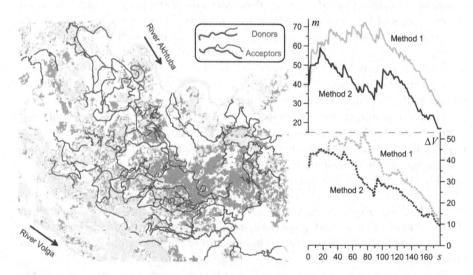

Fig. 8. Left—the donor and acceptor channels positions for $s = 27$. Right—the dependencies $m(s)$ and $\Delta V(s)$ $[10^6 \, \text{m}^3]$ for two different methods. (Color figure online)

In addition, the aggregated state criteria values are determined by not only the respective territory areas, but also evaluation of their state, mainly depended on the flood hydrological regime. The latter, in turn, is governed by both natural processes and hydrotechnical projects. Thus, the development scenarios effectiveness is largely determined by the consistency degree of changes in the hydrological and NSE structures. The possibility and effectiveness of changes in the hydrological structure play the key role in such coordination.

The model of the territory development scenarios consists of a forecast model of channel dynamics and a set of hydrotechnical and socio-economic development project models. To classify them, we draw segments $\mathcal{L}_i$ parallel to the Simplex1 sides (see Fig. 6), corresponding to constant values μ_i ($i = 1, 2, 3$), through the point $\boldsymbol{\mu}(2018)$, segment $\mathcal{L}_4$ corresponding to the threshold value μ_1, and segment $\mathcal{L}_5$ corresponding to the current non-flooded territory share engaged in the socio-economic activity. As a result, in the Simplex1 we identify a number of target regions ($\mathcal{R}_0 - \mathcal{R}_4$, $\mathcal{X}$, Y). Their achievement can be meaningfully interpreted as a result of various socio-economic development scenarios implementation.

Symbol $\mathcal{R}_0$ marks stable development region. The transition to it is primarily the result of the project territory flooding at the minor floods (areas $\mathcal{A}$, $\mathcal{B}$ in Fig. 1), wherein the plot of the function Ψ passes through the threshold area Π in Fig. 4. The strategic projects HP_1 and HP_2 achieve the value $\Delta Q_{\max}$ necessary for this state (see Fig. 4). The projects HP_3–HP_5 contribute to reducing the loss or expansion of the non-flooded territory, its protection from extreme floods as well as stable filling its channels and reservoirs with water. So their implementation can create conditions for the effective socio-economic development. The region $\mathcal{R} = \cup \mathcal{R}_i$ ($i = 1, ..., 4$) differs from the region $\mathcal{R}_0$ by the curve Ψ absence in the threshold area Π in Fig. 4. It means only slowing the pace of the floodplain ecosystem degradation. The regions $\mathcal{R}_1 - \mathcal{R}_4$ can be achieved by complex implementation of the projects HP_1–HP_5 with a limiting resource. The scale of each project and the territorial distribution of project work are determined by a specific region $\mathcal{R}_i$. However, the lack of the strategic projects HP_1 and HP_2 in this complex leads only to tactical or local changes.

The transition to the region $\mathcal{X}$ means the aggressive urbanization strategy adoption. It is followed by the non-flooded territory expansion, the stable and unstable flooded areas reduction through the hydrological safety projects HP_3 and HP_4 implementation with a further $Q_{\max}^{eff}$ decrease. And finally, the transition to the region Y means further prolongation of both the floodplain ecosystem degradation and the spontaneous land development.

4.3   The Models of Goal Setting and Multi-criteria Evaluation

The DSS uses ecological, social and economic territorially localized criteria of state and risk. Their aggregation throughout the territory is carried out by summation. The following functions with the number of grades β are used to calculate the ecological criterion of each DEM cell:

$$I_{ecol}^t = I_{ecol}^k, \quad n^t \geq n_\Pi,$$

$$I_{ecol}^t = \frac{\lambda - 1}{\beta} I_{ecol}^k, \quad \frac{\lambda - 1}{\beta} n_\Pi \leq n^t \leq \frac{\lambda}{\beta} n_\Pi, \tag{4}$$

where $\lambda = 1, ..., \beta$, I_{ecol}^k is a cadastral ecological cell index, n^t is cell flooding frequency for 20-year period preceding the year t. We consider the neighborhood of each cell which size is set by an expert. Such neighborhood is characterized by the total volume of water in the channels V^t, the total length of roads L^t and the average ecological index $I_{ecol,av}^t$. The economic and social criteria values for each cell are calculated by the following formulas:

$$I_{econ}^t = I_{econ}^k \left(\beta_1 n_{can}^t + \beta_2 n_{road}^t \right), \tag{5}$$

$$I_{soc}^t = I_{soc}^k \left(\alpha_1 n_{can}^t + \alpha_2 n_{road}^t + \alpha_3 n_{ecol}^t \right), \quad n_{ecol}^t = \frac{I_{ecol,av}^t}{I_{ecol,av}^0}, \tag{6}$$

where $n_{can}^t = V^t / V_0$, $n_{road}^t = L^t / L_0$, I_{econ}^k and I_{soc}^k are the cadastral economic and social cell indices, a parameter β and weight coefficients α_i and β_i are specified by an expert, symbols with index 0 are initial system state parameters.

Local degradation risks are proportional to the forecast relative reduction values of all criteria after a specified time period. The values of socio-economic territory flooding local risk are equal to their criteria values in the case of corresponding cells flooding by floods from area $\mathcal{F}$ in Fig. 2.

The DSS finds development scenarios characterized by target values of the criteria and risks described above, as well as analyzes their reachability within limited resources. Figure 9 shows a logical scheme of its functioning. We define aggregated criteria and risks by summing social and economic criteria and risks to clarify the analysis of the scenarios types $\mathcal{R}$, $\mathcal{R}_0$, $\mathcal{X}$, $\mathcal{Y}$. Each scenario is characterized by a cost value and five efficiency parameters: the aggregated ecological criterion, the aggregated socio-economic criterion, the aggregated risk of ecological degradation, the aggregated risk of socio-economic degradation, the aggregated risk of socio-economic territory flooding. We use a linguistic static scale ("Low" (L), "Medium" (M), "High" (H) to evaluate each parameter. As a result of simulation experiments, we obtain the following six-tuples of scenarios qualitative evaluations:

$$\mathcal{X} \rightleftharpoons \langle L; L; H; H; L; H \rangle, \quad \mathcal{R} \rightleftharpoons \langle M; M; M; M; H; M \rangle,$$

$$\mathcal{R}_0 \rightleftharpoons \langle H; H; M; L; L; L \rangle, \quad Y \rightleftharpoons \langle \phi; M; L; H; H; M \rangle.$$

5   Discussion and Conclusions

1. The presented DSS for the socio-economic development of the NVAF provides data, algorithmic and instrumental tools for searching, modeling, analyzing and evaluating the scenarios of the socio-economic development and the spatially localized and integral characteristics of the floodplain state.

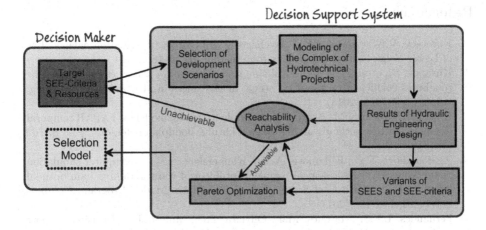

Fig. 9. The logical scheme of the DSS functioning.

2. The mutual dependence of floodplain hydrological and socio-economic structures requires their target changes coherence in the effective scenarios of its development. The main role in these changes is played by hydrotechnical projects. Their implementation creates a new hydrological structure of this territory, contributing to its socio-economic development.

3. Computational experiments showed that even with lowering the thresholds values of flooding frequency and the stable flooded area by 20% the NVAF ecosystem stabilization is impossible without the strategic projects HP_1 or HP_2. A dam on the Volga Channel enables achieving stabilization of the threshold flooding level with the current parameters of the channel system, but with its further degradation the capacity of this dam will not be enough. A bypass canal to the Akhtuba River can potentially be designed for long-term preservation of the NVAF ecosystem threshold stabilization. For this purpose, the project parameters of the canal maximum water discharge should exceed 2000 m^3/s. On the other hand, accounting the VHPS water discharge potential savings to ensure an equivalent territory flooding significantly increases the project efficiency.

4. Despite the high formalization and verifiability level of mathematical NVAF state and project models, the heuristic model of the channel dynamics and the expert model of its hydrological structure are the foundation of the development strategies analysis in the presented DSS. The enhancement of these models based on ecological and hydrological research will significantly increase the analytical and prognostic value of the DSS.

References

1. Korotaev, V.N., Chernov, A.V., Rychagov, G.I.: History of formation palaeodeltas of Lower Volga Deltas. Geogr. Environ. Sustain. **01**, 4–16 (2010)
2. Khrapov, S., et al.: The numerical simulation of shallow water: estimation of the roughness coefficient on the flood stage. In: Advances in Mechanical Engineering, vol. 5, id. 787016 (2013)
3. Kozlov, A., Kozlova, M., Skorik, N.: A simple harmonic model for FAPAR temporal dynamics in the wetlands of the Volga-Akhtuba floodplain. Remote Sens. **8**, 762 (2016)
4. Agafonnikova, E.O., Klikunova, A.Yu., Khoperskov, A.V.: A computer simulation of the Volga river hydrological regime: a problem of water-retaining dam optimal location. Bull. South Ural State Univers. Ser. Math. Model. Program. Comput. Softw. **10**, 148–155 (2017)
5. Fernandes, L.F.S., Marques, M.J., Oliveira, P.C., Moura, J.P.: Decision support systems in water resources in the demarcated region of Douro – case study in Pinhao river basin, Portugal. Water Environ. J. **33**, 350–357 (2019)
6. Ge, Y., Li, X., Huang, C., Nan, Z.: A decision support system for irrigation water allocation along the middle reaches of the Heihe river basin, Northwest China. Environ. Model. Softw. **47**, 182–192 (2013)
7. Wriggers, P., Kultsova, M., Kapysh, A., Kultsov, A., Zhukova, I.: Intelligent decision support system for river floodplain management. Commun. Comput. Inf. Sci. **466**, 195–213 (2014)
8. Voronin, A., Isaeva, I., Khoperskov, A., Grebenuk, S.: Decision support system for urbanization of the northern part of the Volga-Akhtuba floodplain (Russia) on the basis of interdisciplinary computer modeling. Commun. Comput. Inf. Sci. **754**, 419–429 (2017)
9. Weng, S.Q., Huang, G.H., Li, Y.P.: An integrated scenario-based multi-criteria decision support system for water resources management and planning – a case study in the Haihe river basin. Expert Syst. Appl. **37**, 8242–8254 (2010)
10. McCord, J., Carron, J.C., Liu, B., Rhoton, S., Rocha, M., Stockton, T.: Pecos River Decision Support System: Application for Adjudication Settlement and River Operations EIS. Southern Illinois University Carbondale OpenSIUC. 95 (2004)
11. Lamy, F., Bolte, J., Santelmann, M., Smith, C.: Development and evaluation of multiple objective decision making methods for watershed management planning. J. Am. Water Resour. Assoc. **38**, 517–529 (2002)
12. Misganaw, D., Guo, Y., Knapp, H.V., Bhowmik, N.G.: The Illinois River Decision Support System (ILRDSS), Report Prepared for the: Illinois Department of Natural Resources, p. 48 (1999)
13. Han, B., Benner, S.G., Bolte, J.P., Vache, K.B., Flores, A.N.: Coupling biophysical processes and water rights to simulate spatially distributed water use in an intensively managed hydrologic system. Hydrol. Earth Syst. Sci. **21**, 3671–3685 (2017)
14. Boisjolie, B.A., Santelmann, M.V., Flitcroft, R.L., Duncan, S.L.: Legal ecotones: a comparative analysis of riparian policy protection in the Oregon Coast Range, USA. J. Environ. Manag. **197**, 206–220 (2017)
15. Flitcroft, R., et al.: Using expressed behaviour of coho salmon (Oncorhynchus kisutch) to evaluate the vulnerability of upriver migrants under future hydrological regimes: management implications and conservation planning. Aquat. Conserv. Mar. Freshw. Ecosyst. (2019)

16. Lamy, F., Bolte, J., Santelmann, M., Smith, C.: Development and evaluation of multiple-objtective decision-making methods for watershed management planning. J. Am. Water Resour. Assoc. **38**, 517–529 (2002)
17. Presnyakova, A.N., Pisarev, A.V., Khrapov, S.S.: The flooding dynamics of the Volga-Akhtuba floodplain during spring flood using space monitoring. Math. Phys. Comput. Simul. **1**, 66–74 (2017)
18. Klikunova, A.Y., Khoperskov, A.V.: Numerical hydrodynamic model of the lower Volga. J. Phys. Conf. Ser. **1128**, 012087 (2018)
19. Dyakonova, T., Khoperskov, A., Khrapov, S.: Numerical model of shallow water: the use of NVIDIA CUDA graphics processors. Commun. Comput. Inf. Sci. **687**, 132–145 (2016)
20. Khoperskov, A., Khrapov, S.: A numerical simulation of the shallow water flow on a complex topography. In: Numerical Simulations in Engineering and Science. pp. 237–254. Srinivasa Rao, InTechOpen (2018)
21. Dyakonova, T.A.: The method of estimation of the effective roughness coefficient in the meandering channels based on numerical simulation. Math. Phys. Comput. Simul. **21**, 64–69 (2018)
22. Voronin, A., Kharitonov, M.: Model for optimizing the hierarchical structure of artificial canals in floodplain areas. In: International Russian Automation Conference (RusAutoCon), pp. 1–5. IEEE (2018)
23. Voronin, A., Vasilchenko, A., Khoperskov, A.: A project optimization for small watercourses restoration in the northern part of the Volga-Akhtuba floodplain by the geoinformation and hydrodynamic modeling. J. Phys. Conf. Ser. **973**, 012064 (2018)
24. Vasilchenko, A., Voronin, A., Svetlov, A., Antonyan, N.: Assessment of the impact of riverbeds depth in the northern part of the Volga-Akhtuba floodplain on the dynamics of its flooding. Int. J. Pure Appl. Math. **110**, 183–192 (2016)

Modeling and Optimization of Proactive Management of the Production Pollutions in the Conditions of Information Asymmetry

Aleksey F. Rogachev[1,2]([⊠]) [iD] and Maksim S. Lukashin[1]

[1] Volgograd State Agrarian University, Volgograd, Russia
rafr@mail.ru
[2] Volgograd State Technical University, Volgograd, Russia

Abstract. On the basis of the constructed mathematical model, an analysis is made of which of the instruments for regulating industrial emissions of enterprises - environmental standards or quotas sold for industrial emissions of pollutants - allows minimizing the total costs of the strategy of environmental regulation. The necessity of taking into account the asymmetry of information support of the optimization process is shown. It has been proved that the environmental policy regulator, aiming to limit the aggregate level of emissions of a given pollutant by several enterprises, can minimize total costs by applying enterprise-specific environmental standards. The system of quotas sold for production emissions allows minimizing the total costs of the strategy of environmental and economic regulation only if the costs of the environmental audit are the same for all enterprises. It is established that in the event that the cost of implementing penalties varies between enterprises, the competitive market for emission allowances will not minimize the total costs of providing the total amount of emissions for a certain level, allowing a certain degree of non-compliance with environmental requirements.

Keywords: Mathematical modeling · Industrial pollution · Optimization · Proactive control · Asymmetry

1 Introduction

Restriction and regulation of harmful emissions and pollution of industrial and agricultural enterprises is an important government problem, especially in the context of globalization. In the works of M. Buyanova, E. Gushchina, A. Ivashchenko, V. Kamaev, A. Kalinina, A. Kravets, I. Natalukha, E. Petrova, M. Shcherbakov, A. Shokhnekh, N. Skiter and other researchers [1, 9, 13, 18–21] considered the risks and asymmetry of information available to participants in the quota market for pollution. These features of information support further complicate the search for optimal regulatory options.

An effective strategy for regulating industrial pollution is the use of market-oriented tools of environmental and economic policy, including in the field of food security [15–17]. In the study of the problems of proactive management of the structural dynamics of complex technical and social systems, a number of significant theoretical

© Springer Nature Switzerland AG 2019
A. G. Kravets et al. (Eds.): CIT&DS 2019, CCIS 1083, pp. 78–88, 2019.
https://doi.org/10.1007/978-3-030-29743-5_6

results were obtained in various subject areas [8–10, 13]. Among the tools of proactive management, it is possible to note the introduction of fees for industrial emissions, as well as the development of the market for emission quotas of enterprises [2, 3]. However, such a strategy should be complemented by forcing enterprises to comply with the requirements of environmental standards [4, 5].

Reasonable decisions in the field of modernization of the state policy of regulating industrial emissions, as well as the development of an optimal proactive management strategy [3] for industrial pollution by enterprises can be obtained on the basis of fairly rigorous mathematical models of environmental pollution control processes [6, 7, 11, 12, 14, 15]. These circumstances determine the relevance of this work.

2 Methodology

Fundamental methods of constructing, transforming, and studying mathematical models, analytical methods of the classical optimization theory, basic principles of optimal environmental management, proactive management and taking into account the risks of information asymmetry were used in the work. An optimal regulatory strategy based on environmental standards [2, 3] implies the specificity of using environmental standards for enterprises. This allows the enterprises to fully comply with environmental requirements using linear or quadratic penalty functions [10].

Consider the main areas of sustainable development (Fig. 1), focused on improving the quality of life for each person [1].

3 Results and Discussion

The problems of environmental and economic security, as well as free access to relevant information, depicted in the diagram above, are closely related to each other. At the same time, the state, as a regulator of the top level of management, should ensure environmental safety using economically sound methods of proactive management, predicting the possible consequences of the influence of control tools and impacts. Information support and ensuring the management process in the conditions of information asymmetry will directly affect its effectiveness.

Let us formulate the question: which of the regulatory instruments allows minimizing the total costs of the strategy of environmental and economic regulation - environmental standards or quotas [5] sold for industrial emissions of pollutants?

The answer to this question is given by the following statement.

Statement 1. The environmental and economic policy regulator, which aims to limit the total level of emissions of a given polluting substance by several enterprises, can minimize total costs by applying environmental standards specific to enterprises. The system of sold quotas for industrial emissions allows minimizing the total costs of the strategy of environmental and economic regulation only if $\mu_i = \mu_j$ (μ_i - the costs of inspecting the enterprise i) for all enterprises $i \neq j$, i, j = 1, ..., n or $f''(0) = 0$ (f - the function of fines for environmental violations).

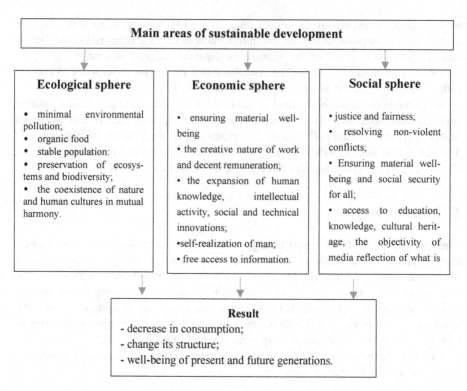

Fig. 1. Ways improving life quality

Evidence that the costs of implementing the strategy of environmental and economic regulation, based on environmental standards, are lower than the total costs of using the system of sold emission allowances, is trivial. By definition, when using an optimal strategy of environmental and economic regulation based on environmental standards, which should ensure full compliance of enterprises with environmental requirements, environmental responsibility (standards) and monitoring probabilities are chosen in such a way as to minimize the total costs of an environmental and economic regulation strategy, limiting aggregate emissions.

Consequently, the total costs of implementing an environmental-economic regulation strategy based on environmental standards should be lower than the implementation of an optimal regulatory strategy using as a tool a system of traded emissions for industrial emissions, which leads to a different distribution of emissions and probabilities of monitoring. In contrast to the strategy of environmental and economic regulation based on environmental standards, an optimal regulatory strategy that uses as a tool a system of sold quotas for industrial emissions does not minimize the total costs of the strategy of environmental and economic regulation that limits the total emissions of divided level, unless monitoring costs differ between enterprises or the marginal penalty is constant.

This last statement we will prove below.

In order to make a task for a regulator, provided that the system of sold emission quotas is used as an instrument of environmental regulation, it is comparable to the task for a regulator, provided that environmental standards are used as an instrument of environmental regulation. When using the strategy of environmental and economic regulation based on the system of quotas on industrial emissions, minimizing costs, the regulator chooses the level of violation v_i and the level of monitoring π_i for each enterprise i, i = 1, ..., n, where v_i = ei − li, and li there are the number of quotas for industrial emissions of pollutants that the enterprise i requires. In formalized form, the task of the regulator is formulated as follows

$$\min_{\substack{(v_1, v_2, \ldots, v_n) \\ (\pi_1, \pi_2, \ldots, \pi_n)}} \sum_{i=1}^{n} c_i(v_i + l_i(p^*, \pi_i)) + \sum_{i=1}^{n} \mu_i \pi_i + \sum_{i=1}^{n} \beta_i \pi_i f(v_i)$$

under the conditions

$$\sum_{i=1}^{n} v_i + l_i(p^*, \pi_i) = Z \text{ и } v_i \geq 0, \quad i = 1, \ldots, n,$$

and, where $l_i(p^*, \pi_i)$ represents the enterprise's demand for quotas for industrial emissions of pollutants and p^* is the equilibrium price of quotas for industrial emissions subject to full compliance of the enterprise's emissions with environmental requirements (i.e., a solution to the equation $\sum_{i=1}^{n} l_i(p^*, \pi_i) = L = Z$ where L − is the number of issued quotas on industrial emissions), c − is a function describing the costs of an enterprise to reduce harmful emissions.

Regardless of the status of an enterprise in terms of the level of compliance of its emissions with environmental requirements in a competitive market for industrial emissions, each company i chooses its level of emissions in such a way $-c_i'(\cdot) = p$. Consequently, the optimal choice of emissions can be represented as a function of the price of quotas for industrial emissions: $e_i = e_i(p)$.

Each enterprise, whose emissions do not meet environmental requirements, has a demand for quotas for industrial emissions of pollutants in accordance with the condition $p = \pi_i f'(v_i = e_i(p) - l_i)$. But provided that the monitoring is effective from the point of view of dejection, it requires equality $\pi_i = \frac{p}{f'(0)}$ for all $i = 1, \ldots, n$, it is also true that equality $p = \pi_i f'(v_i)$ takes place at $v_i = 0$. Thus, this equation determines the enterprise's demand for emissions $l_i(p, \pi_i)$ at $v_i \geq 0$.

For the optimization problem formulated above, the Lagrangian is

$$\Lambda = \sum_{i=1}^{n} c_i(v_i + l_i(p^*, \pi_i)) + \sum_{i=1}^{n} \mu_i \pi_i + \sum_{i=1}^{n} \beta_i \pi_i f(v_i)$$
$$+ \lambda(\sum_{i=1}^{n} v_i + l_i(p^*, \pi_i) - Z).$$

Kuhn-Tucker conditions for this problem are written as follows

$$\frac{\partial \Lambda}{\partial \pi_i} = c_i'(\cdot)\left(\frac{\partial l_i}{\partial p^*}\frac{\partial p^*}{\partial \pi_i} + \frac{\partial l_i}{\partial \pi_i}\right) + \mu_i + \beta_i f(v_i) + \lambda\left(\frac{\partial l_i}{\partial p^*}\frac{\partial p^*}{\partial \pi_i} + \frac{\partial l_i}{\partial \pi_i}\right) \geq 0, \quad (1)$$

$$\pi_i \geq 0, \quad \frac{\partial \Lambda}{\partial \pi_i}\pi_i = 0, \quad i = 1, \ldots, n; \quad \frac{\partial \Lambda}{\partial v_i} = c_i'(\cdot) + \pi_i\beta_i f'(v_i) + \lambda \geq 0, \quad (2)$$

$$v_i \geq 0, \quad \frac{\partial \Lambda}{\partial v_i}v_i = 0, i = 1, \ldots, n; \quad \frac{\partial \Lambda}{\partial \lambda} = \sum_{i=1}^{n} v_i + l_i(p^*, \pi_i) - Z = 0.$$

If it is optimal to ensure full compliance of emissions produced by enterprises with environmental requirements for all i ($v_i = 0$), in the preposition $\pi_i > 0$ for all i, Eq. (1) is written as

$$\frac{\partial \Lambda}{\partial \pi_i} = c_i'(\cdot) + \frac{\mu_i}{\frac{\partial l_i}{\partial p^*}\frac{\partial p^*}{\partial \pi_i} + \frac{\partial l_i}{\partial \pi_i}} + \lambda = 0, \quad i = 1, \ldots, n. \quad (3)$$

Using the condition $-c_i'(\cdot) = p$ and assuming the condition of perfect competition in the quota market for production emissions of pollutants, $\frac{\partial p^*}{\partial \pi_i} = 0$, can be written (3) as

$$-p^* + \frac{\mu_i}{\frac{\partial l_i}{\partial \pi_i}} = -\lambda, \quad i = 1, \ldots, n.$$

This means that when using a cost-minimizing strategy of environmental and economic regulation based on a system of sold quotas for industrial emissions (if the condition of perfect competition in the market for industrial emissions of pollutants is met), the following equality should occur

$$-p^* + \frac{\mu_i}{\frac{\partial l_i}{\partial \pi_i}} = -p^* + \frac{\mu_j}{\frac{\partial l_j}{\partial \pi_j}}$$

at all $i \neq j, i,j = 1, \ldots, n$.

Further, using the relation $p = \pi_i f'(v_i)$, we obtain

$$\frac{\partial l_i}{\partial \pi_i} = \frac{f'(v_i)}{\pi_i f''(v_i)}$$

for all $i = 1, \ldots, n$.

So, if $v_i = 0$, we come to equality

$$-p^* + \mu_i\frac{\pi_i f''(0)}{f'(0)} = -p^* + \mu_j\frac{\pi_j f''(0)}{f'(0)}$$

for all $i \neq j$, $i,j = 1, \ldots, n$.

Replacing the expressions π_i in the last equality $\frac{p^*}{f'(0)}$, we obtain

$$-p^* + \mu_i \frac{p^* f''(0)}{(f'(0))^2} = -p^* + \mu_j \frac{p^* f''(0)}{(f'(0))^2}$$

for all $i \neq j$, $i,j = 1, \ldots, n$.

In the competitive market of quotas for industrial emissions of pollutants (that is, providing a single equilibrium price of quotas for industrial emissions of pollutants p^*), the equality obtained above holds if and only if $\mu_i = \mu_j$ or $f''(0) = 0$. Therefore, it can be concluded that if $f''(0) \neq 0$, and $\mu_i \neq \mu_j$ for any two enterprises $i \neq j$, a competitive system of sold quotas on industrial emissions of pollutants will not minimize the total costs of an environmental and economic management strategy that provides aggregate emissions at a certain level.

As discussed above, in practice often there is a situation when the structure of penalty functions is outside the control of the regulator of environmental-economic policy. Suppose that this is the case and that. In such a formulation, whether the regulator of environmental and economic policy can ensure full compliance of industrial emissions of enterprises with environmental requirements or not depends on the relative amount of monitoring costs and the implementation of penalties.

Suppose that

$$\mu_i \gamma > \beta_i \varphi^2$$

with all i.

Then, in terms of costs, it is effective to determine a strategy that allows you to achieve a given level of non-compliance of industrial emissions of enterprises with environmental requirements for all i. In that case, how are the costs of a strategy based on environmental standards related to the cost of a strategy based on sales quotas for pollutant emissions?

To answer this question, we first characterize a cost-effective strategy based on sales of industrial emissions of pollutants, which provides aggregate emissions at a certain level, when from a cost performance point of view, it is advisable to allow a given degree non-compliance of joint industrial emissions of enterprises with environmental requirements. Next, find out whether this optimal strategy minimizes the total costs of providing total emissions at a certain level that does not exceed Z.

If it is not optimal to ensure full compliance of production emissions of enterprises with environmental requirements for all enterprises ($v_i > 0$), Eqs. (1) and (2) can be converted to the assumption $\pi_i > 0$ for all i as follows

$$\frac{\partial \Lambda}{\partial \pi_i} = c_i'(\cdot) + \frac{\mu_i + \beta_i f(v_i)}{\frac{\partial l_i \partial p^*}{\partial p^* \partial \pi_i} + \frac{\partial l_i}{\partial \pi_i}} + \lambda = 0, \tag{4}$$

$$\frac{\partial \Lambda}{\partial v_i} = c_i'(\cdot) + \pi_i \beta_i f'(v_i) + \lambda = 0, \quad i = 1, \ldots, n. \tag{5}$$

These equations characterize the optimal regulatory strategy based on the sold emission allowances of pollutants, when, from the point of view of cost-effectiveness, it is advisable to allow non-compliance of total emissions of all enterprises with environmental requirements, i.e. $e_i - l_i > 0$. Similarly, the strategy of environmental and economic regulation based on environmental standards in the optimal strategy of environmental and economic regulation based on the sold emission allowances of pollutants, the regulator of environmental and economic policy and sets π_i and v_i, for all i in such a way that:

1. The sum of the marginal costs of reducing harmful emissions, monitoring, and implementation of penalties for changes π_i are the same for all enterprises (Eq. (4))
2. The sum of the marginal costs of reducing harmful emissions and the implementation of penalties for changes v_i are the same for all enterprises (Eq. (5)). From Eqs. (4) and (5) we can also get the equation

$$\frac{\mu_i + \beta_i f(v_i)}{\frac{\partial l_i \partial p^*}{\partial p^* \partial \pi_i} + \frac{\partial l_i}{\partial \pi_i}} = \pi_i \beta_i f'(v_i), \quad i = 1, \ldots, n. \tag{6}$$

Consequently, for the optimal strategy of environmental and economic regulation based on the sold emission allowances of pollutants, when it is reasonable from the point of view of cost-effectiveness, it is reasonable to allow non-compliance of the total emissions of all enterprises with environmental requirements, i.e. their quotas for industrial emissions of pollutants, the regulator of environmental and economic policy sets the amount of marginal costs for monitoring and implementing penalties for changes π_i equal to the amount of marginal costs for penalties for changes v_i for each enterprise i.

Thus, it is possible to build a cost-effective strategy based on tradable emissions allowances for pollutants, which provides cumulative emissions at a certain level. At the same time, from the point of view of cost-effectiveness, it is advisable to allow a given degree of non-compliance of the total production emissions of enterprises with environmental requirements.

It can be shown that this strategy minimizes the total costs of ensuring total emissions at a certain level, not exceeding Z, only under more specific conditions than in the case of full compliance of total production emissions of enterprises with environmental requirements.

We prove this position.

By analogy with the proof of Statement 1, we note that for enterprise i, which exceeds its number of quotas for industrial emissions in the competitive market for industrial emissions, the following is true. The company chooses its level of production emissions in such a way that $-c_i'(\cdot) = p$, and the number of quotas required for production emissions of pollutants from the condition $p^* = \pi_i f'(v_i)$.

Using both of these expressions, we can write Eq. (5) as follows:

$$(-1 + \beta_i)p^* = -\lambda$$

for all $i = 1, \ldots, n$ where we get

$$\beta_i = 1 - \frac{\lambda}{p^*} \quad \text{for all} \quad i = 1, \ldots, n \tag{7}$$

From the equation obtained above, it follows that if the costs of penalties differ between enterprises ($\beta_i \neq \beta_j$ for some $i \neq j$, $i, j = 1, \ldots, n$), then a competitive market of emission quotas will not minimize the total costs of ensuring total emissions at a certain level not exceeding Z. It is the competitive market of quotas on industrial emissions that ensures the only equilibrium price of quotas on industrial emissions of pollutants p^* for all enterprises. At the same time, a certain degree of non-compliance with environmental requirements is allowed.

In addition, the condition $\beta_i = \beta_j$ is sufficient, but not a necessary condition for this statement. If $\beta_i = \beta_j$ for all $i \neq j$, but $\mu_i \neq \mu_j$ for some i, j, it is also fair to assume that the market for quotas on industrial emissions is perfectly competitive, so Eq. (7) can be rewritten as follows

$$\frac{\mu_i + \beta_i f(v_i)}{\frac{\partial l_i}{\partial \pi_i}} = \pi_i \beta f'(v_i) \tag{7'}$$

for all $i = 1, \ldots, n$.

Using equality

$$\frac{\partial l_i}{\partial \pi_i} = \frac{f'(v)}{\pi f''(v)},$$

we get the equation

$$(\mu_i + \beta f(v_i)) \frac{f''(v_i)}{(f'(v_i))^2} = \beta \tag{8}$$

for all $i = 1, \ldots, n$.

This condition will be satisfied only in the special case, when $\mu_i = 0$ for all i, and subject to

$$f(v_i) \frac{f''(v_i)}{(f'(v_i))^2} = 1.$$

Consequently, only if there are no monitoring costs, the costs of the implementation of penalties are the same for all enterprises. In this case, there is equality $f(v_i) \frac{f''(v_i)}{(f'(v_i))^2} = 1$, the system of sold quotas for industrial emissions will minimize the cost of ensuring total emissions at a certain level not exceeding Z. This is true if, in terms of costs, it is effective to allow a certain degree of non-compliance with environmental requirements.

We formalize the result obtained above.

Statement 2. If the environmental policy regulator intends to set a limit on the total amount of harmful emissions and, in terms of costs, effectively allow all enterprises to violate environmental requirements ($\mu_i \gamma > \beta_i \varphi^2$ for all i), then the regulator will minimize the total costs of such a strategy of environmental and economic regulation of environmental regulation using the system enterprise-specific environmental regulations.

Thus, on the basis of the mathematical modeling of the formation of industrial emissions of enterprises processes, an effective strategy has been substantiated that regulates emissions of pollutants using environmental standards and environmental quotas as a tool.

4 Conclusion

The article presents the results of an analysis of proactive control of environmental pollution processes based on mathematical modeling. The necessity of taking into account the information asymmetry for more efficient construction of the process of regulation of environmental pollution processes is substantiated.

The state, as a regulator of the top level of management, should ensure environmental safety using economically sound methods of proactive management, predicting the possible consequences of the influence of control tools and impacts. Information support and ensuring the management process in the conditions of information asymmetry will directly affect its effectiveness.

The system of quotas sold for production emissions allows minimizing the total costs of the strategy of environmental and economic regulation only if the costs of the environmental audit are the same for all enterprises. An effective strategy for controlling emissions of pollutants from the government using environmental standards and environmental quotas as a tool has been proposed.

Acknowledgments. The reported study was funded by RFBR according to the research project № 19-07-01132.

References

1. Gushchina, E.G., Volkov, S.K., Vitaleva, E.M.: Marketing mechanism to overcome the negative effects of information asymmetry in the regional economic system: monograph, p. 136. VSTU, Volgograd (2018)
2. Karakeyan, V.I.: Environmental Economics, p. 576. Yurayt, Lyubertsy (2016)
3. Uhtilev, MYu., Zelentsov, V.A., Potryasaev, S.A., Sokolov, B.V.: The concept of proactive control of complex technical objects and the technology of its implementation. Izv. Univ. Instrument Making **55**(12), 73–75 (2012)
4. Girusov E.V.: Ecology and Economics of Nature, p. 607. UNITY-DANA (2014)

5. Makarov SV., Shagarova L.B.: Ecological audition of industrial productions, NUMC Goskomekologii Russia, p. 144 (2007)
6. Lukashin, M.S., Lukashina, E.V.: Modeling and optimization of strategies for environmental and economic regulation of production emissions. Manag. Econ. Syst. (Electronic Scientific Journal) 11(93), 38 (2010)
7. Gusev, A.A., Guseva, I.G.: Ecological and economic problems of sustainable development. Econ. Environ. Manag. 1, 4–17 (2006)
8. Bobylev, S.N., Khodjaev, A.: Economics of Nature: A Textbook, p. 499. Infra-M, Moscow (2010)
9. Sadovnikova, N., Parygin, D., Gnedkova, E., Kravets, A., Kizim, A., Ukustov, S.: Scenario forecasting of sustainable urban development based on cognitive model. In: Proceedings of the IADIS International Conference ICT, Society and Human Beings 2013, Proceedings of the IADIS International Conference e-Commerce 2013, pp. 115–119 (2013)
10. Anufriev, D., Petrova, I., Kravets, A., Vasiliev, S.: Big data-driven control technology for the heterarchic system (building cluster case-study) studies in systems. Decis. Control 181, 205–222 (2019)
11. Shokhnekh A.V., Skiter N.N., Rogachev A.F., Pleschenko T.V.: Inter-industry externalities. J. Environ. Manag. Tourism 8(17), 100–104 (2017). https://doi.org/10.14505/jemt.v8.1(17).10. Spring 1
12. Rogachev A.F., Melikhova E.V.: Indistinct and multiple simulation. Glob. Nucl. Saf. 1(18) 7–18 (2016)
13. Al-Gunaid, M.A., Shcherbakov, M.V., Skorobogatchenko, D.A., Kravets, A.G., Kamaev, V. A. Forecasting energy consumption with the data reliability estimatimation in the management of hybrid energy system using fuzzy decision trees. In: IISA 2016 - 7th International Conference on Information, Intelligence, Systems and Applications, art no. 7785413 (2016)
14. Melikhova, Elena V., Rogachev, Aleksey F.: Computer simulation and optimization of parameters of configuration of the contour of moistening under drip irrigation of agricultures. In: Popkova, E.G. (ed.) Ubiquitous Computing and the Internet of Things: Prerequisites for the Development of ICT. SCI, vol. 826, pp. 1193–1201. Springer, Cham (2019). https://doi.org/10.1007/978-3-030-13397-9_122
15. Rogachev, A.F.: Computer modeling of the development of russian small towns on the basis of cognitive maps. In: Popkova, E.G. (ed.) Russia and the European Union. CE, pp. 113–118. Springer, Cham (2017). https://doi.org/10.1007/978-3-319-55257-6_16
16. Rogachev, A.F.: Fuzzy set modeling of regional food security. In: Popkova, E.G., Ostrovskaya, V.N. (eds.) ISC 2017. AISC, vol. 726, pp. 774–782. Springer, Cham (2019). https://doi.org/10.1007/978-3-319-90835-9_89
17. Rogachev, A.F., Ostrovskaya, V.N., Natsubidze, A.S., Litvinova, T.N., Yakovleva, E.A.: Tools for sustainability management of socio-ecological systems in the globalizing world. In: Popkova, Elena G. (ed.) HOSMC 2017. AISC, vol. 622, pp. 241–247. Springer, Cham (2018). https://doi.org/10.1007/978-3-319-75383-6_31
18. Afanesyan, M.K., Nataluha, I.A.: Simulation Of optimal regulation of harmful industrial emissions taking into consideration transboundary pollution. Bull. Irkutsk State Tech. Univ. 3(35), 6–11 (2008)
19. Shokhnekh, A.V., Skiter, N.N., Rogachev, A.F., Pleschenko, T.V.: Features of optimal modeling of tax mechanisms in the leveling system of environmental and food security taking into account inter-industry externalities. J. Environ. Manag. Tourism 8(1), 100–104 (2017)

20. Gushchina, E.G., Vitaleva, E.M., Volkov, S.K.: Influence of information asymmetry on sustainability and changeability of region's economy. In: Competitive, Sustainable and Secure Development of the Regional Economy: Response to Global Challenges Proceedings of the International Scientific Conference, pp. 105–108 (2018)
21. Kravets, A.G., Skorobogatchenko, D.A., Salnikova, N.A., Orudjev, N.Y., Poplavskaya, O. V. The traffic safety management system in urban conditions based on the C4.5 algorithm. In: Moscow Workshop on Electronic and Networking Technologies, MWENT 2018 - Proceedings, pp. 1–7, art. no. 8337254 (2018)

Making a Choice of Resulting Estimates of Characteristics with Multiple Options of Their Evaluation

Georgi A. Popov, Irina Yu. Kvyatkovskaya, Olga I. Zholobova,
Anastasia E. Kvyatkovskaya, and Elena V. Chertina[✉]

Astrakhan State Technical University,
16 Tatishcheva Street, 414025 Astrakhan, Russia
{popov, i.kvyatkovskaya}@astu.org,
zholobova_olga@mail.ru, saprikinae_1912@mail.ru,
zima00@list.ru

Abstract. The paper dwells on the analysis of the efficiency of different algorithms for numerical expert data processing. Five methods were chosen for comparison: (1) on the basis of mean values; (2) on the basis of mean values with regard to experts' competence assessment; (3) by means of getting average values on the basis of the maximum likelihood estimation method; (4) by means of getting median values on the basis of the maximum likelihood estimation method; (5) by means of getting median values on the basis of the least squares method. A complex criterion, based on evaluation of the degree of experts' opinion consistency, the degree of closeness of the obtained results to their true values and the degree of convenience of the obtained results for solving specific tasks, is chosen as an efficiency criterion. The paper presents procedures of estimation of the mentioned components of the complex criterion and derivation of a complex estimate on the basis of known estimates of individual components. The experiment showed that, in the context of assessment of importance of individual PC components under the process of information security provision, the best result of the expert data processing is obtained with the use of the maximum likelihood estimation method on the basis of mean values, and the worst result is obtained with the use of the classical processing method on the basis of mean values. It is proposed to apply a procedure of getting a resulting estimate on the basis of a balanced consideration of the estimates obtained through different methods.

Keywords: Expert estimates, methods of estimate processing ·
Efficiency criterion · Information security · Importance of PC components

1 Introduction

When carrying out expert procedures in practice, one often has a choice of expert procedure types that can be conveniently divided into four classes: (1) methods of direct numerical estimation; (2) methods with linguistic, interval and fuzzy estimates;

The reported study was funded by RFBR according to the research project № 18-37-00130.

A. G. Kravets et al. (Eds.): CIT&DS 2019, CCIS 1083, pp. 89–104, 2019.
https://doi.org/10.1007/978-3-030-29743-5_7

(3) pairwise comparison methods; (4) ranking methods. Here the methods are given in the descending order of accuracy of the results, obtained on their basis, in the problems of evaluating the object characteristics. Let us point out the following fundamental difference between methods of the first two classes from methods of the last two classes. The first two classes of methods imply independent evaluation of each object regardless of its connection with other objects, while the methods of pairwise comparison and ranking, on the contrary, are primarily oriented on identifying the place of the object among all other objects, in comparison with other objects and regardless of absolute values of the object characteristics.

Each type of methods has its own specific features, areas of applicability, advantages and disadvantages. In particular, methods of direct numerical estimation are more attractive, as they allow to obtain a numerical value of the parameter (object) under estimation, but the reliability and accuracy of such estimates are often low because of weak structuredness of the object under evaluation. On the other hand, ranking methods do not give such attractive numerical estimates but have a considerably higher level of reliability of their results.

In view of the abovementioned, several problems arise in expert procedure organization and receiving a resulting estimate. Let us mark out the following two marginal approaches to obtaining the resulting estimates: firstly, it is a choice of the most acceptable result under the conditions of carrying out different types of expert procedures in solving a specific problem; secondly, it is a procedure of obtaining a resulting expert estimate based on the use of all the obtained results.

There are a lot of papers dedicated to the analysis of the first problem (see [1, 2]), while there are practically no academic works dedicated to the second problem solution. Papers [3] and [4] are similar by solution methods to this one. The problem described above is fascinating in different applied spheres of technology, and ensuring information security of objects is considered below as an example.

2 Choice of Criteria for Evaluating the Expert Evaluation Results

First of all, let us describe the indicators which will be used for comparing different expert results and choosing the most acceptable one. When comparing different expert results, we will use the following three indicators [6, 7].

1. An indicator p_1 of the expert opinion consistency degree. The lower the value of this indicator, the worse the result is. When these opinions are very poorly consisted, the expert procedure results are usually rejected. For example, if half of the experts recommend painting the product in black, and the second half - in white, it does not mean that the product should be painted in gray. It is necessary to carry out a new session of expert procedure with deeper and more convincing justifications of opinions. The larger the value of p_1, the more preferable the expert evaluation results are, other things being equal.

2. An indicator p_2 of the proximity of the results of evaluating individual objects to their true relative values (that are unknown) or to the rank relations between the

objects. Results obtained on the basis of direct numerical estimation usually appear to be the closest to the true values. Therefore, with a certain combination of the values of the indicators p_1 and p_2, results obtained on the basis of direct numerical estimation can be chosen, even in spite of a relatively low level of the expert opinion consistency. The lower the value of p_2, the more preferable the expert evaluation results are.

3. An indicator p_3 that shows to what extent the obtained estimates are convenient for solving the problems for which the expert procedure was carried out. As an example, we will consider one of the typical tasks of the management process - the problem of resource allocation between different objects in solving various problems. For instance, with high consistency of the expert opinion, results obtained on the basis of the pairwise comparison method may be more preferable than results obtained on the basis of direct numerical estimation. The higher the value of p_3, the more preferable the expert evaluation results are.

Now let us describe possible ways of estimating the values of the indicators p_1, p_2, p_3. Below we will focus on two most common types of expert evaluation methods – direct numerical estimation and ranking method.

In case of direct numerical estimation, the indicator p_1 can be described either on the basis of the coefficient of variation for a small sample size (less than $7 \div 10$) or with the use of Pearson's chi-squared test (with a sample size larger than $20 \div 30$); in case of applying the ranking method, the indicator will be described on the basis of the concordance coefficient. Since the number of experts is often small, the coefficient of variation for direct numerical estimation or the concordance coefficient in case of applying the ranking method are usually used to evaluate the degree of the expert opinion consistency. It is appropriate at this point to recall the expression for the coefficient of variation. Let K be the number of objects given. On the basis of the expert procedure with participation of N experts, a table of estimates $\{x_{ij}\}$ was obtained, where x_{ij} is the estimate of the i-th object by the j-th expert, $\overline{x_1}, \overline{x_2}, \ldots, \overline{x_K}$ and $\overline{\sigma_1}, \overline{\sigma_2}, \ldots, \overline{\sigma_K}$ are the mean value and the standard deviation of the estimates of each object, i.e.

$$\overline{x_i} = \tfrac{1}{N} \sum_{i=1}^{N} x_{ij} \text{ and } \overline{\sigma_i} = \sqrt{\tfrac{1}{N} \sum_{i=1}^{N} (x_{ij} - \overline{x_j})^2}.$$ Then the coefficient of variation of the i-th object estimation is $\rho_i = \tfrac{\sigma_i}{\overline{x_i}}$, and the quantity $p_1 = \max\{\rho_i | i = \overline{1; K}\}$ is proposed as the coefficient p_1.

The indicator p_2 can be estimated in the following way. As a measure of deviation of the j-th expert's estimates from the object true estimates, one can consider the standard deviation of a figure, composed of consecutively arranged rectangles with the base length of 1 and the height x_{ij} for the i-th rectangle, from a similar figure in which the height of the i-th rectangle is equal to $\hat{x}_i$, i.e. the value $\delta_j = \tfrac{1}{K} \sum_{i=1}^{K} |x_{ij} - \hat{x}_i|$, where $\hat{x}_i$ is the resulting estimate of the i-th object obtained after the processing of the expert evaluation results. The example below will present several options for obtaining the resulting estimates. However, this value depends on the absolute values of the estimates x_{ij}, which makes it difficult to compare different sets of objects with different scales of objects. For example, for security systems it is not correct to compare the security protection performance on the basis of the indicators δ_i because they do not take into account the scale of the security systems themselves. Therefore, it is necessary to turn from absolute estimates to relative (dimensionless) ones, which can be obtained on the basis of dividing absolute estimates by their maximum values. In our case, such estimates are the following values (relative proximity measures of j-th expert's estimates to the optimal values):

$$\Delta_j = \frac{\delta_j}{\max_k(\delta_k)} = \frac{\sum_{i=1}^{K}|x_{ij} - \hat{x}_i|}{K \cdot \max_{i,k}(|x_{ik} - \hat{x}_i|)} \tag{1}$$

Let us note that $\Delta_j \in [0; 1]$. Then the best expert estimate of the given set of objects, i.e. the one with the minimum deviation Δ_j is proposed as an estimate for the indicator p_2:

$$p_2 = \min\{\Delta_j | j = \overline{1; N}\} \tag{2}$$

One could consider the mean value of all the deviations Δ_j, i.e. $p_2 = \frac{1}{N}\sum_{j=1}^{N}\Delta_j$, as an alternative to the estimate p_2. If it is also necessary to take into account the experts' competence levels, the estimate (2) can be modified as follows:

$$p_2 = \min\{(\Delta_j)^{\tau_j} | j = \overline{1; N}\}, \tag{3}$$

where τ_j is an assessment of the competence level of the j-th expert on the scale $[0; 1]$, and the more τ_j, the higher the competence level is. In particular, if $\tau_j = 1$ (i.e. the expert is absolutely and completely competent), his/her estimate is used in calculating p_2. As the value of τ_j decreases, the value of the quantity $(\Delta_j)^{\tau_j}$ increases and, as a consequence, reaching the minimum in (3) due to this quantity becomes more and more improbable. Finally, if $\tau_j = 0$ (i.e. the expert is completely incompetent), $(\Delta_j)^{\tau_j} = 1$, and the j-th expert's estimates are not actually taken for calculating p_2 by formula (3).

Let us consider the procedure for estimating the indicator p_3. This indicator should describe to what extent the derived estimates are convenient and acceptable for solving specific problems, provided that these estimates are accurate. The resource allocation problem was chosen as an example. Then, in relation to this problem, the derived estimates of the object can be interpreted as the object importance, and the available resources can be allocated among all the objects in proportion to their importance. Assuming that the indicator p_3 also changes in the interval $[0; 1]$, as well as the indicators p_1 and p_2, one can take the value of $p_3 = 1$ for the purpose of the resource allocation problem. In solving other problems, the estimate p_2 can be based on evaluating the complexity of modifying expert estimates into a form which will be convenient for solving the problem under consideration. In this regard, the evaluation of p_3 requires further analysis.

Therefore, possible ways of estimating the indicators have been described. Then the following quantity is proposed as a resulting estimate of the degree of acceptability of the expert evaluation results for the solution of a particular problem:

$$P^{(r)} = \sqrt[3]{(1.03 - 0.03r)p_1(1 - p_2)p_3} \qquad (4)$$

where r is a number of the class from the above list of four classes to which the considered method belongs. Here, a cube root is added to ensure the same dimensionality and ordinality for the resulting indicator and indicators p_i. Please note that this relation assumes that the method of direct numerical estimation may be more preferable than the ranking method even if its evaluation of the efficiency index $P^{(1)}$ is 2% worse than a similar estimate $P^{(4)}$ for the ranking method: in (4), the estimate for each subsequent class decreases by $1.4\% \approx \sqrt[3]{3}\%$ in relation to the previous one. This is due to the fact that in the present paper, the problems of estimating parameters of characteristics are of primary interest, and the method of direct numerical estimation generally makes it possible to obtain more accurate estimates of the object characteristics than the ranking method that only allows to order objects according to the values of the characteristic under consideration.

Let us point out one more important aspect of the above procedure: the resulting estimate $P^{(r)}$ depends not only on the chosen method of estimation, but also on the procedure of the expert estimates processing that determines the values of the estimates $\{\hat{x}_i\}$. This aspect will be demonstrated through an example below.

3 Example of Estimation of Information Security Object Characteristics

Let us consider the following typical problem related to the information security sphere as an example of the application of the above procedure for selecting the resulting estimates from the available options of expert evaluations.

The following task is considered: to assess the degree of vulnerability of various PC components in terms of information security. Note that any other complex object under protection can be studied similarly instead of a personal computer.

Two methods for conducting the expert evaluation are considered: (1) on the basis of an expert procedure with the use of linguistic variables - the method belongs to the second class; (2) the strict ranking method of the fourth class. First we will carry out the procedure on the basis of the first method [8–10].

In a personal computer (PC), the following six main components are singled out: (1) processor (CPU); (2) random access memory (RAM); (3) read-only memory (ROM); (4) input/output devices (IOD); (5) network facilities (NF); (6) motherboard (MB).

The evaluation process is divided into several stages.

1st stage (data collection). Each expert assesses vulnerability of each PC component using a scale with the following five linguistic rates: (1) undoubtedly (UD) (the component is vulnerable, i.e. an unauthorized leak of information through this component is undoubtedly possible); (2) very likely (VL) (i.e. an unauthorized leak of information through this component is very likely to happen); (3) probably (PB) (i.e. an unauthorized leak of information through this component is probable); (4) unlikely (UL) (i.e. an unauthorized leak of information through this component is unlikely to happen); (5) impossible (IP) (i.e. an unauthorized leak of information through this component is impossible). Senior students of the Information Security Department of Astrakhan State Technical University were involved as experts. Five groups of experts were selected – hereinafter referred to as experts – and the following expert opinions were obtained from them (Table 1) (an assessment by the i-th expert is written in a corresponding column).

Table 1. Expert assessment.

Objects under assessment	1st expert	2nd expert	3rd expert	4th expert	5th expert
1. CPU	UL	IP	UL	UL	UL
2. RAM	VL	VL	PB	VL	VL
3. ROM	VL	UD	IP	IP	VL
4. IOD	UD	PB	UD	UD	UD
5. NF	PB	VL	VL	VL	UD
6. MB	UL	IP	VL	UL	VL

2nd stage. Numerical interpretation of linguistic rates. In order to do this, we will use the Harrington scale [8] that defines a certain interval to each estimate, viz (1) undoubtedly - the interval (0.7; 1); (2) very likely - the interval (0.5; 0.7); (3) probably - the interval (0.25; 0.5); (4) unlikely - the interval (0.05; 0.25); (5) impossible - the interval (0; 0.05). A linguistic rate is replaced by an average value of the interval that is associated with it; i.e. a numerical value of 0.85 is associated to the rate UD, 0.6 – to VL, 0.375 – to PB, 0.15 – to UL, and 0.025 – to IP. Then the table of linguistic estimates obtained at the 1st stage can be replaced by the following numerical Table 2.

Table 2. Numerical interpretation of expert assessments.

Object under assessment	1st expert	2nd expert	3rd expert	4th expert	5th expert
1. CPU	0.15	0.025	0.15	0.15	0.15
2. RAM	0.6	0.6	0.375	0.6	0.6
3. ROM	0.6	0.85	0.025	0.025	0.6
4. IOD	0.85	0.375	0.85	0.85	0.85
5. NF	0.375	0.6	0.6	0.6	0.85
6. MB	0.15	0.025	0.6	0.15	0.6

3rd stage. Processing of the results. Further processing of data can be performed on the basis of various algorithms. Let us consider three possible ways of processing.

1st Processing Method. Average values $\bar{x}_i$ with respect to all the experts are taken as resulting estimates for each component, where i is a serial number of the evaluated object (i.e. average values for each line). Having reordered the objects in descending order of their estimates, we obtain (the resulting estimates of their vulnerability are given next to each estimate in parentheses): IOD (0.755); NF (0.605); RAM (0.555); ROM (0.42); MB (0.305); CPU (0.125). Therefore, the most vulnerable PC component is input/output devices (the resulting estimate is 0.755), and the least vulnerable component is the processor (its estimate is 0.125).

As mentioned above, we have chosen the coefficient of variation to measure the expert opinion consistency degree, since the data volume (5 observations) is small. For this purpose, the standard deviation is calculated for each object. We obtain $\sigma_{CPU} = 0.056$; $\sigma_{RAM} = 0.101$; $\sigma_{ROM} = 0.375$; $\sigma_{IOD} = 0.53$; $\sigma_{NF} = 0.168$; $\sigma_{MB} = 0.174$. Hence, according to formula (1) we obtain the following values for the coefficients of variation, expressed in percent, i.e. the resulting value is multiplied by 100%: $\rho_{CPU} = 44.8\%$; $\rho_{RAM} = 18.2\%$; $\rho_{ROM} = 89.29\%$; $\rho_{IOD} = 70.2\%$; $\rho_{NF} = 27.77\%$; $\rho_{MB} = 89.84\%$.

To interpret and analyze the obtained results, let us use one of the existing scales for interpreting the variation coefficient values. If the calculated value ρ of the variation coefficient is less than 0.3, the expert opinion consistency degree is acceptable, the expert evaluation results are accepted as an estimate of the vulnerability degree of the corresponding component, and the expert procedure on evaluating this component is finished. If the value of the coefficient ρ is within the interval (0.3; 0.7), the opinion consistency degree is average, and a decision on acceptability or unacceptability of the results is taken by the expert procedure organizers. If the value of the coefficient ρ is more than 0.7, the opinion consistency degree is low, and the results of the expert procedure cannot be accepted as estimates of the characteristics under study.

Based on the obtained values of the variation coefficients, we conclude that the experts' estimates of vulnerability of the ROM, I/O devices and motherboard vary enormously, and the consistency degree is low. Therefore, the expert procedure will be continued in relation to these parameters. The results of the expert estimation of the vulnerability degree of the processor, RAM and network facilities are accepted.

To continue the expert procedure, all five experts were asked to give their arguments on estimation of the vulnerability of the ROM, I/O devices and motherboard, for which the consistency degree appeared to be low. Then the expert procedure was repeated over again in relation to these parameters. As a result, the following estimates were obtained (Table 3).

Table 3. Reassessment results.

Object under assessment	1st expert	2nd expert	3rd expert	4th expert	5th expert
ROM	VL	UD	PB	PB	VL
IOD	UD	VL	UD	UD	UD
MB	UL	UL	PB	UL	VL

Having processed the data in a similar way, we obtain the following values of the variation coefficients: $\rho_{IOD} = 13.98\%$, $\rho_{ROM} = 39.54\%$, $\rho_{MB} = 39.32\%$.

The expert opinion consistency degree is now acceptable, and the expert procedure results are accepted as estimates of the vulnerability degree of the respective PC components.

2nd Processing Method. Each of the five PC components will be evaluated with regard to the experts' competence in relation to this task. When assessing the competence degree, we will rely only on the experts' estimates of the PC components. We are based on the following concept: the closer the experts' estimate to the resulting estimate after the processing of all the estimates, the higher his/her competence coefficient is. This requirement can be analytically written as follows. Let x_i be an estimate of the object under consideration by the i-th expert, $\tilde{x}$ is the resulting estimate of the object. Then we accept that the degree of competence of the i-th expert is proportional to the value $(1+|x_i - \tilde{x}|)^{-1}$. Taking the sum $\sum_{ш}(1+|x_i - \tilde{x}|)^{-1}$ as a proportionality coefficient (so that the sum of all the coefficients of competence can be equal to 1), we obtain the following implicit equation to find the resulting estimate $\tilde{x} : \tilde{x} = f(\tilde{x})$, where

$$f(\tilde{x}) \stackrel{def}{=} \frac{\sum_i \frac{1}{(1+|x_i-\tilde{x}|)} x_i}{\sum_i \frac{1}{(1+|x_i-\tilde{x}|)}}$$

The last-mentioned equation can be rewritten in the following form: $\sum_i \frac{x_i-\tilde{x}}{(1+|x_i-\tilde{x}|)} = 0$, which is solved below on the basis of the polyline method, since this method has a very high convergence rate. In relation to the problem under consideration, it was sufficient to do two iterations for each object in order to receive the value of $\tilde{x}$ with the required accuracy. As a result, the following estimates were obtained: $\overline{x_{CPU}} = 0.12643$, $\overline{x_{RAM}} = 0.5595$, $\overline{x_{ROM}} = 0.43337$, $\overline{x_{IOD}} = 0.77355$, $\overline{x_{NF}} = 0.6038$, $\overline{x_{MB}} = 0.29544$. The expert reassessment of the ROM, input/output devices and motherboard allows to obtain the following estimates of these components: $\overline{x_{ROM}} = 0.55728$, $\overline{x_{IOD}} = 0.80551$, $\overline{x_{MB}} = 0.27574$.

The 3rd method is based on building a probability law for a range of estimates using the available set of estimates. This law would describe the spread of estimates of different experts for the given object. In practice, the beta distribution with a distribution density $f_{a,b}(x)$ that depends on two parameters $a > 0$ and $b > 0$ is often chosen as such a distribution law, where

$$f_{a,b}(x) = \begin{cases} (Be(a,b))^{-1} \cdot x^{a-1} \cdot (1-x)^{b-1} & \text{if } x \in (0,1), \\ 0 & \text{in other cases} \end{cases}$$

and the Euler beta function $Be(a,b) = \int_0^1 x^{a-1} \cdot (1-x)^{b-1} dx$.

The desired estimate is found either on the basis of the maximum likelihood estimation method (MLE estimate), or on the basis of the least squares method (LSM estimate).

To find a MLE estimate for this component, the likelihood function is written by the formula

$$L(a, b/x_i, i = \overline{1, n}) = \ln(\prod_i f_{a,b}(x_i))$$

$$= -n \cdot \ln(Be(a, b)) + (a - 1) \cdot \sum_{i=1}^{n} \ln(x_i) + (b - 1) \cdot \sum_{i=1}^{n} \ln(1 - x_i),$$

where $\{x_i\}$ is a set of the expert estimates in numerical form. The function $L(a, b/x_i, i = \overline{1, n})$ is unbounded in the variables a and b, as can be seen by examining the function order at infinity along the direction $a = t \cdot \prod_{i=1}^{n} x_i$, $b = t \cdot \left(1 - \prod_{i=1}^{n} x_i\right)$ when $t \to \infty$. Using Stirling's formula for the gamma function, we will obtain that $L()$ has the order $\sqrt{t}$ when $t \to \infty$. Therefore, in order to find the maximum value of the function $L()$, it is necessary to impose additional restrictions on the variables a and b. It is easy to verify that

$$Var(f_{a,b}(x)) = \int_0^1 |(f_{a,b}(x))'| dx \leq a + b.$$

Since the distribution variance $f_{a,b}(x)$ does not exceed 1, it can be additionally required that the variation of the function $f_{a,b}(x)$ must exceed the dispersion by no more than two orders of magnitude. For this purpose, it is sufficient to impose the condition $a + b \leq c$ with c = 100. This restriction is practically not essential for the final result, since both average and median vulnerability estimates tend to some finite limits. This very restriction will be used in our calculation of the maximum value of the function $L()$.

Let a_0 and b_0 be values of the variables a and b at which $L()$ reaches its maximum value. Then either the mean value $\bar{x}^{MLE} = \frac{a_0}{a_0 + b_0}$ or the median xm^{MLE} of this distribution is taken as the resulting estimate, i.e. the solution of the equation (with $a = a_0$ and $b = b_0$):

$$(Be(a, b))^{-1} \cdot \int_0^m x^{a-1}(1 - x)^{b-1} dx = 0.5.$$

We obtain the following values of the estimates (x_{CPU}^{MLE}, x_{RAM}^{MLE}, x_{ROM}^{MLE}, x_{IOD}^{MLE}, x_{NF}^{MLE}, x_{MB}^{MLE} are the MLE estimates of the mean estimation values for the processor, RAM, ROM, input/output devices, network facilities and motherboard respectively): $x_{CPU}^{MLE} = 0.12361$, $x_{RAM}^{MLE} = 0.55353$, $x_{ROM}^{MLE} = 0.56535$, $x_{IOD}^{MLE} = 0.79787$, $x_{NF}^{MLE} = 0.60731$, $x_{MB}^{MLE} = 0.29024$. The respective MLE estimates obtained on the basis of the medians are: $xm_{CPU}^{MLE} = 0.11267$, $xm_{RAM}^{MLE} = 0.55472$, $xm_{ROM}^{MLE} = 0.57196$, $xm_{IOD}^{MLE} = 0.80793$, $xm_{NF}^{MLE} = 0.61533$, $xm_{MB}^{MLE} = 0.26872$.

LSM estimates of the parameters a and b are found by the formulas $a = \bar{x} \cdot \left(\frac{\bar{x}(1-\bar{x})}{S^2} - 1 \right)$, $b = (1 - \bar{x}) \cdot \left(\frac{\bar{x}(1-\bar{x})}{S^2} - 1 \right)$. In this case, the mean values of the estimates coincide with the values obtained on the basis of the first method, i.e. $x_{CPU}^{LSM} = x_{CPU}$, $x_{RAM}^{LSM} = x_{RAM}$, $x_{ROM}^{LSM} = x_{ROM}$, $x_{IOD}^{LSM} = x_{IOD}$, $x_{NF}^{LSM} = x_{NF}$, $x_{MB}^{LSM} = x_{MB}$. Let us point out that if all the estimates coincide completely for a component, the variance $S^2 = 0$ and the above formulas for the parameters a and b are not applicable. In this case, one of the estimates should be altered by a very small value (for example, by adding 0.0001 to it) so that the condition $S^2 \neq 0$ can be fulfilled.

The estimates obtained on the basis of the medians are:
$$xm_{CPU}^{LSM} = 0.11764, \quad xm_{RAM}^{LSM} = 0.55659, \quad xm_{ROM}^{LSM} = 0.56804, \quad xm_{IOD}^{LSM} = 0.80265,$$
$$xm_{NF}^{LSM} = 0.61488, \quad xm_{MB}^{LSM} = 0.24729.$$

4th stage. Analysis of the results. Combining all the obtained estimates, we obtain the following table of estimates (Table 4):

Table 4. Resulting estimates of the objects.

	Processor	Random access memory	Read-only memory	Input/output devices	Network facilities	Motherboard	Efficiency factor
Estimates based on mean values	0.125	0.555	0.515	0.85	0.605	0.285	0.769774
Estimates based on competence consideration	0.12643	0.5595	0.55728	0.80551	0.6038	0.27574	0.797029
MLE estimates based on mean values	0.12361	0.55353	0.56535	0.79787	0.60731	0.29024	0.798481
MLE estimates based on medians	0.11267	0.55472	0.57196	0.80793	0.61533	0.26872	0.796766
LSM estimates based on medians	0.11764	0.55804	0.56804	0.80265	0.61488	0.24729	0.793112

The last column contains estimates of the efficiency factor obtained on the basis of (4) – in this case $r = 2$, since the evaluation method based on linguistic variables belongs to the second class.

The analysis of the values in Table 4 shows that the estimates obtained on the basis of different methods of expert data processing are numerically different, but generally correspond to the processing main result obtained on the basis of the first method. The best result of the expert data processing was obtained with the use of the maximum likelihood estimation method based on mean values; the worst result is obtained with the use of the classical method of processing based on mean values. The estimation results allow to arrange the PC components in the following descending order of their vulnerability estimates: input/output devices (IOD), network facilities (NF), motherboard (MB), random access memory (RAM), read-only memory (ROM), processor (CPU). However, the efficiency factor estimates of the components differ, which could potentially lead to a different choice of expert evaluation methods based on the procedure described in part 2. Besides, in comparison with mean estimates, median estimates often lessen low-valued estimates.

Now let us carry out the procedure for solving the same problem of expert evaluation of the PC components on the basis of the ranking method.

1st stage. Data collection. The same five experts from the above procedure were selected. The experts were asked to rank six PC components listed above in terms of their vulnerability to all possible threats – the lower the component ranking number, the more vulnerable it is. Note that in this case the criterion differs from the previous case where a higher expert estimate was given to a more vulnerable object. This fact must be taken into account for the estimates comparison. At the same time, a non-strict ranking was allowed, i.e. the experts were allowed to group separate components if they could not rank them among themselves. At the end of the evaluation procedure, the following expert ranking was obtained (estimates given by the i-th expert are written in a corresponding line) (Table 5).

Table 5. Expert ranking.

	1. CPU	2. RAM	3. ROM	4. IOD	5. NF	6. MB
1st expert	6	2	4	1	3	5
2nd expert	5	4	2	1–3	1–3	6
3rd expert	6	1	4	5	3	2
4th expert	6	5	4	3	1	2
5th expert	6	3	2	1	4	5

Next we need to calculate mean values with respect to all the experts for each component, i.e. mean values for the columns. In case of the components grouped together, a mean value for the group is taken as an estimate for each component. For example, the second expert combined the CPU and ROM in one group, placing this group on the 2nd and 3rd positions. Then a mean value of their ranking positions is taken as an estimate for each of these components, i.e. the value $\frac{2+3}{2} = 2.5$. We obtain the following values for the mean values $\bar{x}$ of the estimates for each component: $\bar{x}_{CPU} = 5.8$, $\bar{x}_{RAM} = 3$, $\bar{x}_{ROM} = 3.2$, $\bar{x}_{IOD} = 2.5$, $\bar{x}_{NF} = 2.7$, $\bar{x}_{MB} = 4$.

Thus, the components can be arranged in the following descending order of their vulnerability in terms of importance (a mean ranking number obtained as a result of the expert evaluation processing is given in parentheses): IOD (2.5); NF (2.7); RAM (3); ROM (3.2); MB (4); CPU (5.8).

To assess the expert opinion consistency degree, we will use the following result: if the experts' estimates of a given parameter or object are independent random variables and r_i is a mean value of the parameter estimates given by all the experts, then the value $F = N \cdot (n - 1) \cdot W$ has a χ^2-distribution with $n - 1$ degrees of freedom, where n is a number of ranked parameters, N is a number of experts and $W = \dfrac{12 \sum\limits_{i=1}^{n} [r_i - \frac{1}{2}(n+1)]^2}{(n^3 - n)}$ is the concordance coefficient (concordance coefficient varies from 0 to 1 inclusive, the value

$W = 1$ indicates full coincidence of all the expert estimates; the less the value W, the less consistent the estimates are). In our case $n = 6$, $N = 5$, and the vector $(r_1, r_2, \ldots, r_n)$ is a vector of the mean values calculated above. We find $W = 0.762$, and, consequently, the empirical value of F is equal to $F'_{emp} = 5 \cdot 6 \cdot 0.762 = 22.86$. Using the χ^2-distribution table with $m = 6 - 1 = 5$ degrees of freedom, we find the theoretical value of F with the confidence level of 0.95: $F_{theor} = 12.59$. Since $F_{emp} = 22.86 > F_{theor} = 12.6$, the hypothesis about complete independence of the experts' opinions is rejected, and, therefore, the expert estimates also include a common, jointly agreed understanding of the problem along with individual features. Note that the value $F = 22.86$ corresponds to the level of confidence in the expert procedure results equal to 0.999.

Finally, we will estimate the degree of acceptability of the expert evaluation results by formula (4). In our case, $r = 4$. The value of the coefficient p_1 describing the expert opinion consistency degree is equal to the concordance coefficient $W = 0.762$. The value of the coefficient p_2 is found on the basis of (1), as it was done in the previous case, where the obtained estimates $\{\bar{x}_{CPU}, \bar{x}_{RAM}, \bar{x}_{ROM}, \bar{x}_{IOD}, \cdots, \bar{x}_{NF}, \bar{x}_{MB}\}$ are taken as a set $\{\hat{x}_i\}$, and the ranked estimates of the experts are taken as x_{ij}. We obtain $p_2 = 0.360127$. Then, on the basis of (4), we obtain: $P^{(r)} = 0.643697$. A received value of acceptability of the estimates which were obtained on the basis of the ranking method is worse than any estimate obtained above on the basis of evaluation with the use of the linguistic variables.

It is of interest to estimate the degree of correlation between the results obtained on the basis of linguistic rates and the ranking method. Let us write down the correlation calculation results in the form of the following table (Table 6):

Table 6. Correlation coefficients for all the pairs of methods and components.

	Processor	Random access memory	Read-only memory	Input/output devices	Network facilities	Motherboard
Estimates based on mean values (Mn)	0.125	0.555	0.515	0.85	0.605	0.285
Estimates based on competence consideration (Cmp)	0.12643	0.5595	0.55728	0.80551	0.6038	0.27574
MLE estimates based on mean values (MLE-Mn)	0.12361	0.55353	0.56535	0.79787	0.60731	0.29024
MLE estimates based on medians (MLE-Md)	0.11267	0.55472	0.57196	0.80793	0.61533	0.26872
LSM estimates based on medians (LSM-Md)	0.11764	0.55804	0.56804	0.80265	0.61488	0.24729
Ranking method (Rn)	1.2	4	3.8	4.5	4.3	3

At the same time, as it was mentioned above, in order to ensure the same monotone direction (decreasing order) in evaluation based on the use of linguistic variables and the ranking method, the last line contains values that supplement the obtained ranking numbers to $x_{max} + 1$, where $x_{max} = 6$ is the maximum possible ranking value.

Now we can estimate the results correlation degree on the basis of values of the correlation coefficients between different pairs of lines. The calculation results are shown in Table 7.

Table 7. Coefficients of the results correlation between different methods.

	Cmp	MLE-Mn	MLE-Md	LSM-Md	Rn
Mn	0.994467	0.992627	0.991395	0.989882	0.920522
Cmp		0.999449	0.999484	0.998877	0.935581
MLE-Mn			0.999662	0.998114	0.943591
MLE-Md				0.999302	0.938735
LSM-Md					0.930904

As can be seen from Table 7, the results obtained with the use of different methods have a high level of correlation. At the same time, the correlation level of the ranking numbers is significantly less in comparison with the estimates used in the linguistic variables processing.

4   Comparison of Different Types of Expert Procedures

The procedure for selecting the best result of expert evaluation from all the obtained results was described above. As for all other unselected results, they are discarded and are not used in future. This approach seems irrational, because all other types of expert evaluation usually contain valuable results as well. Therefore, there is an emerging problem of using all the obtained results of expert evaluation. This section is dedicated to this problem.

Let two types of the expert evaluation of N objects be carried out, and the results of the evaluation are represented by two vectors $z_1 = (x_1^{(1)}; x_2^{(1)}; \ldots; x_N^{(1)})$ and $z_2 = (x_1^{(2)}; x_2^{(2)}; \ldots; x_N^{(2)})$. The known values of the acceptability coefficients P for each obtained result will be denoted by P_1 and P_2 respectively. Then, in a first approximation, we can use the point z_L on the segment with the ends z_1 and z_2 as a resulting (combined) estimate that divides this segment in the ratio $P_1:P_2$, counting from the point P_1, i.e.

$$z_L = \frac{P_1}{P_1 + P_2} z_1 + \frac{P_2}{P_1 + P_2} z_2 \tag{5}$$

However, the preconditions, on the basis of which the combined estimate was calculated as a linear combination of the results obtained, are not conclusive. So let us consider another approach that seems more convincing. Namely, let ρ be a correlation coefficient between the vectors z_1 and z_2. Then, as is known, the correlation coefficient ρ in the space of random vectors is interpreted as a cosine of the angle α between the vectors z_1 and z_2 in the plane, passing through the vectors z_1 and z_2. Then we can divide the angle α in the ratio $P_1:P_2$ and take a certain point on this ray l as a combined estimate. The question arises as to how to select this point on the ray l, i.e. which surface passing through the points z_1 and z_2 should be taken if its intersection with l must give the desired point z_*. Since there are no convincing arguments for choosing a surface type, we will take the plane as the simplest possible surface; to be more precise, we will take the interval $[z_1; z_2]$. Since the angle α is usually small (because ρ is close to 1 as it was demonstrated above in Table 7), the error due to the use of a linear function is small with respect almost to any smooth surface.

Then the procedure for finding z_* is described as follows.

We calculate the correlation coefficient ρ between the vectors z_1 and z_2 according to the known formula:

$$\rho = cor(z_1, z_2) = \frac{\sum_{i=1}^{N}(x_i^{(1)} - \overline{x_1})(x_i^{(2)} - \overline{x_2})}{N \sigma_1 \sigma_2}, \quad \overline{x_r} = \frac{1}{N}\sum_{i=1}^{N} x_i^{(r)},$$

$$\sigma_r = \sqrt{\frac{1}{N}\sum_{i=1}^{N}(x_i^{(r)} - \overline{x_r})^2} \quad (r = 1, 2).$$

Let us connect the points z_1 and z_2 with a straight-line segment and then choose a point z that divides the angle α in proportion to the acceptability coefficients of the vectors z_1 and z_2, i.e. if $z = \gamma z_1 + (1 - \gamma)z_2$, the value of γ is chosen according to the condition $cor(z_1, z) = \frac{P_1}{P_1 + P_2}\rho$. Solving this equation with respect to γ, we find the desired value of γ_* and then the value of the evaluation vector $z_* = \gamma_* z_1 + (1 - \gamma_*)z_2$.

Let us demonstrate this procedure using the above example. Two estimates of the PC components were obtained above: an estimate $z_1 = (0.12361; 0.55353; 0.56535; 0.79787; 0.60731; 0.29024)$ (for MLE-Mn, the most efficient data processing method) and $z_2 = (1.2; 4; 3.8; 4.5; 4.3; 3)$ (ranking evaluation), where the estimate based on the mean values was chosen as the resulting estimate. In this case, as it was obtained above, $P_1 = 0.798481$, $P_2 = 0.643697$. From Table 7 we have $\rho = 0.943591$. Hence $\alpha = 0.337482$ rad.

The value γ_* is found from the equation:

$$\cos(z_2; z_*) = \cos\left(\frac{P_2}{P_1 + P_2}\alpha\right), \quad \text{or} \quad \frac{|z_2 \cdot (z_2 + \gamma_*(z_1 - z_2))|}{|z_2| \cdot |z_2 + \gamma_*(z_1 - z_2)|} = \cos\left(\frac{P_2}{P_1 + P_2}\alpha\right).$$

Substituting the values, we get:

$$\frac{|79.62 + \gamma_* \cdot (-17.8621)|}{\sqrt{79.62} \cdot \sqrt{79.62 + (-136.073)\gamma_* + 319.0543(\gamma_*)^2}} = 0.988677$$

Solving the obtained (quadratic) equation, we find $\gamma_* = 0.07827$, whence

$$z_* = (1.115751, 3.730245, 3.546824, 4.210234, 4.010973, 2.787907).$$

In case of a linear approximation we get an estimate

$$z_L = \frac{0.798481}{0.798481 + 0.643697} z_1 + \frac{0.643697}{0.798481 + 0.643697} z_2$$
$$= (0.604042; 2.091816; 2.009093; 2.450267; 2.255493; 1.499705).$$

Let us estimate the relative error δ_i of the vector z_L with respect to z_* for each component and the total error $\delta = \max(\delta_i)$, where $\delta_i = \frac{|z_{*i}^n - z_{L,i}^n|}{z_{L,i}^n} * 100\%$ and z_{*i}^n, $z_{L,i}^n$ are components of the normalized vectors z_* and z_L respectively. It is to be recalled that the vectors z_* and z_L, meant for the resource allocation problem, are used only to determine the proportionality of resource allocation between different objects, and therefore are determined up to a constant. In order to compare them, we normalize them by dividing by the length of a corresponding vector. We obtain (the superscript n indicates normalized values):

$$z_*^n = (0.134004; 0.448012; 0.425982; 0.50566; 0.481728; 0.334835),$$

$$z_L^n = (0.122805; 0.448965; 0.426517; 0.505086; 0.482637; 0.336724).$$

We have: $(\delta_1; \delta_2; \delta_3; \delta_4; \delta_5; \delta_6) = (4.15; 0.72; 3.04; 0.44; 4.76)$ and $\delta = \max(\delta_i) = 4.76\%$. Therefore, the difference in the results appears to be insignificant.

If there are more than two results of the expert evaluation of objects, we can proceed as follows. Let us arrange the results in increasing order of their acceptability coefficients $P^{(r)}$, select the first pair of results from the obtained series and, on the basis of the above procedure, we obtain the resulting combined estimate for this pair. As a result, the number of all the estimates decreases by one. Then the procedure continues in a similar way until eventually we get one estimate.

5 Conclusion

The following results were obtained:

1. The procedure for assessing the degree of acceptability of the expert evaluation results in solving a specific problem is constructed. The composition of indicators characterizing the acceptability degree is formed, expressions for the integral indicator of the acceptability degree are given.

2. Five possible ways of processing expert data are presented. The procedure for using these methods and comparing the obtained results is demonstrated on the example of an information security problem.
3. The paper describes the procedure of forming the final result of expert evaluation with several types of expert evaluation of a set of objects by a given group of indicators.

The described procedures can be used to process the results of expert evaluation of objects of any kind.

References

1. Orlov, A.I.: Matematika sluchaya. Veroyatnosti i statistika – osnovnyye faktory (Mathematics of the Case. Probabilities and Statistics Are the Main Factors), 273 p. Publishing House "Press", Moscow
2. Gutsykova, S.V.: Metod ekspertnykh otsenok. Teoriya i praktika (Method of Expert Estimates. Theory and Practice), 144 p. Institute of Psychology of the Russian Academy of Sciences, Moscow (2011)
3. Popov, G.A., Popova, E.A.: Al'ternativnyy variant koeffitsiyenta konkordatsii (Alternative Type of the Concordance Coefficient). Vestn. Astrakhan. gos. tekhn. un-ta. Ser.: Upravleniye, vychislitel'naya tekhnika i informa-tika (Vestnik of Astrakhan State Technical University. Series: Management, Computer Science and Informatics), no. 2, pp. 158–167 (2013)
4. Popov, G.A., Popova, E.A.: Asimptoticheskoye povedeniye al'ternativnogo varianta koeffitsiyenta konkordatsii (Asymptotic Behavior of an Alternative Type of the Concordance Coefficient). Vestn. Astra- khan. gos. tekhn. un-ta. Ser.: Upravleniye, vychislitel'naya tekhnika i informa-tika (Vestnik of Astrakhan State Technical University. Series: Management, Computer Science and Informatics), no. 1, pp. 153–160 (2014)
5. Makarov, I.M., Vinogradskaya, T.M., Rubchinsky, A.A., Sokolov, V.V.: Teoriya vybora i prinyatiya resheniy (Theory of Choice and Decision-Making), 330 p. Nauka, Moscow (1982)
6. Kvyatkovskaya, I.Y.: Methodology of a support of making management decisions for poorly structured problems. In: Kvyatkovskaya, I.Y., Shurshev, V.F., Frenkel, M.B. (eds.) Creativity in Intelligent Technologies and Data Science. Communications in Computer and Information Science, vol. 535, pp. 278–291. Springer, Cham (2015). https://doi.org/10.1007/978-3-319-23766-4_23
7. Budylsky, A.V., Kvyatkovskaya, I.Yu.: Using coevolution genetic algorithm with Pareto principles to solve project scheduling problem under duration and cost constraints (Текст). J. Inf. Org. Sci. 38(1), 1–9 (2014)
8. Hiep, P.Q., Kvyatkovskaya, I.Yu., Shurshev, V.F., Popov, G.A.: Methods and algorithms of alternatives ranging in managing the telecommunication services quality. J. Inf. Organ. Sci. 39(1), 65–74 (2015)
9. Popov, G.A., Galimova, L.V., Kvyatkovskaya, I.Yu., Shurshev, V.F.: Formation of a system of collection and detection of links between the users based on data from social networks. In: Communications in Computer and Information Science, vol. 535, pp. 603–617 (2015)
10. Popov, G.A., Magomedov, Sh: Comparative analysis of various methods treatment expert assessments. Int. J. Adv. Comput. Sci. Appl. 8(5), 35–39 (2017)

Adaptive Analysis of Merchant Big Data

Oleg Surnin[1], Mariia Sigova[2], Pavel Sitnikov[3],
Anton Ivaschenko[3(✉)], and Anastasia Stolbova[4]

[1] SEC "Open Code", Yarmarochnaya 55, Samara, Russia
[2] International Banking Institute, Nevsky avenue 60, Saint-Petersburg, Russia
[3] Samara State Technical University, Molodogvardeyskaya 244, Samara, Russia
anton.ivashenko@gmail.com
[4] Samara University, Moskovskoe shosse 34, Samara, Russia

Abstract. There is proposed a method and technology for adaptive analysis of demand and supply of regional banking acquiring services based on Big Data processing. The paper introduces a new technology of acquiring services demand and supply monitoring and analysis using specifically designed and developed software solution. The proposed approach and its implementation become a basis for acquiring service marketing, locations perspective search and tariffs calculation considering the individual characteristics of sales and services business. The developed technique is implemented by software for decision-making support system pro-bated on model data of the St. Petersburg financial environment.

Keywords: Digital economy · Merchant acquiring · Big Data · Decision-making support

1 Introduction

Merchant acquiring is a convenient and efficient technology for the interaction of consumers with trade and service outlets nowadays [1]. Its expansion and wide use in various areas of the service industry correspond to the modern trends of economy digitalization [2]. In this regard most acquiring banks (also known as acquires) that process credit or debit card payments on behalf of a merchant express high interest in the development of new digital services using modern technologies.

Practical implementation of merchant acquiring in the real sector is based on the development of digital platforms that force virtual interaction of acquiring services providers and customers and thus help them to find the best options of cooperation [3]. Modern technologies of Big Data processing and analysis can help to solve this complex problem and improve the competitive performance of acquires. In particular, it gives managers a considerably new opportunity to track and monitor payments with plastic bank cards and check it against the potential of banking services development in a certain region. This paper presents a solution and its software implementation for adaptive merchant acquiring using the modern technologies of Big Data analysis.

A. G. Kravets et al. (Eds.): CIT&DS 2019, CCIS 1083, pp. 105–117, 2019.
https://doi.org/10.1007/978-3-030-29743-5_8

2 State of the Art

Merchant acquiring is one of the challenging areas of digitalization. Its advantages in terms of non-cash payments support include [4, 5]: savings of state funds for printing banknotes; the ability to control the cash flow; reducing the number of illegal transactions; the possibility of conducting statistical reporting, planning, forecasting of the state of the economy in the micro- and macro-sections.

Parameters that affect the cost of acquiring, e.g. consumer preferences, are studied in [6]. Benefits for bank service customers include: effective cost management, analysis of consumer spending and control over cash flow; no need to spend own funds, transfer large amounts of cash; an increase in the speed of settlements, since the time to pay with a card should be faster than the cash payment process, issue change; increasing the competitiveness of the enterprise in the occupied market by attracting new customers who actively use card payments; reduction of crime situation, for example, the lack of risk of obtaining counterfeit banknotes.

Modern methods of data analysis and decision-making support for the development of acquiring services should consider ontological features of the financial environment. In particular, the acquiring rate should take into account the geo-referencing and ensure the possibility of analyzing the weighted average cost of the operation depending on the category of the client of the bank.

The conceptual model [7] of acquiring services includes the main ontological concepts and relations between trade and service points of different categories, banks, tariffs, payment systems and cost of operations, areas, and categories of customers. This model was developed to provide an individual approach to the calculation of tariffs, taking into account the peculiarities of individual sales and service outlets, the demand for and the provision of the population with banking services geographically linked to individual territories.

Along with the relevance of the provision of acquiring services, one of the significant problems of acquiring is the lack of a worked out system when choosing trade and service outlets to offer installation of POS terminals, charging service provision, which leads to the fact that acquiring is unprofitable. Thus, there is a need to develop a methodology for developing acquiring services in order to increase the efficiency of acquiring for a bank.

Plastic card transactions form large physical data volume. The number of service calls is big; they vary and require high-speed processing. In this regard, the task of managing the collection and processing of information data in the system of acquisition and processing system with a stratified architecture may be referred to the Big Data problem [8, 9].

One of the solutions can be close to subject-oriented approach for business processes management (S-BPM), which conceives a process as a collaboration of multiple subjects organized via structured communication [10]. There can be proposed a model for the interaction of actors (subjects) in integrated information space, which can be implemented using the multi-agent software [11]. The ideas of indirect and conditional project management generating soft influence over highly motivated autonomous actors are being successfully implemented in Internet communities and social networks [12–14].

To provide effective decision-making support there should be implemented a specialized UI capable of presenting Big Data and put it on map. This task can be solved by contextual data visualization [15, 16] that combines combine several data sets to analyze multiple layers of a complex system at once. The system should interlink all related data sets (e.g., images, text, measured values, scans) and offer visual analytics to support experts. This approach supports the idea of maximum effective visualization of complex data for professionals instead of automatic decision-making. In addition to this, it is proposed to involve the decision maker into the process of data processing and visualization by means of continuous interacting with the system, which helps to optimize the learning behavior of both humans and algorithms.

Based on these approaches there was developed a new concept of adaptive merchant acquiring capable of processing Big Data of transactions to personalize the model of calculating tariffs and consider the features of human behavior.

3   A Model of Adaptive Merchant Acquiring

Market analysis for the provision of acquiring services consists of the selection of potential trade and service outlets (named as "service locations" L). The main strategies for increasing bank profits by acquiring include:

- replacement of terminals owned by competitors, due to the adjustment of tariff making it attractive;
- expanding the coverage area with maximum services coverage by the placement of the terminals in locations where they were previously absent.

Assessment of the prospects of location consists in assessing the priority and efficiency of terminal placement among selected potential customers.

Each location can be a "Location of demand" or a "Location of supply". An example of a demand location is, for example, a university dormitory, a business center, a residential building. The demand location is characterized by the volume of demand Vd (considering the number of citizens in the considered location), the number of cards issued Nc and the rhythm of demand Rd.

Supply location can be illustrated by a retail outlet, for example, a restaurant, a shopping center, a car dealership, a store, a gas station. Supply location is characterized by the volume Vs, which is the turnover per month at a given location; the number of POS terminals Nt installed in the locations and the rhythm Rs. Terminals, in turn, are characterized by the volume Vt – terminal turnover per month.

The proposed solution has 4 stages:

- selecting the market for acquiring services, which consists in identifying a potential client (with terminals and without terminals), on which the development strategy depend;

- assessment of the prospects of a location, the task of which is to select locations that are of the highest priority and potentially beneficial for the placement of the term-fishing;
- calculation of the tariff, which includes the proposal of the tariff on the basis of the similar and analysis of its effectiveness;
- return to the original parameters (this ensures the iterative nature of the modeling and decision making).

The application of this solution allows assisting in the successful arrangement of terminals and the calculation of favorable tariffs due to the possibility of modeling various states of locations.

To be able to compare individual locations and districts, it is necessary to introduce the indicators in relation to the maximum values of the district indicators:

$$V_d^H = \frac{V_d}{V_d^{max}}, \quad N_c^H = \frac{N_c}{N_c^{max}}, \quad V_s^H = \frac{V_s}{V_s^{max}}, \quad N_t^H = \frac{N_t}{N_t^{max}}. \tag{1}$$

Thus, we represent the state of Reg regions and L locations as sets of vectors:

$$Reg\left(\vec{V_d^H}, \vec{V_s^H}\right), \quad L\left(\vec{N_t^H}, \vec{V_s^H}, \vec{N_c^H}, \vec{V_d^H}\right) \tag{2}$$

The prospects of location proposals are characterized by the following indicator. The ratio of the volume of demand to the volume of supply determines the equilibrium coefficient:

$$K_b = \frac{V_d^H}{V_s^H}. \tag{3}$$

If the equilibrium coefficient is less than 1, then with a small number of citizens the turnover of the enterprise is above average. If the equilibrium coefficient is 1, then the demand corresponds to the supply. In these cases, the location is promising.

If the equilibrium coefficient is greater than 1, then, with a large volume of demand, there is a lack of supply location turnover, the causes of which may be various factors. Depending on the causes and magnitude of the deficiency, the location can be reduced as unpromising.

The ratio of the number of cards to the number of terminals determines the ratio of enterprises' security:

$$K_s = \frac{N_c^H}{N_t^H}. \tag{4}$$

If the ratio of the security of the enterprise is less than 1, then there is a shortage of bank cards in the demand locations with an excess of the number of terminals in the supply location. In this case, the supply location is considered unpromising, or a decision should be made about the possibility of providing citizens with bank cards at the respective demand locations.

If the ratio of enterprise security is 1, then the number of bank cards of citizens corresponds to the number of terminals in the location of the offer and this location is estimated as promising for replacing the terminals of competitors.

If the ratio of the security of the enterprise is much greater than 1, then with sufficient availability of cards for citizens, there is a lack of terminals and this location can be considered promising.

The ratio of the number of cards to the number of the population determines the ratio of population security:

$$K_d = \frac{N_c^H}{V_d^H}. \tag{5}$$

If the ratio of the security of the population is 1 or more, then the number of bank cards of citizens corresponds to the number of citizens or exceeds it. If the coefficient of security of the population is less than 1, then not every citizen has a bank card. In this case, it is possible to make a decision on issuing new bank cards.

Table 1 presents a description of the coefficients characterizing the prospects of location offers.

Table 1. Perspective analysis

Indicator	<1	1	>1
K_b	Few consumers, Large turnover	Demand corresponds to supply	Large demand, Low turnover
K_s	Few cards, Many terminals	Enough terminals according to cards	Lack of terminals
K_d	Few cards	Enough cards	Enough cards

4 Decision-Making Support

Based on perspective analysis there is introduced a classification of locations attraction (see Table 2).

The illustration is given in Figs. 1, 2. Let us consider a situation where the location of supply has a small turnover (supply), a small number of terminals, but many citizens around (demand) who have few bank cards (see Fig. 1): L (0.12; 0.23; 0.15; 0.75). Then $K_b = 3.26$; $K_s = 1.25$, $K_d = 0.2$. In this case, the enterprise belongs to class C.1, the recommendation is to provide the population with cards and/or add terminals.

The value of the equilibrium coefficient indicates a shortage of the volume of supply, and the ratio of the lack of terminals with a sufficient volume of demand. In this case, the bank can either leave the location of the offer, as unpromising and go on to consider another location, or assess the possibility of issuing additional cards (as the company's turnover depends, including on the possibility of payment by bank cards) and assess the prospects.

Table 2. Attraction of locations

Attraction class	K	Ks	Kd	Correction measures
A	1	1	–	–
	<1	1		
B.1	>1	>1	≥ 1	Add terminals
	<1	>1	≥ 1	
	1	>1	≥ 1	
B.2	<1	<1	≥ 1	Reduce terminals
	1	<1	≥ 1	
C.1	>1	>1	<1	Issue more cards
	<1	>1	<1	Add terminals
	1	>1	<1	
	>1	1	<1	
C.2	>1	<1	<1	Issue more cards
	1	<1	<1	Reduce terminals
	<1	<1	<1	
C.3	>1	<1	≥ 1	Issue more cards
D	>1	1	≥ 1	No perspective

Then the task comes down to finding the optimal values of these measures: how to change the number of cards issued and increase the number of terminals so that the company's turnover will increase to the prospective level (see Fig. 2).

This problem was solved by a simplex method, which consists in finding a vertex that is optimal among the set of solutions. If the vertex is not optimum, then the simplex method searches for an edge, when moving along which the value of the objective function decreases, and calculates the next vertex.

To assess the impact of the number of terminals registered in the location of the proposal, on the monthly turnover of the location, we introduce the function of turnover:

$$\phi(N_t) = V_s^0 \cdot (1 + \psi(N_t)), \qquad (6)$$

where V_s^0 is the turnover of the client not using POS-terminals for payment,

$\psi(N_t)$ – activation function depending on the number of terminals installed.

The activation function must meet the following requirements. The value of the function at zero must be 0:

$$\psi(0) = 0. \qquad (7)$$

With positive values of the function argument, its value should be less than 1:

$$\psi(x) < 1, \forall x \in [0, +\infty), \lim_{x \to \infty} \psi(x) = 1. \qquad (8)$$

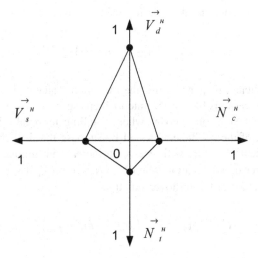

Fig. 1. Supply location current state radar

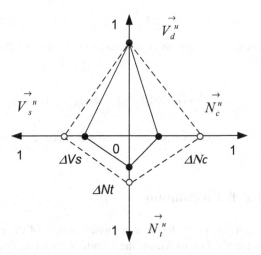

Fig. 2. Supply location changes proposed

The function should be monotonically increasing on the interval $[0, +\infty)$:

$$\forall x, y \in [0, +\infty), x < y \Rightarrow \psi(x) < \psi(y), \tag{9}$$

As the activation function, select the following function:

$$\psi(x) = \begin{cases} \frac{2}{\pi} arctg(x), x \in [0, +\infty), \\ 0, x \in (-\infty, 0). \end{cases} \tag{10}$$

Then the turnover function takes the following form:

$$\phi(N_t) = V_s^0 \cdot \left(1 + \frac{2\alpha}{\pi} arctg(\beta \cdot N_t)\right), \tag{11}$$

where α is the coefficient responsible for the maximum value of the increase in turnover; β – coefficient responsible for the rate of increase in turnover.

To determine the value of turnover when installing terminals, it is necessary to calculate the values of the coefficients α and β. Suppose that if there is installed one POS terminal payment, the store will receive an increase in turnover by $0 < \tau < 1$.

Then the turnover of the location when Nt = 1 will be $V_s^0(1 + \tau)$.

Substitute the values in the turnover function:

$$V_s^0(1+\tau) = V_s^0 \cdot \left(1 + \frac{2\alpha}{\pi} arctg(\beta)\right). \tag{12}$$

Consequently, an increase in turnover when installing one terminal:

$$\tau = \frac{2\alpha}{\pi} arctg(\beta). \tag{13}$$

Similarly, we obtain an increase in the turnover of the location when the nth terminal is installed:

$$\gamma = \frac{2\alpha}{\pi}\left(arctg\left(\beta_{n+1}\right) - arctg(\beta_n)\right). \tag{14}$$

Thus, to determine the coefficients α and β and it is necessary to solve the system of the last two equations.

5 Acquiring Tariff Calculation

The total cost of acquiring (tariff) for an enterprise consists of the cost of equipment (the purchase of the terminal or its lease), the commission for each operation or fixed monthly payment for services and cash and settlement services if a bank needs to open a current account.

When calculating the favourable acquiring tariff, it is necessary to take into account the market. In case when the client does not use the services of acquiring, it is necessary to analyse the tariffs offered by competitors for a similar category of consumers in the area. If a prospective client is already using acquiring, it is necessary to analyse the competitor's rate presented at this location.

In view of the above, the cost of acquiring is determined as follows:

$$E = S + M + C, \tag{15}$$

where S is the cost of acquiring, M – margin of the acquiring bank, C – electronic payment processor commission.

The criterion for the effectiveness of the tariff, in this case, is the size of the marginal revenue received by the bank.

Due to the fact that the bank cannot control the prices for services of third-party organizations, we take S and C as constant values, therefore, when calculating the tariff, the bank may vary the margin M it receives.

There was introduced a function that determines the size of the marginal revenue of the acquiring bank, received from one terminal:

$$M = N_s \cdot A \cdot P_a \cdot P_m, \tag{16}$$

where N_s is the number of transactions that pass through this terminal per month,
A – average transaction receipt of this terminal per month,
P_a – the percentage of acquiring, corresponding to the tariff,
P_m – the percentage of the margin of the acquiring bank.

The objective function is to increase the bank margin on the location of the offer:

$$\begin{cases} \sum_{i=0}^{Nt} N_{s_i} \cdot A_i \cdot P_{a_i} \cdot P_m \to max, \\ P_{a_i} < P^*_{a_i}. \end{cases} \tag{17}$$

where N_{s_i} is the number of terminals installed at the location of the offer,
$P^*_{a_i}$ – percentage of acquiring a competitor bank.

After calculating the tariff and assessing its effectiveness, a tariff adjustment takes place, if necessary, and additional training of the tariff knowledge base.

After changing the conditions of locations, introducing new tariffs and simulating acquiring development situations, the proposed method allows restoring initial values of demand volume, number of cards issued, demand rhythms, supply volume, number of POS terminals, supply rhythms, the volume of terminals and tariffs used by the bank.

6 Implementation

The proposed methodology was implemented in a decision-making support system designed to assist analysts of bank departments responsible for the provision of acquiring services. The system allows processing Big Data of the bank's acquiring system for analyzing the tariffs of other banks with the display of relevant locations on

the interactive map, correlation analysis of offered service options and territory popularity indicators, assistance in calculating the acquiring rate and analyzing the
weighted average cost of acquiring operations.

Decision support system allows solving the following tasks:

- ensuring the possibility of analyzing the parameters affecting the acquiring tariff and
  its growth or decrease;
- determination and analysis of quantitative characteristics of the market of merchant
  acquiring;
- determination of sources of obtaining information on the established parameters;
- comparative analysis of characteristics of tariffs and conditions for the provision of
  trade acquiring;
- building an interactive map of bank service customers with the possibility of
  grouping them by relevant indicators;
- building a model of an information system for a bank's merchant acquiring with the
  ability to analyze the weighted average cost of a transaction depending on the
  profile of the bank's client's activities;
- building a predictive model for the development of acquiring services based on the
  information system of decision-making support.

To provide high usability of acquiring services demand and supply monitoring and
analysis there was proposed a concept of the user interface based on contraposition of
demand and supply on a map (see Fig. 3).

Instead of a classic approach of BI implementation using the dynamical representation of multiple indicators and parameters, there was developed a solution that
provides an analyst with a virtual environment clustered and colored according to
essential benefits, challenges, issues, and constraints.

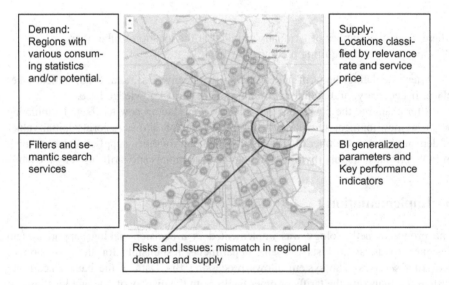

Fig. 3. UI concept for banking services interactive analysis

In order to avoid overload with redundant information, there should be implemented an extensive and flexible system of filtering, prioritization, and semantic search. In addition to this, there was implemented and approach of accented visualization based on highlighting the most important objects that better correspond to the current situation and time.

This approach allows implementing a user-friendly software service for Big Data processing in real time, which allows improving the quality of decision-making based on adaptive analysis of demand and supply of regional banking acquiring.

The proposed concept was implemented by a specifically designed banking acquiring system for decision-making support (see Fig. 4) that implements the following main functions:

- creation and loading of customer data;
- working with bank tariffs and viewing relevant locations on the map;
- correlation analysis of proposals for service options and indicators of the popularity of territories;
- analysis of the weighted average cost of the operation, depending on the profile of the bank's client's activities, with the option to select a particular client category and display the cost value for this category;
- calculation of the most profitable bank acquiring rate;
- work with an interactive map.

The system was developed on Python – a high-level programming language with dynamic typing, supporting object-oriented, functional and imperative programming styles using PyCharm integrated development environment.

Fig. 4. Adaptive acquiring decision-making support system

Analysis of the subject area made it possible to determine the expected data sources. They can be banks, customers of banks (car centers, restaurants, hotels, chain stores), cartographic services.

From such sources, it is possible to obtain data such as a list of bank customers, their binding to geographic coordinates, data on transactions (date, time, transaction amount, type of bank card, payment system), commission of the acquiring bank, bank issuer and payment system, information about the number of terminals. In addition, data can be taken from open sources, such as annual reports from official sites of enterprises, official sites of banks, and official statistics.

The module of intelligent analytics is intended for the correlation analysis of proposals for service options and indicators of the popularity of territories, analysis of the weighted average cost value of the operation depending on the profile of the bank's client's activities with an option to choose a particular client category and display the cost value just for this category.

For customers selected in accordance with the filters, statistics of operations with bank cards with various payment systems are provided. For the correlation analysis of the demand and supply of acquiring services, three independent filterings by participants of acquiring are used: bank customers, acquiring banks, and population categories.

As a result of applying filters to acquiring participants, the correlation between them is displayed on the map using the following layers: bank customers are displayed on the map with dots; areas with selected categories of population are displayed on the map by areas filled with color, the shades of which correspond to the population density of maps for this category.

7 Conclusion

As a result of the work, a model and technology of adaptive analysis of the demand and supply of banking acquiring services in the region based on big data analysis technologies were proposed. The proposed approach includes the selection of the market for the provision of acquiring services, assessment of the prospects of location, calculation of the tariff and return.

To assess the prospects of locations, a system of prospects for location has been developed: an equilibrium coefficient, a population supply ratio, an enterprise supply ratio. Based on these coefficients, customers' classification by attractiveness for a bank offering acquiring services has been developed.

The result of applying this technique is to increase the efficiency of the provision of acquiring services by the bank, which includes assistance in choosing target customers, calculating mutually beneficial tariffs, preventing unprofitable acquiring for the bank.

One of the further directions of development of this topic is the study of the values of the coefficients of prospects and determining the boundaries of the coefficients for the most accurate classification of the attractiveness.

References

1. Kjos, A.: The merchant-acquiring side of the payment card industry: structure, operations, and challenges. Federal Reserve Bank of Philadelphia: Payment Cards Center. No. 07-12, 29 p. (2007)
2. Digital Russia. New Reality Digital McKinsey, July 2017, 133 p. (2017) https://www.mckinsey.com/ru/our-work/mckinsey-digital
3. Ivaschenko, A., Korchivoy, S.: Multi-agent model of infrastructural return for an intermediary service provider. In: Proceedings of the 2018 European Simulation and Modeling Conference (ESM 2018), Ghent, Belgium, EUROSIS-ETI, pp. 192–195 (2018)
4. Stavins, J.: How do consumers make their payment choices? – Federal Reserve Bank Of Boston: Consumer Payments Research Center. No. 17-1, 36 p. (2017)
5. Levine, R., Lin, C., Wang, Z.: Acquiring banking networks. National Bureau of Economic Research, no. 23469, 66 p. (2017)
6. Bounie, D.: Consumer payment preferences, network externalities, and merchant card acceptance: an empirical investigation. Rev. Ind. Organ. **51**(3), 257–290 (2017)
7. Rysman, M., Wright, J.: The economics of payment cards. Rev. Netw. Econ. **13**(3), 303–353 (2014)
8. Baesens, B.: Analytics in a Big Data world: The Essential Guide to Data Science and Its Applications, 232 p. Wiley, Hoboken (2014)
9. Bessis, N., Dobre, C. (eds.): Big Data and Internet of Things: A Roadmap for Smart Environments. SCI, vol. 546, p. 470. Springer, Cham (2014). https://doi.org/10.1007/978-3-319-05029-4
10. Fleischmann, A., Schmidt, W., Stary, C. (eds.): S-BPM in the Wild, p. 282. Springer, Cham (2015). https://doi.org/10.1007/978-3-319-17542-3
11. Gorodetskii, V.I.: Self-organization and multiagent systems: I. Models of multiagent self-organization. J. Comput. Syst. Sci. Int. **51**(2), 256–281 (2012)
12. Ivaschenko, A., Lednev, A., Diyazitdinova, A., Sitnikov, P.: Agent-based outsourcing solution for agency service management. In: Bi, Y., Kapoor, S., Bhatia, R. (eds.) IntelliSys 2016. LNNS, vol. 16, pp. 204–215. Springer, Cham (2018). https://doi.org/10.1007/978-3-319-56991-8_16
13. Surnin, O.L., Sitnikov, P.V., Ivaschenko, A.V., Ilyasova, N.Yu., Popov, S.B.: Big Data incorporation based on open services provider for distributed enterprises. In: CEUR Workshop Proceedings, Session Data Science (DS-ITNT 2017), vol. 190, pp. 42–47 (2017)
14. Ivaschenko, A., Khorina, A., Sitnikov, P.: Online creativity modeling and analysis based on big data of social networks. In: Arai, K., Kapoor, S., Bhatia, R. (eds.) SAI 2018. AISC, vol. 858, pp. 329–337. Springer, Cham (2019). https://doi.org/10.1007/978-3-030-01174-1_25
15. Holzinger, A.: Extravaganza tutorial on hot ideas for interactive knowledge discovery and data mining in biomedical informatics. In: Ślęzak, D., Tan, A.-H., Peters, James F., Schwabe, L. (eds.) BIH 2014. LNCS (LNAI), vol. 8609, pp. 502–515. Springer, Cham (2014). https://doi.org/10.1007/978-3-319-09891-3_46
16. Holzinger, A.: Interactive machine learning for health informatics: when do we need the human-in-the-loop. Brain Inform. **3**(2), 119–131 (2016)

Big Data in the Stochastic Model
of the Passengers Flow at the Megalopolis
Transport System Stops

Elena Krushel[✉], Ilya Stepanchenko[✉], Alexander Panfilov[✉],
and Elena Berisheva[✉]

Kamyshin Technological Institute (Branch of) Volgograd State
Technical University, Kamyshin, Russia
elena-krushel@yandex.ru, stilvi@mail.ru,
elenaberisheva@mail.ru, panfilov@kti.ru

Abstract. The problem of the passengers flow model development is proposed
as the subsystem of the general municipal passengers transport system operation
model of megalopolis. The specific features of the application subject (Volgograd city, Russia) were detected to simplify the big data simulation problem.
The difficulties caused by the high dimensionality were overcome by means of
the double time scaling in passengers' flow estimation. The hour time scale was
accepted to the computation of the hourly flow from each departure stop to the
city district of destination without the pointing of the specific destination
stop. The minute time scale was accepted to distribute the hourly flow between
the destinations stops located in this district. The algorithms of the destination
stops choice simulation were carried out. The follows examples of simulation
results are presented: hourly passengers flow directed to the departure stops;
daily variations of districts population caused by the inter-district passengers'
flows; influence of the of competition on the municipal transport system operation; destination stops choice variants according to the stops' attractiveness
scores designed by experts.

Keywords: Megalopolis · Transport system · Two-time scale simulation ·
Destination choice · Attractiveness scores

1 Introduction

The effective approach to simplify the problem of the megalopolis social passengers
transport simulation is to decompose the general problem on two sub-problems [1].
First sub-problem is formulating as the problem of simulation of passengers' flow
between the stops of the city transport net (i.e. the simulation both of the passengers'
flow to the stops of departure and of the destination stops choice). The second sub-
problem deals with the passengers' transportation accordingly to the chosen route by
means of vehicles of the urban transport system.

Decision of both sub-problems calls for the necessity of the account of multiple
uncertainty factors either stochastic or non-stochastic (including chaotic) nature.
However such account is much more important for the first sub-problem since the real

© Springer Nature Switzerland AG 2019
A. G. Kravets et al. (Eds.): CIT&DS 2019, CCIS 1083, pp. 118–132, 2019.
https://doi.org/10.1007/978-3-030-29743-5_9

passengers' flow depends on the passengers' transport behavior which accumulates in a complicated way the unpredictable preferences of individuals. It is necessary to mention also the existence of links between both of sub-problems via common parameters of the routes net.

One of possible approaches to the passengers' flow modeling based on the agent simulation principles [2, 3] is discussed below. The proposed approach may be considered as the addition and extension of the other approaches (for particularly described in [4–6]) the authors of which emphasize the fundamental difficulties of the passengers' flow simulation.

The purpose of simulation is to receive the data on the passengers transport behavior and on the passengers' flow between the stops of transport net necessary to the second sub-problem decision [7]. For the achievement of this purpose it is necessary, firstly, to simulate the arrival of each agent (below we use the term "passenger" instead of "agent") at each stop of transport net with the pointing of arrival's time moment (hh:mm), and, secondly, for each passenger appearing at the stop of departure to determine the destination stop with the indication of route options (without transfers; with one transfer; with more than one transfer). Some of the results of the trip variant choice are pointed in [8–10].

The main results were obtained during the research of public passenger transport system of Volgograd city (population size in 2018 was 1,013,533 people, Russian Federation).

The discussed problem possesses a number of features inherent to the big data subject of study i.e.:

1. Impressive dimensionality (the examples pointed below were computed for follows parameters of Volgograd city: the number of the stopping zones 535 with up to 6 stops in zone; the number of routs 228, the amount of daily trips about 1,000,000, the duration of working day 900 min). Taking into account the uncertainty presence the patterns of passengers' flow should be of probability nature. Therefore their detection would be carried out only after processing of multiple simulation sessions results for different transport system exploitation periods i.e. for workday/day off/the day before holiday; winter/summer; the different variants of intensiveness of the competitors operating (fixed-route taxis and private motor transport enterprises) etc.
2. The high dimensionality puts practically overpowering obstacles for the large scale examination of the real operating transport system. As the result the heuristics, questioning, and the expert opinions are to be attracted.
3. The demands of discovery-driven data mining [11, 12] techniques application (in addition to well-known statistical methods) for the patterns detections in the raw data (results of restricted real operating transport system observations, reports, statistical information et all).
4. The necessity of the patterns detection [9] for the attempts to following questions answer: is it possible to receive the believable simulation results of the passengers arrivals at the departure stop with the pointing of arrivals time moments with fixation not only hours but minutes also? Do the stereotypes exist in the choices of destination stops for the separate passengers' groups? Is it possible to select the

stable components in passengers' flow under the numerous uncertainty factors influence?

The proposed approach to the passengers' flow simulation carried out with big data methods applications are discussed below in following order:

1. The assumptions accepted for the passengers' flow model implementation are listed, and the algorithmic support elements are annotated.
2. The details of algorithms of the destination stops choices stereotypes for each passenger are described.
3. The simulation results examples with corresponding comments are presented.

2 Assumptions Accepted for the Passengers' Flow Model Implementation and the Algorithmic Support Elements Brief Description

1. The probability distribution functions of the number of passengers choosing the departure stop are estimated in accordance to the information about citizens population nearby the stop's location (the following information sources were attracted: the data about the living buildings placing received by the facilities of Open-StreetMap [13], Google Maps [14], Yandex Maps [15] as well as the statistics about the city population and its distribution between the living zones [16]). For each simulation session the number of passengers' arrival at each departure stop was chosen randomly, in accordance to these probability functions and to the time distribution of the passengers' flow within the working day (see point 4 below).
2. The difficulties caused by the high dimensionality were overcome by means of the double time scaling in the passengers' flow estimation. The hour time scale was accepted to the computation of the hourly passengers' flow from each departure stop to the city district of destination without the pointing of the specific destination stop. The minute time scale was accepted to distribute the hourly flow between the destinations stops located in this district. As the result the passengers' traffic with minute time scale would be obtained for each stop of departure with pointing of destination stop for each passenger.
3. The algorithm for the hourly passengers' flow computation from each stop to every city district is based on the Poisson's random values generator application. In context of the discussed problem the algorithm determines the number of independent events (appearance of generated number of passengers at the departure stop) during the fixed time interval (1 h) with given middle intense.
4. The middle intense of hourly passengers' flow for each working day hour was estimated as follows. The clustering of the different types of citizens' transport behavior assures the possibility of the detection of the passengers' predominant intentions in choosing the destination stops. Respectively the two groups of citizens with similar transport preferences were detected. For the first one (employees and youth 18–24 years old) the predominant passengers' flow is directed in morning hours to the places of work, learning, shopping or entertaining. Since the most of

such places are concentrated in the center of the city the main part of flow of this s' passengers' group is directed to the central district. The remaining part of passengers flow is distributed between the other districts chaotically with small predominance of the residence district. The passengers' flow in the middle of day is distributed predominantly between the stops within the same district. The evening flow corresponds to the passengers' return to the places of living. For the second group (schoolchildren and pensioners) the predominant passengers' flow takes place in the district of residence and remaining flow is distributed between the other districts chaotically.

5. The intensiveness of passengers' flow in morning and middle-day hours was assumed as random and time dependent. The appropriate probabilities were estimated on the base of real system operation observations statistics and expert opinions processing which show the stable existence of morning and evening peaks of traffic intensiveness. The passengers' flow at evening hours was computed as the returning flow of the passengers from the places of trips to the resident places.

6. The distinct values of minutes within each hour for each passenger's arrival at the stop of departure were generated randomly according to the uniform probability distribution.

7. The stop of destination for each passenger appearing on the departure stop is determined by the random choice between all stops of route net. The probability of the distinct destination stop choice is determined with the account of the attractiveness scores assigned for each stop. The latter are appointed via statistics of daily stops' visits and expert opinions. The appropriate algorithm is described below.

3 Algorithm of the Forming of the Destination Stop's Choice Stereotype

3.1 The Purpose of Computation

The purpose of computation: for each passenger outgoing from the departure stop at the pointed time moment (hh:mm) to determine:

1. The chosen destination stop's code and name;
2. The route variant (with no transfers; with single transfer; with two or more transfers);
3. The attractiveness score of destination at the chosen stop.

Figure 1 shows the fragment of computational results of the passengers' flow from certain stop of Volgograd route net to the other stops.

3.2 Main Sections of Initial Data

1. The stops database in which the attractiveness scores are pointed (by experts) for each stop to be chosen as the destination one.

Departure stop's name	Departure district's name	Time moment of departure	Arrival district's name	Arrival stop's name	Approachability 0/ 1/ -1
St_018	Distr_2	6:02	Distr_4	St_054	1
		6:07	Distr_6	St_322	1
		6:09	Distr_2	St_390	1
		6:20	Distr_2	St_310	1
		6:27	Distr_2	St_351	1
		6:27	Distr_8	St_442	1

Fig. 1. Fragment of computational results of the passengers' flow. Designations of approachability: 0 – with no transfers; 1 – with single transfer; −1 –with two or more transfers

2. The database with information about the route net's structure in which for each stop of departure about codes of other stops ordered accordingly to the routes variants (with no transfers; with single transfer; with two or more transfers) are pointed out. Each section of variants is ordered accordingly to the attractiveness scores decreasing (Fig. 2).

Stop's name	Stop allocation's district name	Number of residents nearby the bus stop	Stop's attractiveness score for the destination choice
St_033	Distr_1	7207	1000
St_224	Distr_2	54	500
St_044	Distr_2	3779	400
St_031	Distr_1	3301	300
St_102	Distr_1	4401	300
St_010	Distr_1	3576	200
St_032	Distr_1	2201	150
St_011	Distr_1	3799	100

Fig. 2. Fragment of database with information about route net's stops ordered accordingly to the attractiveness scores decreasing

3. The expert estimations of the probability values of each passenger's preferences in route variant choice (with no transfers; with single transfer; with two or more transfers).

3.3   The Conditions of the Algorithm Execution

The previous computational stages should be completed; the results of them should be present as the traffic of passengers arrivals at each departure stop with the pointing of the district code and arrival's time moment (hh:mm).

3.4   The Description of the Destination Stop Choice Algorithm

Three levels of random elements insertion are provided for the choice algorithm:

Level 1: random choice of the route variant (with no transfers; with single transfer; with two or more transfers); the probabilities of variants choices are shown by experts.

Level 2: for the chosen route variant the random choice of the attractiveness score value of the destination stop.

Level 3: if the attractiveness score determined at the level 2 is inherent to the single stop only then namely this stop should be chosen as the stop of destination. In opposite case (i.e. if several stops possess the equal attractiveness scores) the choice between them is performed chaotically (for example according to the discrete uniform distribution function).

The algorithm of the attractiveness score choice of the destination stop (level 2 of random elements insertion) was worked out by analogy with the algorithm for choosing a crossover participants in genetic optimization algorithms (so called "ruler algorithm" [17]). The analogy is based on the evident similarity between the fitness function in genetic algorithms facilities and the attractiveness score of the stops destination choice.

The steps of algorithm of the attractiveness score choice are shown below.

Step 1. The computing of the attractiveness scores' cumulative sum for the stops of preliminary chosen district of destination.

Step 2. The determination of minimal value of the cumulative attractiveness scores. Due to the ordering of stops according to decreasing of the individual attractiveness scores this minimal value corresponds to the first cortege of stops database of the preliminary chosen district of destination.

Step 3. The generation of random value x from the diapason of values [minimal value, step 2; the cumulative sum of attractiveness scores of all stops in the chosen district of destination]. To avoid the choice variants repeating in the different simulation sessions the randomization procedure is applied [18].

Step 4. If x (step 3) is less the minimum value (step 2) then the stop with maximal value of the attractiveness score among the stops of the preliminary chosen district is assigned as the stop of destination. In opposite case (i.e. if x, step 3, is more or equal to minimal value, step 2) the interval of cumulative attractiveness scores should be found so that x must be within this interval's bounds. This situation meets when several stops possess the equal attractiveness scores. The list of stops which pretend to be chosen corresponds to the upper bound of the detected interval. The choice of the specific stop from the list is chaotic, correspondingly to the mentioned above third level of random elements insertion in the choice algorithm.

As the result the stops with higher attractiveness scores values would be chosen on average more often comparably to the stops with less attractiveness (however the rare choices of the stops with low attractiveness are also possible due to the randomness of the choice mechanism).

4   Illustrations to the Passengers Flow Simulation Results (Volgograd City Transport System)

Illustrations to the Simulation of the Hourly Passengers Flow Directed to the Departure Stops. Figure 3 shows the time distribution of hourly passengers flow during the working day (6:00–21:00) from the stops St_033 (district Distr_2). The computations were carried out for two variants of operating intensiveness of competitors (fixed-route taxis). The left bars of diagrams correspond to the real level of fixed-route taxis flow whereas the right bars correspond to the hypothetic flow (four times less comparably with the existing level).

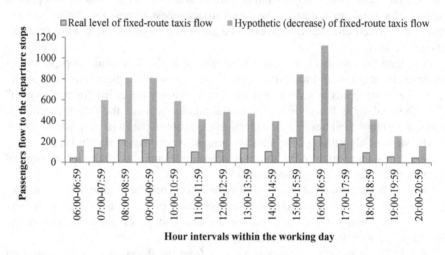

Fig. 3. The example of the hourly passengers flow distribution within the working day hours

Comments to Fig. 3. The model accounts the data on the variations of the passengers flow distributions during the working day achieved from the multiyear statistics of transport system operation observations [7]. Notwithstanding the passengers flow random formation the model stably reproduces the peaks of the morning and evening flows intensity in accordance with the real observations results. The passengers flow intensity between the peaks isn't constant due to stochastic factors accounted in model but the variations of flow are small.

Figure 4 illustrates the two-side passengers flow exchanges between the districts. The flows are formed by the passengers with essentially differing of stereotypes in destination stops choices. Left diagram corresponds to the flow of passengers of group 1 (employees and youth 18–24 years old) whereas right one corresponds to the group 2 (schoolchildren and pensioners). Figure 4 shows the parts (in %) of passengers flow from the stop St_033 of the district Distr_1 to all city districts (including the district of departure namely Distr_1). Figure 5 illustrates the analogous results for the stop St_140 of the district Distr_1.

Comments to Figs. 4, 5. The diagrams illustrate the assumptions about the prevalent passengers flow directions. For the passengers of the group 1 the prevalent direction is from district of residence to center district concentrating the major part of city offices, large educational centers, shopping and entertaining enterprises. For the passengers of group 2 the main part of trips takes place within the residence district; the flows to other districts are essentially less and differences between them are small.

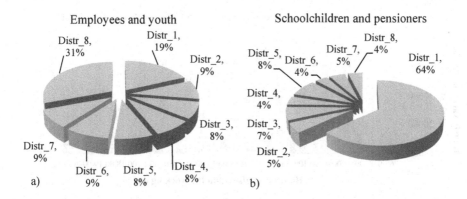

Fig. 4. The distribution of passengers flow from the stop St_033 between the city districts

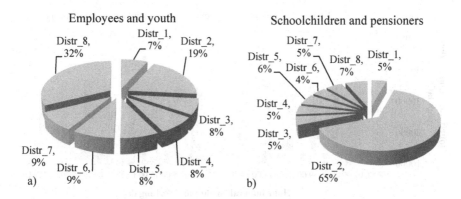

Fig. 5. The distribution of passengers flow from the stop St_140 between the city districts

Illustrations to the Simulation of City Districts Population Changes Due to the Passengers Flows Between the City Districts. Figures 6, 7, 8 show the diagrams of city districts hourly population variations during the working day due to the passengers migrations between the regions (for Distr_2 (Fig. 6), Distr_7 (Fig. 7) and Distr_8 (Fig. 8)). On each diagram the left bars represent the total district population changes; middle and right bars are related to passengers of group 1 (employees and youth) and 2 (schoolchildren and pensioners) correspondingly.

Comments to Figs. 6, 7, 8. The diagrams illustrate the influences of predominant directions of the passengers' flows on the district population changes during the working day. The passengers' flows from the district (except central district, Distr_8) for the passengers of group 1 (employees and youth) directed predominantly to the city center (left of Figs. 4, 5) lead to the decreasing of the district population (Figs. 6, 7) in morning hours. Such decreasing is accompanied of the corresponding increasing of population of the central district (Distr_8, Fig. 8). The passengers' flows in middle-day hours are almost stable. In the evening hours the predominant directions of the flows is reverse comparably with morning one for imitation of the passengers returns to the

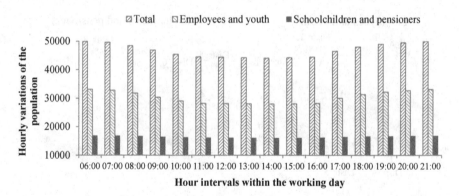

Fig. 6. Hourly variations of the population during the working day (city district 2)

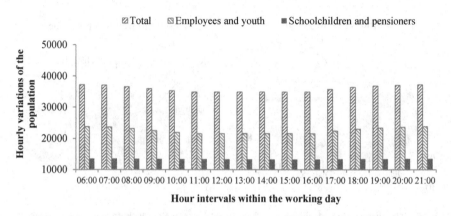

Fig. 7. Hourly variations of the population during the working day (city district 7)

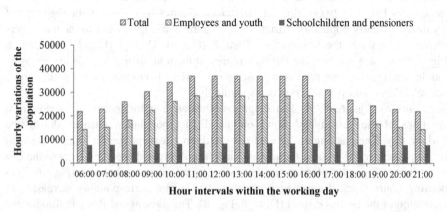

Fig. 8. Hourly variations of the population within the working day (city district Distr_8)

residences. The differences of the population changes in districts vary accordingly to the statistical data on districts total population (compare Figs. 6 and 7). The influence of flows of passengers of group 2 (schoolchildren and pensioners) on the districts population is negligible.

Illustrations of Influence of the Competitors Operating Intensiveness (Fixed-Route Taxis). The citizens migrations between the city districts may be served not only by the municipal transport system facilities but also by the competing variants (own cars, taxis, fixed-route private vehicles etc.). Therefore the income of the municipal transport system is dependent from its competitive ability among different variants of trans-porting service. Figure 9 shows the part of the hourly variations of the district popu-lation (Disrt_2 as the example) which falls to the municipal transport facilities under two variants of competition intensiveness. The Fig. 9a corresponds to the real number of competing transport vehicles (fixed-route taxis) while the Fig. 9b corresponds to the hypothetic four-time decrease of this number.

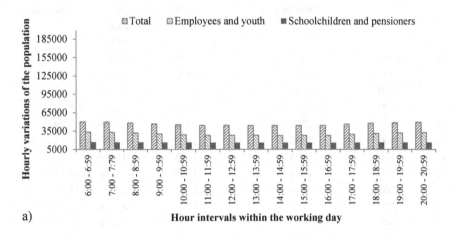

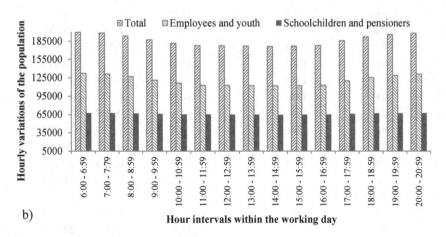

Fig. 9. Competition level influence on the municipal transport system activity: (a) the real number of passengers transported by the facilities of municipal transport system (city district Distr_2 fixed-route taxis, (b) four-time decrease of real number (Distr_2)

Comments to Fig. 9. The diagrams illustrate the possibilities of the essential rise of the municipal transport system income due to the forcing of competition advantages before the private fixed-route taxis.

Illustrations to the Algorithm of the Destination Stops Choice According to the Stops' Attractiveness Scores Designed by Experts. The statistical characteristics of choices were received by the results of 17 simulation sessions. Table 1 shows the data of the expected number of choices with the attractiveness scores 400...1000 comparably with 17 simulation sessions results averaging. Similar computations were carried out for the stops with attractiveness scores of diapasons 150...300 and 10...100.

Table 1. Comparison of the expected choices number with the values achieved by the averaging of simulation results

Stop's code	Attractiveness score	Average number of visits during the working day	Simulated number of visits	Part in the total visits number (%)	
				Of each stop	Cumulatively
33	1000	3676	3596	1,84%	1,84%
299	1000	3731	3596	1,87%	3,70%
85	700	2404	2518	1,20%	4,91%
380	700	2547	2518	1,27%	6,18%
55	600	2218	2158	1,11%	7,29%
83	600	2098	2158	1,05%	8,34%
15	500	1806	1798	0,90%	9,24%
82	500	1784	1798	0,89%	10,13%
105	500	1736	1798	0,87%	11,00%
118	500	1755	1798	0,88%	11,88%
139	500	1780	1798	0,89%	12,77%
204	500	1828	1798	0,91%	13,68%
224	500	1729	1798	0,86%	14,55%
403	500	1762	1798	0,88%	15,43%
22	400	1513	1439	0,76%	16,18%
44	400	1504	1439	0,75%	16,94%
48	400	1452	1439	0,73%	17,66%
57	400	1341	1439	0,67%	18,33%
84	400	1393	1439	0,70%	19,03%
86	400	1346	1439	0,67%	19,70%
93	400	1423	1439	0,71%	20,41%
103	400	1465	1439	0,73%	21,15%
135	400	1490	1439	0,75%	21,89%
145	400	1487	1439	0,74%	22,63%
146	400	1465	1439	0,73%	23,37%
176	400	1495	1439	0,75%	24,11%
200	400	1441	1439	0,72%	24,83%
206	400	1433	1439	0,72%	25,55%

Comments to Table 1. The number of stops' choices varies widely. For example the choices number of the popular stops (Table 1) reaches 31% of the whole choices number (1748 choices per working day) while the number of these stops is less than 8% from total stops number (445). The choices number of the stops with middle attractiveness scores values (of diapason 150…300) reaches 48% (833 choices per working day) while the number of these stops is 26% from total stops number. And the choices number of stops with low attractiveness scores values (of diapason 10…100 reaches 21% only (143 choices per working day) while the number of these stops is 66% from total stops number.

Such computations show that the on-line processing of transport system operation perhaps would be essentially simplified if such processing will be restricted only by the stops with high attractiveness scores (since namely at such stops the stressful situations of traffic occur more often).

The computations show that the variation coefficient (i.e. the ratio of the standard deviation of the choices number to its middle value) rises with attractiveness score decrease. Figure 10 illustrates the transition from the almost deterministic choices between the stops with high attractiveness scores to chaotic, irregular choices of unpopular stops. The dependence of variation coefficient from the attractiveness value can be approximated by polynomial trend of third order if the each following step of abscissa is two times less than previous one (Fig. 10).

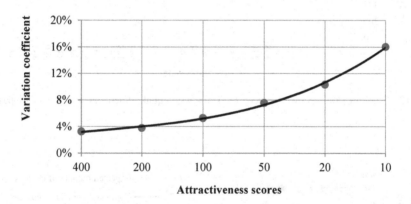

Fig. 10. Increasing of the choices number variation coefficient with the decreasing of attractiveness scores values

Figures 11, 12, 13 illustrate the random mechanism of the destination stops choices (shown by points) between the stops with equal attractiveness scores values.

Comments to Figs. 11, 12, 13. These figures (similarly to Table 1) illustrate the strong correlation between the number of choices computed by the averaging of 17 simulation sessions results (points on figures), on the one hand, and the expected number of choices computed in accordance the attractiveness scores without simulation (solid lines), on the other hand. The random deviations of the middle values of choices number from the expected values are insignificant; the correlation coefficient between these values exceeds 0.99 for the data of Table 1.

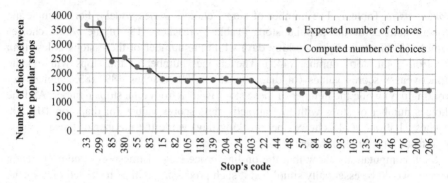

Fig. 11. Random stop's choice between the popular stops with equal attractiveness scores (see Table 1)

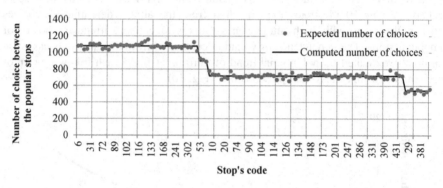

Fig. 12. Random stop's choice between the stops with equal attractiveness scores of diapason 150…300

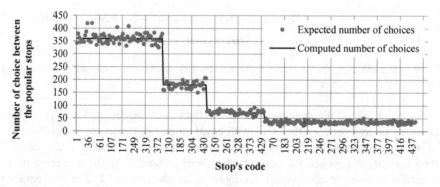

Fig. 13. Random stop's choice between the stops with equal attractiveness scores of diapason 10…100

5 Conclusion

The researches carried out assure the positive answers to the pointed in the introduction questions about big data specifics inherent to the general problem of passengers flow simulation in the municipal passengers transport system:

1. The feasible simulation of passengers' arrivals at the stops of departure with time indication (hh.mm) was implemented. The simulation results correspond to the statistical data of the real transport system operating observations with accuracy about 15%.
2. The stereotypes of the destination stops choices preferences were detected for the two social groups of passengers. First group: employees and youth 18...24 years old, second one: schoolchildren and pensioners.
3. The usefulness of the expert assignation of the attractiveness scopes for the destination stops choice was verified. The choices amount of the popular stops consists up to 40% of the whole choices while the number of such stops is less than 10% of the whole stops number. Consequently the simplification of the on-line processing of the real transport system operation seems to be possible.
4. The decoupling of the total passengers' flow to the relatively stable component (the flow direction to the popular stops) and essentially weaker chaotic component (the flow direction to the rarely visited stops) was applied. Such decoupling assures the reducing of the dimension of the problem of transport system simulation without essential accuracy decreasing as well as the simplifying of real system investigations techniques.

The main results of the presented work are follows:

1. The set of assumptions was proposed suitable to the simulation of passengers' flow as between the city districts as well as between the separate stops.
2. The algorithms of simulation of the hourly passengers' flow from the each stop of municipal transport system to each city district were carried out.
3. The algorithms of the destination stops choice simulation were carried out. These algorithms are suitable to the choice process simulation for each passenger arriving on the stop of departure at the time moments specified with accuracy 1 min.

References

1. Krushel, E.G., Stepanchenko, I.V., Panfilov, A.E., Berisheva, E.D.: An experience of optimization approach application to improve the urban passenger transport structure. In: Kravets, A., Shcherbakov, M., Kultsova, M., Iijima, T. (eds.) JCKBSE 2014. CCIS, vol. 466, pp. 27–39. Springer, Cham (2014). https://doi.org/10.1007/978-3-319-11854-3_3
2. Schelenz, T., Suescun, A., Wikstrom, L., Karlsson, M.: Passenger-centered design of future buses using agent-based simulation. In: Conference on Transport Research Arena, Athens, vol. 48, pp. 1662–1671 (2012)
3. Bai, Y., Sun, Z., Zeng, B., Deng, J., Li, C.: A multi-pattern deep fusion model for short-term bus passenger flow forecasting. Appl. Soft Comput. **58**, 669–680 (2017)

4. Li, D., Yuan, J., Yan, K., Chen, L.: Monte Carlo simulation on effectiveness of forecast system for passengers up and down buses. In: 3RD International Symposium on Intelligent Information Technology Application, Nanchang, pp. 359–361 (2009)

5. Li, W., Zhu, W.: A dynamic simulation model of passenger flow distribution on schedule-based rail transit networks with train delays. J. Traffic Transp. Eng. (English Edition) **3**(4), 364–373 (2016)

6. Dijk, J.: Identifying activity-travel points from GPS-data with multiple moving windows. Comput. Environ. Urban Syst. **70**, 84–101 (2018)

7. Stepanchenko, I.V., Krushel, E.G., Panfilov, A.E.: The passengers' turnout simulation for the urban transport system control decision-making process. In: Kravets, A., Shcherbakov, M., Kultsova, M., Groumpos, P. (eds.) CIT&DS 2017. CCIS, vol. 754, pp. 389–398. Springer, Cham (2017). https://doi.org/10.1007/978-3-319-65551-2_28

8. Maghraoui, O.A., Vallet, F., Puchinger, J., Bernard, Y.: Modeling traveler experience for designing urban mobility systems. Des. Sci. **5**, E7 (2019)

9. Calabrese, F., Diao, M., Lorenzo, G.D., Ferreira Jr., J., Ratti, C.: Understanding individual mobility patterns from urban sensing data: a mobile phone trace example. Transp. Res. Part C **26**, 301–313 (2013)

10. Gärling, T., Axhausen, K.W.: Introduction: habitual travel choice. Transportation **30**, 1–11 (2003)

11. Gecchele, G., Rossi, R., Gastaldi, M., Caprini, A.: Data mining methods for traffic monitoring data analysis: a case study. Procedia Soc. Behav. Sci. **20**, 455–464 (2011)

12. Chen, C., Ma, J., Susilo, Y., Liu, Y., Wang, M.: The promises of big data and small data for travel behavior (aka human mobility) analysis. Transp. Res. Part C Emerg. Technol. **68**, 285–299 (2016)

13. OpenStreetMap Homepage. https://www.openstreetmap.org/. Accessed 30 Mar 2019

14. Google Maps Homepage. https://www.google.com/maps. Accessed 30 Mar 2019

15. Yandex Maps Homepage. https://yandex.ru/maps/. Accessed 30 Mar 2019

16. Regional Office of the Federal State Statistics Service in the Volgograd region, Population Homepage. http://volgastat.gks.ru/wps/wcm/connect/rosstat_ts/volgastat/ru/statistics/population/. Accessed 30 Mar 2019

17. Tang, J., Yang, Y., Qi, Y.: A hybrid algorithm for Urban transit schedule optimization. Physica A Stat. Mech. Appl. **512**, 745–755 (2018)

18. Levin, J.R., Ferron, J.M., Gafurov, B.S.: Additional comparisons of randomization-test procedures for single-case multiple-baseline designs: alternative effect types. J. Sch. Psychol. **63**, 13–34 (2017)

Building a Company's Maturity Management Trajectory Based on the Methods of Optimal Control of Letov-Kalman

Mikhail Dorrer[(⊠)] [iD]

Reshetnev Siberian State University of Science and Technology,
Krasnoyarsky Rabochy Av. 31, Krasnoyarsk 660037, Russian Federation
mdorrer@mail.ru

Abstract. The article proposes a solution to the problem of building optimal management of the maturity level of the company's business processes. The level of maturity is described as a linear dynamic control system. This work is part of the solution to the problem of developing a system for managing the level of maturity of an enterprise's business processes.

A set of indicators of a company's business processes maturity is described as a dynamic model of a control system in discrete time. It is shown that such a model adequately describes the behavior of a system of indicators of the maturity of a company's business processes.

When developing the model, the method of analytical construction of optimal regulators (ACOR) staged on Kalman-Letov's interpretation is used. The constructed model shows plausible behavior in predicting the process of managing organizational maturity. Reproduces the effect of accelerated growth of controlled indicators identified in the model as a priority.

Keywords: Business processes · Organizational maturity · Dynamic system · Linear model · Optimal regulator · ACOR

1 Introduction

Business process management is one of the main technologies of enterprise management in the modern world. ISO 9000 is required to be guided by this approach [1]. The ISO Survey study shows that the number of such enterprises exceeds one million [2]. This fact indicates the high relevance of business process management tasks. The current level of understanding of business process management is BPM CBOK [3].

The history of the process approach to management begins with the work of Philip Crosby "Quality is Free" [4], the approach was further developed in the works of Watts Humphrey [5].

The regulation of business process maturity management is described in a number of international standards – ISO/IEC 15504 [6–9] ISO 9004:2018 [10], ISO 10014:2006 [11].

It should be noted that all the listed standards have a common weak point. All of them are focused on the issues of assessing the level of maturity, but do not contain any decision-making algorithms for managing this indicator.

© Springer Nature Switzerland AG 2019
A. G. Kravets et al. (Eds.): CIT&DS 2019, CCIS 1083, pp. 133–142, 2019.
https://doi.org/10.1007/978-3-030-29743-5_10

The task of improving business processes is solved by reengineering [12], continuous improvement of business processes [13], and also methods of lean manufacturing (Kaizen) [14, 15].

The weakness of these approaches lies in the fact that the decision to invest resources in certain activities is based on an assessment of the expected financial result and may not take into account the systemic impact of activities on the organization as a whole.

To eliminate these weaknesses in business process management methodologies, it is necessary to create an enterprise management system according to a single target indicator - the level of maturity of business processes.

The article proposes to solve this problem by completing the following steps:

1. Description of the set of indicators of the maturity of the business processes of the organization as a dynamic management system;
2. parametric identification of the obtained dynamic control system on the basis of available experimental data of the operating enterprise;
3. development of the maturity level for the constructed model of the algorithm using the Kalman-Letov optimal control method.

It is shown that the model of a linear dynamic system thus obtained in a discrete formulation plausibly describes the dynamics of a system of indicators of the maturity of business processes of an enterprise.

It is shown that by setting target parameters in the Kalman-Letov model, one can obtain a growth trajectory of the level of maturity with a priority increase in the required indicators of the model of maturity.

2 Description of the Level of Maturity of Business Processes as a Control Object

A set of components of organizational maturity will be described as a set of controlled parameters of the organizational system.

A decision-maker in an organization (DM) solves the problem of increasing organizational maturity by spending resources - employees' working time, equipment, materials. Resource consumption can be enlarged to assess a single indicator - the cost. The decision maker is responsible for the efficient use of these resources to ensure the development goal of the organization - raising the level of maturity.

In terms of the theory of automatic control, the task of managing the level of maturity of an organization's business processes is formalized as follows:

- Managed system - the state of maturity of the organization's business processes.
- Management system - a person who makes decisions on projects for the implementation of management technologies.
- Managed indicators - maturity level values for selected management components.
- Control signal - the number of resources invested in the improvement of management technologies.

3   Used Standard of Organizational Maturity

The set of indicators of maturity as a managed system in this work is based on the ISO 9004-2008 standard "Quality management — Quality of an organization — Guidance to achieve sustained success" [10].

This standard is focused on assessing the maturity of the processes of the organization as a whole in terms of achieving sustainable success and contains tools for assessing the maturity of processes.

The standard assumes 6 main (high-level) factors of organizational maturity, respectively, it has sections.

4. Management to achieve the sustainable success of the organization. This section describes the requirements for general management principles.
5. Strategy and policy. This section describes the requirements for ensuring the realization of the mission, vision, and values of the organization.
6. Resource management. This section describes the requirements for the management of internal and external resources required to achieve short-term and long-term goals of the organization.
7. Process management. The section contains requirements for ensuring pro-active management of all processes, including processes transferred to third-party implementers.
8. Monitoring, measurement, analysis, and study. This section contains requirements for monitoring, measuring, studying and analyzing the effectiveness of its activities on the part of the organization.
9. Improvements, innovations, and training. The section contains requirements for the organization's actions to ensure improvements (products, processes, etc.), innovations (development of new products, processes, etc.) and training of participants in the process as a basis for the effectiveness of other actions.

Each of the assessments can take values from 0 to 5. It is these 6 estimates of the levels of maturity of the organization's business processes by sections of the ISO 9004-2008 standard that form the vector of indicators of the controlled system.

4   Research Hypotheses

In this paper, the following hypotheses were adopted.

- The level of maturity of business processes is expressed as a dimensionless value, taking values from 0 to 5. This value is the result of the enterprise's self-assessment by internal experts.
- In the course of an enterprise's activity, the level of a specific element of organizational maturity increases in proportion to the number of resources invested in the development of this element.
- Elements of organizational maturity influence each other, the level of maturity may change during the daily activities of the organization, as well as a result of changes in its corporate values.

- The following indicators influence the planning and implementation of the organizational maturity management process:
  - schedule of increasing the level of maturity of the organization by the elements in time;
  - expenditure of resources (in monetary terms) on projects to increase organizational maturity.

5   A Linear Dynamic Model of Managing the Process of Increasing Organizational Maturity

We describe a linear dynamic system in a deterministic formulation, which simulates the process of increasing organizational maturity. In such an arrangement, the model does not take into account the effect of interference.

$$x(t) = Ax(t) + Bu(t) \qquad (1)$$

Where:

$O = \{O_1, \ldots, O_N\}$ – a list of indicators of organizational maturity, their total number; in this work, the indicators of the top level of the ISO 9004 standard [10] will be used;

t – is the time of implementation of projects for improving organizational maturity, $t \in [0, T]$ where T is the duration of projects in planned periods (months, quarters);

$x(t) = [x_1(t), \ldots, x_N(t)]^T$ is the N-vector of organization maturity values by elements, where $x_i(t)$ – is the level of maturity by the i-th element at time t;

$u(t) = [u_1(t), \ldots, u_M(t)]^T$ is the M-vector of management, where $u_i(t)$ – is the controlling influence on the part of the organization in the form of investing money into resources for the execution of organizational development projects at the moment t;

$A = [a_{ij}]$ – $N \times N$ – the matrix that determines the rate of maturity increase by elements due to factors of the internal environment of the organization;

a_{ij} – the degree of influence of elements of maturity x_i on x_j.

$[b_{ij}]$ – $M \times N$ – the matrix that determines the increase in maturity in the process of strategic development of the management system; b_{ij} is the degree of influence of the control signal $u_j(t)$ on the level of maturity in the j-th element $x_j(t)$.

6   Baseline Data on the State of Maturity of Processes

The baseline data was collected at the Krasnoyarsk Machine-Building Components enterprise (KMK LLC). The company conducted self-assessment in accordance with the standard ISO 9004-2018. The self-assessment procedure consists of interviewing the organization's experts on the questionnaires contained in the ISO 9004-2018 standard. Information on the organizational maturity of the company was compiled based on the results of 2 years of work - for 2016 and for 2017.

$$x_{2016} = [1,250 \quad 1,267 \quad 1,675 \quad 2,000 \quad 1,333 \quad 1,533]$$
$$x_{2017} = [1,950 \quad 1,600 \quad 2,025 \quad 2,600 \quad 1,467 \quad 1,800] \tag{2}$$

This amount of experimental data does not allow a statistically reliable parametric identification of the system. Linear interpolation of these indicators for shorter periods of time also does not solve the problem, since the data in the resulting arrays are linearly dependent.

It should be noted that this problem in economic systems is of a fundamental nature. Such systems are peculiar to:

- The high dimensionality of parameter space in such systems
- Rapid variability of both parameters and system structure
- Long (compared to the time of variability) time step of accumulation of system parameters.

These three properties of economic systems together do not allow for their statistically reliable identification.

To overcome this problem, the following assumptions were made:

1. The linear model is simplified to the diagonal type of the matrix of increments A. At the same time, we neglect the relationship between different indicators of the level of maturity, assuming that each of the indicators changes independently and independently.
2. Let us evaluate two hypotheses about the dynamics of the company's maturity levels:

   - on the linear dynamics of maturity level indicators over time;
   - on the dynamics of maturity indicators in accordance with the exponential law.

Building models of the dynamics of growth indicators of enterprise maturity on the basis of accepted hypotheses will allow you to build an approximate model of the dynamics of management of this process.

7 A Deterministic Model of the Organizational Maturity Management Process

For a deterministic system, the process of formation of organizational maturity can be represented in the form of a linear dynamic system by the formula (1).

Based on formula (2), the calculation of maturity levels increment in discrete time can be described by the following formula:

$$X(t+1) = A * X(t) + B * u \tag{3}$$

The variables $X(t)$, $X(t + 1)$, A, B and u have the same meaning as in formula (1).

8   Linear Interpolation and Extrapolation of Organizational Maturity Indicators

Initially, the calculation will be carried out with a time step of 2 months, i.e. for the year, 6 values of the vector of indicators of maturity levels, linearly distributed between x_{2016} and x_{2017}, are calculated.

It should be noted that hereinafter the formulas are written in vector form, since it is in this way that the parameters were calculated in the Matlab system.

Linear step maturity level:

$$D = \frac{x_{2017} - x_{2016}}{5} \tag{4}$$

$$x_i = x_{2016} + (i - 1) * D \tag{5}$$

The latter value corresponds to the end of the first year.
We extrapolate the dynamics of maturity at a 5-year interval:

$$x_k = x_{2016} + (k * 6 - 1) * D \tag{6}$$

Here k is the year number (2016, 2017, etc.)

9   Exponential Interpolation and Extrapolation of Organizational Maturity Indicators

Similar to the previous item, 6 values of the vector of indicators of the level of maturity are calculated for the year. However, now we take them distributed along an exponential curve between x_{2016} and x_{2017}.

Intermediate index

$$\alpha = \frac{\ln(x_{2017} - x_{2016} + I)}{t} \tag{7}$$

accordingly, when $t = 1$

$$\alpha = \ln(x_{2017} - x_{2016} + I) \tag{8}$$

The latter value corresponds to the end of the first year.

Further, according to the formula (8), the values of the vector x were interpolated during 2016. Then, on the basis of the exponential dependence, the extrapolation of the value of the vector x was carried out with a 5-year interval using formula (9).

The calculation showed that exponential extrapolation provides a more optimistic forecast than linear extrapolation.

10 Deterministic Model of Maturity Level Dynamics

We calculate the deterministic model of the control system by the formula (4).

Based on the calculations performed, we will identify the parameters of the deterministic control model.

Create a matrix A_1 (matrix of increments of the control model in formula (2)), based on the average values of the coefficients of increasing the level of maturity in one step x_{i+1}/x_i for all components of the vector x.

11 Optimal Management of Organizational Maturity by the Quadratic Criterion

The obtained model allows us to solve the optimal control problem with a quadratic quality criterion according to the Kalman-Letov method.

The system equation has the form:

$$x\&(t) = Ax(t) + Bu(t) + v(t) \tag{9}$$

$$y(t) = Hx(t) + w(t) \tag{10}$$

Control Criterion:

$$J = x(T)^T \cdot \psi \cdot x(T) + \int_0^T [x(t)^T \cdot Q \cdot x(t) + u(t)^T \cdot R \cdot u(t)]dt \rightarrow \min \tag{11}$$

Formulas for calculating optimal control:

$$\bar{u}(t) = K(t)x(t) \tag{12}$$

where $K(t)$ is a matrix of dimension $N \times M$, calculated by the formula:

$$K(t) = -R^{-1}B^T P(t) \tag{13}$$

$P(t)$ – the solution of the Riccati equation:

$$\dot{P}(t) = -A^T P(t) - P(t)A + P(t)BR^{-1}B^T P(t) - Q \tag{14}$$

provided that $P(T) = \psi$.

Explain the meaning of the parameters included in the criterion (12).

The matrix ψ determines the significance of the final result of control – a vector of indicators of maturity $x(T)$.

The matrix Q determines the "price" of the organization's costs of increasing the maturity of the relevant components. The matrix R determines the "price" of the organization for managing the levels of maturity.

As is known, the optimal control $\bar{u}(t)$ of the system (5) with a quadratic quality criterion (12) is determined by the formula

$$\bar{u}(t) = K(t)x(t) \tag{15}$$

Here, the gain $K(t)$ is a vector calculated by the formula

$$K(t) = -R^{-1}B^T(t) \cdot P(t) \tag{16}$$

$P(t)-$ is the inverse time solution $t \, \varepsilon \, [T, 0]$ of the scalar Riccati equation:

$$P(t) = -2A(t) + B(t) R^{-1}B^T(t) \cdot P^2(t) - Q \tag{17}$$

The calculation is performed under the condition:

$$P(T) = \psi \tag{18}$$

Having determined the optimal control (16), we can then find the optimal trajectory using formula (5), and calculate the value of the criterion using formula (12).

These calculations for the model identified in clause 10 make it possible to obtain an optimal management plan for the process of increasing organizational maturity and the optimal trajectory of the change in organizational maturity indicators for the selected priorities.

12 Solution of the Problem of Optimal Control of the Process of Increasing Organizational Maturity

With the help of the Matlab system, 6 different variants of organizational maturity growth were calculated. For each of them, on the basis of formulas (15)–(18), the optimal Kalman-Letov regulator was constructed, and then the trajectory was calculated using formula (4). Each of these trajectories corresponds to the priority of one of the components of maturity in accordance with the ISO 9004 standard. The priority is set by increasing the values of the components of the matrix corresponding to the priority components of organizational maturity.

In Fig. 1, it can be seen that when priority is given to each of the components of organizational maturity during the 5-year time interval, the value of the priority component reaches the fifth level of maturity before all other components.

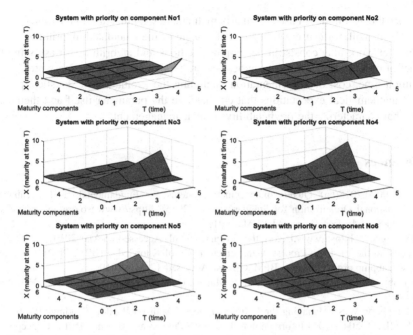

Fig. 1. Trajectories of indicators of levels of maturity of the system with a priority on various indicators.

13 Discussion

Thus, the proposed method of planning and evaluating the process of managing the organizational maturity of an educational system allows one to formulate a mathematical model of organizational development in terms of the theory of control of dynamic systems. The classical dynamic model of the control system allows us to describe the nature of the behavior of such an indicator of an organization as the level of maturity. In this case, the actual data on the dynamics of the level of maturity of the organization allows the identification of control system parameters.

It is shown that in this class of tasks, a workable tool is a deterministic model of a control system in discrete time, using an algorithm for constructing an optimal Kalman-Letov regulator.

The resulting model provides for the construction of trajectories for managing levels of organizational maturity that correspond to the priorities of the decision maker in the process of strategic management. The resulting trajectory ensures that the highest values of maturity levels by priority components are achieved in the first place, reducing the cost of managing lower priority ones.

The proposed model is scalable in terms of the detail of managing indicators of organizational maturity. The same formulas allow you to control

- a single summary measure of the organizational maturity of the entire company;
- self-assessment only for key elements (6 indicators of ISO 9004);
- a detailed self-assessment model (26 indicators).

Since the technique is based on matrix mathematics, an increase in the dimension of the problem will not cause a fundamental change in the calculated algorithms.

Further work may consist in developing methods and algorithms for assessing the impact of organizational maturity indicators on the parameters of business processes - execution time, cost of implementation, including the evaluation of statistical parameters - mathematical expectations that characterize the parameter itself and their variances that characterize the predictability of their management.

References

1. ISO 9000:2015(en) Quality management systems — Fundamentals and vocabulary. International Organization for Standardization (2015). https://www.iso.org/obp/ui/#iso:std:iso:9000:ed-4:v1:en. Accessed 12 Mar 2019
2. ISO Survey. https://www.iso.org/the-iso-survey.html. Accessed 05 Mar 2019
3. Guide to the Business Process Management Body of Knowledge (BPM CBOK®). https://www.abpmp.org/page/guide_BPM_CBOK. Accessed 12 Mar 2019
4. Crosby, P.: Quality is Free. The Art of Making Quality Certain. McGraw-Hill, New York (1979)
5. Humphrey, W.S.: Managing the Software Process. Addison Wesley, Reading (1989)
6. ISO/IEC 15504-1:2004 Information technology – Process assessment – Part 1: Concepts and vocabulary. International Organization for Standardization, https://www.iso.org/standard/38932.html. Accessed 12 Mar 2019
7. ISO/IEC 15504-2:2003 Information technology – Process assessment – Part 2: Performing an assessment. International Organization for Standardization. https://www.iso.org/standard/37458.html. Accessed 12 Mar 2019
8. ISO/IEC 15504-3:2004 Information technology – Process assessment – Part 3: Guidance on performing an assessment. International Organization for Standardization. https://www.iso.org/standard/37454.html. Accessed 12 Mar 2019
9. ISO/IEC 15504-4:2004 Information technology – Process assessment – Part 4: Guidance on use for process improvement and process capability determination. International Organization for Standardization. https://www.iso.org/standard/38932.html. Accessed 12 Mar 2019
10. ISO 9004:2018 Quality management — Quality of an organization — Guidance to achieve sustained success. International Organization for Standardization. https://www.iso.org/obp/ui/#iso:std:iso:9004:ed-4:v1:en. Accessed 12 Mar 2019
11. ISO 10014:2006 Quality management — Guidelines for realizing financial and economic benefits. International Organization for Standardization. https://www.iso.org/obp/ui/#iso:std:iso:10014:ed-1:v1:en. Accessed 12 Mar 2019
12. Hammer, M., Champy, J.A.: Reengineering the Corporation. Nicholas Brealey Publishing, London (1993)
13. Harrington, H.J.: Business Process Improvement: The Breakthrough Strategy for Total Quality, Productivity. Mc-Graw-Hill, New York (1991)
14. Basu, R., Wright, N.J.: Quality Beyond Six Sigma. Elsevier Ltd., Oxford (2003)
15. George, M.L.: Lean Six Sigma for Service. McGraw-Hill, New York (2003)
16. KMC LLC. http://www.krasmach.com/ru/about-us/. Accessed 12 Mar 2019
17. Kwakernaak, H., Sivan, R.: Linear Optimal Control Systems, 1st edn. Wiley-Interscience, New York (1972)

Networkalization of Network–Unlike Entities: How to Preserve Encoded Information

Olga Berestneva[1(✉)] , Olga Marukhina[1(✉)] ,
Alessandra Rossodivita[2(✉)] , Alexei Tikhomirov[3(✉)] ,
and Andrey Trufanov[4(✉)]

[1] Tomsk Polytechnic University, Lenina Ave. 30, 634050 Tomsk, Russia
ogb6@yandex.ru, marukhina@tpu.ru
[2] Medical and University Center Luigi Sacco Hospital, Via GB Grassi 74,
20157 Milan, Italy
italiancare@gmail.com
[3] Inha University, 100 Inharo, Nam-gu, 22212 Incheon, South Korea
alexeitikhomirovprof@gmail.com
[4] Irkutsk National Research Technical University, Lermontova St. 83,
664074 Irkutsk, Russia
troufan@gmail.com

Abstract. More than for twenty years network science with complex networks as its basic component has brought the idea to analyze a wide spectrum of entities through a focus on relations between the actors and has implemented the concomitant powerful instruments of the analysis. Some entities (objects, processes, and data) with their intrinsic web nature might be interpreted as networks naturally. Network ontology of another family, Network–Unlike Entities, e.g. spatial and temporal ones, is severely ambiguous and encounters with tough problems on the way to convert data into networks. We concentrate on separation the properties of data in line with their scale diversity – in the distance, time, and nature and suggested a 3 step algorithm (scale-based technique) to convert Network–Unlike Entities into complex networks. The technique was applied for networkalization of landscape and land use maps representing Olkhon district, Irkutsk region, Baikal Lake territory, RF. It was found that the technique with its coarse-graining and area-like connecting conserves natural information inherent to the entities and imbeds accordingly scale-free and small world properties into output networks, thus making them really complex in their structure.

Keywords: Network-like objects · Network–Unlike Entities ·
Spatial and Temporal Data · Complex networks · Converting · Scaling

1 Introduction

Network science with complex networks as its basic entity has attracted scientific societies with their diverse practical capacities. Domain experts have described successfully Synthetic and Real Data in terms of network structures and design powerful

© Springer Nature Switzerland AG 2019
A. G. Kravets et al. (Eds.): CIT&DS 2019, CCIS 1083, pp. 143–151, 2019.
https://doi.org/10.1007/978-3-030-29743-5_11

applications for further effective analysis with supported by Graph Theory, Probability Theory, and Linear Algebra. The number of actors in a system one observes the more one justifies network approach for the system study. Some systems with their intrinsic web nature have been interpreted as networks, e.g. transportation, communication, and others of critical infrastructures. Tourism [1], commuting [2], trading [3] – activities connected with travels also are presented by networks seamlessly. Similar social contacts [4, 5] and pertinent spread processes for information and infections [6] are of the same profile. Such systems and data are called network-like objects [7].

The exploration of network-like entities [8] becomes of special interest for diverse fields, theoretical and practical both [9, 10]. It is a conventional way to portray those in the formalism of graph theory, and shuffle the words of the latter and network science.

At the same time, it is of sense to put a boundary between math and network science just to clarify which domain the issues focus on. Thus if one uses the terms "connectivity", "nodes", and "links", there is no doubt that network science is represented, not math. The complex networks extend the sub-platform of graph theory by embedding measures, techniques, and instruments based on significant properties of a real system. An instrument to convert so-called Network-Like Entity has been proposed in [8]. However, even Network-Like Entity, such as built-in transportation systems should be thoroughly contemplated. Experts must take into account the fact that not all complex network concepts are applicable to the transportation context and that some adaptation may be required [11]. Thus ambiguous models might be considered for transportation systems, at least those of L- and P- [12] as demonstrated in [13] for Russian railways (see Fig. 1).

Concerning Network–Unlike Entity (NUE) Spatial and Temporal ones, their network interpretations are severely manifold and explorers face with a tough problem which converting algorithm one should apply.

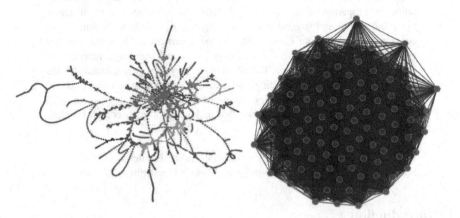

Fig. 1. Russian railways modelled as a network in L-space (a) and P-space (b) respectively.

2 Background

In general, the technique of converting Temporal Data - a time series into complex networks is represented by 3 next steps: the segmentation according to the specified time length, coarsening of the ranges, and linkage of the ranges with necessary weights.

One can find a variety of approaches to transform time series into complex networks, among them as key ones:

- Coarse-graining based on statistics of segments (CBS) [14];
- Visibility Graph (VG) [15], also Multiplex Visibility Graph (MVG) [16];
- Local Sort (LS) [17].

At the same time, there are few dependable works that use the complex networks for Spatial Data (images or maps) analysis and classification.

In the paper [18] it was shown that when a plane is randomly divided into intersecting adjacent blocks it is possible to build a scale-free network in which the nodes are blocks, and connections reflect common boundaries between blocks. This forms a "boundary" approach.

The second approach might be called a "pixel vicinity" one. To interpret the digital image as a complex network: each pixel represents a node; those are linked according to their vicinity in location and similarity in intensity. To reach genuine complex topology while converting image data into networks one might apply a Scale-Level Segmentation Approach [19]. This approach implies grouping components of a multipixel image into 3 categories which correspond to local, proximal, and global regions (super-pixels) and setting specific links among the pixels as nodes respectively to their categories. Figure 2 shows how the approach provides the mapping of a monochromic square into a complex network.

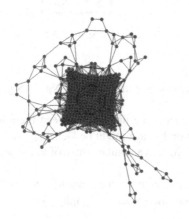

Fig. 2. A network imprint of a monochromic square.

Also set of complex network metrics must be studied to adequately convey key image properties.

Third approach "image visibility graphs (IVG) approach" - (The row of image visibility graphs (IVG/IHVG) have been introduced as simple algorithms by which scalar fields can be transformed into graphs) [20]. It makes sense to apply an approach with the aim to preserve intrinsic information of the studied system (NUE) to the most extent and thus to reveal more specific traits of the system in the appropriate topologic analysis. Comparison of the networking approaches might be qualitative and quantitative (e.g. on entropy metric).

3 Model

Contrary to well-known approaches in converting NUE (presented as Spatial and Temporal Data) into complex networks with one scale, we concentrate on separation the properties of data in line with their scale diversity – in distance, time, and nature. We call this transformation process very simple: "networkalization".

For Spatial Data reflected in a map the networkalization algorithm (scale-based technique, partially similar to the scope [19]) of 3 steps we propose coarsens the areas.

First, inside an area, regular network (lattice of a triangle, polygons, etc.) is constructed with a size that depends on area square and its form (see Fig. 3).

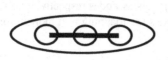 

Fig. 3. Step#1 of the algorithm that converts Spatial Data into a complex network: covering areas with a lattice.

Number of initial lattice nodes within the area Ng $\sim$ S g, g = 1,2...G; G - number of grains.

Two nodes are connected if the distance between them is lesser than a threshold (<dcut). Alternate to polygon linkage might be Delaunay Triangulation. Also, it makes sense to build the local network as a regular lattice of any profile in case of regular node seeding.

At the second step, areas as coarsened entities are portrayed by the node s_g^* or several inside nodes (central nodes), so that numbers of those depends on the pertinent inner network size.

The central nodes of different areas are linked in case of the common border between two areas (see Fig. 4). The number of the links depends on the length of the common border: Number of area grains (supernodes) f: Scale $\rightarrow$ Ng.

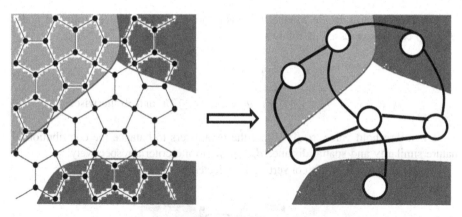

Fig. 4. Step#2 of the algorithm that converts Spatial Data into a complex network: links for coarsened areas.

The number of links between nodes belonged different grains i and j respectively with common border:

$$M_g(i,j) \sim L_g(i,j) / \sum (L_g(i,j)),$$

where Lg (i, j) is a border length between i and j grains (areas).

Third, areas with similar nature of category c have a probability to be linked even with no common border and in the case when their Euclidian distance is significant (see Fig. 5). Thus the difference between the two grains i and j in category c is found by Manhattan distance:

$$|Yg_c(i) - Yg_c(j)|.$$

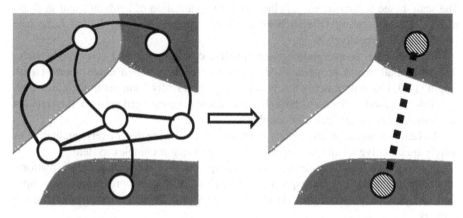

Fig. 5. Step#3 of the algorithm that converts Spatial Data into a complex network: linkage of grains with similar nature.

So, the criteria to decide whether there is or not a link between central grain nodes (v_{ci}, v_{cj}) can be expressed as follows:

$$e_{cij}(v_{ci}, v_{cj}) \, \exists, \text{if}$$

$$\sqrt{(\alpha|Y(v_{ci}) - Y(v_{cj})|)^2 + (\beta d_e(v_{ci}, v_{cj}))^2} \leq Tn, \text{ and } \nexists \text{ otherwise.}$$

T is a threshold value; α, $\beta > 0$ are the parameters to balance the contribution of nature similarity and spatial distance $d_e(v_{ci}, v_{cj})$ to the criteria respectively.

Aggregated result of the converting is reflected by the Fig. 6.

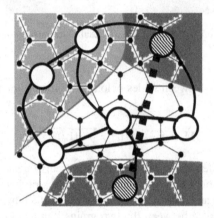

Fig. 6. The algorithm that converts Spatial Data into a complex network: sequence of steps #1, #2, #3.

4   Results and Discussion

The scale-based technique was applied for networkalization of landscape and land use maps [21] representing Olkhon district, Irkutsk region, RF near Baikal Lake (see Figs. 7 and 8 respectively).

We found that coarse-graining and area-like connecting imbed accordingly scale-free and small world properties, "dramatically reducing the average shortest path length" [22], into output networks, thus making them really complex in their structure.

Generalization of the maps brought some details and changed network imprints but not significantly correct network topologies.

As [23] remarked, many experts have sounded the idea that merely qualitative or merely quantitative techniques are aimless for studying a complex system.

It looks like semi-qualitative and semi-quantitative networkalization platform applied in the work and consequent scale-based technique comprises natural component and provide preserving information encoded in NUE while transforming into a network.

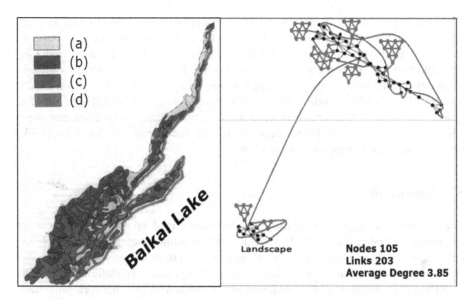

Fig. 7. Networkalization of landscape map [21] representing Olkhon district (Baikal Lake): (a) - Conservation only; (b) - Extensive land use with conservation of sensitive biotopes; (c) - Extensive land use with restoration of damaged biotopes; (d) - Restoration of damaged biotopes.

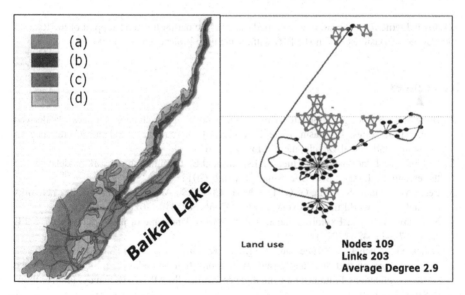

Fig. 8. Networkalization of land use map [21] representing Olkhon district (Baikal Lake): (a) - Improvement with further extensive development; (b) - Extensive development; (c) - Regulated extensive development; (d) - Restricted extensive development.

Similar to Gartner's Digitization [24] and Digitalization [25], we define "networkalization" as "the use of network platform to change a scientific or a business model and provide new advances and revenue and knowledge- or value- producing opportunities; it is the process of moving to a network domain and society in whole". "Networkization" is "the process of changing from direct natural form to network form, not structure". In other words, networkization takes a natural entity (System, process, object) and changes it to a network form without any different-in-kind changes to the entity itself. Thus it is possible to "networkize" only net-like entities, but for network-unlike entities, those need in networkalization.

5 Conclusion

The aggregated research we performed manifests that it is of value to take into account the nature and specificities of Network-Unlike Entity while treating them as networks. This scope provides a researcher with a capacity just not to lose key information and conserve that for analysis and utilization in the field of practice. The information hidden in NUE might be thoroughly transferred into genuine complex network properties, mainly into degree distribution and set of pertinent metrics with realization through scale-based processing.

We trust the scale-based approach to convert NUE into complex networks might be robust for Spatial and Temporal Data both.

Acknowledgements. The study was carried out with the partial financial support of the Russian Foundation for Basic Research (RFBR) within scientific project No. 18-07-00543.

References

1. Baggio, R.: Studying complex tourism systems a novel approach based on networks derived from a time series. In: Yasin, E. (ed.) XIV April International Academic Conference on Economic and Social Development, Moscow (2013)
2. Gargiulo, F., Lenormand, M., Huet, S., Espinosa, O.B.: Commuting network models: getting the essentials. J. Artif. Soc. Soc. Simul. **15**(2), 6 (2012)
3. Lee, J.W., Maeng, S.E., Ha, G.-G., Lee, M.H., Cho, E.S.: Applications of complex networks on analysis of world trade network. J. Phys. Conf. Ser. **410** (2013). ID: 012063
4. Semenov, A., et al.: Exploring social media network landscape of post-Soviet space. IEEE Access **7**, 411–426 (2018)
5. Gadek, G., Pauchet, A., Brunessaux, S., Khelif, K., Grilheres, B.: AI techniques to analyse a social network on text, user and group level: application on Galaxy2. In: 4ème conférence sur les Applications Pratiques de l'Intelligence Artificielle APIA2018 Nancy, France, ffhal-01830922 (2018)
6. Wu, Q., Zhu, W.: Toward a generalized theory of epidemic awareness in social networks. Int. J. Mod. Phys. C **28**(05) (2017). ID: 1750070
7. Newman, M.E.J.: The structure and function of complex networks. SIAM Rev. **45**, 167–256 (2003)

8. Dirnberger, M., Kehl, T., Neumann, A.: NEFI: network extraction from images. Sci Rep. **5** (2015). ID: 15669

9. Costa, L.D.F., Rodrigues, F.A., Travieso, G., Boas, P.R.V.: Characterization of complex networks: a survey of measurements. Adv. Phys. **56**(1), 167–242 (2007)

10. Ruiz-Martin, C., López, A., Wainer, G.A.: Applying complex network theory to the assessment of organizational resilience. IFAC-PapersOnLine **48**(3), 1224–1229 (2015)

11. Zanin, M., Sun, X., Wandelt, S.: Studying the topology of transportation systems through complex networks: handle with care. J. Adv. Transp. (2018)

12. Derrible, S., Kennedy, C.: Transportation research record. J. Transp. Res. Board **21**(12), 17–25 (2009)

13. Tikhomirov, A., Rossodivita, A., Kinash, N., Trufanov, A., Berestneva, O.: General topologic environment of the Russian railway network. J. Phys. Conf. Ser. **803**(1) (2017). ID: 012165

14. Zhang, Z., Xu, J., Zhou, X.: Mapping time series into complex networks based on equal probability division. AIP Adv. **9** (2019). ID: 015017

15. Lacasa, L., Luque, B., Luque, J., Nuno, J.C.: The visibility graph: a new method for estimating the Hurst exponent of fractional Brownian motion. Europhys. Lett. **86**, 30001–30005 (2009)

16. Lacasa, L., Nicosia, V., Latora, V.: Network structure of multivariate time series. Sci. Rep. **5** (2015). ID: 15508

17. Sun, X., Small, M., Zhao, Y., Xue, X.: Characterizing system dynamics with a weighted and directed network constructed from time series data. Chaos: Interdisc. J. Nonlinear Sci. **24** (2014). ID: 024402

18. Hassan, M.K., Hassan, M.Z., Pavel, N.I.: Scale-free network topology and multifractality in a weighted planar stochastic lattice. J. Phys. **12**(9) (2010). ID: 093045

19. Trufanov, A., Kinash, N., Tikhomirov, A., Berestneva, O., Rossodivita, A.: Image converting into complex networks: scale-level segmentation approach. In: Berestneva, O., Tikhomirov, A., Trufanov, A., Kataev, M. (eds.) Proceedings of IV International Conference on Information technologies in Science, Management, Social sphere and Medicine (ITSMSSM 2017) (ACSR), vol. 72, pp. 417–422 (2017)

20. Iacovacci, J., Lacasa, L.: Visibility graphs for image processing. arXiv:1804.07125v1 (2018)

21. Semenov, Y., Antipov, A., Bufal, V., et al.: Ecologically Oriented Land Use planning in the Baikal Region Olkhonsky District. Publishing House of the Institute of Geography. SB RAS, Irkutsk (2004)

22. Vespignani, A.: Twenty years of network science. Nature **558**, 528–529 (2018)

23. Baggio, R., Fuchs, M.: Network science and e-tourism. Inf. Technol. Tourism. **20**(1–4), 97–102 (2018)

24. Gartner IT Glossary. https://www.gartner.com/it-glossary/?s=digitization. Accessed 21 May 2019

25. Gartner IT Glossary. https://www.gartner.com/it-glossary/digitalization/. Accessed 21 May 2019

HR Decision-Making Support Based on Natural Language Processing

Anton Ivaschenko$^{(\boxtimes)}$ ⓘ and Michael Milutkin

Samara State Technical University, Molodogvardeyskaya 244, Samara, Russia
anton.ivaschenko@gmail.com

Abstract. This paper presents an overview and analysis of IT solution of text understanding being applied to a programming professional domain. Conclusions summarize the authors' experience in NLP/NLU in the last years. Binary classification and logistic regression is used to solve typical problems. The results of practical research are presented. The paper develops the ideas of understanding texts in software development domain using standard text processing tools. The proposed solution is recommended for HR professionals who search suitable candidates for a job based on their blogs, online presence and code.

Keywords: Natural language processing · Big Data · Machine learning · Decision-making support

1 Introduction

Natural Language Processing (NLP) is a sub-field of Artificial Intelligence that is focused on enabling computers to understand and process human languages, to get computers closer to a human-level understanding of language. Computers don't yet have the same intuitive understanding of natural language that humans do and can't really understand what the language is really trying to say. In a nutshell, a computer can't read between the lines.

That being said, recent advances in Machine Learning (ML) have enabled computers to do quite a lot of useful things with natural language. Deep Learning gives us an opportunity to write programs to perform things like language translation, semantic understanding, and text summarization. All of these things add real-world value, making it easy for you to understand and perform computations on large blocks of text without the manual effort.

The process of reading and understanding language is far more complex than it seems at first glance. There are many things that go in to truly understanding what a piece of text means in the real-world. In this paper there is presented one of possible cases of deep learning application to improve natural language processing. After brief solutions overview there is presented architecture of a software solution dedicated to search and pick HR candidates for IT jobs based on programming texts analysis available on Internet. Section 4 presents the details of neural network implementation and Sect. 5 describes important aspects of the loss function specification.

A. G. Kravets et al. (Eds.): CIT&DS 2019, CCIS 1083, pp. 152–161, 2019.
https://doi.org/10.1007/978-3-030-29743-5_12

The results of real texts massive analysis are presented in Sect. 6, which finalizes the research and allows making some conclusions on intelligent texts understanding practical use.

2 State of the Art

Natural language processing helps computers communicate with humans in their own language and scales other language-related tasks. For example, NLP makes it possible for computers to read text, hear speech, interpret it, measure sentiment and determine which parts are important [1].

Considering the modern trends of information flows processing and analysis, natural language processing becomes a challenging technology for application in Big Data analysis of social media [2, 3]. Internet users' activity results with various data sets that characterize human behavior [4] and can be treated as promising data sources for natural language processing.

While supervised and unsupervised learning, and specifically deep learning, are now widely used for modeling human language [5], there's also a need for syntactic and semantic understanding and domain expertise that are not necessarily present in these machine learning approaches. NLP is important because it helps resolve ambiguity in language and adds useful numeric structure to the data for many downstream applications, such as speech recognition or text analytics.

Natural language processing includes many different techniques for interpreting human language, ranging from statistical and machine learning methods to rules-based and algorithmic approaches. A broad array of approaches is required because the text- and voice-based data varies widely, as do the practical applications. Basic NLP tasks include tokenization and parsing, lemmatization/stemming, part-of-speech tagging, language detection and identification of semantic relationships. If you ever diagramed sentences in grade school, you've done these tasks manually before.

In general terms, NLP tasks break down language into shorter, elemental pieces, try to understand relationships between the pieces and explore how the pieces work together to create meaning.

These underlying tasks are often used in higher-level NLP capabilities, such as:

- content categorization – a linguistic-based document summary, including search and indexing, content alerts and duplication detection;
- topic discovery and modeling – accurately capture the meaning and themes in text collections, and apply advanced analytics to text, like optimization and forecasting;
- contextual extraction – automatically pull structured information from text-based sources;
- sentiment analysis – identifying the mood or subjective opinions within large amounts of text, including average sentiment and opinion mining;
- speech-to-text/text-to-speech conversion – transforming voice commands into written text, and vice versa;

- machine translation – automatic translation of text or speech from one language to another;
- document summarization – automatically generating synopses of large bodies of text.

In all these cases, the overarching goal is to take raw language input and use linguistics and algorithms to transform or enrich the text in such a way that it delivers greater value. Natural language processing goes hand in hand with text analytics, which counts, groups and categorizes words to extract structure and meaning from large volumes of content. Text analytics is used to explore textual content and derive new variables from raw text that may be visualized, filtered, or used as inputs to predictive models or other statistical methods.

NLP and text analytics are used together for many applications, including:

- investigative discovery – identify patterns and clues in emails or written reports to help detect and solve crimes;
- subject-matter expertise – classify content into meaningful topics so you can take action and discover trends;
- social media analytics – track awareness and sentiment about specific topics and identify key influencers.

A subfield of NLP called natural language understanding (NLU) has begun to rise in popularity because of its potential in cognitive and AI applications [6]. NLU goes beyond the structural understanding of language to interpret intent, resolve context and word ambiguity, and even generate well-formed human language on its own. NLU algorithms must tackle the extremely complex problem of semantic interpretation – that is understanding the intended meaning of spoken or written language, with all the subtleties, context and inferences that we humans are able to comprehend.

The evolution of NLP toward NLU has a lot of important implications for businesses and consumers alike. Imagine the power of an algorithm that can understand the meaning and nuance of human language in many contexts, from medicine to law to the classroom. As the volumes of unstructured information continue to grow exponentially, we will benefit from computers' tireless ability to help us make sense of it all.

Application of information technologies to track and monitor the HR activity represents high efficiency in modern industry. Currently, there are a lot of personnel monitoring systems on the market, Yaware Foreman, and Dispatcher. Yaware is a time tracking system that analyzes human activities at the workplace, by tracking actions behind a PC. Foreman is a system for monitoring industrial equipment with monitoring the efficiency of equipment use in production, by analyzing information from sensors. Dispatcher is a monitoring of industrial equipment.

The problems of human factor influence over the project management technologies are studied by the Agile paradigm that requires organizing the process of adaptive allocation of project tasks in a highly flexible and interactive manner. Due to the high variability of business processes, complexity, and uncertainty of project tasks, and strong request for project team members' pro-activity and motivation the role of tasks performers becomes critical at all stages of project scheduling and execution management.

This requires new approaches for project tasks allocation and scheduling software solutions using modern algorithms and systems of decision-making support, multi-agent technologies and knowledge bases [7, 8].

The problems of project management at modern enterprises with matrix organizational structure including a set of the subdivisions and positions with various relations and subordination are studied in [9, 10]. To provide effective HR management it is necessary to consider specifics of enterprises' activities and features of their interactions with an external environment.

3 HR Analysis Solution Architecture

Considering the results of theoretical overview there was developed a solution for searching and picking HR candidates for IT jobs based on programming texts analysis. Possible solution architecture that has been successfully probated in the area of social media analysis is presented in Fig. 1.

The project was dedicated to development of a "lead generator" for HR team. Resulting solution can be deployed on a DBMS and used by HRs to make the process of finding candidates for IT jobs easy and comfortable. First experiments and practical use of this solution have proven high potential of this application and interest demonstrated by HR professionals.

Technical challenges of implementation are concerned with speed of gathering information from programming resources such as stackoverflow.com, github.com, habr.ru and toster.ru. After that, we have to analyze gigabytes of raw text with elements of code in it. To provide practical solution for HR professionals, the technology should be capable of processing substantial number of raw text in real time.

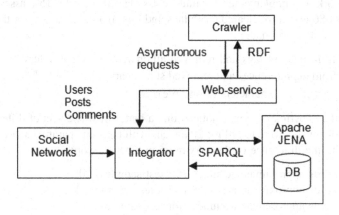

Fig. 1. Ontology based solution architecture

"Lead generator" solution was dedicated to increase the efficiency of the process of finding IT team member candidates. Based on the proposed architecture there was developed special software for decision-making support (see Fig. 2) that can take target skillset as an input and give links to particular portal members as an output based on results of text analysis.

The main condition of the experiment was the use of raw programming texts on different topics (Java/C#/SQL/...) for the task of text understanding and giving conclusions on author's skill set.

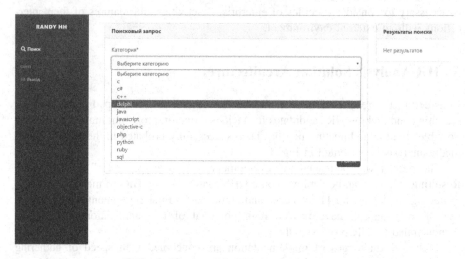

Fig. 2. Front-end for HR Lead Generator

4   Functional Description

Neural network was implemented for multi-class classification by 15 classes. Data set includes 596686 texts (not cleared (with tags and links)) and 15 classes for them. From this set 2 datasets were made:

1. Cleared from links of tags and removed all characters except letters;
2. Cleared from tag references and removed stop_chars = ', "\' / \\? ~! @ # $% ^ & * () {} [] <> №;: = + ' characters (2.png file);

During the experiment, it was noticed that a better fit was 2 sets of difference 1%. 4 different tokenyzers were tested for 20 epochs with the same parameters of the neural network, with the difference of the maximum number of words

3. 10,000 words approximate accuracy (for test samples) 50%
4. 20,000 words approximate accuracy (for a test sample) 51%
5. 30,000 words approximate accuracy (for test sample) 52%
6. 100,000 words approximate accuracy (for a test sample) 53%

In the course of the experiment it was noticed that 4th tokenizer was better suited - only 1% difference. But a further increase in the maximum amount of words leads to the overtraining of the neural network, since for 4th tokenizer the accuracy on the training set was 59%.

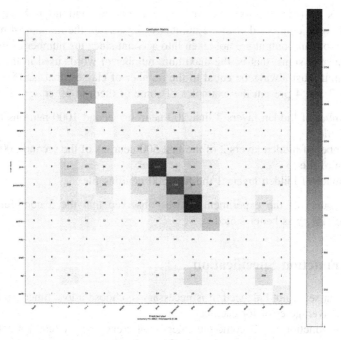

Fig. 3. Confusion matrix, accuracy = 0.4862, misclass = 0.5138

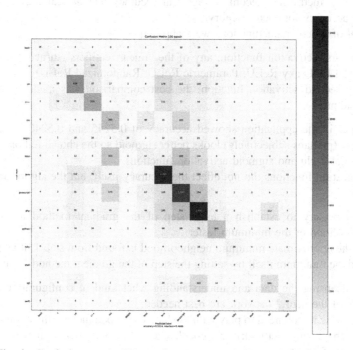

Fig. 4. Confusion matrix 100 epoch, accuracy = 0.5314, misclass = 0.4686

Two sets of balanced marked data were used: test and train. Many different experiments were conducted with the number of layers and the number of neurons on the layers (input and output are not taken into account since the number of inputs must be the number of signs, that is, the maximum number of words used in the tokenizer, and the output must always be equal to the number of classes, that is, 15).

Figures 3 and 4 present the examples of some of them in 50 eras.

7. The number of hidden layers 3 first 200 neurons second 1000 neurons third 2000 neurons file
8. The number of hidden layers 2 of the first 500 neurons of the second 2000 neurons of the third file
9. The number of hidden layers 1 the first 500 neurons file

In the course of the experiment, it was observed that the 3 configuration, the difference of 1%, was better suited.

5 Loss Function Specification

Since the data set is not balanced, it is necessary to choose a loss function that would consider the average error for each category.

This loss function has become the categorical cross entropy (categorical_crossentropy) which calculates the cross entropy for each category. Since the data set is not balanced, it is necessary to choose a metric that would measure the average for each category. This metric has become categorical accuracy (categorical_accuracy) which calculates accuracy for each category.

A total of 2 activation functions were applied.

10. for the first activation function, any of the "linear rectifiers" turned out to be the best (ReLU, Leaky ReLU, Parametric ReLU, Randomized ReLU)
11. for the second activation function, the best comparison was made sigmoid (file sigmoid.png)

Graphics in the application showed accuracy of 0.5245 and 0.5240, respectively, and visually (perhaps subjectively) looks better sigmoid so the choice fell on him. As a result, we got 2 elu and sigmoid activation functions.

Optimization functions did not affect the accuracy itself, but the algorithm of their use is clear.

12. It is necessary to establish a large step of the gradient method to get to the neighborhood of the minimum faster.
13. After the approximate minimum neighborhood is found from step 1, it is necessary to find the minimum itself by setting the step of the gradient method to be less than

After cleansing the data and understanding what kind of configuration and best parameters of the neural network are best needed.

To fine-tune it, you need to play with the batch_size parameters (the amount of data loaded on the neural network) and epoch (the number of neural network training passes) (Figs. 5 and 6).

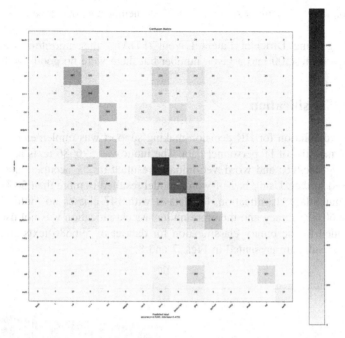

Fig. 5. Confusion matrix, accuracy = 0.5245, misclass = 0.4755 and softmax (file softmax.png)

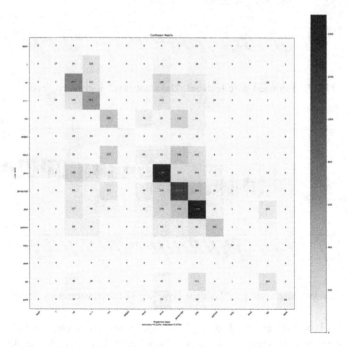

Fig. 6. Confusion matrix, accuracy = 0.5240, misclass = 0.4760

After marking the same texts on 11 tags, the neural network gave an accuracy of 70%.

Clustering using Dirichlet Latent Layout (LDA) - this algorithm was used to combine tags from 4500 into a given number but there were no good results.

6 Texts Classification

The developed solution for HR decision-making support was implemented and tested using a real massive of IT personnel data. The input was 596686 texts and 4500 text classes. Using doc2vec and word2vec initially resulted in 2% accuracy and therefore were not used further. Using bag-of-words model resulted in more than 50% accuracy.

As for multiclass classification, for dataset with 147 classes no multiclass classificator gave 60% accuracy and therefore multiclass classification was not used further. So, we decided to use binary classification for dataset of 596686 texts and 147 text classes. The results are presented in Figs. 7 and 8.

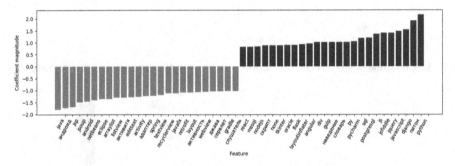

Fig. 7. Stemmed pure texts set, "Java/not Java" logistic regression

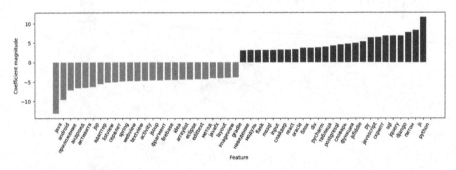

Fig. 8. Stemmed pure texts set, "Java/not Java" logistic regression with TfidfVectorizer

For each class a binary logistic regression classifier was built, resulting in 147 classifiers. Recognition speed is 8 s per 100 texts, without using parallelization of calculations. The average accuracy is 72%. The input is text as processed and resulted in a tag cloud presented by an array of tags and their probability, which made it possible to assign several classes to one text.

7 Conclusion

The results of a presented research illustrate a perspective and challenges of natural language processing using modern technologies of deep learning. The proposed solution helps solving the problems of professionals' skill set identification based on the text analysis, which was written by them. This solution is proposed to be used in practice by HR professionals who constantly search new candidates on special Web platforms.

Being implemented as a part of project management software a combination of the Internet of Things and Big Data technologies provide an effective IT platform for monitoring of employee's activity and HR management decision-making support.

Acknowledgment. This work was supported by the RFBR grant No. 18-47-342003 p_мк "Research of the psycho-physiological health of the driver of a motor vehicle to accompany his professional activity on the basis of a specialized diagnostic hardware-software complex".

References

1. Goldberg, Y.: A primer on neural network models for natural language processing. J. Artif. Intell. Res. **57**, 345–420 (2016)
2. Baesens B.: Analytics in a Big Data World: The Essential Guide to Data Science and Its Applications, 232 p. Wiley, Hoboken (2014)
3. Ivaschenko, A., Khorina, A., Sitnikov, P.: Online creativity modeling and analysis based on big data of social networks. In: Arai, K., Kapoor, S., Bhatia, R. (eds.) SAI 2018. AISC, vol. 858, pp. 329–337. Springer, Cham (2019). https://doi.org/10.1007/978-3-030-01174-1_25
4. Kadushin, C.: Understanding Social Networks: Theories, Concepts, and Findings, 264 p. OUP, New York (2012)
5. Bird, S., Klein, E., Loper, E.: Natural Language Processing with Python, 482 p. O'Reilly Media, Sebastopol (2009)
6. Semaan, P.: Natural language generation: an overview. J. Comput. Sci. Res. (JCSCR) **1**(3), 50–57 (2012)
7. Surnin, O.L., Sitnikov, P.V., Ivaschenko, A.V., Ilyasova, N.Yu., Popov, S.B.: Big Data incorporation based on open services provider for distributed enterprises. In: CEUR Workshop Proceedings. Session Data Science (DS-ITNT 2017), vol. 190, pp. 42–47 (2017)
8. Mouromtsev, D., Pavlov, D., Emelyanov, Y., Morozov, A., Razdyakonov, D., Galkin, M.: The simple web-based tool for visualization and sharing of semantic data and ontologies. In: International Semantic Web Conference, vol. 1486, p. 77 (2015)
9. Simonova, M., Ilyukhina, L., Bogatyreva, I., Vagin, S., Nikolaeva, K.: Conceptual approaches to forecast recruitment needs at the regional level. Int. Rev. Manage. Market. **6**(5), 265–273 (2016)
10. Simonova, M.V., Sankova, L.V., Mirzabalaeva, F.I., Shchipanova, D.Y., Dorozhkin, V.E.: Assessment problems and ensuring of decent work in the Russian regions. Int. J. Environ. Sci. Educ. **11**(15), 7608–7626 (2016)

The Algorithm for the Classification of Methods for Processing Multidimensional Heterogeneous Data in Application to Designing of Oil Fields Development

Alena A. Zakharova[1], Stepan G. Nebaba[2(✉)],
and Dmitry A. Zavyalov[3]

[1] Bryansk State Technical University, Bryansk, Russia
zaa@tu-bryansk.ru
[2] Tomsk Polytechnic University, Tomsk, Russia
stepanlfx@tpu.ru
[3] Keldysh Institute of Applied Mathematics RAS, Moscow, Russia
zda@tpu.ru

Abstract. An algorithm of methods selection for processing multidimensional heterogeneous data based on the general properties of the data used and the methods included in the review is proposed in this paper. The algorithm is implemented in the form of software and a group of interpolation algorithms is compared by the example of the problem of constructing an oil field model for field development designing. It is shown that the proposed algorithm for selecting data processing methods works successfully for a group of data interpolation methods.

Keywords: Algorithms classification · Hybrid data · Heterogeneous data · Interpolation · Data processing · Multisensory systems · Oil field model · Field development designing

1 Introduction

Scientific research directions in the fields of computer vision, robotics, experimental physics, geophysics, numerical and visual modeling of technological and natural processes, as well as many other areas of knowledge, are currently being actively developed. Tasks arising in these areas of knowledge are increasingly associated with processing large arrays of heterogeneous data, that is, in other words, data obtained from detectors and sensors of various types, resolution, accuracy and measurement frequency. A detector, or a sensor, is any source of discrete digital information in the context of this definition, and a specific set of sensors synchronized with each other forms a multisensory system. The importance of the issue dealing with processing and analysis of such type of the data is constantly increasing, while traditional approaches to data processing are no longer relevant because of the growing requirements for the complexity and intelligence of solutions [1, 2].

A. G. Kravets et al. (Eds.): CIT&DS 2019, CCIS 1083, pp. 162–174, 2019.
https://doi.org/10.1007/978-3-030-29743-5_13

The quick and correct selection of a suitable method for processing hybrid (heterogeneous) data has great importance, and an algorithm that can automatically make such a choice can become a major part of intelligent systems working with multidimensional arrays of heterogeneous data. Reliability and accuracy of such systems remain the key issue, especially for such critical areas as autonomous vehicles, security systems, medical technologies, modeling and forecasting of natural and social events [3]. This makes the task of creating an algorithm of the automatic methods selection for processing multidimensional heterogeneous data in specific cases relevant and important.

An attempt to detail and expand the previously proposed algorithm of analysis and classifying data processing methods that would allow selection of the most efficient method for the task, operating solely on the general characteristics of data arrays, such as data type, dimension, sample size, application area and expected processing results, is made in this paper.

2 Classification of Data Types

One of the important steps in the algorithm of methods analysis and classification should be the initial analysis of the types and kinds of data in the array.

There are various classifications of kinds and types of data, these classifications are selected depending on the area of data acquisition and using [4, 5]. The accuracy of the result and the computational complexity of the algorithms aimed at obtaining the final desired result depend on a kind and a type of data that must be processed. Several processing methods do not apply to one or another kind or type of data, or the application does not make sense in the context of the problem being solved. Therefore, it is extremely important to develop an optimal approach to grouping methods according to kinds and types of data being processed, which will allow one not only to structure existing approaches to data processing but also to discover new dependencies and possibilities of applying classical methods and algorithms.

In addition to the classical definition of data types, when data are divided into a logical, numeric, string, in the context of their automated processing, they can be divided into 2 large groups:

- quantitative data, numerical characteristic of parameter amount or change;
- qualitative data, characteristic of the belonging of the studying object to one or another deterministic group.

This separation of data is well suited to automate their processing, as it minimizes the process of analyzing data, reducing it to a simple binary choice of available methods spectrum.

3 Methods, Techniques, and Algorithms for Processing Multidimensional Heterogeneous Data

Methods and techniques of processing multidimensional heterogeneous data can be divided according to several criteria: the subject area of data acquisition (for example: seismic data, chemical analysis data, visual data, etc.), processing principle (for example: reduction of data dimension, calculation of integral and differential characteristics, correlation analysis, visualization and cognitive analysis [6], etc.). In general, the processing method is selected based on the subject area, tasks and amount of data, because different methods have different computational complexity and accuracy.

In addition, different data can have a different way of representation, and it makes sense to represent large-scale data describing time processes in the frequency, phase or time domain. There are specific processing methods for these types of data, for example, Fourier transforms, filtering by band-pass filters, high and low pass filters.

Groups of methods of correlation analysis, regression analysis, interpolation and extrapolation, methods of integral and differential analysis were considered as an object of analysis.

Data interpolation implies an increase in data density due to new synthesized intermediate elements. The question of the accuracy of new data is solved with the help of experimental data in a specific subject area with a high sampling frequency, which makes it possible to compare natural values with values calculated during interpolation.

Data extrapolation is the prediction and addition of data outside the measured interval. Accuracy can also be estimated by full-scale experimental observations.

Algorithm for the classification and selection of specific methods of processing and analyzing data.

The key idea of the previously proposed approach is the attribution of data to a specific group of analysis and processing methods based on their properties, followed by the selection of specific methods. The general scheme of the approach is presented in Fig. 1 and can be expressed by the following algorithm:

1. The data that must be processed is evaluated according to the following criteria: dimension (a number of parameters studied), volume, kinds, and types of data, a problem solved and the form of the result presentation.
2. A group of data processing methods is selected on the assumption of the properties of data defined in the previous step. In particular, while the range of existing methods for numerical data is wide enough, the set of methods for textual and multimedia data is often radically different and requires either data decomposition or their preliminary analysis and conversion into a different presentation type.
3. Almost all variations have their limitations or conditions of applicability within the selected group of methods, such as the dimension of the data being processed, the size of data samples, sensitivity to the nature of data change, speed or computational complexity. At the stage of selecting a specific method, it is necessary to compare existing methods by their properties that are objective and a priori known depending on previously taken into account data properties.

4. It is necessary to obtain a list of properties and parameters of a specific method suitable for the considered task that gives an acceptable solution as a result of the selection of this specific method for processing and analyzing data.

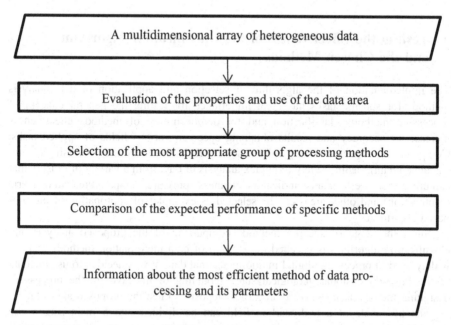

Fig. 1. The basic algorithm for classification and selection of data processing methods.

Comparison of the expected effectiveness of specific methods from the group by the general properties and characteristics of data and processing methods was previously carried out on the task of constructing a 3D model of a human face by interpolation using known points. Data interpolation is a common and flexible tool for processing numerical data of various nature and size.

Many of those who are faced with scientific and engineering calculations often have to operate with sets of values obtained experimentally or by random sampling. As a rule, it is required to construct a function that could relate with values obtained in the future with high accuracy on the basis of these sets [7]. This is known as an approximation. Interpolation refers to such kind of approximation in which the curve of the constructed function passes exactly through the available data points.

There is also a problem close to interpolation, which consists of approximation of a complex function by another, more simple function. If some function is too complex for productive calculations, it is possible to try to calculate its value at several points, and build (interpolate in other words) on it a more simple function. Of course, the use of the simplified function does not allow one to get the exact accurate results that the original function would give. But the achieved increase in the speed of calculations may outweigh a received error in results in some classes of tasks.

By now there are many different interpolation methods. The choice of the most suitable algorithm depends on the answers to the questions: how accurate the chosen method is, how costly it is to use it, how smooth the interpolation function is, how many data points it requires, etc.

4   Testing the Effectiveness of the Classification Algorithm and the Chosen Methods

The implementation of the algorithm of selection and application of data analysis methods for specific tasks has great importance for testing the general concept of processing methods classification and for demonstration of methods effectiveness increase by accuracy and results obtaining speed in various fields of applied tasks. Computer vision (stereo photography using an IR depth sensor and processing of pre-calculated data), facility safety (complex analysis of data from a variety of sensors that capture critical performance indicators: wetness, pressure, temperature, atmospheric composition) and other areas can be selected as examples of approbation of the proposed algorithm.

Since the stage of specific methods comparison of the proposed analysis and classification algorithm is checked on a group of data interpolation methods that are widely used in processing digital multidimensional data, it was decided to use the data of the three-dimensional geological static modeling of the layer in the process of designing the development of hydrocarbon deposits to test the proposed algorithm.

The life cycle of a hydrocarbon field can be divided into 5 main stages: the discovery of a field, the assessment of hydrocarbon volumes, development preparation, production, and liquidation. Each of the stages is characterized by different volumes of research and the reliability of knowledge about the structure of the field. There is a gradual concentration of observation wells points (as they are drilled and researches are conducted in them) and the accumulation of information and knowledge about the object throughout the entire life cycle of any hydrocarbon field. Thus, hydrocarbon production is possible only after assessing the funds of a field based on geological modeling and creating a development project based on predictive modeling (due to Russian laws).

The complexity of solving a geological modeling task is related to the problem of increasing data density in a three-dimensional layer model based on seismic data and geophysical studies in drilled wells by interpolating known values of parameters around wells (Fig. 2). In this case, the initial data are characterized by uneven distribution in the area and different regularity of the observation points. Often, the model is based on data obtained from only a few observation points (in the early stages of the field life cycle), which negatively affects the reliability of the result and it means that the task is characterized by a high rate of geological indeterminacy.

The designing process is repeated many times as new data appears during the drilling of new wells and the knowledge about the geological structure of the field changes. A set of implementations of the geological model is calculated during the design process to select the most reliable model, where the main reliability criterion is the consistency of modeling data with the original data obtained from drilled wells.

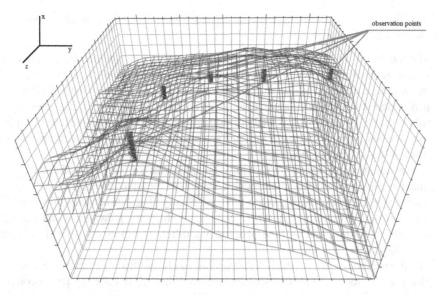

Fig. 2. The task of the distribution of the parameters on the results of studies in drilled wells.

Such tasks as the choice of data interpolation algorithm, as well as its optimal settings depending on the number of observation points, the vertical distribution of properties, on the basis of which the most correct distribution of parameters in the reservoir model volume is obtained, arise at the stage of modeling in the designing of field development. Also, the problem of a small amount of data (insufficient to obtain an adequate model) at an early stage of the field life cycle (a small number of exploration wells are drilled, little research is done) should be taken into account while modeling. Another problem is the uneven distribution of these data due to the specifics of the placement of observation points during the additional research of the fields by drilling new wells and conducting special studies in them because exploration wells are not laid out in a regular mesh but in places of the most probable occurrence of hydrocarbons.

To achieve an acceptable quality of the final field model, it must meet a number of criteria: do not contradict the original data at the observation points; the distribution of parameters must be correct both laterally and vertically in the model volume. The final model of the field is used to assess and estimate hydrocarbon reserves; this model is going through the stages of state expertise and vindication.

Existing software packages for modeling hydrocarbon fields provide an opportunity to assess the results of the distribution of parameters by different algorithms, but it requires calculating these distributions. In this paper, an algorithm for choosing a distribution algorithm according to a number of criteria and depending on the conditions of the problem being solved, as well as on the required degree of accuracy of the result, is proposed. It eliminates the necessity for multiple calculations of various algorithms for the distribution of parameters with different settings to achieve an acceptable result.

The following characteristics, on the basis of which interpolation algorithms are compared, can be singled out:

- The number of adjustable parameters. Each algorithm may require the selection of one or more numerical parameters that affect the accuracy and even correctness of the result in addition to the initial data. Such parameters may have a range of permissible and efficient values depending on other properties of data and algorithm. The algorithm with a smaller number of adjustable parameters and a more formal description of their selection process allows easier and faster automatization of its selection and application.
- Computational complexity. A generally accepted way of comparing the computational complexity of algorithms, which shows the order of the algorithm's work time, or the estimation of algorithm time complexity. The estimation is displayed as a function of T(n) (or O(n)), where a function character indicates computational complexity, so the running time of some algorithms is expressed as O(1) < O(log n) < O(n) < O(n2) < O(n!).
- The dimension of data at which the algorithm can be applied or reaches the greatest efficiency. A lot of data processing algorithms either are not able to give a correct result on initial data of high dimensionality, or their efficiency is significantly reduced.
- The minimum and maximum volumes of data arrays on which the result can be obtained. Some algorithms lose their effectiveness or capacity for work if the volume of input data is too small or too large. This fact should be taken into account during the selection of processing methods.
- Sensitivity to data errors, spikes, remoted values. Excessive sensitivity that is inherent in some algorithms can lead to incorrect results in case of insufficient analysis of data and algorithms general properties.

According to the existing practices in geological modeling, four interpolation algorithms were chosen for testing the effectiveness of the algorithm for classification and selection of data processing methods. These algorithms have different computational complexity and the number of adjustments.

The interpolation with the Kriging interpolation (ordinary Kriging) method can be expressed as follows:

$$z(x_0) = \sum_{i=1}^{n} w_i * z(x_i), \tag{1}$$

where w_i is a weighting value, $z(x_i)$ is an observed value.

Kriging and Kriging by Gslib algorithms have the option of collocated co-kriging and can be expressed as follows:

$$z(x_0) = \sum_{i=1}^{n} w_i * z(x_i) + \left(1 - \sum_{i=1}^{n} w_i * z(x_i)\right) * m, \tag{2}$$

where w_i is a weighting value, $z(x_i)$ is an observed value, m is a local mean.

The next expression describes interpolation with the Moving average algorithm:

$$z(x_0) = \frac{1}{W} * \sum_{i=1}^{n} (w_i * q_i), \tag{3}$$

where q_i is a value included in the summation, w_i is a weighting value, W is a sum of all weights.

Table 1 presents the characteristics of a number of algorithms that were chosen as the main group of interpolation methods. The number of adjustable parameters and computational complexity is taken as key characteristics, the other characteristics are listed in the column "Additional features".

Table 1. Key characteristics of interpolation algorithms.

Method name	The number of adjustable parameters	Computational complexity	Additional features
Kriging interpolation	6	$O(N^4)$ [8]	Does not have the option of Co-kriging but can work in real coordinates rather than simple sim box space and is usually quicker
Kriging	6	$O(N^4)$	The best linear unbiased prediction of intermediate values with correctly selected a priori assumptions; the fastest in terms of performance; the addition of a fast Collocated co-kriging algorithm as well as some additional options to extend user control over the style of Kriging
Kriging by Gslib	6	$O(N^4)$	Uses the external executable and is, therefore, slower, but it has the option for Collocated co-kriging
Moving average	3	$O(N\log N)$ [9]	The algorithm is fast and creates values for all cells, however, it can create "bulls eyes" if the range of the input data is large; the algorithm does not generate values larger or smaller than the min/max values of the input data

As can be seen from Table 1, the interpolation algorithms differ in the accuracy of the result, computational complexity, and the number of parameters that must be selected directly for a specific task. The accuracy of the problem solution, speed of this solution evaluation, its general correctness and accordance with the goal will significantly depend on the method selected.

It is rational to introduce weighting coefficients of significance reflecting the importance of a particular parameter for a specific task as a criterion for the selection of a data processing method for the proposed algorithm besides the obvious restrictions on the size and volume of data. These particular parameters are the accuracy of the result, computation time, complexity of adjustable parameters preparation and setting up.

The following notation was introduced:

PNM is a weighting factor of the parameter that characterizes a particular method, where N is a method number, M is a parameter type. It is set by the user depending on the requirements of the problem being solved. The weights can have any abstract dimension, but for ease of use, it is rational to normalize them in the range [0; 1]. Then the general formula for priorities determination in the use of methods can be written as follows:

$$P_{Nsum} = \frac{\sum_{M=1}^{K} P_{NM}}{K},$$ (4)

where K is the total number of parameters having weight.

By calculating Psum for all N, it is possible to get a one-valued distribution of the value of the methods for the chosen task.

A problem of determining the criteria of algorithms that are difficult to formalize remains in this approach, and if the number of parameters, speed and accuracy are relatively easy to estimate, then it is almost impossible to choose a single scale for such parameters as sensitivity to anomalous data values and boundary conditions.

However, this approach previously was successfully tested in the task of constructing a 3D model of a human face using interpolation methods, and the most efficient algorithms for accuracy and speed were found from a limited set during its solving.

In this paper, a wider set of interpolation methods is considered using the example of a task from the field of designing of oil reservoir development [10].

In the considered problem of building a model of a field, the smoothness and proximity of the interpolated model to the real parameters of the object at the observation points (drilled wells) can be chosen as the final criterion for the quality of interpolation [11]. The comparison was carried out using specialized software for modeling deposits Schlumberger Petrel.

In this paper, a direct comparison is made on a specific field model obtained from raw geological exploration data using various interpolation methods. The characteristics of the data on which the comparison was made are as follows: the size of the field model is 787 cells along the x-axis, 1000 cells along the y-axis, 10 layers in the z-axis, 7870000 cells in total. The vertical layering of the model is selected depending on the characteristics of the source data such as the number of parameter definitions in the drilled wells, thus a lossless distribution and maintaining heterogeneity are achieved. This is especially important since there is a more strict error requirement in the resulting model for vertical dimension than for lateral. Another issue of the parameters distribution task in geological modeling is an uneven distribution of the observation points (the results of studies in drilled wells) over the field area.

It is sufficient to distribute such parameters as porosity, cell volume, and oil saturation in the reservoir model to estimate hydrocarbon reserves using the volumetric method. Oil properties, such as density, volume coefficient, gas factor, are at this moment accepted as a constant. As part of this work, the distribution of the porosity

parameter in the reservoir volume was carried out according to the results of geophysical studies in drilled wells.

Methods that require the specification of interpolation parameters were used with
the recommended parameters for the given conditions, providing the best result in
accuracy [8]. Such parameters were obtained experimentally. 30 distributions were
calculated for each algorithm with parameter variations. Figure 3 shows examples of
visualized field models that were compared inaccuracy: (a) Kriging interpolation (expression 1), (b) Kriging (expression 2), (c) Kriging Gslib (expression 2), (d) Moving
average (expression 3).

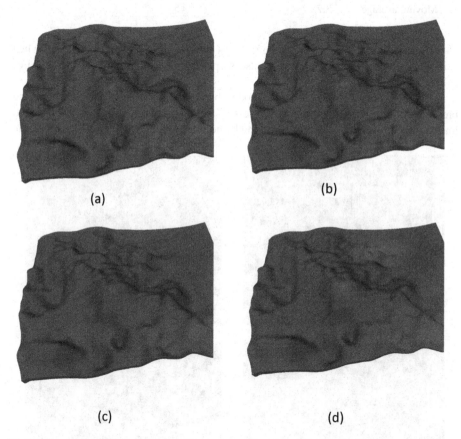

Fig. 3. Parameters distribution according to the results of Kriging interpolation (a), Kriging (b),
Kriging by Gslib (c), Moving average (d).

An estimate of the model's reliability using such parameters as average values,
geological and statistical cross-sections and maps of average values is taken as an

assessment of the accuracy of interpolation. The computation time of all interpolated points of the field model is taken as an assessment of the interpolation rate.

The results of the comparison of the algorithms are presented in Table 2.

Table 2. Property distribution algorithms performance results

Method name	Average interpolation error, %	Average calculation time, sec
Kriging interpolation	4,5	8,35
Kriging	4,9	9,97
Kriging by Gslib	4,8	450,28
Moving average	3,2	5,7

As can be seen from Table 2, the smallest interpolation error was achieved when using the Moving average method; it also surpassed other algorithms in the speed of calculation.

Maps of averages (by layers of the model) based on the results of the algorithms are presented in Fig. 4 to assess the correctness of the lateral distribution. The dash-dotted line shows the region of interest in which the edge of the oil-saturated part of the

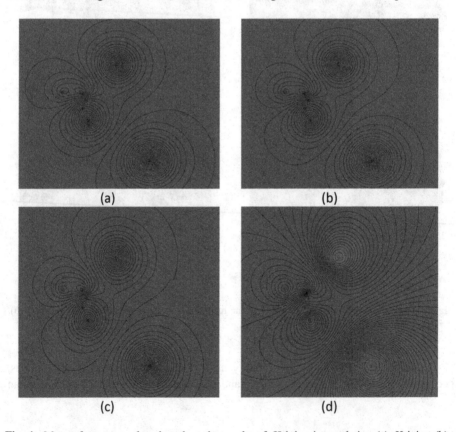

Fig. 4. Maps of average values based on the results of: Kriging interpolation (a), Kriging (b), Kriging by Gslib (c), Moving average (d).

deposit is located and the correctness of the distribution of the model parameters is assessed. Also the locations of observation points (drilled wells), in which geophysical studies were carried out, the results of which were used to interpolate parameters, are marked with crosses in Fig. 4.

The regulated allowed distribution error is 5% [12]. According to the results, all algorithms did not exceed this threshold; however, the Moving average algorithm showed the smallest calculation error by comparison with the original data; it also has the lowest calculation time of all algorithms.

From the comparison made in Tables 1 and 2, it can be concluded that the majority of interpolation methods can be classified according to computational complexity and the number of adjustable parameters. The first criterion affects both the result accuracy and the data processing speed, the second criterion seriously affects the processing time due to the need to iterate over interpolation parameters, and the presence or absence of adjustment parameters directly affects the complexity of data processing automation.

Thus, further work on evaluating the criteria of data processing methods effectiveness and creating an algorithm of automated classification and optimal methods selection seems to be quite relevant.

5 Conclusion

Methods and algorithms of data processing were reviewed in the paper. An extension of the previously proposed algorithm of selecting specific data processing methods based on the general properties of data and algorithms under consideration is extended to the area of geological modeling of oil deposits. A group of interpolation algorithms is compared using the example of building a geological model of an oil field.

The analysis of the results showed that the proposed algorithm of selection data processing methods works successfully for a group of data interpolation methods, identifying a more accurate method than the manual selection and also correctly evaluating the performance complexity of all interpolation methods by calculating a set of realizations of the geological model. The smallest error in constructing and the shortest calculation time was achieved with the choice of the Moving average method as the classification underlying the proposed algorithm predicted. The automatization of this approach and expansion to the more general task of selecting groups of data analysis methods in the future seems rational.

Acknowledgments. The work was supported by RFBR, Grant 19-07-00844 A.

References

1. Klemenkov, P.A., Kuznecov, S.D.: Big data: modern approaches to storage and processing. In: Trudy ISP RAN. Tom: 23, c. 143–158 (2012). (in Russian)
2. Averchenkov, V., Budylskii, D., Podvesovskii, A., Averchenkov, S., Rytov, M., Yakimov, A.: Hierarchical deep learning: a promising technique for opinion monitoring and sentiment analysis in Russian-language social networks. In: Kravets, A., Shcherbakov, M., Kultsova, M., Shabalina, O. (eds.) Creativity in Intelligent Technologies and Data Science. CCIS, vol. 535, pp. 583–592. Springer, Cham (2015). https://doi.org/10.1007/978-3-319-23766-4_46

3. Istomin, E.P., Kolbina, O.N., Stepanov, S.Yu., Sidorenko, A.Yu.: Analysis of models and systems for processing heterogeneous data for use in applied GIS. Sci. Herald **4**, 53 (2015). (in Russian)

4. Pirs, B.: Types in programming languages, 680 s (2012). (in Russian). ISBN 978-5-7913-0082-9

5. Silen, D., Mejsman, A., Ali, M.: The basics of Data Science and Big Data. Python and the science about data. SPb.: Piter, 336 s (2017). (in Russian)

6. Zakharova, A.A., Vekhter, E.V., Shklyar, A.E., Pak, A.Y.: Visual modeling in an analysis of multidimensional data. J. Phys. Conf. Ser. **944**(1), 012127 (2018)

7. Berg, J., Lyofstryom, J.: Interpolation Spaces. Introduction. M.: Mir, 264 s (1980)

8. Srinivasan, B.V., Duraiswami, R., Murtugudde, R.: Efficient kriging for real-time Spatio-temporal interpolation. In: Proceedings of the 20th Conference on Probability and Statistics in the Atmospheric Sciences, pp. 228–235. American Meteorological Society, Atlanta (2010)

9. Perreault, S., Hébert, P.: Median filtering in constant time. IEEE Trans. Image Process. **16**(9), 2389–2394 (2007)

10. Pakyuz-Charrier, E., Giraud, J., Ogarko, V., Lindsay, M., Jessell, M.: Drillhole uncertainty propagation for three-dimensional geological modeling using Monte Carlo. Tectonophysics **747–748**, 16–39 (2018)

11. Yang, L., Hyde, D., Grujic, O., Scheidt, C., Caers, J.: Assessing and visualizing the uncertainty of 3D geological surfaces using level sets with stochastic motion. Comput. Geosci. **122**, 54–67 (2019)

12. Guidelines for the preparation of technical projects for the development of hydrocarbon deposits. Ministry of Natural Resources of Russia. Approved 18 May 2016

Detection of the Patterns in the Daily Route Choices of the Urban Social Transport System Clients Based on the Decoupling of Passengers' Preferences Between the Levels of Uncertainty

Elena Krushel$^{(\boxtimes)}$, Ilya Stepanchenko$^{(\boxtimes)}$, Alexander Panfilov$^{(\boxtimes)}$,
and Tatyana Lyutaya$^{(\boxtimes)}$

Kamyshin Technological Institute (branch of) Volgograd State Technical
University, Kamyshin, Russia
elena-krushel@yandex. ru,
stilvi@mail. ru, panfilov@kti. ru, lyutaya. t. p@gmail. com

Abstract. The ideas of data mining techniques were applied for the problem of municipal passengers transport system simulation and its results interpreting and generalization. The purpose of the presented work is to propose and justify the passengers flow model suitable for the detection of hidden patterns in the processes of flow forming with the application of the available sources for model identification. The patterns of the daily route choices detection are based on the decoupling of the general model between the sub-models according to the different levels of uncertainty of passengers intentions in route choice, and on the following joining of the computational results received for the sub-models. The availability of the approach was illustrated by the examples of the typical patterns in the destination stops choice and in hourly passengers' flow from the departure stops. The model testing shows the high correlation of the simulated passengers' flow with the results of the real observations.

Keywords: Transport system · Daily route · Pattern · Passenger · Simulation

1 Introduction

Modern approaches to improving the urban passenger transport social system's control are based not only on traditional methods including real observations, statistical processing of reports, and operational tracking of citizens' claims but on the application of computational experiments with models of the transport system operation as well. The purpose of such experiments is to forecast the expected values of the activity variants efficiency terms before practical implementation [1–3]. The obvious benefit of such preliminary computer analysis for organizations responsible for the transport system control quality shows the appropriate models' development relevance.

One of the most inapprehensible transport systems' operations mathematical models development problems lays in the necessity of consideration of numerous uncertainty factors inherent to the passengers' flow formation. Such factors are peculiar to practically each general model's component. For example, the private model of forming the

A. G. Kravets et al. (Eds.): CIT&DS 2019, CCIS 1083, pp. 175–188, 2019.
https://doi.org/10.1007/978-3-030-29743-5_14

passengers flow to the departure stops is influenced by follows uncertainty factors: time moments of the passengers' arrival at the stop, their intentions to choose the certain car type, the population in the stop's availability zone, etc. However, overcoming of such difficulties is possible by well-known statistical analysis tools [4–7].

The uncertainties account in the design of private models for destination stops' choosing is much more difficult. The choice of destination stop is individual and unpredictable even for a single passenger. Therefore the flow of numerous passengers from the departure to destination stops receives the chaotic elements.

The different approaches to this problem decision are known [5, 6, 8–12]. However, the attempts of their application to particular megalopolis transport problems solving sometimes may be unsuccessful due to the simulation subject's specific features. In this case, the individual project should be required. If the developed model would be successful it may be added to the existing library of the models and consequently expand the area of known solutions application.

The following presents the results of the development of an approach to the design of passengers flow model as the subsystem of urban passenger transport system operation general model for megalopolis with such specific features:

1. In parallel with thousands of small-sized city enterprises and offices (industrial, commercial, service, educational, medical, etc.) the megalopolis infrastructure includes unique objects of passenger traffic mass attraction – particularly: industrial enterprises of federal importance, large educational centers, shopping and entertaining centers, regional health care enterprises. The total number of such objects is about 2 orders less the number of small enterprises. The difference between the number of daily visits to the smallest of large enterprises and the largest of small enterprises assures the possibility of large enterprises clustering.
2. The form of the megalopolis map is elongated so that the length in the longitudinal direction prevails over the length in the transverse. Such form causes the objective tendency to locate the majority of small enterprises and offices in the central part of the city for the purpose to reduce the summary time consuming for citizens coming from places of residence to places of work and service.
3. The metropolis infrastructure consists of territorially compact districts, therefore, the employers tend to locate shopping and entertaining centers in one-two points of each district in order to maintain the stable flow from the consumers living within the same district.
4. The flow of citizens to large industrial enterprises, universities, specialized healthcare institutions of regional importance is practically independent of the location of district of their living.

The features pointed out above are peculiar to Volgograd city (Russian Federation). The city population exceeds one million. The city is located at the Volga riverside and its length is about 68 km along the river. The average width of city zones in the transverse directions is about 24 km. The daily visits' amount of large enterprises exceeds 2500 and the number of such enterprises is 22. Enterprises with the amount of visits 800...2400 are absent. The amount of daily visits to small and medium enterprises is less than 800. The number of such enterprises exceeds 1200 and for 80% from them, the amount of daily visits does not exceed 100.

The passengers' flow simulation overall problem for any megalopolis conditions possesses the features of big data systems [9, 13, 14]. For example the parameters of the Volgograd passenger transport system are follows: the number of transport stop zones (includes up to 6 stops) is 535, the number of routes is 228, the number of passengers carried out during the working day is about 1,000,000, and the duration of the working day is 900 min. Namely, these city parameters were applied as the base of the developed simulation model.

The detection of hidden patterns of passenger flow formation (in data mining style [15–18]) for megalopolis transport systems is possible only on the basis of analyzing and processing the results of multiple simulation sessions. The computer experiments of such scale are complicated not only by the huge dimensionality of big data processing problems the decision of which requires the application of expensive and non-standard technique. The examples of such projects with the estimation of the expenses are pointed in [10, 13, 17] for other megalopolises conditions.

The main and principal difficulties the developers meet both in the problems of the passengers flow identification and the model adequacy proofing.

2 Problem Statement

The purpose of the presented work is to propose and justify the passengers flow model suitable for the detection of hidden patterns in the processes of flow forming with the application of the available sources for model identification and for the conclusion on its adequacy achieving on the base of the ordinary computers' application with the general purpose software. The achievement of the purpose is based on the simplifications taking into account mentioned above specific features of the simulation subject (therefore we cannot pretend to propose the general problem decision but we hope that the scope of application would be noticeable).

The model implementation is based on the decoupling of total passengers' flow forming model into separate sub-models differing from each other by their inherent levels of uncertainty passengers' preferences in route choice, and subsequent joining of the results received for the sub-models.

The simulation model carried out in the terms of agent simulation theory [6] provides the following information for the transport system control decision makers:

1. The estimation of the daily passengers flow to each departure stop with pointing time moment of each agent arrived at the stop in format hh:mm (below instead of term "agent" we use "passenger").
2. The destination stops for each passenger and appropriate route variant (without transfers; with the single transfer; with two or more transfers).
3. The possibilities to receive the generalized passengers flow characteristics particularly the frequency visits to any stop at any time interval within the working day; the average ratio between the amounts of routes without transfers and with ones; the patterns of the passengers flow forming dependant on the working day interval as well as on the destinations' popularity.

The passengers flow forming model is embedded in the common transport system control simulation model [1]. The latter simulates the transportation of passengers between the transport stops as well as buses movement at the routs with the estimation of following indicators of daily operation effectiveness [4]:

1. Common number of daily bus trips.
2. Daily number of passengers: (1) which appeared at the arrival stops; (2) which used the municipal transport devices to trips; (3) which refused of trips on the municipal transport devices due to the unacceptable waiting time value of their arrival; (4) the number of passengers remaining at the stops of transfers.
3. The average daily effectiveness indicators values: (1) the hour number of passengers trips; (2) transport device load factor; (3) trip distance; (4) daily income.

The details are pointed below in following sections:

1. General description of the proposal essence (main assumption, its utility, implementation steps, project completeness state).
2. Examples of the passengers flow forming patterns.

3   General Description of the Proposal Essence

The assumption accepted for the passengers flow model design follows the concept of the whole flow decoupling on four components:

1. Quasi-deterministic passengers flow from the departure stops to the points of mass passengers' attracting.
2. Stochastic hourly passengers' flow from each arrival stops to city's districts. The probability density of the number of passengers' exchanges between the districts is bimodal. The main mode corresponds to the district concentrating the most of small and medium enterprises location. The second one corresponds to the district of the arrival stop location.
3. Stochastic flow which simulates the distribution of the passengers between the destination stops in accordance to the stops popularity estimations. This flow is directed to middle industry enterprises, educational and healthcare institutions and other plants of district importance level.
4. Chaotic distribution of the passengers flow between the stops with low estimations of the daily visits number.

The general passengers flow model joins the mentioned above components the computing for which may be carried out separately and in parallel.

Several advantages of the proposed approach follow:

1. The model identification can be carried out on the base of statistical processing of reports accumulated in urban transport enterprises during the perennial period of their activity. This advantage is especially important for the megalopolises because the researches of the transport system in conditions of real operating are difficult and expensive and their regular repeating is problematic at all.

2. The possibilities of separate simulation of the passengers flow components allow the reducing of each sub-problem dimensionality to the level acceptable for the low-cost implementation on the ordinary computers with widely applied software.

The implementation of the approach consists of three stages: (1) preliminary data structuring; (2) multiple sessions of passengers flow simulation; (3) the generalization of the simulation results and detecting of the patterns in the daily choices of destination stops.

4 Preliminary Data Structuring

1. The stops of mass passengers flow attraction are selected using the results of the city enterprises clustering. For each such stop, the type of nearing enterprises and the estimations of hourly visits to them during the working day are pointed out.
2. The probabilities of the trips between each transport stop and each city district (including the district of stop's location) are estimated on the base of processing of the data of the multiyear report. The specific form of the city map allows selecting preferable directions of passengers flow between the city districts.
3. In accordance with the multiyear statistics and expert opinions, the stops' clustering is carried out based on the estimation of their daily visits amount. Two clusters are formed: first one – the stops with high (more than 500) and middle (100–500) daily visits numbers; the second one – the stops with low visits amount (less than 100);
4. Each of the stops from the first cluster is marked by the unique estimation of attractiveness for its choice as the destination stop (in score scale of 100...1000 diapasons). The remaining stops from the second cluster receive a low score of attractiveness (less than 100)

5 Multiple Sessions of Passengers Flow Simulation

1. The simulation of the passengers flow from each transport stop to the stops of mass passengers flow attraction is carried out. The variants of each passenger trip to every attractive destination stops are fixed from the moment (hh:mm) of his coming at the departure stop. The contribution of each stop in the whole visits number is esti-mated as the distribution of a given number of attractive stops' visits between the different passengers flows sources at the passengers living zones. The types of enterprises nearby the destination stop are taken into account. Particularly number of visits to universities, specialized regional healthcare institutions, central markets and large enterprises of federal importance is almost independent of the passengers' district of living. In opposite the huge trading and entertaining centers located in a certain district are visited predominantly by the citizens of the same district. The time interval for the trips fulfillment is taken into account.

2. The hourly passengers' flows between the city districts are computed separately for the two passengers groups with different preferences of route choices. The first one joins the employees and youth of 18–24 years old while the second one joins the pensioners and schoolchildren. The main passengers' flows directions are determined separately for the working day fragments: morning flow from the living zones to the district of main small and middle enterprises and offices location; middle day flow mainly between the stops within the same district; evening returning flow from the working places to the living zones with balance of passengers departure and returning.

3. The choice of the destination stop within the district for each passenger at the departure stop is carried out using the destination stop attractiveness score. The choice of the transport stop with certain attractiveness is similar to the known rule of crossover pairs' choice in the genetic algorithms [19]. If the value of the chosen score exceeds the threshold appointed for the stops with low attractiveness the choice of destination stop is carried out between the stops of the 1st group (i.e. with high or middle scores of attractiveness). The choice of such stops is deterministic due to the uniqueness of their attractiveness scores. In the opposite case, the certain stop with low attractiveness is chosen chaotically among the stops of the 2nd group (for example correspondingly to the uniform probability law).

4. The simulation session completes by the joining of the passengers' flows which were previously computed separately. Then the passengers' departures from each stop are sorted correspondingly to the order of increasing of passengers arrivals time moments. Afterwards, the passengers flow simulation results are ready for future processing.

The simulation sessions must be carried out repeatedly for the possibility of simulation results generalization admitting the passengers flow patterns detection.

The support of preliminary data structuring and simulation sessions holding was implemented in the program project "Passengers flow" embedded into the software facilities for Volgograd passenger transport system control simulation. The fragment of the computation results for certain departure stop is shown on Fig. 1. The type feature of the chosen route is pointed in the 6th column (designations of 0, 1, −1 correspond to the route without transfers, with single transfer and with two of more transfers correspondingly).

Departure stop's name	Departure district's name	Time moment of departure	Arrival district's name	Arrival stop's name	Reachability 0/ 1/ -1
St_018	Distr_2	6:02	Distr_4	St_054	1
		6:07	Distr_6	St_322	1
		6:09	Distr_2	St_390	1
		6:20	Distr_2	St_310	1
		6:27	Distr_2	St_351	1

Fig. 1. The fragment of the passengers flow estimation from the departure to the destination stops

6 The Generalization of the Simulation Results and Detecting of the Patterns in the Daily Choices of Destination Stops

This stage is illustrated below by the examples. The simulation results were repeatedly discussed with experts possessing the experience in the passenger traffic control. The consistency of the simulation results with the conclusions of experts confirms the hypothesis of the existence of stable patterns in the transport behavior of citizens.

Example 1. The features of quasi-deterministic passengers flow from the departure stops to the points of mass passengers' attracting. Such stops' data ordered by the average number of daily visits decreasing are shown in Fig. 2 (column 5).

The kind of enterprises located near the stop (column 3) effects on the passengers preferences in its choice as the point of destination. Particularly number of visits to powerful educational centers, citywide markets, industrial enterprises and hospitals of regional importance is almost independent of the passengers' district of living. In opposite the shopping & entertaining centers located in a certain district are visited predominantly by the citizens of the same district.

Attraction stop identifier in the attraction stops database	Attraction stop identifier in the whole transport system database	Kings of the activity at the attraction stops neighborhood	Identifier of the attraction stop location district	Number of average daily attendance (statistical data)	Number of daily attendance (simulation)	Relative error
Attr_03	St_033	Shopping & entertaining center	Distr_1	26000	20613	20,7%
Attr_24	St_380	Powerful educational center	Distr_8	26000	26155	-0,6%
Attr_21	St_299	Shopping & entertaining center	Distr_6	22000	21775	1,0%
Attr_12	St_118	Shopping & entertaining center	Distr_7	20000	20799	-4,0%
Attr_13	St_139	Shopping & entertaining center	Distr_2	20000	24218	-21,1%
Attr_18	St_224	Shopping & entertaining center	Distr_2	20000	24743	-23,7%
Attr_09	St_085	Shopping & entertaining center	Distr_8	15000	12304	18,0%
Attr_07	St_082	Shopping & entertaining center	Distr_8	11300	9235	18,3%
Attr_23	St_335	Shopping & entertaining center	Distr_7	11000	11323	-2,9%
Attr_08	St_083	Citywide market	Distr_8	10000	10182	-1,8%
Attr_26	St_403	Powerful educational center	Distr_6	6900	7139	-3,5%
Attr_15	St_146	Powerful educational center	Distr_8	6000	6248	-4,1%
Attr_22	St_302	Shopping & entertaining center	Distr_2	6000	7608	-26,8%
Attr_20	St_238	Powerful educational center	Distr_6	5100	5302	-4,0%

Fig. 2. Database of powerful passengers' traffic attraction stops

Figure 3 presents the estimations of the number of daily visits to the stops of mass passengers flow attraction received by the simulation results processing. The differences between the simulation results and initial data of statistics are inconsequential (column 7 of Figs. 2 and 3) which proves the success of the simulation (the value of correlation coefficient is 0.97).

We had no need to achieve the exact matching of the simulation results and the available set of field observations due to their principal specificity and incompleteness and sought only to achieve the similarity of stable trends (patterns).

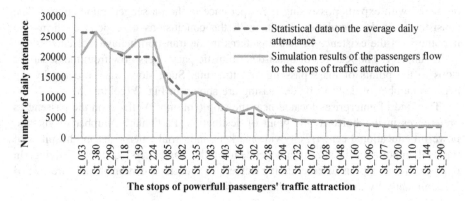

Fig. 3. Correspondence between the simulation results and average data

Example 2. The patterns of the passengers' flow from the stops, which are out of the most attractive stops list. Figure 4 illustrates the pattern 1: hour values of passengers' flow from the certain departure stop of such type (simulation results). This pattern shows the existence of morning and evening peaks of passenger traffic intensity with the predominance of the evening peak (interpretation of visits to shopping and entertainment centers mainly in evening).

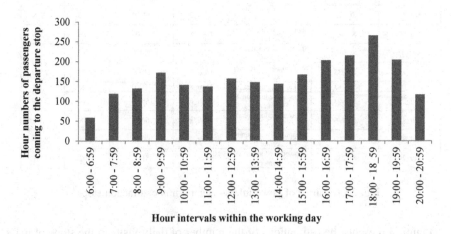

Fig. 4. Pattern 1; Passengers hour flow from the departure stop (St_039, Distr_2, out of list of powerful passengers' traffic attraction stops)

Figure 5 illustrates the pattern 2: the most popular stops of destination chosen by the passengers departing from the stop, which is out of the most attractive stops list.

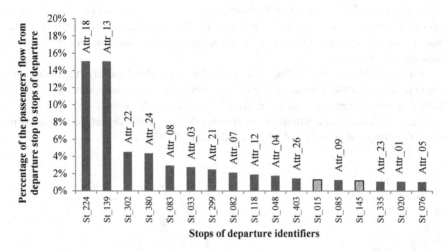

Fig. 5. Pattern 2: Passengers' hourly flow from the departure stop. Joining of the flows to the attractive stops and remaining stops with different attractiveness scores (St_039, Distr_2, out of list of the most attractive stops)

Comments to Fig. 5. The first 3 bars of the diagram in Fig. 5 refer to flows to mass attractive stops located in the district of departure stop placing (codes Attr_18, 13, 22, specialization - shopping and entertaining centers). The 4th bar of the diagram illustrates the value of the to the passengers' flow to the stop located nearby the most powerful educational center of the city (code Attr_24, Fig. 2). The flow to the rest of the destination stops is significantly less, but only 2 stops of them are absent in the list of the most attractive stops (these stops are marked on Fig. 5 by hatched filling).

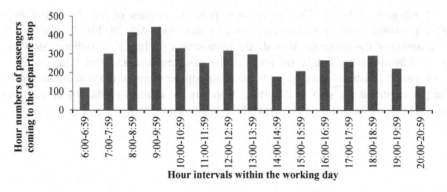

Fig. 6. Pattern 3: Passengers' hourly flow from the departure stop. Joining of the flows to the attractive stops and remaining stops with different attractiveness scores (St_039, Distr_2, out of list of the most attractive stops)

Figure 6 illustrates the pattern 3: the result of joining of the passengers' flows directed to the most attractive stops and to remaining stops (including the stops with the low score of attractiveness).

Comments to Fig. 6. The Fig. 6 illustrates the existence of morning and evening peaks of passenger traffic intensity (similarly to shown at Fig. 4). However, the predominant peak is morning one due to the passengers' flow to the start of classes in the educational center.

Example 3. The patterns of the passengers' flow from the departure stops which are present in the list of the most attractive ones (the group of stops the number of visits for which is almost independent of the citizens' living zones location).

Figure 7 illustrates the pattern 4: passengers flow from the departure stop locating nearby the powerful educational canter (code Attr_24, Fig. 2).

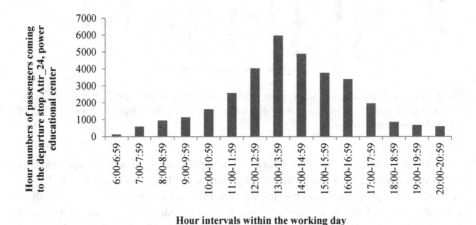

Hour intervals within the working day

Fig. 7. Pattern 4: Passengers hour flow from the departure stop (S_380, Distr_8, element of list of the most attractive stops, Attr_24)

Comments to Fig. 7. The departure stop is the element of the list of the most attractive stops (here – powerful educational center, code Attr_24, Fig. 2). The hourly distribution of the passenger flow differs from shown on Fig. 4 for ordinary stop: the peak of intensiveness falls at the hours of the most learning activities completion.

Figure 8 illustrates the pattern 5: the most popular stops of destination chosen by the passengers at the stop of departure, which is the element of the list of the most attractive stops (the stop type is powerful educational center).

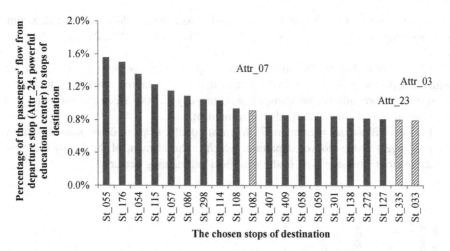

Fig. 8. Pattern **5**: Passengers' hourly flow from the departure stop which is the element of list of the most attractive stops (St_380, Distr_8, powerful educational center, Attr_24)

Comments to Fig. 8. This diagram shows the 20% part of the summary passengers' flow from the departure stop which is the element of the list of the most attractive stops (i.e. the most powerful educational center of the city, code Attr_24, Fig. 2) to the remaining stops with high scores of attractiveness. Comparably with shown on the Fig. 5 the passengers' flow is more uniform. The main part of the destination stops are ordinary (are out of the most attractive stops list), the exceptions are marked on Fig. 8 by the hatched filling. In this case, the intensiveness of passengers' flow to the destination stops depends mainly from the number of citizens living nearby of these stops.

Example 4. The patterns of the passengers' flow from the departure stops which are present in the list of the most attractive ones (the group of stops the number of visits for which is essentially dependent from the citizens' living zones location).

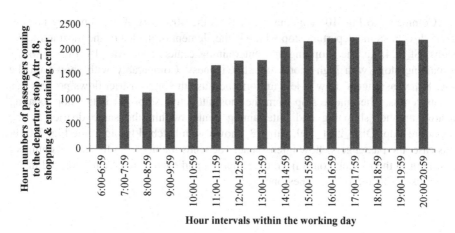

Fig. 9. Pattern **6**: Passengers hour flow from the departure stop (St_224, Distr_2, element of list of the most attractive stops, Attr_18, shopping and entertaining center)

Figure 9 illustrates the pattern 6: the hourly passengers' flow from the departure stop locating nearby the shopping and entertaining center (St_224, code Attr_18, Fig. 2).

Comments to Fig. 9. The intensiveness of passengers' flow is slowly increasing without apparent peaks up to 18:00 and then is slowly falling remaining noticeable even after completion of the transport working day (21:00) since the shopping and entertaining centers are closing after this moment.

Figure 10 illustrates the pattern 7: the most popular stops of destination chosen by the passengers at the stop of departure, which is the element of the list of the most attractive stops (the stop type is shopping and entertaining center).

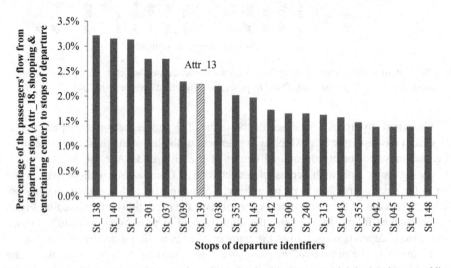

Fig. 10. Pattern 7: Passengers' hourly flow from the departure stop, which is the element of list of the most attractive stops (St_224 Distr_2, shopping and entertaining center, Attr_18)

Comments to Fig. 10. This diagram shows the 40% part of the summary passengers' flow from the departure stop which is the element of the list of the most attractive stops (St_224, i.e. the shopping and entertaining center, code Attr_18, Fig. 2) to the remaining stops with high scores of attractiveness. Comparably with shown on the Fig. 8 the passengers' flow is less uniform because the inter-district flows possess less intensiveness. The unique stop from the most attractive stops list is the stop locating nearby another shopping and entertaining center within the same district as the departure stop (Distr_2 St_119, Attr_13, shown with hatched filling at the Fig. 10). In this case, the passengers' flow intensiveness depends mainly from the citizens number returning to their living zones from the shopping and entertaining center located in the same district as the living zones ones.

7 Conclusion

The account of the megalopolis specific features allowed detecting of the patterns in routes choice in the general problem of simulation of the passengers' flow of the urban social transport system. The patterns detection is based on the decoupling of the general model between the sub-models according to the different levels of uncertainty of passengers intentions in route choice, and on the following joining of the computational results received for the sub-models.

We hope to continue our investigation. One of the promising areas of work may be the design of the inexpensive and simple online passengers' flow tracking system. For such system the tracking of the transport behavior of each passenger (i.e. his entering into the transport device and exiting from it at every stop) perhaps may be replaced by the tracking only at the single typical stop of each pattern with the possibility of the approximate estimate of the passengers' flow at the remaining stops.

The main results of the presented work are the following:

1. We have proposed the assumptions allowing detecting of the hidden patterns in the route choices preferences of the urban transport system passengers.
2. The simulation algorithms of passengers flow to the stops with high attractiveness were carried out and justified by means of comparison with the statistical data of the transport system operation.
3. The feasibility of the approach was illustrated by the examples of typical patterns in the destination stops choice and in hourly passengers' flow from the departure stops.

References

1. Krushel, E.G., Stepanchenko, I.V., Panfilov, A.E., Berisheva, E.D.: An experience of optimization approach application to improve the urban passenger transport structure. In: Kravets, A., Shcherbakov, M., Kultsova, M., Iijima, T. (eds.) JCKBSE 2014. CCIS, vol. 466, pp. 27–39. Springer, Cham (2014). https://doi.org/10.1007/978-3-319-11854-3_3
2. Krushel, E.G., Stepanchenko, I.V., Panfilov, A.E., Haritonov, I.M., Berisheva, E.D.: Forecasting model of small city depopulation processes and possibilities of their prevention. In: Kravets, A., Shcherbakov, M., Kultsova, M., Iijima, T. (eds.) JCKBSE 2014. CCIS, vol. 466, pp. 446–456. Springer, Cham (2014). https://doi.org/10.1007/978-3-319-11854-3_38
3. Horn, M.: An extended model and procedural framework for planning multi-modal passenger journeys. Transp. Res. Part B Methodol. 37, 641–660 (2003)
4. Krushel, E.G., Stepanchenko, I.V., Panfilov, A.E.: The passengers' turnout simulation for the urban transport system control decision-making process. In: Kravets, A., Shcherbakov, M., Kultsova, M., Groumpos, P. (eds.) CIT&DS 2017. CCIS, vol. 754, pp. 389–398. Springer, Cham (2017). https://doi.org/10.1007/978-3-319-65551-2_28
5. Li, D., Yuan, J., Yan, K., Chen, L.: Monte Carlo simulation on effectiveness of forecast system for passengers up and down buses. In: 3RD International Symposium on Intelligent Information Technology Application, Nanchang, pp. 359–361 (2009)

6. Schelenz, T., Suescun, A., Wikstrom, L., Karlsson, M.: Passenger-centered design of future buses using agent-based simulation. In: Conference on Transport Research Arena, Athens, vol. 48, pp. 1662–1671 (2012)
7. Bure, V.M., Mazalov, V.V., Plaksina, N.V.: Estimating passenger traffic characteristics in transport systems. Autom. Remote Control **76**, 1673–1680 (2015)
8. Li, W., Zhu, W.: A dynamic simulation model of passenger flow distribution on schedule-based rail transit networks with train delays. J. Traffic Transp. Eng. (English Edition) **3**(4), 364–373 (2016)
9. Chen, C., Ma, J., Susilo, Y., Liu, Y., Wang, M.: The promises of big data and small data for travel behavior (aka human mobility) analysis. Transp. Res. Part C Emerg. Technol. **68**, 285–299 (2016)
10. Dijk, J.: Identifying activity-travel points from GPS-data with multiple moving windows. Comput. Environ. Urban Syst. **70**, 84–101 (2018)
11. Bai, Y., Sun, Z., Zeng, B., Deng, J., Li, C.: A multi-pattern deep fusion model for short-term bus passenger flow forecasting. Appl. Soft Comput. **58**, 669–680 (2017)
12. Dieleman, F.M., Dijst, M., Burghouwt, G.: Urban form and travel behaviour: micro-level household attributes and residential context. Urban Stud. **39**, 507–527 (2002)
13. Kim, J., Corcoran, J., Papamanolis, M.: Route choice stickiness of public transport passengers: measuring habitual bus ridership behaviour using smart card data. Transp. Res. Part C Emerg. Technol. **83**, 146–164 (2017)
14. Tao, S., Corcoran, J., Mateo-Babiano, I., Rohde, D.: Exploring bus rapid transit passenger travel behaviour using big data. Appl. Geogr. **53**, 90–104 (2014)
15. Gonzalez, M.C., Hidalgo, C.A., Barabasi, A.-L.: Understanding individual human mobility patterns. Nature **453**(5), 779–782 (2008)
16. Maghraoui, O.A., Vallet, F., Puchinger, J., Bernard, Y.: Modeling traveler experience for designing urban mobility systems. Des. Sci. **5**, E7 (2019)
17. Calabrese, F., Diao, M., Lorenzo, G.D., Ferreira Jr., J., Ratti, C.: Understanding individual mobility patterns from urban sensing data: a mobile phone trace example. Transp. Res. Part C **26**, 301–313 (2013)
18. Gärling, T., Axhausen, K.W.: Introduction: habitual travel choice. Transportation **30**, 1–11 (2003)
19. Mühlenbein, H., Zinchenko, L., Kureichik, V., Mahnig, T.: Effective mutation rate for probabilistic evolutionary design of analogue electrical circuits. Appl. Soft Comput. **7**(3), 1012–1018 (2007)

Analysis a Short-Term Time Series of Crop Sales Based on Machine Learning Methods

Mohammed A. Al-Gunaid$^{(\boxtimes)}$, Maxim V. Shcherbakov, Vladislav N. Trubitsin,
Alexandr M. Shumkin, and Kirill Y. Dereguzov

Volgograd State Technical University, Volgograd, Russian Federation
`bilab@vstu.ru`

Abstract. The main goal of this article is to solve the problem associated with identifying sales seasons in time series in order to build the most accurate forecast of sales of various crops and provide decision support and improve the efficiency of business processes of agro-industrial companies. In this regard, the necessity of developing an algorithm that allows to form a time series of sales in accordance with the seasons available in it to improve the accuracy of existing sales forecasting methods is justified. This study provides a detailed description of the problem and its solutions in the form of an algorithm, as well as a comparison of the accuracy of building prediction models before and after its application, which confirms the consistency of the developed method for the formation of time series.

Keywords: Forecasting · Agroindustrial complex · Sales volume · Machine learning

1 Introduction

The agro-industrial complex (AIC) unites branches of the economy involved in the production of agricultural products, their processing and bringing to the consumer. The value of the agro-industrial complex is to provide the country with food and some other consumer goods.

The agro-industrial complex of developed countries is large commodity farms (plantations, farms, etc.) using modern means of production at all stages of economic activity - from the field to storage, processing and packaging of ready-to-use products.

The intensity of agricultural farms in developed countries is determined by significant investments per unit area (in Japan, Belgium, the Netherlands - up to $ 10,000/ha), as well as the extensive use of science and technology [1].

Processes that take place within agribusiness companies produce and operate with large amounts of data: fuel and lubricants costs, procurement costs, field work, sales revenue, and many others. These data can be used for analysis and

© Springer Nature Switzerland AG 2019
A. G. Kravets et al. (Eds.): CIT&DS 2019, CCIS 1083, pp. 189–200, 2019.
https://doi.org/10.1007/978-3-030-29743-5_15

forecasting, thereby allowing you to support decision-making and improve the efficiency of business processes of agro-industrial companies, reduce costs for materials and field work, and minimize the risk of bankruptcy.

Monitoring agricultural production and crop assessment, which can be expected for staple food crops, are essential for balancing trade, correct and stable pricing, and defining a long-term food policy.

With population growth and the negative impact of climate change on world crop production, crop monitoring and yield assessment become important not only for the scientific, but also for the political sphere. If, for example, a deviation from the expected yield is detected at an early stage, this information can be used to adapt strategic and tactical plans for its recovery.

An important feature of agricultural production is seasonality, which leads to an uneven use of labor during the year, makes agriculture dependent on the natural conditions of production, causes uneven flow of products and cash income throughout the year.

This study is aimed at solving the challenge associated with identifying sales seasons in time series to build the most accurate sales forecast for different crops. The study further provides a detailed description of the challenge and its possible solution in the form of an algorithm, as well as a comparison of the accuracy of building prediction models before and after its application.

2   Related Work

One of the main areas of research in the agro-industrial complex is the analysis and forecasting of crop yields and the number of sales of finished products.

Developing and improving methods for predicting crop yields and crop sales in different climates can help stakeholders make important decisions in terms of agronomy and crop selection.

Yield, price and sales data are time series. The time series is a set of observations x_t, each of which is recorded at a specified time t. Next to a discrete time is a set in which the set T_0 of the time at which observations are made is discrete, such as, for example, the case when observations are made at fixed time intervals. Continuous time series are obtained when observations are recorded continuously for a certain time interval, for example, when $T = [0,1]$. For the analysis and forecasting of time series, methods and models of machine learning are used.

Common models for analyzing time series: autoregression (AR) models, integrated (I) models and moving average models (MA). These three classes are linearly dependent on previous data points. Combinations of these ideas provide autoregressive moving average (ARMA) and autoregressive integrated moving average (ARIMA) models [2]. Existing examples and possibilities of applying these methods will be discussed below.

The authors [3] give a comparison of machine learning methods (decision trees, random forest, Bayesian network and naive Bayes classifier, etc.), in relation to forecasting weather conditions for various purposes. As a result of the surveys, among the most accurate methods, the authors indicate neural networks, decision trees, random forest, and fuzzy modeling methods.

In work [4], various data analysis methods are used to predict climate by season, and the forecast results are aggregated with data on the cultivated crop and applied cultivation technologies, which allows you to support decision making on field work by calculating the duration of the various phases of crop development.

For the prediction of NDVI (Normalized difference vegetation index) indicators, linear and quadratic regression methods are used, as well as neural networks [5]. The results obtained as a result of the forecast allow you to track temporary changes in the landscape and vegetation, allowing you to more effectively plan the area of crops.

Time series are also used to predict crop yields [6]. To build models, simple exponential smoothing, double exponential smoothing and linear smoothing are used. However, the authors of the article do not consider the influence of such factors as weather (temperature, precipitation), land management (division into areas), the influence of pests and diseases affecting crop yields.

Based on advances in spectral imaging, the authors [7] consider the potential of artificial neural networks from the point of view of seasonal yield forecasting, modeling and evaluating various soil parameters, while the models built have a high prediction accuracy, but also do not take into account the influence of weather conditions and other factors that affect crop yields.

To obtain a more accurate forecast, it is necessary to study the features and identify the main factors influencing sales volumes in the studied area [8].

At the moment there are a large number of methods for constructing a prognostic model. Many of them are based on fuzzy modeling [9].

Existing studies in this area identify several of the most effective and accurate methods used for analyzing time series: linear regression method (linear regression, LR), random forest method (random forest, RF), building a time series forecast using a neural network (neural network, NN) and Naive Bayes Algorithms [10–12, 17–19].

The article [13] describes the following tasks: minimizing the impact on the environment with a simultaneous increase in production and productivity. The authors selected five different applications illustrating the following: assessment of biomass and yield, monitoring of vegetation and drought tolerance, assessment of the phenological development of the crop, assessment of acreage, and mapping of arable land. The article [13] begins with an overview of the main challenges of agriculture, followed by a brief overview of existing operational monitoring systems. The described applications have their advantages, but they have one common drawback - they are different systems, there is no interaction between them, which leads to a decrease in overall efficiency.

The creation of monitoring systems is one of the most popular areas in the agro-industrial complex. The authors of [14] give an example of designing a system for collecting and processing data from IoT devices. The result is a high-performance system based on an event-oriented architecture, which performs the functions of a data collection and analysis system, decision support and control of IoT devices. To build a network of IoT devices, the ZigBee protocol is used. Event-oriented architecture offers the advantage of flexible scaling of system performance and increased fault tolerance. "Raw" data obtained from IoT devices is stored in a NoSQL solution from Amazon DynamoDB, which are subsequently processed using Amazon Elastic MapReduce and transferred to a relational database (Oracle). This article describes the general principle of operation of the developed system, but does not describe its architecture.

Based on the analysis of the current state of research in this area, it can be concluded that it is necessary to develop and improve methods for constructing models for predicting crop yields, sales and prices for agricultural products in order to increase the efficiency of management in the agro-industrial sector.

3   Problem Statement

The study [15] describes a method for analyzing the time series of sales of sowing crops, based on such machine learning methods as the linear regression method, random forests and the neural network. This method uses as a training set a data set containing gaps and zero values, which can lead to a deterioration in the adequacy of the construction of mathematical models and a decrease in the accuracy of forecasts.

Sales of finished products of each of the sowing crops often have a seasonal nature: sales periods can be repeated for several years in a row. By identifying such seasons in the original training set, you can reduce the amount of noise and anomalies in it.

As can be seen, the predictions constructed by the method described in article [15] have low accuracy. The reason for this may be a small amount of the training sample, as well as a large number of gaps in the data (zero sales and prices during periods when culture sales are not made). Thus, it is possible to formulate the hypothesis that if we identify the seasons in the time series of sales and use only the data of the identified seasons to train mathematical models, we can improve the accuracy of the sales forecasts that are being formed.

This study is aimed at solving the challenge associated with the processing and analysis of short-term time series of sales of sowing crops, namely with the identification of seasons, detection and filtering of anomalies in them to build the most accurate predictions of sales of sown crops.

The time series of sales of crops is a sequence of records, each of which contains the following information:

- date
- cost per kilogram of sunflower (Cost)
- number of centners of sunflower received per hectare (yield, Crop)
- data on the average monthly temperature (Temp)
- the amount of precipitation (Rain), as well as the amount of revenue received from the sale in a given month (Revenue).

The cost of one kilogram is expressed in Russian rubles, the yield is in the number of quintals per hectare and is a constant value for one year. Average monthly temperature and precipitation are measured in degrees Celsius and millimeters, respectively.

In some periods of time (months) sales are not made, respectively, the values of the number of sales and the cost of one kilogram of the product can be 0 rubles.

Applied to this study, the sales season may be a sequence of consecutive records with non-zero sales values, repeated over several years.

In this case, anomalies can be elements of the time series with zero values of culture sales, as well as records with non-zero values that do not have repetitions in the rest of the sample.

Thus, to solve the challenge of identifying the seasons and filtering anomalies, it is necessary to develop and implement criteria and algorithms for their determination.

As mentioned above, the sales season can be considered a periodically repeating sequence of consecutive records (one or more) with non-zero sales values.

The period in this case will be the number of years between repetitions of the season.

The formation of sales seasons is largely influenced by the organizational measures of agricultural enterprises (sowing, harvesting, etc.).

As indicated in [15], the number of sales of sown crops is largely influenced by such factors as price (Cost), yield (Crop), and weather conditions at the place of cultivation - temperature and rainfall (Temp and Rain, respectively). These factors can also influence the seasons and their frequency.

4   Algorithm to Identify Seasons and Anomalies

To identify the seasons in the original sample, you can use the algorithm shown in Fig. 1.

For convenience, the whole algorithm was divided into two stages. The first stage consists in forming a sequence of records with non-zero sales values; the input of the algorithm at the first stage is a list of records; the output returns a list of sequences of records with non-zero sales values. The resulting list is transmitted to the input of the second stage of the algorithm.

The second stage is the formation of sales seasons. The input of this stage is a list of sequences of records with non-zero sales values obtained in the first stage, the output returns the generated list of seasons consisting of repeating sequences.

Algorithm 1: Algorithm for the formation of a seasonal time series

---

1 <u>function GetSeasonalTimeSeries</u> (*Input*);

Input : Item - record of the training sample (date, sales, precipitation, temperature, price, yield);

Input - training set (list Item);

Sequence - sequence (a list of consecutive Item, with non-zero sales values);

Sequences - list of Sequence;

Season - list of repeating Sequence

Output: Seasons - list of Season

2 Sequence = new Sequence();

3 **for** *each Item in Input* **do**

4   **if** *Item.Sales = 0* **then**

5   **if** *Sequence.Length != 0* **then**

6 | Sequences.Add(Sequence);

7   **end**

8   Sequence = new Sequence();

9   **else**

10 | Sequence.Add(Item);

11   **end**

12 **end**

13 Sort Sequences by Month;;

14 Season = new Season();;

15 **for** *each Sequence in Sequences* **do**

16   **if** *Season.Length != 0* **then**

17   **if** *Sequence[0].Month >= Sequence[Sequence.Length-1].Month* **then**

18 | Seasons.Add(Season); Season = new Season();

19   **end**

20   Season.Add(Sequence);

21   **end**

22 **end**

23 **return** Seasons;

Fig. 1. Algorithm of the method

From the list of seasons obtained at the output of the algorithm, it is necessary to form a training sample by arranging records from the obtained groups in ascending order. A fragment of the sample is presented in Table 1. As you can see, the algorithm selected one season: from September to April of each year, there are no rows with data for other months in this table, as they were eliminated by the algorithm.

Table 1. Sample fragment

Date	Revenue	Crop	Temp	Rain	Cost
01.02.2013	10 035 626, 00	20,2	−3,0	13	14,96
01.03.2013	6 051 600,00	20,2	0,3	35	15,60
01.04.2013	900 000,00	20,2	10,3	41	15,00
01.09.2013	168 198,00	20,2	13,7	39	9,70
01.10.2013	2 173 372,00	20,2	7,7	44	9,50
01.11.2013	5 562 870,00	20,2	4,3	16	9,00
01.12.2013	5 112 474,00	20,2	−3,3	45	9,86
01.01.2014	1 154 840,00	15,5	−8,2	32	9,26
01.02.2014	6 744 680,00	15,5	−6,6	23	9,80
01.03.2014	0	15,5	0,8	40	0
01.04.2014	1 126 740	15,5	8,6	15	12,66
01.09.2014	463 080,00	15,5	15,7	12	12,00
01.10.2014	4 500 000,00	15,5	5,4	12	20,00
01.11.2014	1 416 933,00	15,5	−2,5	9	12,56
01.12.2014	10 800 000,00	15,5	−3,7	30	18,00
01.01.2015	0,00	17,6	−7,3	12	0,00
01.02.2015	9 000 000,00	17,6	−4,0	22	21,99
01.03.2015	5 104 815,00	17,6	1,3	34	21,69
01.04.2015	0,00	17,6	9,3	32	0,00

5   Experiment

For the experiment, 4 data sets were formed: a sample containing data on sales of sunflower, a sample containing data on the sale of winter wheat, as well as samples obtained as a result of the operation of the described algorithm for identifying the seasons.

Experiments consist in using the random forest method, the application of which is described in [15].

The main structural element of a random forest is a decision tree, on the construction of which the quality of work and the stability of the final model depend. Consider a sample of objects

$$\{(x_i, y_i)\}_{i=1}^N \tag{1}$$

where $x_i \in R^2$ is the feature description of the object in two-dimensional space, and $y_i \in \{0.1\}$ is the class label. In the process of classification, it is necessary to select the attribute and values of the threshold, according to which the optimal splitting according to a given criterion takes place. In solving applied challenges, the following criteria are often used:

– for classification tasks $iGain$:

$$iGain(S) = H(S) - \sum_{v \in \{L,R\}} \frac{|S_v|}{|S|} H(S_v) \qquad (2)$$

$$H(S) = -\sum_{c \in C} p_c \log_2(p_c) \qquad (3)$$

where S is the set of classes of the challenge under consideration, and p_c is the probability of class c for a set of S objects;
– for regression challenges, the same iGain criterion using variances:

$$iGain(S) = |S|Var(S) - \sum_{v \in L,R} |S_v|var(S_v) \qquad (4)$$

where $Var(S)$ is the variance of the responses of objects from the set S. With each division, all objects are divided into two smaller groups, i.e. The challenge considered in each of the nodes is divided into two smaller subtasks. By specifying the maximum number of objects in the top-list of the tree, one of the possible stopping criteria for the algorithm is established. Thus, it is possible to sufficiently classify the considered sample of objects with just one decision tree, if you give the number of the class most often found in this cell A_i as an answer for a test object that falls into a cell [16].

For the experiment, mathematical models were trained using random forest on each of the 4 data sets described above, with 85% of each sample used for model training and 15% for testing.

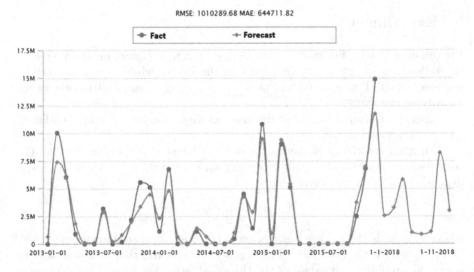

Fig. 2. The result of building a model for a full sample of sales of sunflower

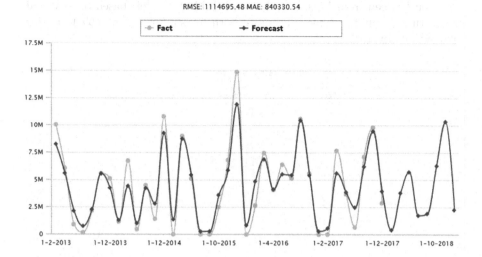

Fig. 3. Result of building a model for seasonal sampling of sunflower sales

RMSE and MAE metrics are used to assess the accuracy of model building.

The results of building a model of sales of sunflower for a full sample and a sample formed according to the identified seasons are shown in Figs. 2 and 3, respectively.

The results of building a model of winter wheat sales for a full sample and a sample formed according to the identified seasons are shown in Figs. 4 and 5, respectively.

6   Discussion of Results

The results of the calculations of the RMSE and MAE metrics for the experiments performed are shown in Table 2.

To compare the quality of the forecast for each model, we compare the accuracy estimates and the operating time of each method.

Table 2. The results of the construction of models of sales

	Sunflower		Winter wheat	
	Experiment 1	Experiment 2	Experiment 1	Experiment 2
RMSE	1114695,48	1010289,68	4625063,02	3891629,89
MAE	840330,54	644711,82	2444650,22	2212011.91

As can be seen from Figs. 2, 3, 4, 5 and Table 2, models based on seasonal samples turned out to be more accurate both for sunflower (by 9.5%) and for winter wheat (by 15%).

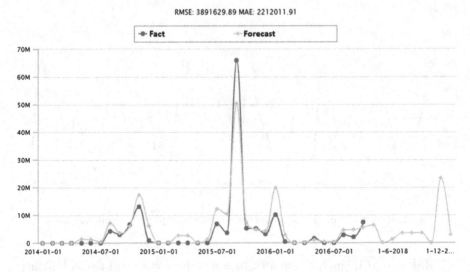

Fig. 4. The result of building a model for a full sample of sales of winter wheat

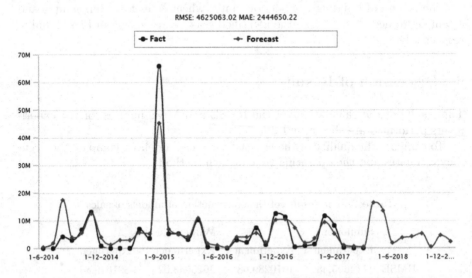

Fig. 5. The result of building a model for a seasonal sample of sales of winter wheat

Thus, the hypothesis formulated in the paper that if you identify seasons in a time series of sales and use only the data of identified seasons to train mathematical models, you can improve the accuracy of sales forecasts by reducing the number of gaps and anomalies in the time series data.

The indicators obtained in these experiments show that when forecasting sales of crops, it is necessary to take into account the seasonality of this phenomenon to improve the accuracy of forecasts, and the developed algorithm is a suitable tool for identifying seasons in time series.

7   Conclusion

This paper describes the challenge of identifying the seasons in the time series of growing sowing crops. In the course of the work, a time series analysis algorithm was developed, allowing it to be converted based on the identified sales seasons.

The time series obtained as a result of the work of the developed algorithm were used to build mathematical models. As a result of comparing models based on the original time series and models based on the transformed series, it was found that the applied analysis methods described in [15] have greater accuracy when used as a training set of time series converted according to seasons detection algorithm.

In the future, the developed method can be improved, including through the use of fuzzy cognitive maps [20] for the analysis of the described time series.

Acknowledgement. The reported study was supported by RFBR research projects (19-47-340010/19).

References

1. Sedova, N.A.: A course of lectures for undergraduates in the discipline "Civil and legal problems in the field of agriculture". Krasnodar, KubGAU (2016)
2. Brockwell, P.J., Davis, R.A.: Time Series: Theory and Methods. Springer Series in Statistics. Springer, New York (1991)
3. Kumar, R.S., Ramesh, C.: A study on prediction of rainfall using datamining technique. In: International Conference on Inventive Computation Technologies (ICICT), Satyabama University Chennai (2016)
4. Han, E., Ines, A.V.M., Baethgen, W.E.: Climate-agriculture-modeling and decision tool: a software framework for climate risk management in agriculture. Environ. Model. Softw. **95**, 102–114 (2017)
5. Xingwang, F., Liu, Y.: A comparison of NDVI intercalibration methods. Int. J. Remote Sens. **38**, 5273–5290 (2017)
6. Choudhury, A., Jones, J.: Crop yield prediction using time series models. J. Econ. Econ. Educ. Res. **15**(3), 53–68 (2014)
7. Uno, Y., Prasher, S.O., Lacroix, R., Goel, P.K., Karimi, Y., Viau, A., Patel, R.M.: Artificial neural networks to predict corn yield from compact airborne spectographic imager data. Comput. Electron. Agric. **47**, 149–161 (2005)
8. Gandhi, N., Armstrong, L.J., Petkar, O.: Predicting rice crop yield using Bayesian networks. In: 2016 International Conference on Advances in Computing, Communications and Informatics (ICACCI) (2016)

9. Natarajan, R., Subramanian, J., Papageorgiou, E.I.: Hybrid learning of fuzzy cognitive maps for sugarcane yield classification. Comput. Electron. Agric. **127**, 147–157 (2016)
10. Al-Gunaid, M.A., Shcherbakov, M.V., Kamaev, V.A., Gerget, O.M., Tyukov, A.P.: Decision trees based fuzzy rules. In: Information Technologies in Science, Management, Social Sphere and Medicine (ITSMSSM 2016), vol. 51, pp. 502–508 (2016)
11. Al-Gunaid, M.A.: Neuro-fuzzy model short term forecasting of energy consumption. Prikaspijskij Zhurnal Upr. I Vysok. Tehnol. **2**, 47–56 (2013)
12. Al-Gunaid, M.A., et al.: Analysis of drug sales data based on machine learning methods. In: Dwivedi, R.K. (ed.) Proceedings of 7th International Conference on System Modeling & Advancement in Research Trends (SMART–2018, IEEE Conference ID: 44078) (23rd–24th November, 2018). College of Computing Sciences & Information Technology, Teerthanker Mahaveer University (Moradabad, UP, India), IEEE UP Section, New Delhi, pp. 32–38 (2018)
13. Atzberger, C.: Advances in remote sensing of agriculture: context description, existing operational monitoring systems and major information needs. Institute for Surveying, Remote Sensing & Land Information (IVFL), University of Natural Resources and Life Sciences, Vienna, Austria (2013)
14. Jinbo, C., Xiangliang, C., Han-Chi, F., Lam, A.: Agricultural product monitoring system supported by cloud computing. Cluster Comput. (2018)
15. Al-Gunaid, M.A., Shcherbakov, M.V., Trubitsin, V.N., Shumkin, A.M.: Time Series Analysis Sales of Sowing Crops Based on Machine Learning Methods. Volgograd State Technical University (2018)
16. Ryzhkov, A.M.: Compositions of Algorithms Based on a Random Forest. MSU, Moscow (2015)
17. Al-Gunaid, M.A., Shcherbakov, M.V., Zadiran, K.S., Melikov, A.V.: A survey of fuzzy cognitive maps forecasting methods. In: 2017 8th International Conference on Information, Intelligence, Systems & Applications (IISA), Larnaca, Cyprus, 27–30 August 2017, Electrical and Electronic Engineers (IEEE), Biological and Artificial Intelligence Foundation (BAIF), University of Piraeus, University of Cyprus, pp. 1–6. IEEE (2017). https://doi.org/10.1109/IISA.2017.8316443. Accessed 15 Mar 2018
18. Al-Gunaid, M.A., Shcherbakov, M.V., Skorobogatchenko, D.A., Kravets, A.G., Kamaev, V.A.: Forecasting energy consumption with the data reliability estimation in the management of hybrid energy system using fuzzy decision trees. In: 7th International Conference on Information, Intelligence, Systems & Applications (IISA), Greece, 13–15 July 2016. Institute of Electrical and Electronics Engineers (IEEE). IEEE (2016). http://ieeexplore.ieee.org/xpl/mostRecentIssue.jsp?punumber=7774711. https://doi.org/10.1109/IISA.2016.7785413
19. Kravets, A.G., Al-Gunaid, M.A., Loshmanov, V.I., Rasulov, S.S., Lempert, L.B.: Model of medicines sales forecasting taking into account factors of influence. In: Journal of Physics: Conference Series 2018, vol. 1015, 8 p. http://iopscience.iop.org/article/10.1088/1742-6596/1015/3/032073/pdf
20. Kosko, B.: Fuzzy cognitive maps. Int. J. Man Mach. Stud. **24**, 65–75 (1986)

A Multifactor Small Business Management Model

Andrey N. Vazhdaev[1(✉)] and Artur A. Mitsel[1,2(✉)]

[1] Department of Digital Technology, Yurga Institute of Technology National
Research, TPU Affiliate, Yurga, Russia
vazhdaev@tpu.ru, maa@asu.tusur.ru
[2] Tomsk State University of Control Systems and Radioelectronics,
Tomsk, Russia

Abstract. The previously existing system of industrial development USSR was aimed at the construction of industries and the arrangement of cities around them. Such cities, which have one or several city-forming enterprises, are called "monotowns". A monotown is a complex structure in which the town and the city-forming enterprises are closely related. The constructed multifactor dynamic model in the article allows to organize the process of managing a small business by influencing all of its microindicators using the monotown's mesoindicators. This approach lets the municipality at every moment influencing indicators of small business with its socio-economic indicators, contribute to the sustainable development of the urban economy.

Keywords: Multifactor dynamic model · Small business · Monotown ·
Microindicator · Mesoindicator

1 Introduction

The previously existing system of industrial development was aimed at the construction of industries and the arrangement of cities around them [1, 2]. Such cities, which have one or several city-forming enterprises, are called "monotowns" [3]. A monotown is a complex structure in which the town and the city-forming enterprises are closely related [4]. At the same time, these enterprises carry not only an economic, but also a social load, thus predominantly creating the conditions for providing public vital activity in the town [4, 5].

Management difficulties, external economic conditions, falling demand and other factors have created economic problems in the city-forming enterprises and problems in monotowns themselves [4, 6]. If the world experience is to be relied on [2, 7–9], then the development of urban small businesses (SB) is one of the few ways to lead the Russian monotowns out of crisis. Small businesses are characterized by the capacity to simultaneously solve both economic and social tasks, a role that city-forming enterprises used to play. At the same time, the monotown, developing its small business, diversifies its economic activity and ensures its own stability when following the strategic course of development.

© Springer Nature Switzerland AG 2019
A. G. Kravets et al. (Eds.): CIT&DS 2019, CCIS 1083, pp. 201–217, 2019.
https://doi.org/10.1007/978-3-030-29743-5_16

2   Background

Yurga (Kemerovo region) has been selected as a monotown for the research. Two sources on the 2007–2016 period were taken as a resource for the economic parameter data of Yurga: annual reports of the Yurga city-manager on the socio-economical city development from the official city website and the website part of the Russian Federal State Statistics Service. This sources contain a many amount of data. Therefore, to conduct research it was necessary to take only those parameters that have the greatest direct impact on the development of small businesses in the monotown and reflect the city economic and social development at most.

To build a multifactor model, the authors in their early work [10] identified factors that have a significant impact on the urban small businesses.

Table 1 shows mesoindicators selected for the study (indicators that are significant for the future multifactor model at the level of the municipality).

Table 1. Mesoindicators of the monotown.

Sequence number	Mesoindicator description	Mesoindicator index
1.	Unified tax on imputed income (UTII) for certain types of activities, thousand rubles	*UTII*
2.	Number of individual entrepreneurs (IE), pcs	*NIE*
3.	Number of small enterprises (SE), pcs	*NSE*
4.	Personal income tax (PIT), thousand rubles	*PIT*
5.	Taxes on total income, thousand rubles	*TTI*
6.	Average monthly nominal income per capita, rubles	*AMNI*
7.	Population, people	*Pl*
8.	Number of large and medium-sized enterprises (LME), pcs	*NLME*

Microindicators of small businesses were taken from the regulated reports: "Balance Sheet Report" (total values from each of 5 sections) and "Report on Financial Results" ("Revenue" indicator). Table 2 shows the microindicators of SB.

Table 2. Microindicators of small businesses.

#	Microindicator description	Microindicator index
1.	The average annual revenue value of small businesses	*Rev*
2.	The ratio of the sum of all the "Total for Section I (Fixed Assets)" indicator values from among the enterprises studied to their total value of the indicator "Balance"	*FAB*
3.	The ratio of the sum of all the "Total for Section II (Current Assets)" indicator values from among the enterprises studied to their total value of the indicator "Balance"	*CAB*

(continued)

Table 2. (*continued*)

#	Microindicator description	Microindicator index
4.	The ratio of the sum of all the "Total for Section III (Capital and Reserves)" indicator values from among the enterprises studied to their total value of the indicator "Balance"	CRB
5.	The ratio of the sum of all the "Total for Section IV (Long-term Liabilities)" indicator values from among the enterprises studied to their total value of the indicator "Balance"	LLB
6.	The ratio of the sum of all the "Total for Section V (Short-term liabilities)" indicator values from among the enterprises studied to their total value of the indicator "Balance"	SLB

3 Methodology

Let's assume that we have selected n mesoindicators of a town that have a significant correlation with six aggregated microindicators of small businesses [10].

Let the values of the aggregated microindicators go beyond the permissible limits. In such a situation, the city administration wants to have a controlled impact on microindicators in order to avoid negative consequences in the functioning of small businesses in the city. If there is a significant correlation relationship between the mesioindicators of the town and the microindicators of its small businesses, a logical question arises: can the town change its mesoindicators in such a way that will enable alterations in the aggregated microindicators of small businesses in the planned form? Also, it is necessary to take into account the important fact of the existence of feedback between the mesoindicators and microindicators: the town plans to influence the microindicators of small businesses by changing its mesoindicators; and microindicators, in turn, affect the urban mesoindicators. When answering these questions, we logically come to the need to create a dynamic model for managing a set of microindicators of small businesses through the controlled change of the monotown's mesoindicators.

Let's take $x_i(t)$, $i = 1,\ldots,n$ for the mesoindicators of the town at the moment of time t, $t = 0,\ldots,T-1$, where T is the planned time for the small business recovering from a crisis; $x_i^0(t)$ – the planned values of the mesoindicators corresponding to the sustainable functioning of small businesses; $V_j(t)$ – the j mesoindicator $j = 1,\ldots,p$; $V_j^0(t)$ – the planned value of the j microindicator corresponding to the sustainable functioning of businesses.

The relationship of microindicators with mesoindicators of the town is represented in the form of a multiple regression:

$$V_j(t) = a_{0j} + \sum_{i=0}^{n} a_{ij}x_i(t), \qquad (1)$$

where a_{ij} – regression coefficients.

The dependency of the planned values of microindicators is set in the following form:

$$V_j^0(t+1) = \left(1 + \mu_j^0(t)\right) V_j^0(t), \tag{2}$$

where $\mu_j^0(t)$ – the desired growth rate of the j indicator. The dependence of $x_i(t)$ on time is presented in the form of:

$$x_i(t+1) = [1 + \mu_i(t)](x_i(t) + y_i(t)), \quad i = 1, \ldots, n, t = 0, \ldots, T-1$$

Then the dependency of $V_j(t)$ on time will be:

$$V_j(t+1) - a_{oj} = \sum_{i=1}^{n} (1 + \mu_i(t)) v_{ij}(t) + \sum_{i=1}^{n} (1 + \mu_i(t)) u_{ij}(t), \tag{3}$$

where $\mu_i(t)$ – the growth rate of the i mesoindicator that has an impact on the j microindicator of SB.

Let's take into account the following fact. All microindicators V_j are associated with the regression dependency with the same mesioindicators $x_i(t)$, $i = 1, \ldots, n$. Therefore, from now we consider only v_1 and u_1 as variables.

Let's introduce a composite vector:

$$z_1(t) = \begin{pmatrix} v_1(t) \\ V_1^0(t) \end{pmatrix}.$$

In this case, the vectors $z_j(t)$ will be:

$$z_j(t) = An_j(t) \cdot z_1(t), \, j = 1, \ldots, p. \tag{4}$$

Define the dependency of the $z_j(t)$ vector as:

$$z_j(t+1) = A_j(t) \cdot An_j(t) \cdot z_1(t) + B_j(t) \cdot Ar_j \cdot Ar_1^{-1} \cdot u_1(t), \\ j = 1, \ldots, p; \, t = 0, \ldots, T-1. \tag{5}$$

Here, the matrices $Ar_j = diag(a_{1j} \quad \ldots \quad a_{nj})$, $j = 1, \ldots p; a_{ij}$, $i = 1, \ldots, n$ are the regression coefficients (1);

$$An_j = diag(a_{1j}/a_{11} \quad \ldots \quad a_{nj}/a_{n1} \quad a_{nj}/a_{n1}), \, j = 1, \ldots p;$$

$$A_j(t) = diag\left((1 + \mu_1(t)), \ldots, (1 + \mu_n(t)); \, 1 + \mu_j^0(t)\right).$$

$$B_j(t) = \begin{pmatrix} (1+\mu_1(t)) & \cdots & 0 \\ \cdots & \cdots & \cdots \\ 0 & \cdots & (1+\mu_n(t)) \\ 0 & \cdots & 0 \end{pmatrix}.$$

Let's take the quadratic functional as the objective function:

$$J = \sum_{t=0}^{T-1} \left[\sum_{j=1}^{p} \left(V_j(t) - V_j^0(t) \right)^2 + \sum_{j=1}^{p} (u_j(t))^T R_j(t)(u_j(t)) \right]$$
$$+ \sum_{j=1}^{p} \left(V_j(T) - V_j^0(T) \right)^2, \tag{6}$$

which characterizes the quality of the process for tracking the planned microindicators. Here $R_j(t)$ – the matrix of the weighting coefficients of the corresponding dimension that takes into account the contribution of the control actions (changes in mesoindicators) on the j indicator of small businesses. By minimizing this functional, we will thereby ensure the operation of small businesses at the planned mode.

Let's introduce the vectors $z_j(t)$ to (6). The value $\left(V_j(t) - V_j^0(t) \right)$ equals $\left(V_j(t) - V_j^0(t) \right) = a_{0j} + c z_j(t)$, where $c = (1, 1, \ldots, 1, -1) \in R^{n+1}$. In view of (4) the quality criterion J will take the form:

In view of the formula (4) the functional (6) will take the form:

$$J = \sum_{t=0}^{T-1} \left(z_1^T(t) A s(t) z_1(t) \right) + 2 \sum_{t=0}^{T-1} \left(A s4(t) z_1(t) \right)$$
$$+ 2 \sum_{t=0}^{T-1} \left(u_1^T(t) A s1(t) z_1(t) \right) + 2 \sum_{t=0}^{T-1} \left(u_1^T(t) A s3(t) \right) \tag{7}$$
$$+ \sum_{t=0}^{T-1} \left(u_1^T(t) (A s2(t) + Rs(t)) u_1(t) \right) \to \min_{u_1(t)}$$

where

$$As(t) = \sum_{j=1}^{p} An_j^T(t) \cdot A_j(t) h \cdot A_j(t) An_j(t),$$
$$As1(t) = Ar_1^{-1} \sum_{j=1}^{p} Ar_j B_j^T(t) \cdot h \cdot A_j(t) An_j(t),$$
$$As2(t) = Ar_1^{-1} \left(\sum_{j=1}^{p} Ar_j B_j^T(t) h B_j(t) Ar_j(t) \right) Ar_1^{-1},$$
$$As3(t) = Ar_1^{-1} \left(\sum_{j=1}^{p} a_{0j} Ar_j(t) B_j(t) \right) c^T,$$
$$As4(t) = c \sum_{j=1}^{p} a_{0j} A_j(t) An_j(t),$$

$$Rs(t) = \sum_{j=1}^{p} \tilde{R}_j(t), \; \tilde{R}_j(t) = Ar_1^{-1} \cdot Ar_j \cdot R_j(t) \cdot Ar_j \cdot Ar_1^{-1}. \tag{8}$$

Let's introduce restrictions on mesoindicators:

$$X^{min}(t) \le Ar_1^{-1}(v_1(t) + u_1(t)) \le X^{max}(t), \; t = 0, \ldots, T-1, \tag{9}$$

Here

$$X^{min}(t) = \left(x_1^{min}(t) \quad x_2^{min}(t) \quad \ldots \quad x_n^{min}(t) \right)^T,$$
$$X^{max}(t) = \left(x_1^{max}(t) \quad x_2^{max}(t) \quad \ldots \quad x_n^{max}(t) \right)^T.$$

The time dependency $v_1(t)$ in the formula (14) has the form:

$$v_1(t+1) = Ax(t) \cdot (v_1(t) + u_1(t)); \; t = 0, \ldots, T-1,$$

where $Ax(t) = diag(1 + \mu_1(t) \quad \ldots \quad 1 + \mu_n(t))$.

Let's consider the limitation on the microindicator:

$$V^{min}(t) \le E \cdot Ap(t-1) \cdot (v_1(t-1) + u_1(t-1)) + a_0 \le V^{max}(t), t = 1, \ldots, T \tag{10}$$

Here

$$V^{min}(t) = \left(V_1^{min}(t) \quad V_2^{min}(t) \quad \ldots \quad V_p^{min}(t) \right)^T;$$
$$V^{max}(t) = \left(V_1^{max}(t) \quad V_2^{max}(t) \quad \ldots \quad V_n^{max}(t) \right)^T;$$
$$a_0 = \left(a_{01} \quad a_{02} \quad \ldots \quad a_{0p} \right)^T.$$

The matrix of dimensions $p \times np$:

$$E = \begin{pmatrix} 1 & \ldots & 1 & 0 & \ldots & 0 & 0 & \ldots & 0 \\ 0 & \ldots & 0 & 1 & \ldots & 1 & 0 & \ldots & 0 \\ \ldots & \ldots & \ldots & \ldots & \ldots & \ldots & \ldots & \ldots & \ldots \\ 0 & \ldots & 0 & 0 & \ldots & 0 & 1 & \ldots & 1 \end{pmatrix}.$$

The matrix of dimensions $np \times n$:

$$Ap(t) = \begin{pmatrix} Ax(t) \cdot Ar_1 \cdot Ar_1^{-1} \\ Ax(t) \cdot Ar_2 \cdot Ar_1^{-1} \\ \ldots \\ Ax(t) \cdot Ar_p \cdot Ar_1^{-1} \end{pmatrix}$$

Let's consider two more restrictions related to the economic meaning of the five microindicators (their balance base): $FAB + CAB = 1$ и $FAB + CAB = CRB + LLB + SLB$.

Let the microindicators be numbered in the following order: $V_1(t)$ – Rev; $V_2(t)$ – FAB; $V_3(t)$ – CAB; $V_4(t)$ – CRB; $V_5(t)$ – LLB; $V_6(t)$ – SLB.

Then the following restrictions are obtained:

$$V_2(t) + V_3(t) = 1,$$
$$V_2(t) + V_3(t) = V_4(t) + V_5(t) + V_6(t). \tag{11}$$

It is necessary to find the optimal solution $(z_1(t), u_1(t))$, $j = 1, \ldots, p$, satisfying the state equation (5) and constraints (9), (10), (11) for which the functional (7) takes the minimum value.

The vector found $z_1(t)$ will enable calculating $z_j(t) = An_j \cdot z_1(t)$, and then estimating the microindicators $V_j(t) = a_{0j} + \sum_{i=1}^{n} z_{ij}(t)$, $j = 1, \ldots, p$.

As mentioned above, the urban mesoindicators themselves depend on the microindicators (feedback). To take this fact into account, let's present the dependence of mesoindicators on microindicators in the form of a regression:

$$x_i(t) = b_{0i} + \sum_{j=1}^{p} b_{ji} V_j(t),$$

where b_{ji} – regression coefficients. We use this fact when building an algorithm for solving the problem.

Thus, we have a dynamic programming problem with a quadratic criterion. Currently, there is no software for solving the general problem of dynamic programming. One possible solution is to reduce this problem to a quadratic programming problem, for whose solution algorithms and software exist. Here we will use another technique, namely, we will look for a suboptimal solution.

Let's set the initial values of microindicators $V_j(0)$, $j = 1, \ldots p$ and their planned values $V_j^0(0)$, $j = 1, \ldots, p$, the parameters of the required increase in the mesoindicators of the town $\mu_i(t)$ and the desired growth rate of microindicators $\mu_j^0(t)$. Let's set the initial values of the mesoindicators $x_i(0)$, $i = 1, \ldots, n$, corresponding to the initial values of the microindicators $V_j(0)$, $j = 1, \ldots p$. We will also set the boundaries of changes in the mesoindicators of the town $x_j^{\min}(t)$, $x_j^{\max}(t)$, $j = 1, \ldots, n$, and the boundaries of possible changes in the aggregated microindicators $V_j^{\min}(t)$, $V_j^{\max}(t)$.

Let's introduce the matrix $h = c^T c$. Then form matrices R_j, Ar_j, Ax, $An_j(t)$, $\tilde{R}_j(t) = Ar_1^{-1} \cdot Ar_j \cdot R_j(t) \cdot Ar_j \cdot Ar_1^{-1}$ as well as matrices:

$$As1(t) = Ar_1^{-1} \sum_{j=1}^{p} \left(Ar_j B_j^T(t) h A_j(t) An_j(t) \right),$$

$$As2(t) = Ar_1^{-1}\left(\sum_{j=1}^{p} Ar_j B_j^T(t)hB_j(t)Ar_j(t)\right)Ar_1^{-1},$$

$$As3(t) = Ar_1^{-1}\left(\sum_{j=1}^{p} a_{0j}Ar_j(t)B_j^T(t)\right)c^T,$$

$$As4(t) = c\sum_{j=1}^{p} a_{0j}A_j(t)An_j(t) \text{ и } Rs(t) = \sum_{j=1}^{p} \tilde{R}_j(t).$$

Form a vector $v_1(0) = (a_{11}x_1(0), a_{21}x_2(0), \ldots, a_{n1}x_n(0))^T$, a composite vector $z_1(0) = \begin{pmatrix} v_1(0) \\ V_1^0(0) \end{pmatrix}$ and vectors $v_j(0) = Ar_j \cdot Ar_1^{-1} \cdot v_1(0)$, $z_j(0) = An_j(0) \cdot z_1(0)$, $j = 1, \ldots, p$. Here a_{i1} – elements of the first column of the regression coefficient matrix.

Form auxiliary vectors $e1 = (0 \quad 1 \quad 1 \quad 0 \quad 0 \quad 0)$ and $e2 = (0 \quad 1 \quad 1 \quad -1 \quad -1 \quad -1)$.

Also form a vector $a_0 = (a_{01} \quad a_{02} \quad \ldots \quad a_{0p})^T$ and a vector $b_0 = (b_{01} \quad b_{02} \quad \ldots \quad b_{0n})^T$.

Step 1. Solve the problem for the moment $t = 0$:

$$J = 2u_1^T(0)As1(0)z_1(0) + 2u_1^T(0)As3(0)$$
$$+ u_1^T(0)(As2(0) + Rs(0))u_1(0) \to \min_{u_1(0)} \tag{12}$$

$$X^{\min}(0) \le Ar_1^{-1}(v_1(0) + u_1(0)) \le X^{\max}(0),$$
$$V^{\min}(1) \le E \cdot Ap(0) \cdot (v_1(0) + u_1(0)) + a_0 \le V^{\max}(1) \tag{13}$$

$$e1 \cdot (E \cdot Ap(0) \cdot (v_1(0) + u_1(0)) + a_0) = 1,$$
$$e2 \cdot (E \cdot Ap(0) \cdot (v_1(0) + u_1(0)) + a_0) = 0 \tag{14}$$

Having found $u_1(0)$, calculate $v_1(1)$ and $z_1(1)$:

$$v_1(1) = Ax(0) \cdot (v_1(0) + u_1(0)) \tag{15}$$

$$z_1(1) = A_1(0) \cdot z_1(0) + B_1(0) \cdot u_1(0) \tag{16}$$

Here the constant $z_1^T(0)As(0)z_1(0) + 2As3(0)z_1(0)$ has been omitted.

Consider the case when mesoindicators themselves depend on microindicators (with the feedback effect):

$$x_i(1) = b_{0i} + \sum_{j=1}^{p} b_{ji}V_j(1), \quad i = 1, \ldots, n.$$

Calculate the vector $V(1) = E \cdot Ap(0) \cdot (v_1(0) + u_1(0)) + a_0$ and then the vector $v_1(1) = Ar_1(0) \cdot x(1)$, and $z_1(1) = \begin{pmatrix} v_1(1) \\ V_1^0(1) \end{pmatrix}$.

Thus, instead of (15) and (16) we will have:

$$
\begin{aligned}
V(1) &= E \cdot Ap(0) \cdot (v_1(0) + u_1(0)) + a_0, \\
x(1) &= b_0 + V^T(1) \cdot b, \\
v_1(1) &= Ar_1(1) \cdot x(1), \\
z_1(1) &= \begin{pmatrix} v_1(1) & V_1^0(1) \end{pmatrix}^T.
\end{aligned}
\tag{17}
$$

Step 2. Solve the problem for the moment $t = 1$.

Omitting the constant $z_1^T(1)As(1)z_1(1) + 2As3(1)z_1(1)$, we have:

$$
\begin{aligned}
J = {}& 2u_1^T(1)As1(1)z_1(1) + 2u_1^T(1)As3(1) \\
& + u_1^T(1)(As2(1) + Rs(1))u_1(1) \to \min_{u_1(0)},
\end{aligned}
$$

$$
X^{\min}(1) \leq Ar_1^{-1}(v_1(1) + u_1(1)) \leq X^{\max}(1),
$$
$$
V^{\min}(2) \leq E \cdot Ap(1) \cdot (v_1(1) + u_1(1)) + a_0 \leq V^{\max}(2)
$$

$$
e1 \cdot (E \cdot Ap(1) \cdot (v_1(1) + u_1(1)) + a_0) = 1,
$$
$$
e2 \cdot (E \cdot Ap(1) \cdot (v_1(1) + u_1(1)) + a_0) = 0
$$

$$
\begin{aligned}
V(2) &= E \cdot Ap(1) \cdot (v_1(1) + u_1(1)) + a_0, \\
x(2) &= b_0 + V^T(2) \cdot b \\
v_1(2) &= Ar_1(2) \cdot x(2), \\
z_1(2) &= \begin{pmatrix} v_1(2) & V_1^0(2) \end{pmatrix}^T.
\end{aligned}
$$

Step T. Solve the problem for $t = T - 1$.

By omitting the constant
$z_1^T(T - 1)As(T - 1)z_1(T - 1) + 2As3(T - 1)z_1(T - 1)$, we have:

$$
\begin{aligned}
J = {}& 2u_1^T(T - 1)As1(1)z_1(T - 1) + 2u_1^T(T - 1)As3(T - 1) \\
& + u_1^T(T - 1)(As2(T - 1) + Rs(T - 1))u_1(T - 1) \to \min_{u_1(0)}
\end{aligned}
$$

$$
X^{\min}(T - 1) \leq Ar_1^{-1}(v_1(T - 1) + u_1(T - 1)) \leq X^{\max}(T - 1),
$$
$$
V^{\min}(T) \leq E \cdot Ap(1) \cdot (v_1(T - 1) + u_1(T - 1)) + a_0 \leq V^{\max}(T)
$$

$$
e1 \cdot (E \cdot Ap(T - 1) \cdot (v_1(T - 1) + u_1(T - 1)) + a_0) = 1,
$$
$$
e2 \cdot (E \cdot Ap(T - 1) \cdot (v_1(T - 1) + u_1(T - 1)) + a_0) = 0
$$

$$V(T) = E \cdot Ap(T-1) \cdot (v_1(T-1) + u_1(T-1)) + a_0,$$
$$x(T) = b_0 + V^T(T) \cdot b$$
$$v_1(T) = Ar_1(T) \cdot x(T),$$
$$z_1(T) = \left(v_1(T) \quad V_1^0(T) \right)^T.$$

4 Data

The multifactor model was used for calculations based on the indicators of the monotown of Yurga. The basis was the collected data on mesoindicators and microindicators for the period from 2007 to 2016, which were previously normalized by the initial value (for 2007). Based on the initial data, the coefficients of multiple regression a_i were calculated by the least square method (Table 3):

$$a = (X^T X)^{-1} \cdot X^T Y, \tag{18}$$

where X – mesoindicator matrix, Y – vector of the aggregated microindicator values.

Table 3. Multiple regression coefficients

Mesoindicators	Microindicators					
	Rev	FAB	CAB	CRB	LLB	SLB
UTII	11.179	5.381	–0.645	–4.066	–1.698	7.096
NIE	2.954	–0.951	0.357	6.671	–5.796	–7.252
NSE	0.958	–0.287	0.108	0.539	–1.349	–0.513
PIT	–0.66	0.266	–0.1	0.444	–0.709	–0.455
TTI	0.26	0.036	–0.014	-0.038	1.343	–0.067
AMNI	–3.419	0.73	–0.274	–7.256	7.29	7.807
Pl	0.12	–0.339	0.127	0.416	–1.599	–0.35
NLME	–9.771	–4.401	1.653	3.641	4.15	–4.565

Figure 1, as an example, compares the model of the normalized microindicator Revenue *Rev* with the original normalized data (horizontal axis – period in years from 2007 to 2016, vertical axis – indicator value in arbitrary units). As follows from the figure, in which the parameter *Pt1* denotes real values, and *Pt1r* – the modeled ones, the agreement is quite acceptable (the maximum deviation was 5.34%, the mean error was 1.72%).

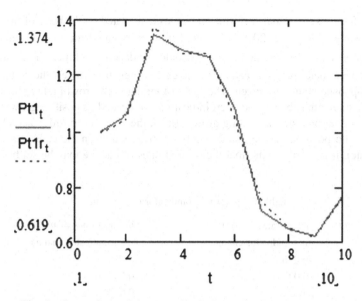

Fig. 1. Comparison of the *Rev* microindicator model with real data.

Calculation of the $\mu_i(t)$ mesoindicator change rate parameters was carried out on the basis of historical data according to the formula:

$$\mu_i(t) = \frac{\sum\limits_{t=2}^{T} x_i(t)x_i(t-1)}{\sum\limits_{t=2}^{T} (x_i(t-1))^2} - 1, i = 1, \ldots, n, \tag{19}$$

Calculation results of $\mu_i(t)$ are shown in Table 4. In this case, the parameters $\mu_i(t)$ do not depend on time. Note that the parameters $\mu_i(t)$ may be given by experts.

Table 4. Parameters of the $\mu_i(t)$ mesoindicator change rate

Mesioindicators	1	2	3	4	5	6	7	8
$\mu_i(t)$	0.038	–0.03	0.064	0.023	0.039	0.08	–0.003	–0.071

The calculation of the $\mu_j^0(t)$ microindicator change rate parameters was carried out on the basis of the data obtained by the formula:

$$\mu_j^0(t) = \frac{\sum\limits_{t=2}^{T} (Pt_j(t)Pt_j(t-1))}{\sum\limits_{t=2}^{T} \left(Pt_j(t-1)^2\right)} - 1, \; i = 1, \ldots, n, \; j = 1, \ldots, p \tag{20}$$

Table 5 shows the actual performance values (calculated on the basis of the original data according to formula (20)) and desired $\mu_j^0(t)$ microindicator change rates. In the case under analysis, the parameters $\mu_j^0(t)$ also do not depend on time. The desired rates of change were determined as actual. In the case of negative values, the actual values with the opposite sign were taken. The logic of taking such growth rate values was as follows: in managing each of the microindicators, we needed its positive growth, which was equal to the previously existing growth (as in the case of a positive actual growth rate) or would be equal to the diametrically opposite value (in the case of a negative growth rate). It is worth noting that the desired rates of change may be set by experts.

Table 5. $\mu_j^0(t)$ microindicator change rates

Microindicators	Actual rates of $\mu_j^0(t)$ microindicator change	Desired rates of $\mu_j^0(t)$ microindicator change
Rev	–0.036	0.036
FAB	–0.047	0.047
CAB	0.013	0.013
CRB	–0.026	0.026
LLB	–0.097	0.097
SLB	0.023	0.023

The desired rates of microindicator change depend on the chosen management strategies [10]. These strategies determine the nature of the microindicator change rate: a positive $(\mu_j^0(t) > 0)$ or negative $(\mu_j^0(t) < 0)$ tendency, as well as zero pace $(\mu_j^0(t) = 0)$.

Next, proceed to the solution of the microindicator management problem. As already mentioned, this microindicator management problem belongs to the class of dynamic programming models with quadratic criteria and constraints. As is known [14], in the absence of constraints, this model has an analytical solution. However, calculations based on such a model sometimes lead to non-interpretable economic results. Therefore, it was suggested to introduce restrictions both on the management $u(t)$ (mesoindicators) and the controlled variable (microindicator). Constraints are determined on the basis of the economic meaning of variables.

Table 6 shows the limitations of mesoindicators, which were defined as the minimum and maximum normalized values, taken by mesioindicators in the past as such. In addition, the table shows the deviations between the lower and upper limitations of the mesoindicators, on the basis of which weighting coefficients w were calculated:

$$w_i = \frac{\delta_i}{\sum\limits_{i=1}^{n} \delta_i},$$

where i – mesoindicator reference number, n – mesoindicator number, δ – deviations of mesoindicators. These weights are used to form a matrix of weighting coefficients $\tilde{R}_j$ (see formula (8)).

Table 6. Limitations of mesoindicators

Mesoindicators	Lower limit	Upper limit	Deviations of mesoindicators, δ	Weighting coefficients, w
UTII	0.994	1.739	0.745	0.132
NIE	0.790	1.239	0.449	0.079
NSE	0.910	1.885	0.975	0.173
PIT	1.000	1.831	0.831	0.147
TTI	0.994	1.751	0.757	0.134
AMNI	1.000	2.261	1.261	0.223
Pl	0.968	1.001	0.033	0.006
NLME	0.400	1.000	0.600	0.106
			$\sum \delta = 5,651$	$\sum w = 1,000$

In turn, the limitations of small business indicators, the parameters of which are given in Table 7, were defined as follows: the minimum values that microindicators took in the study period were taken for the lower limit Lob, and the upper limit Upb was defined as:

$$Upb_i = Lob_i \cdot k,$$

where i - microindicator number.

$$k = \max\left(\frac{MUpb_i}{Lob_i}\right),$$

where $MUpb_i$ – maximum value of the i microindicator for the study period. For the available amount of data it was $k = 3,2$ (LLB microindicator).

Table 7. Parameters of microindicator limitations

Microindicators	Lower limit Lob	Maximum value $MUpb$	Upper limit Upb
Rev	0.623	1.348	1.994
FAB	0.656	1.000	2.099
CAB	1.000	1.129	3.200
CRB	0.795	1.106	2.544
LLB	0.541	1.730	1.731
SLB	0.886	1.258	2.835

5   Results and Discussion

On the basis of this model and the initial data given, a simulation was made that included the management process with all six microindicators taken simultaneously due to a change in the eight mesoindicators of the monotown of Yurga.

Figure 2, as an example, shows a graph of tracking the planned microindicator *Rev* depending on the eight mesoindicators of the town (horizontal axis – period in years from 2007 to 2016, vertical axis – *Rev* indicator value in thousand rubles). The dotted line indicates the desired values of the indicator (VOI_1), the solid line represents the simulated behavior of the indicator studied (VI_1).

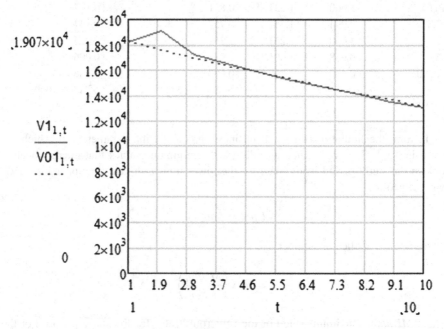

Fig. 2. Results of managing the *Rev* microindicator

According to Fig. 2, the development path of the monotown was chosen so that it would aim at increasing the internal supply by increasing the number of small enterprises. Since the domestic market of the monotown is relatively closed, it will lead to a decrease in the average value of the SB revenues (*Rev* indicator).

Figure 3 has graphs that show the normalized values of all eight mesoindicators which ensure the achievement of the planned values of six microindicators (horizontal axis – period in years from 2007 to 2016, vertical axis – value of mesoindicators in dimensionless units). The conventional symbols of graphs on the figure: xn_1 – for the *UTII* mesoindicator, xn_2 – for the *NIE* mesoindicator, xn_3 – for the *NSE* mesoindicator, xn_4 – for the *PIT* mesoindicator, xn_5 – for the *TTI* mesoindicator, xn_6 – for the *AMNI* mesoindicator, xn_7 – for the *Pl* mesoindicator, xn_8 – for the *NLME* mesoindicator.

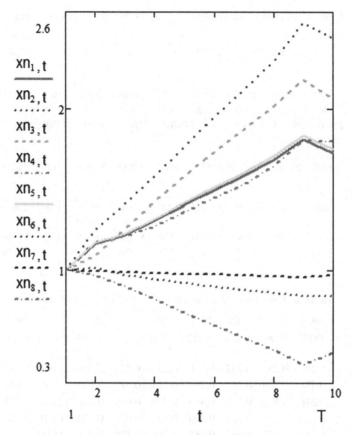

Fig. 3. The graph of changes in mesoindicators (the indicator values are normalized) which ensure the achievement of the planned values of six microindicators

As a result of applying the multifactor model, the values of the urban mesoindicators and microindicators of small businesses were obtained, which must be followed to achieve the planned rates and results of the SB functioning. Table 8 shows the calculated values of the mesoindicators for the monotown of Yurga for the period from 2007 to 2016, at which the planned values of six microindicators are to be achieved.

Table 9 shows the calculated values of the microindicators for the monotown of Yurga for the period from 2007 to 2016. All the microindicator values, except *Rev* are to be measured in dimensionless units.

Table 8. Calculated mesoindicator values of the monotown of Yurga

Indicator	2007	2008	2009	2010	2011	2012	2013	2014	2015	2016
UTII, thousand rubles	31720	36980	38660	41510	44400	47340	50150	53400	57390	54630
NIE, pcs	2100	2129	2032	1979	1930	1886	1845	1806	1763	1764
NSE, pcs	400	436	503	568	631	691	749	805	872	823
PIT, thousand rubles	226600	266200	274600	288300	307600	327800	346900	372300	408100	406700
TTI, thousand rubles	31720	37080	38870	41830	44830	47880	50780	54130	58230	55370
AMNI, rubles	9445	11780	13300	14890	16640	18400	20040	21700	23920	23020
Pl, people	83840	83080	82860	82350	81940	81540	81160	80780	80420	81270
NLME, pcs	25	24	23	21	18	16	14	13	10	12

Table 9. Calculated microindicator values of the town of Yurga

Indicator	2007	2008	2009	2010	2011	2012	2013	2014	2015	2016
Rev, thousand rubles	18182	19069	17265	16495	15805	15216	14668	14106	13516	13075
FAB	0.270	0.255	0.247	0.240	0.229	0.218	0.208	0.197	0.180	0.179
CAB	0.730	0.745	0.753	0.760	0.771	0.782	0.792	0.803	0.820	0.821
CRB	0.516	0.502	0.505	0.489	0.479	0.469	0.458	0.446	0.436	0.471
LLB	0.036	0.036	0.031	0.028	0.025	0.022	0.020	0.020	0.020	0.023
SLB	0.448	0.462	0.465	0.483	0.496	0.509	0.521	0.534	0.544	0.506

6 Conclusion

Thus, the multifactor model enables to simultaneously manage all microindicators of the urban small businesses by means of targeted changes in mesoindicators. Therefore, to manage urban small businesses as an interconnected and interdependent system, the elaborated multifactor (multi-criteria) model should be used which operates all microindicators of small businesses at once.

References

1. Manaeva, I., Kanishteva, A.: Estimation of factors for social and economic inequality of Russia's towns. Reg. Sci. Inq. **9**(2), 147–158 (2017)
2. Manaeva, I., Rastvortseva, S.: Zipf's law as assessment tool of urban inequality. Reg. Sci. Inq. **8**(3), 19–30 (2016)

3. Antonova, I.S., Koptelova, K.S., Popova, S.N., Negodina, O.A., Spitsina, L.Yu., Vavilov, D. D.: Investment attractiveness of closed-end real estate investment funds in Russia: factor score evaluation. In: Proceedings of the 2016 Conference on Information Technologies in Science, Management, Social Sphere and Medicine (ITSMSSM 2016) 2016, pp. 904–907 (2016)

4. Antonova, I.S.: Diversification infrastructure of Russian company towns. In: The European Proceedings of Social & Behavioural Sciences III International Scientific Symposium, pp. 28–36. National Research Tomsk Polytechnic University (2017)

5. Kuznetsov, B.L., Kuznetsova, S.B., Zagitov, I.L.: Economic synergetics: answer to the challenges of the 21st century. Econ. Soc. 2(11), 850 (2014)

6. Korshunov, I.V., Shmatko, A.D., Solovjeva, N.L.: The development of Russian single-industry towns of the industrial regions of Russia: problems and trends. Econ. Bus. **11–3** (76), 528–530 (2016)

7. Zubarevich, N.: Russian agglomerations: trends, resources, and governability. Soc. Sci. **48** (4), 66–80 (2017)

8. Bruening, R.A., Strazza, K., Nocera, M., Peek-Asa, C., Casteel, C.: Understanding the small business engagement in violence prevention programs. Am. J. Health Promot. **30**, 83–91 (2015). https://doi.org/10.4278/ajhp.140221-QUAL-80

9. Hirschman, A.O.: Development Projects Observed, p. 68. Brookings Institution Press, Washington, DC (2011)

10. Vazhdaev, A., Mitsel, A., Grigoryeva, M.: The relationship of city and small business economic parameters. In: Proceedings of the IV International Research Conference Information Technologies in Science, Management, Social Sphere and Medicine, vol. 72, pp. 1–4 (2017). http://doi.org/10.2991/itsmssm-17.2017.1

11. Konnov, A.I., Krotov, V.F.: On the global methods of successive improvement of controllable processes. Autom. Remote Control **60**, 1427 (1999)

Tourism Cluster Enterprises Departments' Resource Management Based on Mobile Technologies

Alla G. Kravets[1]([⊠]) [iD], Aleksandr O. Morozov[1],
Konstantin S. Zadiran[1], Gais Al-Merri[2], and Ekaterina Trishkina[3]

[1] Volgograd State Technical University, Volgograd, Russia
agk@gde.ru, alexmoroz1993@yandex.ru,
konstantin.zadiran@gmail.com
[2] North-Caucasian Federal University, Stavropol, Russia
gaismr2009@mail.ru
[3] Management Academy of the Ministry of the Interior of Russia, Moscow,
Russia
ekaterina.ki@rambler.ru

Abstract. In the conditions of modern management of hospitality facilities, the used approaches and tools for resource management play an important role. The article discusses the use of mobile technologies in resource management of the hotel's housekeeping service. The mobile application «Mobile Housekeeping» is used to manage the resources of the hotel's housekeeping service in addition to the automated PaRM web system. The automated system is based on a proactive methodology, the description of which is given in the article. In the mobile application "Mobile housekeeping" functionality is supported, which requires the operational use of the personnel of housekeeping service at any point of the hotel. The use of integrated software allows you to effectively manage the resources of the enterprise's departments of the tourism cluster.

Keywords: Pro-active management · Hotel · Tourism cluster · Mobile application

1 Introduction

In the sphere of hospitality, an important role is played by the approaches and tools of resource management. Mobile applications are an integral part of modern software and give many advantages to users to work with resource management systems [10]. In this article, the resource management tool for the housekeeping service (HKS) of the hotel, a service that is responsible for the cleanliness of the rooms and the comfort of the guests, will be considered.

The authors [4] propose a proactive method of managing the resources of the hotel's housekeeping service. This technique was used as the basis for the automated system PaRM, which was tested in the network hotel Park Inn by Radisson in the city of Volgograd. The use of only an automated system has a significant drawback: full use of the system is possible only from a personal computer. But the specificity of the work

A. G. Kravets et al. (Eds.): CIT&DS 2019, CCIS 1083, pp. 218–229, 2019.
https://doi.org/10.1007/978-3-030-29743-5_17

of the HKS requires the operational use of the management system, for example, being in one of the hotel rooms [2, 6]. Therefore, it is proposed to use the mobile application "Mobile housekeeping" in addition to the automated system PaRM.

2 The Methodology of Proactive Resource Management

The management of the hotel's housekeeping service is a method of organizing, planning, accounting and controlling the human and material resources necessary for the functioning and coordinated work of this structural unit.

Usually, in the absence or ineffectiveness of a uniform methodology for managing resources in an enterprise, a hotel, in particular, the following problems can occur:

- lack of personnel for cleaning of rooms timely;
- the labor intensity of the scheduling process;
- the complexity of making managerial decisions.

All these factors lead to a decrease in the labor productivity of the personnel of the HKS of the hotel, as well as to a decrease in the efficiency of the management of the resources of the HKS. The hotel company suffers losses, loses potential customers, reduces its own competitiveness.

A new method of proactive management, based on the analysis of the methods used in modern hotels to manage the resources of HKS, is proposed [3, 11].

The management of the resources of the hotel's HKS in most cases is based on the accepted common standards. This is especially true for network hotels. However, there are own corporate standards and rules that are specific to each hotel. The developed method of proactive management of the resources of HKS mainly relies on the needs and specificity of the operation of the Volgograd-based network hotel Park Inn by Radisson.

Based on the needs for managing the resources of the HKS of the Park Inn by Radisson hotel, as well as the problems it contains, the following key models of the proactive management methodology are highlighted:

- HKS personnel management;
- HKS laundry management;
- forecasting needs of HKS resources;
- support for management decisions made by the head of the HKS.

Dedicated models have a number of individual tasks, but, nevertheless, they are all interconnected [5]. In Fig. 1 is a block diagram of the developed methodology, consisting of the highlighted models and their main tasks.

2.1 Model of Managerial Decisions Making Support for the Executive Housekeeper

The most significant for the functioning of the mobile application "Mobile housekeeping" is the model of managerial decisions making support to the head of the HKS department – Executive Housekeeper.

The personnel of the hotel's HKS works in shifts. Therefore, it is necessary to schedule personnel work. The head of the housekeeping service should schedule the work of the staff for the future while not knowing the future occupancy of the hotel and personnel requirements, as well as the need for detergents.

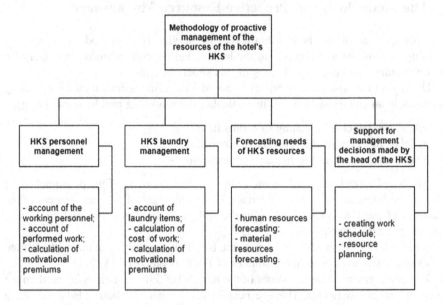

Fig. 1. Structural-functional scheme of the developed methodology

As a consequence, the following problems may occur that require the adjustment of the created schedule and the making of operational management decisions:

- lack of the HKS's personnel;
- excess of the HKS's personnel(no norm, no incentive bonuses);
- lack of capacity for cleaning rooms.

To avoid these problems, a tool to proactively support the management decisions made by the head of the HKS of the hotel is required.

The model of support for managerial decisions making of the hotel HKS department head is shown in Fig. 2. It includes the following tasks:

- storing information about resources spent on cleaning rooms;
- storing information about the work of the staff of the HKS;
- management of cleaning tools database;
- management of the employee work types database;
- human resources planning;
- material resources planning.

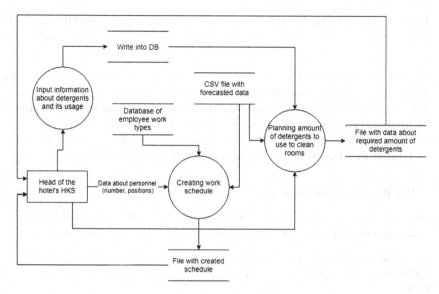

Fig. 2. Model "Managerial decisions making support for the Executive Housekeeper" in the DFD notation

2.2   The Personnel Motivation Procedure

For the functioning of the motivational scheme, it is necessary to have personnel overworking by servicing more numbers than specified by the norm for one work shift.

Table 1 shows the cost of performed works in credits. Hypothetically, it can be assumed that 1 credit is equal to 1 min.

The use of the concept of credit is convenient for calculating the necessary number of maintenance personnel.

Table 1. Works costs

Type of cleaning (work)	Cost of work in credits
Routine cleaning of the standard room	20
Departure cleaning of the standard room	40
Routine cleaning of the luxury room	30
Departure cleaning of the luxury room	50
Deep cleaning of the standard room	120
Deep cleaning of the luxury room	180
Carpet dry cleaning in the standard room	30
Carpet dry cleaning in the luxury room	60

It is necessary to comply with the internal corporate rules of the HKS hotels to schedule the work of the staff. The rules for engaging the personnel of the hotel's HKS are:

- At a low load of the hotel, when each maid has less than 400 credits, the rest of the personnel (janitors, laundry operator, supervisor) is not involved in room cleaning.
- In case of high loading of the hotel, when every maid has from 400 to 520 credits, the head of the HKS engages janitors, a laundry operator, and a supervisor.
- In case of high loading of the hotel, when each employee has more than 520 credits, the head of the HKS engages personnel from the outsourcing company.

2.3   The Personnel Scheduling

Based on the presented rules, the algorithm for supporting the adoption of managerial decisions on scheduling the work of personnel includes the following items:

- Upload information about the number of personnel.
- Building and loading the forecast of the demand for human resources of the hotel's HKS.
- Correction of the forecast of resource requirements by taking into account planned activities.
- Creation of the work schedule for the personnel of the HKS taking into account the above rules, and also with the use of the motivation scheme.

The model being developed directly interacts with the model for forecasting the resource requirements of the hotel's HKS. The forecasting methods used in the methodology [1, 7–9]:

- Support vector regressor.
- Random forest regressor.
- Decision tree regressor.
- K Neighbors regressor.
- Ada boost regressor.
- Gradient boosting regressor.

Support for management decision-making is based on predicted resource requirements.

A fragment of the created work schedule is shown in Table 2:

- A – Housekeepers.
- B – Cleaners of public areas.
- C – Laundry operators.
- D – Supervisor.
- E – Additional personnel from the outsourcing company.

Table 2. Personnel scheduling

Date	Available personnel				Proposed work schedule				
	A	B	C	D	A	B	C	D	E
10.02.2019	5	1	1	1	4	0	0	0	0
11.02.2019	5	1	1	1	4	0	0	0	0
12.02.2019	5	1	1	1	2	0	0	0	0
13.02.2019	4	1	1	1	4	0	0	0	0
14.02.2019	4	1	1	1	4	1	1	1	0
15.02.2019	4	1	1	1	4	1	1	1	2
16.02.2019	4	1	1	1	4	1	1	1	4
17.02.2019	4	1	1	1	4	1	1	1	3

The created schedule shows the minimum number of necessary maintenance personnel. It allows to use the available human resources of the hotel's HKS and, if necessary, additional staff optimally.

Usage of the model of support for making managerial decisions by the head of the HKS will reduce the laboriousness of resource planning.

The head of the HKS of the hotel, knowing the optimal number of personnel, makes a schedule for employees, using the functionality of the mobile application. Survey the architecture and functionality of the mobile application below.

3 The Mobile Application «Mobile Housekeeping»

The application was developed for the Android mobile operating system using the JAVA programming language. The application requires an Android OS version of at least 4.4 for operation. The application consists of a set of screen forms and a local database, in which data about the authenticated user are stored.

3.1 The Architecture of the Mobile Application «Mobile Housekeeping»

To connect the mobile application and the automated system PaRM a single database mechanism is used.

The database uses MySQL database engine. To connect the application to a common database, an additional intermediate level is used in the form of a RESTful web server. The web server was developed using the Python programming language and the Flask web framework. The web server executes queries directly to a single database and provides an external API interface to retrieve and update data. Also, the server validates the data and verifies the user's rights based on his role. Data transfer is performed using the JSON. The application connects to the web server using asynchronous methods built into the Android OS web client. The general scheme of the interaction between system components is shown in Fig. 3.

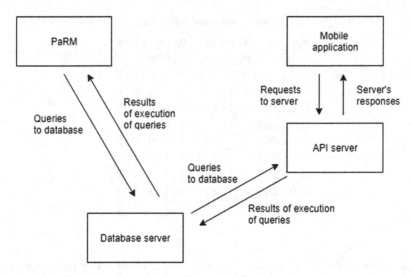

Fig. 3. The general scheme of interaction between system components

The application implements a role system that allows changing the functionality available to the user by assigning a specific role. Data about users and roles are stored in a single database.

The application uses the following roles:

- The head of the housekeeping service of a hotel.
- An employee of the housekeeping service of a hotel (service personnel).

3.2 The Functionality of the Mobile Application «Mobile Housekeeping»

The mobile application implements the following functionality:

- Authorization of the head of the HKS of the hotel.
- Authorization of the staff of the hotel's HKS (maids, janitors).
- Sending personal messages to employees.
- Entering and editing data on washing and ironing property of the hotel with an indication of the employee who performed the job.
- Entering and editing guest laundry and ironing data.
- Entering comments on the room for the current date.
- Creating work orders.
- Performing room inspection.

Depending on the authorized role (manager or maintenance personnel), different functionality is available in the application.

Fig. 4. The interface of the start page of the mobile application

The interface of the mobile application's start page is shown in Fig. 4.
Here is a description of the most important functions of the application.

Performing Room Inspection. In Fig. 5 the interface of the function of performing room inspection is presented. This functionality is available only to the head of the HKS of the hotel. Inspection is performed on the current day. The room fund displays all available hotel rooms. You can move the room between lists and add notes to them. The room with the comment is highlighted in red. The current rooms are displayed in blue. In the "Inspection" category, the numbers checked by the supervisor are displayed. Supervisor puts rooms that require the special following in the "Trace" category. In the category "Nobody" rooms that do not require maintenance are displayed. After the inspection, the head of the HKS of the hotel can quickly check all the notes and eliminate them.

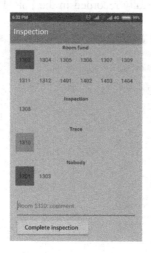

Fig. 5. Room inspection interface (Color figure online)

Housekeeper Work Orders Processing. Figure 6 shows the interfaces for creating, viewing and confirming a work order. From the list, the necessary rooms are marked, the employee for whom the order is made, and the date are selected. The selected rooms are automatically entered in the automated system "PaRM" to account for the serviced rooms and calculate motivational premiums. Executive Housekeeper confirms the completed order of the employee after the inspection of numbers.

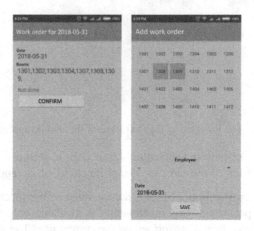

Fig. 6. Work order processing interface

After that, the marked rooms are automatically entered into the automated system PaRM to account for the serviced rooms and calculate the motivational payments.

Entering Information About Laundry and Ironing. Figure 7 presents the interface of the data input function for washing and ironing property of the hotel and guest items. The operator of the laundry can quickly enter information using a mobile application. The entered data are automatically recorded in the PaRM system.

Fig. 7. Entering information about washing and ironing interface

4 Experiments and Results

To ensure the adequacy of the assessment of economic indicators: the productivity of staff, the costs of the hotel' HKS, need to select data for similar periods of 2017 and 2018. To take into account the seasonality factor, the period February-April of each year was chosen. Table 3 shows the reservation data for the Park Inn by Radisson Volgograd hotel.

Thus, the loading of the hotel for the selected period of each year practically coincides (the difference is about 0.05%), therefore the assessment of labor productivity and expenses of the HKS conducted on these data can be considered adequate.

Table 3. Hotel Reservation

Month/year	2018	2017
February	2445	2876
March	2703	2579
April	2798	2487
Total	7946	7942

The main expenses of the SCC, which the head of the service can manage, include:

- Motivation premiums.
- Expenses for cleaning and washing aids.

The new procedure for calculating motivational bonuses allowed not only to increase the transparency and validity of these charges but also to reduce the percentage of daily deficiencies, as well as to take into account additional work as a norm. In general, during the period of 2018, the hotel's expenses for the payment of premiums for processing were reduced by 25.77%, while avoiding staff turnover (Table 4).

Table 4. Cost estimates for motivation payments (rub.)

2018	2017	Odds	%
73076	98450	−25374	−25,77%

The costs of the cleaning and laundry facilities (Table 5) increased in 2018 by 63.4%.

Table 5. Cost estimates for cleaning and laundry facilities (rub.)

2018	2017	Odds	%
74239,09	45432,67	28806,42	63,40%

At the same time, costs for cleaning assets increased by 4688.33 rubles for the period of 2018 with an increase in the number of rooms cleaned at 793, compared to the same period in 2017.

The increase in expenses for laundry facilities in the amount of 17,889 rubles is explained by the introduction of the procedure for calculating motivational bonuses for the laundry division - now the laundry staff is interested in increasing production, both in washing guest items and washing for the internal needs of the hotel. This is confirmed by a significant increase in the amount of work done by the laundry (Table 6) by 290.4% and a decrease in wash orders from outsourcing firms by 24.59%.

Table 6. Laundry volumes

	2018	2017	Odds	%
Outsourcing	357541 RUB	474125 RUB	−116584 RUB	−24,59%
Laundry	245856 RUB	62970 RUB	182886 RUB	290,43%
	7237 kg	2099 kg	5138 kg	244,78%

5 Conclusion

Using the application "Mobile housekeeping" in addition to the automated system of the PaRM allows the complex automation of the resources of the hotel's HKS. The mobile application will make it possible to save HKS employees from the double entry of information about rooms - first on paper, then into the system, thereby increasing productivity.

The proactive methodology allowed to increase the productivity of the personnel of the HKS of the hotel by 20%.

References

1. Cao, S., Du, Q.: The human resource demand forecast based on BP neural network. J. Shandong Univ. Technol. (Nat. Sci. Ed.) 26–29 (2008)
2. Demeke, W.: Adoption of information and communication technologies in the hotel and associated businesses in Addis Ababa, Ethiopia. In: Proceedings of the 7th IADIS International Conference Information Systems 2014, IS 2014, pp. 11–18 (2014)
3. Engel, Y., Etzion, O.: Towards proactive event-driven computing. In: Proceedings of the 5th ACM International Conference on Distributed Event-Based System - DEBS 2011, p. 125. ACM Press, New York (2011)
4. Kravets, A.G., Morozov, A.G., Strukova, I.V.: The pro-active resource management for hotels' housekeeping service. In: Kommers, P. (ed.) International Conference ICT, Society and Human Beings 2017, Lisbon, Portugal, 20–22 July 2017, Part of the Multi Conference on Computer Science and Information Systems 2017. Proceedings. IADIS (International Association for Development of the Information Society), Lisbon, Portugal, pp. 35–42 (2017)

5. Kravets, A.G., Gurtjakov, A.S., Darmanian, A.P.: Enterprise intellectual capital management by social learning environment implementation. World Appl. Sci. J. **23**(7), 956–964 (2013)
6. Kuo, J.-Y., Chen, Y.-C., Chen, C.-Y., Liu, L.-W.: Study on correlation between hotel cleaners' musculoskeletal pain and cleaning pose by RULA (Upper limb assessment) and MSDS checklist: using hot spring hotels and motels in Taiwan as examples. Open Cybern. Syst. J. **9**(1), 1199–1206 (2015)
7. Li, T., Song, G.: Study on regional human resources demand forecast. Yunnan Finan. Econ. Univ. J. Econ. Manage. **3**, 91–95 (2006). (In Chinese)
8. Otava, M.: Regression with enriched random forest. In: Non-Clinical Statistics Conference Brugge, Belgium (2014)
9. Ostertagová, E.: Modelling using polynomial regression, Technical University of Košice, Faculty of Electrical Engineering and Informatics, Department of Mathematics and Theoretical Informatics, NČmcovej 32, 042 00 Košice, Slovak Republic (2012)
10. Park, S., Yaduma, N., Lockwood, A.J., Williams, A.M.: Demand fluctuations, labour flexibility and productivity. Ann. Tourism Res. **59**, 93–112 (2016)
11. Sallam, A., Li, K., Ouyang, A., Li, Z.: Proactive workload management in dynamic virtualized environments. J. Comput. Syst. Sci. **80**(8), 1504–1517 (2014)

The Information and Analytical Platform for the Big Data Mining About Innovation in the Region

Leyla Gamidullaeva ⓘ, Alexey Finogeev$^{(\boxtimes)}$ ⓘ, Sergey Vasin ⓘ,
Michael Deev ⓘ, and Anton Finogeev ⓘ

Penza State University, 40, Krasnaya street, Penza, Russia
gamidullaeva@gmail.com, alexeyfinogeev@gmail.com,
pspu-met@mail.ru, {miqz, fanton3}@yandex.ru

Abstract. The article describes an information and analytical platform for collecting and processing big data for the study of innovative development processes of the constituent entities of the Russian Federation. The toolkit of the platform solves the problem of searching, collecting, processing and downloading data from the Internet for the analysis and prognostic modeling of innovation indicators of economic agents in the region. The results are used to assess the dynamics of changes in the innovative development of enterprises and the region as a whole. The objectives of the research are to select leaders who actively develop and implement innovations, benchmarking analysis of regional enterprises with leaders, develop recommendations for managing innovative development mechanisms, and increase the efficiency of innovative activities of enterprises in the region. It is proposed to create a set of tools for analytic processing of big data in the form of a convergent platform with horizontal scaling. To perform the procedures of loading large data into the cloud storage, the streaming architecture of the data search and integration subsystem is implemented with the possibility of parallel preprocessing of information. The components of the information and analytical platform have been developed and implemented.

Keywords: Information analytical platform · Big data · Intellectual analysis · Innovation system · Convergent platform · ETL procedures

1 Introduction

The universal implementation of the modern technologies of digital economy makes it possible to eliminate barriers that impede the growth of economic entities' activities and to reduce high transaction costs that complicate the interaction of economic process participants. Modern technologies of big data, intellectual analysis and machine learning should be used for the synthesis of mechanisms supporting the processes of innovative development of economic agents in the regions. One of such mechanisms is the innovation development management system with the aim of increasing the competitiveness of enterprises within the framework of the development of the concept of digital economy. The need to introduce an integrated approach to managing innovation

© Springer Nature Switzerland AG 2019
A. G. Kravets et al. (Eds.): CIT&DS 2019, CCIS 1083, pp. 230–242, 2019.
https://doi.org/10.1007/978-3-030-29743-5_18

processes is confirmed by the heterogeneity of the state of enterprises in the regions, the variety of financial and economic conditions for the introduction of new technologies and the creation of an innovative environment. Heterogeneity and diversity are due to such factors as the level of economic development, the availability of qualified personnel, social stratification, level of education, degree of financial security, historical aspects of development, features of the place of residence, preferences and habits of the population. We shall also emphasize a lack of the required level of interaction between participants due to high transaction costs, which, in turn, makes it difficult to efficiently utilize the system's potential and decrease the efficiency of regional innovative development. According to the neo-institutional approach, the regional innovation system should be considered by the concepts of institutional categories and transaction costs [1]. The goal of system optimization is the reduction of economic agents' transaction costs, as a high level of the latter impedes the development of innovation activities.

The development of information and telecommunication technologies has led to the fact that analytical systems can solve rather complex problems using artificial intelligence methods. For example, in the field of economics, such tasks include the tasks of calculating production indicators, planning the volume and timing of production, modeling the indicators of sales of goods and services in accordance with the predicted demand of citizens. The heterogeneity of market conditions is determined by the different behavior of customers in regions and localities, their financial capabilities, preferences, seasonality factors, etc. The process of managing production and sales of goods includes predictive modeling of the dynamics of changes in consumer preferences and shopping potential of stores in regions of the country, taking into account the location and demand indicators in social groups for the categories of the assortment list of goods. To solve the problem of forecasting sales of goods in all outlets in the region and the country as a whole, big data mining methods are needed. The big data here includes the characteristics of shopping facilities in the regions, information about the assortment list of all products of each store and their sales for the previous time intervals. The assortment list of large supermarkets can include tens of thousands of items. In the process of building a predictive model, various factors affecting the sales of specific goods in a given area should be taken into account. Factors of influence in particular include information on household income, transport accessibility of a retail outlet, especially its location, proximity to competitors, the factor of seasonality of demand, etc. At the same time, big data is collected from open sources on the Internet [2], where many data may be heterogeneous, incorrect, duplicated, insufficient and require pre-processing before loading into the repository. The results of prognostic modeling are needed to support decision-making by the administration in the direction of optimizing the assortment matrices, the trading potential and the commercial attractiveness of the commercial enterprise in order to increase its competitiveness.

Similar problems occur in management of innovative development and competitive interaction of any subjects of the digital economy [3]. The most important position here is assigned to the problems of collection and processing of Big Data on all innovation-active companies and investors. The obtained information is required to assess the innovative potential, investment appeal and competitiveness of regional companies, as well as to forecast innovation development dynamics in short-term and long-term perspectives.

The solution of the mentioned problems requires a complex of methods of the intellectual analysis, which includes models and methods of stratification, hierarchic clustering, multifactor variance analysis, ranking of companies, assessment and selection of innovation leaders, benchmarking, forecasting and assessment of innovative development strategies and competitiveness dynamics, etc. Basically, we can see the realization of the convergent approach, which determines the process of convergence of heterogeneous information technologies as a result of their evolutionary development and interaction for the purpose of solving the problem of regional innovation system management [4]. We suggest to implement the complex of models and methods for estimating the innovative potential and competitiveness of companies in modern market conditions, taking account of crisis phenomena, in the form of a convergent system of distributed Big Data processing on the basis of a parallel data flow architecture applying blockchain technologies to secure safe interaction of innovation system's agents.

2 Convergent Approach, Convergent and Hyperconvergent Systems

The convergence between science and technology [5–7] determines the process of interpenetration of technologies and boundary-spanning between them, so that the results and innovations emerge in the interdisciplinary field of knowledge. Sometimes the convergence is regarded as a synonym to the holistic system approach based on the principle of integration and the emergent property, when new features appear in a holistic system as a result of linking of its parts. In our opinion, the convergent approach is a result of synergetic interaction [8] and reciprocal influence of cognitive, social, informational, telecommunication, neurobiological technologies during the synthesis of tools intended for the obtainment of new knowledge and innovations. For example, the convergence between the technologies and systems of fixed line and mobile telephone communication has led to the situation, when subscribers have access to virtually identical services, and the systems themselves are in close interaction between each other, but it doesn't mean that they are integrating.

Convergence defines the integration process of cyber-physical and cyber-social systems and technologies in multimodal infrastructure projects, such as Smart City. Cyber-physical systems are objects of the technogenic sphere with built-in interfaces, sensors and remote access modules for data collection, monitoring and control [9]. Cyber-physical systems interact in the information space of the Internet of Things. An example of cyber social systems are social networks, which designate the concept of a social environment in a virtual space and are tools for managing public consciousness [10]. Each cyber social system represents the knowledge, abilities, socio-cultural characteristics of people as an integral part of the social environment [11].

An innovation system of a region with a multitude of participants and a mechanism for their interaction in the information space will be considered a cyber-social system at the mesoeconomic level. It unites formal and informal institutions of interacting economic agents in the information environment. An analytical platform with instrumental tools is needed to monitor and support decision making on managing the innovative development of these agents.

The concept of convergence is the engine of evolutionary processes in various fields and has an impact on innovation processes in economic systems. Convergent systems of data processing and storage are opening a new stage of the information and telecommunication infrastructure [12, 13]. The convergent infrastructure often refers to network computing complexes containing everything necessary to solve company's problems. Actually, the convergent system is based on such an infrastructure that includes sensor networks and the Internet of things, cloud computing clusters, multiprocessor systems, mobile computing systems. The next stage of the evolution of convergent systems is hyperconvergent infrastructures of the corporate level [14].

The difference between convergent and hyperconvergent systems lies in the fact that convergent structures include specialized interacting components (computing and data storing nodes, etc.). Hyperconvergent systems represent modular solutions developed to simplify scaling by means of inclusion of new modules into the system. The capacity of convergent systems is determined by vertical scalability (scale-in), when computing hardware facilities are increased by adding of special resources. For example, in order to increase storage system capacity one may add new drives and input-output modules when the need arises. Hyperconvergent systems solve the same problem by horizontal scalability (scale out), which means integration of autonomous modules so that they become a uniform complex. Besides, these modules can be geographically remote. New modules may be connected into the system virtually unlimitedly on demand. Autonomous modules merge into clusters connected via an external network. In terms of administration, a cluster is regarded as a logical unit, where information objects are represented in the global namespace or DFS.

According to the research of Forrester Research [15], the hyper-convergent IT infrastructure synthesis principle is crucial for the creation of integrative computing systems. Such systems integrate servers, storage systems, network functions and software in a modular architecture, which provides for common use a single scalable pool of information and computing resources [16]. The modular architecture of hyperconvergent systems includes computational components connected in a horizontally scalable cluster [17]. Each module contains a computing core, a storage resource, a telecommunication component, and a hypervisor for resource allocation. The system represents a software-defined environment. In this environment, resources are defined at the levels of the computing cluster. The components of the data storage and access system and management are implemented at the program level. The architecture provides security and fault tolerance through a single computing infrastructure that includes the same modules. The features of hyperconvergent systems include horizontal scalability and compliance with the needs of the enterprise. Hyperconverged systems are software and hardware systems that are well used for processing big data.

Examples of such systems are hardware-software complexes Oracle Exocomplexes [19, 20], Teradata [18], Hadoop [21] ecosystems, IBM InfoSphere BigInsights, IBM Big Data platform [22], and others. The Blockchain platform can also be attributed to hyperconvergent systems [23].

3 Convergent Information-Analytical Platform

The information and analytical platform includes tools for collecting and mining big data. The platform includes:

- computing power of the data center,
- data collection tools (crawlers),
- data integration subsystem in the storage,
- cloud data storage,
- applications for solving problems of intellectual analysis and predictive modeling,
- expert component for tuning predictive models,
- remote secure access subsystem,
- information security administration subsystem,
- means of monitoring, management and audit of the system

The platform belongs to the class of convergent systems. It implements an automated process for monitoring and decision support. It includes data mining tools, a subsystem for processing, consolidating and storing data, modules for calculating integral indicators, modules for intellectual analysis and predictive modeling, a subsystem for generating reports and presenting it to users in a visual form, an information security administration subsystem. The main function of the platform is to coordinate the work of data processing modules obtained from different sources, with the support of the function of centralized monitoring and auditing of components.

The first stage of the decision-making process using the platform's tools is the consolidation and use of operational and retrospective data on the innovation activities of economic agents in the region. The data after the preprocessing stage is transferred to the cloud storage, from where it is extracted for processing and analysis in data marts. Thus, the process of automating the collection and processing of data on innovations and innovative enterprises in the regions from open sources on the Internet is realized.

The platform tools perform a number of operations, such as:

- search for information about innovations, authors and owners of intellectual property, about innovative enterprises in open sources,
- collection of information on indicators and indicators of innovation,
- collection and analysis of data on factors influencing innovation development processes.
- preliminary processing of data for downloading to the central cloud storage with the implementation of centralized processing of big data.
- monitoring and analysis of innovation indicators of economic agents in the region.
- identification of innovative leaders in the regions in terms of innovation indicators,
- calculation of the values of benchmark indicators of innovation in leaders to assess their competitiveness in the region and in the country as a whole, taking into account the peculiarities of regional development.
- synthesis of forecasting models for predicting the dynamics of indicators of innovation activity and competitiveness of economic agents.

- comparative benchmarking analysis of innovation indicators of economic agents in the region with benchmarks of leaders to develop strategies for innovation development and decision-making to enhance innovation and competitiveness [24].
- formation of analytical reports for stakeholders with the results of the analysis and forecast of the dynamics of innovation activities in order to synthesize recommendations for improving the innovativeness and competitiveness of economic agents and providing personalized access to reference materials.

The main information products of the platform are statistical and analytical reports in digital, text, graphic or mixed presentation. Access to analytical reports is provided to users according to protocols and security policies and. The information repository is filled with data in the process of collecting operational and retrospective information about the state of economic agents and their innovation activities. To make decisions, administrative personnel are centrally provided with the main types of analytical, statistical and forecast reports on the innovation activities of economic agents.

Information and analytical platform implements the functions of:

- centralized processing of data on innovation;
- control the integrity and immutability of data from open sources;
- ensuring consistency and completeness of information for decision-making;
- improving the efficiency of the decision-making process on changing the innovation climate in the regions

The converged computing model is an environment to support the functioning of mining applications and predictive modeling. Applications implement centralized processing, consolidated data storage, report generation and provision to users. The information environment presents the main services for interacting with users, which include:

- providing access to data
- formation of information products and regulations for their use,
- access control for reports,
- quality control of reports,
- collection, accumulation, integration and storage of data,
- management of the functioning of subsystems and the interaction between them.

There are a number of requirements for the platform, including [25]:

1. The platform architecture allows you to connect new data sources with minimal changes to the basic components (system design is determined by the properties of the data model).
2. The platform provides scalability by efficiently allocating resources without software development.
3. The platform allows you to reuse template modular solutions that are customized or refined as needed.

Within the framework of the platform, there are five main levels for data processing:

- level of data sources,
- level of data integration,

- data storage level
- data processing level,
- access level.

The level of data sources is intended for solving problems of collecting and pre-processing data obtained from various sources on the Internet. The data integration level implements the processes of consolidation and loading of data into the repository with the support of procedures for extracting and converting unstructured and weakly structured data, data control, data loading into the cloud storage. The data storage level is represented by the information storage management system. The level of analytical processing includes tools for intellectual analysis and predictive modeling. The data access layer implements access procedures using web services and mobile applications.

The convergent platform's architecture includes the following modular software components:

1. A data storing module on the basis of a cloud storage keeps retrospective data received from the system of integration, integral indicators, reports.
2. A data integration module consolidates and refines data, as well as converts them to be uploaded into a storage and passed into the analytical system.
3. A report making module prepares reports on the basis of the information from a storage according to the regulations or on users' demand.
4. A metadata keeping module synthesizes and describes metadata for primary data, cloud storage entities and data marts. As for the primary data, the module describes an info logical model of data in terms of a subject area. Regarding the storage entities, the module provides description and management at 3 levels: physical, logical and info logical.
5. An interaction module provides users with services of controlled access to information products in accordance with rights and authorization.
6. A module of personal access to data and monitoring results prepares, transforms and publishes data through a web-service or a mobile application.
7. An administrating module automates the activity of system administrators regarding management of modules and platform's hardware functioning and interaction.

The converged platform implements cloud computing models such as Platform-as-a-Service (PaaS) and Infrastructure-as-a-Service (IaaS). The PaaS model provides the consumer with the ability to use the cloud infrastructure to host and launch data processing applications. The IaaS model provides the ability to use the cloud infrastructure to manage processing and storage resources.

A software and hardware complex of virtualization and a complex of terminal access to results are implemented to support the technology of Big Data. The software and hardware complex of virtualization provides as follows:

- functioning of module servers in the virtual environment on architectural platform x86,
- putting new virtual servers into operation during scaling,
- management of computing resources for software module functioning.

The software technical complex of terminal access provides the following:

- the service of cloud access to user's virtual environment using the technology of virtual workstations,
- the service of cloud access to administrator's virtual environment using the technology of virtual workstations;
- the virtual work station interface for mobile devices.

The platform is developed in the Java language in the Java EE environment in a cross-platform version for z/OS, AIX, Linux and Windows OS and is intended for mainframe-class computers (RISC, Intel x86). The data component of the platform in the data center uses UNIX-like OS AIX (Advanced Interactive eXecutive) of IBM and IBM DB2 for AIX. The convergent platform implements the technology of parallel processing of big data during the implementation of ETL procedures and analytical processing procedures. To support the technology, a hypervisor is used with the ability to support: (a) up to 320 logical processors per host server, (b) up to 4 TB of RAM per host server, (c) up to 512 virtual machines per host server, (d) automatic distribution of virtual machines between host servers depending on the load, (e) hot migration of virtual machines between host servers, (f) loading the hypervisor from an external disk array over the network, (g) virtual distributed network switches.

The software and instrumental modules of the platform are located on dedicated resources of the software and technical complex pSeries, running under AIX OS. To organize cloud storage, DB2 10.1 and DB2 Spatial Extender are used, and the data integration module runs on IBM Information Server 9.1.2. Cognos BI 10.2 and IBM HTTP Server 8.0.0.0 are used for generating reports. Interaction with users and administration of the platform is carried out through the application server Websphere Application Server 8.5.5.

4   The Integration System's Architecture for Data Flow Processing

As it has been mentioned previously, the main feature of convergent and hyperconvergent systems is architectural scalability that boosts productivity and increases the amount of processed data without cardinal modernization of the whole system. This feature makes such systems irreplaceable when working with Big Data. For example, let us consider the architecture of a convergent system of data integration or an ETL system. The ETL system performs a number of processes in the field of data processing and processing progress management, including the following:

1. Extraction of data from sources.
2. Convergence of data into a uniform format.
3. Maintaining quality and integrity of data in a storage and their restoration in case of contingencies.
4. Data conversion (refining, standardization and consolidation) when uploaded into a storage.
5. Data uploading and updating of the data previously uploaded into a storage.

6. Monitoring, control and logging of data uploading processes.
7. Detection and handling of errors occurring in data integration processes.

Data extraction is a process, when data are grabbed and shifted into the area of data preparation. Data conversion is a process, when data coming in different formats are unified into one. Next, the data are transformed according to local directories, corresponding to the source of information, and the data identifiers together with the structure of the given data are standardized. Quality assurance is a process, when data in the preparation area are checked for compliance with criteria of correctness, completeness, consistency, uniformity and unification. Data transformation is a process of their refinement, supplement and modification according to the processing logic. When being uploaded the data are transferred from the conversion area into a storage.

The scalability problem is solved by means of convergent architecture synthesis. Such architecture ensures a high level of parallel processing of Big Data with possible controlling of the parallelism degree. Process paralleling enables to efficiently utilize hardware resources and to engage additional resources in case the number of data sources increases. This presupposes linking-up and application of template data processing modules [26, 27]. In this case, the convergent system of data integration may be represented a set of module flows interacting between each other. Each module flow performs the full process of data processing from extraction from sources to uploading into a storage.

The integration system's architecture is designed according to the properties of the corporative model of data in a storage. The regional innovation system's object seems to be a logical concept or a complex. The logical concept may also be represented as an event happened in a data source to one or several objects. Each flow in the architecture performs extraction, transformation and uploading of data on one logical concept. Each component in a flow performs the corresponding transformation of attributes from input metadata into attributes of output metadata. Thus, the flow consists of components that perform the following functions:

1. Collection of data associated with logical concepts;
2. Preliminary transformation;
3. Search for alterations (new data on objects);
4. Transformation of classifier values from sources into storage values;
5. Creation of surrogate keys on the basis of business keys and compilation of a directory of surrogate keys' correspondence to business keys in different sources;
6. Synthesis of links (assignment of correct external keys) between business keys;
7. Final transformation (dismantling of data according to the structure of storage's physical tables);
8. Data uploading into the storage's data base.

Within a single flow ETL procedures are executed consecutively: each procedure processes the result of the previous one. The flows depend on initial data at the "Preliminary transformation" stage and may interact at the stages "Synthesis of links" and "Data uploading". The function "Preliminary transformation" may require an unknown number of operations with data due to the application of algorithms that depend on the sources. The operations executed in other components are known and determined by the system's internal functions. It is possible to create a template for a component that would include a standard set of operations. Thus, the convergent system consists of flows and single-type components differing in input and output metadata. The architecture will be effective in such an informational model, in which the growth of data volumes leads to adding of new objects and doesn't change the existing objects. If the existing objects remain unchanged, than the flows that process these objects are subject to no changes as well. In order to upload new objects it is simply required to add new flows.

In the convergent architecture the flows interact between each other. For example, they wait until the work of the preceding component from another flow is completed. At the same time, the system doesn't stand idle, because other flows operate simultaneously when completing ETL tasks. The flows are executed on distributed physical resources in the GRID architecture solving the problem of scaling. The number of concurrent flows can be regulated to decrease or increase resource utilization.

5   Conclusion

The tools of the information and analytical platform are intended for the analysis and prognostic evaluation of the innovative activity of economic agents in the regions. To solve the problems of analysis and prognostic modeling, a set of indicators of innovative activity of enterprises was proposed. Examples of such indicators are as follows:

- the average and maximum investment for creating and implementing innovations over a period of time,
- the median on the scale of investment values,
- the average and maximum number of innovations implemented in the enterprise over a period of time,
- percentiles (characteristics that show what percentage of an enterprise's investment is below a certain level), etc.

Based on a variety of indicators, integrated criteria for the innovative development of economic agents have been developed, which are also determined for the entire region. The complex criterion for the innovative development of a region is an integral assessment of the innovative potential and investment attractiveness of all enterprises in it.

The calculation of indicators of innovation activity is based on data that are extracted from open sources.

There is a problem of data extraction, which is related to the fact that the number of indicators of innovation development can be many, but in the process of analysis one should select only those to which the integrated criteria have the maximum sensitivity. To assess the sensitivity method is used multivariate analysis of variance. Sensitivity studies have shown that in order to assess the innovation activity of economic agents, it is necessary to select not only direct indicators, but also indirect factors of influence. An example of direct indicators are: (a) the number of registered intellectual property objects in an enterprise, (b) the amount of funding for innovation, etc. Examples of indirect factors include: (a) the state of the transport infrastructure, (b) the income level of the company's employees, (c) the level of development of the information and telecommunications infrastructure in the region, (d) the average cost of Internet access services, etc.

The process of selecting indicators and assessing their impact on the integral characteristics begins with the compilation of their maximum possible list. For the calculation of indicators, data is collected by crawlers using the "curious user" algorithm. After assessing the sensitivity and selection of significant factors of influence, data are collected for each of them, showing the dynamics of their change over a long period of time. This is necessary in order to build graphs of the dynamics of their changes and see how indicators affect the criteria for innovative development.

Many significant factors form the coordinate system of the multidimensional space in which the clustering of economic agents takes place. For each cluster, innovative leaders are determined, the indicators of which form the optimal basis for innovative development. The consolidation of bases for all clusters allows us to determine the optimal vector of innovative development of the region. Before solving the clustering problem, it is necessary to distinguish groups or layers of economic agents that are in approximately equal conditions. Such conditions are determined through data on the location of enterprises, economic, cultural, social and other features of the region. To solve the problem, the stratification technology is used, according to which the allocation of strata of settlements in the region for economic agents is performed. Such criteria as population, number of qualified personnel for the creation and implementation of innovations, development of transport and telecommunications infrastructure, etc. are taken as criteria for stratification.

Examples of source data for solving problems of analyzing the level of innovative development of regions are:

1. Geolocation data on economic agents' positioning;
2. Data on company's resources allocated for innovations;
3. Data on economic agents' financial status;
4. Data on developed, sold and implemented innovations for a set period of time with annual and monthly breakdown;
5. Data on proper financial resources expended on development and implementation of innovations for a set period of time with annual and monthly breakdown;
6. Data on external investments expended on development and implementation of innovations for a set period of time with annual and monthly breakdown;
7. Data on registered intellectual property objects;
8. Data on regional transport infrastructure;
9. Data on regional telecommunication infrastructure, etc.

The most complicated part is the processing of huge data volumes represented in structured and unstructured form on Internet sources. The problem of Big Data collecting and processing can be solved by applying a flow mechanism implemented in the convergent GRID data integration system. The data from open-access sources are extracted by multiple searching agents that collect data on regional innovation objects, including geolocation, designation, financial indicators, data on intellectual property objects, data on company's human resources, tangible and informational resources, etc. The sources of such data are companies' websites, state services' websites, special databases, partner companies' websites. The role of the agents may be performed by special searching crawlers written in Python Scrappy language. The data on the same objects from different sources should be combined. Therefore, in order to exclude duplicated information such elements as addresses, designations and satellite coordinates are compared.

To ensure reliable storage of information about an innovative facility and to realize the possibility of securely sharing this information, the distributed registry technology is used on the blockchain platform Etherium. The platform also allows you to create smart contracts to support the processes of interaction of economic agents and to ensure reliable and safe transfer of intellectual property rights to innovative objects.

Acknowledgments. The reported study was funded by RFBR according to the projects: № 18-010-00204-a, 18-07-00975-a, 19-013-00409-a.

References

1. Vasin, S.M., Gamidullaeva, L.A.: Development of Russian innovation system management concept. Innovations **5**(223), 34–40 (2017)
2. Shmid, A.V., et al.: New methods of working with big data: winning management strategies in business analytics: scientific and practical collection, p. 528. PALMIR, Moscow (2016)
3. Bershadsky, A.M., Berezin, A.A., Finogeev, A.G.: Information support of decision making tools for competitiveness management. Russian J. Manage. **5**(3), 490–493 (2017)
4. Bainbridge, M.S., Roco, M.C.: Managing Nano-Bio-Info-Cogno Innovations: Converging Technologies in Society, p. 390. Springer, Dordrecht (2005). https://doi.org/10.1007/1-4020-4107-1
5. Parygin, D., Shcherbakov, M., Sadovnikova, N., Kravets, A., Finogeev, A.: Proactive urban computing: an active agent-based concept and methods. In: Proceedings of the 6th International Conference on System Modeling & Advancement in Research Trends, Moradabad, India, pp. 219–226 (2017)
6. Roco, M., Bainbridge, W.: Converging Technologies for Improving Human Performance: Nanotechnology, Biotechnology, Information Technology and Cognitive Science. The National Science Foundation, Arlington (2004). http://www.wtec.org/Converging Technologies/Report/NBIC_report.pdf. Accessed 11 Jan 2019
7. Chul, L., Gunno, P., Jina, K.: The impact of convergence between science and technology on innovation. J. Technol. Transf. **43**, 522–544 (2016)
8. Finogeev, A.G.: Modeling research of system-synergetic processes in information environments: Monograph, p. 223. PGU, Penza (2004)
9. Finogeev, A.G., Parygin, D.S., Finogeev, A.A.: The convergence computing model for big sensor data mining and knowledge discovery. Hum.-Centric Comput. Inf. Sci. **7**, 1–11 (2017)
10. Ustugova, S., Parygin, D., Sadovnikova, N., Finogeev, A., Kizim, A.: Monitoring of social reactions to support decision making on issues of urban territory management. Procedia Comput. Sci. **101**, 243–252 (2016). Proceedings of the 5th International Young Scientist Conference on Computational Science, Elsevier, Krakow, Poland
11. Liu, Z., et al.: Cyber-physical-social systems for command and control. IEEE Intell. Syst. **26**(4), 92–96 (2011)
12. Broderick, K., Scaramella, J.: Considering All of IT: Converged Infrastructure Survey Findings. IDC (2010)

13. Weiss, G.J.: Plan now for the future of converged infrastructure. Gartner (2016)
14. Hubbard, P.: Hyper-converged infrastructure forcing new thinking for networks. Techtarget (2016)
15. Taft, D.K.: IBM sees flash, hyper-convergence among top 2016 storage trends. Eweek (2016)
16. Forrester research. http://www.forrester.com. Accessed 18 Dec 2019
17. Whiteley, R.: Forrester research. your next IT budget: 6 ways to support business growth. CIO Magazine Archived, Wayback Machine (2010)
18. Rollason, J.: Introducing NetApp enterprise-scale HCI: the next generation of hyper converged infrastructure. NetApp (2017)
19. Teradata. https://www.teradata.ru/, Accessed 28 Dec 2019
20. Osborne, K., Johnsn, R., Tanel, P.: Exadata, exalogic, exalytics. In: Expert Oracle Exadata, p. 500 (2011)
21. Plunkett, T., Palazzolo, T.J., Joshi, T.: Oracle Exalogic Elastic Cloud Handbook, 432 p. McGraw-Hill, New York (2011)
22. White, T.: Hadoop: The Definitive Guide, p. 600. Sebastopol, O'Reilly Media (2011)
23. Big data analytics. http://www.ibm.com/big-data/us/en/conversations/. Accessed 2 Feb 2019
24. Blockchain platforms. http://smart-contracts.ru/platforms.html. Accessed 2 Feb 2019
25. Mkrttchian, V., Bershadsky, A., Finogeev, A., Berezin, A., Potapova, I.: Digital model of bench-marking for development of competitive advantage. In: Isaias, P., Carvalho, L. (eds.) User Innovation and the Entrepreneurship Phenomenon in the Digital Economy, pp. 279–300. IGI Global, Hershey (2017)
26. Kimball, R., Caserta, J.: The Data Warehouse ETL Toolkit: Practical Techniques for Extracting, Cleaning, Conforming, and Delivering Data. Wiley Publishing Inc., New York (2004)
27. Goma, H.: UML: Design of Real-Time Systems, Parallel and Distributed Applications, p. 704. DMK Press, Moscow (2016). Per. with English

Cyber-Physical Systems and Big Data-Driven World. Design Creativity in CASE/CAI/CAD/PDM

Meta-design of Processes Based on Visualization Tools

Alena A. Zakharova[1] (ID), Anton Krysko[2] (ID), Evgeniya Vekhter[3(✉)] (ID), and Aleksey Shklyar[3] (ID)

[1] Bryansk State Technical University, Bryansk, Russian Federation
zaa@tu-bryansk.ru
[2] Department of Mathematics and Modeling, Yuri Gagarin State Technical University of Saratov, Saratov, Russian Federation
anton.krysko@gmail.com
[3] Tomsk Polytechnic University, Avenue of Lenin, 30, 634050 Tomsk, Russia
{vehter, shklyarav}@tpu.ru

Abstract. Interactive visualization, used to represent and interpret input data, makes it possible to employ visual perception potential to search for and resolve internal contradictions in the studied data, the source of which in many cases is errors made during the development of the program. The purpose of visual analytics in this study is to identify contradictions in the design of an educational process, provided by the curriculum, and to form students' meaningful variable and individual educational trajectories.

Keywords: Visual information · Visual analysis effectiveness · Perception · Meta-design · Educational environment · Educational program

1 Introduction

The concept of meta-design of some process implies its design in such a way that all its participants fulfill the role of active creators of content. Participants in the process are any subjects (people, groups) and objects (regulatory documents, data sources) that influence the final result. An example of applied meta-design is the educational process, which includes three active elements: a teaching subject, a learning subject, and the information environment.

One of the advantages of meta-design is the principle that the basis of any learning is an interpretation of information received through the prism of previously acquired knowledge. This means that learning is much more effective if the learner creates something for others, shares his knowledge and experience. A person ceases to be considered a product of the environment and an idea is formed of a person as of a product of human interaction with the environment. Development of meta-design makes it necessary to formulate and substantiate the fundamental laws, characterizing students' interaction with rich information reality [10].

Educational environment in modern university education acts as a dynamic system which is an integrated set of successively alternating educational situations. A system of psychological, pedagogical and didactic conditions and stimuli arises, confronting a

A. G. Kravets et al. (Eds.): CIT&DS 2019, CCIS 1083, pp. 245–255, 2019.
https://doi.org/10.1007/978-3-030-29743-5_19

person with the necessity of conscious choice, adjustment, formation, and implementation of his own learning model, that is, the realization of independent educational activities. This induces necessity and possibility of forming at the university not only educational trajectories provided by the curriculum, but also students' variable and individual educational trajectories. This is provided for when developing educational programs.

When designing educational environment, one of the significant problems is the creation of tools for collecting, systematizing and analyzing educational information, on the basis of which it is possible to carry out the timely correction of the educational process and educational program components. One of the promising areas in the development of operational data analysis tools is the development of specialized visual analytics tools, which purposefully use the advantage of visual perception.

2 Purpose of Visualization Tools in Educational Process

Transition to the use of visualization tools in design and quality evaluation of an educational program is conditioned by the need to analyze a large number of relationships between elements of this program [13]. Traditional means of analyzing large amounts of information have a number of shortcomings, which include high qualification requirements to the experts involved in the analysis, as well as the necessity for interdisciplinary interaction among them.

The purpose of the use of visualization tools is to identify contradictions in the design of educational process envisaged by the curriculum and formation of meaningful variable and individual educational trajectories of students. In addition, improving the quality of an educational program involves search and elimination of internal contradictions in data under study, the source of which, in many cases, are errors made during the program development. The subjective nature of such contradictions makes it difficult to detect them on the basis of previously defined criteria.

The use of visual analysis tools provides a comprehensive view of a process with the possibility of its dynamic modernization, which creates conditions for achieving maximum performance when finalizing the planned expectations, results and needs between the organizers and consumers of educational services. Efficiency is ensured by obtaining and maintaining professional competencies to the maximum possible extent. The result of the use of visualization tools for the educational process expert evaluation is the identification of opportunities to increase the process intensity while observing all local constraints.

Interactive visualization used to represent and interpret the source data makes it possible to use the potential of visual perception to compensate for the specified difficulties [2, 4]. Benefits include high speed of visual perception necessary for simultaneous comparison of a large array of disparate facts and the possibility to represent data not only in numerical form. Important features of visual perception are the capability to compare several events (options) and the persuasiveness of the received decision-oriented information.

One point of solving problems similar to those under discussion is the assessment of decision consequences. These consequences may include changing the set of related parameters and the total effect of changes on the conformance of the system under study to its goals and boundary conditions. Visualization tools make it possible to simplify the search for a necessary solution as a result of the researcher's forming a common understanding of all relevant relationships in the data under study and ways of implementing them to change the investigated system (educational program) in the required direction [3].

3 Visualization Tool

3.1 Visual Representation Requirements

Variants of information sources involved in visualization ensure availability of information of various origins: input data, interactive data, and pre-stored data. Exclusion of interactive data and preliminary information from consideration forms a visual communication system similar to a conventional communication system [8]. Use of data of interaction between a visual object and a user leads to new data in the process of transferring information and, consequently, to obtain new results. Therefore, one of the requirements for developers of visualization tools is to provide interactive communication with the visual image of the data under study.

Redundancy of Visualization. Observing a three-dimensional object from different angles as it rotates within view corresponds to receiving a sequence of messages informing the recipient about the same event but containing different data sets. Existence of information re-transmission is the basis for evaluating information redundancy, as well as for finding ways to reduce the overall resource-intensiveness of the decision process. According to research results [1], various aspects of visual representation convey different types of information with different cognitive performance. Combination of several ways of data visual representation can be used to improve the overall effectiveness of their interpretation by the user but only if the necessary substantiation is available. Thus, the redundancy of visual information can be considered as a parameter for the rational use of available resources and as a way to obtain additional research results.

Colour Coding. Accuracy of perception and subsequent interpretation of information represented in the form of a color code cannot be reduced to a one-to-one comparison of the digital value, which determines the point of the color range, and the displayed data [6, 7]. For example, an important factor that influences the choice of color-coding scheme is the non-uniform susceptibility of vision to signals having different values of brightness, saturation, and color. Substantiation of the use of a specific color-coding scheme should occur taking into account cultural, physiological and other features of the target audience.

User. The need to use perception capabilities, characterized by empirical principles, sets a developer of visualization tools a task of determining a set of user characteristics that are purposefully involved in interpreting the data visual image [9]. The selection can be made on the basis of preliminary assessment of available resources, which include:

- potential user's characteristics;
- computational resources;
- time resource;
- additional requirements resulting from the research problem formulation.

The set of user characteristics involved in the cognitive visual image interpretation of the studied data is determined as a result of generalizing the existing visualization process schemes [5, 12] and divided into three groups of characteristics:

- Observation. Characteristics that allow the user to obtain visual information (perception of color, space, movement, preferred expressive means, speed of perception).
- Search. Characteristics that allow allocating relevant objects and processes in the initial visual information (spatial thinking, preliminary awareness, motivation).
- Formulation. User characteristics that allow formulating hypotheses for answering a research question (experience in using visual analytics tools, ability to learn and use new language systems).

3.2 Formal Description

Analyzed process E is an ordered set of objects $O = \{O_1..O_n\}$. The number of its elements depends on the target goal and the available resources. Each object O_i has properties $\{P_i\}$, ensuring its interaction with other elements O_j. Order requirement B_k of set O is one of the conditions for the completion of process E, that is, it is an element of boundary requirements set $B = \{B_k\}$. Element properties are divided into two subsets, based on their functional differences:

$$O_i = \{P_i\} = \{In_x, Out_y\},$$

where subset $\{In_x\}$ is processed requirements, the so-called incoming relationships, and subset $\{Out_y\}$ is process results, the so-called outgoing relationships.

The formal purpose of the study is to determine set O, which provides the best results while observing all boundary requirements B:

$$O = \{O_n : n = min, Out = max\} \tag{1}$$

If element properties are defined, then the solution goal becomes ordering set O which ensures the fulfillment of requirement (1). In the opposite case, the solution of the problem is a new set $O^* = \{In^*, Out^*\}$, corresponding to requirements B.

3.3 Visual Data Model

Building a visualization tool designed for studying heterogeneous data, namely, information characterizing any educational program includes a number of mandatory steps [9]. The sequence of necessary actions forms an algorithm aimed at formalizing the development of visualization tools. Existence of formal rules ensures applicability of visualization tools for a wide range of tasks, as well as feasibility assessment of already created visualization tools in new tasks.

Data. Input data are ordered and structured in such a way that description of information objects O_i represented in a visual model is generalized and unified. The information object in the developed visualization tool is an element of an educational program (academic discipline, course, program section). Description of each object includes the following data:

- name;
- course;
- duration of the study;
- volume in hours and credits or as a percentage;
- incoming requirements $\{In_x\}$;
- anticipated results $\{Out_y\}$.

User Perception. As a result of evaluating the supposed advantages of the visualization tool for solving the problem in question, it has been proposed to use representation metaphor [6, 11], based on traditional means of visualization of tabular data (diagrams, graphs). The need for simultaneous visualization of a large (>10) number of objects and their comparison is realized through the use of color coding, rules of which can be changed according to a particular user's perception.

Visualization Metaphor. In 3d-space of the visual model, a cylindrical coordinate system is introduced, allowing to pair three values to each point in space: learning time, volume, result. Scales of measurement units along the *Time* and *Results* axes can be arbitrary. *Volume* is measured as a percent of a maximum possible one. The chosen direction of the time axis allows visualizing the analyzed data on educational programs of any duration (see Fig. 1).

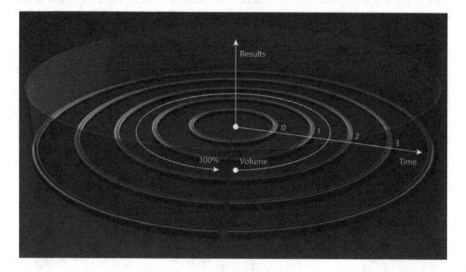

Fig. 1. Visual model space.

Program stages, corresponding to specified time intervals (years, semesters) and sequence of objects $O = \{O_1..O_n\}$, are separated by concentric circular elements used to represent the accumulated results. The radial structure, in this case, is able to represent an increasing number of learning outcomes without disrupting the general perception of data. The visual image of a program stage is accompanied by a volume scale (0–100%) with a common starting point (see Fig. 2).

Fig. 2. Learning time and volume scales.

An information object (see Fig. 3), in accordance with the proposed visualization metaphor, provides an observer with an opportunity to interpret visual attributes as values of corresponding parameters: colour is an identification attribute, dimensions are volumes, the position is learning time.

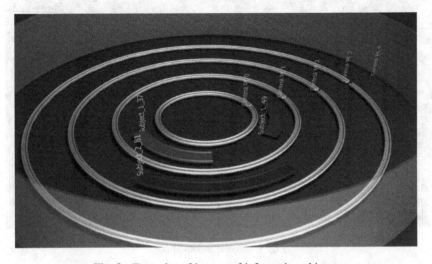

Fig. 3. Examples of images of information objects.

Data on incoming requirements and anticipated results are presented in the form of relationships between information objects. Attributes of such relationships are their direction and number corresponding to the input data. According to the characteristics of the subject area, incoming (requirements) and outgoing (results) relationships are of the same type, i.e. can be interpreted as created or developing competencies (see Figs. 4 and 5).

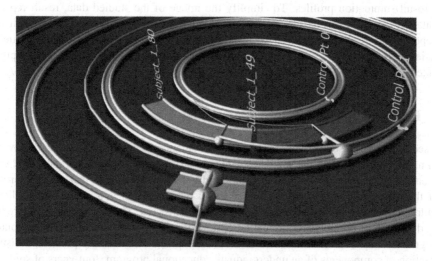

Fig. 4. Incoming and outgoing relationships.

Fig. 5. Visualization of accumulated results.

For a visual representation of accumulated results, simultaneous use of two expressive means has been proposed: a performance rating scale and visual scaling of relationships. In the first case, it becomes possible to effectively use three-dimensional space of the visual model, in the second one, evaluation of educational program results can occur when interpreting two-dimensional visualization.

As a visualization tool using representation metaphor familiar to most users, a means of visualizing intermediate and general results have been developed in the form of result summation profiles. To simplify the image of the studied data, result representation elements can be temporarily excluded from the visual model. Further, it is proposed that result profiles can be used as interactive management tools for visualization tool state. They are designed to select parameters of information objects presented visually.

4   Practical Use of Visualization Tools

Based on the proposed metaphoric visual representation of heterogeneous data, derived from the description of the analyzed educational program, several variants of their visualization have been obtained including individual pieces of data that are of interest for the analysis. The goal of creating a visual representation is a search for implicit contradictions and hidden reserves in the analyzed process. The secondary objective is the definition of possible recombination options for the components of the educational program to improve the achievable results (see Fig. 6). The example presents a visualization of components of an undergraduate educational program (four years of study).

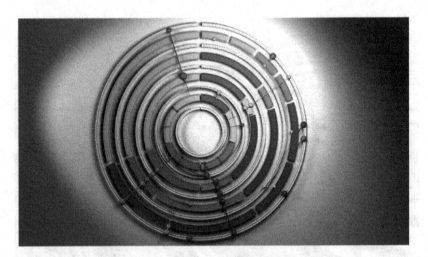

Fig. 6. Visualization of a four-year program.

Radial lines connecting information objects (sectors) are a visual representation of the accumulated learning outcomes (skills and competencies). Simultaneous representation of the time distribution of subjects (sectors) and accumulated results is one of the proposed tools of visual analysis, which allows to assess the level of usefulness of individual subjects, their role in the overall process, as well as to detect errors in the planning of educational programs (loops, gaps in the lines of results, free time ranges, degradation of competencies).

Results Profile. To simplify the assessment of intermediate results, visual representation of a profile is normalized by the value of the planned indicators. This allows determining the direction of control actions quickly in case of discrepancies between real and planned indicators (see Fig. 7).

Fig. 7. Achieved results profile.

Analysis of a set of intermediate results profiles simultaneously with the general idea of the program, which is formed using the developed visualization tool, allows for educational program dynamic correction, aimed at updating the set of final indicators. Possible situations and variants of user interaction with the program are:

- *Identification and elimination of contradictions in the input data.* Several possible situations are identified as input data errors; for their rapid detection, it is advisable to use visualization tools. Such situations include:
- *Lack of input data* is a situation in which incoming requirements are not provided with results, i.e. the requested data are missing.
- *The chronological discrepancy between the incoming requirements of the information object and the results achieved.* The contradiction arises if data which will be obtained later is required at the input of the information object.
- *Results achieved are not considered in the final profile.* The situation corresponds to the unreasonable use of existing resources.
- *Degradation of results.* The proposed visualization tool takes into account the possibility of level decrease of the achieved result with time. The contradiction is the presence in the final profile of results that ignore the level of their decrease.

- *Duplication of results* is the use of resources to repeatedly obtain similar results. The visual image of this contradiction represents divergent lines of accumulated results. The substance of the contradiction is unreasonable use of time and other resources.

Performance Evaluation. Application of the developed visualization tool made it possible to obtain an assessment of advantages of the proposed approach in comparison with traditional methods of interpretation and verification of heterogeneous data contained in documents regulating educational programs (Table 1).

Table 1. Comparison of duration of data research stages.

Comparison parameter (time consumption)	Traditional approach	Visual analysis
Training	Previous experience	Less than 5 min
Forming a general idea	15–20 min	Less than 2 min
Searching contradictions	Up to 30 min	1–5 min
Changing the goal	Impossible	Interactive
Managing data	Impossible	10–20 min

The developed tool of visual analytics of an educational environment can be supplemented by experience maintainability when already formed versions of educational trajectories and corresponding real results are saved [3]. Opportunities for advanced planning for periods of varying duration are expanded by analyzing factors that influence the deviation of real values of achieving professional competencies from those planned during educational program design.

Development of visual analytics in this direction makes a detailed understanding of educational environment functioning patterns possible and obvious. In this case, it is stated that it is necessary to deviate from the model of cognition as a "black box" model with incoming perceptual data and outgoing knowledge integrated into the existing system of human concepts [3]. Combination of visual design tools for educational process and accumulation of knowledge about the results achieved creates unique information environment, access to which can be useful to both "organizers" and "participants" of this process.

5   Conclusion

Search for a common approach to solving the problem of multidimensional data visual analysis allows using visual models as an effective tool for studying characteristics of educational programs. Benefits include high speed of visual perception, necessary for simultaneous comparison of a large array of disparate facts, as well as the possibility to represent data not only in numerical form. Additional perspectives on the use of visual analytics are associated with a full and comprehensive analysis of students' variable and individual educational trajectories. Consumers of visual analysis results can include university education administration, educational program managers and teachers providing the educational process as well as students of an educational program. Data presented in the developed visualizing tool can be applied for correction and development of new educational program trajectories. Thus, the proposed visualization tool performs the role of the main meta-design tool in developing an educational program, which is an example of heterogeneous data.

Acknowledgment. This work has been supported the Ministry of Education and Science of the Russian Federation by the Grant No. 2.1642.2017/4.6.

References

1. Barrett, H.: Perceptual measures for effective visualizations. In: Proceedings of Visualization 1997 (Cat. No. 97CB36155), pp. 515–517 (1997)
2. Batch, A., Elmqvist, N.: The interactive visualization gap in initial exploratory data analysis. IEEE Trans. Vis. Comput. Graph. **24**(1), 278–287 (2018)
3. Chen, C.: An information-theoretic view of visual analytics. IEEE Comput. Graph. Appl. **28**, 18–23 (2008)
4. Matsushita, M., Kato, T.: Interactive visualization method for exploratory data analysis, pp. 671–676. IEEE Computer Society (2001)
5. Pirolli, P., Card, S.: The sense making process and leverage points for analyst technology as identified through cognitive task analysis. In: Proceedings of International Conference on Intelligence Analysis, pp. 2–4 (2005)
6. Podvesovskii, A., Isaev, R.: Visualization metaphors for fuzzy cognitive maps. Sci. Vis. **10** (4), 13–29 (2018)
7. Rogowitz, B.E., Treinish, L.A.: How not to lie with visualization. Comput. Phys. **10**(3), 268–273 (1996)
8. Shannon, C.: A mathematical theory of communication. Bell Syst. Tech. J. **27**(3), 379–423 (1948)
9. Shklyar, A.: Visual modeling in an analysis of multidimensional data. J. Phys: Conf. Ser. **944**(1), 125–128 (2018)
10. Shklyar, A., Zakharova, A., Vekhter, E.: The applicability of visualization tools in the meta-design of an educational environment. Eur. J. Contemp. Educ. **8**(1), 4–24 (2019)
11. Shklyar, A., Zakharova, A.: Visualization metaphors. Sci. Vis. **2**(5), 16–24 (2013)
12. Van Wijk, J.: The value of visualization, 11 p (2005)
13. Vieira, C., Parsons, P., Byrd, V.: Visual learning analytics of educational data: a systematic literature review and research agenda. Comput. Educ. **122**, 119–135 (2018)

Designing Zero-Energy Buildings Using Advanced Fuzzy Cognitive Maps

Theodor Panagiotakopoulos, Nikolaos Zafeirakis,
Iliana-Vasiliki Tsoulea, and Peter P. Groumpos[✉]

Department of Electrical and Computer Engineering,
University of Patras, 26500 Rion, Greece
groumpos@ece.upatras.gr

Abstract. Energy efficient buildings are able to provide effective solutions to reduce energy consumption and carbon emissions, support environmental-friendly energy management and facilitate significant energy savings. The concept of Zero-Energy Buildings is gaining a constant increasing focus. The use of Advanced Fuzzy Cognitive Maps (AFCMs) as a new modelling methodology to provide energy performance indicators in a quantified manner that will drive the appropriate integration of required renewable energy generation, in order to design a (nearly) Zero-Energy Building (nZEB) is considered. The new approach is used to calculate the energy balance of buildings in alternative climate contexts and thus to explore their energy efficiency in six use cases. Simulation results and observations show that AFCMs could provide valuable insight to design and development issues of nZEBs.

Keywords: Advanced fuzzy cognitive maps · Zero energy buildings · Energy efficiency

1 Introduction

Aiming to address contemporary challenges, such as climate change, environmental pollution and fossil fuels shrinking stocks, the energy sector is going through a wide transformation towards more efficient and sustainable approaches. More specifically, energy consumption in buildings has seen a drastic increase over the last twenty years due to various reasons (e.g. population growth and automated building functions demands) resulting in building energy consumption currently accounting for about 40% of the total energy consumption and 36% of all greenhouse emissions in the U.S. and the E.U. However, significant reduction in buildings' energy consumption can be achieved by appropriate design, construction and operation of relative electricity infrastructures. Energy efficient buildings are able to provide effective solutions to reduce energy consumption and carbon emissions, support environmental-friendly energy management and facilitate significant energy savings.

In this context, the concept of Zero-Energy Building (ZEB) is gaining a constant increasing focus since it became a mainstream term in 2006 [1]. A ZEB is a residential or commercial building with greatly reduced energy needs through efficiency gains such that the balance of energy needs can be supplied with renewable technologies [2].

© Springer Nature Switzerland AG 2019
A. G. Kravets et al. (Eds.): CIT&DS 2019, CCIS 1083, pp. 256–266, 2019.
https://doi.org/10.1007/978-3-030-29743-5_20

A zero energy building means a building where, as a result of the very high level of energy efficiency of the building, the overall annual primary energy consumption is equal to or less than the energy production from Renewable Energy Sources (RES). There are two basic functions to achieve a ZEB: (a) deployment and exploitation of renewable generation and (b) dynamic energy-efficient consumption adjustment mechanisms. The first function is mainly applied during the design phase driving construction of or transformation to a ZEB, while the second function is applied during operation for monitoring and control.

The design phase model the energy infrastructure providing the foundation for control optimization of a Complex Dynamic System (CDS), which essentially a ZEB forms [3]. In order to create a ZEB, modelling aims at a select combination of RES based on their availability and physical context, while control includes the mechanisms for energy-efficient operation. All CDSs consist of collections of interacting hetero-geneous components encompassing uncertainties, fuzziness, ambiguity and structural complexities [4]. The underlying collective dynamics of CDSs in conjunction with the scope of a ZEB raise some challenging questions [3, 5]: which combination of RES should we consider and based on what assumptions to meet the total energy demand of a region? How all these are effectively connected to the energy efficiency of buildings? Do we have effective models, methods and software tools to provide qualitative analysis and quantitative indicators of the dynamics and behavior of such systems? Groumpos and Mpelogianni [6] explored the most important factors that affect the overall energy performance of a building and highlighted the lack of a unified math-ematical model to consider all variables and concepts with regards to energy efficient buildings able to address the aforementioned challenges.

This paper proposes the use of Advanced Fuzzy Cognitive Maps (AFCMs) as a modelling methodology for RES requirements to achieve energy efficiency of buildings and realize a nearly ZEB in different contexts. A basic aim of our approach is to provide energy performance indicators in a quantified manner that will drive the appropriate integration of renewable energy generation to compensate for building energy consumption. FCMs comprise a combination of the methods of fuzzy logic and neural networks for modeling a large variety of CDSs [7–10]. They represent knowledge in a symbolic way and model the behavior of systems containing elements with complex relationships, which sometimes can be hidden or illegible.

2 Zero-Energy Buildings

A ZEB is based on the concept of a building which, within its boundaries, produces as much energy as it consumes, usually on an annual basis. The produced energy mainly comes from RES which are located near the building, do not pollute the environment and their cost is reasonable [11]. As with all structures, energy requirements of a ZEB depend on its utility and demands of its habitants/visitors/professional workers. In addition, based on the geographical position of each building, energy demands change due to affiliated climate conditions (e.g. cold places require large amounts of energy for heating). On the other hand, geographical position of a building also affect the integration of RES as less sunny regions will not be able to take full advantage of Photovoltaics (PVs) requiring additional sources to address its loads.

A main classification of ZEBs concerns their connection with the grid. When a ZEB is not connected to the grid it is called autonomous or stand-alone ZEB. This type refers to self-sufficient off-grid ZEBs that meet their energy demands solely from own sources and energy storage mechanisms. Furthermore, off-grid buildings cannot feed their excess energy production back onto the grid to offset other energy uses. As a result, the energy production from RES must be oversized, which implies that in many cases (especially during the summer), excess generated energy cannot be used [1]. Such ZEBs are very challenging to design and operate and are only considered when access to the grid is not available (e.g. rural and isolated areas).

On the contrary, when a ZEB is connected to the grid it may exchange energy with it either exporting excess electricity when on-site generation is greater than the building's loads or importing energy when demand is higher than what it produces. Grid-connected ZEBs are separated in three categories [12]:

- Nearly Zero-Energy Buildings (nZEB) that have nearly zero energy balance in the sense that the energy they consume is slightly higher from what they produce
- Net Zero-Energy Buildings (NZEB) that have zero energy balance (i.e. consumed equals to produced energy)
- Net plus or Positive Energy Buildings that consume less energy than the amount they produce supplying the surplus to the grid

Specifically, according to [13], a nZEB is a building that "has a very high energy performance with a low amount of energy required covered to a very significant extent by energy from RES, including energy from RES produced on-site or nearby". Since the word "nearly" is left somehow abstract without being quantified, there has been a lot of debate around the exact meaning of nZEBs, their characteristics and required infrastructure. The design of each nZEB is made taking into account the energy demands and the potential RES which could be used to meet those demands. Energy demands mainly include heating, ventilation, cooling, lighting, appliances and hot water, while typical examples of renewable technologies available today include PV, solar, wind, hydroelectric, geothermal and biofuels. Required energy is mainly produced by RES, but when those sources are not enough to satisfy the load, conventional energy sources might be used as well. The energy sources may be on the building, on its site or at a distance.

3 Fuzzy Cognitive Maps

3.1 Classical FCM Theory

Fuzzy Cognitive Maps (FCMs) constitute a computational methodology that is able to examine situations during which the human thinking process involves fuzzy or uncertain descriptions. A FCM presents a graphical representation through a signed directed graph with feedback consisting of nodes and weighted arcs. The nodes of the graph stand for concepts that are used to describe, via cause and effect, the relations and behavior of a system in a simple and symbolic way. They are connected by signed and weighted arcs which represent the causal relationships that exist between the concepts (Fig. 1). Each concept C_i (variable) is characterized by a number that represents its values and is calculated through the transformation of a fuzzy value or the fitting of a numeric value, to the desired interval, [0, 1]. The values of the interconnections', weights, are initially linguistically defined by experts and then transformed into values which belong to the interval [−1, 1] through a specially designed algorithm [19]. In this way FCMs embody the accumulated knowledge and experience from experts who know how the system behaves in different circumstances.

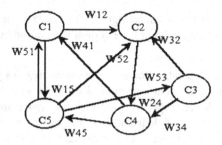

Fig. 1. A simple FCM graph [11]

The sign of each weight represents the type of influence between concepts. There are three types of interconnections between two concepts C_i and C_j:

- $w_{ij} > 0$, an increase or decrease in C_i causes the same result in concept C_j.
- $w_{ij} < 0$, an increase or decrease in C_i causes the opposite result in C_j.
- $w_{ij} = 0$, there is no interaction between concepts C_i and C_j.

Full theories and mathematical models of classical FCMs can be found on references [3] and [19].

3.2   Advanced FCMs Models

Despite the many theoretical developments of FCMs and their application successes, they still have a number of drawbacks and deficiencies. Classical FCM theories do not go into the depth of the dynamic behavior of complex systems. In addition, the initial system structure described by experts and the learning principles-algorithms cannot follow the evolution of a CDS. The mathematical approach of classical FCM theories has several limitations, such as lack of knowledge of the system, dependence on experts, disability of self-learning, definition of the causality, calculation equation, ignorance of time factor and use of the sigmoid function-interpretation of the results [5]. All these limitations have suggest the need of an advanced approach to model FCMs. The full details of the Advanced Fuzzy Cognitive Maps (AFCMs) can be found in references [3, 4] and [16, 17].

Improving the Knowledge of the System. In the classic FCM methods, [4, 19], the concepts are all the parameters which are been examined regardless of their nature. However, in a system even when it is described in a fuzzy way through a FCM the main concept is the same. Each system is described by inputs, states and outputs and since a FCM is a representation of such a system, we should take these characteristics into consideration. For this reason as in the classic control theory methods we shall separate the concepts of a Fuzzy Cognitive Map into the following 3 categories [15].

- **Input** Concepts: The inputs of the system, (**u**)
- **State** Concepts: The concepts describing the operation of the system, (**x**)
- **Output** Concepts: The concepts describing the outputs of the system, (**y**).

In this way we gain a better knowledge of the system. The proposed separation facilitates not only the understanding of the system's operation but also the calculation of the concepts' values.

Calculation Equations. Separating the concepts into categories gives us the ability to calculate their values in a different and more distributed way. For this reason, apart from the separation of the concepts we used the state space approach for one more reason, that of the calculation of their values. After having separated the concepts it became evident that the weight matrix can be divided into smaller ones to correspond them to each concept category. The classic state equations

$$x_{k+1} = Ax_k + Bu_k \tag{1}$$

$$y_k = Cx_k + Du_k \tag{2}$$

are now used to calculate the variation caused by the change in the input and state concepts to the state and output concepts at each time step (k). In this representation, A, B, C and D are individual weight matrices derived from the initial, defined by the experts, weight matrix. The elements of A depend on the states' weights and the elements of B show how each input concept affects the state concepts of the system. C shows how the output concepts are related to the state concepts and D shows how the input concepts directly affect the output concepts [15].

4 Implementing Advanced FCMs to Model an NZEB

This section describes the application of the AFCMs methodology briefly mentioned in Sect. 3.2 to model an nZEB and estimate its energy efficiency over given loads and alternative climate conditions. The full mathematical model of the AFCM, can be found in reference [14]. The constructed model in this paper considers as input concepts the mean wind velocity (m/s), mean solar radiation (kW/m^2), mean external temperature (°C) and electrical appliances (kW). Using these inputs the model infers total energy generation and total energy consumption on a seasonal basis (i.e. autumn/winter and spring/summer) and calculates the building's energy balance (i.e. energy generation vs consumption) to evaluate the adequacy of selected RES, according to the following procedure:

- Step 1: Calculation of the energy production of RES. In this paper, we only consider PVs and wind turbines for simplicity reasons. In addition, estimation of solar water heater potential.
- Step 2: Calculation of the ZEB's internal luminance and temperature
- Step 3: Calculation of the ZEB's energy demands reflected on operation of cooling, heating and lighting equipment.
- Step 4: Calculation of the ZEB's total energy consumption (taking into account results of step 3 along with solar water heater and electrical appliances) and total energy production from its RES to determine the energy balance.
- Step 5: Termination of the algorithm when the variation of the energy balance becomes very small (≤ 0.001).

Based on the description of the advanced FCM model in Sect. 3.2, we classified the FCM's concepts in inputs, states and outputs, as shown in Table 1.

Table 1. FCM concepts

Inputs	States	Outputs
C1: Mean wind velocity	**C5:** Internal luminance	**C13:** Total production
C2: Mean solar radiation	**C6:** Internal temperature	**C14:** Total consumption
C3: Mean external temperature	**C7:** Wind turbine	
C4: Electrical appliances	**C8:** Solar water heater	
	C9: PV	
	C10: Lighting	
	C11: Cooling	
	C12: Heating	

Following the definition of the concepts we determined the interconnection weights between them with the assistance of experts (electrical and mechanical engineers). The (absolute) values of the weights vary among weak, medium, strong and very strong, which were afterwards defuzzified to a corresponding numerical vale [18], as shown in Table 2.

Table 2. Weight matrix

	C1	C2	C3	C4	C5	C6	C7	C8	C9	C10	C11	C12	C13	C14
C1	0	0	0	0	0	0	0,5	0	0	0	0	0	0	0
C2	0	0	0	0	0,6	0	0	0,5	0,7	0	0	0	0	0
C3	0	0	0	0	0	0,3	0	0,3	-0,1	0	0	0	0	0
C4	0	0	0	0	0	0	0	0	0	0	0	0	0	0,8
C5	0	0	0	0	0	0	0	0	0	-0,8	0	0	0	0
C6	0	0	0	0	0	0	0	0	0	0	0,8	-0,7	0	0
C7	0	0	0	0	0	0	0	0	0	0	0	0	0,9	0
C8	0	0	0	0	0	0	0	0	0	0	0	0	0	-0,2
C9	0	0	0	0	0	0	0	0	0	0	0	0	0,9	0
C10	0	0	0	0	0	0	0	0	0	0	0	0	0	0,1
C11	0	0	0	0	0	0	0	0	0	0	0	0	0	0,6
C12	0	0	0	0	0	0	0	0	0	0	0	0	0	0,8
C13	0	0	0	0	0	0	0	0	0	0	0	0	0	0
C14	0	0	0	0	0	0	0	0	0	0	0	0	0	0

According to the separation of the concepts we form the A, B, C and D matrices.

$$A = \begin{bmatrix} 0 & 0 & 0 & 0 & 0 & 0 & 0 & 0 \\ 0 & 0 & 0 & 0 & 0 & 0 & 0 & 0 \\ 0 & 0 & 0 & 0 & 0 & 0 & 0 & 0 \\ 0 & 0 & 0 & 0 & 0 & 0 & 0 & 0 \\ 0 & 0 & 0 & 0 & 0 & 0 & 0 & 0 \\ -0,8 & 0 & 0 & 0 & 0 & 0 & 0 & 0 \\ 0 & 0,8 & 0 & 0 & 0 & 0 & 0 & 0 \\ 0 & -0,7 & 0 & 0 & 0 & 0 & 0 & 0 \end{bmatrix} \quad B = \begin{bmatrix} 0 & 0,6 & 0 & 0 \\ 0 & 0 & 0,3 & 0 \\ 0,5 & 0 & 0 & 0 \\ 0 & 0,5 & 0,3 & 0 \\ 0 & 0,7 & -0,1 & 0 \\ 0 & 0 & 0 & 0 \\ 0 & 0 & 0 & 0 \\ 0 & 0 & 0 & 0 \end{bmatrix}$$

$$C = \begin{bmatrix} 0 & 0 & 0,9 & 0 & 0,9 & 0 & 0 & 0 \\ 0 & 0 & 0 & -0,2 & 0 & 0,1 & 0,6 & 0,8 \end{bmatrix} \quad D = \begin{bmatrix} 0 & 0 & 0 & 0 \\ 0 & 0 & 0 & 0,8 \end{bmatrix}$$

The Fuzzy Cognitive Map produced by the defuzzification process is shown in Fig. 2. Weights and arcs in red indicate that a change of a concept's values results in opposite change to the connected concept's values.

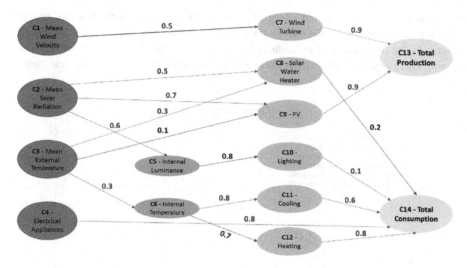

Fig. 2. The constructed FCM

5 Results

To draw conclusions about the behavior of the proposed model, we will look at its response to climate data inputs for a building lying in three different cities for summer and winter. The three cities are Patra, Heraklion and Thessaloniki. The summer season is from March to August and the winter season from September to February and respective climate data (see Table 3) were received from the Greek National Meteo-rological Service[1]. In all 6 use cases (two for each city) we assumed a nominal power of electrical appliances equal to 13 kW.

Table 3. Inputs – climate data

	Mean solar radiation (kWh/m^2)		Mean wind velocity (m/s)		Mean temperature – 24 h (°C)	
	Winter	Summer	Winter	Summer	Winter	Summer
Patra	506	1101	2,4	2,4	14,8	20,9
Heraklion	567	1155	4,5	4,1	16,4	21,2
Thessaloniki	450	1016	2,8	2,9	11,4	20,2

We fit all inputs to the [0, 1] interval and apply the advanced FCM model. The model's outputs are total produced energy and total consumed energy. By subtracting the consumed energy from the produced energy we receive the energy balance. Positive

---

[1] http://portal.tee.gr/portal/page/portal/tptee/totee/TOTEE-20701-3-Final-TEE%202nd.pdf.

energy balance values indicate energy excess, while negative values indicate energy shortage. After calculating the energy balance we can interpret its values by applying a reverse to the normalization procedure. Figure 3 shows the results of our model concerning energy balance estimation obtained through simulations for the six use cases.

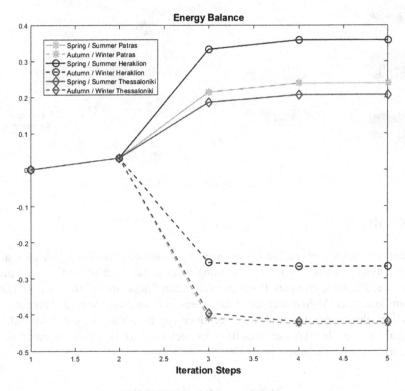

Fig. 3. Energy balance estimation

Summing the results of the algorithm convergence (steady state points) for the energy balances in each season, we can estimate the annual energy balance indicator of a building in the three different cities, as shown in Table 4.

Table 4. Annual energy balance indicator

Cities	Annual energy balance
Patras	−0.1864
Heraklion	0.0914
Thessaloniki	−0.2127

6 Discussion and Concluding Remarks

This paper presents the results of a study that use advanced Fuzzy Cognitive Maps (AFCMs) to model a nZEB and provide quantified performance indicators from an energy efficiency perspective. Based on the simulation results depicted in Fig. 3, we observe that we have excess energy production during the summer period and lack of energy in winter for all three cities. The model reflects the real energy behavior of a building as the main source of energy is solar energy, which helps reduce the energy consumption (water heater), while increasing generation (due to PV). This leads to a positive indicator of the energy balance, which means that on a six-month basis (summer) the house produced on average more energy than it consumed. The opposite applies for the winter season where due to low solar radiation, the generated PV energy is not sufficient to meet the energy needs of the buildings, which are elevated due to low temperature leading in increased energy consumption for heating and hot water. Due to the fact that in all three cities the average wind speed is about the same in both seasonal periods, seasonal variations in energy production are not caused by wind turbine performance.

Moreover, as it is observed from Table 4, the building located at Heraklion approximates more the concept of nZEBs as the annual energy balance indicator is closer to zero. On top of that, in the other two cities, we observe that this indicator is negative, suggesting that on an annual basis the house consumes more energy than it produces. In order to increase the buildings' energy efficiency in these cities, we could increase the power of the wind turbine as its output is relatively constant throughout the year. This significantly increases their energy production and in the winter where the radiation is low. Increasing the power of the wind turbine at FCM is reflected on an increase of the weight of the arc connecting C1 and C7.

It can lie concluded, that, although the developed model is simplified for preliminary investigation of its potential, the simulation results and observations show that advanced FCMs are a promising methodology for modelling nZEBs as complex dynamic systems. FCMs support the acquisition of quantified indicators that could provide valuable information when designing and developing nZEBs, focusing on the integration of appropriate RES with adequate energy generation to meet energy demands under specific environmental contexts. Our future research will aim at enhancing the proposed model by adding more concepts to account for a wider set of variables that will represent a nZEB in a more accurate way, while considering more options for renewable energy generation.

References

1. Torcellini, P., Pless, S., Deru, M., Crawley, D.: Zero energy buildings: a critical look at the definition (No. NREL/CP-550-39833). National Renewable Energy Lab. Golden, CO, United States (2006)
2. Panagiotidou, M., Fuller, R.J.: Progress in ZEBs—a review of definitions, policies and construction activity. Energy Policy **62**, 196–206 (2013)

3. Groumpos, P.P.: Intelligence and fuzzy cognitive maps: scientific issues, challenges and opportunities. Stud. Inform. Control **27**(3), 247–264 (2018)
4. Groumpos, P.P.: Why model complex dynamic systems using fuzzy cognitive maps? Robot. Autom. Eng. J. **1**(3), 555563 (2017)
5. Mpelogianni, V., Groumpos, P.P.: Re-approaching fuzzy cognitive maps to increase the knowledge of a system. AI Soc. **33**(2), 175–188 (2018)
6. Groumpos, P.P., Mpelogianni, V.: An overview of fuzzy cognitive maps for energy efficiency in intelligent buildings. In: 7th International Conference on Information, Intelligence, Systems & Applications (IISA), pp. 1–6. IEEE (2016)
7. Vergini, E., Costoula, T., Groumpos, P.: Modeling zero energy building with a three–level fuzzy cognitive map. In: Recent Advances in Environmental and Earth Sciences and Economics, pp. 275–280 (2015)
8. Bourgani, E., Stylios, C.D., Manis, G., Georgopoulos, Voula C.: Time dependent fuzzy cognitive maps for medical diagnosis. In: Likas, A., Blekas, K., Kalles, D. (eds.) SETN 2014. LNCS (LNAI), vol. 8445, pp. 544–554. Springer, Cham (2014). https://doi.org/10.1007/978-3-319-07064-3_47
9. Mpelogianni, V., Marnetta, P., Groumpos, P.P.: Fuzzy cognitive maps in the service of energy efficiency. IFAC-Papers OnLine **48**(24), 1–6 (2015)
10. Tsadiras, A., Zitopoulos, G.: Fuzzy cognitive maps as a decision support tool for container transport logistics. Evolving Syst. **8**(1), 19–33 (2017)
11. Vergini, E.S., Groumpos, P.P.: A review on zero energy buildings and intelligent systems. In: 6th International Conference on Information, Intelligence, Systems and Applications (IISA), pp. 1–6. IEEE (2015)
12. Voss, K.: Nearly-zero, net zero and plus energy buildings. REHVA J. **49**(6), 23–28 (2012)
13. Directive 2010/31/EU on the Energy Performance of Buildings Recast: Directive 2010/31/EU of the European Parliament and of the Council of 19 May 2010 on the energy performance of buildings (recast). Official Journal of the European Union, 18(06) (2010)
14. Mpelogianni, V., Groumpos, P.P.: Increasing the energy efficiency of buildings using human cognition; via fuzzy cognitive maps. IFAC-Papers OnLine **51**(30), 727–732 (2018)
15. Ogata, K.: State space analysis of control systems (1967)
16. Vergini, E.S., Groumpos, P.P.: A new conception on the fuzzy cognitive maps method. IFAC-Papers OnLine **49**(29), 300–304 (2016)
17. Mpelogianni, V., Groumpos, P.P.: Towards a new approach of fuzzy cognitive maps. In: 7th International Conference on Information, Intelligence, Systems & Applications (IISA), pp. 1–6. IEEE (2016)
18. Runkler, T.A.: Extended defuzzification methods and their properties. In: Proceedings of IEEE 5th International Fuzzy Systems, vol. 1, pp. 694–700. IEEE (1996)
19. Groumpos, P.P.: Fuzzy cognitive maps: basic theories and their application to complex systems. In: Glykas, M. (ed.) Fuzzy Cognitive Maps. STUDFUZZ, vol. 247, pp. 1–22. Springer, Heidelberg (2010). https://doi.org/10.1007/978-3-642-03220-2_1

The Evaluation Method of the Design Department's Information Assets

Svetlana Kozunova[1], Alla G. Kravets[1(✉)] [iD],
and Natalia Solovieva[2] [iD]

[1] Volgograd State Technical University, Volgograd, Russian Federation
one1100n@gmail.com, agk@gde.ru
[2] Volgograd State University, Volgograd, Russian Federation
solovievanataa@gmail.com

Abstract. The activity of the design department (DD) is currently one of the most significant areas in the field of nuclear energy, the defense and rocket, and space industries. This area characterized by large volumes of used economic, technological, industrial and other resources. One of the tasks of the DD is to evaluate information assets (IA) and protect them from threats. The objectives of this article are to develop a method for assessing DD's IA, as well as discussing the possibility of using this method in practice and the risks to which the DD is exposed unless special measures are taken to evaluate IA and threat analysis. Studies related to the assessment of the importance of information IA, the development of a threat model, and damage prediction investigated. The specificity of DD and processing of IA has been determined. In this paper, it is proposed to use the set-theoretic model for evaluating the IA of the DD that takes into account their structure, attributes, and life cycle. To assess the damage caused by the threat, it proposed to use the method of ALE. For the first time, a method for evaluating the IA of DD proposed. This method implemented in software. The software implementation successfully tested in an enterprise that includes the DD. The investigated problem studied quite recently. Therefore, there are open questions such as the classification of information assets of the DD and their categorization (confidentiality stamping), analysis of the life cycle of IA and threats, determination of the criticality level of the DD's IA, assessment of damage from the realization of the threat. The prospect for the development of the research is the development of a threat model for information systems of the DD.

Keywords: Information asset · Design department · Threat ·
Level of criticality · Confidentiality · Evaluation · Damage · PLM · PDM ·
Information system

1 Introduction

Assessment of IA is a difficult task, which is now widely used in DD. The reason for this is the modern development of DD based on the growth of separate bureaus (special or central DD) and the strengthening of composite bureaus that make up the structure of enterprises belonging to the defense industry. The analysis of DD's IA and the assessment of risks and damages in the event of the loss of such assets are complicated

© Springer Nature Switzerland AG 2019
A. G. Kravets et al. (Eds.): CIT&DS 2019, CCIS 1083, pp. 267–277, 2019.
https://doi.org/10.1007/978-3-030-29743-5_21

by the fact that various systems are used to automate the DD's activities, such as PLM, PDM, ERP, CAD, MES systems, electronic document management systems, SIEM, monitoring systems, software modules for calculating the reliability characteristics of the developed complexes and others [1–5]. The direction of this study is new and is studied relatively recently [1, 2]. The main problems of this study include the following: the allocation of protected DD's information; classification and valuation of DD's IA; forecasting the risks and damages that the DD may incur; organizational and technical management of DD's business processes. It is necessary to take into account that modern methods and approaches to the analysis of IA based on an assessment of their value; however, this does not provide a comprehensive assessment of IA and the possibility of distributing IA by levels of criticality. However, most of these techniques cannot be applied to the DD because of the special case management and unique specifics. The arguments given above testify to the high relevance of the area under study.

2 Related Work and Existing Solutions

There are several approaches applied to the valuation of information resources or assets of an enterprise. Generally, these approaches can be divided into several groups: standardized approaches, quantitative methods and a combined approach (using qualitative and quantitative characteristics). Standardized approaches include a management procedure based on the PDCA model («Plan-Do-Check-Act») used to structure management processes. The risk management procedure carried out in accordance with the specific steps and recommendations regulated in the standards [1, 2, 14, 15]. The combined approach determines the assessment process based on a private methodology, oriented enterprise activity. Quantitative methods allow you to evaluate IA using a set of decision criteria and indicators of the values of IA [1, 19].

Based on the results of research [1–8], we can conclude that now the most common methods for evaluating IA (or enterprise resources) are the method for estimating the value of IA, ISO 27002: 2013, a method for evaluating and ranking risks, BS 7799-3: 2006, a method of fuzzy valuation of IA and the construction of fuzzy cognitive maps. The method of IA the value of IA includes a description of the IA by category: human-time resources, IA, software, service and physical (servers, workstations, rooms in which information is processed and stored) resources [7, 8, 14]. Further, each category of IA assessed by a qualification group of experts. The points set by the experts for each category of IA summarized. The category with the highest score is the most valuable. The ISO 27002: 2013 standardized method allows you to manage information security (IS) risks. The authors [1] describe details of the application of this standard for analyzing and managing IS risks. According to [9, 10], the use of ISO 27002 will allow the classification of IA and their management. In [10], an inventory of IA is described, because of which the following classification of assets is built: IA (databases, system documentation), software assets (system software, application software, development tools, and utilities), physical assets (media, technical and computer equipment, premises), and services (computing and communication services). In addition, using this approach, for each level of IA classification, types of information processing took into account in order to label information resources. In Russia, there is an analog of this standard GOST R ISO/IEC 27002-2012, which has gained popularity in the field of IS risk assessment and asset management [11].

The method of risk assessment and ranking reflected in the works of scientists [7, 15, 16]. This method based on the study of risks in terms of their quantitative characteristics [15, 18]. In order to determine which of them more seriously taken into account from the point of view of possible damage, and which less serious, the risks grouped [17] according to the ratio of losses of the organization. This method based on the concept of Total Cost of Ownership (TCO). The initial operations of this method are the identification of probabilistic risks and a description of the probable conse-quences of the occurrence of the detected risks and their valuation, which related to the assessment of IA. According to [15], the method of risk assessment and ranking allows assessing business risks, technical risks, and information security risks. Method BS 7799-3 proposes the use of a process approach to risk assessment [12]. This approach includes sequential procedures: identification of assets, identification of legal and business requirements, assessment of identified assets, taking into account these requirements and the consequences of a breach of confidentiality, integrity, and availability. Method BS 7799-3 proposes the use of a process approach to risk assessment [12]. This approach includes sequential procedures: identification of IA, identification of legal and business requirements, assessment of identified assets, taking into account these requirements and the consequences of a breach of confidentiality, integrity, and availability. In Russia, this method called GOST R ISO/IEC 27001-2006 [13]. A no less common method among research is a risk assessment in corporate networks based on fuzzy logic and the use of cognitive maps [6]. When using this method for each asset, indicators determined by expert means in the form of fuzzy numbers. Cognitive maps at the same time contain links between factors that determine the mutual influence on each other.

However, the current solutions, methods, and approaches described above are not suitable for IA the value of assets for the following reasons: such methods do not take into account the specifics of the DD, the life cycle of the IA, the unique attributes of the design documentation, and the categorization of DD's IA. In addition, foreign methodologies not focused on the Russian document flow and organization of inter-action between DD's automation systems (both with other systems and with infor-mation security system) [1, 15].

3 Business Processes of the Design Department

With regard to the bureau because of its specificity, it is advisable to bring the fol-lowing classification of DD's business processes (BP): typical BP (similar to other enterprises), private BP (inherent in certain departments of the bureau). Typical BP include the following: approval of an order or order, monitoring the execution of an order (order) and tasks assigned to a structural unit, transferring documents between departments, processing incoming and outgoing correspondence, recording personnel movements (admission, dismissal, transfer, etc., personal records), organization of labor and wages, economic analysis of activities, payment of bills, conclusion of contracts, tendering, salary project, work with currency accounts, account management, purchase (receipt and disposal) inventory items. Private BP: the development of a new project, the processing of an incoming application (study, analysis), the development of technical specifications, the development of design documentation (DDC), verification of DDC, coordination and approval of DDC, processing of engineering data, archiving and accounting of DDC, development of design specifications for the product, processing calculations developed complexes.

4 Analysis of the Design Department's Information Assets

Analysis of IA is the main component in terms of not only managing threats and structuring business processes, but also ensuring IS. Categorization and evaluation of IA facilitate the allocation of protected information. From a practical point of view, most of the DD's IA classified as "confidentially". We give a general classification of information. The first class of information includes publicly available information, i.e. information, access to which cannot be limited (well-known information and other information without access restrictions to it) [4, 11, 13, 14]. The second class includes restricted access information, which in turn divided into subtypes: state secrets, confidential information (personal data, trade secrets (classified as "confidentially"), and documents of limited distribution marked "DSP"). The studies conducted in this article do not affect the issues of analyzing information constituting state secrets and documents of limited distribution marked "DSP". Let us analyze the IA, characteristic for DD, and we will describe their life cycle (Table 1).

Table 1. Information assets of the design department and their life cycle.

No.	Information assets of the design department	Life cycle of information assets/Categorization
1	Project documentation	Stages: preparatory, project development, changes to the finished project/ "Confidential"
2	Engineering data: reference books, product design nomenclatures, results of a priori calculations, product specifications, product data	Used for various business processes, as well as an archive, as they are periodically used for analytical and other activities/ "Confidential"
3	Economic: the results of the audit of financial statements, information on the size and conditions for obtaining loans and bank guarantees, the costs incurred by the company, data on the market strategy of the enterprise, investment portfolios	It is used both constantly and for conducting an analytical type of activity/ "Confidential" or "Publicly available"
4	Information about the results of scientific and technical research: various drawings and diagrams, private technological and design solutions	Used for various business processes/ "Confidential"

(continued)

Table 1. (*continued*)

No.	Information assets of the design department	Life cycle of information assets/Categorization
5	Enterprise information infrastructure: physical and logical LAN schemes, classification and composition of automation systems, software, redundancy scheme, information about various network services, testing protocols, information about hardware, organization of a communication system	Used for various business processes/ "Confidential"
6	Information security: access attributes to automation systems and LAN, data on information security measures, a list of protected information, data on applicable information protection systems, lists of protected objects	Used for various business processes/ "Confidential"
7	Archival design documents and design data accounting	Archival storage mode to ensure the relevant requirements of preservation (monitored bodies or higher organization)/ "Confidential"
8	Information about the subjects of personal data	Used for various business processes, as well as an archive, as they are periodically used for analytical and other activities/ "Personal Data"
9	Technological data: information about the design, manufacturing technology and other properties of products, stages of technological processes	Used for various business processes/ "Confidential"
10	Private methods and programs for processing results	Used for various business processes, as well as an archive, as they are periodically used for analytical and other activities/ "Confidential"

Thus, in accordance with the specifics of the DD, ten IA allocated. We also note that for DD characterized by the following IA: the company's charter, authorized capital, equity securities (shares). However, they depend on the typical criteria of economic analysis, which not considered in this article. The life cycle of an IA divided into types. Permanent - continuously used for the implementation of DD's BP. Cyclic is used cyclically for the implementation of DD's BP and periodically for analytical and other activities. Archive is the archival storage mode of IA to ensure the relevant requirements for the safety of documentation of inspection bodies or a higher organization. Multiphase is life cycle, containing a large number of different stages of processing of IA.

5 Description of the Evaluation Method of the Design Department's Information Assets

The method (see Fig. 1) contains several consecutive steps: the structuring of the IA, analyzing the life cycle of the IA, determining the level of criticality of the DD's IA. Based on the attributes inherent in the DD's IA, and the specifics of the DD described in [1, 2], we describe the levels of criticality (significance of the IA). "Level 0" (non-essential IA) - IA with low relevance or not used, IA of this level do not affect DD activities. "Level 1" (useful IA) - the use of such IA saves resources: it is impossible to replace the IA data without spending time, financial and other resources. "Level 2" (important IA) - IA, which are valuable for DD. "Level 3" (critical IA) - if the IA data is lost, the work of the DD can stop, the IA of this level have a significant impact on the activity of the DD. In case of loss of IA Level 3, there is a threat of suspension of the main activities of the DD.

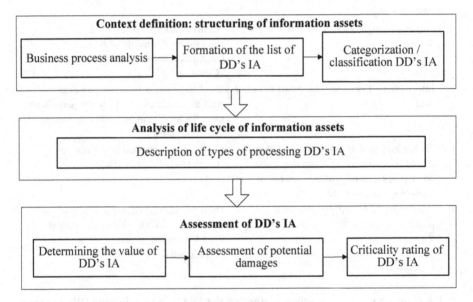

Fig. 1. The evaluation method of the design department's information assets.

We give a formal description of the method. *CONF* – confidentiality, *CONF* = { *conf₁,...,conf₃*}. *CRITIC* – criticality, *CRITIC* = {*critic₁,...,critic₃*}. *VALUE* – value of DD's IA, *VALUE* = {*value₁,...,value₃*}.

To determine the value of information assets we will use a set of rules: R_1: $((CONF = publicly \ available) \wedge (CRITIC = slightly)) \rightarrow (VALUE = very \ low),...,$ R_n: $((CONF = conf_3) \wedge (CRITIC = critic_3)) \rightarrow (VALUE = very \ high)$.

Criticality rating scale of IA *CRITIC* = {0, 1, 2} = {*minor, significant, critical*}. Asset Privacy Rating Scale: *CONF* = {0, 1, 2} = {*publicly available, confidential, trade secret*}. Information asset value assessment scale: *VALUE* = {1, 2, 3, 4, 5} = {*very low,*

low, medium, high, very high}. To assess the damage caused to the information asset of the DD due to the realization of a risk or threat, we will use the method of Annualized Loss Expectancy (ALE).

6 Software Implementation of the Proposed Solution and the Results of Its Testing

6.1 Software Architecture Design

The software architecture designed based on the concept of distributed service-oriented architecture (SOA). The architecture (see Fig. 2) of the proposed solution includes a GUI, a client module, a DLL, and virtual data storage.

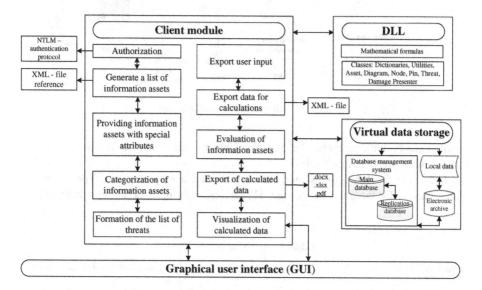

Fig. 2. Software architecture.

Designed architecture is the basis for software development. Software implementation made in C# in the environment of Microsoft Visual Studio 2017.

6.2 Software Testing and Experimental Results

The software tested in a real LAN environment of the "ITC SKON" enterprise (Volgograd, Russian Federation). The scheme of the testing stand is shown in Fig. 3.

Using the built-in software tool, the researcher compiles a list of IA that need to assess. Next, the expert sets the value of each of these IA. The value of IA calculated in rubles. After that, the IA categorized, their life cycle classified and analyzed. Next, the software performs a comprehensive assessment of DD's IA according to the criteria:

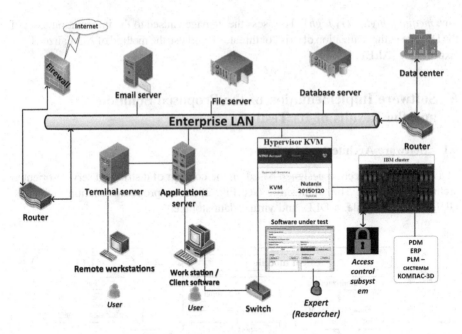

Fig. 3. Scheme of the testing stand

significance (value), potential damage, level of criticality. The results of the experimental study presented in Table 2.

Thus, a very high score scored three assets and a very low one. The following assets may suffer the greatest damage: IT, DP, engineering data, enterprise shares.

Table 2. Software test results.

Information asset (asset type)	Value/asset category	Criticality/potential damage/asset value
Engineering data (Reference books, design product nomenclatures, calculation results, product specifications, product data)	4200000/trade secret	Substantially/247800000/average
Economic data (economic information)	60000/trade secret	Slightly/540000/low
Design data (design documentation)	700000/confidentially	Slightly/3500000/average
Archival documents (archives)	600000/publicly available	Critical/7200000/very high
IT (information infrastructure)	4500000/confidentially	Critical/40500000/very high

(*continued*)

Table 2. (*continued*)

Information asset (asset type)	Value/asset category	Criticality/potential damage/asset value
Private design methods of calculation (patented techniques)	120000/publicly available	Slightly/360000/very low
Audit of financial statements (accounting information)	70000/trade secret	Substantially/400000/average
Process data (technological documentation)	60000/trade secret	Substantially/900000/average
Draft technical assignment (project documentation)	10000/confidentially	Slightly/1200000/average
Personal information (about employees and customers)	250000/confidentially	Substantially/80000/low
Economic information (enterprise shares)	6000000/confidentially	Critical/36000000/very high
DP (information Security)	1200000/confidentially	Critical/14400000/average
Scientific research	520000/trade secret	Substantially/1560000/average

7 Conclusion

According to the results of the study of the problem, the main scientific result obtained, consisting of the development of an evaluation method of DD's IA. Based on this method, software developed that allows for a comprehensive assessment of IA in real time. The software proposed by the authors passed the test tests with the data of the "ITC SKON" enterprise under conditions of a real LAN. In the course of testing, software showed its effectiveness.

The conclusions regarding the development of the method are as follows:

- the developed method differs from others that solve similar problems in that it is oriented for use in DD for IA valuation since this method allows to take into account the attributes of IA and their life cycle;
- as a result of using the developed software that implements the valuation method, it is possible to estimate the value, criticality and potential damage to DD's IA, as well as to build an IA dependency diagram.
- The developed method described in the text of this publication, and the experimental studies conducted, in turn, are the basis for subsequent research. Thus, the prospect of the development of this study is to conduct development in the field of analysis and risk management of DD automation systems.

Acknowledgment. The study was supported by the Russian Fund of Basic Research (grant No. 19-07-01200 A).

References

1. Kravets, A., Kozunova, S.: The risk management model of design department's PDM information system. In: Kravets, A., Shcherbakov, M., Kultsova, M., Groumpos, P. (eds.) CIT&DS 2017. CCIS, vol. 754, pp. 490–500. Springer, Cham (2017). https://doi.org/10. 1007/978-3-319-65551-2_36
2. Kozunova, S., Kravets, A.: The risk management system of the design department's corporate information system. In: VII All-Russian Scientific and Practical Conference Topical Issues of Information Security of Regions in the Conditions of Russia's Transition to a Digital Economy, pp. 244–249. Volgograd State University, Volgograd (2018)
3. Kondratiev, S., Ulyanin, O., Abakumov, E.: Improving data exchange processes between the PLM-system and the corporate information management system in an integrated information environment. In: XV - International Youth Conference Systems of Design, Technological Preparation of Production and Management of the Stages of the Life Cycle of the Industrial Product CAD/CAM/PDM. Institute of Management Problems named after Trapeznikova V. of the Russian Academy of Sciences, Moscow (2015). http://lab18.ipu.ru/projects/conf2015/ 1/8.htm. Accessed 29 Mar 2019
4. Shevtsov, V., Babenko, A., Kozunova, S., Kravets, A.: Information security management system of workflow at the enterprise. Caspian J. Control High Technol. 1(41), 161–172 (2018)
5. Buldakova, T., Korshunov, A.: Ensuring the information security of ERP-systems. Cyber Secur. Issues 5(13), 41–44 (2015)
6. Kravets, A.G., Belov, A.G., Sadovnikova, N.P.: Models and methods of professional competence level research. Recent Patents Comput. Sci. 9(2), 150–159 (2016)
7. Kopyltsov, A.V., Kravets, A.G., Abrahamyan, G.V., Katasonova, G.R., Sotnikov, A.D., Atayan, A.M.: Algorithm of estimation and correction of wireless telecommunications quality. In: 9th International Conference on Information, Intelligence, Systems and Applications, IISA 2018 (2019). https://doi.org/10.1109/iisa.2018.8633620
8. Finogeev, A.G., Parygin, D.S., Finogeev, A.A.: The convergence computing model for big sensor data mining and knowledge discovery. Hum.-Centric Comput. Inf. Sci. 7(1), 11 (2017)
9. ISO 31000:2009. Risk management – Principles and guidelines
10. ISO/IEC 27002:2013. Information technology – Security techniques – Code of practice for information security controls
11. GOST R ISO/IEC 27002-2012. Information technology. Methods and means of security. Code of practice and information security management rules. Standartinform Publications, Moscow (2014)
12. BS 7799-3. Information security management systems. Guidelines for information security risk management
13. GOST R ISO/IEC 27001-2006. Information technology. Methods and means of security. Information security management system requirements. Standartinform Publications, Moscow (2008)
14. Campbell, T.: The information security manager. In: Practical Information Security Management, pp. 31–42 (2016)
15. Shcherbakov, M., Groumpos, P., Kravets, A.: A method and IR4I index indicating the readiness of business processes for data science solutions. In: Kravets, A., Shcherbakov, M., Kultsova, M., Groumpos, P. (eds.) CIT&DS 2017. CCIS, vol. 754, pp. 21–34. Springer, Cham (2017). https://doi.org/10.1007/978-3-319-65551-2_2

16. Kiseleva, I., Iskadjyan, S.: Information risks - methods of evaluation and analysis. ITportal **2** (14), 1–9 (2017)
17. GOST R ISO/IEC 27005-2010. Information technology. Security techniques. Information security risk management. Standartinform Publications, Moscow (2011)
18. Finogeev, A., et al.: Methods and tools for secure sensor data transmission and data mining in energy SCADA system. In: Kravets, A., Shcherbakov, M., Kultsova, M., Shabalina, O. (eds.) Creativity in Intelligent Technologies and Data Science. CCIS, vol. 535, pp. 474–487. Springer, Cham (2015). https://doi.org/10.1007/978-3-319-23766-4_38
19. Yanovsky, T., Kirichuk, A., Bales, A., Scherbakov, M., Sokolov, A., Brebels, A.: The technique of extracting knowledge about buildings' and constructions' day energy consumption models. In: Kravets, A., Shcherbakov, M., Kultsova, M., Groumpos, P. (eds.) CIT&DS 2017. CCIS, vol. 754, pp. 441–451. Springer, Cham (2017). https://doi.org/10.1007/978-3-319-65551-2_32

Technology Model to Support the Initiation of Innovation Artefacts

Maria-Iuliana Dascalu[1]([⊠]), Elisabeth Lazarou[1],
and Victor Florin Constantin[2]

[1] Department of Engineering in Foreign Languages,
University POLITEHNICA of Bucharest, Bucharest, Romania
{maria.dascalu, elisabeth.lazarou}@upb.ro
[2] Department of Mechatronics and Precision Mechanics,
University POLITEHNICA of Bucharest, Bucharest, Romania
victor.constantin@upb.ro

Abstract. The current paper proposes a technology model to support the process of creating innovative artefacts, where artefact is any project proposal, business plan, business solution, article with a high degree of innovation. The model is based on an advanced technology stack, in which the central role is played by semantic high-performance computing. Several functionalities are available both for academic researchers and business consultants, from validating the innovation degree of an idea, to supporting its development with useful bibliographical recommendations or building research proposals based on that idea.

Keywords: Innovative artefact · Semantic search ·
High-performance computing · Technological model

1 Introduction

The current paper proposes a technology model – InnovRes, which can be used to implement a support product for shaping and validating innovative ideas by identifying and recommending valuable bibliographic resources (articles, patents, project descriptions, websites, etc.), and partially automating the writing process of research or statup projects. The model is useful both for academia researchers and business consultants, as they are trying to enter in a new cutting-edge domain. The model is based on semantic and Big Data processing technologies, as well as on the use of Application Programming Interfaces (APIs) for access the various scientific warehouses, thus providing a very current technological stack. The InnovRes model respects the digitization trend of the European Union: digital and large data platforms are becoming more widespread, impacting almost all industries [1]. Large data volumes generated by equipment, machines and people bring special opportunities for innovation, new business models, smart products and services, leading to industrial progress and adding value to the European society and beyond. There are digital tools for researchers and consultants - collaborative writing and visualization tools, search engines [2], but no tool combines both directions (search for relevant resources to create an innovative

A. G. Kravets et al. (Eds.): CIT&DS 2019, CCIS 1083, pp. 278–287, 2019.
https://doi.org/10.1007/978-3-030-29743-5_22

artefact and the creation itself), where artefact is any project proposal, business plan, business solution, article with a high degree innovation. The current papers presents the functions of the model, the technologies necessary to implement it, as well as the state-of-the-art related to its development. From the scientific point of view, the model has two directions of innovation: the semantic computing (as a new computational model) and the high performance computing, the real challenge being the realization of the interoperability between the semantic technologies and the high performance computations, thus optimizing the processing, searching and recommending relevant resources for innovative artefacts. In the context of the model, the semantic technologies are the ones that make the Big Data processed by the high-performance computing to be truly smart and useful.

2 Semantic Technologies, Potentiator of High-Performance Computing for Innovation Seekers

There are several types of tools which can be used by researchers or innovation seekers [2]:

- dedicated search engines (BibSonomy, Biohunter, DeepDyve etc.);
- article visualization tools (ACS ChemWorx, Colwiz, eLife Lens etc.);
- research data sharing instruments (BioLINCC, Code Ocean, ContentMine etc.);
- virtual communities (AcademicJoy, Addgene, AssayDepot etc.);
- crowdfunding (Benefunder, Consano, Experiment etc.) and so on.

Of course, dedicated tools to search for patents are developed or still in development [3, 4], but no tool offers integrated services for checking the validity of an innovative idea, supporting it with relevant resources, initiating the process of writing it, as our model proposes. In order for all those services to be successfully interconnected, a proper mix of advanced technologies is necessary. The context of these necessary technologies is further described.

High performance computing means the use of supercomputers and parallel processing techniques to solve complex computational problems [1]. In the case of our model, high-performance computation is necessary for large data collections of articles, project descriptions, scientific web resources, etc., needed to generate new ideas and innovation artefacts. In order to select the most relevant data, semantic models have to be applied to high-performance computing.

In a search engine, a keyword-based search returns documents, taking into account the greatest number of matching words in the query with the text of the documents. Semantic search seeks to improve search precision by understanding the intent of the seeker and contextual meaning of terms as they appear in the search data space, either on the Web or in a closed system, to generate more relevant results [5]. Semantic search represents the capacity of a search engine to determine what the user thought of in the moment of query and also to offer the user results that do not fully match the words that are typed in, but are equivalent in meaning. For a better understanding of the concept of semantic search, it must be placed, comparatively, in the context of another concept: keyword search. Semantic search intelligently understands the meaning of the words that are typed in, to be more exact, it focuses on the context. Semantic search provides accurate and relevant results based on the queries. This approach is ontology-based, which is faster due to association between contents. Keyword search engines come in handy when the meaning of terms is not necessarily needed and the results are displayed within a decent amount of time. Surveys indicate that there are a lot of people not receiving accurate results in the first set of URLs returned, due to the fact that several words have the same meaning and one word could mean several thing, therefore it might lead to confusion. A clear comparison between semantic and keyword search is available in Fig. 1.

Keyword Search Engine	Semantic Web Search Engine
1. It is a traditional search engines that produce results of given query within the given context.	1. It works on Semantic based approach which is useful for having accurate and relevant information about the given query.
2. The information which is retrieved is dependent on keywords and page ranking algorithms that can produce spam results.	2. The information retrieved is independent of keywords and page rank algorithms that produce exact results rather than any irrelevant results.
3. It does not focus on stop words like is, or, and, how because it does not give accurate results what user is searching to get information.	3. It focuses on stop words and punctuation marks because it takes into account each and every small character as it affects search results.
4. It displays all web pages that may or may not satisfy user's query and to select relevant page from many pages is difficult task.	4. It will show only those results that will answer our query.
5. It does not highlight any words or phrases which are useful in answering getting accurate results.	5. It highlights the sentences or words that give answer to query asked by the user.
6. It makes use of keywords to expand query instead of using any methodology.	6. It uses ontology to get relations between the keywords.
7. It uses HTML, XML language for creation of metadata.	7. It uses Semantic Web languages like OWL, RDF for creation of metadata.

Fig. 1. Comparison between keyword search and semantic web search

To implement semantic searches, unstructured text needs to be transformed into a structured, easy-to-process computer form. Such form is the ontology, which models concepts and relationships within a domain, allowing an application to make automatic inferences, similar to the human way of thinking [6]. Although there are semantic search applications – OSSSE [7] or IBRI-CASONTO [8], these were developed only in the laboratory without being tested in an industrial environment: semantic search is not completely explored, thus an emergent direction of research nowadays. There are many criteria that classify approaches of semantic search proposals [9]: architecture (stand-alone search engine or meta-search engine), coupling (tight coupling, loose coupling), transparency (transparent, interactive, hybrid), user context (learning, hardcoded), query modification (manual, query rewriting or graph-based), ontology structure (anonymous properties, standard properties, domain specific properties) and ontology technology. Some examples of semantic search approaches are the following ones:

- Simple HTML Ontology Extensions (SHOE) is a form based semantic search engine;
- Inquirus2;
- TAP;
- Hybrid spreading activation;
- Intelligent Semantic Web Retrieval Agent (ISRA);
- Librarian agent;
- Semantic Content Organization and Retrieval Engine (SCORE);
- TRUST;
- Audio data retrieval;
- Ontogator.

There are also some approaches proposed by researchers which are based on ontologies or XML and we will mention the most relevant ones. In [10], it is presented an engine for semantic search which would be used for tourism domain, which is able to provide precise and relevant results based on the input query. It is ontology based. The main modules are: Query Controller, Query Prototype, Query Similarity Mapper, State Parser, City-State Parser, Ontological Synset Parser, Distance Parser, Service Finder and Caller, Service Modules, Metaprocessor, and URL Generator. XSEarch [11] is a semantic search engine based on XML (eXtensive Markup Language) and the implementation of it was challenging due to the numerous steps that needed to be taken for the engine to return favorable and relevant results. SemSearch [12] is an ontology based search engine which distinguishes from the others with: low barrier to access for ordinary end users, dealing with complex queries, precise and self-explanatory results, quick response, along with the following layers: the Google-like User Interface Layer, the Text Search Layer, the Semantic Query Layer, the Formal Query Language Layer and the Semantic Data Layer.

Closely related to semantic search are recommender systems, which primarily aim to provide suggestions useful to the user [13]. There are three main types of such systems: (1) content-based systems - artefacts similar to previously-appreciated ones are suggested; (2) collaborative filtering based systems - are suggested artefacts which were appreciated by users with a similar profile; (3) hybrids - in which ontologies often play an important role in optimizing the performance of the recommendation model [13]. An extensive classification of recommender systems is available in Fig. 2. Creating suitable recommendation algorithms for an innovative artefacts will add value to this research direction. Another current trend to which the model can contribute is that of chatbots (conversational agents) - computer programs designed to simulate conversations with human users [14]. The InnovRes model requires the use of a conversational engine that will assist in identifying the right innovative resources.

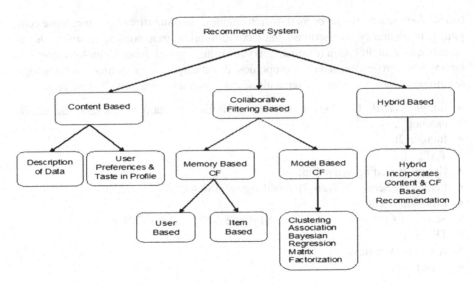

Fig. 2. Taxonomy of recommender systems

In terms of large data searches, high-performance computing will ensure the speed of response to the users. For this purpose, the Hadoop component for data storage – Hadoop Distributed File System (HDFS) [15] and the Apache Spark data processing framework [16] will be used. Unlike the MapReduce mechanism offered by Hadoop for data processing and used in a previous project [17], Apache Spark uses a resilient distributed data set that makes processing faster [18]. At the same time, Apache Spark is adapted to ontological data, which can be seen as a graph. The big data processing, as well as the graph/triplestores databases, are on the rise: the Neo4j Graph platform (ontological graph database) announced its collaboration with Apache Spark [19], so the interoperability between the two types of technologies (semantics, large data processing using high performance calculations) is doable.

3   Functional Description of the Model for Innovative Artefacts

The model will offer several functions via five services (see Fig. 3), from validating the innovation degree of an idea, supporting its development with useful bibliographical recommendations to building proposals for innovative artefacts based on that idea.

The first functionality is the **checking of the innovation degree of an idea**. This is possible using advanced data analytics: e.g., statistics of the number of similar reports, projects, patents, articles and the date of their publication. If none related references exist, then the idea is challenging: it might be very good, or not feasable. If old references exist, for sure the idea can't be the starting point to an innovative artefact. If a lot of recent references exist, then the idea respects a trending research direction and should be further exploited and so on.

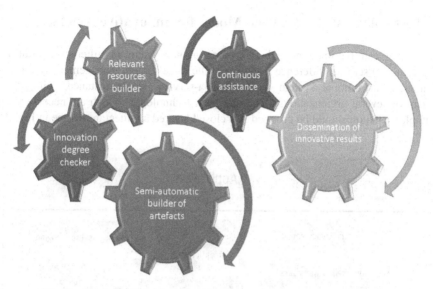

Fig. 3. Services offered by the technology model for innovative artefacts

The second functionality is the **building of relevant resources for the innovative artefact development**, through semantic search, recommendations and creation of resources, which let the users build personal innovation repositories. By combining semantic search and recommendation functionalities, our users will be able to obtain, in an integrated way, a relevant set of bibliographical resources, according to a specific research domain, abstract or keywords. Each resource could be evaluated for relevance by the user and thus further exploited in recommendations in next steps of the innovation process. The documents, links and other text-based artefacts will be transformed into data streams, then into ontologies (structured text), which can be interrogated by SPARQL questies processed by Apache Jena [20].

The third functionality is **the semi-automatic building of artefacts**, which will allow the user (researcher, business consultant, teacher, student) to customize some existent templates or to propose new ones, which will be available to the users after the administrator's acceptance.

The forth functionality is the **dissemination of own innovation results**: the users will be able to publish their own research, which will be searchable in the system after admin's validation.

The last functionality is **continuous assistance** via a trained chatbot and via a virtual forum community.

4   Technological Stack of the Model for Innovative Artefacts

The model can be implemented as a stand-alone system in different institutions (platform-as-a-service, difference instances of the same content management system) or as a cross-institutional system (software-as-a-service, single instance, joining the content of several organizations). The emergent technologies which are necessary for its implementation should be grouped in a closed layered architecture (as see in Fig. 4).

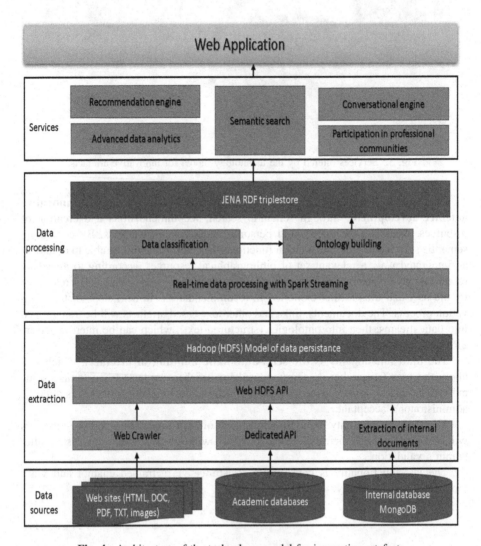

Fig. 4. Architecture of the technology model for innovative artefacts

The layer exposed to the users is given by the web application, which is in the form of a portal. This layer has access to the service layer, which allows the implementation of the functionalities described in second section. The main components of the service layer are: the advanced analytics engine, the semantic search and recommendation engine, the conversational and the forum engine.

The service layer has access to the data processing layer, where the real time processing of data with Spark Streaming API [21] is done. Spark processing runs 10 times faster on disk and 100 times faster in memory than normal processing. For implementing recommendations and semantic search, ontologies will be built from extracted data, using several technologies: GATE, WordNet, Text2Onto, OpenNLP, Jena API [22]. The transformation of resources from plain text/natural language to structured text/ontologies, for them to be queried by computer-based applications, is not an easy task and advanced algorithms are needed [18], e.g. the ones for semantic similarity [23]. The ontologies will be saved in a semantic repository, e.g. JENA RDF triplestore [20]. Pre-processing of documents might be necessary and, for this purpose, the open-source Apache Kafka will be used.

The processing layer has access to the modules which deal with data extraction. Here, in data extraction layer, dedicated APIs for scientific databases are used, e.g. Springer APIs, IEEE Xplore API, Nature OpenSearch API [24] etc. All the data are saved in the files distributed system Hadoop – HDFS, using the Web HDFS API [25]. Various sources of data (as seen in Fig. 4) will be interrogated:

- websites;
- academic databases;
- an internal repository of innovative resources.

5 Conclusions

In this article, we propose a technological model for innovation seekers. Although there are many semantic search products [5], there are no tools which integrate the smart search of resources, the validation of an innovative idea and the initiation of its description, like our model proposes. Also, there are no search engines for business consultants, which makes our model a necessary documentation tool for them to make as many valuable project proposals as possible and to increase the absorption rate of European funds. We described a full technological stack and argument the interoperability of all proposes technologies, thus we claim that our model is feasible and implementable.

Acknowledgements. This work has been partially supported by a grant of the Romanian Ministry of Research and Innovation, CCCDI - UEFISCDI, project number PN-III-P1-1.2-PCCDI-2017-0689/"Lib2Life - Revitalizarea bibliotecilor si a patrimoniului cultural prin tehnologii avansate"/"Revitalizing Libraries and Cultural Heritage through Advanced Technologies", within PNCDI II. Also, the work has partially received funding from the European Union's Erasmus+ Capacity Building in Higher Education program under grant agreement No. 586060-EPP-1-2017-1-RO-EPPKA2-CBHE-JP for the EXTEND project.

References

1. European Commission. https://ec.europa.eu/growth/industry/policy/digital-transformation_en. Accessed 2018
2. Digital tools for researchers. http://connectedresearchers.com/online-tools-for-researchers/. Accessed 2018
3. Alves, T., Rodrigues, R., Costa, H., Rocha, M.: Development of an information retrieval tool for biomedical patents. Comput. Methods Programs Biomed. **159**, 125–134 (2018)
4. Ribeiro Nogueira Ferraz, R., Quoniam, L., Reymond, D., Maccari, E.A.: Example of open-source OPS (Open Patent Services) for patent education and information using the computational tool Patent2Net. World Pat. Inf. **46**, 21–31 (2016)
5. Elbedweihy, K.M., Wrigley, S.N., Clough, P., Ciravegna, F.: An overview of semantic search evaluation initiatives. J. Web Semant. **30**, 82–105 (2015)
6. Bodea, C.N., Lipai, A., Dascalu, M.I.: An ontology-based search tool in the semantic web. In: Advancing Information Management through Semantic Web Concepts and Ontologies, pp. 221–249. IGI Global (2013)
7. Bošnjak, A., Podgorelec, V.: Upgrade of a current research information system with ontologically supported semantic search engine. Expert Syst. Appl. **66**, 189–202 (2016)
8. Sayed, A., Muqrishi, A.A.: IBRI-CASONTO: ontology-based semantic search engine. Egypt. Inform. J. **18**(3), 181–192 (2017)
9. Mangold, C.: A survey and classification of semantic search approaches. Int. J. Metadata Semant. Ontol. **2**(1), 23–34 (2007)
10. Laddha, S., Jawandhiya, P.M.: Semantic search engine. Indian J. Sci. Technol. **10**(23), 1–6 (2017)
11. Cohen, S., Mamou, J., Kanza, Y., Sagiv, Y.: XSEarch: a semantic search engine for XML. In: Proceedings of the 29th VLDB Conference, Berlin (2003)
12. Lei, Y., Uren, V., Motta, E.: SemSearch: a Search Engine for the Semantic Web. Knowledge Media Institute. Accessed 2018
13. Ricci, F., Rokach, L., Shapira, B., Kantor, P.B.: Recommender Systems Handbook. Springer, London (2011). https://doi.org/10.1007/978-0-387-85820-3
14. Stanica, I., Dascalu, M.I., Bodea, C.N., Moldoveanu, A.: VR job interview simulator: where virtual reality meets artificial intelligence for education. In: Zooming Innovation in Consumer Technologies Conference (ZINC), Novi Sad, pp. 9–12. IEEE (2018)
15. HADOOP – HDFS. https://hadoop.apache.org/docs/r1.2.1/hdfs_design.html. Accessed 2018
16. Apache Spark. https://spark.apache.org/. Accessed 2018
17. Paraschiv, I.C., Dascalu, M., Banica, C., Trausan-Matu, S.: Designing a scalable technology hub for researchers. In: Proceedings of the 13th International Scientific Conference "eLearning and Software for Education", Bucharest, pp. 13–18 (2017)
18. Noyes, K.: Five things you need to know about Hadoop v. Apache Spark (2015). https://www.infoworld.com/article/3014440/big-data/five-things-you-need-to-know-about-hadoop-v-apache-spark.html
19. Burt, J.: Connecting The Dots With Graph Databases (2017). https://www.nextplatform.com/2017/10/24/connecting-dots-graph-databases/
20. Apache Jena. https://jena.apache.org/. Accessed 2019
21. Spark Data Sources. https://jaceklaskowski.gitbooks.io/mastering-apache-spark/content/spark-data-sources.adoc. Accessed 2019

22. Dascalu, M.I., Bodea, C.N., Marin, I.: Semantic formative e-assessment for project management professionals. In: Proceedings of the 4th Eastern European Regional Conference on the Engineering of Computer Based Systems (ECBS-EERC), Brno, pp. 1–8. IEEE (2015)
23. Rus, V., Lintean, M., Banjade, R., Niraula, N., Stefanescu, D.: SEMILAR: the semantic similarity toolkit. In: Proceedings of the 51st Annual Meeting of the Association for Computational Linguistics, Sofia (2013)
24. APIs for scholarly resources. https://libraries.mit.edu/scholarly/publishing/apis-for-scholarly-resources/. Accessed 2019
25. HADOOP – HDFS. https://hadoop.apache.org/docs/r1.2.1/hdfs_design.html. Accessed 2019
26. Apache Kafka. https://kafka.apache.org/. Accessed 2019

Solving the Inverse Kinematics of Robotic Arm Using Autoencoders

Konstantinos D. Polyzos⬤, Peter P. Groumpos$^{(\boxtimes)}$⬤,
and Evangelos Dermatas

Department of Electrical Engineering and Computer Technology,
University of Patras, Patras, Greece
k.polyzos@upnet.gr, groumpos@ece.upatras.gr,
dermatas@upatras.gr

Abstract. In the modern era, robotics is an attractive field for many researchers since robots are involved in many aspects of everyday life due to the conveniences and solutions that they provide in various daily difficulties. For this reason, the inverse kinematics of robotic arms is a challenging problem that seems more appealing to researchers as years pass by. In this paper, a novel approach to solve this problem is assessed, which is based on autoencoders. In our implementation the goal is not only to find one random (of the infinite solutions) of this problem, but to determine the one that minimizes both the position error between the actual and desired position of the end-effector of the robotic arm and the joint movement. For the training of the Neural Network of the autoencoder, four different types of the loss function and their corresponding results are examined. A robotic arm with three Degrees of Freedom is used for the evaluation of our implementation and the accurate results demonstrate the efficiency and effectiveness of our proposed method.

Keywords: Autoencoders · Inverse kinematics of robotic arm ·
Neural Networks · Machine Learning · Robotics

1 Introduction

The field of robotics and robotic manipulators gains the attention of many researchers since they provide assistance in ameliorating the main difficulties and improving time-consuming and computationally demanding tasks of everyday life. Therefore, there have been copious efforts of attempting to solve the inverse kinematics problem of the robotic arm, which is the determination of a set of angles/joint-variables such that the end-effector of the robotic arm moves to the desired position. However, this is a challenging and not easily solved task, since there is no unique solution but an infinite number of solutions.

Considering $\underline{X}$ as the coordinates of the end-effectors position and $\underline{Q}$ the set of angles/joint variables then:

© Springer Nature Switzerland AG 2019
A. G. Kravets et al. (Eds.): CIT&DS 2019, CCIS 1083, pp. 288–298, 2019.
https://doi.org/10.1007/978-3-030-29743-5_23

$$\underline{X} = f(\underline{Q}) \tag{1}$$

The inverse kinematics problem can be expressed mathematically as:

$$\underline{Q} = f^{-1}(\underline{X}) \tag{2}$$

One initial approach is to seek for closed-form solutions to Eq. (2). Nonetheless, the number of robots, in which closed-form solutions are applied, is very limited and thus closed-form solutions are not available. One common method which is used for this problem and relies on the Jacobian matrix is the pseudoinverse method. Details about the pseudoinverse method are explained in detail in [1].

One other approach is presented in [2], in which a modified Newton-Raphson iterative technique is used to solve the system of non-linear kinematic equations. Though, the convergence to the desired point depends on a good initial condition.

Many researchers resorted to genetic algorithms to solve this problem due to the fact that the computation of the Jacobian matrix is not needed in order to move the end-effector to the desired position minimizing also the joint displacement from the initial position. In [3, 4], typical works in which genetic algorithms are utilized for the solution of this problem can be found. One drawback is that genetic algorithms alone cannot lead to the desired accuracy and therefore they should be combined with other methods. A genetic algorithm approach combined with Adaptive Niching and Clustering is shown in [13].

Many numerical approaches which employ optimization techniques for the solution of the Inverse Kinematics problem are presented in [11, 12].

During the last two decades, in which Artificial Intelligence and Machine Learning have greatly developed, Neural Networks gained the attention of many researchers and therefore many approaches in this problem are closely related to Neural Networks. For instance, in [5], a Neural Network with end-effector position and end-effector orientation as inputs is used in order to predict the joint angles $\underline{Q}$. Other similar approaches regarding Neural Networks are presented in [6–8]. In [9], a different Neural Network configuration is employed in which, feedback of current joint angles with the desired position and orientation of the end-effector are used as inputs of the Neural Network. In [10], Elman Neural Networks are combined with genetic algorithms to solve the inverse kinematics problem of a six-joint robotic manipulator.

Some other recent approaches in this field are presented in [14–20].

In this paper, a novel approach for solving the inverse kinematics of the robotic arm is presented which is based on autoencoders. Unlike an initial and similar to our attempt, which was introduced by Dermatas et al. in [4], no non-linear activation function was used in our approach and thus the output of the neural network is a linear function of the input reducing the computational cost. However, the main difference is that in our implementation, the goal is to determine a valid solution to the inverse kinematics problem in which both the error between the actual and desired position of the end-effector and the joint movement are minimized. The proposed multi-objective technique leads to accurate results regarding both criteria.

This paper is structured as follows: In Sect. 2, the proposed method which is based on autoencoders is described, in Sect. 3 four different case studies and their corresponding results are presented and in Sect. 4 some remarkable conclusions and a summary of the contribution of the paper are provided.

2 Analysis of the Autoencoder Based Solution

In our presentation of the proposed method, a simple robotic arm with 3 Degrees of Freedom is used, as it is shown in Fig. 1, and the goal is to find the proper angles q_1, q_2, q_3 so that the end-effector of the robotic arm moves to the desired positions in the xy plane.

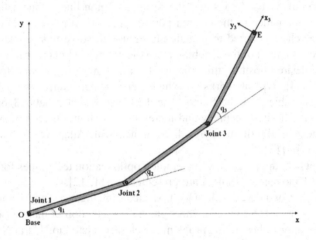

Fig. 1. Illustration of a Robotic arm with 3 Degrees of Freedom

The forward kinematics equations of this robotic arm are the following:

$$x_E = l_1 \cdot cos(q_1) + l_2 \cdot cos(q_1 + q_2) + l_3 \cdot cos(q_1 + q_2 + q_3) \tag{3}$$

$$y_E = l_1 \cdot sin(q_1) + l_2 \cdot sin(q_1 + q_2) + l_3 \cdot sin(q_1 + q_2 + q_3) \tag{4}$$

where l_1, l_2, l_3 are the lengths of the 1st, 2nd and 3rd link respectively and q_1, q_2, q_3 are the angles that are presented in Fig. 1 and each range in the following values:

$$q_1 \in [0, \pi] \tag{5}$$

$$q_2 \in [-\pi, 0] \tag{6}$$

$$q_3 \in \left[-\frac{\pi}{2}, \frac{\pi}{2}\right] \tag{7}$$

The estimation of the angles q_1, q_2, q_3 is achieved utilizing an autoencoder, the structure of which is shown in Fig. 2:

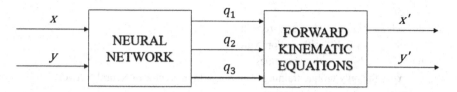

Fig. 2. Structure of the autoencoder

The first part of the Autoencoder consists of an Artificial Neural Network with 2 inputs in the input layer, two hidden layers with 50 hidden units each and an output layer with 3 outputs. The inputs are the (x, y) coordinates of the end-effector position and the outputs are the aforementioned angles: q_1, q_2, q_3. In both layers and in all hidden units the linear function: $f(x) = x$ is used as activation function, which means that the output $\overline{Q} = [q_1\ q_2\ q_3]$ is a linear function of the input: $\underline{X} = [xy]$. In the second part, the forward kinematics equations (3) and (4) are used, in order to compute the end-effector coordinates: (x', y') from the angles q_1, q_2, q_3 which are the outputs of the Neural Network. For the training of the Autoencoder based system, the Gradient Descent method is used for the minimization of the loss function. Thus, the weights and biases of the Neural Network are updated according to the following equations:

$$w_{ij} = w_{ij} - \alpha \frac{\partial L}{\partial w_{ij}} \tag{8}$$

$$b_{ij} = b_{ij} - \alpha \frac{\partial L}{\partial b_{ij}} \tag{9}$$

where α is the learning rate and is chosen to be equal to 0.003, and L is the loss function.

In the present work, four different types of loss function are assessed, which are presented in the case studies of Sect. 3 with their corresponding results. A comparison between them is discussed in Sect. 4.

In the experimental evaluation, 500 different and randomly chosen sets of angles $\underline{Q} = [q_1\ q_2\ q_3]$ are taken, according to the constraints (5), (6) and (7), in order to compute from Eqs. (3) and (4), 500 different (x, y) position coordinates of the end-effector, which are depicted in Fig. 3.

In the training procedure, each of these 500 end-effector positions is used separately from the others, to estimate the angles q_1, q_2, q_3 and is the only unique example used for training. One final detail is that the lengths of the links are: $l_1 = l_2 = l_3 = 1$. The algorithm that is used for the implementation of our proposed method is the following:

Algorithm

Input: Set of 500 different (x,y) position coordinates of the end-effector: x_i , $i=1,...,500$

FOR each position x_i, $i=1,...,500$ repeat:

  Initialize W_1, W_2, W_3 with random values.

  Initialize b_1, b_2, b_3 with zero values.

  Use x_i as the only unique training example → Input vector of Neural Network contains only this specific vector x_i

  FOR each iteration t, $t=1,....,k$ repeat:

    Compute the output of the 1st hidden layer: $y_1 = W_1^T x_i + b_1$

    Compute the output of the 2nd hidden layer: $y_2 = W_2^T y_1 + b_2$

    Compute the output of the Neural Network: $y_3 = W_3^T y_2 + b_3$

    Use y_3 that contains the estimated q_1, q_2, q_3 as the input of the forward kinematic equations according to constraints: (5), (6), (7).

    Compute the output y of the forward kinematic equations according to Eq. (3),

(4).

    Define the loss function: Use Eq. (10), (11), (14), (15) for case study I, II, III, IV respectively

    Compute the position error from Eq. (10)

    Use Gradient Descent optimizer for the minimization of the loss function with learning rate: $\alpha=0.003$

    Update weights and biases according to Eq. (8), (9).

  END FOR

  Print/Estimate the joint angles/parameters from the last value of y_3 for the specific position vector x_i.

  Print the last value of the loss function and the position error for x_i.

END FOR

Plot the results

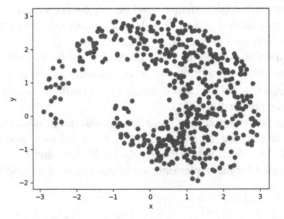

Fig. 3. 500 different (x, y) position coordinates of the end-effector

3 Case Studies and Results

In the first case study, the goal is to find any set of angles q_1, q_2, q_3 so that the end-effector of the robotic arm moves to the desired position. For this reason, for the training of the Neural Network, the squared-Euclidean distance between the actual and desired end-effector position is used as loss function:

$$L = (x - x')^2 + (y - y')^2 \tag{10}$$

One worth-mentioning detail is that this loss function takes into account the output of the forward kinematic equations in the second part of the Autoencoder-based system, and not the output of the Neural Network of the first part.

The results of the proposed method are presented in Fig. 4:

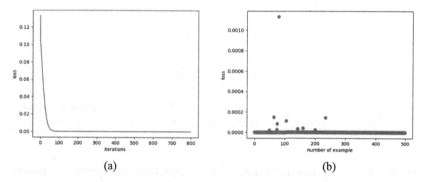

(a)   (b)

Fig. 4. (a) The loss function of a randomly selected example during training, (b) The value of the loss function (from Eq. 10) for all 500 examples after convergence.

However, in a real-life application, it is desired to estimate a proper set of angles q_1, q_2, q_3 in order for the end-effector to move to the anticipated point in the xy plane, minimizing the joint movement. For this reason, an autoencoder with the same structure with the one of the previous case is used, but the loss function is altered as follows:

$$L = k \frac{\|\underline{X} - \underline{X'}\|^2}{R} + (1 - k) \cdot \|\underline{Q} - \underline{Q_{in}}\|^2 \tag{11}$$

where $\underline{X} = [x\ y]$ is a vector containing the desired positions coordinates, $\underline{X'} = [x'\ y']$ is the vector output of the autoencoder which should be equal or very close to $\underline{X}$, $\underline{Q}$ is the vector which contains the looked-for angles q_1, q_2, q_3, that are the outputs of the Neural Network, and $\underline{Q_{in}}$ is a vector comprising the joint angles of the initial position of the robotic arm. R is a constant number used for normalization and is equal to:

$$R = \sqrt{l_1^2 + l_2^2 + l_3^2} \tag{12}$$

where l_1, l_2, l_3 are the lengths of the 1st, 2nd, and 3rd link respectively. Finally, k is a factor used to weight the two aforementioned optimizing criteria and should increase the significance of the position error, which is the squared difference between the desired and actual position, when the actual position is close to the desired one. Therefore, it is described by the equation:

$$k = 0.5 \cdot e^{-|\underline{X} - \underline{X}'|} + 0.5 \tag{13}$$

The results are summarized in Figs. 5 and 6:

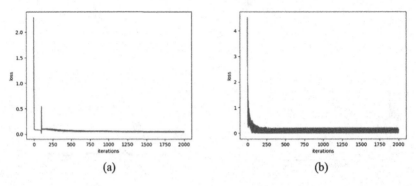

Fig. 5. The loss function (Eq. 11) of two randomly selected examples during training

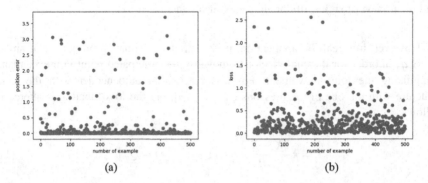

Fig. 6. (a) The value of the position error for all 500 examples, (b) The value of the loss function (Eq. 11) for all 500 examples.

In order to improve the performance of the proposed method, in case study III, an alternative loss function is employed which takes into account minimizing both the position error between the actual and desired position and the joint movement, as optimizing criteria:

$$L = \frac{\|X - X'\|^2}{R^2} + \frac{1}{t} \cdot \|Q - Q_{in}\|^2 \tag{14}$$

where R is the constant number from Eq. (12) and t represents the tth iteration. Using this loss function, less significance is given to the second minimizing criterion when the end-effector approaches the desired position. The results are depicted in Figs. 7 and 8.

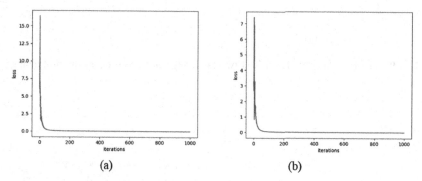

(a)   (b)

Fig. 7. The loss function (Eq. 14) of two randomly selected examples during training

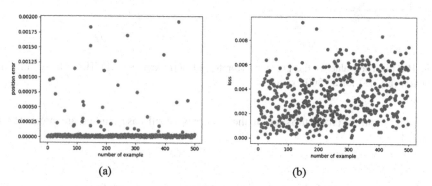

(a)   (b)

Fig. 8. (a) The value of the position error for all 500 examples, (b) The value of the loss function (Eq. 14) for all 500 examples.

Finally, for further improvement of both position error and loss function, in case study IV, the loss function is modified as follows:

$$L = \frac{\|X - X'\|^2}{R^2} + \frac{1}{t} \cdot log(\|Q - Q_{in}\|^2 + 1) \tag{15}$$

where R is the constant number from Eq. (12) and t represents the tth iteration. The results are shown in Figs. 9 and 10.

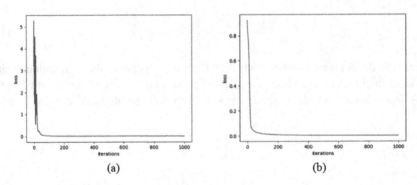

(a)   (b)

Fig. 9. The loss function (Eq. 15) of two randomly selected examples during training

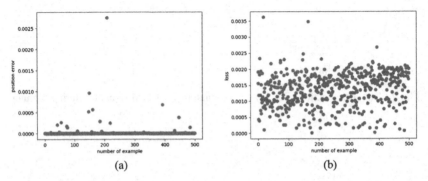

(a)   (b)

Fig. 10. (a) The value of the position error for all 500 examples, (b) The value of the loss function (Eq. 15) for all 500 examples

Some detailed characteristics of the accuracy of all case studies are presented in Table 1:

Table 1. Accuracy characteristics of all case studies

	CS I	CS II	CS III	CS IV
Mean loss value	$1.42 \cdot 10^{-14}$	0.269	0.0033	0.0014
Median loss value	$1.36 \cdot 10^{-14}$	0.163	0.0031	0.0015
Max. loss value	0.0011	2.598	0.0095	0.0036
Mean position error	$1.42 \cdot 10^{-14}$	0.179	$6.19 \cdot 10^{-5}$	$1.69 \cdot 10^{-5}$
Median position error	$1.36 \cdot 10^{-14}$	0.0127	$1.87 \cdot 10^{-5}$	$8.9 \cdot 10^{-7}$
Max. position error	0.0011	3.519	0.0019	0.0027

4 Conclusion

The best performance regarding the position error is reached in the case study I, in which only the position error is considered as minimizing criterion. However, in real-life applications, the minimum joint movement is also desired and therefore in case of studies II, III and IV it is taken into account as well as the position error. In case study IV, less significance is given to the minimization of the joint movement, compared to the other case studies, when the end-effector of the robotic arm approaches the desired position. The results of case study IV are relatively close to the ones of case study I regarding the position error, which implies the effectiveness of our proposed method.

In this paper, a novel approach for the solution of the inverse kinematics problem of robotic arm is proposed, which is based on autoencoders. Unlike many other Neural Networks based approaches in this problem, in our implementation, the only input needed is the end-effector position. Furthermore, the output of the Neural Network is a linear function of the input which significantly reduces the computational complexity and most importantly our method takes into account minimizing both the position error and the joint movement. The proposed method provides accurate results since both the position error between the actual and desired position and the joint movement are minimized.

References

1. Klein, C.A., Huang, C.H.: Review of pseudoinverse control for use with kinematically redundant manipulators. IEEE Trans. Syst. Man Cybern. **SMC-133**, 245–250 (1983)
2. Goldenberg, A., Benhabib, B., Fenton, R.: A complete generalized solution to the inverse kinematics of robots. IEEE J. Robot. Autom. **RA-1**(1), 14–20 (1985)
3. Parker, J.K., Khoogar, A.R., Goldberg, D.E: Inverse kinematics of redundant robots using genetic algorithms. In: Proceedings of IEEE Conference on Robotics and Automation (1989)
4. Dermatas, E., Nearchou, A., Aspragathos, N.: Error-back-propagation solution to the inverse kinematic problem of redundant manipulators. Robot. Comput. Integr. Manuf. J. **12**, 303–310 (1996)
5. Duka, A.V: Neural network based inverse kinematics solution for trajectory tracking of a robotic arm. In: Proceedings of 7th International Conference Interdisciplinarity in Engineering. Procedia Technology, vol. 12, pp. 20–27 (2014)
6. Jha, P., Biswal, B.B.: A neural network approach for inverse kinematic of a SCARA manipulator. Int. J. Robot. Autom. (IJRA) **3**, 52–61 (2014)
7. Daya, B., Khawandi, S., Akoum, M.: Applying neural network architecture for inverse kinematics problem in robotics. J. Softw. Eng. Appl. **3**, 230–239 (2010)
8. Koker, R., Oz, C., Cakar, T., Ekiz, H.: A study of neural network based inverse kinematics solution for a three-joint robot. J. Robot. Auton. Syst. **49**(3–4), 227–234 (2004)
9. Almusawi, A.R.J., Dulger, L.C., Kapucu, S.: Computational intelligence and neuroscience (2016)
10. Koker, R.: A genetic algorithm approach to a neural-network-based inverse kinematics solution of robotic manipulators based on error minimization. Inf. Sci. **222**, 528–543 (2013)

11. Courty, N., Arnaud, E.: Inverse kinematics using sequential Monte Carlo methods. In: Proceedings of the 5th International Conference on Articulated Motion and Deformable Objects, pp. 1–10 (2008)

12. Wang, L.-C.T., Chen, C.C.: A combined optimization method for solving the inverse kinematics problems of mechanical manipulators. IEEE Trans. Robot. Autom. **7**(4), 489–499 (1991)

13. Tabandeh, S., Clark, C., Mellek, W.: A genetic algorithm approach to solve for multiple solutions of inverse kinematics using adaptive niching and clustering. In: 2006 IEEE International Conference on Evolutionary Computation, Vancouver, BC, Canada (2006)

14. Mahanta, G.B., Deepak, B.B.V.L., Dileep, M., Biswal, B.B., Pattanayak, S.K.: Prediction of inverse kinematics for a 6-DOF industrial robot arm using soft computing techniques. In: Bansal, J.C., Das, K.N., Nagar, A., Deep, K., Ojha, A.K. (eds.) Soft Computing for Problem Solving. AISC, vol. 817, pp. 519–530. Springer, Singapore (2019). https://doi.org/10.1007/978-981-13-1595-4_42

15. Momani, S., Abo-Hammour, Z.S., Alsmadi, O.M.K.: Solution of inverse kinematics problem using genetic algorithms. Appl. Math. Inf. Sci. **10**(1), 225–233 (2016)

16. Chen, Q., Zhu, S., Zhang, X.: Improved inverse kinematics algorithm using screw theory for a Six-DOF robot manipulator. Int. J. Adv. Robot. Syst. **12**(10) (2015)

17. Dereli, S., Köker, R.: A meta-heuristic proposal for inverse kinematics solution of 7-DOF serial robotic manipulator: quantum behaved particle swarm algorithm. Artif. Intell. Rev., 1–16 (2019)

18. Gong, Z., Cheng, J., Hu, K., Wang, T., Wen, L.: An inverse kinematics method of a soft robotic arm with three-dimensional locomotion for underwater manipulation. In: Proceedings of the 2018 IEEE International Conference on Soft Robotics (RoboSoft), Livorno, pp. 516–521. IEEE (2018)

19. Li, S., Wang, Z., Zhang, Q., Han, F.: Solving inverse kinematics model for 7-DoF robot arms based on space vector. In: Proceedings of the 2018 International Conference on Control and Robots (ICCR), Hong Kong, pp. 1–5. IEEE (2018)

20. Zaplana, I., Basanez, L.: A novel closed-form solution for the inverse kinematics of redundant manipulators through workspace analysis. Mech. Mach. Theory **121**, 829–843 (2018)

Structural and Parametrical Model of the Physical Functional Principle of the Microelectronic Capacitive Pressure Sensor

Mikhail Shikulskiy[1], Olga Shikulskaya[2(✉)] ⬤, Irina Yu. Petrova[2] ⬤,
Gennady Popov[2], Issa Bogatyrev[2], Victor Samsonov[2],
and Alla Kachalova[2]

[1] Astrakhan State Technical University, Astrakhan, Russia
[2] Astrakhan State University of Architecture and Civil Engineering,
Astrakhan, Russia
shikul@mail.ru

Abstract. In this paper it is shown that one of the most important problems of technical progress development is productions automation. The leading place in the world on production and the number of the granted patents is occupied by microelectronic sensors of pressure. The retrospective analysis of patent, scientific and technical literature was made by authors. Importance of initial design stages was proved. The solution of a formalization problem of the processes description of information transformation in microelectronic capacitive pressure sensors by means of model's development on the basis of the theory of energy and information circuit models is proposed. The parametric structural scheme is developed. Mathematical dependences of its quantities and parameters on actual physical quantities are defined. The adequacy of model is proved. The developed model is intended for the automated synthesis of new technical solutions at a stage of search design and for predesign of sensors' output parameters at a stage of outline design.

Keywords: Microelectronic capacitive pressure sensor ·
Energy and information circuit model · Parametric structural scheme ·
Physical and technical effect · Operational characteristic · Parameter · Quantity

1 Introduction

One of the most important problems of technical progress development is productions automation. The possibility of automation of any technological production is defined by existence of the corresponding control devices.

Recently sensors on the microelectronics basis develop intensively. The leading place in the world on production and the number of the granted patents is occupied by microelectronic sensors of pressure [1].

The retrospective analysis of patent, scientific and technical literature allowed to reveal basic designs of microelectronic pressure sensors which can be used at synthesis

A. G. Kravets et al. (Eds.): CIT&DS 2019, CCIS 1083, pp. 299–308, 2019.
https://doi.org/10.1007/978-3-030-29743-5_24

of new technical solutions. One of such elements is the basic design of the micro-electronic capacitive pressure sensor [1–13].

The variety of the measured parameters, design features, the functional principles, the used materials, continuous growth of operational characteristics requirements, scale and complexity of modern sensors design problems, requirements to accounting of the increasing number of the interconnected factors, to reduction of time for these tasks solution demand system approach to the analysis and synthesis of sensors. On the other hand, mathematical language specifics of the description of the various phenomena and processes on which the sensors' functional principle is based, limitation of access to information on physical effects and a possibility of its full use owing to a human factor significantly complicate development of new sensors with the required operational characteristics.

The quality of design decisions in many respects is defined by results of the initial design stages (a stage of the specification and the technical offer) on which fundamental decisions on structure and the functional principle of a designed project are made. The initial stages of design are characterized by processing of considerable quantity of information, a large number of the studied realization options. The solution of these tasks in many respects depends on how the developer will be provided with the new information technologies strengthening his intellectual opportunities, allowing to automate processes of search and information processing on the basis of application of system approach to development of bases of the theory of sensitive elements of control systems including general concept about a class of objects.

2 Materials and Methods

Analysis of the works devoted to the sensors development decisions synthesis and choice the best one problem solution showed following: in the works of R. Koller, E. M. Shmakov, S. Lu, V.M. Tsurikov poorly structured models created, intended for the limited tasks area solution; in the works of A.I. Polovinkin, V.A. Kamayev, V.N. Glazunov, A.M. Dvoryankin, S.A. Fomenkov [14–18] created systems intend for the technical multipurpose devices synthesis, however there are difficulties in creation of mathematical models of the synthesized physical functional principle (PFP) variants description and an assessment of their operating characteristics that does not allow to carry out quantitative comparison of these variants.

The greatest efficiency of new technical design devices is reached due to a uniform approach to the tasks solution from different areas, transferring of potent decisions from one area to another. The theory of energy and information circuit models (EICM) and the parametric structural schemes (PSS) technique realize such approach. The EICM theory enables one to formalize the description of PFP of converters by the means of equations invariant under physical nature of the transformations (mechanical, electrical, thermal and so on): [19–23]. The PSS technique is intended for graphical interpretation of PFP for technical devices. The EICM theory operates with elements such as quantities, parameters and physical and technical effects (PTE). The quantities are variable in time and are denoted in PSS by arrows. The parameters and PTE are rather constant in time. The parameter describes transforming quantities of the same physical nature by the means of elementary analytical dependence, while the PTE characterizes elementary transforming quantities of one physical nature into quantities of a different physical nature or parameters into quantities of any physical nature. The parameters and PTE are denoted as rectangles in the PSS. Branching of quantities in the PSS is denoted by points and merging by circles separated into four sectors. On merging, quantities may be added or subtracted. If the quantity should be subtracted, then summation element sector in which it occurs is colored in the PSS. EICM represent the set of analytical dependences between quantities and parameters in an idealized circuit of the certain physical nature, similar to the sets of dependences between quantities and parameters in circuit of the other physical nature. PFP of any converter is based on the circuits interaction of various physical nature that allows to formalize description of converter's PFP in the form of the PSS.

The EICM theory is particularly effective for computerized systems for locating new technical designs (NTD). In computerized sensor PFP synthesis the program constitutes PSS with given input and output. The input quantity for each circuit component coinciding with output quantity of the presiding element. For the providing of successful synthesis, the constraints supplied by the user or the software are used. When the PFP circuits have been generated for a technical device (TD) one performs multivariate optimization and determines the target function in terms of the operating characteristics.

3 Modelling of the Microelectronic Capacitive Pressure Sensor

The general element of the majority of microelectronic pressure sensors is the flat membrane performing function of a sensitive element. The functional principle of such sensors is based on transformation of the membrane deformation arising under the influence of pressure to an electric signal. On a way of such transformation it is possible to allocate three basic designs of microelectronic sensors: capacitive, vibration and tensoresistor ones.

This work is devoted to development of the structural and parametrical model describing processes of transformation in the capacitive pressure sensor.

For the solution of this task the theory of energy and information circuit models (EICM) is used. EICM not only allows to consider the phenomena of various physical nature by means of the equations invariant to the most physical nature, but also gives the chance to shift the powerful device of the analysis and synthesis of electrical circuits to a research of the phenomena of other physical nature.

The microelectronic capacitive pressure sensor is executed from the semiconductor crystal (Fig. 1).

It consists of a membrane and the motionless plate interacting through a spring. The membrane and a motionless plate are electrodes of the capacitive sensor. Under the pressure influence the membrane caves in. As a result of it the distance between plates and respectively the electric capacity of the sensor changes. Therefore, the electric capacity of the sensor depends on a membrane deflection.

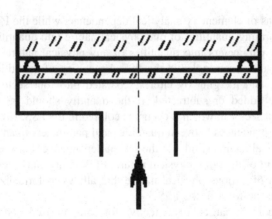

Fig. 1. Scheme of the capacitive microelectronic pressure sensor

EICM of a flat membrane deflection was developed earlier [24, 25]. The following step is the description of transformation process of a membrane deflection to change of the sensor capacity on which the output voltage of the sensor depends.

The scheme of the functional principle of the pressure capacitive sensor is provided on Fig. 2.

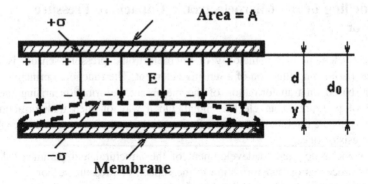

Fig. 2. Scheme of the functional principle of the capacitive pressure sensor

The capacity of the flat condenser is directly proportional to the area of plates and is inversely proportional to distance between them (1).

$$C = \frac{\varepsilon_0 A}{d} \tag{1}$$

As the distance between plates of d is changeable for various sections, it is expedient to break a surface of plates into elementary sites for which conditionally d can be considered constant.

Distinctive feature of semiconductor materials of which microelectronic sensors are manufactured is their anisotropic properties. If not to consider anisotropic properties of the membrane material, then a deflection it in points equally spaced from the center it is possible to consider identical. For this case the element in the ring form allocated with two cylindrical sections was considered. For capacity determination of the sensor taking into account anisotropic properties of material the element allocated with two cylindrical and two radial sections was considered (Fig. 3).

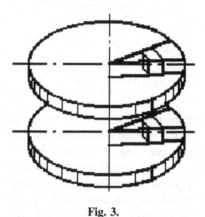

Fig. 3.

As the capacity of the flat condenser is directly proportional to the area of plates, and the plates area is equal to the sum of the areas of the allocated elements, and the capacity of the pressure sensor is equal to the sum of all elements capacities and, therefore, it can be presented how a chain in parallel the connected elementary condensers.

Now we will consider any element. The distance between plates of d can be determined by formula (2).

$$d = d_0 - y \tag{2}$$

where y is a deflection of the considered membrane element.

Having substituted this expression in a formula (1) we receive

$$C = \frac{\varepsilon_0 A}{d_0 - y} \tag{3}$$

Now we will consider rigidity. It is inversion of capacity. We will execute necessary transformations.

$$W = \frac{d}{\varepsilon_0 A} = \frac{d_0 - y}{\varepsilon_0 A} = \frac{d_0}{\varepsilon_0 A} + \frac{(-y)}{\varepsilon_0 A} \tag{4}$$

For the formalization purpose of the process description we will conditionally consider quantity $\frac{d_0}{\varepsilon_0 A}$ as quantity, that is inversion of the constant capacity, and quantity $\frac{(-y)}{\varepsilon_0 A}$ as variable negative rigidity.

$$W = \frac{(-y)}{\varepsilon_0 A} \tag{5}$$

$$\frac{1}{C} = \frac{d_0}{\varepsilon_{0A}} \tag{6}$$

From here we receive:

$$W = \frac{1}{C_0} + W \tag{7}$$

It follows from this that any sensor element on the scheme can be presented how a connection of two consistently connected condensers. The first has a constant capacity, the second has a variable negative capacity, or, more precisely, rigidity.

The analysis and synthesis of technical solutions is significantly facilitated if to consider the corresponding technical device as set of simple links, each of which characterizes elementary dependence of quantity or parameter on quantity of the same or other physical nature. The functional principle of any converter is based on chains interaction of various physical nature.

It allows to formalize the description of the functional principle of the considered converter and to present it in the form of the parametric structural schemes (PSS).

For simplification of development of PSS at the beginning we will display the received dependences on the equivalent circuit (Fig. 4).

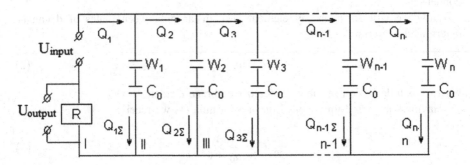

Fig. 4. Equivalent circuit of the capacitive pressure sensor

1. Quantities

   U_{input} — input impact

   U_{output} — output impact

   Q_i — charge of any i-th link

   $Q_i \sum$ — summary charge of any i-th link

2. Parameters

C_0 — capacity of any 0-th link
W_i — rigidity of any i-th link

The developed parametric structural schemes (PSS) of the microelectronic capacitive pressure sensor is submitted in Fig. 5.

The mathematical dependences determining parameters and quantities of PSS of the capacitive pressure sensor using actual physical quantities are received.

The developed model allowed to automate calculation of output characteristics of the sensor.

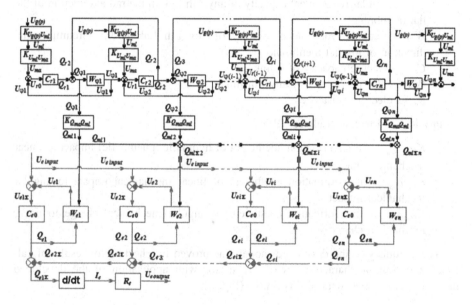

Fig. 5. PSS of the capacitive pressure sensor

The Designations Applied in the Scheme

1. Quantities

$U_{ig(p)}$ — hydraulic (pneumatic) impact

U_{mi} — linear mechanical impact

U_{ma} — angular mechanical impact

Q_{ri} — angular mechanical charge of any i-th link in the radial direction of the flat membrane

$Q_{\varphi i}$ — angular mechanical charge of any i-th link in the circumferential direction of the flat membrane

$Q_{mi} \sum i$ — summary charge of any i-th link

$U_{b\,input}$ — input electric impact

$U_{b\,output}$ — output electric impact

U_{bi} — electric impact of any i-th link

$U_{bi} \sum$ — summary impact of any i-th link

U_{ri} — angular mechanical impact of any i-th link in the radial direction of the flat membrane

$U_{\varphi i}$ — angular mechanical impact of any i-th link in the circumferential direction of the flat membrane

Q_{bi} — electric charge of any i-th link

$Q_{bl} \sum l$ — summary charge of the 1-th link

I_b — electric reaction

2. Parameters

C_{ri} — angular mechanical capacity of any i-th link in the radial direction of the flat membrane

$W_{\varphi i}$ — angular mechanical rigidity of any i-th link in the circumferential direction of the flat membrane

$C_{\varepsilon 0}$ — electric capacity of 0 link

W_{bi} — electric rigidity of any i-th link

R_e — electric resistance

3. Physical and technical effects (PTE)

$K_{U_{R(U)}U_{ml}}$ — transformation coefficient of hydraulic (pneumatic) impact to linear mechanical impact

$K_{U_{ml}U_{ma}}$ — transformation coefficient of linear mechanical impact to angular mechanical impact

$K_{Q_{ml}Q_{ma}}$ — transformation coefficient of angular mechanical charge to linear mechanical charge

The adequacy to the developed model was proved by checking of results of calculation of output characteristics of the sensor with application of the developed method with passport data of this sensor (Fig. 6).

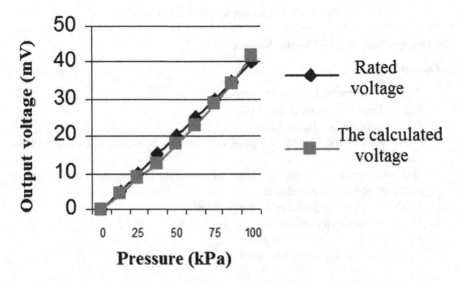

Fig. 6. Diagram of output voltage of the microelectronic pressure sensor

Check showed that use of the developed model at early design stages is quite acceptable.

4 Conclusion

Modeling of a basic design of the microelectronic capacitive pressure sensor is based on new approach to the automated synthesis of the physical functional principle of sensors and their elements at the initial stages of design which allowed to broaden area of synthesized technical devices and to increase the models accuracy.

The received results are applicable, both at a stage of search design, and at a stage of outline design.

The developed model of the microelectronic capacitive pressure sensor can be used in the form of the structural generalized technique at the automated synthesis of new technical solutions at a stage of search design.

Computer-aided design (CAD) system of microelectronic capacitive pressure sensors has been developed for its use at a stage of outline design. Application of this system allowed to reduce sensors' prime cost.

References

1. Shikulskaya, O., Petrova, I., Shikulskiy, M.: The methods analysis of achievement of the required operational characteristics of microelectronic pressure sensors. Int. J. Eng. Sci. Res. Technol. (IJESS7) 6(4), 347–354 (2017)
2. Balzar, R., Krasnogenov, E., Abbasov, S.: Semiconductor vibrational frequency response sensor for pressure measurement. Phys. Tech. High Press. 2, 25–27 (1993). Pap. 30 Annu. Meet. Eur. High Pressure Res. group
3. Bao, M.-H., Yu, L.-Z., Wang, Y.: Micromachined beam-diaphragm structure improves performances of pressure transducer. In: Transducers 1989: Proceedings of the 5th International Conference on Solid-State Sensors and Actuators and Eurosensors III, Montreux, Lausanne, vol. 2, pp. 137–141, 25–30 June 1989
4. Bai-zar, R., Voronin, V., Krasnogenov, E., Bogdanova, N.: Operation of monocrystalline silicon resonator in a measuring circuit. Sens. Actuators A 30(1–2), 175–178 (1991). Pap. East-West Workshop Microelectron. Sens, Sozopol
5. Zook James, D., Burns David, W.: Resonant gauge with microbeam driven in constant electric field. Patent 5275055 USA. Honeywell Inc. - No 937068; Appl. 31.08.92; publish 04.01.94
6. Tilmans Hendricus, A.C.: Resonant mechanical sensor. Patent 5165289 USA, Johnson Service Co. - No 551523; appl. 10.07.90; publish 24.11.92
7. Ryan, K., Bryzek, J.: Sensor with new configuration of a touch element. Flexible miniature packaging from Lucas Nova sensor provides low-cost pressure sensor solutions to a wide variety of hostile media applications. Electron. Compon. News 39(4), 118–120 (1995)
8. Frische Richard, H.: Semiconductor pressure sensor. Patent 5142912 USA, МКИ5 G 01 L 9/06. Honeywell Inc. No 538956; Patent 15.06.90; publish 01.09.92
9. Keiichi, S., Osamu, T., Susumu, S., Toyota Chuo Kenkyusho, K.K.: Semiconductor pressure sensor. Patent 5163329 USA, No 635953; Patent 28.12.90; publish. 17.11.92.; НКИ 73/721

10. Tetsuo, F., Yoshitaka, G., Susumu, K.: Fabrication of microdiaphragm pressure sensor utilizing micromachining. Sens. Actuators A **34**(3), 217–224 (1992)

11. Tehn, R., Werthschutzky, M.: Silizium sensoren inprozeB-meBgeraten, Zar Druckmessung-Stand and Tendenzen, No. 9, pp. 340–346 (1992)

12. Wilfried, G., Gunter, K.: Mechanical decoupling of monolithic pressure sensor in small plastic encapc. In: Transducers 1989: Proceedings of the 5th International Conference on Solid-State Sensor and Actuators and Eurusensors III, Montreux, Lausane, vol. 2, pp. 1065–1069 (1989)

13. Wang, Y., Liu, L., Zheng, X., Li, Z.: A novel pressure sensor structure for integrated sensors. In: Transducers 1989: Proceedings of the 5th International Conference on Solid-State Sensors and Actuators and Eurosensors III, Montreux, Lausanne, 25–30 June, vol. 2, pp. 62–64 (1989). Appl. 2235773 1989, 1990

14. Dvoryankin, A.M., Polovinkin, A.I., Sobolev, A.N.: Automating the search for operation principles of technical systems on the basis of a bank of physical phenomena. Cybernetics **14**, 79–86 (1978)

15. Andreychikov, A.V., Dvoryankin, A.M., Polovinkin, A.I.: Using expert systems in an automated bank of engineering knowledge for development and design by search. Sov. J. Comput. Syst. Sci. **27**, 41–46 (1989)

16. Fomenkov, S.A., Korobkin, D.M., Kolesnikov, S.G., Kamaev, V.A., Kravets, A.G.: The automated methods of search of physical effects. Int. J. Soft Comput. **10**, 234–238 (2015)

17. Korobkin, D.M., Fomenkov, S.A., Kolesnikov, S.G., Kizim, A.V., Kamaev, V.A.: Processing of structured physical knowledge in the form of physical effects. In: Proceedings of the European Conference on Data Mining 2015, ECDM 2015 and International Conferences on Intelligent Systems and Agents 2015, ISA 2015 and Theory and Practice in Modern Computing 2015, TPMC 2015 - Part of the Multi Conference on Computer Science and Information Systems 2015 (2015)

18. Fomenkova, M.A., Kamaev, V.A., Korobkin, D.M., Fomenkov, S.A.: The methodology of semantic analysis for extracting physical effects. J. Phys. Conf. Ser. **803**, 1–6 (2017)

19. Petrova, I., Shikulskaya, O., Shikulskiy, M.: Conceptual modeling methodology of multifunction sensors on the basis of a fractal approach. Adv. Mater. Res. **875–877**, 951–956 (2014)

20. Shikul'skaya, O.M., Nezametdinova, É.R.: Modernization of a conceptual model of a data bank for physicotechnical effects based on contemporary information technology. Meas. Tech. **50**(1), 7–9 (2007)

21. Shikul'skya, O.M., Konstantinova, O.S.: Synthesis of new designs based on modern technologies. Meas. Tech. **52**(8), 829–832 (2009)

22. Zaripova, V., Petrova, I., Lezhnina, Y.: Designing the module "Methods for activating engineering creativity" on basis of competence approach. Recent Pat. Comput. Sci. **9**(2), 160–165 (2016)

23. Zaripova, V., Petrova, I.: Knowledge-based support for innovative design on basis of energy-information method of circuits. In: Kravets, A., Shcherbakov, M., Kultsova, M., Iijima, T. (eds.) JCKBSE 2014. CCIS, vol. 466, pp. 521–532. Springer, Cham (2014). https://doi.org/10.1007/978-3-319-11854-3_45

24. Shikul'skaya, O.M.: A recurrent model for a line with distributed parameters and quantities. Meas. Tech. **50**(3), 245–248 (2007)

25. Shikulskaya, O.M., Shikulskiy, M.I.: Energy-information modelling of the flat membrane on the fractal approach basis. J. Phys. Conf. Ser. **803**(1), 1–6 (2017). Article id: 012145, Open Access

Theoretical Bases of the Application of Various-Color Graphs in the Solution of Intellectual Chemical Tasks

Ilya V. Germashev[1] (ID), Evgeniya V. Derbisher[2](✉) (ID), and Vyacheslav E. Derbisher[2] (ID)

[1] Volgograd State University,
University Avenue, 100, Volgograd 400062, Russia
germasheviv@mail.ru
[2] Volgograd State Technical University,
V.I. Lenin Avenue, 28, Volgograd 400131, Russia
derbisherl@yandex.ru

Abstract. The paradigm of using artificial neural networks (ANN) for solving intellectual problems of chemistry and chemical technology is considered: classification, identification, design, modeling, optimization, and others. Using the example of studying the applicability of colored graphs in the neural network analysis of chemical structures at the site «structure-property-application» relationship, the possibility of identifying chemical structures when creating actual substances is shown. Artificial neural network learning to identify graphs is shown. The results obtained are mathematical software that allows solving creative problems and creating decision rules when choosing chemical-technological systems formalized in terms of graph theory and intended to support decision-making.

Keywords: Intellectual task · Identification · Artificial neural network · Chemical structure · Multi-colored graphs · "Structure - property" dependence · Statistics · Decision making

1 Introduction

One of the most important purposeful intellectual tasks of modern chemical science, and on its basis technology, is the design and identification of structures of compounds with desired properties. Here actualized methods of discrete mathematics can be used, in particular, the theory of graphs, which are increasingly used in research and development of technologies in various fields of science and technology [1–5], including chemistry and chemical technology [1, 6–8]. Here, in some cases, to identify the structure of chemical compounds, they are modeled using graphs, which allows not only to apply mathematical methods to analyze and design these structures in an academic sense but also to allow the selection of promising substances with desired properties to promote them to the technology market. At the same time, one of the most promising ways is a statistical analysis of the descriptors of chemical structures.

© Springer Nature Switzerland AG 2019
A. G. Kravets et al. (Eds.): CIT&DS 2019, CCIS 1083, pp. 309–318, 2019.
https://doi.org/10.1007/978-3-030-29743-5_25

The mathematical solution of such a cluster of intellectual problems from our point of view includes six stages: formalization of the initial data, construction of a profiled mathematical model, analysis of the model, including algorithmized, selection of a set of decision rules, decision making, updating the decision.

The following areas of intellectual tasks from the field of analysis and synthesis of chemical-technological systems (CTS) and in particular chemical structures and substances can be identified on this beachhead: analysis, approximation, classification, identification, modeling, optimization, prediction, pattern recognition, which ensure the adoption of high-tech making. The information space and information flows in this part are constantly growing and differentiating [9, 10]. It also draws attention to the fact that the algorithms that simulate the processes occurring in relation to this article in a real artificial neural network (ANN) are associated with training networks to solve specific problems, including CTS [1, 6–8, 11–13].

Infogrames 1 shows the current approximate distribution of research activity in various branches of science and technology (based on data processing of 4031 publications for the period 1990–2018) associated with the use of ANN. It should be mentioned that over the past 10 years, the activity in solving applied problems in the field of chemistry and chemical technology [14–16], ecology, and transport has slightly increased and slightly decreased in cybernetics. In all these areas, there is a rapid convergence of academic ideas about ANN and practice. Here empirical, semi-empirical and theoretical approaches are used, of which the latter is the most economical, which is purely intellectual and requires mostly mental and information resources obtained from practice [17, 18]. The empirical approach is increasingly being used only as the penultimate link in the transition from theory to practice, followed by a decision supported by the corresponding theory (Fig. 1).

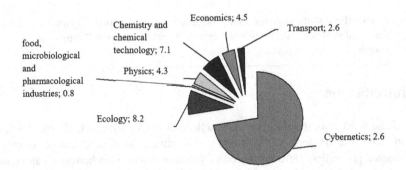

Fig. 1. The distribution of information fields in the space of artificial neural networks.

Now let us consider in more detail the objective problem of identification for creating intelligent solutions in the field of chemical structures (formulas) with the use of ANN, which is the leading topic of this article. As a simple example, let us point out that the chemical formula of a well-known substance (compound), ethyl alcohol (C_2H_5OH) has the form:

$$
\begin{array}{ccccc}
& H & H & & \\
& | & | & & \\
H- & C & -C & -O & -H \\
& | & | & & \\
& H & H & &
\end{array}
$$

and is conveniently analyzed in the form of multicolored graphs in the ANN. In this case, chemical bonds, atoms, and groups of atoms are colored. The same applies to any chemical compounds.

2 Theoretical Solution of the Identification Problem of Chemical Structures in Terms of Multi-colored Graphs

2.1 Formalization

The task of analyzing and synthesizing chemical structures in terms of graphs can be formally presented as follows. The universal of G graphs is given. We select in it a subset of G+ ⊂ G- -graphs with the "given" property. Accordingly, the set G+/G- is denoted by G-. We consider that many elements of the set G- are not known, and only some of them that make up the set G+ ⊂ G+ are established. Similarly to G− ⊂ G−. Thus, the set G = G+ ∪ G is a learning sample. Moreover, let the graph G0 ⊂ G+/G- be given. It is required to determine which one of the two sets (G+ or G−) it belongs to.

To solve the problem, we use the basic concepts of graph theory [19]. We use the statistics of simple chains and in the simulation of the chemical structure of the following provisions:

- each atom (or functional group of atoms) we will represent as vertex painted in the color corresponding to a chemical element (or functional group).
- quantity of colors of vertices will be designated as k_v (k_v can reach several thousand: chemical elements plus groups of elements).
- for identification of atoms in a molecule we will mark all vertices in the graph: v_1, ..., v_n, where n-quantity of vertexes in the graph.
- color of vertex v_i we will designate as c_i, i = 1, ..., n.

chemical bonds between atoms in a molecule will be represented by edges, and the edges will be painted in colors corresponding to different types of chemical bonds in accordance with established scientific knowledge in this area. Quantity of colors of edges we will designate k_e (k_e can reach several units, depending on considered types of a chemical bond). Colour of an edge incidental to vertices v_i and v_j we will designate c_{ij} (color 0 designates lack of an edge).

As a result, we will receive simple (without loops and multiple edges) marked graph G both with vertices and with an edge coloring. Moreover, the degree of any vertex doesn't exceed the maximum valency of a chemical element - 8, i.e.

$$\Delta(G) \leq 8, \qquad (1)$$

where $\Delta(G)$ - maximum degree of a vertex of the graph G [19].

2.2   Routing

In this case, we are talking about the definition of all possible simple chains (hereinafter referred to as chains) in the graph G. To consider the problem, we use the search wide [19].

1. Define the set $H = \varnothing$ chains, the set $V_0 = \varnothing$ of the considered initial vertices of chains and $V_n = VG$ of yet not considered initial vertices.
2. Fix initial vertex $v_{i0} \in VG\backslash V_0$ of the chain, suppose that $V_0 = V_0 \cup \{v_{i0}\}$, $V_n = V_n\backslash\{v_{i0}\}$, sets $H_k = \varnothing$ of chains of length k = 0, ..., n with initial vertex v_{i0}.
3. Suppose that the considered chain $h_c = v_{i0}$ and vertex $v_c = v_{i0}$, the set $V_h = \{v_{i0}\}$ of vertices of chain h_c, k = 1.
4. Define the set $V_c \subset VG\backslash V_h$ of vertices adjacent to the vertex v_c. If $V_c = \varnothing$, then we should move on to the 6th step.
5. Suppose that $H_k = H_k \cup \{h_c.v | v \in V_c\}$ and $H = H \cup \{h_c.v | v \in V_c\}$, where «.» is a concatenation operation (clutch).
6. If $H_{k-1} = \varnothing$, then move on to step 7, otherwise let us take $h_c \in H_{k-1}$, make v_c be the last vertex of the chain h_c, and inset V_h take all the vertices of the chain h_c, also let us suppose that $H_{k-1} = H_{k-1}\backslash\{h_c\}$ and move on to step 4.
7. Suppose that k = k + 1. If k < n + 1, then move on to step 6.
8. If $V_n = \varnothing$, then finish algorithm, differently move on to step 2.

Evidently, the coloring was not considered any way in the algorithm. Therefore the algorithm is applicable to a wider class of graphs (and to inconsistent too).

Now it should be shown that the given algorithm really finds all chains in the graph. Let us consider in the graph G some chain $V_{i_1} V_{i_2} \ldots V_{i_m}$, where $2 \leq m \leq n$. According to steps 2 and 8, the vertex of V_{i_1} obligatory becomes initial in the chain and, according to step 3, the vertex of V_{i_1} becomes considered. Further, as V_{i_2} is adjacent t V_{i_1}, then V_{i_2} in step 4 will be placed in the set Vc and then in step 5 the chain $V_{i_1} V_{i_2}$ will be placed in sets H1 and H. Then in step 6 the chain $V_{i_1} V_{i_2}$ and the vertex V_{i_2} will become considered. After that, we should repeat given above arguments for a bunch of vertices $V_{i_2} - V_{i_3}$ and the chain $V_{i_1} V_{i_2} V_{i_3}$ will be placed in the set H.

Continuing our reasoning the same way, we will achieve that the chain $V_{i_1} V_{i_2} \ldots V_{i_m}$ will be placed in the set H. As the chain $V_{i_1} V_{i_2} \ldots V_{i_m}$ was chosen randomly, it means that, as a result of the algorithm work, in the set H will be placed all the chains of the graph G.

Let us evaluate the complexity L of the algorithm.

Step 1 is carried out only once and it consists of the initialization of the empty sets H, V0 (complexity – constant c_0), and also of the sets Vn (complexity c_{1n}). Steps from 2 to 8 are carried out, until each vertex of the graph G takes part as the initial vertex of the chain, i.e. n times:

$$L = c_0 + c_{1n} + nL_1, \tag{2}$$

where L_1 - the complexity of the steps 2–8.

In turn, L_1 constitutes step 8 (complexity c_2) and steps 2 through 7 (complexity L_2). Steps 2 through 7 are repeated until we consider all the lengths of the chains k, i.e. n times. We get that $L_1 = c_2 + nL_2$. Substituting the obtained equality in (2), we get

$$L = c_0 + (c_1 + c_2)n + n^2 L_2, \tag{3}$$

Further L_2 form step 7 (complexity c_3), step 2 where H0, ..., Hn are initialized and some operations are carried out (complexity $c_4 + c_{5n}$), step 3 where we create the set Vh of k vertices, considering that $k \leq n$, plus some more operations, we will obtain the 3rd step complexity of no more than $c_6 + c_{7n}$, and steps from 4 to 6 (complexity L_3). Steps from 4 to 6 repeat until we consider all the chains of the set Hk (the number of such chains we will designate Nk). We obtained that $L_2 \leq c_3 + c_4 + c_6 + (c_5 + c_7)n + NL_3$, where $N = \max_{k=1,...,n} N_k$. Substituting the received inequality in (3), we receive

$$L \leq c_0 + (c_1 + c_2)n + (c_3 + c_4 + c_6)n^2 + (c_5 + c_7)n^3 + n^2 NL_3, \tag{4}$$

In step 4 some operations and search of adjacent vertices are realized. All adjacent vertices can be found no more than for n operations. Therefore complexity of this step can be evaluated, as not exceeding value $c_8 + c_{9n}$.

In step 5 we add new chains to the sets Hk and H. The number of these chains equally to the number of adjacent vertices, and the number of adjacent vertices cannot be more than 8 for a considered class of graphs, i.e. complexity of this step is a constant c_{10}.

In step 6 some operations and formation of the set Vh are realized, where can be necessary up to n operations. Consequently, the complexity of this step can be estimated as $c_{11} + c_{12n}$.

Summing up aforesaid, we will receive $L_3 \leq c_8 + c_{10} + c_{11} + (c_9 + c_{12})n$ and substitute this inequality in (4), we receive:

$$L \leq c_0 + (c_1 + c_2)n + (c_3 + c_4 + c_6)n^2 + (c_5 + c_7)n^3 + (c_8 + c_{10} + c_{11})n^2 N \\ + (c_9 + c_{12})n^3 N \leq c_{13}n^3 N \tag{5}$$

From this assessment, it is already visible that the complexity of the algorithm is polynomial concerning a number of vertices and number of chains that allows making the conclusion about sufficient efficiency of the algorithm.

Now it is necessary to estimate the value of N.

It is obvious that $N1 \leq \Delta(G)$. Further, as one adjacent vertex is that from which we got to the following one, then the number of adjacent vertices which are absent in the chain will be no more than $\Delta(G)-1$ and we receive $Nk \leq \Delta(G)(\Delta(G)-1)k-1$. Wherefrom considering (1) we get:

$$N = \max_{k=\overline{0,n}} N_k \leq \Delta(G)(\Delta(G) - 1)^{n-1} = \frac{\Delta(G)}{\Delta(G) - 1}(\Delta(G) - 1)^n \leq c_{14} 7^n. \qquad (6)$$

Substituting this assessment in (5), we will receive

$$L \leq cn37n. \qquad (7)$$

It is obvious that the total number of chains in the graph does not exceed the value $n(\Delta(G))n$. Let us make sure that among the graphs under consideration there are indeed those that have an exponential number of chains. A small example is the graph of order n shown in Fig. 2.

Let n be a multiple of 7. Then take a series of 7-clicks (altogether there will be n/7), successively connect them with edges (bridges), so that these edges are not adjacent, and connect extreme edges with an edge in the same way. In each 7-clique, you can select $\sum_{k=0}^{5} A_5^k$ chains of length from 1 to 6, starting from the top, incident to one bridge, and ending with the top, incident to the other bridge. Connecting chains from neighboring clicks you can make up $\left(\sum_{k=0}^{5} A_5^k\right)^{\frac{n}{7}}$, and we did not take into account all the chains, so this is the lower estimate of the number of chains of the graph. We also take into account that $\sum_{k=0}^{5} A_5^k \geq \sum_{k=0}^{7} C_7^k$ (as can be verified by direct calculation). Therefore, the total number of chains will exceed the following value (8):

$$\left(\sum_{k=0}^{5} A_5^k\right)^{\frac{n}{7}} \geq \left(\sum_{k=0}^{7} C_7^k\right)^{\frac{n}{7}} = (2^7)^{\frac{n}{7}} = 2^n. \qquad (8)$$

I.e. generally it is impossible to construct a polynomial algorithm for the solution of this task and the offered decision is effective.

Thus, we considered the algorithm of search of all chains in the graph and now it is possible to pass actually to the solution of a problem of graph's identification.

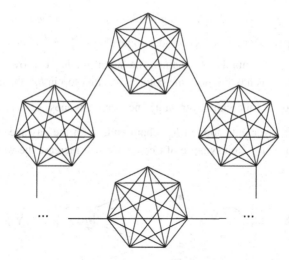

Fig. 2. A graph with an exponential number of chains.

2.3   Identification

Let there be two classes of the painted graphs G+ and G−. It is presented some graph $G0 \notin G+ \cup G-$. We need to define to which of the two classes it is necessary to attribute this graph. Let us dwell on the formal side of the question.

Let $G^+ = \{G_1^+, .., G_{s^+}^+\}$, $G^- = G+ = \{G_1^-, .., G_{s^-}^-\}$, and let for each graph $G_1^+, 1 = 1, \ldots, s^+, G_1^-, 1 = 1, \ldots, s-$ and G0 respectively, a set is obtained, and H_1^+, H_1^- and H0 of all its chains and $H^+ = \bigcup_{l=1}^{s^+} H_l^+$, $H^- = \bigcup_{l=1}^{s^-} H_l^-$ and $H = H^+ \cup H^-$.

Let us build ANN of m layers, where m - the maximum length of all received chains. Working principle of ANN is following. On input synapses, we will give chains of the graph G0, and on output, we will read out signals. If the sum of these signals is positive, we will suggest that $G0 \in G+$, and if it is negative, then $G0 \in G-$. As on entrances of ANN we will submit chains, then we will accept that the neuron corresponds to the top, and synapse - to an edge. Thus the number of neurons in each layer will be identical and equal to the number of all tops' colors (plus one for zero color) meeting among graphs from $G = G+ \cup G-$. All neurons in one layer are painted in various colors (including a zero color).

Let each of m of layers of ANN consists of kv + 1 neurons u_p^j, where p = 0, ..., kv (the neuron with the number p = 0 is fictitious and serves for the solution of some problems when signal is passing through ANN) – color of neuron, j = 1, ..., m. Also, we will agree to consider that any pair of neurons located in two next layers, is connected by ke synapses (each synapse corresponds to an edge of a certain color) with weight $\omega_{pq_r}^j$ – the weight of synapse (for an edge of r color) between neurons u_p^j and u_p^{j+1} as illustrated in Fig. 3.

The weight $\omega_{pq_r}^j$ is formed by training ANN as follows. At the beginning of training $\omega_{pq_r}^j = 0$ for all p, q, r, and j. Let's consider some chain $h_{lt}^+ = \left(u_{i_1^{lt}} ... u_{i_{a_{lt}}^{lt}} \right) \epsilon H_1^+$, where a - length of a chain, t – number of chains. The signal for h_{lt}^+ is provided on neuron's entrance $u_{c_{i_1^{lt}}}^1$ (which is having the same color as the first top in h_{lt}^+ the chain). Further, the signal goes to the following layer on $u_{c_{i_2^{lt}}}^2$ neuron on synapse of color $c_{i_1^{lt} i_2^{lt}}$ and so on from a layer to a layer until tops in h_{lt}^+ chain end. With the passage of signals from neuron u_p^j to neuron u_q^{j+1} on synapse of r color, we will increase the weight ω_{pqr}^j by 1.

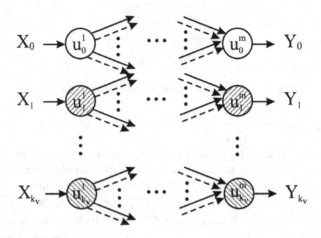

Fig. 3. Schematic diagram of the ANN: X - input signal; Y - output signal; u - neuron; m - the number of layers ANN; k - the number of colors of the vertex of the original graph.

So we do for each chain of H_1^+. Further, we will repeat this procedure for each l = 1, ..., s + . Let us similarly arrive with chains from sets H_l^-, l = 1, ..., s− only with the difference that with the passage of the signal we will not increase the weight of the synapse ω_{pqr}^j, but decrease by one. As a result, we obtain a decision rule in the form of ANN, which identifies the presented G0 graph as follows.

We provide on ANN entrances all chains from H0. On an entrance, each signal has value 0. The signal for each chain passes through ANN how it was described above, but now when the signal is passing on synapse, there is no updating of its weight ω_{pqr}^j, but reading. Read value is added to signal value. If the length of a0t chain is less than m, then after the last top of this chain the signal goes to the fictitious neuron $u_0^{a_{0t}+1}$ and further the signal goes through fictitious neurons up to u_0^m. As the weight of synapses between fictitious neurons is zero, the signal is unchanged to its output.

Let's designate as yt the turned-out value of a signal on output from a signal $X_{C_{i_1^t}}$ on an entrance of ANN for the chain $h_t^+ = \left(u_{i_1^t} \ldots u_{i_{a_t}^t} \right) \epsilon H^0$. Then

$$y_t = \sum_{j=1}^{a_t-1} \omega^j_{C_{i_j^t} C_{i_j^t} \ C_{i_{j+1}^t} C_{i_{j+1}^t}}$$

The total signal Y at the output of the ANN will be reflected by the Eq. (9):

$$Y = \sum_{p=0}^{k_v} Y_p = \sum_{t=1}^{|H^0|} y_t = \sum_{t=1}^{|H^0|} \sum_{j=1}^{a_t-1} \omega^j_{C_{i_j^t} C_{i_j^t} \ C_{i_{j+1}^t} C_{i_{j+1}^t}}, \tag{9}$$

where Yp - output value of the signal.

As a result, if $Y > 0$, we identify graph G0 as G+. If $Y < 0$ we identify graph G0 as G–.

3 Conclusion

The ideas proposed here, so far selectively tested in the "manual" mode on the structures of additives to polymer composites, on the "structure-property" platform, with the algorithmization, substances can be invested in neurocomputer technologies to solve the intellectual problems of creating and identifying new chemical structures by conducting statistical analysis of simple colored graphs in accordance with the theory discussed above. Our proposals should be understood as mathematical software to generate subject-matter decision rules, including by introducing activation functions, perceptions, and other components into the ANN, which will allow the ANN to analyze and synthesize graph structures, such objects as formulas of chemical compounds, including virtual substances.

It should be noted that today the direct synthesis of chemical compounds within the framework of creating a profiled intellectual (expert) system due to the rapid expansion of the information space, without their prior selection, is becoming more and more expensive and less promising. Work on the creation of an information system for this profile will continue.

This work was supported by the Russian Foundation for Basic Research grant "Managing the quality of polymer products based on the optimization of formulation of composite materials". Form of the project 18-48-340011 (Application 2018).

References

1. Glebov, M.B., Galushkin, A.I.: The use of neural networks in chemistry and chemical technology. Neurocomput. Dev. Appl. (3–4), 66–107 (2003)
2. Smith, K.A.: Neural networks for combinatorial optimization: a review of more than a decade of research. Inf. J. Comput. **11**(1), 15–34 (1999)
3. Hung, D.L., Wang, J.: Neurocomputing **51**, 447–461 (2003)
4. Devillers, J. (ed.): Neural Networks in QSAR and Drug Design. Academic Press, London (1996)
5. Halbershtam, N.M., Baskin, I.I., Palyulin, V.A., Zefirov, N.S.: Neural networks as a method of finding dependencies structure - a property of organic compounds. Successes Chem. **72**(7), 706–727 (2003)
6. Tumanov, V.E.: The use of an artificial neural network to predict the reactivity of molecules in radical reactions. Inf. Technol. **5**, 11–15 (2010)
7. Stasyuk, V.V.: Prediction of sensitivity to impact of explosives by neural networks with preliminary grouping of data. Fundam. Res. **12–6**, 1139–1143 (2015)
8. Baskin, I.I., Madzhidov, T.I., Antipin, I.S., Varnek, A.A.: Artificial intelligence in synthetic chemistry: achievements and prospects. Chem. Adv. **86**(11), 1127–1156 (2017)
9. Heung, B.K., Sung, H.J., Tag, G.K., Kyu, H.P.: Fast learning method for learning. Neurocomputing **11**, 101–106 (1996)
10. Qian, N.: On the dynamic algorithms. Neural Netw. **12**, 145–151 (1999)
11. Skorobogatchenko, D.A.: Methods of predicting the operational condition of roads based on the representation of fuzzy sets by neural networks. Proc. High. Educ. Inst. Build. **2**(626), 72–77 (2011)
12. Germashev, I.V., Derbisher, E.V., Alexandrina, A.Y., Derbisher, V.E.: Hazard evaluation of organic substances using artificial neural networks. Theor. Found. Chem. Technol. **43**(2), 225–231 (2009)
13. Germashev, I.V., Derbisher, V.E.: Use of fuzzy sets for computer processing of information on chemical structures and substances. Control Syst. Inf. Technol. **2**, 76–80 (2008)
14. Germashev, I.V., Derbisher, V.Ye.: Solving problems in chemical technology using fuzzy sets: monograph, p. 142. GOU VPO Volgograd State Pedagogical University, Peremena, Volgograd (2008)
15. Germashev, I.V., Derbisher, V.E., Losev, A.G.: Analysis and identification of the properties of complex systems in the natural sciences: monograph. FSAEI of HE, 271 p. Volgograd State University Publishing House, Volgograd (2018)
16. Derbisher, V.E., Germashev, I.V., Derbisher, E.V.: Fuzzy sets in chemical technology. Proc. High. Educ. Inst. Chem. Chem. Technol. **1**, 104–110 (2008)
17. Germashev, I.V., Derbisher, V.Ye., Derbisher, E.V.: Making decisions on the choice of ingredients of polymeric compositions in conditions of fuzzy information. Plastics **7**, 24–27 (2007)
18. Germashev, I.V., Derbisher, V.E., Tsapleva, M.N., Derbisher, E.V.: Sorting of additives to polyethylene based on the non-distinct multitudes. Russ. Polym. News **6**(2), 53–57 (2001)
19. Emelichev, V.A., Melnikov, O.I., Sarvanov, V.I., Tyshkevich, R.I.: Lectures on graph theory. Science, 384 p. (1990)

Cyber-Physical Systems and Big Data-Driven World. Intelligent Internet of Services and Internet of Things

Forecasting and Optimization Internet of Things System

Yakov Lvovich[1], Igor Lvovich[1], Andrey Preobrazhenskiy[1]($\boxtimes$) (iD),
and Oleg Choporov[2] (iD)

[1] Information Systems and Technologies Department, Voronezh Institute
of High Technologies, Lenina str. 73a, 394043 Voronezh, Russia
komkovvivt@yandex.ru
[2] Information Security Department, Voronezh State Technical University,
Moscow district 14, 394026 Voronezh, Russia

Abstract. Currently many methods and approaches related to the management of Internet of Things systems are associated with the collection of large amounts of information. The results of the rating assessment from the management point of view are limited. In many cases we need to involve modeling and optimization techniques in the management process. This paper shows how an integral assessment of the efficiency of Internet of Things systems is formed. The optimization model of the problem is developed and the procedures of expert evaluation of management decisions are formed. On the basis of the methods used, the results demonstrating their efficiency are obtained.

Keywords: Optimization · Internet of Things systems · Model · Management

1 Introduction

Currently, one can observe the development of Internet of Things systems. Different methods should be used to describe them [1, 2]. The Internet of things is a complex heterogeneous network. At present, we cannot talk about a generalized approach, which can take into account the heterogeneity of network technologies and provide appropriate modes of operation. The aim of the work is to develop a set of problem-oriented modeling and optimization procedures that are associated with the results of monitoring and rating evaluation, which will improve the efficiency of the Internet of Things system. The paper proposes the development of an algorithm based on optimization and expert modeling, with the involvement of monitoring information.

2 Optimization-Expert Modeling in the Problem of Manage Resource Efficiency

When managing the resource efficiency of Internet of Things systems, the problem of making a rational decision is essential. In this case, information from two sources is used: a formalized solution of the problem using optimization modeling and expert evaluation of its results [3, 4].

© Springer Nature Switzerland AG 2019
A. G. Kravets et al. (Eds.): CIT&DS 2019, CCIS 1083, pp. 321–333, 2019.
https://doi.org/10.1007/978-3-030-29743-5_26

The need for combining it is determined by the nature of the multicriteriality of the choice of resource support in the case of taking into account in this problem the set of monitored performance indicators of the Internet of Things systems [5, 6]. Moreover, in most cases, the solution of the problem of resource efficiency by one criterion is reduced to a linear programming problem with continuous or integer variables. In the situation of using monitoring information for many indicators [7, 8], it is required to organize the search for the optimally compromise solution of the multicriteria optimization problem based on the vector criterion.

$$F = (F_1, \ldots, F_s, \ldots, F_S) \rightarrow \max, \ s = \overline{1, S} \tag{1}$$

The effectiveness of the solution (1) is based on the transformation by means of the operator $\Psi = (\Psi_1, \ldots, \Psi_s, \ldots, \Psi_S)$ of the criterion $F = (F_1, \ldots, F_S)$ into an equivalent vector criterion $\Psi(F) = (\Psi_1(F_1), \ldots, \Psi_S(F_S))$ which characterizes the same properties of the control object as F, and defines in the area of acceptable solutions $x = (x_1, \ldots, x_i, \ldots, x_I) \in \Omega$ the same ratio of non-strict preference O as and vector criterion F: for any $x', x'' \in \Omega$ takes place $F(x') \ OF(x'')$ if and only if

$$\Psi(F(x')) \ O \ \Psi(F(x'')). \tag{2}$$

The case when the mathematical model of effective decision-making is given by the multi-criteria optimization problem (1), in which the particular optimality criteria $s = \overline{1, S}$ either have a single measurement scale or are homogeneous criteria, is considered [4, 9]. The mechanism for selecting the optimal compromise solution can be reduced to a sequence of the following two procedures:

selection of the domain of Pareto $\overline{\Omega}$ optimal solutions (not necessarily explicitly), which also includes optimal solutions $x_i^*, i = \overline{1, I}$ obtained from the solution of parametric optimization problems for each of the particular optimality criteria $F_s, s = \overline{1, S}$;

the introduction of a compromise agreement between the partial optimality criteria $F_s, s = \overline{1, S}$, which allows the search for an optimal compromise solution $x^0 \in \Omega$ using a specially constructed scalar generalized optimality criterion Φ as a function of the partial optimality criteria $\Phi(F) = \Phi(F_1, \ldots F_S)$, satisfying the condition [10]:

for any $F(x'), F(x'')$ we can see: $\Phi(F(x')) \leq \Phi(F(x''))$ if and only if

$$F(x') \ OF(x'')$$

Thus, introducing the generalized optimality criterion $\Phi(F(x))$ on the basis of the compromise agreement, according to the condition (2), the search for the optimal compromise solution $x^0 \in D$ in the original multi-criteria optimization problem is reduced to the problem of parametric optimization of the following form

$$\min_{x \in \Omega} \Phi(F(x)).$$

In the case where the set $\overline{\Omega}$ consists of a single vector of weight coefficients, the convolution of the vector optimality criterion $F = (F_1, \ldots, F_s)$ is reduced to a summation operation with known weight coefficients that implements the additive generalized optimality criterion:

$$\Phi(x) = \Phi(F(x)). \tag{3}$$

The generalized optimality criterion (3) can be used to collapse the vector optimality criterion F only if the partial optimality criteria $F_s, s = \overline{1, S}$ satisfy the following requirements [11]:

particular optimality criteria $F_s, s = \overline{1, S}$ are commensurate in importance, i.e. each of them can be assigned a certain non-negative number, which characterizes its relative importance in relation to other particular criteria;

particular optimality criteria $F_s, s = \overline{1, S}$ are homogeneous criteria or have a single measurement scale.

For the generalized optimality criterion (3), even in the nonconvex domain of feasible solutions Ω and any functions $F_s, s = \overline{1, S}$, the following statement is true:

if an acceptable solution $x^0 \in \Omega$ is an effective solution, and everything $F_s(x^0) > 0, s = \overline{1, S}$, then there is a vector of weight coefficients such that the optimal solution to the problem of parametric optimization:

if an acceptable solution $x^0 \in \Omega$ is an effective solution, and everything $F_s(x^0) > 0, s = \overline{1, S}$, then there is a vector of weight coefficients such that the optimal solution of the parametric optimization problem is achieved in an effective solution $x^0 \in D$. At the same time, for the fixed values of the vector of positive coefficients ρ, the optimal solution of the problem is the optimal compromise solution $x^0 \in D$.

Another form of generalized criterion of optimality for homogeneous partial criteria of optimality can be represented using the average of the exponential function:

$$\Phi_p(x) = \Phi_p(F(x)) \tag{4}$$

For any modification of the average power generalized optimality criterion, i.e. for any $-\infty \leq p \leq \infty$ optimal solution of the parametric optimization problem

$$\Phi_p(x^0) = \min_{x \in \Omega} \Phi_p(x) = \min_{x \in \Omega} \left\{ \left(\frac{1}{S} \sum\nolimits_{s=1}^{S} \hat{F}_S(x) \right)^{1/p} \right\}, \tag{5}$$

it an optimal compromise solution $x^0 \in \Omega$.

Having accepted the agreement that particular optimality criteria are equivalent criteria, i.e. criteria between which it is impossible to establish priority by importance, thereby we set the same values of weight coefficients:

$$\lambda_s = 1/S, \text{ for all } s = \overline{1, S}. \tag{6}$$

For unequal criteria, i.e. criteria for which priority can be established by importance, the values of the weight coefficients are chosen in accordance with their priority (a more "important" criterion should correspond to a greater value of the weight coefficient) so that the search for optimal compromise solutions with the help of parametric optimization is carried out (3). Let us consider a number of compromise agreements based on the information about the minimum Φ_s^{min} and maximum Φ_s^{max} values of particular optimality criteria in the field of acceptable solutions Ω, the values of partial criteria of optimality $F_s(x), s = S$ which are obtained by solving parametric optimization problems [12]. If we accept the agreement that the particular optimality criteria, for which the minimum F_s^{min} and maximum F_s^{max} values are very different from each other, are more priority, then the weights can be determined in the following way. For every private criterion of optimality $F_s(x) > 0$ of the calculated coefficient of relative variation

$$\delta_s = \frac{(F_s^{max} - F_s^{max})}{F_s^{max}}. \tag{7}$$

which determines the maximum possible relative deviation according to the s-th partial criterion of optimality in the field of admissible solutions. Weight coefficients λ_s are the most important for those criteria whose relative spread in the area of acceptable solutions D is the most significant:

$$\lambda_s = \delta_s / \sum_{k=1}^{S} \delta_k, s = \overline{1, S}. \tag{8}$$

From expressions (7)–(8) it can be seen that the closer the minimum value F_s^{min} to the maximum value F_s^{max}, the smaller the value of the weight coefficient λ_s. In $F_s(x) =$ const i.e., $F_s^{min} = F_s^{max}$ we get that $\lambda_s = 0$. With a strong difference in the limit values of S-th partial criterion $(F_s^{max} \gg F_s^{min})$, the value of the weight coefficient is chosen to be large, since in this case the relative spread coefficient δ_s is close to one. Let all $F_s^{min} \neq 0, s = \overline{1, S}$. Then, instead of the coefficients of the relative spread δ_i, it is possible to introduce the coefficients of stability of the minimum value in the consideration [13]:

$$\beta_i(x) = (F_s(x) - F_s^{min})/F_s^{min}, s = \overline{1, S},$$

which give information about the deviation of the value of S-th particular optimality criterion calculated in an admissible solution $x \in \Omega$ from its minimum possible value F_s^{min}. Let us accept the agreement that the priority of S-th particular criterion depends on the implementation of inequality

$$\beta_s(x) \leq \varepsilon_s \tag{9}$$

where parameter ε_s is selected in such a way that the "more important" S-th particular criterion, the less select its value. The agreement on the compromise between the particular optimization criteria can be obtained with the help of the relative loss matrix

C, the lines of which correspond to the optimal solutions of the parametric optimization problem (5) for each particular optimality criterion, and the columns-the particular optimality criteria themselves:

$$
\begin{vmatrix}
 & F_1 & F_2 & \cdots\cdots & F_s \\
x_1^* & 0 & c_{12} & \cdots\cdots & c_{1s} \\
x_2^* & c_{21} & 0 & \cdots\cdots & c_{2s} \\
\cdot & \cdot & \cdot & & \cdot \\
\cdot & \cdot & \cdot & \cdots\cdots & \cdot \\
\cdot & \cdot & \cdot & & \cdot \\
\cdot & \cdot & \cdot & & \cdot \\
x_s^* & c_1 & c_2 & \cdots\cdots & 0
\end{vmatrix}
\tag{10}
$$

The value of the coefficient c_{dk} characterizes the relative influence of the optimal solution x_s^* on the value of $k-$th particular criterion. Obviously, that $c_{kk} = 0$, and the rest $c_{dk} \geq 0$. Let us consider the matrix of relative losses (10) as a matrix of payments in the game of two persons with a zero sum, in which each party is reduced to the fact that the first player chooses one of the optimal solutions x_s^* (this is the net strategy of the first player), and the second player, regardless of the choice of the first player, indicates $k-$th particular criterion of optimality F_s (this is the net strategy of the second player). Due to the fact that all the elements $c_{dk} \geq 0$, the first player pays the second player a penalty c_{dk}. It is obvious that the first player seeks to minimize the loss by choosing the optimal solution, which should be expected in relation to all possible particular criteria QF_k, $k = \overline{1, S}$.

$$
\min_{1 \leq l \leq s} \max_{1 \leq k \leq s} c_{lk} = \min_{1 \leq l \leq s} \max_{1 \leq k \leq s} \left| \frac{F_k - F_k(x_l^*)}{F_s^*} \right|.
$$

In this sense, in this formulation, they understand the agreement on compromise between particular criteria of optimality. The structure of the relative loss matrix (10) shows that it does not have a saddle point. Therefore, the optimal solution of the constructed game for each player will be given in the form of mixed strategies: for the first player: $\mu_l \geq 0, l = \overline{1, S}, \sum_{l=1}^{S} \mu_l = 1$; for the second player: $\lambda_k \geq 0, k = \overline{1, S}, \sum_{k=1}^{S} \lambda_k = 1$. In this case, the probabilities μ_l choose big for those x_l^*, for which the values of the coefficients c_{lk} are less. Similarly, probabilities λ_k more for those particular criteria F_k, for which values c_{lk} are greater. We present one of the algorithms for individual examination, which implements the Churchman-Akof logical ordering method, which is based on a systematic check of the expert's judgments about the relationship of preference k – private criterion over all remaining $(F_{k1}, F_{k2}, \ldots, F_s)$ particular criteria and consists of the following sequence of actions.

1. Linear ordering of partial optimality criteria is carried out $F_k, k = \overline{1, S}$ in order of decreasing their importance by using the ordinal scale of natural numbers (index 1 is assigned to the particular criterion with the greatest importance, and index S - to a particular criterion with the least importance): $F_1 \ F_2, \ldots, \ F_s$.

2. Partial criterion of optimality F_s score matching $\mu_s = 1$. Then, using a nonlinear scale of orders, assign different numbers to the estimates μ_i reflecting the expert's judgments about the relative importance i – private criterion, observing the condition: $\mu_{i-1} > \mu_s$ $i = S, S - 1, \ldots, 2$.

3. Considering columns one through $(S - 2)$ From top to bottom of Table 1, called the table of options for a logical choice, the expert fixes his judgments about preferences between the left (x) and right part of the relationship. For this purpose, instead of the sign V, the sign > is placed between the left and right parts of the relationship if x is strictly more respectable than y; sign < if y is strictly preferable to x and sign $\sim$ if x is equivalent to y. In this case, as soon as one of the following relations is fulfilled: x > y or x $\sim$ y, then they switch to viewing the new column.

Table 1. Table of options for logical choice

1		2		.	$(S-2)$	
y		x	y	.	x	y
		$F_2 v$	$F_3 + F_4 + \Lambda + F_S$	.	$f_{S2} v$	$F_{S-1} + F_S$
$F_2 + F_3 + \Lambda + F_{S-1}$	$F_2 v$	$F_3 + F_4 + \Lambda + F_{S-1}$		.		
....				.	....	
.				.	.	
$F_2 + F_3$	$F_2 v$	$F_3 + F_4$		.	View finished	
Move to the second column		Move to the third column		.		

Here is the view ratio $F_k \vee F_{k-1} + F_{k-2} + \cdots F_S$ means that for an expert criterion F_k strictly preferable (not preferable, equivalent) combined criteria $(F_{k-1}, F_{k-2}, \ldots, F_S)$.

4. Grades $\mu_i, i = \overline{1, S}$ obtained in the second step are put in the relationship of logical choice, which were recorded in the third step, starting with $(S - 2)$. In addition, each column is viewed from the bottom up. If the total value of the estimates of the right-hand side does not correspond to the value of the left estimate in the sense of fulfilling one of the inequalities:

$$\mu(x) > \sum_s \mu_s(y), \text{if } x > y; \mu(x) > \sum_s s\mu_s(y), \text{ if } x < y;$$
$$\mu(x) > \sum_s \mu_s(y), \text{ if } x \sim y,$$

then the left estimate $\mu(x)$ is adjusted to the minimum possible extent so that the inequalities correspond to the decisions of the expert, affixed in the relationship table of options for logical choices. In checking each subsequent relationship, the already adjusted estimates are used μ'_s.

5. For refined values $\mu_s', s = \overline{1,S}$, among which there are not adjusted estimates μ_s, obtained in the second step, calculate the weighting coefficients of the relative importance of the partial optimality criteria $F_3, i = \overline{1,s}$:

$$\lambda_s = \mu_i' / \sum\nolimits_{k=1}^{S} \mu_k', s = \overline{1,s}.$$

3 Evaluation of Expert Procedure

The expert assessment procedure begins with the formation of the personal composition of the group of experts. One of the most common methods for solving this problem is the snowball method. The procedure of the method assumes the known number of initial participants of the expert group. P_0 – "Core expert group." Among them, a survey is conducted to identify their views on possible candidates for the expert group, then let each d – the respondent calls $m_1(d)$ persons, among which $p_1(d) \notin P_0$. As a result of the first round of such a survey, we get: $P_1^0 = P_0 + \sum_{i=1}^{P_0} p_1(d) = P_0 + P_1$, where P_1 – the number of new individuals named in the first round. Then the process continues, revealing on each k – step set: $P_k^0 = \sum_{j=0}^{k} \sum_{i=1}^{P_0} p_j(d)$.

If taken as unknown $(D+1)$ – the number of all participants in the expert group, the number of persons called by each interviewed candidate, then for the case of complete uncertainty, when any m persons from D may be called a candidate (excluding himself), we are likely to be named L new faces based on combinatorial considerations:

$$P(L) = \frac{C_{D+1-P_0}^L C_{P_0-1}^{m-L}}{C_D^m},$$

where L varies from 0 before m. The resulting distribution is a hypergeometric, expectation of a random variable p' – numbers of new faces:

$$M(P') = m(N+1-P_0)/D.$$

We equate the expectation of the sample mean: $M(P') \approx \frac{1}{P_0}, \sum_{d=1}^{P_0} \mu(d)$, where $\mu(d) = 1$ – if d– candidate from P_0 calls the person not entering P_0 and 0 - otherwise. Hence, an approximate estimate of the possible number of candidates: $D^* = \frac{mP_0(P_0-1)}{mP_0 - \sum_{d=1}^{P_0} \mu(d)} + 1$. Based on the primary set of experts obtained, for example, using the snowball method, we can distinguish groups of non-conflicting experts, "clans" of experts. To determine the competence of experts, a "test" method can be applied or peer evaluations of experts can be used. The essence of the latter method is as follows: each expert fills in a matrix $A = \|a_{ij}\|$, each element of which is an integral assessment of competence j – an expert with the help of j – an expert. If the division of experts into groups ("clusters") is set $G_1, \ldots, G_q$, then, using the average value of competence assessments by groups as measures of the "conditional" competence of an expert, we have:

$$u_i = \frac{1}{n_s} \sum_{i \in G_s} a_{ij},$$

where n_s – number of experts in the group G_s. Denote $\Delta_j^{(H)}$ – lower bound of the confidence interval for the mean u_j. If for given thresholds a and b it turns out $u_j < a, \Delta_j^{(H)} < b$ then j – the expert is considered incompetent in the group G_s With $u_j \geq a$ и $\Delta_j^{(H)} \geq b$, the expert is considered competent in the group G_s This method allows you to leave in each "clan" sufficiently competent experts in the relevant field. Expert assessments are also applied, the use of which should take into account the fact that "if it is human nature to make mistakes, then first of all when trying to evaluate oneself." A measure of the consistency of expert assessments may be the coefficient of concordance:

$$W = \frac{\sum_{i=1}^{n} \Delta_i^2}{\left[\sum_{i=1}^{n} \Delta_i^2\right]_{max}},$$

introduced by M. Kendall. As a quantity Δ_i^2 consider the difference of the sum of ranks σ_i attributed by experts i – object, and the average value of such a sum σ_{CP} Number n determines the number of objects of expert ranking. Magnitude varies from 0 to 1. With $W = 0$ There is no consistency between the assessments of various experts, and with $W = 1$ the consistency of expert opinions is complete. There are other estimates of the consistency of expert estimates. After determining the composition of the group of experts, it is necessary to form a mechanism for group expert assessment based on the following stages of its implementation: organization of group expertise, processing the results of examinations, management decision making.

Formation of models of an integrated assessment of the performance of objects of distributed electrical systems based on monitoring information. A procedure for the formation of an integral assessment is proposed. Y based on the transformation of monitoring data and focused on specific management objectives. By structural identification, we will understand the choice of the structure of the integral assessment model and the method of rationing indicators Y_s.

To solve the first problem of the structural identification goal of management, it is advisable to assess the possibility of using variants of the model structure of the global target multicriteria optimization function, allowing to determine the optimal-compromise management solution (Table 2). Let us analyze the conformity of the models.

Table 2. Structures of integral estimation models

Option designation	Model name	Kinds of math models
1	2	3
Structure 1	Additive convolution with variable weights	$Y = \sum_{s=1}^{S} \lambda_s \hat{y}_s$, where $\hat{y}_s$ – normalized values of monitoring indicators, λ_s – weighting factors that meet the conditions $0 \leq \lambda_s \leq 1, \sum_s^S \lambda_s = 1$.
Structure 2	Additive convolution with constant weights	$Y = \frac{1}{S} \sum \hat{y}_s$
Structure 3	Average power convolution	$Y = \left(\frac{1}{S} \sum_{s=1}^{S} \hat{y}_s^u \right)^{1/u}$, where $-\infty < u \leq \infty$
Structure 4	Geometric mean convolution	$Y = \frac{1}{S} \left(\prod_{s=1}^{S} \hat{y}_s \right)$
Structure 5	Multiplicative convolution	$Y = \prod_{s=1}^{S} \hat{y}_s$
Structure 6	Logical convolution on the principle of "maximum risk"	$Y = \max_{1 \leq s \leq S} \hat{y}_s$
Structure 7	Logical convolution according to the principle of "maximum caution"	$Y = \min_{1 \leq s \leq S} \hat{y}_s$

In Table 3 summarizes the main objectives of each of these management tasks and provides a rationale for the adequacy of options for the structures of the integral assessment model.

All considered models operate with normalized values of monitored indicators $\hat{y}_s$. The choice of the rationing method is the second stage of the structural identification. Next, we study the effect of individual methods in the orientation of the integral assessment model on the task of managing resource supply. The problem of parametric optimization is to determine the weighting coefficients in the case of choosing the structure 1 of the model of the integral estimate. The mechanism of selection of specific options is explored in the next section. Next, we will use the procedure to build basic models of integral estimation: on the basis of rationing by (rating) ranking sequences of monitoring indicators; based on the valuation of the minimum and maximum values of the indicators in the statistical sample.

Table 3. Adequacy of integral assessment structures for management objectives and objectives

Management task based on the use of monitoring	Main management objective	Option structures models	The adequacy of the task and objectives of management
Information	Increasing the importance of objects of a distributed electrical system	Structure 4 Structure 5 Structure 1	Reflects the synergistic effect of the impact of achievements in one direction on other
Significance Management	Improving the efficiency of activities in promising areas through rational budgeting	Structure 3 Structure 6 Structure 7	Reflects the varying degrees of priority of achievements in individual areas.
Development Management (Budgeting)	Achieving the greatest resource efficiency	Structure 1 Structure 2	Strengthens the importance of promising areas

4   Determination of the Potential of Objects of a Distributed Electrical System Based on an Integrated Assessment

The introduction of basic models of integrated assessment allows you to proceed to the definition of an integrated assessment of objects of a distributed electrical system, which characterizes their potential for the effective development of resource support. It is proposed to use a multi-method approach to processing monitoring information to obtain an estimate of the potential of a distributed electrical system: excluding after-effects; with limited aftereffect; with prediction. In case of determining the potential of a distributed electrical system π_i statistical samples are used in the form without consequence y_{tsi} current time period τ^1. Magnitude π_i calculated on a given interval (O, P) using the integral estimation model. Along with models of rank sequences and additive convolution of indicators $y_{tsi}, i = \overline{1,I}, s = \overline{1,S}, t_s = \overline{1,T_S}$ considered the combined option. In this case, the most significant indicator is selected for each direction. $y_s, s = \overline{1,S}$ and calculated by approximating the rank sequences y_i continuous scale α with values on the interval $[A, O]$ normalized values of indicators $\hat{y}_{si} = \alpha(i_s')$. Definition π_i carried out on the basis of additive convolution $\pi_i = \sum_{s=1}^{S} \lambda_s \hat{y}_{si}$, where $\lambda_s -$ weights. The option of limited aftereffect is focused on the formation of monitoring information related either to the previous time interval τ_2, or to current τ_1 and the previous τ_2 temporary periods. In addition, for each time period a set of indicators from $s = \overline{1,S}$ directions

$$\tau_1 - s^{\tau_1} = \overline{1.S^{\tau_1}}, \tau_2 - s^{\tau_2} = \overline{1.S^{\tau_2}}.$$

These sets determine $\pi_i^{\tau_1}$, or

$$\pi_i^{\tau_1 \tau_2} = \lambda^{\tau_1} \pi_i^{\tau_1} + \lambda^{\tau_2} \pi_i^{\tau_2}, \tag{11}$$

where are the weights $\lambda^{\tau_1}, \lambda^{\tau_2}$ determine the priorities of time intervals in assessing the potential of the educational organization. The method of obtaining an estimate of the potential of Internet of Things systems with prediction is based on processing or statistical selections y_{ts} either time series $y_{ts}(\tau)$ [14]. In the first case, the prediction is carried out using numerical characteristics i – sampling (expected value $m(y_{si})$, standard deviation $\sigma(y_{si})$, as well as the standard deviation of the sample values of the indicator y_s on set $i = \overline{1, I} \; \sigma(y_s)$:

$$\pi_i = \sum_{s=1}^{S} \lambda_s (y_{si} - m(y_{si})) \frac{\sigma(y_{si})}{\sigma(y_s)}. \tag{12}$$

When accumulating monitoring information for several time periods $k = \overline{1, K}$, that is, the formation of statistical time series $y_{si}(\tau_k), s = \overline{1, S}$ it also becomes possible to determine the prognostic value of the potential. This is especially important given the fact that resources are distributed one and a half years before the beginning of the planned period.

In this case, we will use the integral estimation model (11), but the definition of the normalized values of the indicators can be carried out as follows:

$$\hat{y}_{si}(\tau_k) = \begin{cases} \frac{y_{si}(\tau_k) - y_s^{gr}}{y_{max}(\tau_k) - y_s^{gr}} & \text{if } y_s(\tau_k) > y_s^{gr} \\ 0, & \text{otherwise} \end{cases}$$

where y_s^{gr} threshold value of performance evaluation by indicator y_s;

$y_s^{max}(\tau_k)$ – maximum value of the indicator in the selection $y_{si}, i = \overline{1, I}$ for k time period.

In determining the prognostic evaluation, it is necessary to take into account that the time series $\pi_i(\tau_k)$ displays the changes in the integral estimate (11), which depend on the changes of each indicator $\widehat{y_{si}}$: $\pi_i(\tau_k) = \sum_{s=1}^{S} \lambda_s \widehat{y_{si}}(\tau_k)$. For this class of social systems - time series of individual indicators $\widehat{y_{si}}(\tau_k)$ possess certain properties: monotony and gradual change over time. These properties are determined by the inertia of educational systems. On the other hand, these time series are heterogeneous, because differ in the rate of change of indicators $\widehat{y_{si}}(\tau_k)$. Given the monotony of functions and the need for their changes, it is proposed to build a prognostic estimate in the form of a sum of polynomials of various degrees $v = \overline{0, V}$, where the value of the degree of a polynomial: $\pi_i(\tau_k) = \sum_{s=1}^{S} \lambda_s \sum_{v=0}^{V} \gamma_{v_s} \delta_{v_s} Y_{v_s}(\tau_k)$ where $y_{v_s}(\tau_k)$ - time functions $(Y_0(\tau) = 1, Y_1(\tau) = \tau, Y_2(\tau) = \tau^2, \ldots, Y_v(\tau) = \tau^v); \gamma_{v_s}$ - participation factors $y_v(\tau)$ in a mathematical time series model $\hat{y}_{si}(\tau_k)$ and determined by expert,

$$\gamma_{v_s} = \begin{cases} 1, \text{if function } Y_{v_s} \text{ a time series model } Y_{v_s}(\tau_k), \\ 0, \text{otherwise} \end{cases}$$

δ_s - coefficients determined by the exponential smoothing method by the values of the time series $\widehat{y_{si}}(\tau_k)$ for time periods from 1 to k. Then the forecast estimate for the time period k + k_1 is defined as follows $\pi_i(\tau_{k+k_1}) = \sum_{s=1}^{s} \lambda_s \sum_{v=0}^{V} \gamma_{v_s} \delta_{v_s} Y_{v_s}(\tau_{k+k_1})$. The multi-method approach to assessing the potential allows determining the criterion for the distribution of resources, which differs from the previously proposed in [10, 11], according to two components: the potential of the Internet of Things systems based on the monitoring results and the corresponding GHS using expressions (11) and (12).

5 Results

To select the structure of the criteria for making management decisions on the establishment of parameter values, a comparative analysis of the capabilities of several models of integrated assessment of the efficiency of Internet of Things systems is carried out. As alternative structures of the model (Table 1) consider the additive convolution variable (structure 1) and permanent (structure 2) weighting factors, and alternative ways of rationing is based on rating order in the ranking order of the translated discrete scale $i_s = \overline{1, S}$, where $s = \overline{1, S}$, - the performance of system components ys, y_s' the rating of i-th component of the s-th indicator and by conversion in a dimensionless form a single continuous scale [A, O]. Comparative analysis is carried out by means of a computational experiment. The following key indicators s = (1, 3) were considered (1): y1-energy characteristics (average power); y2-research activities (income from research and development activities per employee); y3-infrastructure (total area of premises per employee). Comparison of rating i' and expert rating i" by value (determined that its highest value corresponds to the model 2, so in the future it is advisable to use such a model mainly to assess the potential of Internet of Things systems.

6 Conclusion

The paper presents optimization and expert modeling for the problem related to the management of resource efficiency of Internet of Things systems based on monitoring information. The analysis of the possibilities of optimizing resource management in the Internet of things is carried out. The possibility of using the information of monitoring and rating evaluation to build a model and develop procedures for intellectual decision support is shown. A combination of optimization methods and expert approaches in monitoring information with a focus on optimizing resource management is carried out. Optimization models and algorithmic procedures for the formation of decision-making options have been developed to improve the efficiency of the Internet of Things system are developed. The results of the calculation based on the developed algorithm are presented. In the result part of the paper the recommendations for the use of different models are given.

References

1. Minerva, R., Biru, A., Rotondi, D.: Towards a definition of the Internet of Things (IoT). IEEE Internet Initiative, Torino, Italy (2015) https://iot.ieee.org/images/files/pdf/IEEE_IoT_Towards_Definition_Internet_of_Things_Revision1_27MAY15.pdf
2. Stankovic, J.A.: Research directions for the internet of things. IEEE Internet of Things J. 1 (1), 3–9 (2014). https://doi.org/10.1109/jiot.2014.2312291
3. Broadband Internet Technical Advisory Group. Internet of Things (IoT) Security and Privacy Recommendations (2016). https://www.bitag.org/documents/BITAG_Report_-_Internet_of_Things_(IoT)_Security_and_Privacy_Recommendations.pdf
4. Lutakamale, A.S., Kaijage, S.: Wildfire monitoring and detection system using wireless sensor network: a case study of Tanzania. Wirel. Sens. Netw. 9, 274–289 (2017). https://doi.org/10.4236/wsn.2017.98015
5. Groefsema, H., van Beest, N.R.T.P.: Design-time compliance of service compositions in dynamic service environments. In: International Conference on Service Oriented Computing & Applications, pp. 108–115 (2015)
6. Groefsema, H.: Business process variability: a study into process management and verification. Ph. D. thesis (2016)
7. Object Management Group. Business Process Model and Notation, version 2.0. http://www.omg.org/spec/BPMN/2.0/. Accessed 10 Mar 2019
8. Weber, I., Xu, X., Riveret, R., Governatori, G., Ponomarev, A., Mendling, J.: Untrusted business process monitoring and execution using blockchain. In: La Rosa, M., Loos, P., Pastor, O. (eds.) BPM 2016. LNCS, vol. 9850, pp. 329–347. Springer, Cham (2016). https://doi.org/10.1007/978-3-319-45348-4_19
9. Bertone, G., et al.: Accelerating the BSM interpretation of LHC data with machine learning. arXiv preprint arXiv:1611.02704 (2016)
10. Odu, G.O., Charles-Owaba, O.E.: Review of multi-criteria optimization methods - theory and applications. IOSR J. Eng. (IOSRJEN) 3, 1–14 (2013)
11. Sorokin, S.O.: Optimization modeling of the functioning of the system of homogeneous objects in a multidimensional digital environment. Model. Optim. Inf. Technol. 6(3), 153–164 (2018). (in Russian)
12. Orlova, D.E.: Stability of solutions in ensuring the functioning of organizational and technical systems. Model. Optim. Inf. Technol. 6(1), 325–336 (2018). (in Russian)
13. Neittaanmäki, P., Repin, S., Tuovinen, T. (eds.): Mathematical Modeling and Optimization of Complex Structures. CMAS, vol. 40. Springer, Cham (2016). https://doi.org/10.1007/978-3-319-23564-6
14. Rios, L.M., Sahinidis, N.V.: Derivative-free optimization: a review of algorithms and comparison of software implementations. J. Glob. Optim. 54, 1247–1293 (2013)

Modeling a Microgrid Using Fuzzy Cognitive Maps

Vassiliki Mpelogianni, George Kosmas, and Peter P. Groumpos[✉]

Electrical and Computer Engineering Department,
University of Patras, 26500 Rion, Greece
{v.mpelogianni,groumpos}@ece.upatras.gr

Abstract. The energy problem is among the most important issues in the global community over the last decades. Worldwide researchers have focused their attention and work to the increased use of renewable energy sources as a solution to the greenhouse effect. The reduction of the emitted pollutants, as well as managing, controlling and saving energy, are key research items. This paper attempts to cover part of the load of the studied microgrid, which consists of three buildings of the University of Patras using the method of Fuzzy Cognitive Maps. The goal is using renewable energy sources to cover 20% of their total load, aiming to decongest the network at peak times.

Keywords: Fuzzy cognitive maps · Decision making · Energy efficiency · Human cognition

1 Introduction

In recent years the rapid increase of low or high consumption electrical appliances in conjunction with the major production lines of factories and sensitive systems that require continuous and quality power supply have led to increased energy demand, which cannot often be met by the grid. Since energy production cannot meet the increased demand a collapse of the network causes activities that are very important for our everyday life to be paralyzed. One of the most important goals for any developed country today is to replace at a large percentage the energy produced from conventional energy sources with environmentally friendly energy produced by renewable energy sources (RES). To this end, many countries have developed appropriate legislation and financial incentives to increase the use of RES from both large, small and domestic operators.

According to a directive of the European Union, by 2020, 20% of the total energy consumed in each country should come from RES [1]. The incorporation of these sources into the existing network faces several problems both because of the nature of renewable energy sources and of its structure which is hierarchically allowing the flow of energy from the big power plants to final consumers. This is the reason why bidirectional energy flow stresses the network; it is not built under such conditions. In order to address the aforementioned issues is very important to study the different elements of nowadays power grids (RES, conventional energy sources, small and large power plants) as a whole keeping always in mind the many differences they present.

© Springer Nature Switzerland AG 2019
A. G. Kravets et al. (Eds.): CIT&DS 2019, CCIS 1083, pp. 334–343, 2019.
https://doi.org/10.1007/978-3-030-29743-5_27

A very promising method of combining the various new elements of a power grid is the development of microgrids which are very promising in becoming a vital part of the new grids. A microgrid is a localized group that consists of loads and small-scale energy sources. Most of the time it operates while being connected to the synchronous grid (macrogrid) but it can also operate disconnect as a standalone smaller grid (microgrid). The microgrid can function autonomously according to physical or economic conditions. As the need of enabling microgrids to effectively integrate various sources of distributed energy generation, especially RES as well as changing between the island and connected modes so that they can meet the needs of the consumers, emerges control and protection of the microgrid become a challenge. In such a system uncertainty is a critical factor that makes the task of controlling a microgrid very challenging. Modeling such a complex system using a classic control systems approach can be a rather demanding and time-consuming task. The formulation of a mathematical model to describe such a system is a task that demands a lot of time and resources and can sometimes prove to be next to impossible [2]. In the effort of simplifying the modeling process while maintaining high-end results, the authors of this paper propose the use of the Fuzzy Cognitive Maps (FCM) methodology.

FCM belong to the field of computational intelligence. They offer an alternative way of modeling a complex system by using the knowledge and experience of experts. FCM approach a problem and attempt to solve it in a way similar to the human mind; they can take into consideration situations and descriptions with ambiguity and fuzziness [3]. FCMs were initially proposed Kosko in 1986 as a means to describe the relationships between concepts/ideas and analyze the patterns that arise among them [4–7]. FCM were originally used to describe political decision-making processes. Since then they have been widely used to model systems that belong to a great variety of research fields such as economy, medicine, geology, engineering and environmental research, etc. [8–18]. FCMs were developed to combine the robust characteristics of two other widely known, used and respect modeling and control methods, Fuzzy Logic and Neural Networks. After creating the FCM of a system can be used to perform simulations and experiments and gain qualitative as well as quantitative results and useful insights into the operation of the modeled system.

In this paper, the authors attempt to model a microgrid using. The goal is to cover 20% of the energy needs of three buildings in the University of Patras. The outline of the paper goes as follows: In Sect. 2 the State Space FCM methodology is briefly being presented. In Sects. 3 and 4 the microgrid modeling and the results of the new method are presented. Finally, in Sect. 5 some useful conclusions are made and future research topics are proposed.

2 State FCM

As mentioned in Sect. 1 the use of FCM for modeling complex systems has proven to be very promising especially in systems involving non-linearities and/or uncertain situations [19–22]. State Fuzzy Cognitive Maps are a new approach of the classic FCM method that offered a more qualitative approach They are a newly developed approach which is thoroughly analyzed in [23, 24] is briefly presented in this section. The new systemic approach proposed by State FCM is shown in Fig. 1.

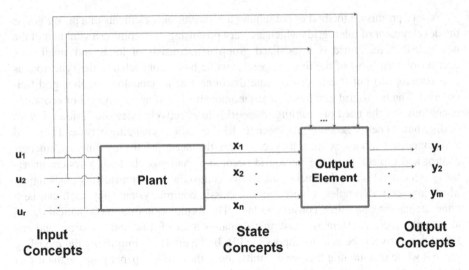

Fig. 1. Block diagram of the separated concepts

The input, state, and output concepts describe the inputs, characteristics and outputs of the system respectively.

The State FCM are described by new equations (Eqs. 1–4) which help achieve higher convergence speed and more accurate results.

$$x[k+1] = x[k] + \frac{\Delta x[k+1]}{\sum_{j=1, j \neq i}^{n} |w_{ji}|} \tag{1}$$

$$y[k+1] = y[k] + \frac{\Delta y[k+1]}{\sum_{j=1, j \neq i}^{n} |w_{ji}|} \tag{2}$$

Where

$$\Delta x[k+1] = A\Delta x[k] + B\Delta u[k] \tag{3}$$

$$\Delta y[k] = C\Delta x[k] + D\Delta u[k] \tag{4}$$

$\Delta x[k+1], \Delta x[k], \Delta y[k]$ *and* $\Delta u[k]$ are column vectors which describe the variation of input, state and output concepts.

The process of calculating the variation (Eqs. 3–4) and then the final values of the concepts (Eqs. 1–2) is terminated when the concepts meet the following conditions (Eqs. 5–6).

$$F_1 = \sqrt{\sum_{i=1}^{m} (C_i(k) - T_i)^2} \tag{5}$$

$$F_2 = \left| C_j^{n+1} - C_j^n \right| \le \varepsilon \tag{6}$$

where T_i is the optimal value and

ε is the optimal difference between the values of two concepts (C)

For the State FCM methodology to be applied the values of all the concepts, inputs and initial conditions, must belong to [0, 1], with 0 being the smallest and 1 the largest values of a concept. However, the real values of the concepts do not usually belong to the desired interval, to achieve that Eq. 7 is used. This equation offers, on the one hand, the ability to change the slope of the curve depending on the limits of each variable and once inverted (Eq. 8) allows to gain back the real value of the concept thus having accurate and interpretable results.

$$f(x) = m + \frac{M - m}{1 + e^{-r(x-t_0)}} \tag{7}$$

where $x \in R$ and $f(R) = (m, M)$

$$f^{-1}(x) = t_0 - \frac{1}{r} \ln \left(\frac{M - x}{x - m} \right) \tag{8}$$

where $x \in (m, M)$ and $f^{-1}((m, M)) = R$

In Eqs. 7–8:

- m: lowest limit of the sigmoid curve
- M: upper limit of the sigmoid curve
- r: the slope of the curve and
- t_0: the point of symmetry with the y-axis

In Sect. 3, the State FCM modeling method will be used to model a microgrid developed to help cover the energy needs of three high consumption buildings in the University of Patras.

3 Microgrid Modeling

3.1 The Model

In this section, the model used to describe the operation of a microgrid used to cover 20% of the needs of three of the biggest buildings of the engineering school of the University of Patras.

The buildings of the departments of electrical and computer, mechanical and civil engineering consume about 1103790 kWh a year. Because of the large amounts of energy consumed it is of utmost importance to introduce RES to energy production. The goal is to cover 20% of the total consumption on a monthly basis. In this paper, we model a microgrid which by using climate data calculates the energy produced by the pv array and the wind turbine as well as the part of the energy production which will be used to charge the batteries used in critical situations.

A microgrid is a system that can constitute of many smaller systems and has to combine efficiently the production and consumption of electrical energy [25, 26]. In order to efficiently model the microgrid which is presented in this paper, the authors studied previous attempt in modeling microgrids [25–34] and interviewed experts regarding the needs and potential of such a microgrid. After taking into consideration the opinions of the experts, the fuzzy cognitive maps of the microgrid was formulated. In this case study, the inputs of the system will be the shading of the pv array, the wind speed, the environmental temperature, the solar radiation and the pitch of the wind turbine.

3.2 Fuzzy Cognitive Maps Construction

System Concepts:
  INPUTS

- C1: Shading, the shading of the pv arrays
- C2: Wind Speed, the wind speed in m/s
- C3: Temperature, the temperature of the environment
- C4: Solar Radiation, used to calculate the production of the pv arrays
- C5: Pitch, the the pitch of the blade of the wind turbine

  STATES

- C6: Photovoltaic Production
- C7: Wind Turbine Production
- C8: Batteries, used for emergency situations

  OUTPUTS

- C9: Total Energy Production

Interconnections between concepts: The weights that show how one concept affects another are defined by experts (electrical, mechanical, civil engineers) who cooperate with each other and decide the optimal values. The procedure followed for exporting the numerical values is explained in [35].

The initial weight matrix of the system is shown in Table 1.

Table 1. Weight matrix

	C1	C2	C3	C4	C5	C6	C7	C8
C1	0	0	0	0	0	−0.625	0	0
C2	0	0	0	0	0	0.375	0.7916	0
C3	0	0	0	0	0	−0.375	0	0
C4	0	0	0	0	0	0.7916	0	0
C5	0	0	0	0	0	0	−0.5	0
C6	0	0	0	0	0	0	0	1
C7	0	0	0	0	0	0	0	1
C8	0	0	0	0	0	0.32	0.15	1
C9	0	0	0	0	0	0	0	0

As described in [11] when separating the concepts one has to also separate the weight matrix into the following matrices.

$$A = \begin{bmatrix} 0 & 0 & 0 \\ 0 & 0 & 0 \\ 0.32 & 0.15 & 0 \end{bmatrix}$$

$$B = \begin{bmatrix} -0.625 & 0.375 & -0.375 & 0.7916 & 0 \\ 0 & 0.7916 & 0 & 0 & -0.5 \\ 0 & 0 & -0.375 & 0 & 0 \end{bmatrix}$$

$$C = \begin{bmatrix} 1 & 1 & 1 \end{bmatrix}$$

The graphical representation of a Fuzzy Cognitive Map is presented in the following figure (Fig. 2).

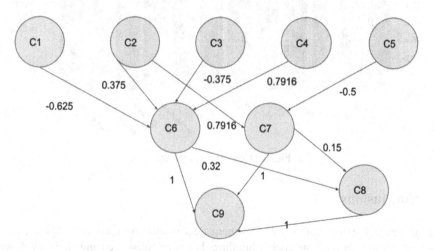

Fig. 2. System's fuzzy cognitive map

4 Results

The proposed methodology was used and a number of simulations were performed. The new Fuzzy Cognitive Maps (FCM) Construction been defined above in Sect. 3.2 clearly show the different approach been used here from the classical Fuzzy Cognitive Maps (FCMs) methodology. Here the total number of concepts are classified as state concepts, input concepts and output concepts. This classification provides us a better understanding of the behavior of the overall system.

After fitting the inputs and initial conditions of the system to the desired interval using Eq. 6 and apply the State FCM methodology we gain the results of the simulation. The final values of the concepts are calculated after following the reverse procedure, by applying Eq. 7. The following figure shows the results of the simulation (Fig. 3).

The results show the annual coverage of the energy consumed by the buildings participating in the microgrid. The power plant in most cases achieves the goal of the 20% coverage and in some months, reaches 30%. From the energy produced from the renewable energy sources, the majority of the load is covered from the wind turbine and a much smaller percentage from the photovoltaic array. Even though we achieve to reach our goal the overall consumption is still very high and it needs to be reduced.

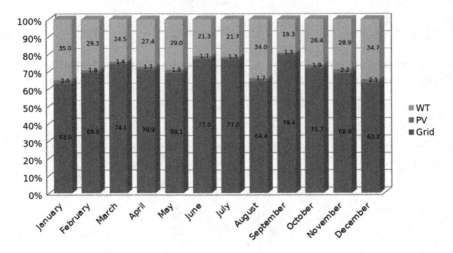

Fig. 3. Consumption coverage

5   Conclusions

In this paper the formulation of a mathematical model to describe complex energy systems, especially for large energy buildings has been considered and analyzed. It was defined, in the introduction that such a task is not only difficult but might turn to be next to impossible demanding a lot of time and resources. In the effort of simplifying the modelling process while maintaining high end results this paper propose the use of the Fuzzy Cognitive Maps (FCM) methodology. They offer an alternative way of modelling a complex system by using the knowledge and experience of experts.

FCM approach this problem and attempt to solve it in way similar to human mind; they can take into consideration situations and descriptions with ambiguity and fuzziness. The new methodology is different than the classical Fuzzy Cognitive Maps (FCMs) approach. In the beginning it seems as an utopia to use the state space approach to model complex nonlinear energy buildings.

The purpose of this paper was to propose a novel methodology of modelling microgrids, one that can use the uncertainties of such complex systems in the most effective way and produce promising results. Fuzzy Cognitive Maps is a methodology that has not been used extensively in energy systems but once used can offer flexible and dynamic system modelling. The authors of this paper do not only aim in offering alternative ways of modelling complex systems but also want to help reduce the energy consumption of buildings thus addressing the problem of high energy consumption of the building sector and the environmental disaster and greenhouse effect in general.

The model proposed in this paper includes only three buildings, but it can easily be expanded to include more energy sources and buildings. It can also be easily and effectively combined with systems that offer a better management of a buildings automation in the effort of reducing the energy consumption of each building participating in the microgrid.

The results been presented here clearly show the advantage of the state space approach been used to model microgrids. The classification of the Fuzzy Cognitive Maps concepts to state concepts, input concepts and output concepts have clearly shown the advantages of this new approach. The new novel proposed methodology can address many issues of the European Energy policy been set the so call Energy 20-20-20.

6 Future Research

The future research directions in the field of microgrids for the academic and research communities is quite open and very promising. Here are some: modify the current complex energy system in order to be able to disaggregate the loads of the buildings in order to be able to cover the most demanding of the loads and cut off excessive loads in an effort to reduce the consumption of the buildings. Investigate a techno-economic analysis to prove how the use renewable energy sources (RES) and automated control actions can help not only the environment but can also save money that can be invested in new research goals. Use the new novel methodology been proposed here to study very large and complex energy buildings. The use of the state space Fuzzy Cognitive Maps (FCM) approach can provide numerous research studies. Then new software tools based on the new novel methodology can be developed. Simulation studies should be performed for large energy buildings such as Hospitals, University and School buildings, state and government ones, large malls and energy driven manufacturing infrastructure.

References

1. Europäische Union. Directive 2009/28/EC of the European Parliament and of the Council of 23 April 2009 on the promotion of the use of energy from renewable sources and amending and subsequently repealing Directives 2001/77/EC and 2003/30/EC. Official Journal of the European Union 5 (2009)
2. Aguilar, J.: A survey about fuzzy cognitive maps papers. Int. J. Comput. Cognit. 3(2), 27–33 (2005)
3. Bourgani, E., Stylios, C.D., Manis, G., Georgopoulos, V.C.: Time dependent fuzzy cognitive maps for medical diagnosis. In: Likas, A., Blekas, K., Kalles, D. (eds.) SETN 2014. LNCS (LNAI), vol. 8445, pp. 544–554. Springer, Cham (2014). https://doi.org/10.1007/978-3-319-07064-3_47
4. Kosko, B.: Fuzzy cognitive maps. Int. J. Man-Mach. Stud. 24(1), 65–75 (1986)

5. Kosko, B.: Neural networks and fuzzy systems: a dynamical systems approach to machine intelligence. No. QA76. 76. E95 K86 (1992)
6. Kosko, B.: Fuzzy Engineering, vol. 13. Prentice Hall, Upper Saddle River (1997)
7. Kosko, B.: Global stability of generalized additive fuzzy systems. IEEE Trans. Syst. Man Cybern. Part C (Appl. Rev.) **28**(3), 441–452 (1998)
8. Ntarlas, O.D., Groumpos, P.P.: Unsupervised learning methods for foreign investment using fuzzy cognitive maps. In: 2015 6th International Conference on Information, Intelligence, Systems and Applications (IISA). IEEE (2015)
9. Anninou, A.P., Groumpos, P.P., Panagiotis, P.: Modeling health diseases using competitive fuzzy cognitive maps. In: Papadopoulos, H., Andreou, A.S., Iliadis, L., Maglogiannis, I. (eds.) AIAI 2013. IAICT, vol. 412, pp. 88–95. Springer, Heidelberg (2013). https://doi.org/10.1007/978-3-642-41142-7_10
10. Vergini, E.S., Groumpos, P.P.: A critical overview of net zero energy buildings and fuzzy cognitive maps. Int. J. Monit. Surveill. Technol. Res. (IJMSTR) **3**(3), 20–43 (2015)
11. Glykas, M. (ed.): Fuzzy Cognitive Maps: Advances in Theory, Methodologies, Tools, and Applications. STUDFUZZ, vol. 247, 1st edn. Springer, Heidelberg (2010). https://doi.org/10.1007/978-3-642-03220-2
12. Poczeta, K., Papageorgiou, E.I., Yastrebov, A.: Application of fuzzy cognitive maps to multi-step ahead prediction of electricity consumption. In: 2018 Conference on Electrotechnology: Processes, Models, Control and Computer Science (EPMCCS). IEEE (2018)
13. de Maya, B.N., Kurt, R.E.: Application of fuzzy cognitive maps to investigate the contributors of maritime grounding accidents. Human Factors. Royal Institution of Naval Architects (2018)
14. Amirkhani, A., et al.: A novel hybrid method based on fuzzy cognitive maps and fuzzy clustering algorithms for grading celiac disease. Neural Comput. Appl. **30**(5), 1573–1588 (2018)
15. Mohr, S.T.: Modelling approaches for multilayer fuzzy cognitive maps (2019)
16. Amirkhani, A., et al.: A review of fuzzy cognitive maps in medicine: Taxonomy, methods, and applications. Comput. Methods Progr. Biomed. **142**, 129–145 (2017)
17. Salmeron, J.L., Froelich, W., Papageorgiou, E.I.: Application of fuzzy cognitive maps to the forecasting of daily water demand. In: Proceedings of 2015 ITISE (2015)
18. Papageorgiou, E.I., Poczęta, K., Laspidou, C.: Application of fuzzy cognitive maps to water demand prediction. In: 2015 IEEE International Conference on Fuzzy Systems (FUZZ-IEEE). IEEE (2015)
19. Giabbanelli, P.J., Gray, S.A., Aminpour, P.: Combining fuzzy cognitive maps with agent-based modeling: frameworks and pitfalls of a powerful hybrid modeling approach to understand human-environment interactions. Environ. Model Softw. **95**, 320–325 (2017)
20. Osoba, O., Kosko, B.: Beyond DAGs: modeling causal feedback with fuzzy cognitive maps. arXiv preprint arXiv:1906.11247 (2019)
21. Demertzis, K., Anezakis, V.-D., Iliadis, L., Spartalis, S.: Temporal modeling of invasive species' migration in greece from neighboring countries using fuzzy cognitive maps. In: Iliadis, L., Maglogiannis, I., Plagianakos, V. (eds.) AIAI 2018. IAICT, vol. 519, pp. 592–605. Springer, Cham (2018). https://doi.org/10.1007/978-3-319-92007-8_50
22. Mpelogianni, V., Groumpos, P.P.: A comparison study of fuzzy control versus fuzzy cognitive maps for energy efficiency of buildings
23. Mpelogianni, V., Groumpos, P.P.: Re-approaching fuzzy cognitive maps to increase the knowledge of a system. AI & Soc. **33**(2), 175–188 (2018)
24. Vassiliki, M., Peter, G.P.: Increasing the energy efficiency of buildings using human cognition; via fuzzy cognitive maps. IFAC-PapersOnLine **51**(30), 727–732 (2018)

25. Pogaku, N., Prodanovic, M., Green, T.C.: Modeling, analysis and testing of autonomous operation of an inverter-based microgrid. IEEE Trans. Power Electron. **22**(2), 613–625 (2007)
26. Ahamed, M.H.F., et al.: Modelling and simulation of a solar PV and battery based DC microgrid system. In: 2016 International Conference on Electrical, Electronics, and Optimization Techniques (ICEEOT). IEEE (2016)
27. Kitson, J., et al.: Modelling of an expandable, reconfigurable, renewable DC microgrid for off-grid communities. Energy **160**, 142–153 (2018)
28. Fathima, A.H., Palanisamy, K.: Optimization in microgrids with hybrid energy systems–a review. Renew. Sustain. Energy Rev. **45**, 431–446 (2015)
29. Kyriakarakos, G., et al.: Design of a fuzzy cognitive maps variable-load energy management system for autonomous PV-reverse osmosis desalination systems: a simulation survey. Appl. Energy **187**, 575–584 (2017)
30. Kottas, T., et al.: New operation scheme and control of smart grids using fuzzy cognitive networks. In: 2015 IEEE Eindhoven PowerTech. IEEE (2015)
31. Hawkes, A.D., Leach, M.A.: Modelling high level system design and unit commitment for a microgrid. Appl. Energy **86**(7-8), 1253–1265 (2009)
32. Abu-Sharkh, S., et al.: Can microgrids make a major contribution to UK energy supply? Renew. Sustain. Energy Rev. **10**(2), 78–127 (2006)
33. Li, Z., Yan, X.: Optimal coordinated energy dispatch of a multi-energy microgrid in grid-connected and islanded modes. Appl. Energy **210**, 974–986 (2018)
34. Ferreira, R.A.F., et al.: Analysis of voltage droop control method for DC microgrids with Simulink: modelling and simulation. In: 2012 10th IEEE/IAS International Conference on Industry Applications. IEEE (2012)
35. Groumpos, P.P.: Fuzzy cognitive maps: basic theories and their application to complex systems. In: Glykas, M. (ed.) Fuzzy Cognitive Maps. STUDFUZZ, vol. 247, pp. 1–22. Springer, Heidelberg (2010). https://doi.org/10.1007/978-3-642-03220-2_1

Data-Driven Framework for Predictive Maintenance in Industry 4.0 Concept

Van Cuong Sai[(✉)], Maxim V. Shcherbakov, and Van Phu Tran

Volgograd State Technical University, Lenin Avenue 28, 400005 Volgograd, Russia
svcuonghvktqs@gmail.com
http://www.vstu.ru

Abstract. Supporting the operation of the equipment at the operational stage with minimal costs is an urgent task for various industries. In the modern manufacturing industry machines and systems become more advanced and complicated, traditional approaches (corrective and preventive maintenance) to maintenance of complex systems lose their effectiveness. The latest trends of maintenance lean towards condition-based maintenance (CBM) techniques. This paper describes the framework to build predictive maintenance models for proactive decision support based on machine learning and deep learning techniques. The proposed framework implemented as a package for R, and it provides several features that allow to create and evaluate predictive maintenance models. All features of the framework can be attributed to one of the following groups: data validation and preparation, data exploration and visualization, feature engineering, data preprocessing, model creating and evaluation. The use case provided in the paper highlights the benefits of the framework toward proactive decision support for the estimation of the turbofan engine remaining useful life (RUL).

Keywords: Condition-based maintenance (CBM) ·
Predictive maintenance (PdM) · Industry 4.0 ·
Internet of Things (IoT) · Remaining useful life (RUL) ·
Data-driven method · Machine learning · Deep learning

1 Introduction

In the current manufacturing world, systems are becoming more and more complex, especially for the machine system. This complexity is a source of various incidents and faults that cause considerable damage to items, the environment, and people. Failure of some parts of the system could affect all of the operations. The classical maintenance approaches (corrective and preventive maintenance) under such conditions largely lose their effectiveness.

In corrective maintenance, the interventions are performed only when the critical component is fully worn out and failure. It minimizes the number of unnecessary part replacements or repairs since maintenance is only carried out as needed. However, this approach can also lead to unexpected and lengthy

The reported study was supported by RFBR research projects 19-47-340010 r_a.

losses of production, safety risks as a system nears failure, or expensive repairs and replacements.

In preventive maintenance (time-based maintenance or planned maintenance), the interventions are placed according to periodic intervals regardless of the assets' health condition and thus the service life of the critical components are not fully utilized [11].

Therefore, in order to prevent risks, another efficient strategy for preventive maintenance needs to be carried out system. One effective strategy to enhance the reliability of the system is to develop and utilize intelligent systems that perform the functions of predictive analytics and predictive maintenance. This strategy allows for the transition from time-based preventive maintenance to condition-based maintenance (CBM). Condition-based maintenance, known as Predictive Maintenance (PdM), is a maintenance strategy that provides an assessment of the system's condition, based on data collected from the system by continuous monitoring to optimize the availability of process machinery and greatly reduce the cost of maintenance.

The key to implementing predictive maintenance is the ability to assess equipment health and discover detail information about current or future faults through collected data. Nowadays, with the trend of smart manufacturing and the rapid development of information and communication technologies (ICT), companies are increasingly applying types of sensors and information technologies to capture data at all stages of production. It allows for collecting large amounts of data about the health condition of the equipment. Simultaneously, technologies such as Internet of Things (IoT), Internet of Services (IoS), Artificial intelligence (AI), and data mining (DM), which are all inherent in Industry 4.0, are being leveraged with "Big Data" to facilitate a more adaptable and smart maintenance policy.

Remaining useful life (RUL) prediction of the equipment is the key technology for realizing condition-based maintenance (CBM). Accurate prediction of RUL plays an important increasingly crucial role in the intelligent health management system for the optimization of maintenance decisions. Thus, RUL prediction of equipment has important significance for guaranteeing production efficiency, reducing maintenance cost, and improving plant safety [9,10].

At present, the main methods used for RUL estimation is physics-based failure models (model-based methods) and data-driven methods. Model-based methods attempt to set up mathematical or physical models to describe degradation processes of machinery, and update model parameters using measured data [3,4]. The commonly used models include the Markov process model [2], the Wiener process model [12], etc. Hence, the model-based method is difficult to be put into use for complex systems as damage propagation processes and equipment dynamic response are complex. To address this issue, data-driven prognostic methods represent the system degradation process using machine learning algorithms. These methods rely on the assumption that the statistical characteristics of data are relatively consistent unless a fault occurs. Literally hundreds of papers propose new machine learning algorithms, suggesting methodological advances and accuracy improvements for RUL prediction. Methods such as the autoregressive model (AR) [8], deep neural network [7,17], and support vector machine [5,15] are used. Yet their conclusions are based only on a certain situation and on specific data.

In machine learning, there's something called the "No Free Lunch" theorem which basically states that no one-size-fits-all machine learning algorithm is best for all problems and every dataset. It is difficult to determine which or what type of learning algorithm should be selected among many competing learning algorithms. Moreover, accurate model today could become inaccurate tomorrow and the model's predictive accuracy depends on the relevance, sufficiency, and quality of the training and test data. Therefore, proper preprocessing strategies and model selection are the foundation of the construction of a robust accurate model.

This paper presents a developed framework (a package in R) for predictive maintenance in Industry 4.0 concept (PdM framework). The PdM framework helps engineers and domain experts to easily analyze and utilize multiple multivariate time series sensor data to develop and test predictive maintenance models based on RUL estimation using machine learning algorithms and deep learning algorithms in a rapid for decision support proactive systems for optimizing the maintenance and service of the machine.

R is a free software environment for statistical computing and graphics supported by the R Foundation for Statistical Computing [13]. R is one of the most powerful machine learning platforms and is used by the top data scientists in the world. There are so many algorithms and so much power sits there ready to use. It has a large number of packages that expand the functionality for processing and predictive modeling. One of them is caret [6], which implements the functions to streamline the model training process for complex regression and classification problems.

2 Proposed Framework

2.1 Task Statement and Methodology

We assume to have sensor readings over the total operational life of similar equipment (run-time to failure data). We denote the set of instances by ID. For an instance $i \in ID$, we consider multi-sensor times series $X^{(i)} = \{X_1^{(i)}, X_2^{(i)}, ..., X_{T^{(i)}}^{(i)}\}$, where $T^{(i)}$ is length of time series that corresponds to the total operational life (from start to end of life), $X_t^i \in \mathbb{R}^{(n+k)}$ is an $(n+k)$-dimensional vector corresponding to the n sensors related to the equipment state and k sensors related to operational conditions at time t: $X^{(i)} = \{s_1^{(i)}, s_2^{(i)}, ..., s_n^{(i)}, c_1^{(i)}, c_2^{(i)}, ..., c_k^{(i)}\}$.

In Table 1 we presents the data table schema for storing such data allowing the implementation of the proposed framework. Figure 1 shows the architecture of the proposed framework.

Table 1. The data Table schema for predictive maintenance framework.

Column	Description
id	Unit identifier - a unique number that identifies an instance
timestamp	A timestamp (days, cycles, ..) when data was obtained
$s_1, s_2, ..., s_n$	The n sensor columns related to the equipment state at each time step
$c_1, c_2, ..., c_k$	The k sensor columns related to the operating conditions

Here is how data can look like in this format:

id	timestamp	c1	c2	c3	s1	s2	s3	s4	s5	s6	s7	s8
1	1	-0.0007	-4e-04	100	518.67	641.82	1589.70	1400.60	14.62	21.61	554.36	2388.06
1	2	0.0019	-3e-04	100	518.67	642.15	1591.82	1403.14	14.62	21.61	553.75	2388.04
1	3	-0.0043	3e-04	100	518.67	642.35	1587.99	1404.20	14.62	21.61	554.26	2388.08
1	4	0.0007	0e+00	100	518.67	642.35	1582.79	1401.87	14.62	21.61	554.45	2388.11
1	5	-0.0019	-2e-04	100	518.67	642.37	1582.85	1406.22	14.62	21.61	554.00	2388.06
1	6	-0.0043	-1e-04	100	518.67	642.10	1584.47	1398.37	14.62	21.61	554.67	2388.02

Because we know when each instance in ID will fail, for a instance i, we can compute a RUL at each time step t, defined as an instance's elapsed life at that time minus its total lifetime: $RUL_t^{(i)} = T^{(i)} - t^{(i)}$.

In order to produce RUL estimates, we must still determine the models $f(.)$ of the form described below that captures a functional relationship between the sensor values and RUL at time t for a instance i:

$$RUL_i(t) = f\big(s_{i,1}(t), s_{i,2}(t), ..., s_{i,n}(t), c_{i,1}(t), c_{i,2}(t), ..., c_{i,k}(t)\big)$$

Once we have the historical run-to-failure data with RUL labels at each time step, we can build and train models using machine learning and deep learning technologies. The next step is to find a predictive model that can accurately predict the RUL from new sensor data coming in from the currently monitored operating instances similar to the historical monitored instances in ID.

For the currently monitored operating instance similar to the historical monitored instances in ID, the length $T^{(i)}$ corresponds to the elapsed operational life till the latest available sensor reading (measurements are truncated some (unknown) amount of time before it fails.).

2.2 Predictive Maintenance Framework (PdM)

The proposed framework (PdM) for predictive maintenance in the concept of Industry 4.0 implements some tools shown on Fig. 1. The PdM framework helps engineers and domain experts to easily analyze and utilize multiple multivariate time series sensor data to develop and test predictive maintenance models that to estimate remaining useful life (RUL) to prevent equipment failures. These models are developed by accessing historical failure data that is stored in local files, in SQL database, on cloud storage systems such as Amazon S3, or on a Hadoop Distributed File System, etc in the format presented in Table 1. The following assumptions are required to create accurate predictive maintenance models: (1) historical data should contain degradation evolution of the critical component over time, (2) historical data should contain sufficient number of training instances to build representative models of the desired critical component's behavior.

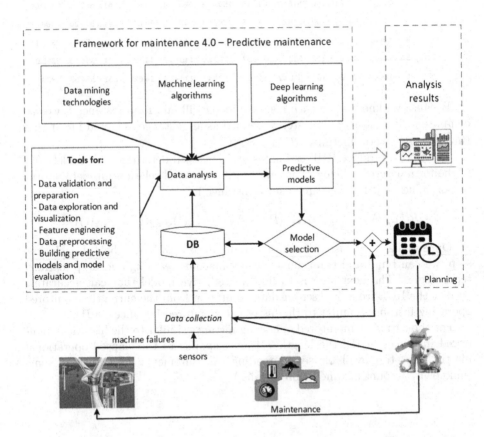

Fig. 1. System architecture for predictive maintenance in concept of Industry 4.0.

This framework is developed to solve following tasks for predictive maintenance:

1. Analyze data: to load, summarize and visualize multiple multivariate time series data,
2. Prepare data: for data preparation including data cleaning, feature engineering and data transforms,
3. Build and evaluate predictive maintenance models: for using a large number of machine learning algorithms which are available in R, including linear, non-linear, trees, ensembles for regression; for re-sampling methods, algorithm evaluation metrics and model selection, for algorithm tuning and ensemble methods.

The advantage of all functions implemented in the PdM framework is using a universal interface for different tasks. The proposed framework can be used for any multiple-component system.

The schematic diagram implementing this framework is shown in Fig. 2. The predictive maintenance routine starts with data acquisition using sensors and data acquisition boards. Appropriate signal processing techniques will then be applied to extract representative features and/or system model parameters from the collected data. These features will be used to create accurate predictive maintenance models. These obtained models utilize the current health status of a given critical component to predict its future condition and plan maintenance actions before breakdown for the optimal use of the equipment in real time.

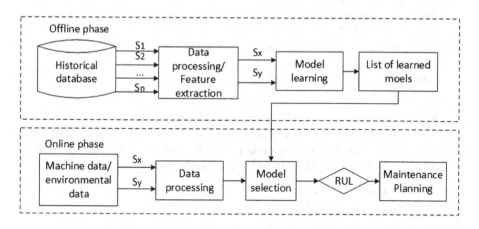

Fig. 2. The schematic diagram of the predictive maintenance system.

Downloading and Installation. To install and use the PdM framework, run this code:

```
> install.package(devtools)
> devtools::install_github("forvis/PdM")
> library(PdM)
```

3   Use Case Example

In this section we present end-to-end use case applying some key features of the PdM framework to analyze multiple multivariate time series sensor data, to build and evaluate predictive maintenance models for remaining useful life (RUL) estimation of a turbofan engine.

The framework has several built-in datasets available as data frames. For illustrations, we will use the *Turbofan Engine Degradation Simulation data set FD001* that was released by the Prognostics Center of Excellence at NASA's Ames research center [14]. It contains simulated sensor data for different turbofan engines generated over time. It consists the training dataset (train_data1), testing dataset (test_data1), and ground truth data (truth_data1). The training dataset includes the run-to-failure sensor measurements from degrading turbofan engines of the same type, recorded as multiple multivariate time series. However, the testing data only have aircraft engine's operating data without failure events recorded. Both the training set and the test are stored using data table schema presented in Table 1. The ground truth data is a vector containing the information of true remaining useful life for each engine in the testing data. Both training set and testing set data have 100 turbofan engines.

The first step is to load and check if the input datasets are correctly formatted in accordance with the data table schema presented in Table 1:

```
> library (PdM)
> data ( train_data1 )
> data ( test_data1 )
> data (( truth_data1 )
> validate_data ( train_data1 )
[1]  TRUE
> validate_data ( test_data1 )
[1]  TRUE
```

The function validate_data() checks that the input data necessary column and the composite primary key values are not duplicated. When input data is loaded successfully and corresponds to the format required, we can look at descriptive statistics using the function summarize_data():

```
> summary_data ( train_data1 )
 ++++ Summary  statistics  ++++
════════════════════════════════════════
− Number  of  observations :  20631
− Number  of  variables :  26
════════════════════════════════════════
```

variable	type	complete	missing	min	quartile_25	mean	median	quartile_75	max	skew
id	numeric	20631	0	1.000	26.000	51.507	52.000	77.000	100.000	-0.068
timestamp	numeric	20631	0	1.000	52.000	108.808	104.000	156.000	362.000	0.500
c1	numeric	20631	0	-0.009	-0.002	0.000	0.000	0.002	0.009	-0.025
c2	numeric	20631	0	-0.001	0.000	0.000	0.000	0.000	0.001	0.009
c3	numeric	20631	0	100.000	100.000	100.000	100.000	100.000	100.000	NaN
s1	numeric	20631	0	518.670	518.670	518.670	518.670	518.670	518.670	NaN
s2	numeric	20631	0	641.210	642.325	642.681	642.640	643.000	644.530	0.316
s3	numeric	20631	0	1571.040	1586.260	1590.523	1590.100	1594.380	1616.910	0.309
s4	numeric	20631	0	1382.250	1402.360	1408.934	1408.040	1414.555	1441.490	0.443
s5	numeric	20631	0	14.620	14.620	14.620	14.620	14.620	14.620	NaN
s6	numeric	20631	0	21.600	21.610	21.610	21.610	21.610	21.610	-6.916
s7	numeric	20631	0	549.850	552.810	553.368	553.440	554.010	556.060	-0.394
s8	numeric	20631	0	2387.900	2388.050	2388.097	2388.090	2388.140	2388.560	0.479
s9	numeric	20631	0	9021.730	9053.100	9065.243	9060.660	9069.420	9244.590	2.555
s10	numeric	20631	0	1.300	1.300	1.300	1.300	1.300	1.300	NaN
s11	numeric	20631	0	46.850	47.350	47.541	47.510	47.700	48.530	0.469
s12	numeric	20631	0	518.690	520.960	521.413	521.480	521.950	523.380	-0.442
s13	numeric	20631	0	2387.880	2388.040	2388.096	2388.090	2388.140	2388.560	0.470
s14	numeric	20631	0	8099.940	8133.245	8143.753	8140.540	8148.310	8293.720	2.372
s15	numeric	20631	0	8.325	8.415	8.442	8.439	8.466	8.585	0.388
s16	numeric	20631	0	0.030	0.030	0.030	0.030	0.030	0.030	NaN
s17	numeric	20631	0	388.000	392.000	393.211	393.000	394.000	400.000	0.353
s18	numeric	20631	0	2388.000	2388.000	2388.000	2388.000	2388.000	2388.000	NaN
s19	numeric	20631	0	100.000	100.000	100.000	100.000	100.000	100.000	NaN
s20	numeric	20631	0	38.140	38.700	38.816	38.830	38.950	39.430	-0.358
s21	numeric	20631	0	22.894	23.222	23.290	23.298	23.367	23.618	-0.350

The function summarize_data() provides a solution to show key descriptive stats for each column, e.g. the number of observations and variables, a data frame containing the descriptive stats of each of the columns: data types, number of missing values, min, max, mean, median, percentiles, and skewness.

After using summarize_data() function if we've seen that the dataset has few missing values across all columns, we may to do well to impute it using handle_misv() function. This function provides different imputation algorithms: remove rows with missing values, replace the missing values with the mean, median, mode of the column, k-Nearest Neighbors (knn), bagging of regression, etc.

Here is an example of using knn algorithm to impute missing data in training dataset:

```
> train_data1 <- handle_misv(train_data1, method = 'knn')
```

Now that the missing values are handled, our dataset is now ready to visualize by using the universal function visualize_data(). This function allows us to plot different types of charts, e.g. scatter plots, line graphs, both line and point graphs, boxplot, histogram, etc for the multiple multivariate time series sensor data with the results appearing as panels in a larger figure. Each panel plot corresponds to a set value of the variable (sensor channel).

Here is an example of using the function visualize_data() to plot the line graphs for training dataset:

```
> visualize_data(train_data1, id = 1:10, type = 'l')
```

The Fig. 3 shows all 24 sensor channels (21 sensors – about the health condition of the engines and 3 sensors – about the conditions in which engines are

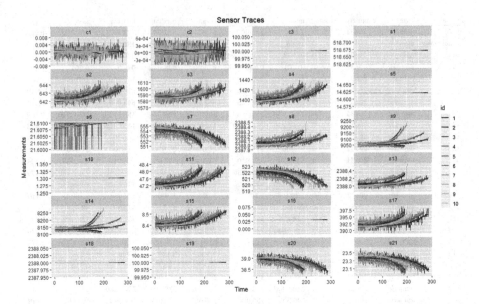

Fig. 3. Sensor readings over time for the first 10 engines in the training set

operating) for the first 10 engines (10 lines in each subplot-one for each engine) from the training set, plotted against time.

From the results of the data summary and visualization we can draw the following conclusions:

- The variables have not the same scale and sensor readings have noise. It means that we should transform this data in order to best expose its structure to machine learning algorithms.
- The following variables are constant in the training set, meaning that the operating condition was fixed and/or the sensor was broken/inactive: c3, s1, s5, s10, s16, s18, s19.
- The sensor s6 is practically constant.

We can check and discard these variables from the analysis for both training and testing datasets by using the function process_data():

```
# Check and remove variables with a zero variance
> c(train_data1,test_data1) %<-% process_data(train_data1,
                          test_data1, method='zv')
## The following variables with a zero variance are
## removed: c3, s1, s5, s10, s16, s18, s19

# Check and remove variables with a near zero variance
> c(train_data1,test_data1) %<-% process_data(train_data1,
                          test_data1, method='nzv')
## The following variables with a near zero variance are
## removed: s6
```

The function process_data() also provides a number of useful data transform methods supported in the argument to the process_data() function in PdM framework, e.g. Box-Cox transform, Yeo-Johnson transforms, MinMax normalization, divide values by standard deviation, subtract mean from values, transform data to the principal components, etc.

Before building any predictive maintenance model for predicting RUL, we should check that our data should contain enough useful information to allow us to distinguish between healthy and failing states of the engines. If they don't, it's unlikely that any model built with sensor data will be useful for our purposes. The function visualize_data() also allows us to compare the distribution of sensor values in "healthy" engines to a similar set of measurements when the engines are close to failure:

```
> visualize_data(train_data1, id = 1:100, type = "hf",
                  n_step = 20)
```

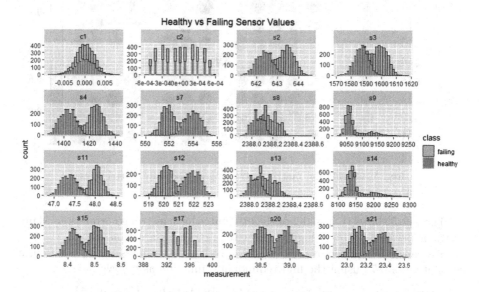

Fig. 4. Distribution of the healthy vs failing sensor values.

The Fig. 4 shows the distribution of the values of all sensor channels for each engine in the training set, where healthy values (in green) are those taken from the first 20 time steps of the engine's lifetime and failing values are from the last 20 time steps (n_step = 20). It's apparent that these two distributions are quite different for some sensor channels.

Also, the correlation between attributes can be calculated using the visualize_correlation() function.

```
> visualize_correlation(train_data1, method='circle')
```

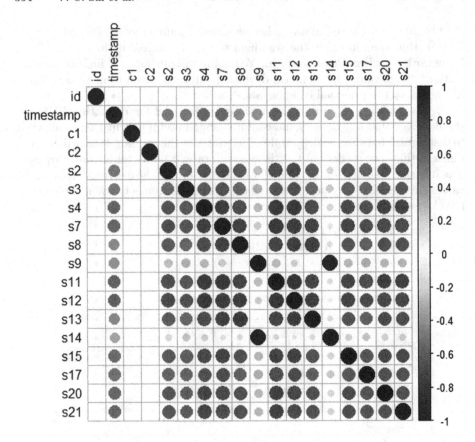

Fig. 5. Correlation matrix of training dataset input attributes

The Fig. 5 shows that many of the attributes have a strong correlation. Many methods perform better if highly correlated attributes are removed.

We can find and remove the highly correlated attributes with an absolute correlation of 0.75 using the find_redundant() function as follows:

```
> train_data1 <- find_redundant(train_data1, cf = 0.75)
## The following highly corrected features are removed: s4,
## s7, s11, s12, s13, s14
```

With the missing values handled and redundant features removed, our datasets is now ready to undergo variable transformations if required. Here is an example of using the process_data() function to transform the training and testing datasets (MinMax normalization):

```
# MinMax normalization
> c(train_data1, test_data1) %<-% process_data(train_data1,
                             test_data1, method='range')
```

Before building predictive maintenance models we should generate labels for the training data which are remaining useful life (RUL) by using the calculate_rul() function:

```
> train_data1 <- calculate_rul(train_data1)
```

After this step, the dataset is ready to build any predictive maintenance model, but we have no idea what algorithms will do well on this task. Let's check several different algorithms, e.g. linear regression (lm), regression trees (rpart), support vector machines (svm), random forest (rf)) using a unified function train_model():

```
> models <- train_model(RUL~, train_data1, method = c('lm',
                        'rpart', 'svmRadial', 'rf'))
```

The train_model() function is based on train() function from the caret package [6]. It means that the train_model() function allows using any available in R algorithm and can be used to: evaluate, using re-sampling, the effect of model tuning parameters on performance; choose the "optimal" model across these parameters; estimate model performance from a training set. To know that models train_model() supports, run the following:

```
# Looking for available algorithms in caret
> models <- paste(names(getModelInfo()), collapse = ', ')
> models
```

To make a prediction based on data omitted in training data set, we use the following sentence:

```
> predictions <- create_predciction(models,
                        new_data = test_data1)
> evaluation <- evaluate_model(truth_data1, predictions)
```

The evaluate_model() function returns a list with the following variables: accuracy – data frame with accuracy table, plot – visualization of predicted and actual values, prd – a prediction-realization diagram showing a scatterplot with forecast vs actual values (Figs. 6 and 7).

```
> evaluation$accuracy
```

## Model	MAE	MdAE	RMSE	sMAPE
## lm	25.97517	31.25047	31.25047	19.54203
## rpart	21.69112	18.12015	28.31998	34.15792
## svm	17.52203	14.60832	23.60905	24.27818
## rf	19.47539	13.66242	26.49968	25.18338

```
> evaluation$plot
```

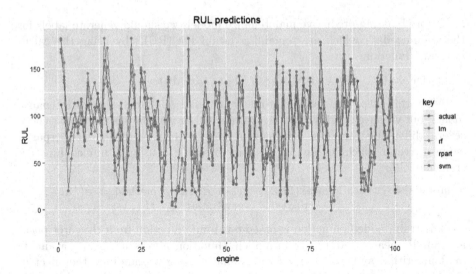

Fig. 6. Visualisation of machine id vs. RUL covering both predicted and actual values of dataset.

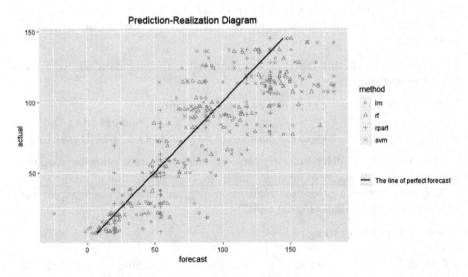

Fig. 7. Prediction-realization diagram for FD001 data. Different colors and marks to show forecasts relating to different forecasting methods.

> evaluation$prd

The result shows that SVM has the lowest errors (MAE, MdAPE, RMSE, sMAPE). We can look at the default parameters of this algorithm:

> print(models$svm)

We can improve the accuracy of this best algorithm (svm in this case) by tuning their parameters using grid search:

```
# Tune SVM sigma and C parametres
# Use the expand.grid to specify the search space
> grid <- expand.grid(sigma=c(.01, .015, 0.2),
                       C=seq(1, 10, by=1))
# Train the svm
> svm_grid <- train_model(RUL, train_data1,
                          method="svm",
                          tuneGrid=grid)
```

Using print(svm_grid) we can see the optimal model with final values of parameters selected for this model (sigma and C in this case). Once we have an accurate model on our test harness we can save it to a file so that we can load it up later and make predictions by using the saveRDS() and readRDS() function:

```
# save the model to disk
> saveRDS(svm_grid, "./final_model.rds")
# Load the model
> model <- readRDS("./final_model.rds")
```

In addition to machine learning algorithms, the PdM framework also provides some tools for building deep learning predictive maintenance models based deep learning algorithms, e.g. create_tensor(), train_lstm(), train_cnn(), etc. More details about all functions of the PdM framework use following code to access to the documentation pages:

```
> help(package = "PdM")
```

4   Conclusion

We conclude, that the proposed framework PdM in this study can be applied for proactive decision support. The proposed method was applied to predict the remaining useful life of the equipment in the concept of industrial predictive maintenance.

In future work, we wrap the functionalities of the proposed predictive maintenance framework PdM into a graphical user interface. This enables the user to conduct all steps of the predictive maintenance building workflows from his browser without using codes.

References

1. Allaire, J., Chollet, F.: R Interface to 'Keras'. R package version 2.2.4 (2018). https://CRAN.R-project.org/package=keras
2. Dui, H., Si, S., Zuo, M., Sun, S.: Semi-Markov process-based integrated importance measure for multi-state systems. IEEE Trans. Reliab. **64**(2), 754–765 (2015)

3. Hanachi, H., Liu, J., Banerjee, A., Chen, Y., Koul, A.: A physics-based modeling approach for performance monitoring in gas turbine engines. IEEE Trans. Reliab. **64**(1), 197–205 (2015)

4. Huang, Z., Xu, Z., Wang, W., Sun, Y.: Remaining useful life prediction for a nonlinear heterogeneous Wiener process model with an adaptive drift. IEEE Trans. Reliab. **64**(2), 687–700 (2015)

5. Khelif, R., Chebel-Morello, B., Malinowski, S., Laajili, E., Fnaiech, F., Zerhouni, N.: Direct remaining useful life estimation based on support vector regression. IEEE Trans. Industr. Electron. **64**(3), 2276–2285 (2017)

6. Kuhn, M.: caret: Classification and Regression Training. R package version 6.0-82 (2019). https://CRAN.R-project.org/package=caret

7. Li, X., Ding, Q., Sun, J.: Remaining useful life estimation in prognostics using deep convolution neural networks. Reliab. Eng. Syst. Saf. **172**, 1–11 (2018)

8. Long, B., Xian, W., Jiang, L., Liu, Z.: An improved autoregressive model by particle swarm optimization for prognostics of Lithium-Ion batteries. Microelectron. Reliab. **53**(6), 821–831 (2013)

9. Malhi, A., Yan, R., Gao, R.: Prognosis of defect propagation based on recurrent neural networks. IEEE Trans. Instrum. Meas. **60**(3), 703–711 (2011)

10. Qian, Y., Yan, R., Hu, S.: Bearing degradation evaluation using recurrence quantification analysis and Kalman filter. IEEE Trans. Instrum. Meas. **63**(11), 2599–2610 (2014)

11. Soh, S., Radzi, N., Haron, H.: Review on scheduling techniques of preventive maintenance activities of railway. In: Fourth International Conference on Computational Intelligence, Modelling and Simulation. IEEE, pp. 310–315, Kuantan, Malaysia, September 2012. https://doi.org/10.1109/CIMSim.2012.56

12. Si, X., Wang, W., Chen, M., Hu, C., Zhou, D.: A degradation path-dependent approach for remaining useful life estimation with an exact and closed-form solution. Eur. J. Oper. Res. **226**(1), 53–66 (2013)

13. The Comprehensive R Archive Network. https://cran.r-project.org/. Accessed 20 Jan 2019

14. Turbofan engine degradation simulation data set. https://c3.nasa.gov/dashlink/resources/139/. Accessed 18 Jan 2019

15. Wang, S., Zhao, L., Su, X., Ma, P.: Prognostics of Lithium-Ion batteries based on battery performance analysis and flexible support vector regression. Energies **7**(10), 6492–6508 (2014)

16. Wickham, H.: ggplot2: Elegant Graphics for Data Analysis. Springer, New York (2016). https://doi.org/10.1007/978-0-387-98141-3

17. Yu, J., Mo, B., Tang, D., Liu, H., Wan, J.: Remaining useful life prediction for Lithium-Ion batteries using a quantum particle swarm optimization-based particle filter. Qual. Eng. **29**(3), 536–546 (2017)

Method of Acquiring the Video Conference Using the Skill in Investigative Actions

Evgeny Kravets[1]($\boxtimes$), Svetlana Gladkova[2,4], Vladimir Shinkaruk[3] ⓘ,
Vladimir Ovchinnikov[1], and Nikolai Bukharov[4]

[1] Volgograd Academy of the Russian Ministry of Internal Affairs, Volgograd,
130 Istoricheskaya Street, Volgograd 400089, Russia
80kravez@gmail.com, gimnast-69@yandex.ru
[2] State Institute of Economics, Finance, Law and Technologies,
5 Roschinskaya Street, Gatchina, Leningrad reg. 188350, Russia
gladkovas@rambler.ru
[3] Volgograd State University, 100 Universitetskiy Avenue,
Volgograd 400062, Russia
shinkarukvm@gmail.com
[4] Saint-Petersburg University of the Ministry
of the Interior of the Russian Federation, 1 Letchika Pilyutova Street,
Saint-Petersburg 198206, Russia
russkif@mail.ru

Abstract. The current law does not directly establish the possibility of remote investigative actions. However, it does not contain direct bans on the introduction of this progressive procedural form. Nevertheless, the practice of using information and communication technologies by an investigator in his work will inevitably lead to the need for detailed regulation of such improvements. The decision of the legislature on the full legal regulation of this problem is brewing. It is necessary to supplement the content of the training of the official's persons, who will be in charge of criminal cases, at the expense of developing the skill to use the video conference system as needed during a number of investigative actions.

Keywords: The video conference system · Crime investigation ·
Professional training of investigators ·
Information and communication technologies · Business game

1 The Informational Origin of Evidence as a Prerequisite to the Use of the Video Conferencing in the Production of Investigative Actions

The use of scientific and technical means for fixing and getting information plays the most important in the process of collecting evidence [1]. The capture (mention, fixing) of evidence strictly immanent to the legal proceedings, is a mandatory attribute. Any participant of the investigative action may have the initiative to use scientific and technical means. This is a fundamental competence and only guided by the

© Springer Nature Switzerland AG 2019
A. G. Kravets et al. (Eds.): CIT&DS 2019, CCIS 1083, pp. 359–368, 2019.
https://doi.org/10.1007/978-3-030-29743-5_29

informational approach we can truly appreciate it. The search character of each investigative action prompts the investigator not to include in the protocol the information that is irrelevant, as well as repetitions, minor details, vague and incomprehensible expressions; the information that is not expressed in the word directly, but enclosed in the context of oral message, may be included in the text of the protocol [2].

Strengthening the idea, we note that the video allows you to objectively capture everything that is in the camera lens, and the protocol of the investigative action does not always reflect the completeness of the picture, much at the time of its compilation may not yet be clarified by the investigator [3]. Provided that a protocol is drawn up perfectly, reflecting the entire required aggregate of the data it contains, possessing such an application as video recording (made with varying degrees of reduction during shooting and from different angles) contributes to a more correct assessment of the information collected, accurate perception of the event under study.

Factors in the development of technical and forensic support for the investigation of crimes at the present stage predetermined the possibility of conducting separate investigative actions remotely. Video conferencing (hereinafter referred to as VC) is a preferred way of communication especially applicable for, primarily, to such investigative actions as interrogation, confrontation, presentation for identification and examination.

Let's make a reservation that we offer to confine ourselves to four investigative actions precisely at the present stage, starting from the ideas about the realism of scientific forecasting and the formulation of production problems. The listed investigative actions have a high coefficient of repeatability in law enforcement practice. For interrogation, confrontation, presentation for identification and certification, there are enough stationary premises for VC with standard technical settings and communication requirements. Further expansion of the list of investigative actions that are possible with the use of information and communication technologies (hereinafter - ICT), by including a dredging, investigative experiment, checking evidence on the spot, as some researchers suggest, is irrelevant today due to the lack of economic and legal prerequisites such a step, since it involves the use of mobile installations of VC and expensive high-speed communication settings [4].

2 Remote Investigative Actions in European and Russian Crime Investigation Practice

The practice of remote investigative actions has become every day for law enforcers in many countries. And if in most of them (Germany, Switzerland, Belgium, and others) innovative technologies are applying in court, our closest geographical and mental neighbor, Ukraine, has advanced further than others in this matter: art. 232 of the Criminal Procedure Code of Ukraine, adopted in 2012, allows remote interrogation and person presentation for identification. Despite the fact that only on the basis of the ratio of geopolitical indicators (size of the territory, population density), Russia's need for this technology is much higher. A similar opportunity is provided for in the CPC of Kazakhstan, which has been in force since 2015.

It should be noted that even in the absence of a sufficient regulatory framework, Russian law enforcers have already used VC systems in investigative actions. Guided by the provisions of the European Convention on Mutual Legal Assistance in Criminal Matters, General Prosecutor's Office of the Russian Federation for the first time in 2006 executed a request for legal assistance in a criminal case via video conferencing, which resulted in the creation of a precedent for this type of legal assistance. In 2006, the Prosecutor General's Office of the Russian Federation executed a petition from the Court of Hamburg (Germany), Klaus Wille, to provide legal assistance in the criminal case on charges of a number of persons as part of a transnational organized criminal group in illegal drug traffic. The initiator petitioned for the witnesses interrogation who was serving a sentence of imprisonment in the Republic of Mordovia, via videoconference with the court. Witness interrogations were in the communication center in the Yavas village in the Zubovo-Polyansky District of the Republic of Mordovia during three video conferencing sessions with the Hamburg State Court and the investigator of the Prosecutor's Office of the Republic of Mordovia on the basis of the laws of both states on judicial proceedings in Germany and preliminary investigation in Russia. Video conferencing was provided by VolgaTelecom at the expense of the requesting party.

In a criminal case against a citizen of Germany and Russia K. Wiese (Perepyatenko) in the period from December 2008 to February 2009 the Investigation Department of the Omsk region was overloaded with German side requests. In total, were 7 video conferencing sessions, where testified 11 witnesses who were in Russian Federation.

In 2009, with the participation of representatives of the General Prosecutor's Office of the Russian Federation and Finnish colleagues, the interrogation was conducted using video conferencing during the court case in the Leningrad Region [5].

We are aware of cases of use in practical activity of local networks consisting of two successively connected personal computers to identify the person in conditions that preclude visual observation of the identifier [5]. In this way, it is most appropriate to conduct a practical exercise aimed at the acquisition by future investigators of the skills of producing such an investigative action as the presentation of a person for identification in conditions precluding visual observation of the identifier.

3 Training Students for the Educational Presenting to Identify the Person in Conditions of Excluding Visual Observation of the Identifier

At the beginning of the class, it is necessary to conduct a brief theoretical survey on the nature of the presentation for identification, procedural order, and rules of a specific investigative action. Preparation for the procedure of presenting a person for identification with a thorough examination of the material of the criminal case, the results of which determine the content of the preparatory stage of the investigative action: time of the beginning of investigative action; place of investigation; participants of the investigative action (measures are being taken to ensure their attendance); relevant tactics; definition of a set of technical equipment to be applied [6].

Preparation for identification includes the following steps:

- psychological preparation of the identifying person for the investigative action;
- selection of relevant objects;
- determining the time and place of the investigative action;
- preparation of technical equipment;
- the choice of tactics for identification.

It is necessary to take a responsible attitude towards the choice of figurant, that is, persons who will be presented simultaneously with an identifiable person. They must not differ from a recognizable person by race, age, height, build, hairstyle, hair or eye color. The color and style of clothing, the degree of wear and tear should also be as similar as possible. It is necessary to exclude the presence of signs of detention in a penitentiary institution for an identifiable person (overalls, means of restriction of movement). According to Part 4 of art. 193 of the Code of Criminal Procedure of the Russian Federation, the total number of persons presented for identification must be at least three.

When performing the exercise, it is necessary to draw the attention of the listeners to the advisability of participating in the investigative activities of a specialist, and to the using of additional means of recording evidentiary information used in the conduct of investigative actions, their significance for the criminal case, as well as to the issues of registration in the protocol of participation of a specialist.

The participation of a specialist in the identification procedure is due to the need for additional fixation of the identification process. The main means of fixation in criminal proceedings is the protocol of investigative action. The main means of fixation in the criminal process is the protocol of the investigative action, however, during such investigative actions as a presentation for identification, it is desirable to visually fix the progress and results of the identification, confirming the observance of the rights of all the persons involved. When challenging the results of identification in court, video filming of this investigative action, duly included in the materials of the criminal case and recognized as physical evidence, will be additional evidence.

In the protocol of the investigative action, it is necessary to indicate the technical means used by the specialist with a description of their brand and model. At the request of the identifiable or his counsel, the investigator should be given the opportunity to get acquainted with the video recording of the investigative action indicating this fact in the identification protocol. When performing the exercise, students need to understand the content of the identification of persons, its goals and objectives, to achieve which the investigator develops tactics and an investigative action plan. In preparation for the production of an investigative action, the following are determined: the time of the beginning of the investigative action, the place of its production, its participants (the way to ensure their attendance), the content of the investigative action (traditionally with the preparation of a plan), a set of technical means to be applied.

All these issues are resolved on the basis of a thorough examination of the materials of the criminal case [7].

The identification procedure includes the following steps:

1. Invitation of witnesses.
2. Inviting persons among who will be presented identifiable.
3. The invitation (delivery) of the identifiable, the offer of the identifiable to choose the place among other identifiable persons (figurants).
4. Clarification of the purpose and order of the investigative action, their rights and obligations to all the persons involved.
5. Inviting the person identifying, explaining to him the purpose and procedure for conducting the investigative action, his rights and obligations; warning of the person recognizing a criminal liability for refusing to testify or giving knowingly false testimony.
6. The offer to the identifier to inspect the persons being presented and to report whether he identifies anyone, if so, to whom and by what grounds the person was identified.
7. Provided that the person is identified, a proposal to the identified person to give his last name, first name, and patronymic.
8. Fixation of the course and results of the presentation for identification (can be carried out from the very beginning of the investigative action as far as obtaining relevant information).

The results of the identification are recorded in the protocol of the investigative action by all the persons involved by signing the protocol and indicating in it any comments or statements (if any).

When performing the exercise, it is necessary to draw the attention of the cadets (listeners) to the fact that before starting identification the investigator must ensure the rights of the suspect (an accused person) and the safety of the participants of the investigative action [8].

Before the start of the identification, the main task of the investigator is to exclude the visual contact between the identifiable person and identified person. The process of identification begins only after clarification of the rights and obligations of all those involved in the investigative action.

The total number of persons submitted cannot be less than three. An identifiable person should be invited to take any place among the presented persons. This is noted in the protocol of the investigative action.

If the identifying person is a witness or a victim, they are warned about criminal liability for refusal or evasion from testifying and for giving knowingly false testimony, as noted in the protocol. In addition, these persons are being informed about their rights under art. 51 of the Constitution of the Russian Federation.

During the presentation for identification, leading questions to the identifying person and the announcement of his preliminary interrogation data are excluded.

The identifying person should list the signs by which he recognized the person. Witnesses are located in a place that is most suitable for a full view of the identification process. The defender is located near the identifying person. The investigator must warn the defender about the inadmissibility of any impact on the identifying person and ensure that this requirement is met. The identification person is best summoned to the identification procedure by telephone.

If it is necessary to ensure the safety of the identifying person and his close relatives, it is advisable to carry out the identification procedure in conditions that preclude visual observation (the identifying person sees the identifiable person, and the identifiable person does not see the identifying person). In this case, the identifiable person and the identifying person may be located in the same or in different premises, the identifying person identifies the person through tinted glass or glass, which excludes bilateral observation. In this case, the witnesses and the defender of the identifiable are near the identifying person. An identifiable person and persons involved are in a place that excludes their visual observation of an identifying person.

4 The Process of Student's Education During Business Game

Students are invited to participate in the business game to present a person for identification in conditions that preclude visual observation of the identifier.

During the business game, the identifying and identifiable persons will be located in different rooms, each of them has personal computers interconnected by a local computer network with the installed automated system "Investigative actions in video conferencing". Software tools can be installed on a personal computer, laptop or mobile device. Camera, microphone and speaker or external devices, such as a webcam, headset or speakerphone can be used as hardware for capturing and playing video and sound [9].

In addition to the investigators, on both sides should be specialists to provide a communication session. They will be responsible for the preservation and transmission of data, the work of computer and video equipment. Investigative actions should take place after the technical communication session through the information and communication network, the purpose of which will be to coordinate the activities of the technical support services. Before starting an investigative action, the investigator should ascertain the competence of involved specialist, to ensure that he is familiar with the software and aware of his upcoming work process. He should be further instructed, and also in advance to inquire about possible technical problems. Instructing should concern specific manipulations (changing the view angle, stopping the transmission of a video stream, etc.) and their sequence [10].

The spatial arrangement of the participants of the investigative action depends on the technical characteristics of using hardware. Naturally, if possible all of them should be in sight, in the lens of a video camera. The software should implement the function of simultaneously finding images from both connection points in a picture so that participants actions don't look scattered.

In necessary cases, the personal data of the interrogated person, who will participate in the presentation for identification in the condition of excluding visual observation, may be classified as secret, to provide the person's confidentiality by Part 3 of Art. 11 and Part 9 of Art. 166 Code of Criminal Procedure.

For a business game, students determine who will get the roles of investigators, specialists, identifiable and identifiable, figurant. In addition, the teacher assigns the functions of arbitrators to several students - they will have to monitor the actions of the investigator and determine the mistakes made by him (procedural, organizational, tactical). The work of the arbitrators and the investigator is assessed. All participants of the business game should be instructed in detail by the teacher. There may be a certain conflict game scenario in which the participants create additional difficulties for the investigator, which will most fully evaluate the preparedness of the student performing the role of the person conducting the investigation.

Before the start of the investigative action, the identifier must be questioned about the signs of the identifiable. As part of a business game, you can offer the listener who plays the role of an identifier, according to the rules for creating a verbal portrait, describe one of the students in the group who will later play the role of an identifiable.

Next, participants in a business game are divided into two rooms: an identifiable person with figurant and a second teacher go to an audience which has been prepared in advance for the remote person identification, and the main part of the group, including the remaining participants of the business game - an investigator who identifies (who leaves the audience just before the start), arbitrators - stay in the original room, which also technically prepared for the needs of the class [11].

In modern conditions, the key component of the process of fixing evidence in the course of investigative actions is computer software [12]. It is necessary to dwell on the capabilities of the software used - the automated system "Investigative actions in the mode of video conferencing". The system realizes the possibility of mutual observation of participants in both points of the connection. Herewith, the presence of the "face recognition" function, as well as the option providing the ability to turn off the image at one of the points with voice communication preservation, allow for the person to be presented for identification in conditions that preclude visual observation of the identifying person. All processes at both points of communication are synchronized. The investigator at this time has the opportunity in a text editor to draw up a protocol of the investigative action taken, which by his decision at any time can be available for reading at the peripheral point of contact.

The proposed approach implements a three-level client-server architecture consisting of the following modules:

- common component library - implements the functions available to the client and server parts of the system software, such as encryption (Fig. 1);
- server - transfers information between clients;
- client - captures video and sound, recognizes the face and retouching it, transfers audio- and video- streams, files to the server.

The following tasks are solved:

- receiving video from a webcam;
- streaming audio and video over the network;
- transfer of the protocol of investigative action and other documents;
- encryption of transmitted traffic - for security reasons and ideas about ensuring the secrecy of the preliminary investigation;
- recognition and concealment of the face of the participant of the investigation if necessary.

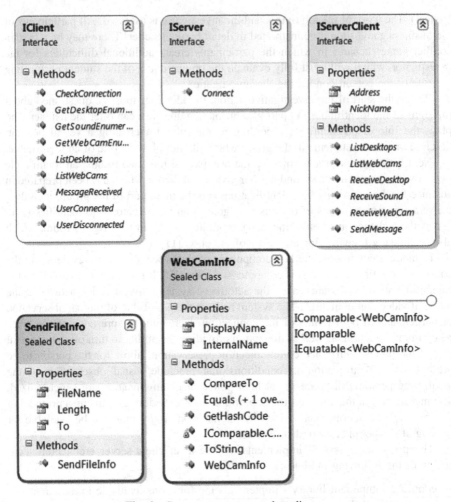

Fig. 1. Common component class diagram

After establishing the connection, the investigator proceeds to explain the peculiarities of the legal status of the participants in the investigation. All duties assigned to the investigator in accordance with the requirements of articles 161, 164 of the Code of Criminal Procedure of Russian Federation must also be fulfilled with respect to the participants of the investigative action, which are also located at the peripheral points of communication.

After explaining the peculiarities of the legal status of the participants and the completion of all procedural measures, the investigator asks the specialist to limit the video stream to a remote location, or, using the program function "face recognition", to hide the appearance of the identifiable person from the persons in the peripheral station. Next, the investigator proceeds to the working stage of the identification process. An identifiable person is given the opportunity to choose any place among the figurants.

Then, at the request of the investigator, one of the attesting witnesses invites an identifying person to the premises. He is also being informed about the features of his procedural status and is invited to carefully look at the persons submitted to him to determine which of them he had previously seen and under what circumstances. His explanations are entered in the protocol, the result of identification is recorded in the same place.

In the final part of the investigative action, the investigator asks the participants if they have any statements in the course of the conducted investigative action. Upon receipt of such indications are entered in the protocol. After this, the investigative action is declared finished, a protocol is made and presented to all participants for review, the investigator also records possible comments on the protocol. At the request of the participants, a video of the investigative action is played.

A CD/DVD disc with a recorded file containing video recording is also attached to the criminal case file.

At the end of the business game, a discussion takes place involving the maximum number of students in the group. The first with their observations are the students who acted as arbitrators, they can be asked to record the comments in writing and pass them on to the teacher. The teacher comments on the students' performances, sums up the lessons, gives marks.

5   Conclusion

In conclusion, I would like to note: there is no doubt that in the future, video conference technology can form a scientific and technical basis for remotely conducting a number of investigative actions (interrogation, confrontation, presentation for identification, inspection). As the relevant legal framework is formed, the methodological developments cited above can be extended to acquire investigative skills of a larger spectrum.

The evidentiary information obtained by video conferencing is of high quality and is a factor of tactical advantage of the preliminary investigation bodies, that is, such a dynamic characteristic of the investigation as a whole or its separate stage, in which the investigator has access to a greater number of permissible tactical techniques in a particular investigative situation, by reducing the period of time before its procedural consolidation and reducing its losses and distortions.

References

1. He, J.: The rules of judicial proof. In: He, J. (ed.) Methodology of Judicial Proof and Presumption. Masterpieces of Contemporary Jurisprudents in China, pp. 89–122. Springer, Singapore (2018). https://doi.org/10.1007/978-981-10-8025-8_4
2. Bulgakova, E., Bulgakov, V., Trushchenkov, I., Vasilev, D., Kravets, E.: Big data in investigating and preventing crimes. In: Kravets, Alla G. (ed.) Big Data-driven World: Legislation Issues and Control Technologies. SSDC, vol. 181, pp. 61–69. Springer, Cham (2019). https://doi.org/10.1007/978-3-030-01358-5_6

3. Luo, Y., Cheung, S.S., Lazzeretti, R., et al.: Anonymous subject identification, and privacy information management in video surveillance. Int. J. Inf. Secur. **17**, 261 (2018). https://doi.org/10.1007/s10207-017-0380-2

4. Kravets, A.G., Kravets, A.D., Korotkov, A.A.: Intelligent multi-agent systems generation. World Appl. Sci. J. **24**(24), 98–104 (2013)

5. Vasilev, D., Kravets, E., Naumov, Y., Bulgakova, E., Bulgakov, V.: Analysis of the data used at oppugnancy of crimes in the oil and gas industry. In: Kravets, A.G. (ed.) Big Data-driven World: Legislation Issues and Control Technologies. SSDC, vol. 181, pp. 249–258. Springer, Cham (2019). https://doi.org/10.1007/978-3-030-01358-5_22

6. Dronova, O., Smagorinskiy, B.P., Yastrebov, V.: Counteraction to e-commerce crimes committed with the use of online stores. In: Kravets, A.G. (ed.) Big Data-driven World: Legislation Issues and Control Technologies. SSDC, vol. 181, pp. 121–131. Springer, Cham (2019). https://doi.org/10.1007/978-3-030-01358-5_12

7. Kravets, E., Birukov, S., Pavlik, M.: Remote investigative actions as the evidentiary information management system. In: Kravets, A.G. (ed.) Big Data-driven World: Legislation Issues and Control Technologies. SSDC, vol. 181, pp. 95–103. Springer, Cham (2019). https://doi.org/10.1007/978-3-030-01358-5_9

8. Smith, C.J.: Research on crime and technology. In: Savona, E.U. (ed.) Crime and Technology, pp. 105–110. Springer, Dordrecht (2004). https://doi.org/10.1007/978-1-4020-2924-0_10

9. Saltykov, S., Rusyaeva, E., Kravets, A.G.: Typology of scientific constructions as an instrument of conceptual creativity. In: Kravets, A., Shcherbakov, M., Kultsova, M., Shabalina, O. (eds.) Creativity in Intelligent Technologies and Data Science. Communications in Computer and Information Science, vol. 535, pp. 41–57. Springer, Cham (2015). https://doi.org/10.1007/978-3-319-23766-4_4

10. Klimmt, C.: Virtual worlds as a regulatory challenge: a user perspective. In: Cornelius, K., Hermann, D. (eds.) Virtual Worlds and Criminality, pp. 1–18. Springer, Heidelberg (2011). https://doi.org/10.1007/978-3-642-20823-2_1

11. Shabalina, O., Mozelius, P., Malliarakis, C., Tomos, F.: Creativity-based learning versus game-based learning. In: Kravets, A., Shcherbakov, M., Kultsova, M., Shabalina, O. (eds.) Creativity in Intelligent Technologies and Data Science. Communications in Computer and Information Science, vol. 535. Springer, Cham (2015). https://doi.org/10.1007/978-3-319-23766-4_57

12. Pocar, F.: New challenges for international rules against cyber-crime. In: Savona, E.U. (ed.) Crime and Technology, pp. 29–38. Springer, Dordrecht (2004). https://doi.org/10.1007/978-1-4020-2924-0_3

Development the Methodology of Urban Area Transport Coherence Assessment

Danila Parygin$^{(\boxtimes)}$ ⓘ, Alexander Aleshkevich, Alexey Golubev,
Natalia Sadovnikova ⓘ, Maxim V. Shcherbakov ⓘ,
and Oksana Savina

Volgograd State Technical University,
28, Lenina Avenue, Volgograd 400005, Russia
dparygin@gmail.com, deck344@gmail.com,
ax.golubev@gmail.com, maxim.shcherbakov@gmail.com,
npsnl@ya.ru, nov1984@yandex.ru

Abstract. The present paper analyzes modern approaches to assessing the balance of urban infrastructure. The definition of transport coherence is given. The developed methodology of urban area transport coherence assessment is described. The method of localized assessment of transport provision has been tested in cities of various shapes and sizes: positive results and limits of the method applicability are analyzed by example of Volgograd, St. Petersburg, Novosibirsk, Moscow, Elista, Astrakhan, Uryupinsk and Kamyshin. The features of application of technologies and data of OSRM and OSM are highlighted. Checking options for calculating the coefficient of coherence for cells was held. Verification of the results obtained by the four methods of calculating the average is performed by comparing the estimates of connectedness with the length of roads in the corresponding cells. For this, a method for calculating the local density of the road network has been proposed. It is proposed to use a transport plasmograph of the territory for a visual demonstration of the coherence of space and the possibility of assessing its main structural features. The paper describes the method of creating a plasmograph and provides examples of the analysis with its help of the territory of Novosibirsk and St. Petersburg. Conclusions are drawn about the possibilities of formalizing the infrastructure integrity of cities based on an analysis of their transport coherence and suggest promising areas for further research using the established methods for analyzing other types of infrastructure, as well as comparative analysis of cities.

Keywords: City transport provision · Urban area connectedness ·
City boundaries · Transport coherence assessment · Coherence coefficient ·
Road network density · Localized assessment · Transport plasmagraph ·
OSRM · Transport infrastructure balance

1 Introduction

The main goal of the city's transport system is to ensure transport accessibility. It is necessary to solve a variety of tasks related to the organization of traffic, the formation of a route network of urban passenger transport, parking policies, etc. to achieve it. But all these tasks are directly related to transport planning [1]. The high level of

© Springer Nature Switzerland AG 2019
A. G. Kravets et al. (Eds.): CIT&DS 2019, CCIS 1083, pp. 369–381, 2019.
https://doi.org/10.1007/978-3-030-29743-5_30

uncertainty and ambiguity of the situation in different cities makes it impossible to define uniform requirements for the formation of transport infrastructure [2]. Significant difficulties are associated with uneven settlement and structural complexity of the territories, geographical features of the location of the city, etc. There is a need to create tools to assess the quality and effectiveness of management decisions made in the field of transport planning in terms of their impact on the quality of life of the population [3].

The transport provision of the city is a characteristic of its territory, reflecting the relationship between the need for movement and the availability of the necessary transport network [4]. Industry experts suggest using a number of indicators that allow to estimate the density of the road and route network, taking into account the area of the territory, the length of networks, the number of vehicles and the population in various combinations [5]. In this case, a distinction is introduced when applying these indicators for objects of different scale: at the level of a region or a whole city, an individual district or a city block. However, this approach carries a significant simplification, which consists in reducing the assessment of the provision of transport conditions, firstly, to obtaining averaged values for the territory under consideration, and secondly, it does not reflect the main property of the transport infrastructure, which consists in its ability to connect spatially separated from each other plots.

In this regard, it is necessary to develop an integrated approach to assessing the state of communication channels of the elements of a distributed system, allowing to take into account the structure of the territory, the composition and geographical binding of infrastructure objects. Such methods and technologies should allow exploring the parameters of the transport system in a spatial reference and identify their relationship with environmental conditions, which will contribute to the formation of a balanced approach in making decisions about the transformation of infrastructure [6].

2 Urban Infrastructure Balance Assessment

The integrity of the city is determined by the infrastructure balance, which, in turn, depends on how each element of the urban space is included in the overall system of communications and services. At the same time, the notion of a balanced territory is most often found in studies related to urban design, and, as a rule, is evaluated using a variety of indicators. For example, in [7], questions of morphological consistency of a territory are considered. Spatial proximity and consistency are proposed as two key indicators for measuring the coherence of an urban structure.

Salingaros paper provides a comprehensive analysis of the concept of connectedness. It is suggested that the urban structure should be formed on the basis of the rules that underlie the construction of any complex systems, such as, for example, the organism or a large computer program, where certain assembly rules are followed for the normal interaction and functioning of the parts [8, 9]. In his opinion, there is a slight formal difference between the general type systems and the urban structure. Now studies of such complex systems are reinvented in the context of computer programming [10].

One of the key components of infrastructure balance is the transport connectivity of territory. Issues of its quality are investigated in works representing approaches to transport planning and building public transport routes [11, 12]. Guidelines for assessing the security of the transport zones of the city are formed [13].

Moscow Region's accessibility model is an example of an approach to assess the balance of infrastructure by taking into account a number of parameters in relation to space. The model takes into account the connectivity of blocks and districts, the density of road network in different sections and the grid of blocks [14].

In [4, 15], an approach was proposed for calculating localized transport provision, which is the basic component of transport coherence assessment. The concept of coherence is used by the authors of a number of studies as one of the basic characteristics of urban space [7, 10, 16]. In this regard, it is proposed to determine the transport coherence, as the mutual transport proximity of all elements, ensuring the total equilibrium internal connectivity of settlement territory.

An attempt to form a system of criteria for transport connectivity assessment and city territory balance is made in this paper. It is necessary to propose methods for determining and visualizing the values of these criteria.

3   Transport Coherence Assessment Methodology

The research and development conducted earlier by the authors formed the basis of the created methodology of urban area transport coherence assessment. At present, the methodology includes a number of methods, approaches and algorithms for assessing the transport provision of cities and a comparative analysis of the transport coherence of urbanized territories:

1. Approach to the extraction and use of data on the boundaries and road network of a particular city.
2. Method of scalable structurisation of polymorphic geospatial object.
   a. Grid generation algorithm in accordance with a city boundaries.
   b. Empty cell removal algorithm.
3. Method of city transport provision localized assessment.
   a. Algorithm for constructing adjacency matrices based on data about the length of transport routes between cells.
   b. Algorithm for calculating the coherence coefficient of cells based on the adjacency matrix.
4. Method of calculating the road network local density.
5. Method of creating a transport plasmograph of the territory.

This paper proposes to consider in more detail some features of these methods. In particular, the problems of forming a route between points on the map using OSRM [17, 18], taking into account the natural obstacles of the territory, require clarification. And it is also necessary to make experimental calculations of urban area connectedness with different spatial-dimensional parameters to verify the applicability of principle used to obtain of provision assessments.

4 Testing the Method of City Transport Provision Localized Assessment in Cities of Different Shapes and Sizes

Eight cities with different spatial-dimensional structure were selected in order to study the possibilities of the method. It was decided to cover a number of key features of the objects of study when forming the requirements for selection:

1. Size range by cities area:
   a. Small (Astrakhan, Elista, Kamyshin, Uryupinsk).
   b. Middle (Volgograd, Novosibirsk).
   c. Large (St. Petersburg, Moscow).
2. Features of shapes:
   a. Correct or evenly distributed (Elista, Kamyshin, St. Petersburg, Moscow).
   b. Curvilinear or stretched in space (Astrakhan, Volgograd, Novosibirsk, Uryupinsk).
3. The presence of complex internal obstacles, such as large rivers, which break up the territory into several parts and create narrow communication channels (Novosibirsk, Astrakhan, St. Petersburg).
4. Administrative status:
   a. State capitals and high-level resource concentration centers (St. Petersburg, Moscow).
   b. The capitals of regions (Astrakhan, Volgograd, Novosibirsk, Elista).
   c. Small cities (Kamyshin, Uryupinsk).

The coordinates of the boundaries of cities were extracted [19, 20] from files in the ".shp" format, which store relevant geodata about the contours of many objects of the macroregion in accordance with the developed approach to the processing of data on the boundaries of settlements in the process of preparing the base of the study. Coordinates for the selected city are saved in the ".geojson" file, which the newly created program works with.

Files ".shp" format data from OpenStreetMaps [21] on Russia are available for download online in archives by federal districts [22]. Coordinates of borders and data on their belonging to a specific city are stored in different ".shp" files, the line-by-line procedure for storing information in which is the same.

Testing conducted on selected cities showed the applicability of the method for almost all research conditions. (see Fig. 1). The revealed restrictions mainly concerned the settlements belonging to group 4(c).

Problems due to the lack of complete coordinates of the boundaries of the city of Uryupinsk arose during the preparation of the initial data [23]. The subsequent analysis showed that this situation is typical for small settlements (the area of the territory is up to 50 sq.km), which introduces a restriction on the use of the methodology in terms of using the proposed approach to the automated processing of open map data.

Another unobvious problem of small cities turned out to be related to the size of road network [24]. The calculated coherence coefficient is almost the same for the entire settlement for a grid step of 250 m selected according to the method of transport provision localized assessment. That creates a monotonous and non-informative map of results.

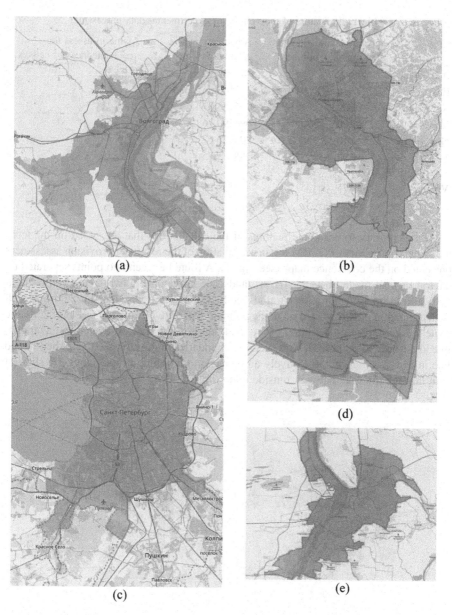

Fig. 1. Results of provision assessment for cities of different in shape and size: a. Volgograd; b. Novosibirsk; c. St. Petersburg; d. Elista; e. Astrakhan.

The developed software solutions and the applied equipment of the computing cluster of VSTU showed satisfactory performance indicators (see Table 1). Although for cities from groups 1(b) and 1(c) the calculation time took from 2 to 8 days.

Table 1. Indicators of the volume of experimental data processing.

City	Area, sq.km	Grid cells number	Adjacency matrix calculation time, s	Time to assess the connectedness of cells, s
Astrakhan	208.69	3667	41683.55	23.58
Elista	92.36	911	2146.66	1.38
Kamyshin	81.00	2186	15153.07	6.41
Moscow	2511.00	17266	696590.76	437.58
Novosibirsk	502.10	8062	203936.62	108.43
St. Petersburg	1439.00	9984	288718.75	149.10
Volgograd	859.35	14519	464596.337	331.41

It is necessary to designate features of the calculations that are based on the technological capabilities of OSRM for an explanation of the results of provision assessment presented on the coherence maps (see Fig. 1). A route between two points separated by natural or man-made obstacles (river, landscape curvature, railway, etc.) can be built with a bridge, a tunnel or a ferry traffic (see Fig. 2, a). Otherwise (see Fig. 2, b), as well as in a situation if there is no road to the point of departure/destination (see Fig. 2, d), the route will terminate on a section of the road that is at the shortest distance in a straight line to the desired point [25]. However, the boundaries of the city (see the dashed-dotted line in Fig. 2, c) are not objectively an obstacle to building a route along the shortest path through the road network outside its territory.

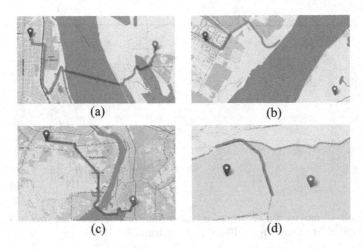

(a)   (b)

(c)   (d)

Fig. 2. Features of calculating the distance between points using OSRM: a. Through the water barrier with a ferry; b. Through the water barrier in the absence of a ferry; c. Outside the settlement boundaries; d. Away from roads.

5 Verification of Options for Calculating the Coherence Coefficient for Cells

One of the key objectives of the study is to ensure the invariance of coherence assessments of the territory. It is required to find a method for calculating the values of the coefficients of coherence, taking into account the territorial distribution of cities, as an essential feature of their systemic consideration.

The evaluation was carried out using the algorithms for calculating the average using the arithmetic mean, median, mean square and geometric mean to identify an adequate level of sharpness of the boundaries of the connectivity coefficient values. The visualization of the coherence maps for the resulting calculations is shown in the figure (see Fig. 3). Here are the following logic of reasoning, verification calculations and conclusions for interpreting the obtained results from a mathematical point of view.

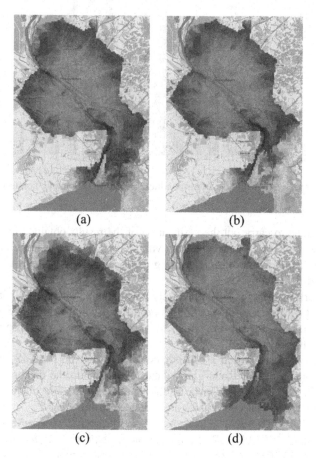

(a)   (b)

(c)   (d)

Fig. 3. The results of applying various options for calculating the coherence coefficients for cells (coherence maps): a. Arithmetic mean; b. Median; c. Mean square; d. Geometric mean.

Using the arithmetic mean, as a classical approach to finding the average gave uniformly distributed results in terms of the number of cells for a certain value of the coherence coefficient (see Fig. 4). In this case the limitations of the scale provide a fairly stable result despite the possibility of the influence of a large number of extreme values on the superiority of the final grade.

The results obtained by calculating the mean square and median have similar in form and smoother distributions. At the same time, the median also covers an extended range of estimates, showing its robustness characteristic, which is independent of emissions and the influence of "heavy" tails of distribution.

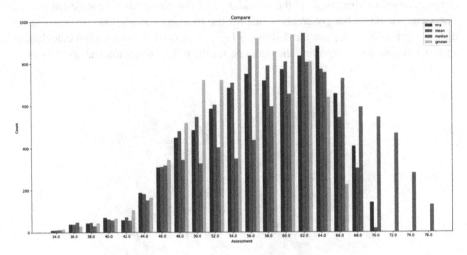

Fig. 4. Number of cells with the corresponding estimates of mutual connectedness of the territory.

It was decided to carry out the verification of the results obtained in four ways by comparing the estimates of connectedness with the length of roads in the corresponding cells. (see Fig. 5). A method for calculating the local density of the road network has been proposed for this.

The network of cells for the studied city was obtained using the algorithms of the method of scalable structurisation of polymorphic geospatial object. The grid structure and cell size corresponded to the parameters specified earlier for transport coherence assessment of the territory.

The length of roads inside a cell is calculated using the PostGIS library for the PostgreSQL database [26]. Road graph data is loaded into the database from Open-StreetMap [27, 28]. A query is made to the database to directly obtain the length of roads in the cell. The cell coordinates are indicated in this query:

```
"SELECT SUM(ST_LENGTH(ST_Intersection(ST_GeomFromText('PO
LYGON((" + p_t + ")))',4326), ST_GeomFromText(ST_AsText(ST_Tra
nsform(way,4326)),4326))))) FROM planet_osm_line WHERE ST_
Intersects(ST_GeomFromText('POLYGON((" + p_t + ")))',4326), ST_
GeomFromText(ST_AsText(ST_Transform(way,4326)),4326)))"
```

and "p_t" is an array with coordinates of cell borders.

Lighter tones on the resulting road network density map of the (see Fig. 5, b) show areas with a greater length of roads per unit area. A comparative analysis of the average network density relative to the transport provision assessment reveals a number of trends characteristic of different ways of calculating the coherence coefficient. Thus, the geometric mean showed large emissions in both graphs (see Figs. 4 and 5, a), as well as overestimated shift of final values in the rating scale compared with other methods of calculation.

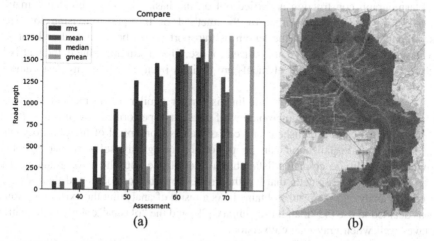

(a)   (b)

Fig. 5. Assessment the local density of the road network of Novosibirsk: a. The length of roads in the cells (in meters) corresponding to estimates of territory interconnectedness obtained in various ways; b. Road Density Map.

Other evaluation options that have uniform distributions and wide ranges form a more representative gradation of values based on the logic of this study. At the same time, the calculation results using the median correlate most adequately with the network density indicators for the test case under consideration.

Another important conclusion that can be made on the basis of the analysis of the figure (see Fig. 5, a) is the absence of a linear relationship between the density of the road network and the assessment of its connectivity. In this regard, it was decided not to take into account the types of roads and the number of lanes in the framework of the studies, since the ability of roads to take more traffic does not actually determine their importance in the balance of transport provision.

6 Method of Creating a Transport Plasmograph of the Territory

It is proposed to investigate the correspondence matrix of the city territory at the stage of assessing the balance of transport provision within the framework of the developed methodology. In the first approximation the method of creating a plasmograph is intended to visually demonstrate the coherence of space, to give an opportunity to evaluate its main structural features.

Plasmograph construction is carried out on the basis of a correspondence matrix created using the first algorithm of the method of transport provision localized assessment based on data on the length of transport routes between grid cells of the city. Source route data must be normalized for use. The maximum value in the matrix is searched for and all the other elements are divided by it, since the smallest value is always 0.

The process of plasmograph building is further similar to the methods for constructing heat maps. But the interpolation of data is not performed in contrast to them, but an exact match is established: one cell of values - one pixel of the plasmograph.

Plasmograph visualization can be performed using any software package that provides the ability to color the data table in accordance with the color gradient. It is preferable to choose a palette that has the greatest number of colors and their shades, for ease of analyzing the results obtained. As a result of analyzing the existing options, it was decided to use the "matplotlib" library [29] and the "plasma" color palette, which behaves well when grayscale conversion.

A rectangular map (see Fig. 6) is obtained at the output as a result of building a plasmograph, where the main diagonal (or secondary depending on the construction method) has the smallest value - the distance from the cluster to itself has zero length (purple color), and the largest value (yellow color) is the longest distance in the correspondence matrix. The abscissa and ordinate scales indicate the correspondence matrix dimension. The separate scale, located to the right of the plasmograph, is a color legend reflecting the transport proximity of the cells in meters - the larger the value so the more distant one cell is from another.

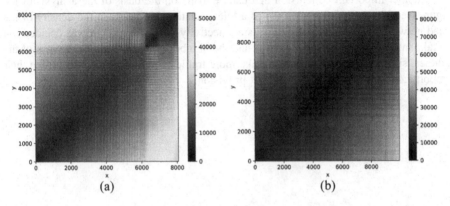

Fig. 6. Transport plasmograph of the territory: a. Novosibirsk; b. St. Petersburg. (Color figure online)

In Fig. 6 presents examples of plasmograph of the territory of Novosibirsk and St. Petersburg. It can be seen that the matrix has a symmetric form relative to the main diagonal, on which the zeros are located. The normalized distances between the grid cells, constructed along the roads of the city, are represented at the intersection of x and y by color.

The plasmograph of St. Petersburg characterizes the relative uniformity of the distribution of transport provision values, high coherence and large sizes of the urban core, as well as the growth of urban suburbs that are less connected with the rest of the territory. The situation can be visually examined in the coherence map (see Fig. 1, c).

The picture of a different nature can be observed on the plasmograph of Novosibirsk. The spatial isolation of the southern appendix is pronounced in this case. Almost a quarter of the urban area is actually fenced off by narrow transport channels and has an internally balanced transport connection. At the same time, the urban core itself is fairly uniform, although discharged because of suburbs that are poorly provided with transport links. These factors can be visually assessed on the coherence map (see Fig. 1, b) and the road network density map (see Fig. 5, b).

7 Conclusions and Future Work

The conducted research implements a formal definition of infrastructure integrity based on an analysis of transport coherence. This characteristic makes it possible to assess the living conditions of the settlement, to compare territories and cities. The proposed methodology can be used to analyze and select the most effective design decisions in the process of urban development management.

The issues of assessing the transport provision and density of the road network are most closely considered at the moment. Successful results of testing the applicability of the developed methods for analyzing cities of various shapes and sizes were obtained. The method of morphologically independent comparative assessment of the transport infrastructure balance was created and tested.

It is supposed to analyze the approaches to the assessment of integrity from the point of view of other subsystems of the city, separately and in combination with the transport system, in the framework of continuing research. It is planned to compare the provision of social infrastructure and public transport in a specific city.

In addition, it is necessary to solve the issues of presenting the results [30]. This concerns the development of adequate visual tools for visual demonstration of estimates and tools for remote access and viewing "heavy" calculation results.

Acknowledgments. The reported study was funded by Russian Foundation for Basic Research (RFBR) according to the research project No. 18-37-20066_mol_a_ved, and by RFBR and the government of the Volgograd region of the Russian Federation grant No. 18-47-340012_r_a. The authors express gratitude to colleagues from UCLab involved in the development of UrbanBasis.com project.

References

1. Sadovnikova, N.P., Parygin, D.S., Potapova, T.A., Sobolev, V.O.: Support of decision-making in the urban logistics tasks based on traffic congestion data. Casp. J.: Control High Technol. 1(41), 94–102 (2018)
2. Sadovnikova, N., Parygin, D., Kalinkina, M., Sanzhapov, B., Ni, T.N.: Models and methods for the urban transit system research. Commun. Comput. Inf. Sci. 535, 488–499 (2015)
3. Parygin, D.S., Sadovnikova, N.P., Shabalina, O.A.: Information and analytical support for city management tasks (Информационно-аналитическая поддержка задач управления городом). Volgograd (2017)
4. Aleshkevich, A.A., Parygin, D.S., Sadovnikova, N.P., Golubev, A.V.: Algorithmic support for the method of city transport provision localized assessment. Proc. Volgogr. State Tech. Univ.: Ser. Actual Probl. Control Comput. Eng. Inform. Tech. Syst. 13(223), 29–33 (2018)
5. Parygin, D., Golubev, A., Sadovnikova, N., Shcherbakov, M.: Method GAND: multi-criteria analysis for choice the most preferable geodata-based transport network. Commun. Comput. Inf. Sci. 745, 329–340 (2017)
6. Golubev, A., Chechetkin, I., Parygin, D., Sokolov, A., Shcherbakov, M.: Geospatial data generation and preprocessing tools for urban computing system development. Procedia Comput. Sci. 101, 217–226 (2016)
7. Caliskan, O., Mashhoodi, B.: Urban coherence: a morphological definition. Urban Morphol. 21(2), 123–141 (2017)
8. Korobkin, D., Fomenkov, S., Kravets, A., Kolesnikov, S.: Methods of statistical and semantic patent analysis. Commun. Comput. Inf. Sci. 754, 48–61 (2017)
9. Korobkin, D., Fomenkov, S., Kolesnikov, S., Lobeyko, V., Golovanchikov, A.: Modification of physical effect model for the synthesis of the physical operation principles of technical system. Commun. Comput. Inf. Sci. 535, 368–378 (2015)
10. Salingaros, N.A.: Complexity and urban coherence. J. Urban Des. 5, 291–316 (2000)
11. Mees, P., Stone, J., Imran, M., Nielsen, G.: Public transport network planning: a guide to best practice in NZ cities. NZ Transport Agency research report 396 (2010)
12. Golubev, A.V., Chechetkin, I.A., Solnushkin, K.S., Sadovnikova, N.P., Parygin, D.S., Shcherbakov, M.V.: Strategway: web solutions for building public transportation routes using big geodata analysis. In: 17th International Conference on Information Integration and Web-based Application & Services, pp. 91:1–91:4, 665–668. ACM, New York (2015)
13. Yakimov, M.R.: Assessment of transport provision of urban areas on the basis of predictive transport models: guidelines. Transport Planning Institute of the All-Russian Public Organization Russian Academy of Transport, Moscow (2016)
14. Planiformica. https://www.fb.com/1054321067983339/posts/2314758378606262/. Accessed 22 Dec 2018
15. Parygin, D.S., Aleshkevich, A.A., Golubev, A.V., Smykovskaya, T.K., Finogeev, A.G.: Map data-driven assessment of urban areas accessibility. J. Phys: Conf. Ser. 1015, 042048 (2018)
16. Rahaman, K.R., Afrin, S., Rahman, M.A.: Modeling system coherence to know the pedestrian's level-of services in Dhaka city. Khulna Univ. Stud. 8(1), 13–19 (2007)
17. Open Source Routing Machine. http://project-osrm.org/. Accessed 21 Nov 2018
18. Zilske, M., Neumann, A., Nagel, K.: OpenStreetMap for traffic simulation. https://svn.vsp.tu-berlin.de/repos/public-svn/publications/vspwp/2011/11-10/2011-06-20_openstreetmap_for_traffic_simulation_sotm-eu.pdf. Accessed 24 Feb 2019
19. Fomenkova, M., Korobkin, D., Fomenkov, S.: Extraction of physical effects based on the semantic analysis of the patent texts. Commun. Comput. Inf. Sci. 754, 73–87 (2017)

20. Korobkin, D., Fomenkov, S., Kravets, A., Kolesnikov, S., Dykov, M.: Three-steps methodology for patents prior-art retrieval and structured physical knowledge extracting. Commun. Comput. Inf. Sci. **535**, 124–136 (2015)
21. OpenStreetMap. http://openstreetmap.ru/. Accessed 05 Dec 2018
22. Geofabrik Download Server. https://download.geofabrik.de/russia.html. Accessed 29 Nov 2018
23. Gil, J.: Using OSM data for street network analysis - from data to model to graph(s), https://doi.org/10.13140/rg.2.2.23099.87846. Accessed 15 Jan 2019
24. Boeing, G.: A multi-scale analysis of 27,000 urban street networks: every US city, town, urbanized area, and Zillow neighborhood. Environ. Plan. B: Urban Anal. City Sci. https://doi.org/10.1177/2399808318784595. Accessed 17 Mar 2019
25. Poppinga, M.: Large-scale accessibility analysis using OpenStreetMap data. https://hps.vi4io.org/_media/research/theses/martin_poppinga_large_scale_accessibility_analysis_using_openstreetmap_data.pdf. Accessed 3 Mar 2019
26. Network analysis in Python. https://automating-gis-processes.github.io/2017/lessons/L7/network-analysis.html. Accessed 14 Dec 2018
27. Cohen, A.: Building a weighted graph based on OpenStreetMap data for routing algorithms for blind pedestrians. https://pdfs.semanticscholar.org/e7cb/a6fb5565afa11e0b89f466f0-481699bfb59e.pdf. Accessed 27 Mar 2019
28. Janakiev, N.: Loading data from OpenStreetMap with Python and the Overpass API. https://towardsdatascience.com/loading-data-from-openstreetmap-with-python-and-the-overpass-api-513882a27fd0. Accessed 02 Apr 2019
29. Matplotlib: Python plotting—Matplotlib 3.0.2 documentation. https://matplotlib.org/. Accessed 02 Feb 2019
30. Parygin, D., Sadovnikova, N., Kalinkina, M., Potapova, T., Finogeev, A.: Visualization of data about events in the urban environment for the decision support of the city services actions coordination. In: 5th International Conference on System Modeling & Advancement in Research Trends, pp. 283–290. IEEE (2016)

Cryptographic Protection of Data Transmission Channel

Arina Nikishova$^{(\boxtimes)}$, Ekaterina Vitenburg, Mikhail Umnitsyn[ID],
and Tatiana Omelchenko

Department of Information Security, Volgograd State University,
Volgograd, Russia
{nikishova.arina,infsec,umnitsyn,
omelchenko.tatiana}@volsu.ru

Abstract. Data transmission over the network is the most vulnerable stage of the information life cycle in the information system. The main way to protect data when transmitting over a communication channel is to hide its content. For this purpose, cryptographic means of information protection are used. Among the cryptographic means, encryption and digital signature are distinguished. There are different algorithms that allow performing encryption or digital signature. So which one is better? What algorithms should be used to make cryptographic protection the most effective? The study of the effectiveness of approaches to the construction of encryption algorithms is carried out. SP-network is recognized as more efficient than Feistel network. The study of the effectiveness of approaches to the construction of digital signature algorithms is carried out. The study took into account how the algorithm is used in conjunction with SP-network. Algorithm of the elliptic curve is recognized as the most efficient. As a result, the protocol of secure data transmission over the network is developed.

Keywords: Data transmission · Encryption · Digital signature · SP-network · Elliptic curve

1 Introduction

The next stage of the technological revolution, which is currently taking place in the world, entails serious changes in the economy and social structure of society. Mass application of new technological means, on the basis of which informatization is carried out, erases geopolitical borders, changes the way of life of millions of people. At the same time, the information sphere becomes not only one of the most important spheres of international cooperation but also an object of competition.

Currently, most managers of enterprises and organizations are taking measures to protect information that is important for them. Different information protection means are applied. But despite this, there are incidents of information security violations. According to Infowatch company report, data leakage through the network is the most common (Fig. 1) [1].

© Springer Nature Switzerland AG 2019
A. G. Kravets et al. (Eds.): CIT&DS 2019, CCIS 1083, pp. 382–391, 2019.
https://doi.org/10.1007/978-3-030-29743-5_31

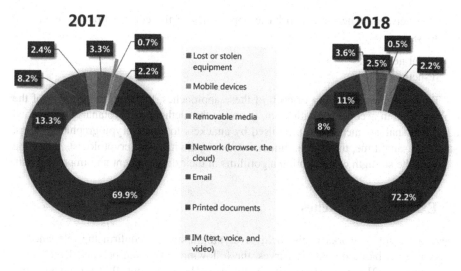

Fig. 1. Breakdown by channel in 2017–2018.

Intentional leaks are most often associated with the network channel. Almost 90% of intentional leaks are related to illegal transfer or disclosure of information via the Internet (including web services, e-mail, and other online resources).

The most common protection means using to protect data during its transfer over the network is cryptography. There are two directions of cryptographic protection of information: symmetric cryptography and asymmetric cryptography.

Asymmetric cryptography came later, but it has no theoretical strength, unlike symmetric cryptography. All asymmetric cryptosystems offered today rely on one of the following types of one-way transformations:

- decomposition of large numbers into Prime factors;
- the computation of the discrete logarithm and discrete exponentiation;
- the problem of laying a backpack;
- calculation of roots of algebraic equations;
- the use of finite state machines;
- the use of code structures;
- using the properties of elliptic curves.

Due to the lack of theoretical strength of such systems, they are used to solve problems such as authentication and integrity of the received data. Currently, cryptosystems using the properties of elliptic curves are actively developing. The current standard of Russian Federation for digital signature (GOST R 34.10-2012. "Information technology. Cryptographic protection of information. Processes of formation and verification of electronic digital signature") uses elliptic curves. So it is only natural to use elliptic curves for data authenticity and integrity protection during its transmission over the network.

On the other hand, symmetric cryptosystems have theoretical strength and are used to protect the contents of a large amount of data during its storage and transmission over the network. There are two basic approaches to the construction of symmetric cryptosystems:

- Feistel network;
- SP-network.

To determine the quality of each of these approaches, the study of strength of the ciphers, built in accordance with them, to one of the methods of cryptanalysis is carried out. Cryptanalysis methods can be used by attackers to attack cryptographic systems, but at the same time, they are an important tool in the hands of cryptologists, allowing to assess the strength of encryption algorithms in their development and improve them.

2 Existing Approaches

There are a lot of works in the field of cryptography. To confirm the relevance of cryptosystems based on elliptic curves, the following works can be considered.

Author of [2] considers security in Internet. He points out, that nowadays commercial structures can no longer run their business without using the Internet and cloud technologies. Electronic transactions conducted through the global Internet play an increasing role in the modern global economy, and their importance is rapidly increasing every year. However, the reality is the Internet is quite vulnerable in terms of threats of most diverse types. So commercial organizations increasingly focus on Web security. The author explores the encryption of Web pages using encryption based on elliptical curves. Even a simple transformation of information is a very effective means, making it possible to hide its meaning from the majority of unskilled offenders. Additionally, the algorithm of constructing an electronic-digital message signature based on encryption using elliptic curves is considered.

Author of [3] suggests the expansion of the use of elliptic curves. He defines a finite field of elements that exceeds one in the common algorithm. This work allows using computer technology for purposes of cryptography more efficiently.

Author of [4] presents a new digital signature scheme with message recovery based on elliptic curve cryptography on the base of the State standard 4145-2002. Elliptic curve cryptosystem provides greater security compared to integer factorization system and discrete logarithm system, for any given key size and bandwidth. The main difference between the proposed scheme and the current standard is the replacement of the hash function with the hash token function, which makes the signature and verification procedure reversed and allows to recover messages from the signature r-component.

Author of [5] considers data protection in Egyptian optical network. The physical layer of the optical transport network (OTN) is the weakest layer in the network, as anyone can access the optical cables from any unauthorized location of the network and stat his attack by using any type of the vulnerabilities. To protect data new security layer is added to the OTN frames for the first time since the network infrastructure has been installed. The proposed model is implemented on the basis of protecting the important client signals only over the optical layers by passing these signals into an extra layer called security layer, and before forming the final frame of the OTN system. The proposed model is only suitable for optical networks.

Author of [6] presents a novel secure medical image transmission scheme using hybrid visual cryptography and Hill cipher (HVCHC) between sender and receiver. The grayscale medical images have been considered as a secret image and split into different shares by visual cryptography (VC) encryption process. The split shares are once again encoded by Hill cipher (HC) encode process for improving the efficiency of the proposed method.

Analysis of modern research in the field of cryptography shows that in relation to elliptic curves, active research is conducted, which makes its use relevant [7]. Research on symmetric cryptosystems is mainly aimed at improving the cryptographic protocols that use them, rather than at changing the algorithms themselves. Therefore, it is important to study the existing symmetric cryptosystems [8].

3 Cryptographic Systems

There are universal methods of hacking cryptosystems, such as the method of brute force, key attack, the method of "meeting in the middle", frequency analysis.

Brute-force method involves iterating through all possible keys until you find one that allows you to decrypt the intercepted message. This attack is practically impossible on modern ciphers due to the immensity of the time or computing power required for this [9].

The key attack involves the presence of weak keys in the algorithm that does not provide the necessary level of protection, and its success depends on the correctness of the configuration of the system parameters.

The method of "meeting in the middle" assumes that the cipher key can be represented as a composition of keys, and offers to pick up not the whole key, but a set of keys equivalent to the main key.

But these methods are universal and are used without taking into account the internal structure of the cipher, so are not of interest in this work. Frequency analysis is a linguistic method based on the assumption that there is a nontrivial statistical distribution of symbols and their combinations in the text, which is stored both in plain text and in the ciphertext. Thus, analyzing a sufficiently long encrypted text, it is possible to make a reverse replacement and restore the original text by the frequency of appearance of symbols. Frequency analysis can also be used as a universal, but especially vulnerable to this type of cryptanalysis replacement ciphers, i.e. based on simple S-blocks, as well as in various modifications, it is applied to permutation ciphers, i.e. based on P-blocks.

The methods of cryptanalysis those are specific for block ciphers should be considered. The most common and universal method of cryptanalysis of block ciphers is differential (difference) cryptanalysis and linear cryptanalysis.

The basic idea of linear cryptanalysis is to use (existing for any non-linear transformations) hidden linear equations connecting some bits of input and output. When performing this attack, it is assumed to use a lot of open texts and corresponding cryptograms. However, such equations will not always exist, but only for some part of the input messages. Therefore, it is possible to speak only about some probability of their execution. To determine the numbers in the linear equation, the ones that provide the highest probability of equations performing on all possible inputs must be selected.

Differential cryptanalysis uses abnormally increased probabilities of some cryptogram differences occurring for certain differences between open messages. Differential cryptanalysis is based on the hypothesis that there are certain output differences that have increased or decreased probabilities.

Another universal, but a less common method is cryptanalysis by the method of solving systems of nonlinear equations uses the fact that the block cipher can be described using Boolean functions that connect the bits of the public message, the bits of the cryptogram and the bits of the unknown key. These Boolean functions can be represented as a Zhegalkin polynomial, i.e. as equations containing products and sums of these products modulo 2. Then, having compiled a system of equations for a complete cipher with several known blocks of open messages and corresponding cryptograms obtained using the same key, this system can be solved with respect to the values of the key bits.

There are attacks aimed at one of the operations used in block ciphers - gamming operation. One of them is an attack based on the Berlekamp-Messi algorithm. Let the structure of the cipher be unknown, but it is assumed that it is based on the use of one or more shift registers and the linear equivalent complexity of the encryption gamma is an observable value. Then, to perform the attack, there is a segment of the encryption gamma of sufficiently large length N. To obtain it bits of the message and the corresponding bits of the cryptogram must be known. Further, the Berlekamp-Messi algorithm is applied to this gamma, which allows finding the length of the equivalent shift register, as well as its bends and initial filling and, consequently, to calculate an arbitrary continuation of this gamma. Knowing the continuation of the gamma allows, in turn, to decrypt the message outside the known N bits.

Methods of cryptanalysis are analyzed according to the criteria:

- cryptographic operations that are vulnerable to the method;
- the complexity of method implementation;
- method operation speed [10].

The final comparison of cryptanalysis methods is given in Table 1.

Table 1. Comparison of cryptanalysis methods characteristics.

	Affected transactions	Method's complexity	Method's speed	Overall assessment
Linear cryptanalysis	S-block	Low	Medium	1,25
Differential cryptanalysis	S-block P-block Gamming	Medium	High	0,25
Cryptanalysis by the method of solving systems of nonlinear equations	S-block	High	Medium	2,25
Attack based on the Berlekamp-Messi algorithm	Gamming	High	Medium	2,25

It can be concluded that the most rational method for carrying out an attack on a symmetric cryptographic system of block encryption is the method of differential cryptanalysis.

Differential cryptanalysis is an attack based on open texts, that is, involves the ability to encrypt in the attacked cryptosystem any messages in any quantity. As objects for cryptanalysis simulated cryptosystems built on the principle of SP-network and Feistel network will be used.

Since only half of the block is converted during a single round of Feistel network encryption, the Feistel network-based cipher is designed with twice as many rounds as the SP network-based cipher to achieve a level of protection equivalent to that of the SP network.

The architecture of the software that allows differential cryptanalysis of simulated cryptographic systems of block encryption is shown in Fig. 2 and consists of the following modules:

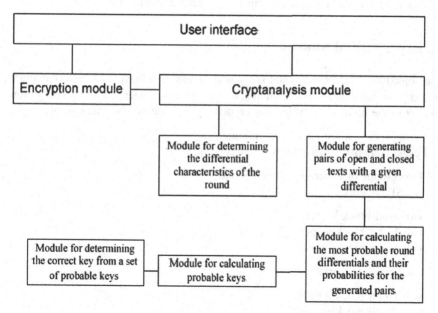

Fig. 2. The architecture of software for cryptanalysis of block ciphers.

- The user interface provides interaction between the user and the program modules through a graphical interface, provides tools for data input and output of the results.
- Encryption module performs cryptographic conversion of the input plaintext using the specified key.
- The module of cryptanalysis carries out the procedure of cryptanalysis and combines the work of other modules.
- Module for determining the differential characteristics of the round builds a table of frequencies of input and output differentials for the round and on the basis of the

constructed table searches for pairs of differentials with the highest frequency of occurrence.

- Module for generating pairs of open and closed texts with a given differential generates a specified number of open texts with a specified differential, as well as corresponding closed texts formed by encryption of open texts on a randomly generated encryption key.
- Module for calculating the most probable round differentials and their probabilities for the generated pairs searches for the most likely differentials for each round based on the generated open text pairs.
- Module for calculating probable keys iterates through the rounds subkeys based on the information received about the most likely differentials of the rounds and makes a list of possible encryption keys.
- Module for determining the correct key from a set of probable keys checks each key in the list of possible keys and determines the encryption key used for encryption.

Using developed software experimental studies are carried out.

4   Experimental Studies

The objective of the experimental study is to assess the effectiveness of cryptographic protection of information using simulated cryptographic systems of block encryption in relation to the method of differential cryptanalysis, built on the principle of:

1. SP-network – n rounds of encryption;
2. Feistel Networks – 2n rounds of encryption.

Two groups of experiments are defined:
For SP-network

- with 8-bit block length;
- with 12-bit block length;
- with 16-bit block length.

For Feistel network:

- with 16-bit block length;
- with 24-bit block length;
- with 32-bit block length.

For example in experiment 1 where SP-network has blocked with a length of 8 bit the following steps are performed:

1. Parameters of the cryptosystem "block length – 8 bits, key length 16 bits" are selected.
2. The random encryption key for the cryptosystem is generated. Round subkeys are computed from the encryption key. As a result of generation, the following key was received: 18388 and the following subkeys: (71, 212).
3. Some plain text: 123 is entered, and the encryption procedure is started.

4. The encryption result: 32 is received, and the encryption time $T_{ch} = 0.011$ ms is estimated.
5. The best input differentials for generating open text pairs are determined. In this experiment, the best input differentials equal to 10 and 160 are obtained.
6. The parameters of cryptanalysis are set: the number of generated pairs is set to 10; the input differential value obtained in step 2 is set to 10.
7. The process of cryptanalysis is started. As a result, the encryption key matching the valid key is found in $T_{cr} = 3{,}7392$ ms.

Thus, the value of the effectiveness of cryptographic protection of information using a single round of cipher, based on the SP-network, with a block length of 8 bits and a key length of 16 bits is equal to the division of T_{cr} to T_{ch} and is $T_{cr}/T_{ch} = 3{,}7392/0{,}011 = 339{,}92$.

As a result of all experiments, the following values of the effectiveness of cryptographic protection of information in relation to the method of differential cryptanalysis are received (Table 2).

Table 2. Results of experimental studies.

		Encryption time	Cryptanalysis time	Effectiveness
SP-network	Block length - 8 bit, key length - 16 bit	0,011 ms	3,7392 ms	339,92
	Block length - 12 bit, key length - 24 bit	0,0168 ms	76,1266 ms	4531,35
	Block length - 16 bit, key length - 32 bit	0,0207 ms	1683,9672 ms	81351,07
Feistel Network	Block length - 8 bit, key length - 16 bit	0,0209 ms	8,6342 ms	413,12
	Block length - 12 bit, key length - 24 bit	0,0234 ms	137,2908 ms	5867,13
	Block length - 16 bit, key length - 32 bit	0,0273 ms	2679,0894 ms	98135,14

As the results of the experiments it is shown, that the effectiveness of cryptographic protection of information in relation to the method of differential cryptanalysis using a cipher, built on the principle of the Feistel network, on average 24% higher than the same indicator for the SP-network, which allows us to consider the use of this type of cipher in the threat of differential cryptanalysis more effective.

5 Conclusion

The analysis of symmetric block cryptographic systems is carried out, as the result of the basic cryptographic operations from which symmetric block cryptographic systems are constructed are revealed:

- substitution (S-block);
- permutation (P-block);
- gamming.

The analysis of block ciphers is carried out. As a result it is revealed that the vast majority of block ciphers are built on two principles:

- SP network;
- Feistel network.

The analysis of existing methods of cryptanalysis, such as the method of linear cryptanalysis, the method of differential cryptanalysis, cryptanalysis by the method of solving systems of nonlinear equations, an attack based on the use of the Berlekamp-Messi algorithm is carried out. As a result it was found that the most rational for application to block ciphers is the method of differential cryptanalysis.

The architecture of the software for differential cryptanalysis of block ciphers, including the following modules: user interface; encryption module; cryptanalysis module; module for determining the differential characteristics of the round; module for generating pairs of open and closed texts with a given differential; module for calculating the most probable round differentials and their probabilities for the generated pairs; module for calculating probable keys; module for determining the correct key from a set of probable keys; is developed. The algorithms of the modules of the software for cryptanalysis of block ciphers are developed.

The user interface of the software for cryptanalysis of block ciphers, consisting of a switch of cryptosystem type, switch of cryptosystem parameters, encryption and cryptanalysis areas is developed.

The results of experimental studies have shown that the effectiveness of cryptographic protection of information using a single round of cipher, built on the principle of the Feistel network is higher than the same indicator for the SP-network.

However, it is worth noting that the new standard of symmetric encryption of the Russian Federation involves the use of SP network instead of Feistel network used in the old standard. What raises the question of the effectiveness of the encryption algorithm of the new standard.

Acknowledgment. The reported study was funded by the Council for grants of Russian Federation President, according to the research project No. MK-6404.2018.9.

References

1. A Study on Global Data Leaks in 2018. https://infowatch.com/sites/default/files/report/analytics/Global_Data_Breaches_2018.pdf. Accessed 14 Apr 2019
2. Belej, O.: The cryptography of elliptical curves application for formation of the electronic digital signature. In: Hu, Z., Petoukhov, S., Dychka, I., He, M. (eds.) ICCSEEA 2019. AISC, vol. 938, pp. 43–57. Springer, Cham (2020). https://doi.org/10.1007/978-3-030-16621-2_5
3. Boulbot, A., Chillali, A., Mouhib, A.: Elliptic curves over the ring R *. Boletim da Sociedade Paranaense de Matematica **38**(3), 193–201 (2020)

4. Kazmirchuk, S., Anna, I., Sergii, I.: Digital signature authentication scheme with message recovery based on the use of elliptic curves. In: Hu, Z., Petoukhov, S., Dychka, I., He, M. (eds.) ICCSEEA 2019. AISC, vol. 938, pp. 279–288. Springer, Cham (2020). https://doi.org/10.1007/978-3-030-16621-2_26

5. Rahoma, K.H., Elsayed, A.A.: Applying cryptographic techniques for securing the client data signals on the Egyptian optical transport network. In: Hassanien, A.E., Azar, A.T., Gaber, T., Bhatnagar, R., Tolba, M.F. (eds.) AMLTA 2019. AISC, vol. 921, pp. 609–622. Springer, Cham (2020). https://doi.org/10.1007/978-3-030-14118-9_61

6. Almutairi, S., Manimurugan, S., Aborokbah, M.: A new secure transmission scheme between senders and receivers using HVCHC without any loss. EURASIP J. Wirel. Commun. Netw. **2019**, 88 (2019)

7. GOST R 34.10-2012. Information technology. Cryptographic protection of information. Processes of formation and verification of electronic digital signature (2012)

8. GOST R 34.12-2015. Information technology. Cryptographic protection of information. Block cipher (2015)

9. Luptáková, I., Pospíchal, J.: Community cut-off attack on malicious networks. In: Kravets, A., Shcherbakov, M., Kultsova, M., Groumpos, P. (eds.) CIT&DS 2017. CCIS, vol. 754, pp. 697–708. Springer, Cham (2017). https://doi.org/10.1007/978-3-319-65551-2_50

10. Li, H., Ding, M., López-Pérez, D., Fotouhi, A., Lin, Z., Hassan, M.: Performance analysis of the access link of drone base station networks with LoS/NLoS transmissions. In: Duong, T.Q., Vo, N.-S. (eds.) INISCOM 2018. LNICST, vol. 257, pp. 111–121. Springer, Cham (2019). https://doi.org/10.1007/978-3-030-05873-9_10

Use of Fuzzy Neural Networks for a Short Term Forecasting of Traffic Flow Performance

Skorobogatchenko Dmitry[1(✉)] and Viselskiy Sergey[2]

[1] Chair "Systems of Computerized Design Engineering
and Exploratory Engineering", Volgograd State University, Volgograd, Russia
dmitryskor2004@gmail.com
[2] Chair "Construction and Operation of Transport Facilities",
Volgograd State University, Volgograd, Russia
ps8808@mail.ru

Abstract. The method for a short term forecasting of the traffic in the urban road network and of the average vehicle speed is suggested. The author's method is based on a regulatory approach to the calculation of the traffic capacity of the city road network. This method is completed with the methodology of forecasting the changes in the hourly traffic intensity. As the mathematical tool for the implementation of the forecasting methodology, the fuzzy neural networks are taken. It is suggested to make the forecast of short-term traffic intensity taking into account time of day, day of the week and season. On the basis of the data on the traffic capacity, the authors provide the relationships of an average speed change. The example of the calculation of transport flow performance is made in one of the motorways in the city of Volgograd.

Keywords: Forecasting · Fuzzy neural networks · Transport flow ·
Average speed · Traffic capacity · Traffic intensity · City road network

1 Introduction

The effective operation of road transport is largely determined by the transport and operational conditions of roads [1]. One of the most significant transport and operational indicators is the traffic intensity and traffic capacity. Using these indicators the load coefficient of automobile roads is calculated which presents the main characteristics of technical and economic efficiency of the city road network [2]. At the same time, it should be noted that a significant increase in the traffic intensity and a qualitative change of the composition of the traffic flow which is observed in the past decade led to the situation that the largest part of the urban road network is reaching its capacity limits. This situation results in traffic jams, a significant reduction of traffic speed, growth of road accidents' number, increased wear of road infrastructure and ecological load on the urban environment [3].

One of the ways to solve the problems mentioned above is the use of methods of transport flow processes' modeling, software use, information gathering, and transport systems' management in real time [4]. The development of such an intelligent management system of road traffic is an integrated, complex task solved with the use of the modeling of transport systems and traffic regulation.

A. G. Kravets et al. (Eds.): CIT&DS 2019, CCIS 1083, pp. 392–405, 2019.
https://doi.org/10.1007/978-3-030-29743-5_32

It is known that the measures for improvement of traffic organization, safety growth, average speed growth and the productivity growth of road transport vehicles are based on the study and timely analysis of intensity, directions, and character of traffic [5]. However, currently, the issues dealing with the determination of transport flow performance such as intensity and traffic capacity of an urban road network are insufficiently analyzed [6]. So the average annual daily traffic intensity is often recorded not in compliance with the data of continuous automated records and numerical methods, but in compliance with the recommendations [7] according to which the daily traffic intensity on the roads in use is determined as a result of the extrapolation of direct hourly observations during the peak period. The situation is worsened by the facts that in many large cities the possibilities of extensive development of transport networks have exhausted or are close to exhausting [8]. In this regard, the solution of the issues connected with the forecasting of the load of the city road network is currently becoming particularly relevant. The management of the city road network on the basis of an effective method of forecasting and estimating its load will also contribute to the solution of the problems of creation of "smart cities" [9] and intelligent transport systems [10].

The purpose of this research is to forecast the traffic performance in order to create the control systems of the traffic capacity of an urban road network.

2 Literature Review

A significant number of researches is devoted to the study of short-term forecasting of traffic flow performance in the domestic and foreign scientific journals. At the same time, the forecasting methods are based on taking into account the various factors which in the opinion of their authors have a significant impact on the traffic intensity and the traffic capacity of the urban road network. Among the researchers, there is no unified approach to the selection of such factors. These factors can be: the information about road users (demographic indicators, income level per capita and data on users' benefit analysis, car ownership, data on the analysis of points of departure and destination for road users and also macroeconomic indicators affecting the business activity) and also the data about the road network [11]. Because of the instability of road conditions, the attempts are made to decompose the forecasting problem. So, in the scientific paper [12], the authors used the short-term observations in accordance with the ideas mentioned in the article [13] to determine the average annual daily traffic intensity. In the paper [14] at the determination of performance, the authors confine themselves with the conditions of the urban environment of specific cities.

In a number of papers [15], the authors try to combine, when modeling, both physical concepts of transport flows with the mathematical tools, in particular, with graph theory.

It can be stated that despite a lot of research in the field of the forecasting of traffic intensity and traffic management, the overall level of their practical use is not sufficient due to the abundance of determining factors and input information, which sometimes cannot be formalized due to the instability of road conditions and road traffic.

When analyzing the mathematical approaches to the solution of the problem of forecasting and estimating the parameters of traffic flows, we can enumerate regression models [16], models based on time series [17], models based on neural networks [18] and models based on vectors [19]. The establishment of the relations between different pairs of the main characteristics of the traffic flow led to the establishment of two main approaches to the modeling of traffic flows (Fig. 1).

The macroscopic approach considers the vehicle flow as a weakly compressible liquid [20]. This can be seen fair for large distances, much larger than the dimensions of the vehicles themselves and sufficiently large densities (the so-called "limited" movement), when all drivers are forced to obey the same rules, restrictions and, therefore, develop the same or similar strategies [21]. The comparison of traffic flow with the flow of a compressible fluid taking into account the shock wave began in the paper [22]. Within the macroscopic approach, the traffic flow is described by a non-linear system of hyperbolic equations (for density and flow velocity) with the diffusion [23]. A significant generalization of macroscopic hydrodynamic models describing the traffic of vehicles is presented in the article [24]. The microscopic approach considers each car as a separate particle with its own speed and an ultimate goal. The vehicle traffic is an interaction between separate parts according to certain laws that ensure the safety of vehicles, the possibility of acceleration, brake function, etc. This approach is most effective in the simulation of traffic at short distances like at the crossroads and which are comparable with the size of cars. With the development of computer technologies, the micromodels were significantly expanded up to the analysis of the movement of each driver in the stream of vehicles [25].

Quite a lot of researches were devoted to the modeling and forecasting the traffic speed both in the domestic road science and in international literature. In particular, the developed model is published in the paper [26] allows showing the distribution of flow speeds on a traffic diagram.

In the article [27] with the use of multivariate regression analysis the models were developed that allow forecasting the average instantaneous speed of mechanical transport vehicles on multi-lane highways. In the research [28], on the basis of a multifactor correlation and regression analysis, a relationship was established between the technical speed and the intensity of traffic flow reflected by a power function.

A specific characteristic of all the analyzed models is that they, as a rule, miss the forecasting of the average speed of motor vehicles in the hours of the day and days of the week mainly focusing on the relationships between the density and intensity or on making a multifactor vehicle speed estimate. The climatic factors are taken into account only at the assessment of the ratio of the estimated speed.

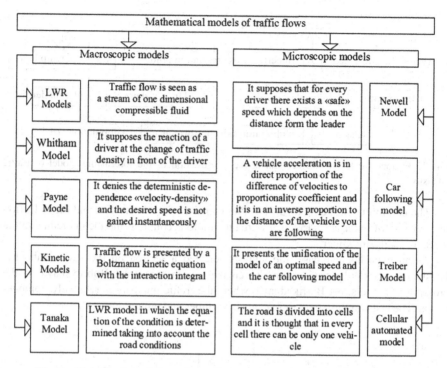

Fig. 1. Classification of the main mathematical models describing traffic flows

According to a number of observations made by the authors in the article [29] when forecasting the traffic capacity the choice of mathematical tools was made in favor of artificial neural networks. Since it is necessary to carry out a short-term forecast of traffic intensity for the vehicle stream intensity, this mathematical apparatus allows using the parameters of the studied indicator for previous years increasing the objectiveness of the forecast results. It should be noted that artificial neural networks are widely used to predict various processes associated with the changes in the transport and operational indicators of roads in the road transport industry [30].

3   Forecasting Methodology of the Load of an Urban Road Network

The methodology suggested for the estimation of the load of the urban road network is based on the regulatory approach to the calculation of the load ratio [31], complementing the industrial norm taking into account the seasonality and short term forecasting of the average annual hourly traffic intensity.

At the first stage, the authors developed a forecasting methodology of the hourly intensity using fuzzy neural networks. The following factors determine the traffic flow intensity (Fig. 2).

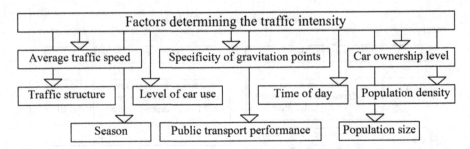

Fig. 2. Factors are taken into account at the construction of the forecasting model of traffic intensity

The conditions of the road surface, the intensity of road services, and the reduction of the width of outer lanes [32, 33] were taken into account, as the factors reducing the traffic capacity in winter.

As an experimental base, the authors selected a section on the street Raboche-Krestyanskaya (Volgograd) from the crossing with the street Bobruyskaya to the crossing with the street Barrikadnaya, where the traffic intensity is relatively homogeneous. The tests on this street took place in summer and winter during the year (Fig. 3).

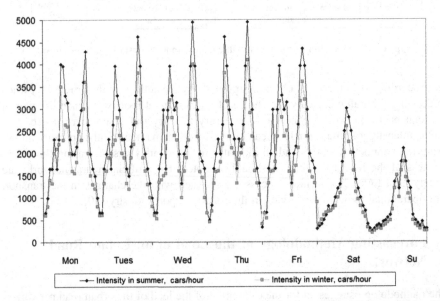

Fig. 3. The general trend of hourly intensity changes during a week on the street Raboche-Krestyanskaya (Volgograd) in various seasons

For the simulation of the process, a neural network has created the structure of which is experimentally modified depending on the number of input signals and the number of tests. The general view of the neural network used in the work can be shown in Fig. 4.

The elements denoted by the symbol Π are multiplied by all the input signals characterizing the state of a complex object of the energy industry and its environment. The elements marked with the symbol $\sum$ are summed up, and the element a/b produces one signal on another. The black dots placed on the lines indicate the weights of these relations. The elements of Layer 1 implement the Gauss function with parameters $\bar{x}_i^k$ и $\bar{\sigma}_i^k$ characterizing the center of the function and its width respectively.

The expressions and arrows put above the diagram show the direction of signal propagation and its interpretation. In the diagram presented above, there are four layers. Each element of Layer 1 implements a membership function to a fuzzy set A_i^k, $i = 1, \ldots, n \ k = 1, \ldots, N$.

The input signals $\bar{x}_i$ come into this layer and the output values of the membership function for these signals are created, i.e. $\mu_{A_i^k}(\bar{x}_i)$. In fact, in this layer, the degree of belonging of the input data $\bar{x}_i$ characterizing the initial state of external factors to the corresponding fuzzy sets A_i^k is estimated. The functional relationship between the input and the output at the nodes of this network is determined by the Gauss function. Its characteristics $\bar{x}_i^k$ and $\bar{\sigma}_i^k$ will be modified in the process of research what which will improve the results of forecasting.

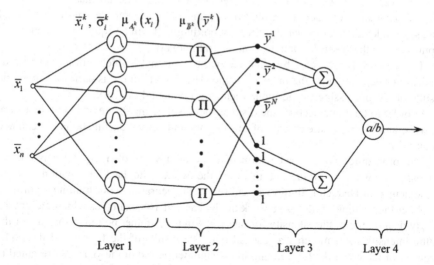

Fig. 4. The general structure of fuzzy neural nets used in the forecasting model of the condition of the state of a complicated object in the energy industry

The number of elements in Layer 1 is equal to the number of all sets belonging to A_i^k. In case of N of fuzzy rules ($k = 1, \ldots, N$) and n input variables ($i = 1, \ldots, n$), taking into account that in each rule any input variable is associated with another fuzzy set, the number of nodes (elements of Layer 1) will be equal to the multiple of the number of input variables n and the number of fuzzy rules N.

At the output of Layer 2, the result of output as a value of the function of belonging to the integral index of the final state of the object $\mu_{\bar{B}^k}(\bar{y}^k)$ is formed. The number of elements of this layer is equal to the number of rules N.

Layer 3 and Layer 4 represent the implementation of the dephasing block. The weights of relations reaching the upper node of Layer 3 and indicated $\bar{y}^k$ are interpreted as the centers of the membership functions to fuzzy sets Bk. These weights as well as the values of the parameters $\bar{x}_i^k$ and $\bar{\sigma}_i^k$ in Layer 1 will be modified during the training process. At the output of Layer 4, the output value of the state of the object $\bar{y}$ will be formed. The structure shown in Fig. 3 is a combination of a neural multi-layer network with the idea of fuzzy inference.

The procedures for the calculation of the output value of yi by the network are standard and therefore are not given in this research. The gradient descent is chosen as the algorithm for training of the neural network.

Practically a fuzzy neural network was selected with five inputs, two hidden layers containing six and twelve neurons respectively. The output layer is presented by a single neuron, the output of which will be the value of the predicted traffic intensity. A general view of the neural network used in the work is shown in Fig. 3.

The input neurons take the values of the vector variables of the input action X = (x1, x2, ..., xn), where n is the number of vector components equal to the number of input parameters characterizing the average annual hourly intensity of traffic (time of day, season, level of car ownership, etc.). Accordingly, it will be equal to the number of input neurons that form the input of the neural network.

The network is presented by only one output neuron Y, which will accept various final values depending on the intensity value. The output neuron is used to display the results of the processing of the input vector by the neural network.

In order to take into account the displacement, single inputs are added to the neural network and all the first elements of the vectors and activation functions are equated to one.

The procedures for the calculation of the output value of Y by the network are standard, so we do not present them in the work. The backpropagation method implemented in Deductor Studio was chosen as the neural network training algorithm.

After the training of neural network on the basis of 168 examples which present the hourly data on the traffic intensity for one week in the summer period, a forecast of the traffic intensity for a month was carried out. The results of the forecast of the traffic intensity of the network after training in the summer period of the year are presented in Fig. 5.

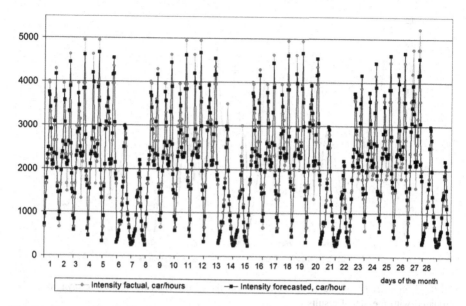

Fig. 5. The results of the forecast of the hourly traffic intensity on the street Raboche-Krestyanskaya for a summer month in comparison with the factual test data obtained after the training of neural nets.

The similar results were obtained at the application of the neural network training on the intensity data collected in winter.

It is obvious that the forecast of the average annual hourly intensity of traffic approximates closely enough the factual information obtained from the tests on the road.

So the mean absolute percentage error at the forecast for a month does not exceed 10% in the summer period and 12–15% in winter (depending on the cumulative impact of negative factors: rain, snow, and ice on roads). Consequently, the quality of the calculation results of the load coefficient based on the forecast of the data on the traffic intensity will be high enough.

The data for the calculation of the forecast of traffic intensity of the road in comparison with actual results for the street Raboche-Krestyanskaya (Volgograd) are presented in Figs. 6 and 7.

At the second stage of tests, the authors processed the results of the traffic intensity forecast and determined the traffic density. In order to verify the convergence, the main diagram of the state of the traffic flow was constructed after the processing of the data on traffic intensity and traffic density of motor vehicles.

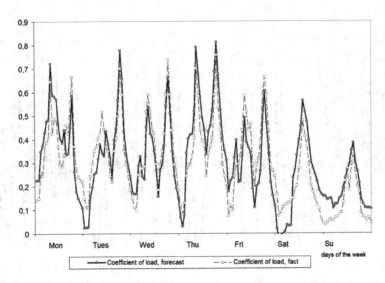

Fig. 6. Data forecast of the load coefficient on the street Raboche-Krestyanskaya in winter compared with the actual results

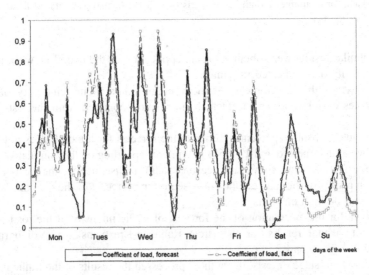

Fig. 7. Data forecast of the load coefficient in the street Raboche – Krestyanskay in the winter period in comparison with the actual test results obtained under the influence of adverse weather and climatic factors

At the third stage, the authors calculated the relationship of the average speed and the traffic intensity of motor vehicles (Fig. 8). The functional relationship of the average speed and the traffic intensity was obtained on the basis of the correlation and regression analysis with the use of the data obtained:

$$v = 138,17 \cdot e^{-0,0008 \cdot N} \tag{1}$$

where v – an average speed of motor vehicles at a road section, km/h; N – forecasted traffic intensity, car/hour.

It should be noted that the obtained relationship corresponds to the results of the paper [34] where the nonlinear dependences of the average traffic speed on the traffic density were also obtained.

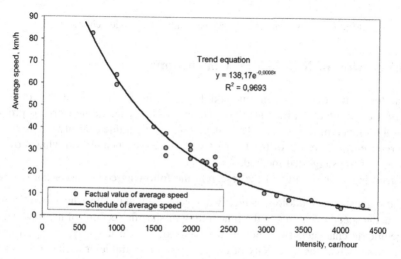

Fig. 8. Data on the relationship of average vehicle speed and the traffic intensity with the trend diagram and functional dependence

At the final stage the authors, using the model of traffic intensity forecast and the functional relation of the average speed and the traffic intensity, obtained an hourly forecast of the traffic average speed in the section under analysis which showed a good convergence with the factual information obtained on the basis of the experimental data on the road (Fig. 9).

Thus, having the data on the structure of the traffic flow on a particular highway of the city's road network, the data on time and season, it is possible to obtain the hourly forecast of the average motor vehicle speed of the traffic flow on the basis of the suggested methodology. The methodology of obtaining the forecasting data about the motor vehicle speed will allow purposefully approaching the development of models for the analysis of the condition of the objects on the road network and correcting the routes of road users using the information about their current situation and forecasting the changes in road conditions in real time.

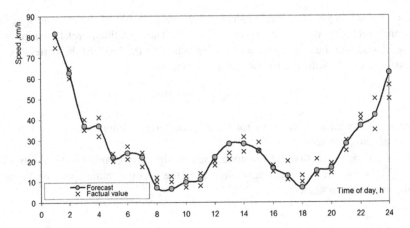

Fig. 9. Assessment of the forecast results of average vehicle speed

4   Discussion of Results and Conclusions

The authors have developed the methodology for the forecasting of the traffic flow performance of the urban road network. The use of fuzzy neural networks is proposed as a tool for this type of research. The calculations of the traffic capacity showed a good convergence of the results of the forecast with the experimental data what proves the efficiency of the suggested method.

According to the results of the research, the following conclusions can be drawn:

1. The suggested methodology is highly adaptable. When training the network in other parts the specific features of the functioning of specific sections of the road network (geometric characteristics, such as the width of the carriageway, transport characteristics, such as the specificity of the composition of traffic or social and economic characteristics, for example, the proximity of shopping malls to which the traffic flows are directed), the suggested methodology can form the basis for the management system of traffic capacity of the urban road network.
2. The author's approach allows taking into account the changes in the traffic capacity of the urban road network not only within an hour or weekdays but also it reflects seasonal changes, including the occurrence of adverse weather and climatic factors.
3. The authors obtained the functions that allow making an hourly forecast of the average traffic speed within the urban road network on the basis of the data on the traffic density taken from the web cameras online and on the basis of the intensity assessment according to the model of fuzzy neural networks, to make an hourly forecast of the average speed of traffic on the city's road network.
4. The method of an hourly forecast of the traffic speed is suggested which takes into account a number of additional factors such as seasonal effect of weather and climatic factors, network load, length of sections, days of the week, time of day and traffic time within a part of a route, places of a mass congestion of vehicles, location of road sections.

On the basis of the suggested methodology, it is possible to plan the specific measures for the traffic management and the operational management of city traffic taking into account the seasonality and the adverse weather and climate factors. One of the future directions of the research is to develop a decision support system at the operational management of the traffic capacity of the urban road network using the suggested forecasting methodology as one of the components. In addition, it is possible to work at the application of the author's approach as a component of technologies for the creation of "smart cities", intelligent transport systems and Internet services for road users, allowing to analyze the development of the transport situation when planning the itinerary in a city.

References

1. Skorobogatchenko, D.A.: Model for the assessment of the operational condition of roads taking into account the qualitative information. Bulletin of the Volgograd State University of Architecture and Civil Engineering. Series: Construction and Architecture, No. 21, pp. 60–66 (2011). (in Russian)
2. Methodical recommendations for the assessment of the traffic capacity of motor highways. Approved by the Ministry of Transportation of the Russian Federation 17.02.2012. Introduced into effect 17.02.2012, 135 p. Moscow (2012). (in Russian)
3. Yu, S.E.: Possible ways of increase of the capacity of the city's road network. Bulletin of the Volgograd State University of Architecture and Civil Engineering. Series: Construction and Architecture, vol. 46, no. 65, pp. 84–94 (2016). (in Russian)
4. GOST R ISO 14813-1-2011 Intellectual transport systems. Scheme of the system construction of intelligent transport systems. Part 1. Service domains in the field of intelligent transport systems, service groups and services, 51 p. « Standartinform » Publications, Moscow (2011). (in Russian)
5. Gasnikov, A.V., Klenov, S.L., Nurminskiy, E.A., Kholodov, Ya.A., Shamrai, N.B.: Introduction into the mathematical modeling of transport flows: study manual. Applications: Blank M.L., Gasnikova E.V., Zamyatin A.A. Malyshev V.A., Kolesnikov A.V., Raigorodskiy A.M; Edited by A.V. Gasnikov, 362 p. MFTI Publ., Moscow (2010). (in Russian)
6. Akulov, V.V.: Analysis of methods of traffic intensity calculation on highways. Internet Journal « Naukovedeniye » , 4 (2012). https://naukovedenie.ru/PDF/1trgsu412.pdf. Accessed 23 Oct 2017. (in Russian)
7. VSN 42-87. The guidelines for the economic studies at the design of roads. TsBNTI Minavtodora Publications, Moscow (1989). (in Russian)
8. Inose, Kh., Khamada, T.: Traffic management, 248 p. Transport Publications, Moscow (1983). (in Russian)
9. Batty, M., et al.: Smart cities of the future. Eur. Phys. J. Spec. Top. 214(1), 481–518 (2012)
10. Hall, R.W.: Handbook of transportation science, p. 737. Kluwer Academic Publishers, Dordrecht (2003)
11. Pingasov, D.V.: Forecast of traffic flows in the regions of the Siberian Federal District of the Russian Federation. Computerized methods and design technologies, vol. 4, no. 43, pp. 82–84. « KREDO- DIALOG » Publ., (2011). (in Russian)
12. Ermachenko, K.A., Shakina, E.I.: Forecasting of traffic flows on the streets of the city of Chita with short-term tests. Graduate student. Supplement to the Scientific Journal "Bull. Transbaikalian State Univ.", 1(13), 86–91 (2013). (in Russian)

13. Isakov, V.G.: Application of the method of hierarchy analysis in the assessment of the traffic capacity of urban roads in winter. Bulletin of the Izhevsk State Technical University named after M.T. Kalashnikov, vol. 2, pp. 170–172 (2011). (in Russian)
14. Gasanov, T.G., Batmanov E.Z., Guseinov M.R.: Determination of the city traffic intensity in the Republic of Dagestan. Bulletin of Moscow Automobile and Road Construction of Technical University (MADI), vol. 3, no. 34, pp. 98–102 (2014). (in Russian)
15. Agafonov, A.A., Myasnikov, V.V.: Assessment and forecasting of traffic flow parameters using the methods of machine training and models of time series forecasting. Computer optics, vol. 38, no 3, pp. 539–549 (2014). (in Russian)
16. Sun, H., Liu, H., Xiao, R., He, R., Ran, B.: Short term traffic forecasting using the local linear regression model. J. Transp. Res. Board **1836**, 143–150 (2003)
17. Box, G.E., Kenkins, G.M., Reinsel, G.C.: Time Series Analysis: Forecasting and Control, 4th edn, p. 784. Wiley, Hoboken (2008)
18. Min, W., Wynter, L.: Real-time road traffic prediction with spatiotemporal correlations. Transp. Res. Part C: Emerg. Technol. **19**(4), 606–616 (2011)
19. Zhang, X., He, G.: Forecasting Approach for Short-term Traffic Flow based on Principal Component Analysis and Combined Neural Network. Syst. Eng. Theory Pract. **27**(8), 167–171 (2007)
20. Haith, F.: Mathematical theory of traffic flows, 287 p. Mir Publishers, Moscow (1966). (in Russian)
21. Buslaev, A.P., Novikov, A.V., Prikhodko, V.M., Tatashev, A.G., Yashina, M.V.: Probabilistic and simulation approaches to the traffic optimization. Edited by the Academician of the Russian Academy of Sciences V.M. Prikhodko, 368 p. Mir Publishers, Moscow (2003). (in Russian)
22. Lighthill, M.J., Whitham, G.B.: On kinematic waves: II. Theory of traffic flow on long crowded roads. In: Proceedings of the Royal Society of London, Series A, vol. 229, pp. 281–345 (1955)
23. Payne H.J.: Models of freeway traffic and control. In: Simulation Council Proceedings 28, Mathematical Models of Public Systems. Edited by G. A. Bekey, vol. 1, pp. 51–61, 22 (1971)
24. Morozov, I.I., Gasnikov, A.V., Tarasov, V.N., Kholodov, Ya, A., Kholodov, A.S.: Numerical study of traffic flows based on hydrodynamic models. Comprehensive research and modeling, vol. 3, no. 4, pp. 389–412 (2011). (in Russian)
25. Eremin, V.M., Fedorov, N.V., Morgachev, K.V.: Some aspects of the combination of uncertainty models. Inf. Anal. Bull. Min. Ind. (Sci. Tech. J.). **56**, 571–575 (2011). (in Russian)
26. Volkov, D.O., Garichev, S.N., Gorbachev, R.A., Moroz, N.N.: Mathematical modeling of the load of the transport network for the calculation of the construction feasibility of new types of transport systems. Production upon Moscow Physical and Technical Institute, vol. 7, no. 3, pp. 69–77 (2015). (in Russian)
27. Car transportation and traffic management. Translated from the English Language. Edited by V.U. Rankin, P. Clafy, S. Halbert and others, 592 p. Transport Publ., Moscow (1981). (in Russian)
28. Chernova, G.A., Vlasova, M.V.: Determination of the relationship between the changes in the technical speed and traffic intensity of motor vehicles. Bulletin of the Volgograd State Technical University. Series: ground transport system, vol. 10, no. 70, pp. 110–113 (2010). (in Russian)
29. Zheng, W., Lee, D.-H., Shi, Q.: Short-term freeway traffic flow prediction: a bayesian combined neural network approach. J. Transp. Eng. **132**(2), 114–121 (2006). (in Russian)

30. Shcherbakov, M.V., Skorobogatchenko, D.A., Avdeev, A.A., Al'-Gunaid, M.A.: Problems of design of systems for the forecasting of the operational state of highways based on the basis of fuzzy neural networks. Bulletin of the Volgograd State Technical University, vol. 10, no. 3 (76), pp. 82–87 (2011). (in Russian)
31. Methodical recommendations on the assessment of traffic capacity of roads: ОДМ 218.2.020-2012: approved by the Ministry of Transportation of the Russian Federation 17.02.2012: introduced into effect since 01.03.2012, 135 p (2012). (in Russian)
32. Bobrova, T.V., Sleptsov, I.V.: Simulation of snow removal solutions for the urban road network in a multi-agent system. Bulletin of Siberian Automobile and Road Institute, vol. 5, no. 33, pp. 51–57 (2013). (in Russian)
33. Isakov, V.G., Dyagelev, M.Y.: Application of the method of hierarchy analysis in the assessment of the traffic capacity of urban roads in winter. Bulletin of the Izhevsk State Technical University named after M.T. Kalashnikov, vol. 2, pp. 170–172 (2011). (in Russian)
34. Zimina, L.A., Berezovskii, A.B.: Assessment of the traffic capacity of the road network. Bulletin of the Scientific Center of Life Security, vol. 1, no. 27, pp. 28–32 (2016). (in Russian)

Effective Quaternion and Octonion Cryptosystems and Their FPGA Implementation

Andrey Andreev[1]($\boxtimes$), Mikhail Chalyshev[1], Vitaly Egunov[1] (iD),
Evgueni Doukhnitch[2], and Kristina Kuznetsova[2] (iD)

[1] Volgograd State Technical University, Volgograd, Russia
andan2005@yandex.ru, mchalyshev@gmail.com,
vegunov@mail.ru
[2] State Maritime University, Novorossiysk, Russia
evgenydukhnich@gmail.com, 1415923@rambler.ru

Abstract. An approach for effective hardware implementation of the proposed quaternion encryption algorithm (HW-R4) as well as modifications for known quaternion HW-QES and octonion HW-OES schemes are discussed. Instead of 3-D rotations as usually, 4-D transformations for encryption with quaternions and 8-D with octonions are suggested. Such size of transformation matrices increases the size of plaintext/ciphertext blocks and eliminates the need to calculate elements of rotation matrices. To speed up an encryption process the HW-R4, HW-QES, and HW-OES include mainly addition and shift operations with modular arithmetic. In our experiments, we used a product Intel (former Altera) OpenCL SDK (AOCL), which allows compiling OpenCL programs for FPGAs. The launch of the developed algorithms was carried out on two devices: the Intel Core i7 920 CPU and the Terasic DE5-Net FPGA (Stratix V). Experimental results show that the proposed algorithms and modifications are about 30–50% more effective in the encryption speed of signals than the original HW-QES/HW-OES. Additionally, HW-R4 is shown to be more effective in the encryption quality of images than the original QES. Our approach can also be used for robustness increasing when the Feistel network is added to the system.

Keywords: Quaternion · Octonion · Encryption ·
Known plaintext-ciphertext attack · Image/Signal encryption · HW-QES ·
HW-OES · HW-R4 · Altera/Intel OpenCL SDK · FPGA

1 Introduction

Increasingly growing amounts of information transfers, especially with the development of the Internet of things (IoT), require fast encryption algorithms. On the other hand, the increasing performance of computing devices reduces the cryptographic strength of the encryption algorithms used. This problem causes the relevance of constant developments in the field of information security.

© Springer Nature Switzerland AG 2019
A. G. Kravets et al. (Eds.): CIT&DS 2019, CCIS 1083, pp. 406–419, 2019.
https://doi.org/10.1007/978-3-030-29743-5_33

In the field of computing, the technology of programmable logic integrated circuits (FPGAs) is particularly well suited for streaming information processing, for example, data encryption.

With its reconfigurable architecture and low power consumption, FPGAs can compete with graphics coprocessors in performance and energy efficiency. It is also worth noting that not all algorithms have the ability to apply massive parallelism, which means that graphics accelerators may be inferior to the pipeline processing on FPGA (especially when the calculation results are formed on the basis of the previous).

This paper considers the implementation of encryption algorithms HW-R4 (the new one), HW-QES, HW-OES, using Intel (Altera) OpenCL SDK, and the results of their testing in DE5-Net device.

The quaternion number system is widely used to control rotations in three-dimensional space. The quaternion number system may be applied in computation models due to its matrix representation. The use of quaternion apparatus in building cryptosystems has become widespread due to their relatively high encryption speed. In addition, it is explained by the simplicity of constructing the decrypting matrix by transposing the key matrix. It has been applied as a mathematical model in encryption by several researchers. In [1, 2], a new quaternion encryption scheme (QES) is proposed for signal encryption providing good hiding properties. These schemes and other ones [4] are used on their own or are supplemented with a Feistel network [6, 7] to increase their robustness. Another advantage of these ciphers is the possibility of their modification, suitable for hardware implementation [4].

The QES works as follows, a sequence of signal samples is arranged as a sequence of frames containing three three-component vectors, represented as a 3×3 matrix B, i-th column B_i of which is the i-th mentioned above sample-vector ($i = 1, 2, 3$). Each vector Bi in a frame is encrypted by applying to it the same transformation represented by its multiplication from one side by some quaternion q and the other side by its inverse q^{-1} producing the ciphertext vector B_i':

$$B_i' = q^{-1}B_iq, \ i = \overline{1,3} \tag{1}$$

or, in the terms of plaintext-ciphertext matrices, (1) may be rewritten as

$$B' = q^{-1}Bq \tag{2}$$

Transformation (2) may be also represented using matrix multiplication of the plaintext matrix B by a secret key matrix depending on q and producing the ciphertext matrix B'. It was expected that QES provides high security due to using dynamic key matrix obtained by changing the next quaternion components. But, this algorithm is a particular case of the well-known Hill cipher (HC) [3]. The Hill cipher is susceptible to the known plaintext-ciphertext attack (KPCA), therefore QES can be broken with the KPCA, and the secret key matrix can be obtained.

The aim of the paper [4] was to show that QES is susceptible to KPCA and to overcome (repair) this weakness of QES by adjusting the frame size and the quaternion update procedure. In addition, hardware-oriented implementation of the QES modification (HW-QES) was proposed (see also [8]) based on the ideas from [5]. In [6, 7] it was suggested to improve the cryptographic security by adding the Feistel network to QES with the implementation of modular arithmetic [9]. Despite the fact that proposed quaternion model features fast computation advantages over others, yet its encryption speed is not always sufficient for many applications.

In this paper, we propose a hardware-oriented algorithm and fast FPGA implementation of the modified QES (HW-R4) with 4×4 matrix B and modular arithmetic which can be used singly or with followed Feistel network as in [6, 7]. Such size of matrix B increases the size of plaintext/ciphertext blocks (frames) and eliminates the need to calculate elements of rotation matrices. This modification significantly speeds up the process and simplifies its implementation.

Alongside the HW-R4 we consider an FPGA-implementation of octonion crypto algorithm HW-OES [4], similar to the implementation of a quaternion-based hardware-oriented algorithm, described in [8], and some improvements of such implementation, which also can be applied to all mentioned algorithms (HW-QES, HW-R4, and HW-OES).

The rest of the paper is organized as follows. Section 2 introduces the main notions for quaternion and provides necessary details for QES. Section 3 shows proposed QES modification (R4) and contains a description of the effective hardware implementation of the proposed HW-R4 using mainly operations of addition and shift. Section 4 is devoted to octonion-based OES and HW-OES. Description of FPGA implementation for HW-R4 and HW-OES is given in Sect. 5. Details of implementation, as well as modifications of formerly known implementation of HW-QES, experimental results of signal and image encryption quality of the proposed HW-R4 algorithm versus the original QES, are presented in Sect. 6. Security and statistical analysis of the proposed HW-R4 are discussed in Sect. 7. Conclusions are given in Sect. 8.

2   QES Details

The quaternion q is a hyper-complex number represented by

$$q = w + xi + yj + zk, \tag{3}$$

where w, x, y, z are real numbers, i, j, k forms an orthonormal basis in $\mathbb{R}^3$,

$$i^2 = j^2 = k^2 = ijk = -1. \tag{4}$$

Inverse q^{-1} of the quaternion q is a quaternion such that

$$q^{-1}q = qq^{-1} = 1, \tag{5}$$

and

$$q^{-1} = \frac{w - xi - yj - zk}{|q|^2}, \tag{6}$$

where

$$|q| = \sqrt{w^2 + x^2 + y^2 + z^2} \tag{7}$$

is the norm of q. Vector transform (1) is a rotation of vectors of data in a three-dimensional space if $|q| = 1$, and may be represented as a matrix-vector product

$$B'_i = \Gamma(q)B_i, i = \overline{1,3}, \tag{8}$$

where the rotation matrix is

$$\Gamma(q) = \frac{1}{|q|^2} \begin{bmatrix} |q|^2 - 2(y^2 + z^2) & 2(xy + wz) & 2(xz - wy) \\ 2(xy - wz) & |q|^2 - 2(x^2 + z^2) & 2(yz + wx) \\ 2(xz + wy) & 2(yz - wx) & |q|^2 - 2(x^2 + y^2) \end{bmatrix} \tag{9}$$

Equation (8) may be written similar to (2) as

$$B' = \Gamma(q)B. \tag{10}$$

Plaintext matrix B can be restored from (10) using (9)

$$B = (\Gamma(q))^{-1}B', \tag{11}$$

where $(\Gamma(q))^{-1}$ is the inverse of $\Gamma(q)$, i.e.

$$(\Gamma(q))^{-1}\Gamma(q) = \Gamma(q)(\Gamma(q))^{-1} = E, \tag{12}$$

where E is 3×3 unity matrix such that $e_{ij} = \begin{cases} 1, i = j \\ 0, i \neq j \end{cases}$; note that $(\Gamma(q))^{-1} = \Gamma(q)'$, where X' is a transpose of the matrix X. The QES assumes that each next frame is enciphered using another quaternion, three components (x, y, z) of which are obtained as three row elements of the matrix (9) used for encryption of the previous frame whereas its scalar component w, is set to zero, that is

$$q_m = \begin{cases} w + xi + yj + zk, m = 0 \\ 0 + x_mi + y_mj + z_mk, m > 0 \end{cases}, \tag{13}$$

where $x_m = (\Gamma(q_{m-1}))_{11}$, $y_m = (\Gamma(q_{m-1}))_{12}$, $x_m = (\Gamma(q_{m-1}))_{13}$, $m > 0$ and the key matrix used for the m-th frame is $\Gamma(q_m)$. The next quaternion components may be taken not from the first row as shown above but from the other rows of the matrix (9) as well, or its columns. Hence, encryption algorithms [1, 2, 4, 6, 7] use dynamically changing matrices of the form (9) in (10), (11) that are claimed to increase its security contrary to the usage of the static matrix (9).

3 Algorithm R4 and Its Hardware Orientation (HW-R4)

The quaternion (3) can be represented in matrix form as

$$\Gamma(q) = \frac{1}{|q|} \begin{bmatrix} w & x & y & z \\ -x & w & -z & y \\ -y & z & w & -x \\ -z & -y & x & w \end{bmatrix} \tag{14}$$

Then the transformations (10) and (11) can be considered as a matrix cipher (algorithm R4) for 4×4 frame B of data. In contrast to QES, it has a simple way to form a matrix (14) using components of quaternion and greater size of blocks of data to speed up the process.

Since a hardware-oriented algorithm is understood as a transformation using simple and fast operations such as addition and shift, algorithm HW-R4 uses quaternions like

$$q = w + t(xi + yj + zk),$$

where $w^2 = x^2 + y^2 + z^2$, $t = 2\tau$, $(\tau \in Z+)$ and

$$w = 2^p + 1, tx = 2^{p+\tau}\alpha, ty = 2^{\frac{p+1}{2}+\tau}\beta, tz = 2^\tau\gamma,$$
$$p = 2f + 1, |d| = (2^p + 1)\sqrt{(1 + 2^{2\tau})}, \tag{15}$$
$$\alpha, \beta, \gamma \in \{-1, 1\}, F > f \geq 0, T > \tau \geq 0$$

Therefore a key matrix is looked as:

$$\Gamma(q) = \frac{1}{|q|} \begin{bmatrix} 2^p + 1 & 2^{p+\tau}\alpha & 2^{\frac{p+1}{2}+\tau}\beta & 2^\tau\gamma \\ -2^{p+\tau}\alpha & 2^p + 1 & -2^\tau\gamma & 2^{\frac{p+1}{2}+\tau}\beta \\ -2^{\frac{p+1}{2}+\tau}\beta & 2^\tau\gamma & 2^p + 1 & -2^{p+\tau}\alpha \\ -2^\tau\gamma & -2^{\frac{p+1}{2}+\tau}\beta & 2^{p+\tau}\alpha & 2^p + 1 \end{bmatrix} \tag{16}$$

Decryption matrix $(\Gamma(q))^{-1} = \Gamma(q)'$ is a transpose of the matrix (16). Elements of (16) belong to the set Z^+_N, where $N = 2^n$. They are integer numbers if $\tau > 0$. Performing all operations modulo 2^n allows to hold all operands of the algorithm in the specified format.

The division by the quaternion norm in (16) and the same for decryption can be replaced by single multiplication by the multiplicative inverse of $|q|^2$ modulo 2^n after decoding:

$$M = \frac{1}{(2^p + 1)^2(1 + 2^{2\tau})} \mod 2^n \tag{17}$$

Division by square of the norm in (17) is correct since according to (15) square of the norm is an odd number having multiplicative inverse modulo 2^n. Calculating this value can be replaced by reading it from the read-only memory (ROM) with $2^{n-1} \times n$-bits size.

As far as entries of (16) contain contributors being powers of two when these powers exceed n, they vanish modulo 2^n, and matrix (16) degenerates to the unity matrix and does not provide hiding the plaintext. This degradation can be avoided if the following conditions are fulfilled for the elements of the matrix (16):

$$\max\left(p, \tau, (p+\tau), \left(\tau + \frac{p+1}{2}\right)\right) < n \text{ or } (p+\tau) < n \qquad (18)$$

Since p, $\tau > 0$, it can be written from (15) and (18):

$$p, \tau < \frac{n}{2} \text{ and } f < \frac{n}{4} \qquad (19)$$

For example, if $n = 8$, $\tau = 3$, $f = 1$, p = 3, the matrix (16) looks like:

$$\Gamma(q) = \frac{1}{185} \begin{bmatrix} 2^3 + 1 & 2^6\alpha & 2^5\beta & 2^3\gamma \\ -2^5\alpha & 2^3 + 1 & -2^3\gamma & 2^5\beta \\ -2^5\beta & 2^3\gamma & 2^3 + 1 & -2^6\alpha \\ -2^3\gamma & -2^5\beta & 2^6\alpha & 2^3 + 1 \end{bmatrix} \qquad (20)$$

Key quaternion generation can be organized as mentioned above by using a rotation matrix (9) applied for constructing an "infinite encryption keyspace" [6, 7]. For HW-R4, it will be less computation-intensive to use a pseudo-random number generator (PRNG) to form components of q according to (15). Output bits of PRNG the number can be grouped as following: log_2 n/2 bits for τ, log_2 n/4 bits for f, and 1 bit per each for α, β, γ.

4 Octonion-Based HW-OES

The octonion encryption system (OES) algorithm, as well as its hardware orientation modification HW-OES, are discussed in [4], so this paper provides only a brief description.

The OES algorithm assumes that each point of the image can be represented as a quaternion which elements are components of the color of that point:

$$B(x, y) = 0 + r(x, y)i + g(x, y)j + b(x, y)k \qquad (21)$$

Octonion, in this case, can be obtained by presenting two pixels of the image with one vector of dimension 8. One 8×8 frame B of plaintext consists of 8 such vectors.

Actually, the octonion is as follows:

$$o = w + xe_1 + ye_2 + ze_3 + ae_4 + be_5 + ce_6 + de_7 \tag{22}$$

where w, x, y, z, a, b, c, d are real numbers, and e_i are numbers forming an orthonormal basis.

Similarly to the previous algorithms, we chose the parameter values such as:

$$o = w + t(xe_1 + ye_2 + ze_3 + ae_4 + be_5 + ce_6 + de_7)$$

where $x^2 + y^2 + z^2 + a^2 + b^2 + c^2 + d^2 = w^2$ and $t = 2^{-i}$.

The resulting key-matrix for HW-OES would be:

$$\Gamma(o) = \begin{bmatrix} 2^m+1 & \alpha 2^{m-1-i} & \beta 2^{m-1-i} & \gamma 2^{m-1-i} & \delta 2^{m-1-i} & \lambda 2^{m/2-i} & \mu 2^{m-1-i} & -\rho 2^{-i} \\ -\alpha 2^{m-1-i} & 2^m+1 & -\delta 2^{m-1-i} & -\rho 2^{-i} & \beta 2^{m-1-i} & -\mu 2^{m-1-i} & \lambda 2^{m/2-i} & \gamma 2^{m-1-i} \\ -\beta 2^{m-1-i} & \delta 2^{m-1-i} & 2^m+1 & -\lambda 2^{m/2-i} & -\alpha 2^{m-1-i} & \gamma 2^{m-1-i} & -\rho 2^{-i} & \mu 2^{m-1-i} \\ -\gamma 2^{m-1-i} & -\rho 2^{-i} & \lambda 2^{m/2-i} & 2^m+1 & -\mu 2^{m-1-i} & -\beta 2^{m-1-i} & \delta 2^{m-1-i} & -\alpha 2^{m-1-i} \\ -\delta 2^{m/2-i} & -\beta 2^{m-1-i} & \alpha 2^{m-1-i} & \mu 2^{m-1-i} & 2^m+1 & -\rho 2^{-i} & -\gamma 2^{m-1-i} & \lambda 2^{m/2-i} \\ -\lambda 2^{m/2-i} & \mu 2^{m-1-i} & -\gamma 2^{m-1-i} & \beta 2^{m-1-i} & \rho 2^{-i} & 2^m+1 & -\alpha 2^{m-1-i} & -\delta 2^{m/2-i} \\ -\mu 2^{m/2-i} & -\lambda 2^{m/2-i} & \rho 2^{-i} & -\delta 2^{m-1-i} & \gamma 2^{m-1-i} & \alpha 2^{m-1-i} & 2^m+1 & -\beta 2^{m-1-i} \\ -\rho 2^{-i} & -\gamma 2^{m-1-i} & -\mu 2^{m-1-i} & \alpha 2^{m-1-i} & -\lambda 2^{m/2-i} & \delta 2^{m/2-i} & \beta 2^{m-1-i} & 2^m+1 \end{bmatrix}$$

$$\tag{23}$$

where $\alpha, \beta, \gamma, ..., \rho \in \{-1, 1\}$, $m = 2k$, $K \geq k > 0$, $|i| < I$.

Octonion encryption algorithm uses a larger number of parameters compared to the quaternion algorithms (9 to 5), which determines the greater encryption strength, and also means a smaller number of rounds of encryption to achieve adequate protection of the source text/signal. However, one round of encryption can take more time due to the larger size of the matrix and data vector.

5   FPGA Implementations of HW-R4, HW-QES and HW-OES

The structure of the hardware implementation of HW-R4 (similar to HW-QES, and HW-OES) is shown in Fig. 1. There are EC (encrypting circuit) and DC (decrypting circuit) for computations (15) and matrix multiplication by (16) for EC (without division by norm) or its transpose for DC. This multiplication of 4-component column vector of the plaintext by the matrix (16) in the EC takes time about 4 additions with shifts. On the decryption side, there is a circuit for calculating a value $|q|^2 mod(2^n + 1) = \left(2^p + 1\right)^2 (1 + 2^{2\tau}) mod(2^n + 1)$ as an address for the ROM.

Decrypted text from DC is multiplied by ROM output number. It should be noted that the PRNG on the transmitting and receiving sides must have the same large pool containing random information, and the same seed value (the parameter specifying the beginning of the pseudo-random numbers in the sequence) for their synchronization.

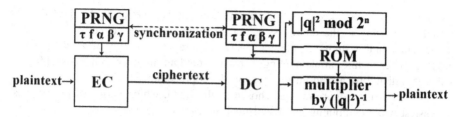

Fig. 1. Structure of FPGA implementation.

As an example of a hardware implementation of mentioned algorithms, we used FPGAs in contrast to fast but very expensive specialized application-specific integrated circuits (ASICs).

6 Experimental Results

In our experiments, we used Intel (former Altera) OpenCL SDK (AOCL) product, a high-level synthesis (HLS) technology, which allows compiling high-level OpenCL (mostly C-like) programs to register-transfer logic (RTL), suitable for FPGAs, via intermediate representation in the hardware-descriptive language (HDL). In a few words, the process of preparing a hardware wiring for FPGA includes writing an OpenCL representation of future scheme (core), then its pre-optimization using special AOCL compiler key – c, and afterwards – compiling the binary image for the FPGA (takes many hours) and its testing using host C (OpenCL) program. Pair of core and host programs can be located on FPGA co-processor and host PC (as in our case) or inside one chip in case of system-on-crystal (SoC) implementation. In the process, the described key stage is writing and optimizing OpenCL core source code.

The general implementation scheme is similar for all algorithms (except stage 5). It looks as follows:

1. Selection of random parameters α, β, γ, ..., ρ;
2. Construction of the matrix Γ, based on the quaternion q (octonion in the case of OES);
3. Multiplying the data vectors of input frame B by the key matrix;
4. Steps 1–3 are repeated l times for the current data frame;
5. (For the HW-QES algorithm each encoded frame vector is
6. multiplied by a factor $K_q = 1/|q|^2$);
7. Steps 1–5 are performed for each frame of plaintext.

Decrypting occurs in the same way, except that the matrix Γ must be transposed. Decrypted frames for HW-R4 and HW-OES must be multiplied by a factor M (17) or $Ko = 1/|o|^2$ correspondently. The number of rounds of encryption 1 for different algorithms is different: for HW-QES - 14, HW-R4 - 13, HW-OES – 2. This number provides an optimal cryptographic strength of the algorithm.

As it was mentioned above, FPGA implementation of HW-QES using AOCL was considered in [8].

In previous works, a sequence of random numbers was generated by the CPU and passed as an array to the coprocessor, but this approach is not effective in terms of performance. In this study, an attempt was made to replace an array of numbers with a single number, while implementing a pseudo-random number generator (PRNG), which is initiated by a random number, on the coprocessor.

The Park-Miller algorithm was chosen as the RNG, which is one of the simplest and fastest while combining good statistical indicators [10].

The testing of the developed algorithms was carried out on two devices: the Intel Core i7 920 CPU and the Terasic DE5-Net FPGA (Stratix V). On the CPU, the program was run on a single core. Hardware implementation of HW-R4 together with PRNG took up about 79% of the FPGA chip area. The test compared the performance of different devices.

The encryption time measured for all the mentioned algorithms are given in Table 1.

The original HW-QES algorithm on the FPGA took about 80% of the device memory, while the modified one took 89% of the logic gates. The transfer of the PRNG to the FPGA scheme helped to achieve an acceleration of about 30% relative to the previous version of the algorithm (see Table 1). However, the selected simplified version of the PRNG (Park-Miller generator [10]) may have a negative impact on the quality of statistical tests and cryptographic stability.

In general, the results show that the cipher implementation in the FPGA circuit has helped to achieve acceleration of approximately 35–37 times relative to one CPU core, HW-R4 let us achieve acceleration up to 1,16 times compared to HW-QES. The main improvement is likely to be faster construction of the key matrix, despite the fact that its size is larger because only 4 different elements are required to fill it.

PRNG implementation in FPGA lets us obtain 1,3 times gain, so common speed-up for HW-R4 compared to HW-QES is about 1,5 times.

Table 1. Encryption time (s) of the devices.

Plaintext size (bytes)	QES (CPU)	HW-QES (FPGA) old version	HW-QES (FPGA)	R4 (CPU)	HW-R4 (FPGA)	HW-OES (FPGA)
1024 × 1024	0.366	0.015	0.012	0.278	0.011	0.038
8 × 1024 × 1024	2.924	0.113	0.089	2.233	0.077	0.329
16 × 1024 × 1024	5.895	0.226	0.176	4.470	0.156	0.455
32 × 1024 × 1024	11.808	0.449	0.351	8.984	0.311	0.633
64 × 1024 × 1024	23.493	0.901	0.703	17.845	0.622	0.830

The HW-OES algorithm also shows efficiency of a hardware implementation of the algorithm compared to the CPU implementation. In addition, it demonstrates a non-linear dependence of the operating time on the amount of data, working almost 4 times slower than HW-R4 to 16 MB of data, and about 30% slower at 64 MB of data. It should be noted that HW-OES has the best statistical indicators in comparison with other algorithms.

For a fair comparison of the quality of the encryption algorithms, the number of iterations $l = 1$ was used. First, the values of the function were used as plain text:

$$function(t) = (int)(10 * (\sin t - \cos 3t))modN. \tag{24}$$

The first 300 signal values (24), encrypted using algorithms, are graphically represented in Fig. 2. It is clear from the visual inspection of Fig. 2 that the algorithm HW-R4 gives better encryption quality than the original QES. The inter-pixel correlation coefficient was used to evaluate the quality of encryption. Table 2 presents the test results. Note that the closer correlation coefficient to zero the better.

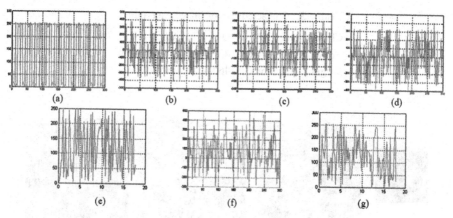

(a)   (b)   (c)   (d)

(e)   (f)   (g)

Fig. 2. Encrypting of plaintext (a) by QES (b), M-QES (c), R4 (d), HW-QES (e), HW-R4 (f) and HW-OES (g).

Table 2. Correlation coefficients of encryption when processing 0.25 GB of data (24).

	QES	M-QES	R4	HW-QES	HW-R4	HW-OES
Correlation coefficients	−0,1197	0,077509	−0,0000001	0,0604	0,09024	0,0044

Additionally, an analysis of the quality of the algorithms was performed when working with images. Figure 3 and Table 3 demonstrate the quality of software-oriented algorithms and Fig. 4 and Table 4 – of hardware-oriented algorithms. Quality indicators are the correlation coefficient and irregular deviations. For an equivalent evaluation of the algorithms, a single iteration was used for the analysis.

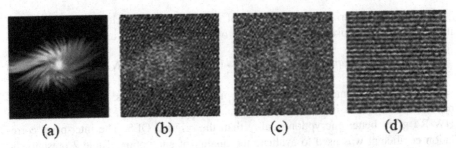

Fig. 3. Encryption of the original image (a) using: QES (b), M-QES (c), R4 (d).

Table 3. Characteristics of image encrypting.

Characteristics	QES	M-QES	R4
Correlation coefficient	0,1920	0,1043	0,0039
Irregular deviations	46062	47452	46914

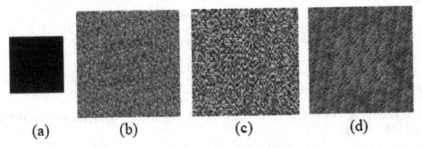

Fig. 4. Encryption of the original image (a) using: HW-QES (b), HW-R4 (c), HW-OES (d).

Table 4. Characteristics of image encrypting.

Characteristics	HW-QES	HW-R4	HW-OES
Correlation coefficient	0,02457	0,0155	−0,0728
Irregular deviations	22805,03	27054	10521,33

7 Security and Statistical Analysis

To prove the robustness of the proposed scheme, the statistical analysis has been performed. It is usually evaluated by histograms of the encrypted images. The results (Figs. 5 and 6) presented below show that our proposed modifications strongly withstand statistical attacks. The histograms of the encrypted by our proposed HW-R4, and by HW-QES images are very close to uniform distribution; they are significantly different from those of the original image and bear no statistical resemblance to the original image.

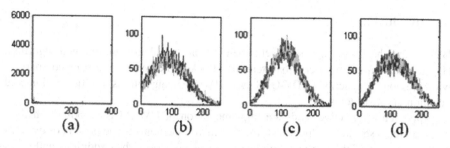

Fig. 5. Histograms: source image (a), QES (b), M-QES (c), R4 (d).

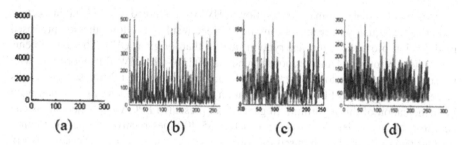

Fig. 6. Histograms: source image (a), HW-QES (b), HW-R4 (c), HW-OES (d).

It should be noted that, as in the case of the M-QES algorithm, before encrypting, an exclusive OR operation is applied to plaintext elements with quaternion elements. The HW-R4 algorithm dynamically generates transformation matrices, the number of variants of which determines the degree of security of the cryptographic system. This number is calculated as the number of possible combinations of parameters from the set (15), which contains five parameters: α, β, $\gamma \in \{-1,1\}$, $\tau \in \{0, ... T-1\}$, $f \in \{0, ... F\}$. These parameters can be formed, for example, using a pseudo-random number generator [11].

We estimate the number of possible combinations of five parameters. Taking into account (18), this number will be equal to 2^C where

$$C = log_2 \frac{n}{2} + log_2 \frac{n}{4} + 3, \tag{25}$$

since the values are binary. If $n = 32$, the total number of combinations is 2^{10}. If the plaintext is subjected to $l = 13$ consecutive transformations, then the number of possible combinations will be 2^{130} and is considered to be a sufficient number of searches, which provides minimal sufficient protection against hacking and is a parameter of the AES algorithm. Thus, the degree of security of such a cryptographic system is quite high. It is possible to raise the level of protection with a smaller number of iterations l due to the subsequent use of the Feistel network, by analogy with [6].

8 Conclusion

We present the results of the development of the new hardware-oriented algorithm HW-R4 of the quaternion cryptosystem, its FPGA implementation and its comparison with previously described HW-QES and HW-OES algorithms for quaternion and octonion cryptosystems.

Approach to effective hardware implementation of HW-R4 is proposed which is based on the restriction of the transformation matrix elements to the powers of two that allows escaping of the use of multiplications and divisions when additions and shifts are necessary only. Algorithm HW-R4 showed good results for signal and image encryption.

Quality of signal and image encryption of HW-R4 is studied using visual inspection and numerical quality measures. From the obtained results, it follows that the proposed modification provides higher encryption quality than original QES. The experiments show the advantage of the proposed versions of HW-QES/HW-R4 algorithms with internal PRNG relative to the host array of random numbers in 1,3 times. New results presented for HW-OES FPGA implementation also show the efficiency of the hardware implementation of this algorithm. In general, all presented FPGA implementations can help to achieve acceleration of approximately 35-40 times relative to one CPU core.

Our approach can also be used for robustness increasing when the Feistel network is added to the cipher.

Acknowledgments. Work is performed with the financial support of the Russian Foundation for Basic Research - project # 18-47-340010 ra and the financial support of the Administration of Volgograd region.

References

1. Nagase, T., Komata, M., Araki, T.: Secure signals transmission based on quaternion encryption scheme. In: Proceedings 18th International Conference on Advanced Information Networking and Application (AINA 2004), pp. 35–38. IEEE Computer Society (2004)
2. Nagase, T., Koide, R., Araki, T., Hasegawa, Y.: A new quadripartite public-key cryptosystem. In: International Symposium on Communication and Information Technology (ISCIT 2004), Sapporo, Japan, pp. 74–79, 26–29 October 2004
3. Stallings, W.: Cryptography and Network Security, pp. 41–46. Prentice Hall, Upper Saddle River (2006)
4. Doukhnitch, E., Chefranov, A., Mahmoud, A.: Encryption schemes with hyper-complex number systems and their hardware-oriented implementation. In: Theory and Practice of Cryptography Solutions for Secure Information Systems, pp. 110–133. IGI Global, Pennsylvania (2013)
5. Doukhnitch, E., Ozen, E.: Hardware-oriented algorithm for quaternion valued matrix decomposition. IEEE Transactions on Circuits and Systems–II: Express Briefs, **58**(4), 225–229, 2011
6. Dzwonkowski, M., Rykaczewski, R.: A quaternion-based modified feistel cipher for multimedia transmission. Telecommun. Rev. + Telecommun. News **8**(9), 1177–1181 (2014)

7. Dzwonkowski, M., Papaj, M., Rykaczewski, R.: A new quaternion. based encryption method for DICOM images. IEEE Trans. Image Process. **24**(11), 4614–4622 (2015)
8. Andreev, A., Doukhnitch, E., Egunov, V., Zharikov, D., Nozdrenkov, S.: Implementing encryption with quaternions on the basis of programmable logic using Altera OpenCL SDK/ (CEUR Workshop Proceedings; Vol. 1576), pp. 396–401 (2016)
9. Sastry, V.U.K., Kumar, K.A.: A modified feistel cipher involving modular arithmetic addition and modular arithmetic inverse of a key matrix. Int. J. Adv. Comput. Sci. Appl. (IJACSA 2012) **3**(7), 40–43 (2012)
10. A Fast High Quality Pseudo Random Number Generator for nVidia CUDA W. B. Langdon https://pdfs.semanticscholar.org/9ed6/10a88217feedda2b8fe1286cd3b7e47cc604.pdf
11. Ismail, A.I., Amin, M., Diab, H.: How to Repair the Hill Cipher. J. Zhejiang Univ Sci. A **7** (12), 2022–2030 (2006)

Smart Contracts for Multi-agent Interaction of Regional Innovation Subjects

Leyla Gamidullaeva[1] ⓘ, Alexey Finogeev[1(✉)] ⓘ, Sergey Vasin[1] ⓘ,
Anton Finogeev[1] ⓘ, and Sergey Schevchenko[2] ⓘ

[1] Penza State University, 40, Krasnaya str, Penza, Russia
gamidullaeva@gmail.com, alexeyfinogeev@gmail.com,
pspu-met@mail.ru, fanton3@yandex.ru
[2] National Technical University «Kharkiv Polytechnic Institute»,
2, Kyrpychova str, Kharkiv, Ukraine
s.v.shevchenko55@gmail.com

Abstract. The main obstacle to effective interaction between innovation agents is high innovation transaction costs. The development of innovation requires the continuous interaction of participants at all stages of the innovation process, from idea to commercialization. The article discusses the creation of a safe and reliable way to support such interaction in regional innovation systems based on blockchain technology and smart contracts. This approach is recommended to exclude unfair and fraudulent actions on the part of participants. Another feature is the transfer of third-party functions to a smart contract to ensure safe communication. The smart contract will allow, on the one hand, to realize trustful and reliable relationships between the project participants themselves, and, on the other hand, between participants and stakeholders. The article discusses the possibilities of the Ethereum blockchain platform, with the help of which the main components of a smart contract were synthesized for concluding contracts for creating and introducing innovations, transferring intellectual property rights, using licenses, etc. The basis of the smart contract is a distributed registry of transactions and a database with descriptions of innovative objects.

Keywords: Smart contract · Blockchain · Ethereum platform · Big data ·
Cyber-social system · Innovation system · Data mining

1 Introduction

The regional innovation systems existing nowadays are uncoordinated due to insufficient interaction between them. The main barrier impeding efficient interaction of innovation activity subjects (agents) in Russia is high transaction costs. It is necessary to simulate interactions of regional activity participants to have a qualitative and quantitative understanding of the role of relationships between environment's components, their impact on the development of a concrete region. One of the ways to develop innovation is the growth of interactions between the participants of the regional innovation system in the process of creating an idea before being implemented in a real commercial project. There are certain problems of innovative enterprises

© Springer Nature Switzerland AG 2019
A. G. Kravets et al. (Eds.): CIT&DS 2019, CCIS 1083, pp. 420–434, 2019.
https://doi.org/10.1007/978-3-030-29743-5_34

associated with the growth of instability and uncertainty of relations and relations between them. This causes an increase in transaction costs and, consequently, an increase in the cost of creating and promoting innovation. Innovation costs are not associated with resource changes. They have a transactional nature, which is determined by the interactions of the participants to enter into mutually beneficial contacts. Such transaction costs will be considered the main barrier to the innovative development of enterprises, since they actually reduce the owners' interest in the introduction and use of innovations [1, 2].

It is known that the process of innovation creation is a result of interactions between innovation activity agents, It depends both on transactions within a company and on established relations of an economic agent with the institutional environment. The institutional environment creates conditions for cooperation of economic agents with other innovation activity participants in terms of searching for information and other resources, experience sharing. It determines the behavior of economic agents by shaping their behavior sets, formal institutional structures that are crucial when making decisions on creation and implementation of innovations. According to the neoinstitutional approach the innovation system is a complex open structure providing interaction of economic agents, formal and informal regional institutions.

Innovation process participants should interact freely to gain experience of joint projects aimed at development and commercialization of innovations. This requires efficient coordinated relations within the "subject-project-medium" continuum. Regarding the intensification of interactions of a subject, a project and a medium the key process is self-organization providing a decrease of transaction costs, which is based on promoting the emergent effect unavailable to some innovation activity participants. Minimization of transaction costs means determination of their optimal level, which is reasonably necessary for economic system functioning [3]. Consequently, the innovation system management should be focused on development and realization of a strategy identifying socioeconomic structures with investment appeal that can be called innovation attractors. Such structures most precisely correspond to main paths of regional development and take into account a current situation and participants' capacities.

At present, various cyber-social technologies are being successfully developed, which can also be used to support the interaction of participants in the innovative regional system. An example of the use of such technologies is the creation of a social network for communication among the participants of the innovation environment. The network allows you to develop a community of people interested in creating and promoting innovation. These include universities and research centers, industrial enterprises, government agencies, ordinary citizens. The use of cyber-social technologies will allow turning the innovative system of a region into an adaptive intellectual environment due to synergistic effect [4].

The cyber-social system may be considered as an intellectual system focused on lowering the barriers to implementation of innovations (transaction costs of innovation activity subjects' interaction) by engaging a larger amount of participants in the innovation process and ensuring their intensive interaction. Its synthesis requires a mechanism that will enable different agents of innovation interaction having common development goals to create new knowledge and exchange it in a safe intelligent network.

2 Blockchain, Smart Contracts and Decentralized Applications for Multi-agent Interaction

The implementation of secure transactions during the exchange of information between participants in economic interaction is a necessary condition for supporting transactional processes, including in innovative systems. The objective is to reduce the influence of interested parties in concluding contracts and fulfilling contractual obligations, as well as their possible interference in the interaction processes between economic agents. One of the mechanisms for secure interaction is distributed registry technology (blockchain), the creation and implementation of smart contract algorithms.

The main problem of the safe use of e-commerce technology is to ensure trust relationships between users, online trading platforms and financial structures. Here is widely used method of attracting a third trusted party to confirm the guarantees of the transaction. But this method can not fully guarantee the reliability and security of transactions. At this stage of development, the blockchain technology or a distributed registry with hashing algorithms can replace the certification mechanism using a third party to completely eliminate the possibility of fraudulent activities on the part of the parties to the transaction. In fact, the functions of a third party are transferred to some intellectual agent, f namely, the smart contract algorithm [5].

As is known, the blockchain technology involves the synthesis of a sequential chain of blocks, which is called a distributed registry, according to a given algorithm. The registry stores information about participants in transactions, transactions and objects of the transaction, in our case, participants in innovative interactions and innovations [6]. In this case, copies of the blocks are placed on the computing devices of the participants themselves, where they are processed [7, 8]. The technology was created to create and conduct operations with cryptocurrencies and was first implemented in the Bitcoin system. As it turned out, it can be used to organize and support any information interactions. All data in the system is stored on user nodes as a distributed database, and not in a centralized repository. At the same time, only one part of information (block) or several copies of blocks is contained on one node. The principle of decentralized storage does minimizes system vulnerabilities to information attacks. The information blocks themselves are encrypted using hash functions (Fig. 1).

As is known, the blockchain technology involves the synthesis of a sequential chain of blocks, which is called a distributed registry, according to a given algorithm. The registry stores information about participants in transactions, transactions and objects of the transaction, in our case, participants in innovative interactions and innovations [6]. The copies of the blocks are placed on the computing devices themselves. An important feature of the distributed registry is the fact that each participant in the transaction actually has information about the actions of other parties by copying and distributing blocks with transactions throughout the network. This ensures transparency of transactions and serves as a confirmation of trust relationships between all subjects of innovation activity. The decentralized repository stores all the data to ensure innovative interactions. Examples of such data are:

- personal data of participants,
- information about legal entities,

- intellectual property rights and description of protected objects,
- digital copies of various documents (contracts, invoices, invoices, etc.),
- records of financial transactions (copy payment orders, cash checks), etc.

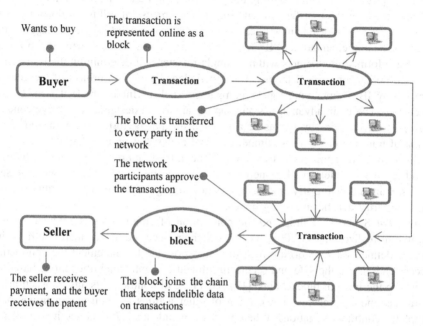

Fig. 1. A transaction scheme using the distributed register

In the information space, authenticity and rights to virtual objects are most often realized through the use of digital certificates, which are issued by a third trusted party. The blockchain technology allows you to opt out of a third party, for example, to confirm the right of authors and intellectual property owners to innovative objects. In addition, the technology will help to control the life cycle of innovations from their creation to implementation and obtaining a commercial result [9]. As an example, we give scientific publications. In many countries, scientists who work in universities and other educational institutions exhibit the greatest publication activity. They are not always participants in economic interactions and often are not associated with the actual production process. However, they are the main sources of innovation. Enterprises, in turn, cannot use their research in economic activity. The author of innovations must register the intellectual property right and then he can transfer it to a company that is interested in putting the innovation into practice or in its refinement and further transfer to the next participant in the innovation process. Thus, a chain of innovative transactions arises, where at each step it is necessary to guarantee the security and reliability of the transfer of intellectual property rights. At the same time, it is required to provide information on the completed operations of all previous owners up to the primary author's source. To implement such a chain of interactions, a distributed registry mechanism is needed. The blockchain technology will allow you to follow the process of creating, modifying, transferring and using innovations, as well as help in obtaining and distributing fair remuneration between all owners and authors. An example of the use of such an approach is the creation of a distributed register of created objects of art, with assigning unique hash identifiers to authors and their works and then tracking the transfer of ownership in the process of selling or donating [10].

An example of blockchain application in intellectual property rights management in Russia is the implementation of IPChain on HyperLedger Fabric allowing to work with different information channels within a single register and determining the transaction approval policy for each of them [11]. Hyperledger Fabric is a project of the consortium led by IBM embracing top IT companies, such as Intel, Oracle, Cisco, Digital Assets, etc. The main advantage is an adaptive algorithm designed to achieve concord between trusted nodes by means of a mechanism that performs decentralized registration of transactions in a set number of equal nodes and, in case the authenticity of results is proved, confirms a transaction. The infrastructure of IPChain includes a bound register of intellectual property objects and a transaction register with the said objects, transaction registry nodes, transaction fixing nodes, network administration nodes and trust certificate issuing nodes.

In 1994 Szabo [12] proposed the conception of smart contracts, which became possible to realize only in 2008, when blockchain occurred. As a smart contract, this concept defines some algorithm by which it is possible to implement the contracting process and ensure the safe and secure fulfillment of contractual obligations based on records in the form of blockchains. [13]. This type of contracts fits any transactions. It guarantees money transfer or execution of other actions as soon as all parties have completed contract obligations. When parties conclude a smart contract, it is similar to transferring of cryptocurrency blockchain funds. After that the contract comes into effect. In order to have contract's obligations automatically complied with there is required a special environment enabling automatic execution of all contract's clauses. Thus, a smart contract can exist only within such environment, where the program code executing the contract's algorithm has access to its objects. Therefore, all relationships between parties within the contract should be mathematically formalized and feature a clean execution logic. According to transaction conditions, the smart contract's algorithm tracks accomplishments or breaches of its clauses and makes a corresponding decision automatically to ensure authenticity of contract obligations.

To ensure interaction between interested parties, the algorithm should describe the following objects:

- information about the parties to the transaction, which can accept, change or withdraw from the terms of the contract, using electronic digital signatures to identify themselves,
- the conditions and subject of the contract for innovative objects and objects of intellectual property, information about which is placed in a distributed registry,
- description of the procedures and operations of the contract execution in the form of a formalized algorithmic description that can be programmed in the blockchain environment.

The operation of the smart contract algorithm is based on the following technologies and platforms:

- digital signature and certification technologies using asymmetric encryption cryptographic algorithms,
- blockchain tools platforms like Codius, Ethereum, Counterparty,
- distributed database technologies for decentralized storage of transaction information.

It should be noted, the use of blockchain platforms for the development of decentralized applications that are similar to smart contracts, but are not only intended to provide contractual and financial obligations [14]. Such applications can be used to provide any informational interactions, are not limited to the parties to the transaction, and are used in various fields, for example, in online games.

All platforms can be conditionally divided into global and private ones. Global platforms make it possible for users and application developers to use an open blockchain network, which represents a network of peer-to-peer nodes, containing a transaction log replicated on many nodes.

The tools with which you can implement a smart contract include platforms Aeternity, Cardano, Ethereum, Hyperledger Fabric [15].

The Aeternity blockchain platform is based on the Lightning Network payment protocol [18, 19]. The protocol works with block chains to conduct fast transactions between nodes. However, he himself solves the problem of scaling and the developed algorithms do not affect the system performance. Computational load with the increase in the number of the transaction is transferred to the logical level, where transactions between participants are implemented in separate logical channels. The entire block chain is not involved, but is used as a distributed database to control financial transactions and as an arbitrator in case of disagreement to resolve disputes.

The Cardano system [21] was designed to transfer the cost of cryptocurrency with the scaling property. It represents the third generation of blockchain platforms. For the synthesis of a chain of blocks, the Haskell programming language is used. The main feature of the system is the logical separation of computational layers into the main layer for working with ADA cryptocurrency and the layer of synthesis and functioning of smart contracts. Here too, a special mechanism for reaching agreement through evidence of the share of ownership of an information object (cryptocurrency, intellectual property, etc.) is implemented. For example, for cryptocurrency, the number of units of a user's own cryptocurrency determines the probability of synthesizing its block in a chain. Thus, the owners of cryptocurrency can control all operations with cryptocurrency in the network.

The Ethereum system not only works with cryptocurrency, but is also intended for the synthesis and implementation of smart contracts, as well as for the development and implementation of decentralized applications [16]. Moreover, the platform can use the network for operations of any level of complexity through synthesized decentralized applications. In fact, the platform is a network virtual machine for conducting secure operations. The ability to create and use a smart contract is implemented by advanced tools and the presence of an embedded Solidity programming language [17], which allows developing smart contracts for various ownership conditions, with many transaction formats and state transition functions. Smart contracts allow you to register transactions with assets in a distributed database, and security is ensured by using hashes in blockchain chains. Calculations hash of block sums is implemented on the computational tools of the users themselves.

The project Hyperledger Fabric is implemented with the support of IBM and JP Morgan and is designed to synthesize an open distributed registry for universal use [20]. The system allows you to develop decentralized applications with the possibility of multilayer blockchain configuration. As well as the Aeternity platform, the system implements custom transaction channels with increased data transfer speed, security and reliability.

3 Choosing a Blockchain Platform for Regional Innovation Systems

In the process of working on the project, a comparative analysis of these systems was made and tools were chosen for synthesizing smart contracts and supporting secure interactions between the participants of the innovation system based on the blockchain platform Ethereum. The platform contains many tools for solving specific tasks: CPP-Ethereum, Solidity, Remix, Webpack, Geth, Web3.js, Parity, etc.

The smart contract algorithm is programmed in the Solidity language as a decentralized application. This is an object-oriented language similar to javascript. Synthesis of the contract is performed in the Remix cloud environment. The environment implements the process of debugging the application by running the generated code directly in the browser. The code is broadcast and executed on the Ethereum virtual machine on distributed computing nodes.

As already mentioned, the system has implemented a way to prove that the Proof-of-Work has been completed in order to achieve consensus. The authenticity of completed transactions is confirmed by the computing power of network nodes. The disadvantage of the approach is that the probability of synthesizing a new unit directly depends on the power of the network node. Therefore, to eliminate this dependence, the Proof-of-Stake method is used, in which the probability of block formation is proportional to the share that the cryptocurrency calculation units belonging to the participant constitute of their total number.

The CPP-Ethereum, Geth and Parity tools are used to connect new network nodes to the circuit. They are loaded as clients on user nodes and are responsible for implementing the Ethereum protocol. Work with the blockchain can be performed via a website using special browsers or standard browsers with the installation of MetaMask and Mist extensions to execute programs and send commands. The Web3.js library provides operation with network nodes via the Remote Procedure Call (RPC) protocol via the HTTP protocol.

Another tool is the Truffle framework. It supports contract management, their placement on the blockchain and migration. To access the blockchain, network nodes are used that interact with each other via the Ethereum protocol.

4   Results

In the process of working on the synthesis of a smart contract algorithm to describe and support secure interactions of participants in a regional innovation system, components were developed for performing transactions. The main system requirements are:

- ensuring the conclusion of contracts,
- support the fulfillment of contractual obligations in the creation and transfer of innovative solutions,
- ensuring compliance with the terms of license agreements,
- implementation of the safe transfer of intellectual property rights,
- monitoring the use of intellectual property rights and licenses in innovation activities
- ensuring the transparency of transactions and the immutability of data on innovations and participants.

The main component is a distributed transaction database (registry) with digital descriptions of innovations and participants in interactions. The registry is a virtual chronological notary. The database describes the main transactions. Examples of transactions are: (a) granting access rights to the innovation passport; assessment of (b) innovation objects; (c) examination of innovations; (d) registration of intellectual property rights; (e) registration of innovation; (f) fixing the transfer of property rights; (g) financial transactions; (h) payment of remuneration; (i) intellectual property rights dispute, etc.

Smart contracts perform various tasks to support interaction and information exchange between users of the innovation system. These tasks include:

- Identification of participants and innovative assets;
- Synthesis of digital copies of innovative assets
- Confirmation of authenticity of documents;
- Verification and validation of intellectual property rights;
- Use of cryptocurrency for mutual settlements between participants;
- Raising funds to support the development, promotion and implementation of innovations;
- Maintaining a decentralized exchange of innovations, etc.

Let us consider the blockchain system performance by the example of issuance of a smart contract for transfer of rights on intellectual activity results (IAR) between innovation participants.

The process of working with a distributed register of innovations begins with the creation of a contract for each result of innovation activity (IAR). The contract is synthesized using a client web application. IAR information is entered into the blockchain and is a smart contract. According to this algorithm, only its owner of the

IAR can transfer the rights to the IAR into ownership to another user. The owner is specified in the "Current owner" variable. The owner pays a commission for placing information about the IAR in the registry. After the innovation description is placed in the registry, the IAR is assigned a unique hash identifier by calculating the hash function. To visualize the information on the IAR, the identifier is translated into a QR code, which is placed on the web page of the website with the name and a brief description of the information. This is how a showcase of innovative solutions is formed available for exchange or sale (Fig. 2).

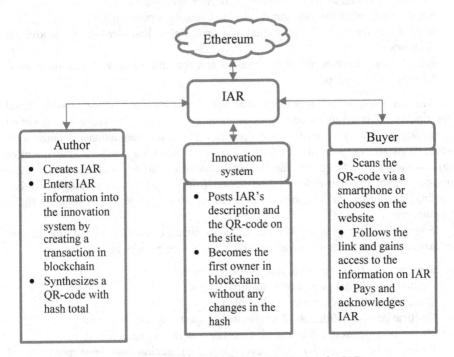

Fig. 2. A scheme of smart contract functioning for IAR

The new owner can access the detailed description of the innovation through the installed mobile application by scanning the QR code. Traditional access via a browser and search box is also supported. Available on request information about the IAR includes: description of information with drawings and diagrams, information about the author, information on intellectual property rights (patent, certificate of registration), date of creation and registration of the IAR in the registry, information on all owners of the IAR, etc.

For registration of the process of selling IAR and the transfer of intellectual property rights, a functionality has been implemented that establishes a new owner. When a IAR is transferred to the ownership of a new owner, the procedure for confirming ownership is implemented, and information about the new owner is added to the blockchain, after which the information block is synthesized and the new hash sum is calculated as an identifier of innovation. To confirm ownership, the new owner must also pay a reward to the previous owner and a commission for the transaction made.

The smart contract is synthesized using the tools of Git, VisualStudio Code, Ganache, Node.js v6 + LTS, truffle and web3.js libraries. For web applications, the lite-server web server is used. Compilation and debugging of smart contracts is implemented in the IDE Remix software.

The compiled and debugged smart contract is transferred to the blockchain system using Ethereum client Ganache. To access and work with the contract, you must add the Metamask extension to the standard browser.

Thus, the process of interaction of subjects of innovation in the region is recorded in the form of a smart contract, and all transactions between participants are recorded in the blockchain.

To complete the functions it is necessary to create a Product.sol smart contract in the Remix environment. The smart contract must include an IAR's creation function, a function of IAR's transfer to a new owner, a property rights confirmation function. To create IAR there is developed an IARItem function with such parameters as IAR's name, author, model (description), price, date, next owner's address.

Having synthesized IAR's description in blockchain the only one, who is authorized to transfer IAR to a new owner, is the one specified in _currentOwner. The function of IAR ownership transfer by a current owner is performed for an input variable _nextOwner with the next owner's address:

```
function setNextOwner(address
nextOwner) public returns(bool set) {
    if (_currentOwner != msg.sender) {
        return false;
    }
    _nextOwner = nextOwner;
    return true;
}
```

Ownership confirmation for the next IAR owner is performed through the function confirmOwnership, which features the new owner's name at the input. The IAR owners' array _owners is appended by a variable _nextOwner, and this address is assigned to a variable _currentOwner. Until the new owner remains unknown, the variable _nextOwner has a zero address. The name of the new owner is added to the owners' array. In order for buyers to check authenticity of IAR the function of full IAR's owners list acquisition is provided for:

```
function confirmOwnership(string customer)
public returns(bool confirmed) {
    if (_nextOwner != msg.sender) {
        return false;
    }
    _owners.push(_nextOwner);
    _currentOwner = _nextOwner;
    _nextOwner = address(0);
    _customer.push(customer);
    return true;
}
```

Following the synthesis of main functions, the contract should be compiled using Truffle and its performance should be checked in the IDE Remix testing network. In the course of compilation a JSON file is created with Application Binary Interface (ABI) of the smart contract, which is used for the contract placement in blockchain.

The operation with smart contracts in the blockchain system requires a web interface based on the bootstrap library that includes the following pages: create.html – IAR creation, confirm.html – IAR receipt confirmation, etc. The work with the web interface and the interaction with blockchain are carried out by means of the web3.js library. The work with the smart contract requires an event service function. An example of a concrete event is the creation of an IAR's digital copy in blockchain. The creation algorithm can be launched by pressing the corresponding button on the web page. It includes the following steps:

- IAR Contract synthesis,
- Contract deployment in blockchain (specification of a contract owner's address, an IAR data line and an amount of gas required for the deployment. The term "gas" defines units of payment for completion of common tasks in blockchain. For example, an addition of numbers costs 3 gas, a multiplication – 5 gas. A transition of IAR ownership rights to another user demands a certain amount of gas. Using Metatask users set prices and amounts of gas),
- If a contract is successfully added in blockchain, it launches the smart contract's function ProductItem with parameters from input fields,
- A QR-code is generated by the qrcode.js library to identify IAR.

Below is the function of IAR's digital copy creation:

```
$(#makeIAR)'.click(function() {
    var IARContract = web3.eth.contract(abi);
    var IAR = IARContract.new(
    {
        from: web3.eth.accounts[0],
        data:'
0x60806040523480156100105760008fd5b50611253806... ',
        gas: '4700000'
    }, function (e, contract){
        console.log(e, contract);
        if (typeof contract.address !== 'undefined') {
            console.log('Contract mined! address: ' +
contract.address + ' transac-tionHash: ' +
contract.transactionHash);
            addr=contract.address;
            var code=http://localhost:3000/check.html#'+addr;
con-tract.IARItem($('#nameIAR').val(),$('#manufacturer').val
(),$('#modelIAR').val(),$('#priceIAR').val(),String($('#create
Date').val()),$('#nextOwner').val(),function(e,contract){
            $('#bigText').qrcode(code);
            console.log(e,contract);
    });
    }
})
```

The function of IAR ownership reception is initiated by the corresponding button on the web interface. The IAR sale function operates with the new owner's address or in the absence of the latter with the address «0x00000000000000000000000000000000000000000000».

The execution of transactions in functions cost gas with exception of the IAR checking function, which is launched when jumping to the page/check.html with the address of a contract to be checked and gives information on IAR as a result of script execution:

```javascript
$(location='http://localhost:3000/app/view/check.html').click(func
tion(){
    var checkIAR = web3.eth.contract(abi);
    var check = checkIAR.at(codeIAR);
    check._nameProduct(function(error, result){
        if(!error)
            {
                $('#nameProduct').text(result);
            }
        else
            console.error(error);
    });
    check._model(function(error, result){
        if(!error)
            {
                $('#model').text(result);
            }
        else
            console.error(error);
    });
    check._color(function(error, result){
        if(!error)
            {
                $('#color').text(result);
            }
        else
            console.error(error);
    });
    check._createDate(function(error, result){
        if(!error)
            {
                $('#createDate').text(result);
            }
        else
            console.error(error);
    });
    check.getOwnersCount(function(error, result){
        if(!error)
            {
                var countOwner=result;
                $('#ownersCount').text(result);
                for (var i = 0; i < countOwner; i++) {
                    check.getOwners(i,function(error, result){
                        if(!error)
                            {
                                $('<div class=flex-container row'+<span
id=owner'+i+'>'+result+'</span></div><br>').appendTo($('#ow
ners'));
                            }
                        else
                            console.error(error);
                    });
                }
            }
        else
            console.error(error);
    });
});
```

Similarly, smart contracts are created to accomplish any operations on informational interaction of regional innovation system's participants. Having smart contracts created and deployed in the blockchain system it is necessary to run automatic testing implemented by the Truffle framework tools. The testing targets are individual functions of each smart contract, as well as its functioning in general and its web interface.

5   Conclusion

The article describes the process of a component of a smart contract for its use as a system to support the secure interaction of participants in innovative regional systems. In the course of the system development the following tasks were completed:

- adjustment of the smart contract environment based on the Ethereum platform, installation and testing of the required tools and creation of the blockhain testing network to work with smart contracts,
- development of the web interface to work with smart contracts,
- development of scripts running basic functions for a number of smart contracts. In particular, the intellectual property rights transfer contract,
- development of event processing scripts for users to work with smart contracts through the web interface, etc.

The technology of smart contracts on the blockchain platform represents a new mechanism for managing regional innovation development. This allows you to combine the efforts of scientific researchers and business to create and implement innovative solutions based on safe and transparent interaction within the framework of cooperation efforts to promote, commercialize innovative projects, reduce transaction costs of participants and investors.

Acknowledgments. The reported study was funded by RFBR according to the projects: № 18-010-00204-a, 18-07-00975-a, 19-013-00409-a.

References

1. Gamidullaeva, L.A.: About formation of innovation management system in Russia. Econ. Revival Russia **4**(50), 74–84 (2016)
2. Vasin, S.M., Gamidullaeva, L.A.: Development of Russian innovation system management concept. Innovations **5**(223), 34–40 (2017)
3. Gamidullaeva, L.A., Tolstykh, T.O.: Transaction costs, institutions and regional innovation development: the case of Russia. In: Proceedings of the 30th International Business Information Management Association Conference (IBIMA), Vision 2020: Sustainable Economic development, Innovation Management, and Global Growth, Madrid Spain, pp. 2121–2135, 8–9 November 2017
4. Finogeev, A.G.: Simulation of systems-synergistic processes in information environments, p. 223. Penza State University, Penza (2004)

5. Blockchain in Russia (2018). http://www.tadviser.ru/index.php/Статья:Блокчейн_в_России#cite_note-7. Accessed 17 April 2019

6. Swan, M.: Blockchain: Blueprint for a New Economy, 152 p. O'Reilly Media, Inc., Sebastopol (2015). ISBN 978-1-4919-2047-3

7. Franco, P.: The Blockchain. In: Understanding Bitcoin: Cryptography, Engineering and Economics, 288 p. Wiley, Hoboken (2014). ISBN 978-1-119-01916-9

8. Antonopoulos, A.M.: The Blockchain. In: Mastering Bitcoin. O'Reilly Media, Inc., Sebastopol (2014). ISBN 978-1-4493-7404-4

9. Matveev S.: Blockchain will provide a fair reward for scientists. https://4science.ru/articles/Sergei-Matveev-blokchein-obespechit-uchenim-spravedlivoe-voznagrazhdenie. Accessed on 17 April 2019

10. Official site of Ascribe company https://www.ascribe.io/. Accessed on 17 April 2019

11. In Russia may appear a blocking analogue of eBay in the field of intellectual property management. http://forklog.com/v-rossii-mozhet-poyavitsya-blokchejn-analog-ebay-v-sfere-upravleniya-intellektualnymi-pravami/. Accessed on 17 April 2019

12. Szabo, N.: Smart contracts: formalizing and securing relationships on public networks. First Monday 2, 9 (1997). http://firstmonday.org/ojs/index.php/fm/article/view/548/469

13. Smart Contracts, Explained. Partnership Material. https://cointelegraph.com/explained/smart-contracts-explained. Accessed on 17 April 2019

14. Decentralized platforms for smart contracts: challenges and solutions. https://forklog.com/detsentralizovannye-platformy-dlya-smart-kontraktov-vyzovy-i-resheniya/. Accessed on 17 April 2019

15. Blockchain platforms. http://smart-contracts.ru/platforms.html. Accessed on 17 April 2019

16. Blockchain app platform. https://www.ethereum.org/. Accessed on 17 April 2019

17. Solidity is a contract-oriented, high-level language for implementing smart contracts. http://solidity.readthedocs.io/en/v0.4.24/

18. Aeternity blockchain. https://aeternity.com/. Accessed on 17 April 2019

19. Poon, J., Dryja, T.: The Bitcoin Lightning Network: scalable off-chain instant payments (2016). http://lightning.network/lightning-network-paper.pdf

20. Hyperledger Fabric is a platform for distributed ledger solutions. http://hyperledger-fabric.readthedocs.io/en/release-1.1/. Accessed on 17 April 2019

21. Cardano is a decentralised public blockchain and cryptocurrency project and is fully open source. https://www.cardano.org/en/home/. Accessed on 17 April 2019

Author Index

Printed in the United States
By Bookmasters